Episcopal Networks in Late Antiquity

Arbeiten zur Kirchengeschichte

Founded by
Karl Holl † and Hans Lietzmann †

Edited by
Christian Albrecht and Christoph Markschies

Volume 137

Episcopal Networks in Late Antiquity

Connection and Communication Across Boundaries

Edited by
Carmen Angela Cvetković and Peter Gemeinhardt

DE GRUYTER

ISBN 978-3-11-073662-5
e-ISBN (PDF) 978-3-11-055339-0
e-ISBN (EPUB) 978-3-11-055251-5
ISSN 1861-5996

Library of Congress Cataloging in Publication Control Number: 2018964953

Bibliographic information published by the Deutsche Nationalbibliothek
The Deutsche Nationalbibliothek lists this publication in the Deutsche Nationalbibliografie;
detailed bibliographic data are available on the Internet at http://dnb.dnb.de.

© 2020 Walter de Gruyter GmbH, Berlin/Boston
This volume is text- and page-identical with the hardback published in 2019.
Printing & binding: CPI books GmbH, Leck

www.degruyter.com

Table of Contents

Abbreviations —— VII

Introduction —— 1

Part 1: **The Ties That Bind**

Volker Menze
Episcopal Nepotism in the Later Roman Empire (c. 350–450) —— 19

Ariane Bodin
A New Approach to Ambrose of Milan's Kinship —— 43

Gillian Clark
Influential Friends? Augustine's Episcopal Networks —— 63

Madalina Toca & Johan Leemans
The Authority of a 'Quasi-Bishop:' Patronage and Networks in the Letters of Isidore of Pelusium —— 83

David M. Gwynn
Patronage Networks in the *Festal Letters* of Athanasius of Alexandria —— 101

Peter Gemeinhardt
Bishops as Religious Mentors: Spiritual Education and Pastoral Care —— 117

Sigrid Mratschek
Crossing the Boundaries: Networks and Manifestations of Christian Hospitality —— 149

Carmen Angela Cvetković
Niceta of Remesiana's Visits to Nola: Between Sacred Travel and Political Mission —— 179

Part 2: Episcopal Networks in Context

Daniel K. Knox
The Impact of the Laurentian Schism on Ennodius of Pavia's Participation in Episcopal Networks —— 207

Jamie Wood
Building and Breaking Episcopal Networks in Late Antique *Hispania* —— 227

Erika Manders
Macedonius, Constantius and the Changing Dynamics of Power —— 249

Jakob Engberg
Caring for African Confessors in Exile: The Ministry of Numeria and Candida during the Decian Persecution (Cyprian, *Epistulae* 21–22) —— 267

Daniëlle Slootjes
The Impact of Geographical and Administrative Boundaries on Late Antique Bishops —— 295

Andrea Sterk
Bishops and Mission Beyond the Frontiers: From Gothia to Nubia —— 313

List of Contributors —— 339

Index of Authors and Texts —— 343

Index of Ancient Places —— 357

Index of Modern Authors —— 361

Abbreviations

Abbreviations for journals, series and reference works are given according to Siegfried M. Schwertner, *Internationales Abkürzungsverzeichnis für Theologie und Grenzgebiete* (Berlin, De Gruyter, ³2014). When the works of Christian ancient works are abbreviated, these abbreviations follow *Lexikon den antiken christlichen Literatur,* eds. Siegmar Döpp/Wilhelm Geerlings (Freiburg: Herder, ²1999).

Introduction

Recent studies on the development of early Christianity emphasize the important role played by the regional or local contexts in what is nowadays commonly regarded as an increasingly fragmented late ancient world. However, despite the political fragmentation of the late Roman Empire, one distinctive feature of the Christianity of this time that needs to be taken more into consideration is its 'inter-connectivity.'[1] As Peter Brown has observed, the basic module of Christianity consisting of a bishop, clergy, people and a place to worship was remarkably stable and easily transferrable to any region. Once established, such basic structures did not develop in isolation but remained closely connected, thus leading to the emergence of a web of Christian belief and practice that spread over much of the later Roman Empire. Both local and trans-regional networks of interaction contributed to the expansion of Christianity in this age of fragmentation.

The present volume investigates a specific aspect of the 'inter-connectivity' that characterizes the late ancient Christianity in the area of the Mediterranean by focusing on the formation and operation of *episcopal networks*. The gradual rise of the bishop as a key figure of authority in the late antique city has been explained based on multiple converging factors,[2] such as: an increase in the number of episcopal responsibilities facilitated by the vacuum of local power, well documented throughout the Roman empire beginning with the third century; the recognition of the bishop as the highest moral and spiritual authority within Christian communities which required ecclesiastical leaders to set an example of moral and virtuous conduct to their congregation; the transfer in the bishops' hands of the management of funds and economic resources. Thus, at a local level, the bishops in their various roles as patrons, teachers, defenders of faith, pastoral counselors, managers of economic resources etc. were expected to interact with individuals of diverse social background that formed their congregations as well as with secular authorities.

To the above mentioned factors, one must also add the official recognition of Christianity as *religio licita* in the Roman Empire which was followed by a number of privileges granted by Constantine to bishops, which strengthened the role

---

1 Peter Brown, *The Rise of Western Christianity: Triumph and Diversity AD 200–1000* (Cambridge Mass.: Blackwell, 1996) 14.
2 Rita Lizzi Testa, "The Late Antique Bishop: Image and Reality," in *A Companion to Late Antiquity*, ed. Philip Rousseau (Malden, MA: Wiley-Blackwell, 2012) 527.

of the bishop as a major public figure of the late ancient city.³ Among these privileges, the permission to travel by imperial post (the *cursus publicus* usually reserved for imperial officials) in order to attend church synods and councils resulted in a marked increase in long-distance communication among church elites coming from different geographical areas and belonging to distinct ecclesiastical cultures and theological traditions. The hustle and bustle of ecclesiastical travel prompted Ammianus Marcellinus' famous complaint about "the throngs of bishops hastening hither and thither on the public post horses to various synods."⁴ Other reasons for long-distance ecclesiastical mobility included, missionary voyages, disciplinary hearings or pilgrimage, a phenomenon that saw an outstanding growth as a result of Constantine's ambitious building program in the Holy Land.⁵ Finally, bishops also travelled against their will to more or less remote locations either fleeing barbarian invasions or because of imperial banishment.⁶

The ability of bishops to interact at local level with different segments of the late ancient society as well as episcopal long-distance interactions will be under scrutiny in this volume. The papers assembled here explore the nature and quality of various types of episcopal relationships in Late Antiquity attempting to understand how they were established, cultivated or put to use across cultural, social or geographical boundaries. These papers are revised versions of the lectures presented at a conference dealing with the topic of "Episcopal Networks in Late Antiquity: Connection and Communication across Boundaries," held in Göttingen from 28 to 30 September 2016 at the University's Historical Observatory, and generously funded by the Fritz Thyssen Foundation. The conference brought together researchers working in various disciplines (ancient history, church history, theology and classics) and belonging to different academic traditions (Britain, Germany, Denmark, France, the United States, Belgium, Switzerland and Hungary). In addition to the contributors to this volume, the conference included also Kate Cooper (London), Julia Hillner (Sheffield), David Lambert (Rome/Oxford), Seraina Ruprecht (Bern) and David Natal (London).

The meeting offered the opportunity to address a number of questions in order to assess an array of issues regarding the bishops' rise to or fall from

---

3 Lizzi Testa, "The Late Antique Bishop," 528.
4 Ammianus Marcellinus, *Res gestae* 21.16.18.
5 See, e.g., Georgia Frank, *The Memory of the Eyes. Pilgrims to Living Saints in Christian Late Antiquity* (Berkeley: The University of California Press, 2000).
6 For a survey of religious travel in Late Antiquity, see Blake Leyerle, "Mobility and the Traces of Empire", in *A Companion to Late Antiquity*, ed. Philip Rousseau (Malden, MA: Wiley-Blackwell, 2012) 112–113.

power, transfer of knowledge, development of religious disputes, long-distance mobility and connectivity, the nature of ancient sources and their suitability for a study of networks. Some of the main questions raised by the participants in the conference and which also shape the contributions to the present volume are:
a. How did episcopal networks come into being, how were they maintained, how did they function and what role did they play in specific situations?
b. How an investigation of episcopal networks enables us to gain new insights about interpersonal connection in the late ancient world?
c. Were episcopal networks different from other types of networks such as trade or elite networks, and if so, in which way?
d. How useful is the concept of 'networks' for studying the social interactions of bishops in late antiquity?

During the last century, in particular the social and exact sciences manifested a steady growing scholarly interest in the concept of networks, which came to be applied in a variety of ways. For a long time, scholars made extensive use of the image of 'network of social relations' in a metaphorical sense in order to represent the interconnections of social relationships without specifying the properties of these interconnections which could help to interpret social actions.[7] The work of the anthropologist J. Barnes about a Norwegian island parish represents a landmark in the studies of networks due to his use of the notion of 'social networks' as an analytical rather than a metaphorical concept.[8] The use of the concept in an analytical way developed in the following decades especially in anthropological studies (Elizabeth Bott, J. C. Mitchell, Jeremy Boissevain)[9] where networks have been defined as: "a specific set of linkages among a defined set of persons, with the additional property that the characteristics of these linkages may be used to interpret the social behavior of the persons involved."[10] In sociological contexts the term has been used initially more often

---

[7] J. Clyde Mitchell, "The Concept and Use of Social Networks", in *Social Networks in Urban Situations: Analyses of Personal relationships in Central African Towns*, ed. J. Clyde Mitchell (Manchester: Manchester University Press, 1969).
[8] J. A. Barnes, "Class and Committees in a Norwegian Island Parish," *Human Relations* 7 (1954): 39–58.
[9] Elizabeth Bott, *Family and Social Network: Roles, Norms and External Relationships in Ordinary Urban Families* (New York: Free Press, 1957); J. C. Mitchell, ed., *Social Networks in Urban Situations*; Jeremy Boissevain and J. C. Mitchell, eds., *Network Analysis: Studies in Human Interaction* (The Hague: Mouton, 1973); Jeremy Boissevain, *Friends of Friends: Networks, Manipulators, Coalitions* (Oxford: Blackwell, 1974).
[10] Mitchell, "The Concept and Use of Social Networks," 2.

than not in a metaphorical way,[11] a situation that lasted until the 1970s when the studies of Stanley Milgram[12] on what has come to be designated as "six degrees of separation" or "small world" theory and those of Mark Granovetter on "the strength of weak ties" became highly influential in the discussion of social networks.[13] Milgram conducted an experiment, which showed that, in average, six social ties were needed in order to connect any two randomly selected people. Defining interpersonal ties as "strong" (high-level of interaction, e.g., friends), "weak" (low-level of interaction, e.g., acquaintances) and "absent", Granovetter identified the weak ties as responsible for the transmission of information to a larger number of people than those accessible via strong ties. Additionally, the information that flows through weak ties traverses greater social distance and is more novel than that diffused by strong ties. For social scientists network description is based on comprehensive data collected through direct observation, questionnaires, interviews etc. that allow a precise and thorough documentation of social connectivity.

In parallel with these theoretical perspectives developed in the fields of anthropology and sociology, mathematical work on graph theory was also concerned with the functioning of networks.[14] Already in the 1950s, Paul Erdös demonstrated that only a relatively small percentage of a network's potential links was needed in order to connect every element in a network. Building on Stanley Milgram's findings about the surprising connectivity of the American society, the mathematicians Steven Strogatz and Duncan J. Watts have discovered in 1998 a graph, which provides a key to understanding the "small world" mystery, or how it is possible that "six degrees of separation" exist between any two people on this planet.

Historians have been slow in drawing on network theory as developed in the social and exact sciences contexts despite the fact that the concept of networks has been used rather early in a metaphorical way by historians working on the Mediterranean. Fernand Braudel spoke of the lines crisscrossing the Mediterranean in terms of networks (*réseaux*) and insisted that the Mediterranean needs

---

11 Mitchell, "The Concept and Use of Social Networks," 2.
12 Stanely Milgram, "The Small World Problem," *Psychology Today* 6 (1967) 60–67.
13 Mark S. Granovetter, "The Strength of Weak Ties," *American Journal of Sociology* 78 (1973) 1360–1380.
14 For this brief summary I am indebted to Giovanni Ruffini, *Social Networks in Byzantine Egypt*, (Cambridge: Cambridge University Press, 2006) 9 and Mark Buchanan, *Nexus: Small Worlds and the Groundbreaking Science of Networks* (New York: Norton, 2002) 13–15.

to be regarded as an exchange.[15] Among historians of the ancient world social network theory has had a limited use with varying degrees of success. An important work for the application of the network theory approach to the history of early Christianity and of its Hellenistic-Roman environment is the 1992 issue of the journal *Semeia* edited by L. Michael White. In particular Elizabeth Clark's contribution to this issue offers an excellent example of how network theory yields new insights when applied to the study of the fourth and fifth century Origenist theological debate.[16] Following the lead of social anthropologists such as J. C. Mitchell who claim that structures of relationships rather than issues of content, motivation or belief are responsible for the behavior of persons,[17] Clark concludes that it was not so much theological exchange that determined the development of the Origenist controversy as the social relationships of the participants. Also drawing on the work of early social anthropologists, such as Mitchell and Jeremy Boissevain, is Margaret Mullet's study of the epistolary corpus of the twelfth century Byzantine bishop Theophylact of Ochrid.[18] Her focus, however, is not on *whole-* or *group-networks* but on the analysis of an individual's set of social relationships also termed as an *egocentric* or *personal network*. Another example of an egocentric network analysis is Sigrid Mratschek's study of the social contacts of Paulinus of Nola based on evidence deriving both from his letters and poems. As Paulinus has never met some of his correspondents in person (e. g., Augustine) his web of social contacts has been described as a "literary network".[19] More recently, Adam Schor analysed the social network of the well-documented bishop Theodoret of Cyrrhus against the backdrop of fifth century religious conflicts.[20] Like Elizabeth Clark in her study of the Origenist controversy, he argues that doctrinal partisanship was not purely a matter of theology but

---

15 Fernand Braudel, *La Méditerranée et le monde méditerranéen à l'époque de Philippe II* (Paris: Colin, 1949).
16 Elizabeth A. Clark, "Elite Networks and Heresy Accusations: Towards a Social Description of the Origenist Controversy," *Semeia* 56 (1992) 79–97, republished as part of the monograph *The Origenist Controversy: The Cultural Construction of an Early Christian Debate* (Princeton: Princeton University Press, 1992).
17 Mitchell, "The Concept and Use of Networks", 46: "The variations in behaviour of people in any one role relationship may be traced to the effects of behaviour of other people, to whom they are linked in one, two or more steps, in some other quite different relationship."
18 Margaret Mullet, *Theophylact of Ochrid: Reading the Letters of a Byzantine Archbishop* (Aldershot: Variorum, 1997).
19 Sigrid Mratschek, *Der Briefwechsel des Paulinus von Nola: Kommunikation und soziale Kontakte zwischen christlichen Intellektuellen* (Göttingen: Vandenhoeck & Ruprecht, 2002).
20 Adam Schor, *Theodoret's People: Social Networks and Religious Conflict in Late Roman Syria* (Berkeley: University of California Press, 2011).

that, in addition to issues of faith, it depended heavily on bonds of patronage and friendship.

While other historical studies have used the concept of networks as a theoretical lens for their analysis of the social structures of the ancient world in a Hellenistic-Roman, Christian or Judaic context,[21] they often stay away from the quantitative side of network analysis. Among some exceptions to this tendency, one ought to mention the study of Giovanni Ruffini on the social structures of two locations, Oxhyrynchos and Aphrodito, in the sixth century Byzantine Egypt. He observes that network analysis provides us with the possibility "to measure the extent of a society's centralization, to identify topographical patterns in the formation of large estates, and to identify the most central – and yet frequently unstudied- figures in its social networks."[22] More recently, Julia Hillner, the coordinator of the collective international research project *Migration of Faith: Clerical Exile in Late Antiquity*,[23] has described the project as adopting a "big data" approach to the phenomenon of clerical exile. This approach rests primarily on the collection of all empirical evidence in a relational, digitally available database which records information about the lives and after-lives of exiled clerics, their social relationships, the form of interaction, etc. These data will eventually be visualized as network graphs, which will be able to reveal larger patterns of social and cultural transformation triggered by clerical exile.[24]

Despite this recent effort, there is an important reason why historians avoid the quantitative approaches in their analysis of networks, as emphasized by many papers in this volume, and this has to do, to a great extent, with the precarious nature of ancient evidence. The extant sources are often scarce, fragmentary, unreliable or tendentious making it difficult for the historian to identify who is related to whom and how individuals in a group are linked to each other by social relationships. In addition to the fragmentary survival of ancient evidence, there is also the problem of omission. For example, the everyday relationships of an individual are almost always absent from historical sources which manifest a tendency to exclude the domestic and the banal rather focusing on what is per-

---

[21] See Ariane Bodin, Tiphaine Moreau, eds., *Réseaux sociaux et contraintes dans l'Antiquité Tardive. Actes de la journée d'études*, Révue des Études Tardo-Antiques 3 (2014) Supplément 1.
[22] Ruffini, *Social Networks* 3.
[23] This project is an interdisciplinary and international collaboration between scholars from the University of Sheffield (UK), Halle (Germany), Aarhus (Denmark) and Vienna (Austria).
[24] Julia Hillner, "Approaches to Clerical Exile in Late Antiquity: Strategies, Experiences, Memories and Social Networks," in *Clerical Exile in Late Antiquity*, eds. Julia Hillner, Jörg Ulrich, Jakob Engberg (New York: Peter Lang, 2016).

ceived as extraordinary.²⁵ Also rarely mentioned are significant agents, such as scribes and letter-carriers, who remain largely unnoticed by modern scholars despite the important role they played in various networks.²⁶ Therefore, this kind of historical evidence cannot measure up to the more ample and well-documented contemporary data on which quantitative approaches to social network theory have been developed. Other difficulties may be encountered when attempting to detect the type of a relationship. While evidence about interpersonal bonds may be provided by a wide range of literature, from archives of letters, to prosopographical collections, conciliar records, historiographical material, theological and even literary sources, awareness about the conventions and limitations of each genre is needed in order to assess the quality of specific relationships. Although letter collections are regarded as more adequate for the investigation of relationships than any other type of sources, letters may often mislead because of the illusory charge of intimacy that is characteristic of the epistolary genre.²⁷ In sources which record religious conflict, social relationships may often be represented in a biased way in order to suit particular agendas. At the same time, types of sources considered less reliable, such as literary sources may provide significant evidence for the existence of social relationships when dealt with circumspectly. Confronted with such difficulties in datamining their sources in search for the presence or absence of social relationships, it is important that the historians pay attention to the way in which the individuals studied portrayed their own social relationships. In other words, historians only have access to the structure of the ancient social world as it is presented in the written records (and in material remains) and in their own description of the social links identified they should not depart from the textual representation of these links.²⁸ This in turn will enable them to further reflect on why ancient authors construct social relationships the way they do or why do they mention particular relationships while ignoring others.

While reconstructing social networks and quantifying social relationships in late antiquity may prove, most often than not, a difficult task to achieve given the problematic nature of the historical sources, it has been observed that not

---

25 Mullet, *Theophylact* 166; Hillner, "Approaches," 35.
26 On the important role played by letter-carriers, see Catherine Conybeare, *Paulinus Noster: Self and Symbols in the Letters of Paulinus of Nola* (Oxford: Oxford University Press, 2000) in particular the first chapter "*Ipsae litterae:* the actual letters." On this aspect see also Gillian Clark's contribution in the present volume, pp. 66–67.
27 Mullet, *Theophylact* 167.
28 Tiphaine Moreau, "Réseaux sociaux et contraintes dans l'Antiquité Tardive: Réflexions préliminaires," *Révue des Études Tardo-Antiques*, Supplément 1 (2014) 10.

only the number but also the quality of ties is of great significance in order to understand the functioning of networks.[29] This is precisely one of the main aspects under scrutiny in the present volume, which is structured in two parts. The first part, entitled "The Ties that Bind," includes chapters that investigate the nature and quality of the late antique bishops' various social relationships. In the second part, entitled "Episcopal Networks in Context", attention is focused on understanding how bishops drew on their respective networks in handling particular situations. The chapters from the first part of the volume detect and analyze the variety of links that bishops established both horizontally with other fellow bishops, and also vertically with religious or secular individuals. Therefore, in this volume, "episcopal networks" designate the social links of a bishop to a variety of people from the ecclesiastical as well as the "secular" sphere, rather than networks formed exclusively of bishops. These links are regarded as potential communication channels that are used in order to transmit information from one person to another. Who was connected to whom and in which way they were related are important questions that will be addressed in order to detect the type of a relationship, to distinguish it from others by understanding the norms and expectations governing a given relationship, and to explain how such relationship may have influenced a certain behavior. Thus, these contributions explore relationships established between kin or kin like individuals, friends, patron and clients, teachers and disciples, hosts and guests. Of course, it is assumed that frequently individuals are related in a multiplicity of ways (kin, patron, friend etc.), but for the sake of understanding the way of functioning of each relationship, the papers focus, as far as possible, on one type of relationship at a time. Consequently, in the first part of the volume are discussed relationships of kinship (Volker Menze, Ariane Bodin), friendship (Gillian Clark), patronage (Madalina Toca / Johan Leemans, David Gwynn), religious mentorship (Peter Gemeinhardt) and hospitality (Sigrid Mratschek, Carmen Cvetković).

The volume opens with the study of **Volker Menze** (Budapest) on episcopal families and nepotism in the Eastern Roman Empire over a period of roughly one hundred years, from the mid fourth to the mid fifth century. Although canonical texts demonstrate that there have been some attempts to prevent the interference of family bonds in episcopal matters, a survey of significant examples from Cappadocia, Jerusalem, Edessa and Egypt demonstrate that nepotism (understood in a narrow sense as employing family members to episcopal office) not only did not have a pejorative connotation, but it was quite spread and rather common

---

[29] Hillner, "Approaches," 39.

especially in rural areas. The examples provided clearly indicate however, that episcopal (family) dynasties did not last for longer than two generations.

Family ties are also under scrutiny in the paper of **Ariane Bodin** (Paris) on Ambrose of Milan's kinship. Investigating a variety of sources that document Ambrose' family connections, paying attention to the kinship terminology employed and also to the geographic background of Ambrose's family, she reaches the conclusion that the bishop of Milan was most likely related on his mother side to the pagan aristocrat Symmachus.

In the following chapter, **Gillian Clark** (Bristol) turns her attention to Augustine of Hippo and his friendship networks. While, at first glance, Augustine's impressive body of literature may seem ideal for a study seeking to trace his social relationships, Gillian Clark ponders on the difficulties involved in the reconstruction of Augustine's social networks. She observes that even if one focuses on Augustine's letter-collection, as the obvious place where to start the search for networks, problems concerning the survival, omission, organization, dating of the letters and the practicalities of letter-exchange make it difficult to answer basic questions about Augustine's relationship with any of his correspondents.

The next chapter by **Madalina Toca** and **Johan Leemans** (Leuven) investigates the patronage networks of the monk Isidore of Pelusium on the basis of his extensive letter-collection, which consists of more than 2000 surviving letters. Although Isidore was never a bishop, the analysis of his letters shows him taking on a number of roles that were also adopted by contemporary bishops, such as patron, pastoral counselor, benefactor, defender of doctrine etc. Toca and Leemans argue that Isidore's succesful networking owes much to the networks he built when pursuing a secular career in Pelusium as a *sophistes*, before becoming a monk. Due to his connections with the secular elites Isidore, a simple monk, proved more influential than many other local bishops.

The contribution of **David Gwynn** (London) offers a convincing explanation for one of the most intriguing puzzles of Athanasius' career who although was five times banished from his episcopal see in Alexandria has managed to strengthen the Alexandrian authority within Egypt and came to be hailed as a champion of orthodoxy. Gwynn's investigation is largely based on an essential, yet often neglected source, the *Festal Letters*, which delivered Athanasius' Easter message to the Egyptian churches. He claims that the control and cultivation of patronage networks that the *Festal Letters* reveal played a crucial role in Athanasius' success as he maintained and increased his standing despite years in exile and numerous rivals in Alexandria and beyond.

In his paper entitled "Bishops as Religious Mentors: Spiritual Education and Pastoral Care", **Peter Gemeinhardt** (Göttingen) endeavours to explain networking strategies by employing two other concepts: the mentor-mentee relationship which can be found not only in anchorite contexts but also between bishops and other people, and the notion of 'pastoral care' which comprises aspects of spiritual counselling as well as of educating someone with regard to his or her religious thought and practice. He chooses three typical addressees of such episcopal activities, namely pagans in the course of conversion (including individuals, like Volusianus, to whom Augustine wrote letters, or groups like the hearers of Zeno of Verona's sermons), virgins (like Olympias, the head of a female ascetic community in Constantinople, to whom John Chrysostom wrote many letters), or monks (like Dracontius whom Athanasius tried to convince not to resign from the bishopric). These examples reveal different strategies of establishing and enforcing networks, be it by episcopal authority or by rhetorical persuasion. Bishops thus became tighter interconnected with different social strata as well as with groups within the Church and, in doing so, maintained and stabilized their own position.

Sigrid Mratschek (Rostock) turns her attention to Christian views on and practices of hospitality. She observes that contrary to previous research claims, the classical concepts of *philoxenia* and *hospitalitas* with the obligation to reciprocity have endured in Late Antiquity, albeit in an altered form. Based on various biblical models (Lot, Abraham, the widow of Sarepta etc.) and especially on the biblical verse Mt 22:35–40, Christian bishops like Ambrose, Augustine, Paulinus of Nola and John Chrysostom devised a competing model of hospitality that replaced the pagan tradition of the gift-exchange with the promise of a reward in a non-material form: the much more attractive 'treasure in heaven'. The author argues that these innovative perceptions and social practices initiated the fourth century "communications revolution" that united Christian centers around the Mediterranean, leading to the emergence of a networked world, criss-crossed by visitors, messengers, refugees and guests.

The contribution of **Carmen Cvetković** (Göttingen) deals with the relationship between Paulinus of Nola and the little known Illyrian bishop Niceta of Remesiana. Niceta's visits to Nola on at least two occasions have been recorded by Paulinus in his *Epistula* 27, *Carmen* 17 and *Carmen* 18. Despite Paulinus' intentions to present Niceta in an idealized form as a "holy bishop" and despite wrapping up their host-guest relationship in the noble language of Christian friendship, the author argues that peering through the heavy rhetoric and the display of Christian ideology enables us to perceive Niceta as a well-connected bishop involved in more mundane issues, such as ecclesiastical business between the Illyrian churches and the church of Rome. She also identifies Niceta as a messenger of ecclesiastical news to his fellow bishops, whom he informs about recent works produced in the regions he visited as well as about the results of important events, such as episcopal elections in Rome.

The chapters from the last half of the volume attempt to understand what kind of relationships were mobilized in particular situations and explain the behavior of the bishop(s) involved in that given situation not only through an understanding of the role a bishop was expected to play in the late ancient society, but also in light of the position he occupied in a social network. Through the study of the web of social connections we expect, for instance, to identify which ecclesiastical leaders were in a position to manipulate others, to differentiate which were more likely to control the flow of information or services for their own benefit, or to shed new light on how the actions and decisions of bishops in a given moment of crisis is affected by the position they occupy in a social network. Thus, these chapters investigate the way in which various types of episcopal relationships were put to use in specific situations, such as ecclesiastical affairs (Daniel Knox), religious violence (Jamie Wood, Erika Manders), exile (Jakob Engberg), negotiating geographical boundaries (Daniëlle Slootjes) and Christian mission (Andrea Sterk).

Daniel Knox (Budapest) investigates "The Impact of the Laurentian Schism on Ennodius of Pavia's Network Participation" by way of a quantitative analysis of the interconnectedness of this deacon and later bishop in North Italy around 500 CE. Both writing letters to certain individuals and naming other persons (or groups) in these letters are telling in this respect, and the literary corpus of Ennodius provides enough material to undertake such a study. Of special interest is the functioning of 'triadic closure', that is, active participation in networks tends to increase the number of people with which one stays in touch without oneself writing to them – of course a well-known phenomenon in social networks, but obviously a successful strategy for a late ancient bishop, too. As Knox demonstrates, the supporters of Pope Symmachus "were a part of a dense web of correspondents with whom Ennodius corresponded frequently and who were frequently mentioned in his letters to others". Thus, epistolary actions can well be revealing with regard to political controversies of the day, even in Late Antiquity.

With the paper of **Jamie Wood** (Lincoln), the regional focus shifts to the Iberian peninsula. While scrutinizing the dynamics of "Building and Breaking Episcopal Networks in Late Antique *Hispania*", he highlights not the networking of (and between) individuals but much rather the interrelations of groups of bishops and other members of the clergy. In late antique *Hispania*, as attested in the seventh century hagiographical corpus of the *Vita Sanctorum Patrum Emeritensium*, conflicts over episcopal office can be frequently observed. In principle, councils were the place and means of negotiation of such conflicts (especially concerning the election of bishops) and should have strengthened the ties between individual bishops by displaying and stabilizing ecclesiastical networks. In reality, this was not a given, not the least due to the fact that, in most cases, bishops participated in other (e.g., aristocratical) networks and had to come to terms with different ties and obligations. Until the end of the sixth century there were competing Nicene and Homoian bishops who strove for support of the king but also of local elites, and also economic power and family relationships came into play. Wood concludes "that the neat networks of bishops described by the normative sources were rather more ephemeral in practice". While bishops participated in a variety of networks, the specific episcopal networks were often not to be presupposed but in fact created in conflicts.

Erika Manders (formerly Göttingen, now Nijmegen) turns her attention to "Macedonius, Constantius [II] and the Changing Dynamics of Power" under the auspices of an empire which became increasingly dominated by Christianity during the fourth century. By focusing on this emperor's relationship to one of the first bishops of the newly established capital in the East, she highlights the practical and conceptual challenges which were posed by the rise of a new religious authority which would eventually replace the emperor's role in religious affairs. Thus, the paper deals with networks between emperors and bishops, but not in terms of a formal 'state-church-relationship' but much rather of a practical level. Macedonius' election as bishop was highly contested because his predecessor Paul had been expelled (and appealed, together with Athanasius of Alexandria, to Constantius' brother Constans) but, at least in the 340s, we do not only observe a struggle between imperial brothers but also an emperor who decidedly interfered in the ecclesiastical affairs in the East: "The emperor was pulling the strings!" As reported by later Church historians, he supported the persecution of rivalling pro-Nicene and Novatian groups, but as it seems, Macedonius' influence grew successively, and in fact, he disposed over the military troops he needed. Relationships deteriorated slowly, but it was only the removal of the tomb of Constantine from the Church of the Holy Apostles that broke the ties between Constantius and Macedonius: "the bishop no longer considered the emperor's authority as self-evident", and the emperor reacted by deposing his rival. This story therefore reveals the aspect of religious power which could be assigned to networks and also the changing conditions under which such rivalry was negotiated.

Jakob Engberg (Aarhus) brings another region with intensified religious conflicts to the fore: third century North Africa ("Caring for African Confessors in Exile. The Ministry of Numeria and Candida during the Decian Persecution [Cyprian, Ep. 21–22]"). In this letter exchange between a group of North African refugees in Rome and a confessor who was imprisoned in Carthage, we can observe an epistolary network between different regions of the Church as well as the strife for spiritual and material support of refugees, provided by the confessor Celerinus and his sisters Numeria and Candida who had previously apostatized (or sacrificed, respectively, following the emperor Decius' decree of 250) but now were respected, even leading figures in the community of refugees. The letters hint at the situation of Christianity in mid-third century: Christians who refused to obey to the emperor's edict had to face severe threats to possession and life, but there was the possibility to find refuge among the large community in Rome (and also in the anonymity of this big city). Beyond this very practical aspects, we can also gain insights into Cyprian's communication of Christian behaviour in these difficult times: the episcopal network in North Africa served as means of transmission of letters and thus helped to uphold Christian ideals of confessorship. Interestingly, the joint origin and background of people held such groups together even in exile – which is telling not only with respect to Late Antiquity but also to very present debates about refugees.

The following paper of **Daniëlle Slootjes** (Nijmegen) deals with "the impact of geographical and administrative Boundaries on late antique bishops". With regard to the changed structures of imperial and ecclesiastical administration in the fourth century, she asks "if, and to what extent the wide-ranging changes of the administrative structures in the fourth century had an effect on the functioning of church institutions and leadership". She underlines that the expectation of "stable, life-long and regional appointments of bishops" had no parallel in imperial offices, but it was the basis on which bishops could create local and regional networks (and thus gain lasting prominence in a city and/or province); in the course of time, they even took over some duties of urban or imperial officials. Moreover, she points to a structural discrepancy between the organization of imperial and ecclesiastical organization; while cities and provinces were roughly similar, dioceses and prefectures did not mirror the structure of episcopal power and jurisdiction (as displayed in conciliar debates and decisions). Against previous scholarship, Slootjes argues that 'dioceses' were something different with respect to the Church, and were by no means congruent with civic entities of the same designation. This means that for the sake of ecclesiastical administration, sometimes terms and spaces were adopted, but not in every case and certainly not slavishly. We thus should not infer, Slootjes concludes, from medieval regulations how the late antique church was structured and how such structures were instrumental in shaping the limits of episcopal networks.

Finally, **Andrea Sterk** (University of Minnesota) takes the reader beyond the frontiers of the Roman Empire ("Bishops and Mission beyond the Frontiers: From Gothia to Nubia") in order to investigate missionary networks. Against a striking predominance of "imperially-sponsored mission" in recent research, she sets out to highlight the role of bishops in such endeavours. It is interesting to note the differences between the parts of the Empire (in the West, there was very few episcopal missionary initiative) and perceptions of culture (for regions beyond the borders of the empire, it seemed sufficient to appoint bishops for whole peoples, while in more urbanized and cultivated regions, mission was a more individual affair). While Gothia was converted by Ulfila (who greatly contributed to the Goth's Homoian profile in the fourth century) and John Chrysostom, by way of sending letters, directed a missionary network from Constantinople, the mission in Nubia followed other conditions. Long before Justinian and his wife took the initiative in the sixth century, there had been missionary activities (documented in hagiographic sources which renders the interpretation quite difficult). Missionaries appeared, at least in Gothia and Nubia, as primordial episcopal candidates: "those already involved in missionary activity, whether as monks or priests, were more readily ordained as bishops for the people they served or for other unevangelized areas"; in other terms, they had already had the opportunity to establish networks on which they could base their conduct of office. Thus it should be kept in mind that "'episcopal networks' included not only bishops but a diverse cast of characters too easily dismissed as 'accidental' evangelists". Here, we face the question of how to discern networks which were made up exclusively by bishops and networks in which the latter participated together with other people – which was most probably the regular case.

The contributions to this volume cover a large geographical area of the former Late Roman Empire extending from Iberia to Cappadocia and from Egypt and Nubia to Illyricum and North Italy. In addition to focusing on major late ancient bishops from the Latin West and the Greek East, such as Augustine, Ambrose, John Chrysostom or Athanasius, attention is also paid to less studied ecclesiastical figures, such as Niceta of Remesiana, Ennodius of Pavia, Macedonius or the "quasi-bishop" Isidore of Pelusium. While the evidence for episcopal connectivity derives from a wide range of material, e.g. historiographical (Menze, Manders, Sterk), conciliar (Slootjes), literary (Cvetković), hagiographical (Wood), most chapters in this volume rely largely on letters (Bodin, Clark, Toca and Leemans, Gwynn, Knox, Engberg) which may be used in combination with other type of material. This indicates that letters are in general perceived as better suited for a study of human connectivity due undoubtedly to their interactive nature, its emphasis on emotion and affect and the existence of named correspondents.[30] However, even letter collections need to be well-documented in order to be approached by means of quantitative social network analysis. In this volume, Daniel Knox applies this method to the epistolary corpus of the

---

30 Mullet, *Theophylact* 167.

bishop Ennodius of Pavia. The rest of contributions rely on qualitative textual analysis and they do not reconstitute whole networks, but usually study human interactions by focusing on segments of episcopal networks.

Overall all contributors to this volume reflect on what makes episcopal networks different from other types of networks extant in the late ancient world such as trade or elite networks. They also seek to understand how Christian ideals of doctrinal normativity, ecclesiastical unity and spiritual perfection governed, shaped and affected interpersonal relationships leading towards cooperation or conflict. This perspective thus unites both parts of this volume, which presents new insights into the characteristic traits of episcopal networks, compared to other late antique modes of inter-connectivity in political, cultural, or philosophical contexts.

Last but not least, it is our pleasure to extend our thanks to people and institutions who supported, first, the conference in Göttingen and, then, the publication of the present volume. Of course, our heartfelt thanks go to the participants in the conference and authors of this book who presented and elaborated their papers. Holding this conference would not have been possible without the generous financial support of the Fritz Thyssen Foundation, for which we are very grateful. The editors of the series "Arbeiten zur Kirchengeschichte", Christoph Markschies and Christian Albrecht, also deserve our thanks for accepting this volume for publication, and Albrecht Döhnert and the team of de Gruyter publishers for their collaboration in the process of copy-editing and type-setting. Furthermore, we thank Laura Fee Brand for her assistance while formatting the papers for print, and Louisa Meyer for helping us with preparing the index.

Göttingen, August 2018   Carmen Cvetković and Peter Gemeinhardt

Bibliography

Barnes, J.A. "Class and Committees in a Norwegian Island Parish." *Human Relations* 7 (1954): 39–58.

Bodin, Ariane and Tiphaine Moreau eds. *Réseaux sociaux et contraintes dans l'Antiquité Tardive. Actes de la journée d'études. Révue des Études Tardo-Antiques* 3 (2014) Supplément 1.

Boissevain, Jeremy. *Friends of Friends: Networks, Manipulators and Coalitions*. Oxford: Blackwell, 1974.

Boissevain, Jeremy and J. Clyde, Mitchell, eds. *Network Analysis: Studies in Human Interaction*. The Hague: Mouton, 1973.

Bott, Elizabeth. *Family and Social Network: Roles, Norms and External Relationships in Ordinary Urban Families*. New York: Free Press, 1957.

Braudel, Fernand. *La Méditerranée et le monde méditerranéen à l'époque de Philippe II*. Paris: Colin, 1949.

Brown, Peter. *The Rise of Western Christianity: Triumph and Diversity AD 200–1000*. Cambridge Mass.: Blackwell, 1996.

Buchanan, Mark. *Nexus: Small Worlds and the Groundbreaking Science of Networks*. New York: Norton, 2002.

Clark, Elizabeth A. "Elite Networks and Heresy Accusations: Towards a Social Description of the Origenist Controversy." *Semeia* 56 (1992) 79–97.

Clark, Elizabeth A. *The Origenist Controversy: The Cultural Construction of an Early Christian Debate*. Princeton: Princeton University Press, 1992.

Conybeare, Catherine. *Paulinus Noster: Self and Symbols in the Letters of Paulinus of Nola*. Oxford: Oxford University Press, 2000.

Granovetter, Mark S. "The Strength of Weak Ties." *American Journal of Sociology* 78 (1973) 1360–1380.

Hillner, Julia. "Approaches to Clerical Exile in Late Antiquity: Strategies, Experiences, Memories and Social Networks." In *Clerical Exile in Late Antiquity*, edited by Julia Hillner, Jörg Ulrich, Jakob Engberg, 11–47. New York: Peter Lang, 2016.

Leyerle, Blake. "Mobility and the Traces of Empire." In *A Companion to Late Antiquity*, edited by Philip Rousseau, 110–125. Malden, MA: Wiley-Blackwell, 2012.

Lizzi Testa, Rita. "The Late Antique Bishop: Image and Reality." In *A Companion to Late Antiquity*, edited by Philip Rousseau, 527–538. Malden, MA: Wiley-Blackwell, 2012.

Milgram, Stanley. "The Small World Problem." *Psychology Today* 6 (1967) 60–67.

Mitchell, J. Clyde. "The Concept and Use of Social Networks." In *Social Networks in Urban Situations: Analyses of Personal Relationships in Central African Towns*, edited by J. Clyde Mitchell, 1–51. Manchester: Manchester University Press, 1969.

Mratschek, Sigrid. *Der Briefwechsel des Paulinus von Nola: Kommunikation und soziale Kontakte zwischen christlichen Intellektuellen*. Göttingen: Vandenhoeck & Ruprecht, 2002.

Moreau, Tiphaine. "Réseaux sociaux et contraintes dans l'Antiquité Tardive: Réflexions préliminaires." *Révue des Études Tardo-Antiques*, Supplément 1 (2014) 7–28.

Mullet, Margaret. *Theophylact of Ochrid: Reading the Letters of a Byzantine Archbishop*. Aldershot: Variorum, 1997.

Ruffini, Giovanni. *Social Networks in Byzantine Egypt*. Cambridge: Cambridge University Press, 2006.

Schor, Adam. *Theodoret's People: Social Networks and Religious Conflict in Late Roman Syria*. Berkeley: University of California Press, 2011.

Part 1: **The Ties That Bind**

Volker Menze
Episcopal Nepotism in the Later Roman Empire (c. 350–450)

> Dona Lucrezia: *Gennaro! Sais-tu qui tu es? Sais-tu qui je suis? Tu ignores combien je te tiens de près! Faut-il tout lui dire? Le même sang coule dans nos veines, Gennaro!*[1]

1 Introduction

The nineteenth century explorer and writer Isabella Bird was the first woman to be elected fellow of the Royal Geographical Society in 1892. She was celebrated for her extensive travel reports from around the globe: maybe most famous was her *A Lady's Life in the Rocky Mountains* from 1879 but she also travelled extensively the Far East as well as today's southeastern Turkey. The letters she wrote from her trip to the Ottoman Empire in 1890 are published in her *Journeys in Persia and Kurdistan*. In one of them she reports from her stay at the patriarchal residence of the Holy Apostolic Assyrian Church of the East in Kochanes/Qudshanis (today: Hakkâri):

> To realize what this house is like, one must go back four centuries, to the mode of living of the medieval barons of England. Mar Shimun is not only a spiritual prince, but the temporal ruler of the Syrians of the plains and valleys, and of the Ashirets or tribal Syrians of the mountains of Central Kurdistan, as well as a judge and a salaried official of the Turkish Government. He appoints the *maleks* or lay rulers of each district, where the office is not hereditary, and possesses ecclesiastical patronage. For over four centuries the Patriarch has been of the family of Shimun, which is regarded as the royal family.[2] [...]
>
> The succession to the Patriarchate and Episcopate is the subject of a peculiar arrangement, which makes these offices practically hereditary. In the Mar Shimun family there has been

---

My sincere thanks go to Carmen Cvetković and Peter Gemeinhardt (Göttingen) for inviting me to the conference "Episcopal Networks in Late Antiquity: Connection and Communication across Boundaries." It was an excellently organized conference with stimulating discussions. My thanks go also to Madalina Toca (Leuven) and Andra Jugănaru (Budapest) for references and literature, and to Rudolf Haensch (Munich) for reading the revised version and correcting mistakes.

1 Victor Hugo, *Lucrèce Borgia*, 2nd edition (Paris: Eugène Renduel, 1833), 174.
2 Letter 29, Kochanes, Oct. 27, 1890: Mrs Bishop (Isabella L. Bird), *Journeys in Persia and Kurdistan*, Vol. 2 (London: John Murray, 1891), 288.

provided for more than three centuries a regular succession of youths called *Nazarites*, who have never eaten meat or married, and whose mothers ate no meat for many months before they were born. One of these is chosen by the Patriarch as his successor, and then some of the disappointed youths take to eating meat like other men.[3]

Bird continues to vividly describe the daily life at the patriarchal residence of patriarch Shimun, the twentieth patriarch of this name. She provides a fascinating inside into the routine of this isolated tribal society with its theocratic rulership, portraying for example the bishop of Urmia as a caring but bold and undiplomatic *pater familias* who visited the patriarchal residence in order to betroth his fourteen-year-old nephew to the patriarch's eight-year-old niece.[4]

Bird meticulously analyzes the microcosm of the patriarchal family: "Intrigues are rife. In some ways every man's hand is against his fellow, and the succession to the Patriarchate, although nominally settled, is a subject of scheming, plotting, rivalries, and jealousies."[5] Bird also met the Patriarch-designate Mar Auraham thirteen years before the patriarch in power Shimun XX actually died in 1903.[6] A few years later, World War I changed the fate of this small tribal Church: many Assyrians, including the patriarch Shimun XXI, were killed, and the Church exiled. The last patriarch of the patriarchal house of Shimun, Mar Shimun XXIII, ordained as a twelve-year-old boy in a refugee camp in Iraq, was shot in San Jose/California in 1975. Since then the Church of the East no longer follows a hereditary succession but elects its patriarchs.[7]

Canon lawyers may turn up their noses at such uncanonical tradition but the hereditary patriarchate of the Church of the East remained a stable institution from the fourteenth to the twentieth century. As such it is unrivalled throughout Christendom but not without parallels in other Christian Churches. The term "nepotism" was originally coined for the Medieval and Early Modern institution of the cardinal-nephew of a ruling Roman-Catholic pope.[8] Therefore ecclesiasti-

---

[3] Mrs Bishop, *Journeys*, 308–309.
[4] Mrs Bishop, *Journeys*, 304–5. Bishoprics were hereditary within the episcopal families as well.
[5] Mrs Bishop, *Journeys*, 288–9.
[6] This line of succession was, however, a few years later changed, and Benyamin, fifteen years old and another nephew of the ruling patriarch, became patriarch in 1903 as Shimun XXI. Auraham converted to Catholicism in 1904.
[7] Although it should be noted that the Church of the East still maintained "episcopal families": Shimun XXIII's successor Dinkha IV (1976–2015) was from a family that had brought forth 17 bishops. See in general Wilhelm Baum and Dietmar W. Winkler, *The Church of the East. A Concise History* (London: Routledge Curzon, 2003), 135–157, and James F. Coakley, "The Church of the East since 1914," *Bulletin of the John Rylands Library of Manchester* 78 (1996): 179–198.
[8] Georg Schwaiger, "Nepotismus," *Lexikon des Mittelalters* 6 (1993): 1093–1094.

cal family dynasties may be expected in other churches as well; not the least for the period of late antique Christianity when the ecclesiastical canons were just being established. Wolfgang Reinhard spoke of a "factual hereditability" of the episcopal office in ancient Christianity, and scholars like Luce Pietri, Claire Sotinel and most recently Peter Kritzinger pointed out that "episcopal dynasties" were a familiar feature of the late antique Church.[9] Other scholars like Claudia Rapp and Peter Norton remain more skeptical, and warn against overemphasizing such episcopal dynasties or families as dominant phenomenon in Late Antiquity.[10]

In the following, the most contextualized cases of episcopal families and nepotism from fourth- and especially fifth-century churches in the Eastern Roman Empire will be presented and discussed to the extent that the surviving material allows. Most attention will be paid to narrative sources but no claim to completeness can be made.[11]

"Nepotism" is narrowly understood here as appointing family members to episcopal offices – not in the broader sense of favoring (also) non-relatives for such positions.[12] Most of the time an uncle ordained his nephew (also brothers or cousins can be found) but in other cases the circumstances of ordination are

---

[9] Wolfgang Reinhard, "Nepotismus. Der Funktionswandel einer papstgeschichtlichen Konstanten," *ZKG* 86 (1975): 145–185, here 147; Luce Pietri, "Das Hineinwachsen des Klerus in die antike Gesellschaft," in *Die Geschichte des Christentums. Religion, Politik, Kultur. Altertum Vol. 2. Das Entstehen der einen Christenheit (250–430)*, eds. Charles and Luce Piétri, (Freiburg: Herder, 1996): 633–666, here 652. Claire Sotinel, "Le Recrutement des Évêques en Italie aux IVe et Ve Siècles. Essai d'Enquête Prosopographique," in *Vescovi e Pastori in Epoca Teodosiana. In Occasione del XVI Centenario della Consacrazione Episcopale di S. Agostino, 396–1996* (Rome: Institutum Patristicum Augustinianum, 1997): 193–204. Peter Kritzinger, *Ursprung und Ausgestaltung bischöflicher Repräsentation* (Stuttgart: Franz Steiner, 2016), 265.
[10] Claudia Rapp, *Holy Bishops in Late Antiquity. The Nature of Christian Leadership in an Age of Transition*, The Transformation of the Classical Heritage 37 (Berkeley: University of California Press, 2005), 195–99, although actually herself overstating the case when she believes (p. 196) that in "fifth-century Spain, bishoprics were passed on from father to son as if they were a piece of property" with reference to Pope Hilarius, *ep.* 15. The letter criticizes indeed that bishoprics are passed from present office holders to successors without popular vote but nothing is said about the relationship of office holder to successor. Peter Norton, *Episcopal Elections 250–600. Hierarchy and Popular Will in Late Antiquity*, OCM (Oxford: Oxford University Press, 2007), 209.
[11] Inscriptions add surprisingly little to the overall picture. See below, pp. 22 and 25 n. 24.
[12] Cf. the meaning 1a) in the *Oxford English Dictionary:* "The showing of special favour or unfair preference to a relative in conferring a position, job, privilege etc.; *spec.* such favour or preference shown to an illegitimate son by a pope or other high-ranking ecclesiastic" (accessed online www.oed.com).

unknown or an independent committee elected the younger relative. The focus will be on episcopal families, that is, families that produce at least two bishops, not families that may have had several family members joining the church but in sub-episcopal positions.[13] Although the evidence is sketchy, the conclusion is inevitable that within the context of the Eastern Roman empire, hereditary successions were no viable option for more than two generations.

2 The legal framework and historical setting

Since Martin Heinzelmann's *Bischofsherrschaft in Gallien* scholarship often points to (post-) Roman Gaul to show the establishment of episcopal dynasties.[14] Besides the fifth-century bishop Rusticus of Narbo (c. 420–460) who was the son of a bishop and the nephew of another, and whose epigraphic self-representation is preserved, scholars refer first of all to the sixth-century Gregory, bishop of Tours 573–594.[15] Gregory claimed that a majority of his predecessors as bishops of Tours were his blood relatives,[16] and even if this is an exaggeration, as Walter and Patzold in a recent article reconstruct "only" nine bishops as ancestors, this may certainly count as a dynasty.[17] Gregory also reports that Felix, bishop of Nantes, requested (because of sickness) to have his nephew consecrated as his successor. Felix's colleagues agreed but Gregory denied this – however, not

---

[13] Evidence for sub-episcopal positions most often stem from inscriptions, which are occasionally used here.

[14] Martin Heinzelmann, *Bischofsherrschaft in Gallien. Zur Kontinuität römischer Führungsschichten vom 4. bis zum 7. Jahrhundert. Soziale, prosopographische und bildungsgeschichtliche Aspekte*, Francia.B 5 (Munich: Artemis 1976). In addition, scholarship pointed to some examples from Late Roman Italy: Pietri, "Das Hineinwachsen des Klerus," 652: reference to a Cypriotic family dynasty in Subaugusta close to Rome: *Inscriptiones Christianae urbis Romae septimo saeculo antiquiores: nova series Vol. 6. Coemeteria in viis Latina, Labicana et Praenestina*, ed. Antonio Ferrua, (Rome: Pontificio Instituto di Archeologia Cristiana 1975): 280–1 (17293–17297); see also Sotinel, "Le Recrutement des Évêques."

[15] Henri Irénée Marrou, "Le Dossier Épigraphique de l'Évêque Rusticus de Narbonne," *Rivista di Archeologia Cristiana* 3–4 (1970): 331–349; RVSTICUS 3 in *PCBE* 4 (2013), 1657–1663.

[16] Gregory of Tours, *The History of the Franks* 5.49 (*Gregorii Episcopi Turonensis Libri Historiarum X*, ed. Bruno Krusch and Wilhelm Levison (Hannover: Hahn, 1951), 262; Gregory of Tours, *The History of the Franks*, trans. Lewis Thorpe (London: Penguin, 1974), 321; see also here introduction p. 8).

[17] Not to mention that Gregory also had relatives who were bishops of Lyon, Langres and Clermont; Conrad Walter and Steffen Patzold, "Der Episkopat im Frankenreich der Merowingerzeit," in Steffen Patzold and Karl Ubl (eds.), *Verwandtschaft, Name und Soziale Ordnung (300–1000)*, RGA 90 (Berlin: de Gruyter, 2014): 109–139, here 127.

because it was nepotism but because the uncle was still alive. In other words, the only obstacle raised here (although Gregory clearly saw that the boy was hardly fit to become the next bishop of Nantes) was canon 23 of the Council of Antioch (341) which forbade appointing a successor while the bishop was still alive.

Canon 23 seems to be the earliest testimony that implies that bishops may have tried to find a successor themselves while still being alive. This, however, refers to any successor, independent of the question if the possible successor was a relative. Normative sources that discuss the possibility of succession within the family are rare in Antiquity – only two clear canonical regulations are attested. The earliest comes from the second half of the fourth century with canon 76 of the so-called *Apostolic Canons*, an appendix to the *Constitutions of the Apostles*. It stipulates that:

> (it) is decreed that no Bishop shall be allowed to ordain whomsoever he wishes to the office of the Episcopate as a matter of concession to a brother, or to a son, or to a relative. For it is not right for heirs to the Episcopate to be created, by subjecting God's things to human passion; for God's Church ought not to be entrusted to heirs.[18]

The collection probably stems from Antioch from around 380, and it is a clarification of canon 23 from 341 by forbidding not just generally the ordination of a successor but particularly referring to the possibility of ordaining a relative as successor. "Ordination" of course should not be mixed up with designating a successor in the bishop's lifetime. It seems that bishops often did name the person whom they wished to succeed, and if the bishop was respected, it was likely that this candidate became the new bishop after the former's demise.[19]

---

18 Ὅτι μὴ χρὴ τὸν ἐπίσκοπον τῷ ἀδελφῷ ἢ τῷ υἱῷ ἢ ἑτέρῳ συγγενεῖ χαριζόμενον τὸ ἀξίωμα τῆς ἐπισκοπῆς ἢ ἑτέρῳ συγγενεῖ χαριζόμενον τὸ ἀξίωμα τῆς ἐπισκοπῆς χειροτονεῖν οὓς αὐτὸς βούλεται· κληρονόμους γὰρ τῆς ἐπισκοπῆς αὐτοῦ ποιεῖσθαι οὐ δίκαιον, τὰ τοῦ Θεοῦ χαριζόμενον πάθει ἀνθρωπίνῳ· οὐ γὰρ τὴν τοῦ Θεοῦ Ἐκκλησίαν ὑπὸ κληρονομίαν ὀφείλει τιθέναι. *Ecclesiastical Canons of the Same Holy Apostles* 76; *Les Constitutions Apostoliques*, Vol. 3, ed. and trans. Marcel Metzger, SC 336 (Paris: Éditions du Cerf, 1987), 302–305; English trans. in *The Rudder (Pedalion) of the Metaphorical Ship of the One Holy and Apostolic Church of Orthodox Christians*, ed. Denver Cummings (Chicago: Orthodox Christian Educational Society 1957): 136. For a short overview of the *Canons* see Heinz Ohme, "Sources of the Greek Canon Law to the Quinisext Council (691/2). Councils and Church Fathers," in *The History of Byzantine and Eastern Canon Law to 1500*, eds. Wilfried Hartmann and Kenneth Pennington, (Washington, D.C.: Catholic University of America Press, 2012): 24–114, here 28–33.
19 Episcopal saints' lives proudly record that the office holder – maybe even from his deathbed – enlightened a wavering job committee of who would be worthy to succeed him. It shows the foreknowledge of the saint to take care of his bishopric and his flock even after his death. See Norton, *Episcopal Elections*, 204–214, especially 204 where Norton refers to Paulinus' *Vita Am-*

Successions within one family nevertheless happened as a canon from the Quinisext Council confirms at the very end of antiquity (691/2):

> Since we know that, in the region of the Armenians, only those are appointed to the clerical orders who are of priestly descent (following in this Jewish customs) [...] we decree that henceforth it shall not be lawful for those who wish to bring any one into the clergy, to pay regard to the descent of him who is to be ordained.[20]

Several 'patriarchs' of the early Armenian Church in the fourth and fifth centuries had stemmed from the same family of Gregory the Illuminator, but it remains unknown how much a hereditary principle was adopted in the late antique Armenian Church in general.[21] The canon here is not just concerned about episcopal dynasties but about clerical families in general. However, it clearly refers to a specifically regional problem, and no other general canons or rules are known from antiquity. As legal regulations did play a prominent part for late antique Christianity – both laymen, monks as well as clergy found themselves subjected to increasingly detailed legislation –, the fact that only two canons were composed against episcopal family dynasties within three centuries, speaks against the perception that episcopal family dynasties played a major role. Or, that the Church did not regard this as a problem for church life.

Looking at the narrative sources, one of the earliest evidence for a possible episcopal family stems from Eusebius' *Church History:* Eusebius quotes from a letter of bishop Polycrates of Ephesus (c. 160–196) in which Polycrates reports proudly that seven of his relatives (συγγενεῖς) had been bishops.[22] He unfortunately did not specify the sees of these relatives but even if only less than half of them were bishops of Ephesus, it would constitute an impressive local family dynasty. Be this as it may, Polycrates brought up his episcopal relatives in the discussion of the date of Easter, and the mentioning of his episcopal kinsmen

---

brosii 46; an example not mentioned here can be found in the *Vita Dioscori:* Dioscorus of Alexandria pointed to Timothy Aelurus as his successor.

20 Ἐπειδήπερ ἔγνωμεν ἐν τῇ Ἀρμενίων χώρᾳ μόνους ἐν κλήρῳ τοὺς ἐκ γένους ἱερατικοῦ κατατάττεσθαι, ἰουδαϊκοῖς ἔθεσιν ἐπομένων τῶν τοῦτο πράττειν ἐπιχειρούντων [...] ὥστε ἀπὸ τοῦ νῦν μὴ ἐξεῖναι τοῖς εἰς κλῆρον βουλομένοις προάγειν τινὰς εἰς τὸ γένος ἀποβλέπειν τοῦ προχειριζομένου; Council of Trullo in 692, can. 33; *ACO* II.2.4, 38; *Nicene and Post-Nicene Fathers Vol. II.14. The Seven Ecumenical Councils,* trans. Henry R. Percival (New York: Charles Scribner's Son, 1900), 381.

21 Timothy Greenwood, "Armenia," in *The Oxford Handbook of Late Antiquity,* ed. Scott Fitzgerald Johnson (Oxford: Oxford University Press 2012): 124–125.

22 Eusebius, *h.e.* 5.24.6 (Eusebius, *Kirchengeschichte,* ed. Friedrich Winckelmann, GCS 6 (Berlin: Akademie 1999), 492).

is obviously intended to prove his Christian pedigree. In other words, seven bishops as relatives signaled the reader that the bishop was qualified, and he had intimate knowledge of Christian rules and regulations. Nepotism as derogative prejudice is apparently neither on the author's nor the reader's mind.

Such perception of pride for an episcopal breeding could go as far as inventing an episcopal ancestry. Zachariah Rhetor, the biographer of Severus, the sixth-century patriarch of Antioch (512–518), made up a Christian pedigree for Severus, including a grandfather of the same name who supposedly was bishop of Sozopolis, Severus' home town.[23] In other words, whatever the late antique legal regulations stipulated, bishops did take pride to be the offspring or relatives of bishops, and they shared this perception with their flock and audience.

3 Episcopal nepotism in the Eastern Roman Empire (350–450)

I do not know of any ecclesiastical family dynasty in the Eastern Roman empire in Late Antiquity if "dynasty" would encompass members from more than two successive generations. A case like Polycrates of Ephesus in the second century is not recorded, and can at least be ruled out for the most prominent episcopal sees for which information is available. However, sources are very limited, and already for many metropolitan sees, the possibility cannot be excluded that family dynasties existed without leaving a lasting record in narrative sources.[24]

---

[23] *Vie de Sévère par Zacharie*, ed. M. A. Kugener, in *Patrologia Orientalis* 2 (1904), 11; *Two Early Lives of Severus, Patriarch of Antioch*, trans. Sebastian Brock and Brian Fitzgerald (Liverpool: Liverpool University Press, 2013), 35; see also p. 3 for Severus' information of his pagan family background.

[24] Inscriptions would be the only way to trace more possible dynasties but examples remain rare. I am grateful to Rudolf Haensch for discussing this issue with me via e-mail. For the West, Rusticus of Narbo has been mentioned above, and another well-known example was the Italian bishop Pancratius who informed the reader on his tombstone that his father Pancratius was also bishop as was his brother Herculus; *Inscriptiones Latinae Christianae Veteres*, ed. Ernst Diehl, Vol. 1 (Berlin: Weidmann, 1925): 197; however, there is no information if this lasted for more generations than the two mentioned. For the east see the inscription from Resafa that was set up by a deacon John from Antioch, who was the nephew of the metropolitan Sergius of Resafa, who in turn was related to the *chorepiscopos* Maronios: Pierre-Louis Gatier, "Inscriptions grecques de Résafa," *Damaszener Mitteilungen* 10 (1998): 237–241. Sergius and the *chorepiscopos* Maronios appear on a number of inscriptions from Resafa; see for example Pierre-Louis Gatier, "Les Inscriptions grecques," in *Resafa II. Die Basilika des Heiligen Kreuzes in Resafa-Sergiupolis*, ed. Thilo Ulbert (Mainz: von Zabern, 1986): 161–169. For Egypt, see Ewa Wipszycka, *Études sur le*

Bishops from the same family within one or over two generations, and clear cases of nepotism, were not uncommon. The most prominent examples from the fourth century offer the Cappadocian fathers Basil of Caesarea (370–379), Gregory of Nazianzus (372–390), and Gregory of Nyssa (372–394) and their families. Basil's family already had a Christian pedigree – persecuted in the last great persecution under Diocletian – when the three men came of age and made their career as bishops and theologians in the second half of the fourth century.[25]

Basil became metropolitan in Cappadocia with the help of Gregory the Elder, who was bishop of Nazianzus (328–374) and the father of Gregory of Nazianzus.[26] Basil appointed his brother Gregory as bishop for the newly created bishopric Nyssa (372–395) as well as his friend Gregory of Nazianzus – the just mentioned son of Gregory the Elder – as bishop of Sasima (372–380).[27] Basil also ordained his youngest brother Peter priest who years later in 380 became metropolitan of Sebaste in Armenia II. Atarbius, metropolitan bishop of Neocaesarea (368–381) in Pontus, was also a relative of Basil.[28] Gregory of Nazianzus' cousin, Amphilochius became metropolitan of Iconium in Lycaonia in 373/4. In as much family relations were responsible to ensure that the candidate successfully advanced to episcopal rank, is not known in all cases. However, scholars have argued that Basil created suffragan bishoprics in order to broaden the basis of his episcopal followers after emperor Valens (364–378) divided the province of Cappadocia.[29] Also the other ordinations – even when they happened beyond the provincial borders – were facilitated by family bonds: not Gregory of Nazianzus but Basil had lobbied for Amphilochius's election as metropolitan of Iconium.[30]

Christianisme dans l'Égypte de l'Antiquité tardive (Rome: Institutum Patristicum Augustinianum, 1996), 215 n. 42 and 43.

25 Philip Rousseau, *Basil of Caesarea*, The transformation of the classical heritage 20 (Berkeley: University of California Press, 1994), 1–16.

26 Raymond van Dam, *Families and Friends in Late Roman Cappadocia* (Philadelphia: University of Pennsylvania Press, 2003), 34. I am heavily indebted to his excellent account on the family relations of the Cappadocians.

27 The older Gregory had already ordained his son as priest; for the father-son relationship see van Dam, *Families and Friends*, 40–58.

28 Van Dam, *Families and Friends*, 27.

29 For example Paul Jonathan Fedwick, *The Church and the Charisma of Leadership in Basil of Caesarea*, STPIMS 45 (Toronto: Pontifical Institute of Medieval Studies, 1979), 47–48 n. 48, and Anthony Meredith, *Gregory of Nyssa* (London: Routledge, 1999), 4. However, Basil argued against appointments of relatives and friends in *ep.* 54; see *Saint Basil. The Letters*, Vol. 1, ed. Roy J. Deferrari (Cambridge, MA: Harvard University Press, 1926): 344–45.

30 Van Dam, *Families and Friends*, 39 and 54.

This may not be called nepotism but rather shows the close-knitted relationship of two prominent Cappadocian family clans.

Sometimes such inter-family bonds provided more support than one's own blood relatives: while Gregory the Elder and father of his friend Gregory of Nazianzus lobbied for Basil to become metropolitan in 370, Basil's own uncle Gregory, bishop in Cappadocia as well, opposed his election.[31] Also Gregory of Nazianzus who had a close and dear relationship with his father (and assisted his father in his father's later years instead of administering his own see in Sasima), reports upsetting issues that affected the family's work for the Church. Gregory's younger brother Caesarius served at emperor Julian's court in Constantinople. Thereby he embarrassed the whole family and undermined the authority of his father as bishop: what sermons was a bishop to offer to his flock when the own son affiliated himself with an apostate?[32] Families may have provided the best network that a son, nephew, cousin etc. could rely on for advancing his career but occasionally they also developed unforeseen dynamics that caused family-internal tensions and rifts.

Besides the Cappadocians, there are a few other individual cases of family relatives that opted for ecclesiastical careers. Cyril of Jerusalem (350–387) ordained his nephew Gelasius c. 367 as bishop of Caesarea in order to end a conflict with the metropolitan see of Palestine, and to have a loyal ally ordained for this important see.[33] Antiochos, nephew of Eusebius, bishop of Samosata (361–379), was elected successor of his uncle as bishop of Samosata – but after his uncle's death![34] The church historian Sozomenos noted that emperor Theodosius I chose to everybody's surprise the unbaptized *clarissimus* Nectarius to be ordained the bishop of Constantinople in 381. After the banishment of Nectarius' successor John Chrysostom (398–404), people remembered that Nectarius had

---

[31] Rousseau, *Basil of Caesarea*, 6–7; Van Dam, *Families and Friends*, 31; the two may have come to terms later as Basil tried to set things right: Basil *ep.* 59 and 60; *Saint Basil. The Letters*, Vol. 2, ed. and trans. Roy J. Deferrari, Loeb Classical Library (Cambridge, MA.: Harvard University Press, 1928), 2–13. The see of this Gregory is not known – maybe he was a *chorepiscopos*; Van Dam, *Families and Friends*, 197 n.38.
[32] Gregory of Nazianzus, *ep.* 7; Van Dam, *Families and Friends*, 49. However, also Basil and his brother Gregory had their issues: Rousseau, *Basil of Caesarea*, 6–7.
[33] Epiphanius *Adv. Haer.* 73.37 (PG 42, 472); Ernst Honigmann, "Juvenal of Jerusalem," *DOP* (1950): 209–79, here 215–16 rightly speaks of Cyril's nephew but Edward Yarnold mistakes it for Cyril's brother: Edward Yarnold, *Cyril of Jerusalem*, The early church fathers (London: Routledge, 2000), 6; see also Jan Willem Drijvers, *Cyril of Jerusalem: Bishop and City* (Leiden: Brill, 2004), 43 and 45.
[34] Theodoret, *h.e.* 4.15 (Theodoret, *Kirchengeschichte*, ed. Leon Parmentier & Günther Christian Hansen (3rd edition Berlin: Akademie Verlag, 1998), 237).

a brother, Arsacius. The eighty-year old Arsacius ruled as bishop for a little more than a year (404–405).[35] The famous Theodore of Mopsuestia (392–428) had a (probably younger) brother Polychronius, who was metropolitan of Apamea in Syria II (428–431?).[36]

For the fifth-century, the best-known examples of nepotism stem from the acts of the second Council of Ephesus in 449. Emperor Theodosius II (408–450) convoked the council as the third ecumenical council in order to settle quarrels that disturbed the ecclesiastical peace in the Near East in wake of the Nestorian controversy after the first Council of Ephesus in 431. The emperor requested patriarch Dioscorus of Alexandria (444–451) to preside over the council, and the patriarch launched a full-scale attack against bishops who opposed Alexandrian theology as well as the ecclesiastical politics of the see of St Mark.[37]

Incidentally, the reader of the acts also learns about Ibas of Edessa's (435/6–449 and 451–457) kinsmen who made ecclesiastical careers: his nephew Daniel as bishop of Harran, and his cousin Sophronius as bishop of Tella.[38] As Edessa was the metropolitan see of Osrhoene, and both Harran/Carrhae as well as Tella/Constantina its suffragan sees, it seems more than likely that Ibas had ordained his (younger) relatives to these posts in order to strengthen his own position as metropolitan. In 449, the council charged Ibas of being jealous of Christ, hating Christ, heresy, Nestorianism, company with Jews, being a Jewish bishop etc. etc., Daniel of Harran of fornication and theft from the church,[39] and Sophronius of

---

[35] Maybe because Nectarius managed the difficult see so well, it was believed that his brother would also do a good job; Socrates Scholasticus, *h.e.* 5.8 and 6.19; *Sokrates Kirchengeschichte*, ed. Günther Christian Hansen, GCS 1 (Berlin: Akademie, 1995), 280 and 343; trans. *Nicene and Post-Nicene Fathers* 2.2, 121–122 and 151; Sozomenos, *h.e.* 7.8 and 8.23; Sozomenos, *Historia Ecclesiastica*, Vol. 3 and 4, ed. and trans. Günther Christian Hansen (Turnhout: Brepols, 2004), 854–59 and 1028–29.

[36] Theodoret, *h.e.* 5.40 (ed. Parmentier & Hansen, 348).

[37] This was first of all Theodoret of Cyrrhus, the most prolific dyophysite theologian of his time and stern opponent of Alexandrian patriarchs and their theology as well as ecclesiastical policy.

[38] For Ibas see Claudia Rammelt, *Ibas von Edessa. Rekonstruktion einer Biographie und dogmatischen Position zwischen den Fronten* (Berlin: de Gruyter, 2008). The council deposed Daniel and investigated Sophronius: according to the acts of Council of Ephesus, the decision about Sophronius was left to the new bishop of Edessa. According to the *Chronicle of Edessa* 63 the Council condemned him together with Ibas, Flavian, Domnus, Irenaeus of Tyre, Eusebius of Dorylaeum, Theodoret and Daniel of Harran (*Untersuchungen über die Edessenische Chronik*, ed. Ludwig Hallier, Texte und Untersuchungen zur Geschichte der altchristlichen Literatur 9.1 (Leipzig: J. C. Hinrichs, 1892), 111). If deposed, it was only temporary as Sophronius reappeared at the Council of Chalcedon as bishop of Tella/Constantina.

[39] *Acts of the Council of Ephesus 449*; *Akten der Ephesinischen Synode vom Jahre 449*, ed. and trans. Johannes Flemming (Berlin: Weidmannsche Buchhandlung, 1917): 69–73.

Tella of paganism, astrology, fortune-telling and Nestorianism that he "learned from his relative Ibas".[40] It is notable that not a single bishop at the Council regarded nepotism as an issue and brought up such charges against Ibas, nor were Ibas' kinsmen accused of incompetence because they earned the positions more to an influential relative than personal merits.[41]

If the *Apostolic Canons* had been a widely accepted collection, it seems likely that the council would have charged Ibas of acting against canon 76 as well.[42] However, the accusations against Ibas did include the misappropriation of church property for his clan – first of all in Edessa but supposedly also Sarug suffered.[43] As Ibas' brother is mentioned as well to be judged by Edessa's *boule*, the metropolitan obviously shared the profit of his elevated position with his family. Furthermore, the bishops accused Sophronius of heresy because being related to Ibas implied for the council members that he adhered to the same faith. This may be a likely – or, for the intentions of the accusers: convenient – conclusion but the case of the Cappadocians show that this was not necessary always the case. Basil the Great was not only estranged from his relative Atarbius of Neocaesarea because of theological quarrels but they actually broke off communion for good.[44]

The most distinguished bishop that the Council condemned in 449 was Domnus, patriarch of Antioch (442–449 CE) who had succeeded his uncle John (429–441 CE) as patriarch, and was condemned in 449 for opposition to Cy-

---

40 *Acts of the Council of Ephesus 449*, ed. and trans. Flemming, 80–81. Presbyter Simeon, his son as well as another relative of Simeon, the deacon Abraham, who all worked in the household of the bishop brought testimony concerning fortune telling against Sophronius: *Acts of the Council of Ephesus 449*, ed. and trans. Flemming, 80–81 (Simeon in the *libellus* is probably the presbyter Simeon who brought forth the accusation as he is otherwise not specified). Sophronius had a son, Habbib, who was accused of eating with Jews in the bishop's residence (*Acts of the Council of Ephesus 449*, ed. and trans. Flemming, 82–83).
41 Incompetence or lacking merits would be difficult to prove but considering the wide range of accusations brought up (most of which hardly had any factual basis), the plausibility of the charges were hardly an issue.
42 For the usage of the *Apostolic Canons* in Late Antiquity see Ohme, "Sources of the Greek Canon Law to the Quinisext Council (691/2)," 32–33.
43 *Acts of the Council of Ephesus 449*, ed. and trans. Flemming, 18–19; now discussed with a focus on finances and canonical proceedings by Thomas Graumann, "Synodale Praxis und administratives Handeln in der spätantiken Kirche: Einige Schlaglichter," in *Was ist Kirche in der Spätantike?* ed. Peter Gemeinhardt, Studien der Patristischen Arbeitsgemeinschaft 14 (Leuven: Peeters, 2017): 123–24 and 138–39.
44 Van Dam, *Friends and Family*, 27–28 and Thomas Graumann, *Die Kirche der Väter. Vätertheologie und Väterbeweis in den Kirchen des Ostens bis zum Konzil von Ephesus (431)* (Tübingen: Mohr Siebeck, 2002), 223.

ril's *Twelve Chapters* and "Nestorianism".[45] Cyril of Scythopolis reports that Domnus was a disciple of the famous Euthymius in the Holy Land.[46] It can therefore be assumed that he was a well-educated monk when elected patriarch. However, the acts are completely silent about Domnus' relationship with the former patriarch but surprisingly question the canonicity of Domnus' ordination from an unexpected angle: supposedly a high-ranking pagan, Isocasius, and people of questionable reputation favored Domnus but no bishop supposedly ordained him in a proper ordination ceremony.[47]

In other words, in Domnus' case nepotism was not only *not* an issue but it was even implicitly denied. The most likely reason for this was that Domnus' uncle had concluded the important union between Antioch and Alexandria in 433 with Cyril of Alexandria (412–444). If now a condemned heretic would be connected to John, this would not only blacken John's rule (the bishops at the Council of Ephesus II were fine with that!) but implicitly also make the venerated Cyril an accomplice of a questionable ally. It seems that the council attempted to avoid this by constructing an ordination that was questionable for other reasons.

4 The episcopal succession in Alexandria (373–451)

Cyril and his family present a (comparatively) well-documented case to analyze the succession of bishops and its implications for ecclesiastical politics. The see of Alexandria was next to Rome the most important see of ancient Christianity, and not only the names of all bishops are known but sometimes also information concerning their family relations. Sozomenos narrates that Athanasius of Alexandria (328–373) designated Peter II (373–380) as his successor who then "at his death appointed his brother Timothy (380–384) to succeed him."[48] The famous Athanasius as well as his successors were probably from modest backgrounds, and Timothy is remembered as being "without possessions" – maybe

---

[45] *Acts of the Council of Ephesus 449*, ed. and trans. Flemming, 146–151.
[46] Cyril of Scythopolis, *The Lives of the Monks of Palestine* 16 and 20, ed. Eduard Schwartz (Leipzig: J. C. Hinrichs 1939): 26 and 33; trans. Price, 21 and 29.
[47] This *libellus* is one of the texts charging Domnus with crimes that led to his condemnation: *Acts of the Council of Ephesus 449*, ed. and trans. Flemming, 126–129; for Isocasius, who later became the *quaestor sacri palatii*, and was a well-known pagan, see *PLRE* II, 633–34.
[48] If Peter was already ordained before Athanasius' death is not clear from the account: Sozomenos, *h.e.* 6.19 (ed. and trans. Hansen, 732–33); Socrates Scholasticus, *h.e.* 4.37 (ed. Hansen, 272; trans. *Nicene and Post-Nicene Fathers* 2.2, 117).

a reference to an ascetic background like Athanasius. Before being elevated to the throne of St Mark, the brothers Peter and Timothy were part of Athanasius' entourage to which probably also their successor Theophilus (384–412) belonged. According to later sources Theophilus was an orphan, brought together with his sister by a slave to Alexandria where he came into the custody of the church. Athanasius became aware of him, and enrolled him in the clergy. [49] Eva Wipszycka noted that the "sources never mention a bishop coming from any of Egypt's most powerful families (big landlords or higher state functionaries). It is true that the *argumentum ex silentio* is often deceptive, but in this case it can be taken seriously, for the amount of evidence on the church and the monastic milieu is enormous." [50]

This is clearly the case with the patriarchs of Alexandria in the two centuries from Constantine to Justinian, and although Theophilus is not as well-known as some other late antique patriarchs, he was the leading ecclesiastical figure of his time.[51] Theophilus was the first patriarch of Alexandria who earned himself the questionable fame of being compared to Pharaoh, later also used by Pope Leo (440–461) against Dioscorus.[52]

The Church also took care of Theophilus' sister, and, after having been married to a Christian husband, she became the mother of Theophilus' nephew Cyril. The medieval *History of the Patriarchs* narrates how Theophilus took care of his

---

[49] John of Nikiu, *Chronicle*, 79 (trans. Robert Henry Charles, 75–76). "Athanasius took him into his household and arranged for him to complete his studies under his supervision. As a highly intelligent Christian with no family ties, Theophilus could evidently be of service to the Church of Alexandria." Norman Russell, *Theophilus of Alexandria* (London: Routledge, 2007), 4; however, some parts of the orphan story may be legendary embellishment; see also Norman Russell, *Cyril of Alexandria* (London: Routledge, 2000), 4.

[50] Eva Wipszycka, *The Alexandrian Church. People and Institutions* (Warsaw: University of Warsaw and Raphael Taubenschlag Foundation, 2015), 114. Cf. also Arnold Hugh Martin Jones, *The Later Roman Empire 284–602*, Vol. 2 (Oxford: Basil Blackwell, 1964), 923–26 that bishops were usually not from the senatorial but from the middle class (*curiales*).

[51] Norman Russell, "Theophilus of Alexandria as a Forensic Practitioner", StPatr 50 (2011): 235–243, here 243; see also Russell's *Theophilus of Alexandria*.

[52] Sozomenos, *h.e.* 8.18 (ed. and trans. Hansen, 1016–17) narrates that John Chrysostom compared Theophilus to Pharaoh after his return from exile; see also Palladius' *Dialogue on the Life of John Chrysostom: Dialogue sur la vie de Jean Chrysostome* 6.62, ed. and trans. Anne-Marie Malingrey and Philippe Leclercq, Vol. 1, SC 341 (Paris: Éditions du Cerf, 1988), 132–33. In modern times, Edward Hardy picked up on this with his chapter on "The Pharaohs of the Church – Theophilus to Dioscorus"; Edward Rochie Hardy, *Christian Egypt: Church and People. Christianity and Nationalism in the Patriarchate of Alexandria* (New York: Oxford University Press, 1952).

nephew – as uncles were supposed to do.⁵³ The patriarch sent Cyril to the Nitrian desert, and entrusted him to Abba Serapion the Wise for five years to study in solitude.⁵⁴ Similarly, a few decades later John of Antioch may have sent his nephew Domnus to Saint Euthymius in Palestine although the sources are silent about how Domnus met Euthymius.⁵⁵

Cyril learned all the canonical books by heart, and after he returned to Alexandria, he stayed with his uncle and enjoyed a privileged relationship. However, this was not enough to allow a smooth succession after Theophilus' death in 412 as Socrates Scholasticus mentions riots that broke out in Alexandria over Theophilus' succession:

> A great contest immediately arose about the appointment of a successor, some seeking to place Timothy the archdeacon (ἀρχιδιάκονον) in the episcopal chair; and others desiring Cyril, who was a nephew of Theophilus. A tumult having arisen on this account among the people, Abundantius, the commander of the troops in Egypt, took sides with [Cyril].⁵⁶ Whereupon on the third day after the death of Theophilus, Cyril came into possession of the episcopate, with greater power than Theophilus had ever exercised. For from that time the bishopric of Alexandria went beyond the limits of its sacerdotal functions, and assumed the administration of secular matters.⁵⁷

In other words, the nephew competed for the succession of his uncle with the patriarch's archdeacon, a position that is often regarded as the springboard for the succession to the episcopal throne.⁵⁸ Cyril had the better end but appa-

---

53 Compare also the close-knit family relations of the Cappadocians where Basil the Elder teaches his supposed son-in-law; van Dam, *Friends and Family*, 18–22.
54 *History of the Patriarchs of the Coptic Church of Alexandria*, ed. and trans. Basil Evetts, *Patrologia Orientalis* 1 (1907), 383–518, here 427–28.
55 See above, pp. 29–30.
56 The manuscript (and also the nineteenth century translation; see n. 57) reads "Timothy" – not "Cyril". However, cf. Günther Christian Hansen's edition (*Sokrates: Kirchengeschichte*, ed. Hansen, 352–53) and Susan Wessel, "Socrates' Narrative of Cyril of Alexandria's Episcopal Election," *JThS* 52 (2000): 98–104.
57 ἐπιμάχου δὲ γενομένης καὶ ἐνταῦθα τῆς ἐπισκοπῆς οἱ μὲν ἐζήτουν ἐνθρονισθῆναι Τιμόθεον ἀρχιδιάκονον, οἱ δὲ Κύριλλον, ὃς ἦν ἀδελφιδοῦς Θεοφίλου. στάσεως δὲ διὰ τοῦτο μεταξὺ τοῦ λαοῦ κινηθείσης συνελαμβάνετο τῷ μέρει Κυρίλλου ὁ τοῦ στρατιωτικοῦ τάγματος ἡγεμὼν Ἀβουνδάντιος. διὸ τρίτῃ ἡμέρᾳ μετὰ τὴν τελευτὴν Θεοφίλου ὁ Κύριλλος ἐνθρονισθεὶς ἐπὶ τὴν ἐπισκοπὴν ἀρχικώτερον Θεοφίλου παρῆλθεν. καὶ γὰρ ἐξ ἐκείνου ἡ ἐπισκοπὴ Ἀλεξανδρείας πέρα τῆς ἱερατικῆς τάξεως καταδυναστεύειν τῶν πραγμάτων ἔλαβε τὴν ἀρχήν; Socrates, *h.e.* 7.7, trans. A. C. Zenos, in *Nicene and Post-Nicene Fathers* 2.2, 156 (modified).
58 For Rome see Bernhard Domagalski, "Der Diakonat als Vorstufe zum Episkopat," *StPatr* 29 (1997): 17–24, but close relations between bishop and their deacon is also attested for other sees like Alexandria. Bishops and deacons were earlier professionalized than presbyters which gave

rently only because he could rely on the support of the imperial army.⁵⁹ Contemporaries noted the kinship with Theophilus and expected that Cyril would continue the ecclesiastical politics of his uncle. Isidore of Pelusium warned Cyril in a letter that episcopal colleagues may believe he fought a personal vendetta against Nestorius of Constantinople because he was the nephew of Theophilus who had quarreled with the bishop of Constantinople, John Chrysostom, as well.⁶⁰ The insinuation that kinsmen continue the politics of their relatives is the same as in the case of Ibas of Edessa and his cousin Sophronius regarding Christology.

When Cyril died in 444, Dioscorus became his successor but his election may have been contentious as well. No contemporary sources survive but from the time of Dioscorus' downfall at the Council of Chalcedon in 451, Cyril's nephew as well as two other Alexandrian clerics who presented themselves as confidants of Cyril, and a layperson brought forth serious accusations against Dioscorus that shed some light on Cyril's succession in 444.

The first, Theodore, had been deacon in Alexandria for 15 years, and had accompanied Cyril to the Council of Ephesus I in 431 CE. He bitterly complained that

> Dioscorus, at the beginning of the episcopate that he obtained I know not how, expelled me from the clergy and threatened to drive me out of that great city, for no other reason than because I had been honoured with the friendship and favour of Cyril of sacred memory; for his plan was to chase out of that city, or even deprive of life, not only the members of Cyril's family but also all those who had been on familiar terms with him, whom he hated because of the orthodoxy of his [Cyril's] faith.⁶¹

---

deacons advantage over presbyters; see Georg Schöllgen, *Die Anfänge der Professionalisierung des Klerus und das kirchliche Amt in der syrischen Didaskalie* (Münster: Aschendorff, 1998). However, also presbyters could succeed their bishops; for Alexandria see for example Eusebius *h.e.* 7.11.26, stating that presbyter Maximus (bishop: 264–82) succeeded Dionysius (248–64) as bishop of Alexandria.

59 Considering his ruthlessness as patriarch, it is not surprising to see that already the early Cyril defeated a formidable competitor like his uncle's archdeacon.

60 Isidore of Pelusium, *ep.* 310 (*PG* 78, 361 C); obviously, Isidore knew that the cases of Nestorius and John Chrysostom were different.

61 ἐκτός με τοῦ κλήρου πεποίηκεν ἐν προοιμίοις τῆς οὐκ οἶδ' ὅπως ἔλαχεν ἐπισκοπῆς, ἀπειλήσας καὶ τῆς μεγάλης ἐκείνης διώκειν πόλεως δι' οὐδὲν ἕτερον εἰ μὴ διὰ τὸ τῆς οἰκειότητος καὶ εὐμενείας τοῦ τῆς ὁσίας μνήμης Κυρίλλου ἠξιῶσθαί με. σκοπὸς γὰρ αὐτῶι οὐ μόνον τοὺς ἀπὸ γένους αὐτοῦ ἐλάσαι ἐκείνης τῆς πόλεως ἢ γοῦν περιελεῖν τοῦ ζῆν, ἀλλὰ γὰρ καὶ τοὺς προσοικειωθέντας αὐτῶι, ἀπεχθανομένωι πρὸς τὴν ὀρθὴν ἐκείνου πίστιν; *ACO* 2.1.2, 212 (trans. Gaddis – Price II, 52).

According to his own words, Theodore had further ambitions and expected a more elevated position in the Church.[62] Another deacon, Ischyrion, who also claimed to have been a confidant of Cyril, and having being entrusted with many missions especially to Constantinople, accused Dioscorus for not only driving him out from the clergy but having sent monastics to burn down his property.[63] Like Theodore, he adds that he could also attest to the fact that Dioscorus was a heretic, and blasphemed against the Holy Trinity.

The third accusation comes from Cyril's nephew, Athanasius, a former priest in Alexandria, who narrates a longish complaint of his family's odyssey after Dioscorus dispossessed the whole Cyrillian family clan, and drove them out of the city – Athanasius, his brother Paul with his family as well as unspecified aunts. "In his [Cyril's] will he made when about to die he honoured his successor as bishop, whoever that might be, with many large legacies from his own estate, adjuring him in writing, by the venerable and awesome mysteries, to comfort his family and not to cause it any trouble."[64] Dioscorus turned the family houses into churches, and stripped Athanasius off his position as presbyter in the church of Alexandria. The extended family came to Constantinople but even there, Dioscorus had the government go after them and extract 1400 pounds of gold from them.[65] Athanasius confirmed his written statement in person, and added that Dioscorus had plotted and schemed against him for eight whole years. If taken at face value, the Cyrillian family clan and Dioscorus started to fight over Cyril's succession, his legacy and inheritance the year before Cyril's death in 443.[66]

---

62 *ACO* 2.1.2, 212 (trans. Gaddis – Price II, 52).
63 As he actually speaks of buildings in the plural and various fruit trees and land that was devastated, it seems to have been some kind of estate; *ACO* 2.1.2, 214–15 (trans. Gaddis – Price II, 55).
64 οὗτος μέλλων τελευτᾶν διαθήκας θέμενος ἐτίμησε τὸν μετ' αὐτὸν γενόμενον ἐπίσκοπον, ὅστις ἐὰν ᾖ, πλείστοις καὶ μεγάλοις λεγάτοις ἐκ τῆς ἰδίας ἑαυτοῦ ὑποστάσεως, ὁρκώσας τοῦτον ἐγγράφως κατὰ τῶν σεπτῶν καὶ φρικτῶν μυστηρίων ὥστε θάλψαι τὸ αὐτοῦ γένος καὶ ἐν μηδενὶ κάματον αὐτῶι παρασχεῖν; *ACO* 2.1.2, 216 (trans. Gaddis – Price II, 58).
65 Athanasius complained about hunger, destitution, strained circumstances so that he was "short of the necessities of life from every angle" because Dioscorus took everything from him and his family clan; *ACO* 2.1.2, 217–18 (trans. Gaddis – Price II, 59–60).
66 Athanasius makes the statement probably October 13th, 451 and Cyril died June 27th, 444, see John McGuckin, *Saint Cyril of Alexandria and the Christological Controversy. Its History, Theology, and Texts*, (Crestwood, NY: St Vladimir's Seminary Press, 2004), 123. Taking eight full years at face value would mean that ecclesiastical factions in Alexandria started to quarrel over Cyril's succession and inheritance more than eight months before Cyril's death.

Skipping here the account of the fourth accuser,[67] the record shows three ambitious members of the city's ecclesiastical elite who first of all lamented their own unfortunate fate. All three clerics could have realistically hoped (and actually *had* expected as Theodore confessed) to advance their ecclesiastical careers. The unmarried Athanasius may have even speculated to become his uncle's successor. Being exiled must have been particular hard for him because his family had ruled the city for almost 60 years. Considering both the requisition of buildings in Alexandria as well as the money that Dioscorus requested from him and the other clerics, the Cyrillian family clan and its minions had accumulated an enormous amount of wealth for themselves throughout Theophilus' and Cyril's tenures.[68] As in the case with Ibas, the bishop provided for the family clan which caused resentment among those community members not favored by the ruling family.

What is known about the successful candidate Dioscorus? According to Coptic hagiography of the sixth century, Dioscorus had accompanied Cyril as one of his junior secretaries to the first council of Ephesus, and later became deacon.[69] According to Liberatus of Carthage, Dioscorus was Cyril's archdeacon, and as such, in an excellent position to succeed Cyril as next patriarch.[70] The only contemporary sources for his accession to the throne of St Mark are a letter by Pope Leo (*ep.* 9) and one by Theodoret of Cyrrhus (*ep.* 60). While Leo's letter conveys no insight into Dioscorus' personality, Theodoret called the main characteristic of Dioscorus as having "humility" (ταπεινοφροσύνη).[71] Maybe Dioscorus had an ascetic background, as Zacharias Rhetor called him in the sixth century "a serene man and a champion (ἀγωνιστής)".[72]

---

[67] Sophronius, a layperson, accused Dioscorus to have intervened in secular legal affairs. Of course he also accused the patriarch of blasphemy as well as adultery etc.
[68] Late bishops may have regarded accumulated property as their personal bargain; see the example of Paul of Merida in Norton, *Episcopal Elections*, 207. See now also Graumann, "Synodale Praxis und administratives Handeln," 123–24.
[69] *A Panegyric on Macarius, Bishop of Tkôw. Attributed to Dioscorus of Alexandria* X, ed. and trans. D. W. Johnson, CSCO 415/416 (Louvain: Secrétariat du CorpusSCO, 1980), 78 (60).
[70] Liberatus, *Breviarium* x, in: *ACO* II.5, 113; note that at the time of the Council of Ephesus a certain Epiphanius was Cyril's archdeacon (*ACO* I.4, 222).
[71] Pope Leo pointed to the inferiority of the see of St Mark in comparison to the see of St Peter, and lectured the newly appointed bishop of Alexandria; Theodoret, *ep.* 60 (*Théodoret de Cyr, Correspondance*, Vol. 2, ed. and trans. Yvan Azéma (Paris: Éditions de CERF, 1964), 136–39). While scholars consider the letter to be friendly flattery, it might indicate a characteristic feature of Dioscorus.
[72] It might be a stereotypical compliment but more likely it refers to Dioscorus's orthodoxy (= a champion of faith) or to an ascetic/monastic context; Zachariah Rhetor, *h.e.* 3.1, ed. *Historia ec-*

Be this as it may, we can conclude that in 444 the succession to the throne of St Mark was again contentious. Like Timothy in 412, as archdeacon Dioscorus was not the undisputed candidate to succeed Cyril but the latter's family clan intended to play a major role. However, in contrast to Timothy in 412, Dioscorus had the better end and was elected patriarch – maybe because of his Christian virtues, or maybe because the sixty year-rule of one family had caused strong opposition and resentments. Dioscorus immediately secured his position by removing Cyril's clan and minions from the clergy, and repatriate their property to the church of Alexandria.

5 Conclusions

The material remains meager for any systematic treatment of episcopal families and nepotism in the Eastern Roman Empire.[73] Furthermore, I discussed here only a segment of roughly 100 years but it has been chosen exactly because we find in these years significant examples of episcopal families and nepotism in the narrative sources. Therefore, some tentative concluding remarks are possible.

1) If "episcopal (family) dynasties" mean bishops of the same family for more than two generations, they cannot be regarded a common feature of the ecclesiastical landscape in the Later Roman Empire. Maybe that changed dramatically in Gaul after the end of the Roman Empire but the sample of cases discussed here clearly indicate that episcopal families lasted for two generations only.

2) Nepotism as nepotism was never an issue: a pejorative connotation did not exist. If canon 76 of the *Apostles Canons* intended to rule out nepotism (although without specifically banning kinsmen from pursuing ecclesiastical careers), it does not seem to have been an empire-wide known or accepted canon. No imperial legislation concerning the prevention of clerical nepotism

---

clesiastica Zachariae Rhetori vulgo adscripta, Vol. 1, ed. Ernest W. Brooks, CSCO 83 (Paris: E Typographeo Reipublicae, 1919), 147 (*The Chronicle of Pseudo-Zachariah Rhetor. Church and War in Late Antiquity*, ed. Geoffrey Greatrex, trans. Robert R. Phenix and Cornelia B. Horn (Liverpool: Liverpool University Press, 2011), 99).

73 More kinsmen could be discussed among the fifth-sixth-century patriarchs in Alexandria but information is too limited to understand the specifics behind the elections; cf. Patriarch Timothy Aelurus (457–460; 475–77) had a nephew, Dioscorus who succeeded later as patriarch of Alexandria (516–17). Patriarch John Hemula (496–505) had a relative, John Niciotas, who immediately succeeded him as patriarch (505–516). See also Ewa Wipszycka, "Les élections épiscopales en Égypte aux VIe–VIIe siècles," in *Episcopal Elections in Late Antiquity*, eds. Johan Leemans et al., AKG 119 (Berlin: de Gruyter, 2011): 259–291.

is known. The trials in 449 against Ibas, Daniel and Sophronius included many made-up charges but nepotism was not brought up as possible misdemeanor. However, the enrichment of the episcopal family could cause resentments, probably depending on the scrupulousness of the ruling clan.

3) Kinship-bonds mattered – often probably not just for blood relatives but befriended families would mutually look after their offspring as the Cappadocians prove. Particularly in rural backwater areas, important offices and positions – and being bishop was arguably the most important office in many cities – may have been distributed among the most prominent families.[74] The importance that the family played in the ancient world was of course not exclusive to Christians but received a Christian context in the case of the episcopal office. The right pedigree helped potential candidates to be accepted as qualified candidate for the episcopate. Furthermore, the first episcopal office holder within a family could ensure that his younger relative received the best possible education, maybe also including exposure to asceticism as the examples of Theophilus-Cyril and John-Domnus indicate. The see holder functioned as mentor and provided the younger kinsman with an ecclesiastical position that would allow him to advance to the episcopal office himself one day.

4) However, even if an eastern bishop wished to appoint a blood relative as bishop in another see or designate him as his successor, his options may have been rather limited because of reproduction. Sophronius of Tella did have a son, and other married bishops are known from the East but remain exceptions.[75] While the fifth century Gallo-Roman aristocrat Sidonius Apollinaris complained that people objected to a monk becoming bishop as the monk-bishop would rather be helpful for their souls with a heavenly judge but not saving their bodies with an earthly judge, in the east, clerics with an ascetic background seemed to have been preferred candidates for episcopal appointments.[76] Maybe also imperial legislation that asked bishops to rely on monks if they are in need of clerics rather than taking candidates from the *curiales* did play a role here.[77]

---

74 Which may have led to clerical families in late antique/early Byzantine Armenia.
75 I am not aware of any empirical study on this issue.
76 Sidonius Apollinaris, *Ep.* 7.9.9; the decisive criterion for becoming bishop was *nobilitas*, not *humilitas*; Bernhard Jussen, "Über ‚Bischofsherrschaften' und die Prozeduren politisch-sozialer Umordnung in Gallien zwischen ‚Antike' und ‚Mittelalter'," *Historische Zeitschrift* 260 (1995): 673–718, here 706. Concerning ascetics in the East: we obviously only have information about a minority of bishops but they were often acclaimed for having practiced asceticism before being entrusted with the episcopal office.
77 *C. Th.* 16.2.32; see also Karl Leo Noethlichs, "Zur Einflussnahme des Staates auf die Entwicklung eines christlichen Klerikerstandes," *JbAC* 15 (1972): 136–153, here 145–46. See also Jones, *The Later Roman Empire*, Vol. 2, 927 for Constans' law on the clergy.

Monks could not have a family of their own, and therefore, when they became bishops, had to rely on their extended family for possible nepotism.[78] However, no source indicates that any of these episcopal families planned to establish a dynasty as this was the case with the hereditary patriarchate of the Church of the East since the fourteenth century. On the contrary, Gregory of Nazianzus did not even wish to become bishop in the first place. And although Basil of Caesarea who came from a prominent Cappadocian family had numerous siblings, hardly any married and no episcopal dynasty was established. Last but not least, Basil also shows that family quarrels could effectively prevent family nepotism.[79]

5) The case study of Alexandria indicates that it was impossible to establish a position within the Church that predetermined the succession to the episcopal throne. The succession of Theophilus – Cyril – Dioscorus, and their fights for the succession offer a glimpse on the archdeaconate as VIP-position to advance to the throne but it was not a given. Alexandria, and probably all major sees, had a pool of able candidates who competed with each other, and although a late bishop might have designated a successor, the designated candidate could fail to succeed, especially in times of doctrinal controversies. For example, it is highly unlikely that Rabbula, the miaphysite bishop of Edessa (411–435/36), designated the dyophysite Ibas as his successor. On the contrary, here it was probably not only a faction within the city that had opposed the former bishop and now succeeded with installing their own candidate, but it is seems likely that the patriarch of Antioch played a role in choosing Ibas as new bishop.[80]

6) In other words, different groups (including the extended family of the late bishop) within the civic communities and within the clergy competed, and if the factions within the city were unable to find a suitable solution, the framework of the empire always allowed for calling in external reinforcements. As nephew of Theophilus, Cyril had a privileged position at the time of his uncle's death but without imperial troops, the archdeacon Timothy might have succeeded in 412. For the time after the Council of Chalcedon in 451, some scholars perceive an antagonism between Alexandria and the Chalcedonian court in Constantinople but in fact, it was an Alexandrian cleric, Proterius, who called in the military for his own protection as patriarch.[81]

---

[78] Which in most known cases meant the sister's sons.
[79] For Basil's peculiar personality see van Dam, *Families and Friends*.
[80] As argued by Claudia Rammelt, "Bischofswechsel in Edessa zur Zeit der christologischen Auseinandersetzung," in *Episcopal Elections in Late Antiquity*, eds. Johan Leemans et al., AKG 119 (Berlin: de Gruyter, 2011): 499–513.
[81] Proterius had been priest or steward of the Church of Alexandria throughout the tenure of Dioscorus. In other words, he may have been a confidant of Dioscorus before turning on him;

This is in stark contrast to Bird's depiction of the Church of the East in nineteenth-century Kochanes which had established the institution of a hereditary patriarchate over centuries in an isolated environment without the competition of other qualified candidates. In the Eastern Roman Empire, no family could hope to completely eliminate competition between able clerics, nor could any major see exist in isolation from the rest of the empire.[82] At smaller sees, competition was certainly less fierce, and local benefactors and their family may have established themselves more easily but overall, various groups and interests – being that doctrinal questions or the advancement of personal careers – as well as an imperial framework prevented the prominent establishment of lasting family dynasties in the Later Roman Empire.

Bibliography

Primary Sources

Acta Conciliorum Oecumenicorum. Tomus Primus. Volumen Quartum. Ed. Eduard Schwartz. Berlin: de Gruyter, 1922–23.
Acta Conciliorum Oecumenicorum. Tomus Alter. Volumen Primum. Pars Alter. Ed. Eduard Schwartz. Berlin: de Gruyter, 1933.
Acta Conciliorum Oecumenicorum. Tomus Alter. Volumen Quintum. Ed. Eduard Schwartz. Berlin: de Gruyter, 1936.
Acta Conciliorum Oecumenicorum. Series Secunda. Volumen Secunda. Pars Quarta. Ed. Heinz Ohme. Berlin: de Gruyter 2013.
Akten der Ephesinischen Synode vom Jahre 449. Ed. and trans. Johannes Flemming. Berlin: Weidmannsche Buchhandlung, 1917.
Saint Basil. *The Letters*, Vol. 2. Ed. and Roy J. Deferrari. Loeb Classical Library. Cambridge, MA.: Harvard University Press, 1928.
Mrs Bishop (Isabella L. Bird). *Journeys in Persia and Kurdistan including a Summer in the Upper Karun Region and a Visit to the Nestorian Rayahs.* Vol. 2. London: John Murray, 1891.
Les Constitutions Apostoliques. Vol. 3. Ed. and trans. Marcel Metzger, SC 336. Paris: Éditions du Cerf, 1987.
Eusebius. *Kirchengeschichte.* Ed. Friedrich Winckelmann, GCS 6. Berlin: Akademie, 1999.
Gregory of Tours. *Gregorii Episcopi Turonensis Libri Historiarum X.* Ed. Bruno Krusch and Wilhelm Levison. Hannover: Hahn, 1951.

---

on the different sources for Proterius' status before becoming patriarch see Gereon Siebigs, *Kaiser Leo I.: Das oströmische Reich in den ersten drei Jahren seiner Regierung (457–460 n. Chr.)*, Vol. 1, (Berlin: de Gruyter, 2010), 111–112.

82 I have left aside here the question of legal obligations that influenced who joined the ranks of the church; see Noethlichs, "Zur Einflussnahme des Staates."

Inscriptiones Christianae urbis Romae septimo saeculo antiquiores: nova series Vol. 6. *Coemeteria in viis Latina, Labicana et Praenestina.* Ed. Antonio Ferrua. Rome: Pontificio Instituto di Archeologia Cristiana, 1975.
Inscriptiones Latinae Christianae Veteres. Vol. 1. Ed. Ernst Diehl. Berlin: Weidmann, 1925.
Palladius. *Dialogue sur la vie de Jean Chrysostome.* Vol. 1. Ed. and trans. Anne-Marie Malingrey and Philippe Leclercq, SC 341. Paris: Éditions du Cerf, 1988.
A Panegyric on Macarius, Bishop of Tkôw. Attributed to Dioscorus of Alexandria. Ed. and trans. D. W. Johnson, CSCO 415/416. Louvain: Secrétariat du CorpusSCO, 1980.
Sokrates. *Kirchengeschichte.* Ed. Günther Christian Hansen, GCS 1. Berlin: Akademie, 1995.
Sozomenos, *Historia Ecclesiastica*, 4 Vols. Ed. and trans. Günther Christian Hansen. Turnhout: Brepols, 2004.
Theodoret. *Kirchengeschichte.* Ed. Leon Parmentier & Günther Christian Hansen. 3rd edition Berlin: Akademie Verlag, 1998.
Théodoret de Cyr. *Correspondance*, Vol. 2. Ed. and trans. Yvan Azéma, SC 98. Paris: Éditions de CERF, 1964.
Vie de Sévère par Zacharie. Ed. M. A. Kugener. In *Patrologia Orientalis* 2 (1904), 1–115.
Zachariah Rhetor. *Historia ecclesiastica Zachariae Rhetori vulgo adscripta*, Vol. 1. Ed. Ernest W. Brooks, CSCO 83. Paris: E Typographeo Reipublicae, 1919.

Secondary Literature

Coakley, James F. "The Church of the East since 1914." *Bulletin of the John Rylands Library of Manchester* 78 (1996): 179–198.
Domagalski, Bernhard. "Der Diakonat als Vorstufe zum Episkopat." *StPatr* 29 (1997): 17–24.
Drijvers, Jan Willem. *Cyril of Jerusalem: Bishop and City.* Leiden: Brill, 2004.
Fedwick, Paul Jonathan. *The Church and the Charisma of Leadership in Basil of Caesarea.* STPIMS 45. Toronto: Pontifical Institute of Medieval Studies, 1979.
Gatier, Pierre-Louis. "Inscriptions grecques de Résafa." *Damaszener Mitteilungen* 10 (1998): 237–241.
Gautier, Pierre-Louis. "Les Inscriptions grecques." In *Resafa II. Die Basilika des Heiligen Kreuzes in Resafa-Sergiupolis*, edited by Thilo Ulbert, 161–169. Mainz: von Zabern, 1986.
Graumann, Thomas. *Die Kirche der Väter. Vätertheologie und Väterbeweis in den Kirchen des Ostens bis zum Konzil von Ephesus (431).* Tübingen: Mohr Siebeck, 2002.
Graumann, Thomas. "Synodale Praxis und administratives Handeln in der spätantiken Kirche: Einige Schlaglichter." In *Was ist Kirche in der Spätantike?*, edited by Peter Gemeinhardt, 117–143. Leuven: Peeters, 2017.
Greenwood, Timothy. "Armenia." In *The Oxford Handbook of Late Antiquity*, edited by Scott Fitzgerald Johnson, 115–141. Oxford: Oxford University Press, 2012.
Hardy, Edward Rochie. *Christian Egypt: Church and People. Christianity and Nationalism in the Patriarchate of Alexandria.* New York: Oxford University Press, 1952.
Heinzelmann, Martin. *Bischofsherrschaft in Gallien. Zur Kontinuität römischer Führungsschichten vom 4. bis zum 7. Jahrhundert. Soziale, prosopographische und bildungsgeschichtliche Aspekte.* Munich: Artemis, 1976.
Honigmann, Ernst. "Juvenal of Jerusalem." *DOP* (1950): 209–279.

Jones, Arnold Hugh Martin. *The Later Roman Empire 284–602*. Oxford: Basil Blackwell, 1964.

Jussen, Bernhard. "Über ‚Bischofsherrschaften' und die Prozeduren politisch-sozialer Umordnung in Gallien zwischen ‚Antike' und ‚Mittelalter'." *Historische Zeitschrift* 260.3 (1995): 673–718.

Marrou, Henri Irénée. "Le Dossier Épigraphique de l'Évêque Rusticus de Narbonne." *Rivista di Archeologia Cristiana* 3–4 (1970): 331–349.

McGuckin, John. *Saint Cyril of Alexandria and the Christological Controversy. Its History, Theology, and Texts*. Crestwood, NY: St Vladimir's Seminary Press, 2004.

Meredith, Anthon. *Gregory of Nyssa*. London: Routledge, 1999.

Noethlichs, Karl Leo. "Zur Einflussnahme des Staates auf die Entwicklung eines christlichen Klerikerstandes." *JbAC* 15 (1972): 136–153.

Norton, Peter. *Episcopal Elections 250–600. Hierarchy and Popular Will in Late Antiquity*. OCM. Oxford: Oxford University Press, 2007.

Ohme, Heinz. "Sources of the Greek Canon Law to the Quinisext Council (691/2). Councils and Church Fathers." In *The History of Byzantine and Eastern Canon Law to 1500*, edited by Wilfried Hartmann and Kenneth Pennington, 24–114. Washington, D.C.: Catholic University of America Press, 2012.

Pietri, Luce. "Das Hineinwachsen des Klerus in die antike Gesellschaft." In *Die Geschichte des Christentums. Religion, Politik, Kultur. Altertum Vol. 2. Das Entstehen der einen Christenheit (250–430)*, edited by Charles and Luce Piétri, 633–666. Freiburg: Herder, 1996.

Rammelt, Claudia. *Ibas von Edessa. Rekonstruktion einer Biographie und dogmatischen Position zwischen den Fronten*. Berlin: de Gruyter, 2008.

Rammelt, Claudia. "Bischofswechsel in Edessa zur Zeit der christologischen Auseinandersetzung." In *Episcopal Elections in Late Antiquity*, edited by Johan Leemans et al., 499–513. Berlin: de Gruyter, 2011.

Rapp, Claudia. *Holy Bishops in Late Antiquity. The Nature of Christian Leadership in an Age of Transition*. Berkeley: Berkeley University Press, 2005.

Rousseau, Philipp. *Basil of Caesarea*. Berkeley: University of California Press, 1994.

Russell, Norman. *Cyril of Alexandria*. London: Routledge, 2000.

Russell, Norman. *Theophilus of Alexandria*. London: Routledge, 2007.

Russell, Norman. "Theophilus of Alexandria as a Forensic Practitioner." *StPatr* 50 (2011): 235–243.

Schöllgen, Georg. *Die Anfänge der Professionalisierung des Klerus und das kirchliche Amt in der syrischen Didaskalie*. Münster: Aschendorff, 1998.

Schwaiger, Georg. "Nepotismus," *Lexikon des Mittelalters* 6 (1993), 1093–1094.

Siebigs, Gereon. *Kaiser Leo I.: Das oströmische Reich in den ersten drei Jahren seiner Regierung (457–460 n.Chr.)*. Berlin: de Gruyter, 2010.

Sotinel, Claire. "Le Recrutement des Évêques en Italie aux IVe et Ve siècles. Essai d'Enquête Prosopographique." In *Vescovi e Pastori in Epoca Teodosiana. In Occasione del XVI Centenario della Consacrazione Episcopale di S. Agostino, 396–1996*, 193–204. Rome: Institutum Patristicum Augustinianum, 1997.

Walter, Conrad and Steffen Patzold. "Der Episkopat im Frankenreich der Merowingerzeit." In *Verwandtschaft, Name und Soziale Ordnung (300–1000)*, edited by Steffen Patzold and Karl Ubl, 109–139. Reallexikon der Germanischen Altertumskunde 90. Berlin: de Gruyter, 2014.

Wessel, Susan. "Socrates' Narrative of Cyril of Alexandria's Episcopal Election." *JThS* 52.1 (2000): 98–104.
Wipszycka, Ewa. *Études sur le Chrstianisme dans l'Égypte de l'Antiquité tardive*. Rome: Institutum Patristicum Augustinianum, 1996.
Wipszycka, Ewa. "Les élections épiscopales en Égypte aux VIe–VIIe siècles." In *Episcopal Elections in Late Antiquity*, edited by Johan Leemans et al., 259–291. Berlin: de Gruyter, 2011.
Wipszycka, Ewa. *The Alexandrian Church. People and Institutions*. Warsaw: University of Warsaw and Raphael Taubenschlag Foundation, 2015.
Yarnold, Edward. *Cyril of Jerusalem*. London: Routledge, 2000.

Ariane Bodin
A New Approach to Ambrose of Milan's Kinship

Despite all the biographies written about Ambrose of Milan,[1] his family history remains something of an enigma, as the data available to us does not answer the entire scope of our questions. Until Neil McLynn's thesis, it was generally admitted that Ambrose of Milan was a relative of Symmachus. This paper aims at gathering all the data about Ambrose's family that is currently available to us, so as to pinpoint sources that suggest kinship between Ambrose and Symmachus. The intent behind establishing this connection is to provide a more detailed understanding of the relationships between two major political actors of the second half of the fourth century. The implications of this suggested kinship between Symmachus and Ambrose would be many. They would not only practice friendship in exchanging letters, but they would be members of the same family, avoiding to confront publicly. It would also show that several members of the prominent pagan and aristocratic family of Symmachus were already Christians, as early as in the first half of the fourth century. First of all, we shall start with a historiographical overview of Ambrose's family. We shall then examine Ambrose's social background and analyse the merits of the theory of his kinship to Symmachus.

---

[1] Jean-Rémy Palanque, *Saint Ambroise et l'empire romain. Contribution à l'histoire des rapports de l'Église et de l'État à la fin du quatrième siècle* (Paris: De Boccard, 1933); Angelo Paredi, *S. Ambrogio e la sua età* (Milan: Ampliata, 1960); Yves-Marie Duval, *Ambroise de Milan, XVIe centenaire de son élection épiscopale: dix études* (Paris: Études augustiniennes, 1974); Giuseppe Lazzati, *Ambrosius episcopus* (Milan: Vita e pensiero, 1976); Neil McLynn, *Ambrose of Milan: Church and Court in a Christian Capital* (Berkeley-Los Angeles: University of California Press, 1994); Hervé Savon, *Ambroise de Milan (340–397)* (Paris: Desclée, 1997); John Moorhead, *Ambrose. Church and Society in the Late Roman World* (London-New York: Longman, 1999).

1 A historiographical overview of Ambrose's family

According to the inscription found in the Milanese church of Saint Nazarius, the man who became bishop in 374 AD bore the name of *Aurelius Ambrosius*.[2] However, little is known about the life of Ambrose prior to his becoming a bishop. Giovanni Battista de Rossi considered in a rather logical manner that the *gentilicium Aurelius* borne by Ambrose came from the imperial *gentilicium* of Marcus Aurelius.[3]

1.1 Ambrose's birth

Ambrose was probably born early in 339 AD since he himself has stated that he was 53 years old in the letter 49,[4] which Jean-Rémy Palanque contends was written in 392 AD.[5] If this contention is correct, we can state that Ambrose was born in the year 339.

In an attempt to *provide more details* about his birth, we can rely on the *Vita* of Ambrose written by Paulinus the Deacon, which dates back to 412–422,[6] in which the author stated that "[a]nd so, when his father Ambrose was administering the prefecture of the Gauls, Ambrose was born."[7] Ambrose was born either when his father was serving at the court of Constantine II, or when he was administrating the provinces of Gauls, Britanny and Hispania, in the name of the

---

[2] ILCV¹ 1800 [= *Inscriptiones Latinae Christianae Veteres*, vol. 1, ed. Ernestus Diehl, inscription no 1800]: *Aur. Ambrosius episc.*

[3] Giovanni Battista de Rossi, "Osservazioni sul nome gentilizio Aurelius di S. Ambrogio e di S. Agostino," *Bulletino di Archeologia Christiana* 3 (1865): 15–16, 15.

[4] Ambrose of Milan, *Epistula* 49 (Maur. 5) 4, CSEL 82/2, ed. Otto Faller and Michaela Zelzer (Vienna: Hölder-Pichler-Tempsky, 1968), 55: *cum ad annum tertium et quinquagesimum iam perduxerim.*

[5] Palanque, *Saint Ambroise*, 480–481.

[6] Stéphane Gioanni, "Augustin, Paulin, Ennode et les origines de la mémoire d'Ambroise," in *La mémoire d'Ambroise de Milan. Usages politiques d'une autorité patristique en Italie (V^e–XVIIIe siècle)*, eds. Patrick Boucheron and Stéphane Gioanni (Rome: École française de Rome, 2015): 235–252, 237.

[7] Paulinus of Milan, *Vita Ambrosii* 3.1, ed. Antoon A. R. Bastiaensen, *Vite de santi* 3, ed. Christine Mohrmann, (Milan: Fondazione Lorenzo Valla: A. Mondadori, 1974), 56: *Igitur posito in administratione praefecturae Galiarum patre eius Ambrosio natus est Ambrosius*; translation Boniface Ramsay, *Ambrose* (London-New York: Routledge, 1997), 197.

Emperor as praetorian prefect of the Gauls. Nevertheless, the notion that Ambrose of Milan would have borne the name of his father is confronted by a major obstacle, in that in most cases only the eldest son would bear the father's name.

1.2 Ambrose's father

Indeed, Santo Mazzarino identified the father of Ambrose as the Uranius to whom Constantine II sent a directive to implement a law on February 3rd of 339.[8] This theory is based on two main factors: a straightforward comparison with the identity of Ambrose's older brother, Uranius Satyrus, as well as the chronological concordance between the possible position of Ambrose's father and the supposed year of Ambrose's birth. As a consequence, Santo Mazzarino holds that this man would have been called *Uranius* and would definitely be praetorian prefect of the Gauls under Constantine II.[9]

However, the exact name of Ambrose's father still eludes us, since he cannot possibly bear both the names of Ambrosius and Uranius. Santo Mazzarino's theory is very appealing for three reasons. According to Alan Cameron, "in the later empire a man was in most contexts called by only one of the often quite numerous names he might possess: and normally (if not invariably) by the last."[10] Ambrose's father would thus have been known as *Uranius*. As his father's first son, Uranius Satyrus would have inherited his father's name. Timothy Barnes considered Santo Mazzarino's theory to be "indisputable."[11] Still, we know that in Late Antiquity men did not systematically take on their fathers' *gentilicium*.[12] As a consequence, it is possible that Ambrose bore his mother's *gen-*

---

[8] Santo Mazzarino, *Storia Sociale del Vescovo Ambrogio* (Rome: "L'Erma di Bretschneider", 1989), 11 and 81.
[9] *Codex Theodosianus* 11.1.5, ed. Theodor Mommsen and Paul Meyer (Berlin: Weidmannos, 1954), 572: *Idem A. Ad. Uranium. Omnes omnino ad oblationem "pecuniarum" oportet urgueri. Lege enim nostra signatum est nec esse extraordinaria nec vocari, quae specialiter a provincialibus devotissimis conferenda sunt.*
[10] Alan Cameron, "The Date and Identity of Macrobius," *JRS* 56 (1966): 25–38, 26.
[11] Timothy Barnes, "The Election of Ambrose of Milan," in *Episcopal Elections in Late Antiquity*, eds. Johan Leemans, Peter Van Nuffelen, Shawn W. J. Keough and Carla Nicolaye (Berlin/Boston: De Gruyter, 2011): 39–59, 45.
[12] Ollies Salomies, "Réflexions sur le développement de l'onomastique de l'aristocratie romaine du Bas-Empire," in *Les stratégies familiales dans l'Antiquité tardive*, eds. Christophe Badel and Christian Settipani (Paris: De Boccard, 2012): 1–26, 5.

tilicium, which would then explain why Uranius Satyrus and Ambrose had different *gentilicia*.

Barnes further adds that "Ambrose could be a later gloss," since the name of the father is usually bestowed upon the elder son.[13] Santo Mazzarino and Barnes' theories are both very alluring, although as far as Barnes is concerned, the critical apparatus available to us does not support any evidence corroborating this hypothesis.

What is certain is that Ambrose was born in Trier, and his father was a member of the administration of the Praetorian prefect of the Gauls, and perhaps even the praetorian prefect himself. We can however agree on the importance of a reliable identification of Ambrose's father and therefore we tend to consider that Barnes' hypothesis, *i.e.* the name "Ambrose as a later gloss", would be highly satisfactory as it could be an easy way to reconstruct the family's onomastic.

1.3 The name Uranius

The name *Uranius*, which Ambrose's brother bore and which his father might have borne too, may hold the key to uncovering his family's background. The name *Uranius* may be proof he belonged to the *Urania* family. According to Christian Settipani, its members bore this very unique name because priesthood of the Phenician goddess Astarte (Urania) was hereditary in the family.[14] Zenobia the Palmyrian queen could well be an ancestor of Ambrose's, as she may have been the daughter or the niece of Iulius Aurelius Zenobius, kin to Palmyra and Emesa's Sun-priests. He could also have been related to Iulius Aurelius Uranius Antoninus, and may well be descended from the union between Cleopatra and Marc Anthony.[15]

Even if Ambrose considered himself a true Roman, his family could have had a Hellenistic background, and this theory is supported by his very name and his brother's *gentilicium*. Indeed, although the name of his father remains uncertain, the fate of Ambrose's father is well-known, despite the lack of mentions.

---

13 Barnes, "The Election," 46.
14 Christian Settipani, *Continuité gentilice et continuité familiale dans les familles sénatoriales romaines à l'époque impériale. Mythe et réalité* (Oxford: Unit of the prosopographical research, 2000), 438.
15 Settipani, *Continuité*, 436–440.

1.4 The death of Ambrose's father and its aftermath

Paulinus did not mention the death of Ambrose's father, but he may have been killed soon after the birth of his son Ambrose, either during the infamous ambush outside Aquileia in 340 AD, or disgraced and executed by Constans I.[16] As Timothy Barnes has stated, if Ambrose's father was acting as praetorian prefect of the Gauls, he would therefore have headed Constantine II's troops and died on the battlefield.[17]

Paulinus spoke neither of the disappearance of Ambrose's father nor of its consequences for his family. Paulinus omits the years elapsed after the death of his father altogether and only mentions that:

> Afterwards, in fact, when he had grown up and was living in Rome with his widowed mother and his sister (who had already professed her virginity and had another virgin as her companion, which virgin's sister was Candida, who had made the same profession and is now already an old woman living in Carthage).[18]

Just as Barnes did, we can suggest that Paulinus did not mention the aftermath of the death of Ambrose's father so as not to soil the memory of the son, who did not know his father and whose properties would have been seized by Constans I as an enemy of the new emperor.[19] This sentence by Paulinus is very enlightening. Indeed, Jean-Rémy Palanque understood that the widow of the possible praetorian prefect had left Trier and had headed back to Rome with her family where she had remained a widow.[20] However, there is no clear evidence indicating that this woman remained widowed for the rest of her days. She could have married again, which would explain why Ambrose never once mentioned his mother. Had she remained a widow, Ambrose would most likely have been as proud of his mother as he was of his famously virginal sister Marcellina[21] and

---

16 Arnold H. M. Jones, John R. Martindale and John Morris, eds., *The Prosopography of the Later Roman Empire, T. I (260–395)* (Cambridge: Cambridge University Press, 1971), 51.
17 Barnes, "The Election," 45.
18 Paulinus, *Vita Ambrosii* 4.1, ed. Bastiaensen, 54–56: *Postea vero, cum adolevisset, et esset in urbe Roma constitutus cum matre vidua et sorore, quae virginitatem iam fuerat professa, comite alia virgine– cuius virginis soror Candida et ipsa est eiusdem professionis, quae nunc Carthagine degit iam anus*; translation Ramsey, *Ambrose*, 197.
19 Barnes, "The Election," 48.
20 Palanque, *Saint Ambroise*, 4.
21 Ambrose of Milan, *Epistula* 77 (Maur. 22), *CSEL* 82/3, ed. Michaela Zelzer (Vienna: F. Tempsky, 1982), 126: *Dominae sorori vitae atque oculis praeferendae frater*; Ambrose of Milan, *De virginibus* 3.1, ed. Franco Gori (Milan-Rome: Cità Noua Editrice, 1989), 204: *Quoniam quae habuimus diges-*

of Sothera, an issue we will address later. Palanque suggested his mother was a pious Christian, as her Roman house was always filled with bishops whose hands she kissed, and because of Marcellina's veiling.[22] Regardless, at the time of Marcellina's veiling, Ambrose's mother was most certainly a widow.

What we do know for certain is that Ambrose was criticized since the Milanese priest Donatus is said to have "slandered the reputation of the bishop."[23] Furthermore, Bishop Muranus of Bolita in Africa is also known "slandering the holy man."[24] Paulinus wrote the life of Ambrose to protect his memory and so as to portray him as a saint. This means we have to be careful when reading Paulinus of Milan's life, even if the prosopographical sources such as the *Prosopographie chrétienne du Bas-Empire* takes his word for granted.[25]

The theory that the mother entered a second marriage could be supported further by the fact that Ambrose was a fierce opponent of second marriages. Remarriages were widely rejected by the Church fathers, particularly by figures such as Jerome of Stridon, Zenon of Verona, John Chrysostom and Ambrose of Milan. They are well known for arguing that a mother who remarries is likely to neglect the children born from the first union.[26] Indeed, in 377 AD the Milanese bishop condemned the widowed mothers who marry again, in his *De viduis*:

> And what advice shall I give to you who have children? What reason have you for marrying? Perhaps foolish light-mindedness, or the habit of incontinence, or the consciousness of a wounded spirit is urging you on. But counsel is given to the sober, not to the drunken, and so my words are addressed to the free conscience which is whole in each respect. [....] You wish to give birth to offspring who will be not the brothers but the adversaries of your children. For what is to bring forth other children other than to rob the children

---

simus superioribus libris duobus, tempus est, soror sancta, ea quae mecum conferre soles beatae memoriae Liberii praecepta revoluere, ut quo uir sanctior eo sermo accedat gratior. Namque is, cum Saluatoris natali ad apostolum Petrum virginitatis professionem vestis quoque mutatione signares.

22 Palanque, *Saint Ambroise*, 8; Paulinus, *Vita Ambrosii* 4.1, ed. Bastiaensen, 58: *[...] cum videret sacerdotibus a domestica, sorore, vel matre manus osculari;* translation Ramsey, *Ambrose*, 197: "he would see his sister and his mother's servant girl kissing the hands of bishops".

23 Paulinus, *Vita Ambrosii* 54.1, ed. Bastiaensen, 120–122: *Donatus [...] detraheret memoriae Sacerdotis*.

24 Paulinus, *Vita Ambrosii* 54.2, ed. Bastiaensen, 122: *tunc Murano episcopo detrahenti Sancto viro*.

25 Charles and Luce Pietri, eds. *Prosopographie chrétienne du Bas Empire, 2, Prosopographie de l'Italie chrétienne (314–604)*, vol. 1 (Rome, École française de Rome, 1999), 104; Jones, Martindale and Morris, *Prosopography*, 51.

26 Michel Humbert, *Le remariage à Rome: étude d'histoire juridique et sociale* (Milan: Giuffrè, 1972), 238; Dominique Lhuillier-Martinetti, *L'individu dans la famille à Rome au IVe siècle d'après l'œuvre d'Ambroise de Milan* (Rennes: PUR, 2008), 183–184.

which you have, who are deprived alike of the offices of affection and of the profit of their possessions.[27]

Ambrose may even have been influential in the implementation of the Theodosian law code of January 21st, 390 AD which stated that mothers could only serve as their own children's guardians provided they declare they would not remarry.[28] This clear opposition to second marriages could be a reflection of Ambrose's personal experience, as well as those of Marcellina and Satyrus.

To summarize, we can assert that Ambrose was born before 340 AD, since his father passed away in this very year. Later on, at an unknown date, his mother fled Trier with her three children in order to go to Rome. We can also take for granted that his father, whose name remains unknown to this day, served at the praetorian prefecture. His mother also remains somewhat of a cypher. We know Ambrose's father died young and left behind a widow and three children: a girl

---

[27] Ambrose of Milan, *De viduis* 15.88, ed. Franco Gori (Milan-Rome: Biblioteca Ambrosiana, 1989), 316–318: *Nam tibi quid consilii tribuam, quae liberos habes? Quae tibi causa nubendi? Forte levitatis error, et intemperantiae usus, et saucii cogit pectoris conscientia. Sed consilium sobriis, non ebriis datur; et ideo apud liberam conscientiam mihi sermo est, cui utrumque integrum est. [...] Generare liberos vis, non fratres futuros tuorum, sed adversarios filiorum. Quid est ergo generare alios liberos, nisi spoliare quos habes liberos: quibus pariter auferuntur et pietatis officia, et compendia facultatum?* Translated by Augustus Henry Eugene de Romestin, Eugene de Romestin and Henry Thomas Forbes Duckworth. *Nicene and Post-Nicene Fathers*, Second Series, Vol. 10, eds. Philip Schaff and Henry Wace (Buffalo-New York: Christian Literature Publishing Co., 1896), 406–407.

[28] *Codex Theodosianus* 3.17.4, ed. Mommsen and Meyer, 159–160: *IDEM AAA. TATIANO P(RAEFECTO) P(RAETORI)O. Matres, quae amissis viris tutelam administrandorum negotiorum in liberos postulant, priusquam confirmatio officii talis in eas iure veniat, fateantur actis ad alias se nubtias non venire. Sane in optione huiuscemodi nulla cogitur, sed libera in condiciones quas praestituimus voluntate descendat; nam si malunt alia optare matrimonia, tutelas filiorum administrare non debent. Sed ne sit facilis in eas post tutelam iure susceptam inruptio, bona eius primitus, qui tutelam gerentis affectaverit nubtias, in obligationem venire et teneri obnoxia rationibus parvulorum praecipimus, ne quid incuria, ne quid fraude depereat. His illud adiungimus, ut mulier, si aetate maior est, tum demum petendae tutelae ius habeat, cum tutor legitimus defuerit vel privilegio a tutela excusetur vel suspecti genere submoveatur vel ne suis quidem per animi aut corporis valetudinem administrandis facultatibus idoneus inveniatur. Quod si feminae tutelas refugerint et praeoptaverint nubtias neque quisquam legitimus ad pares possit causas vocari, tunc demum vir inlustris praefectus urbi adscito praetore, qui inpertiendis tutoribus praesidet, sive iudices, qui in provinciis iura restituunt, de alio ordine per inquisitionem dari minoribus defensores iubebunt. DAT. XII KAL. FEBR. MEDIOL(ANO) VALENT(INIANO) A. IIII ET NEOTERIO CONSS.*

named Marcellina and two boys, the older called Uranius Satyrus, and the younger, Ambrose.[29] Neither of them ever married nor had any issue.

Neil McLynn posited that Ambrose's family did not come from the upper echelons of the senatorial ranks.[30] Peter Brown confirmed McLynn's theory, stating that "[u]nlike Symmachus, Ambrose did not represent old money."[31] According to them, Ambrose of Milan would have been no more than a man belonging to the rich and late Roman Christian nobility. However this notion is not based on any straightforward evidence.

2 The social background of Ambrose

As stated earlier, Ambrose was unable to summon any memory of his father, probably for a twofold reason. First, he never knew him, since he died when Ambrose was still so young, and second, his father might have died a traitor, meaning his properties would have been seized by the new emperor Constans I. Despite the fact that Ambrose never disclosed any information about his parents, Marcellina's life can be used to shed light on the family's networks.

2.1 Marcellina's life in Rome

Between December of 352 and January of 355 AD,[32] Marcellina took a vow of perpetual virginity in the presence of Pope Liberius. She lived as a virgin in her mother's *domus*, with Candida's sister. According to Paulinus, their house was a favourite among priests and bishops (*Vita Ambrosii* 4). We also know that Marcellina belonged to the Roman virgin Asella's network, as Asella received a letter from Jerome of Stridon in August of 385 AD asking her to give his salutations to several virgins and widows, including a woman named Marcellina.[33] Neil Adkin

---

[29] Ambrose states explicitly that he was younger than Satyrus, who was younger than Marcellina, who survived him. Ambrose of Milan, *De Excessu Fratris* 1.54, CSEL 73, ed. Otto Faller (Vienna: Hoelder-Pichler-Tempsky, 1955), 238: *Quis igitur non miretur virum inter fratres duos alterum virginem, alterum sacerdotem, aetate medium.*
[30] McLynn, *Ambrose*, 1994, 31.
[31] Peter Brown, *Through the Eye of a Needle. Wealth, the Fall of Rome, and the Making of Christianity in the West, 350–550* (Oxford: Princeton University Press, 2012), 123.
[32] Barnes, "The Election," 42.
[33] Jerome of Stridon, *Epistula* 45.7, trans. Jérôme Labourt, *Jérôme: Lettres (Epistulae)*, tom. 2 (Paris: Les Belles Lettres, 1951), 100: *Saluta Paulam et Eustochium – uelit nolit mundus in Christo*

states that she could not possibly have been Ambrose's sister as Jerome was feuding with Ambrose from 384 AD onwards.³⁴ However, Jerome and Ambrose had many enemies and Marcellina, although she loved her brother, had to make a life for herself in the Christian environment of Rome. She could have had to visit people who disliked her brother. Moreover, Jerome was not particularly friendly towards Marcellina. He merely mentioned her as being a sister, which is not the most affectionate of titles. It simply meant that she adopted the *sanctum propositum*. In one way or another, Marcellina had to frequently see Asella or Marcella.

Marcellina could very well have lived in Rome together with her aristocratic cousins, with whom she lived the perfect life. Even though we know very little about Ambrose's life, Ambrose nonetheless mentioned having an aristocratic ancestor named Sothera.

2.2 Ambrose and the virgin Sothera: An aristocratic ancestor?

Ambrose claimed to be descended from Sothera, a young girl martyred in February 304 AD, under the reign of Emperor Diocletian. Instead of taking pride in their shared lineage and underlining it, Ambrose chose to praise her choice to give precedence to Christianity rather than nobility.³⁵ Ambrose regularly mocked aristocrats who prided themselves of their nobility, since it is merely a family inheritance rather than a personal virtue.³⁶ However, Neil McLynn considers that

---

meae sunt –, *saluta matrem Albinam sororesque Marcellas, Marcellinam quoque et sanctam Felicitatem.*
34 Neil Adkin, "Is the Marcellina of Jerome Ep. 45.7 Ambrose's sister?," *Phoenix* 45 (1995): 68–70, 69.
35 Ambrose of Milan, *Exhortatio virginitatis* 12.82, ed. Franco Gori (Milan-Rome: Cità Noua Editrice, 1989), 262: *At non sancta Soteris, ut domesticum piae parentis proferamus exemplum (habemus enim nos sacerdotes nostram nobilitatem praefecturis et consulatibus praeferendam; habemus, inquam, fidei dignitates, quae perire non norunt).*
36 Ambrose of Milan, *De Nabuthae* 13.54, CSEL 32 (2), ed. Charles Schenkl (Prague-Vienne-Leipzig: F. Tempsky, 1897), 499: *quid te iactas de nobilitatis prosapia? soletis et canum vestrorum origines sicut divitum recensere, soletis et equorum vestrorum nobilitatem sicut consulum praedicare. ille ex illo patre generatus est et ex illa matre editus, ille auo illo gaudet, ille se proauis adtollit. sed nihil istud currentem iuvat; non datur nobilitati palma, sed cursui. deformior est victus, in quo et nobilitas periclitatur. cave igitur, dives, ne in erubescant tuorum merita maiorum, ne forte et illis dicatur: 'cur talem instituistis, cur talem elegistis heredem?' non in auratis laquearibus nec in porphyrectis oribus heredis est meritum.*

this family link cannot be taken for granted, because it would be highly unusual for such a noble girl to go ignored by the Roman and Christian aristocracy.[37] Cécile Lanéry does not even mention McLynn's theory, implying that this connection is trust worthy.[38]

Nevertheless, a cult to the martyr Sothera was consecrated inside the Appian cemetery. Constantine I even erected the Basilica Apostolorum over the catacombs of San Sebastiano, on the Appian way. Located around the basilica, the cemetery of the Appian way was the focal point of early Christian worship. A circular mausoleum was discovered there, bearing inscriptions that recorded burials as early as the 340s AD. Among these, one inscription helped identify the owner of this monument. Written in fairly tall letters (0,28 m high), it reads *Urani* (the rest has faded).[39] According to Marucchi, it could stand for *Uraniorum makari*.[40] As it is located close to Sothera's resting place, this mausoleum may have belonged to Ambrose's family on his father's side. Cécile Lanéry suggested that the mausoleum housing Ambrose's family, on the *Aurelii*'s side, lies also on the Appian way.[41]

This monument may demonstrate that his family has Roman roots through the paternal branch. Furthermore, when Ambrose was a young man, he lived and studied in Rome. He also most certainly considered himself to be a Roman from Rome.[42] Regardless, we know that his family had extensive connections outside the *Vrbs* as well as inside.

---

[37] McLynn, *Ambrose*, 34.
[38] Cécile Lanéry, *Ambroise de Milan Hagiographe* (Paris: Collection des Études augustiniennes, 2008), 121.
[39] Carlos Machado, "Roman aristocrats and the Christianization of Rome," in *Pagans and Christians in the Roman Empire: The Breaking of a Dialogue*, eds. Rita Lizzi Testa and Peter Brown (Münster: Lit-Verlag, 2011): 493–516, 497–498.
[40] Horace Marucchi, *Éléments d'archéologie chrétienne, t. II. Itinéraire des Catacombes* (Paris-Rome: Desclée, Lefebre & Cie, 1900), 185.
[41] Lanéry, *Ambroise*, 121.
[42] Paulinus, *Vita Ambrosii* 9.4, ed. Bastiaensen, 64: *Igitur post annos aliquot ordinationis suae ad urbem Romam, hoc est, ad proprium solum, perrexit ibique sanctam puellam, de qua supra memoravimus, cui manum offerre solitus erat, in domo propria cum germana, sicut reliquerat, invenit, iam matre defuncta;* translation Ramsey, *Ambrose*, 199: "A few years after his ordination he went to the city of Rome – in other words, to his own home – and there in his own house he found the holy servant girl, whom we previously mentioned, to whom he used to offer his hand, along with his sister, just as he had left them. (His mother had died meanwhile.)"

2.3 The geographic background of Ambrose's family

Even if we know extremely little about Ambrose's family, his close relatives were Christians. Indeed, his mother always hosted plenty of clerics at her Roman *domus*. Then, there is the matter of his sister being a consecrated virgin. Moreover, the *cognomen* borne by Ambrose's brother, Uranius Satyrus, echoes that of Saturus, one of the martyrs persecuted along with the matrona Perpetua and her slave Felicity in Carthage in 203 AD. It may also suggest that Ambrose's family had some roots in Africa. As a matter of fact, we do know that the family owned a few estates in Africa and Sicily.[43] Just like Yves-Marie Duval suggested, Ambrose's family could have had some properties and other interests around the area of Cherchell in Mauretania.[44] Furthermore, as soon as Ambrose was elected bishop in 374 AD, his brother Uranius Satyrus went to Africa to collect a debt that a man called Prosper had contracted towards Ambrose and that he did not wish to repay.[45] Symmachus recommended Uranius Satyrus to his brother, the African vicarius Celsinus Titianus.[46] We also happen to know that in 377 AD, a number of young African girls from Mauretania lived in Milan.[47] These African estates might have been owned by Ambrose's mother, since the father's possessions were most likely seized after his hypothetical execution or death in battle. Moreover, through reading the *Life of Ambrose*, we are already aware that an old virgin by the name of Candida, who lived in Carthage at the time when the *vita* was written, had a sister who lived in Rome with Marcellina and whose identity is unknown.[48] It is common knowledge that after 410 AD, a lot of aristocrats or

---

[43] Ambrose of Milan, *De Excessu fratris* 1.17, ed. Faller, 218: *quod amantissimi fratris ex Siculis Africanisve regionibus exoptatum nobis reditum contulisti*.
[44] Yves-Marie Duval, "L'influence des écrivains africains du IIIe siècle sur les écrivains chrétiens de l'Italie du nord dans la seconde moitié du IVe siècle", in *Aquileia e l'Africa, Antichità altoadriatiche* 5, 191–225 (Udine: Arti grafiche friulane, 1974); McLynn, *Ambrose*, n. 67, 71.
[45] Ambrose of Milan, *De Excessu fratris* 1.24, ed. Faller, 222–223: *Plaudebat sibi, ut audio, Prosper, quod sacerdotii mei occasione redditurum se, quae abstulerat, non putabat: sed vehementiorem tuam unius efficaciam expertus est, quam duorum. Itaque solvit omnia, nec moderationi ingratus tuae, nec illudens pudori, sed et modestiae gratus nec insolens efficaciae. Sed cui, frater, illa quaesisti?*
[46] Symmachus, *Epistula* 1.63, Letttres, t. 1, trans. Jean-Pierre Callu (Paris: Les Belles Lettres, 1972), 121.
[47] Ambrose of Milan, *De virginibus* 1.59, ed. Ignazio Cazzaniga (Turin: In aedibus Io. Bapt. Paraviae, 1948), 30–31: *Contuemini quam dulcis pudicitiae fructus sit, qui barbaricis quoque inolevit affectibus. Ex ultimis infra ultraque Mauritaniae partibus deductae virgines hic sacrari gestiunt; et cum sint omnes familiae in vinculis, pudicitia tamen nescit esse captiva.*
[48] Paulinus, *Vita Ambrosii* 4.1, ed. Bastiaensen, 54–56: *Postea vero, cum adolevisset, et esset in urbe Roma constitutus cum matre vidua et sorore, quae virginitatem iam fuerat professa, comite*

noble Romans left the *Vrbs* to take refuge in Africa. We know for certain that Candida was the name given to a Roman martyr,[49] and we can suggest that this unknown virgin, Candida, could have come from Africa, since her name was borne by several other martyrs such as a Carthaginian martyred virgin who died who died under the rule of Emperor Maximian, on the 20th of September, in the beginning of the fourth century.[50] Yet another Candida was martyred in Mauretania on the 2nd of December, along with ten men and nine other women.[51] This is intriguing since we know that under the bishopric of Ambrose, a few Mauretanian virgins lived in Milan. Candida could also have lived in Milan along with these Mauretanian virgins around 377 AD and moved back to Africa after 410.

We know that Ambrose's family had many interests in Africa, which could shed light on a possible African background on the mother's side, since it is almost certain that Ambrose, his brother and his sister could not have inherited any of their father's estate. We are aware that Ambrose owned properties in Sicily as well. Interestingly enough, Symmachus' family, one of the great pagan families of Rome, also owned estates in Italy, Sicily, Africa and Mauretania Caesariensis.[52] Even if Ambrose's status as a member of Symmachus' family has recently been contested, a number of elements can be used to further substantiate this hypothesis.

---

alia virgine– cuius virginis soror Candida et ipsa est eiusdem professionis, quae nunc Carthagine degit iam anus.

49 *Candida 6*, in *Dictionnaire d'histoire et de géographie ecclésiastiques*, ed. Alfred Baudrillart, T. XI, (Paris: Letouzey et Ané), 1949, 726.

50 *Bibliotheca Hagiographica Latina Antiquae et Mediae Aetatis* 1537, ed. Socii Bollandiani (Brussels: Via dicta des "Ursulines", 1898–1899), 230; *Acta Sanctorum septembre VI* (Brussels-Anvers: Société des Bollandistes, 1867), 104: *Carthagine sanctae Candidae, virginis et martyris, quae sub Maximiano Imperatore plagis toto corpore dilacerata, martyrio coronatur*. But several researchers doubt of the veracity of this Vita: *Candida 4*, in *Dictionnaire d'histoire et de géographie ecclésiastiques*, ed. Alfred Baudrillart, T. XI, (Paris: Letouzey et Ané, 1949), 724–725.

51 *Candida 9*, in *Dictionnaire d'histoire et de géographie ecclésiastiques*, ed. Alfred Baudrillart, vol. 9, (Paris: Letouzey et Ané, 1949), 726; *Martyrologium Hieronymianum*, ed. Giovanni Battista de Rossi and Louis Duchesne (Brussels: Acta Sanctorum, 1894), II nov. 1a, 150: *Nonas dec civi togora nt iuli potamiae crispinae et alioru | vii . in misita nt crispini in aff humili felicis eracli misi victo | ris trofimi serapioni et alioru viii. candonani pauli marci | sussi privati fulgenti matronae feladi scae mariæ! et alibi amanti epi.*

52 We have many letters written by Symmachus concerning the estates administered by his family: Symmachus *Epistula* 3.23, *Lettres, t. 2*, trans. Jean-Pierre Callu (Paris: Les Belles Lettres, 1982), 35–36; *Epistula* 5.87, tr. Callu, 219; *Epistula* 6.81, *Lettres, t. 3*, trans. Jean-Pierre Callu (Paris: Les Belles Lettres, 1995), 46; *Epistula* 7.66, tr. Callu, 80; *Epistula* 9.130, *Lettres, t. 4*, trans. Jean-Pierre Callu (Paris: Les Belles Lettres, 2002), 55.

3 Ambrose's kinship with Symmachus

A family link between Ambrose and Symmachus has already been suggested. According to Giovanni Battista de Rossi, Ambrose and Symmachus were related through Aurelius Celsinus, who was the urban prefect of Rome in 341 AD and may have been an uncle to Symmachus' father, Lucius Aurelius Avianius Symmachus Phosphorius.[53] Unfortunately, he does not offer a basis for his claim.

3.1 The sources suggesting this theory

Symmachus belonged to Ambrose's episcopal network. *Amicitia* was essential for participation in late antique society. As a consequence, eight letters were written by Symmachus and sent to Ambrose,[54] attempting recommendations, but they do not provide any information regarding their kinship, or lack thereof. Unfortunately, Ambrose's answers are missing.

Just like Ambrose, Symmachus is related to the *gens Aurelia*, but there is no point in suggesting a connection between these two men as a great number of Romans had borne the *gentilicium Aurelius* since the year 212 AD. Be that as it may, we do know that Symmachus inherited his *gentilicium* through his father.[55]

In *Letter* 1.63, Symmachus wrote to his own brother Celsinius Titianus and mentioned Uranius Satyrus as being their "common brother."[56] However, aristocratic conventions can be highly ambiguous when it comes to describing family bonds. The meaning of the term *frater* is quite broad and may refer to a brother, a half-brother, a cousin or even a brother-in-law.[57] Archie C. Bush and Steven Cerutti posited that *frater* could stand for a cousin, a husband or a lover, whereas J. P. Wilson convincingly demonstrated that it necessarily indicated a family link, either that of brother or cousin.[58] And yet Neil McLynn considers that this expression does not prove any actual kinship between Symmachus and Ambrose. McLynn shows, for instance, that Symmachus regularly used the term *frater*, even when he had absolutely no blood ties with the people whom he was refer-

---

53 Giovanni Battista de Rossi, "Osservazioni," 15. See figure 1, family tree.
54 Symmachus, *Epistulae* 3.30–37, tr. Callu, 41–45.
55 Family Tree 1.
56 Symmachus, *Epistula* 1.63, tr. Callu, 12: *nostras Saturus frater communis*.
57 Settipani, *Continuité*, 13.
58 Archie C. Bush, Steven Cerutti, "A Use of the Term *Frater* in *Pro Caelio*," *CJ* 82 (1) (1986): 37–39; Joseph P. Wilson, "Three Non-Uses of Frater in *Pro Caelio* 32," *CJ* 83 (3) (1988): 207–211.

ring to.⁵⁹ McLynn's arguments are perfectly sensible since the term *frater* is indeed often used by a senator when he addresses another member of the Senate. Symmachus is no exception in this regard, and frequently used the term to establish equal standing with another man.⁶⁰ When reading the correspondence of Symmachus as translated by Jean-Pierre Callu, we come across 103 times the word *frater*. Notwithstanding, when referring to an actual brother, Symmachus seems to always go back and forth between the terms *germanus* and *frater* within the same missive.⁶¹ But in some letters sent to his own daughter and to Nicomachus Flavianus, his step-son, *frater* is used to mean both step-brother and brother.⁶² However, in two instances the reference to a "brother" seems dubious as far as blood relations are concerned. In his *Letter* 7.109 sent to Petronius, Symmachus is seemingly talking about Petronius' brother.⁶³ Through *Letter* 8.57,⁶⁴ we learn that Flavius Pisidius Romulus and Valerius are related, but we cannot be more specific when it comes to the nature of their kinship. As a consequence, *Letter* 1.63 is not particularly helpful in clearing up the exact nature of Ambrose and Symmachus' family bond.

Luckily, the analysis of Ambrose's own corpus yields more meaningful results. The main sources dealing with Ambrose's life are the *De Excessu fratris*, written by Ambrose of Milan himself after the death of his beloved brother Uranius Satyrus in 378 AD, as well as the *Vita Ambrosii* of Paulinus of Milan. In the *De Excessu fratris*, Ambrose states that his brother, Uranius Satyrus, is related to "Symmachus, your kinsman."⁶⁵ If we look at Ambrose's correspondence, it appears that the term *parens* is used 39 times by the bishop, and it always describes either a religious filiation⁶⁶ or a genuine family link. We can divide the family links that *parens* stands for according to Ambrose's letter into six distinct categories. Twenty-eight occurrences of the term *parens* refer to an ancestor, a

---

59 McLynn, *Ambrose*, 262.
60 Mireille Corbier, "Épigraphie et parenté," in *Épigraphie et histoire: acquis et problèmes. Actes du congrès de la Société des professeurs d'histoire ancienne, Lyon-Chambéry, 21–23 mai 1993*, eds. Yann Lebohec and Yves Roman (Lyon: De Boccard, 1998): 101–152, 117.
61 Symmachus, *Epistula* 1.46, tr. Callu, 111: *germanus meus / frater*; *Epistula* 4.30, tr. Callu, 112: 2. *excelsi germani tui / frater*; *Epistula* 5.16, tr. Callu, 165: *Sancto Lampadio germano tuo /Fratre meo praefecto*.
62 Symmachus *Epistula* 6.26, tr. Callu, 17; *Epistula* 6.34, tr. Callu, 22; *Epistula* 6.35, tr. Callu, 22; *Epistula* 6.37, tr. Callu, 23.
63 Symmachus *Epistula* 7.109, tr. Callu, 101.
64 Symmachus, *Epistula* 8.57, tr. Callu, 140.
65 Ambrose of Milan, *De Excessu fratris* 1.32, ed. Faller, 227: [...] *Symmacho, tuo parente*.
66 In one case only: Ambrose of Milan, *Epistula* 75 (Maur. 21), 14, ed. Zelzer, 79.

father or a mother.[67] One mention pertains to a childminder.[68] Ambrose ends his letters by stating that he loves his addressee as a father loves his son six times[69]. The term *parens* can also mean a step-brother,[70] a family as a whole,[71] or an individual member of a family.[72] As a consequence, it seems that for Ambrose, *parens* always refers to a member of the same family. If Ambrose and Symmachus both practiced *amicitia*, it is striking that the terms they used do not describe the same reality. Symmachus uses the vocabulary of family relationships to describe friendships in a broad sense, including people of his own family, while Ambrose kinships' vocabulary refers either to the inner circle of the family or in the broader sense to members of the Christian community he is connected to.

We can thus safely conclude that Ambrose and Symmachus are truly related in one way or another. Unfortunately, none of the known members of Ambrose's family appear in the Stemma *Symmachorum*.[73] Therefore, the only remaining question is that whether and how we can reach back far enough to find out where their lineages merge.

3.2 Timothy Barnes' theory

As many women's names are missing from the stemma of Symmachus' family, Timothy Barnes has suggested that Ambrose and Satyrus could have been first

---

67 Ambrose of Milan, *Epistula* 57 (Maur. 6), 4, 8, 16, 17, CSEL 82/2, ed. Michaela Zelzer (Vienna: Hölder-Pichler-Tempsky, 1990), 100–111; *Epistula* 52 (Maur. 16), 3, ed. Zelzer, 68; *Epistula* 72 (Maur. 17), 12, ed. Zelzer, 17; *Epistula* 62 (Maur. 19), 10, 13, 14, 18, ed. Zelzer, 126–131; *Epistula* 77 (Maur. 22), 18, ed. Zelzer, 137; *Epistula* 40 (Maur 32), 6, 7, ed. Zelzer, 39; *Epistula* 7 (Maur. 37), 13, CSEL 82/1, ed. Michaela Zelzer (Vienna: F. Tempsky, 1968), 49; *Epistula* 8 (Maur. 39), 2, ed. Zelzer, 67; *Epistula* 34 (Maur. 45), 16, ed. Zelzer, 237; *Epistula* 58 (Maur. 60), 7, ed. Zelzer, 115; *Epistula extra coll.* 14 (Maur. 63), 2 and 99, ed. Zelzer, 236; 289; *Epistula* 48 (Maur. 66), 1 and 7, ed. Zelzer, 49–51; *Epistula* 18 (Maur. 70), 8, ed. Zelzer, 135; *Epistula* 20 (Maur. 77), 1, ed. Zelzer, 132; *Epistula* 67 (Maur. 80), 3, ed. Zelzer, 166; *Epistula* 35 (Maur. 83), 4, ed. Zelzer, 240; *Epistula* 59 (Maur. 84), 1, ed. Zelzer, 117; *Epistula* 46 (Maur. 85), 3, ed. Zelzer, 47.
68 Ambrose of Milan, *Epistula* 56 (Maur. 5), 23, ed. Zelzer, 97.
69 Ambrose of Milan, *Epistula* 68 (Maur. 26), 20, ed. Zelzer, 178; *Epistula* 11 (Maur. 29), 24, ed. Zelzer, 92; *Epistula* 45 (Maur. 52), 2, ed. Zelzer, 45; *Epistula* 25 (Maur. 53), 2, ed. Zelzer, 176; *Epistula* 15 (Maur. 69), 7, ed. Zelzer, 113; *Epistula* 2 (Maur. 65), 10, ed. Zelzer, 19.
70 Ambrose of Milan, *Epistula* 56 (Maur. 5), 17, ed. Zelzer, 93.
71 Ambrose of Milan, *Epistula extra coll.* 14 (Maur. 63), 101, ed. Zelzer, 290.
72 Ambrose of Milan, *Epistula* 74 (extra coll. a) (Maur. 40), 28, ed. Zelzer, 71.
73 Otto Seeck, "Symmachos IV (2)," in *Paulys Real-Encyclopädie der Classischen Altertumswissenschaft. Neue Bearbeitung*, eds. Wilhelm Kroll and Karl Mittelhaus, Stuttgart: J.B. Metzlersche Verlagsbuchhandlung, 1931): 1135–1161, 1143.

cousins to Quintus Aurelius Symmachus Eusebius. Ambrose's mother would thus be the sister of Lucius Aurelius Avianius Symmachus Phosphorius, who was Symmachus the Orator's father.[74] This theory bolsters the idea that Ambrose could have inherited his place in the *Aurelia* family from his mother. Ambrose's father, Uranius, would then be son-in-law to Lucius Aurelius Valerius Tullianus Symmachus, consul in 330 AD. As a consequence, when his mother went back to Rome with her three children either right after the death of her husband or later on, she could have reunited with Avianius Symmachus Phosphorius, her assumed brother. In reading the *Symmachorum* family tree, I suggest she might bear the name of *Aurelia Valeria*. This woman would be a Christian aunt of Symmachus the Orator. It would perhaps confirm the intriguing theory of Michele R. Salzman, suggesting either that an uncle of Symmachus, M. Aurelius Valerius Valentinus, or one of his brother, Avianius Valentinus, would be Christians as they could be recognized as the author of the Codex-Calendar of 354.[75] If an uncle or a brother of Symmachus was indeed a Christian, the Orator could have had both Christian cousins and a faithful aunt. As Symmachus was born around 340 AD, Ambrose could have played with Symmachus when they were young children.

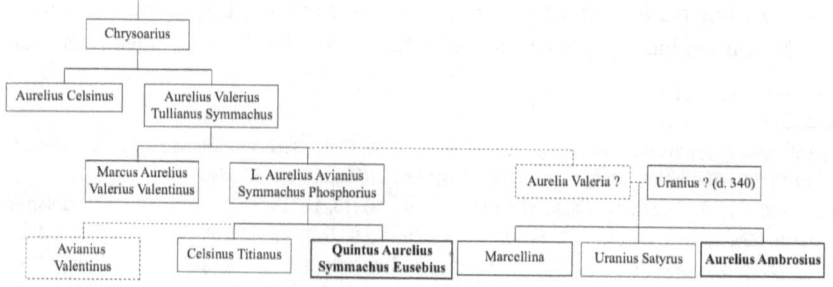

Fig. 1: Ambrose as Symmachus' first cousin.
As for the Symmachi family, this stemma is based on: Christian Settipiani, *Continuité gentilice et continuité familiale dans les familles sénatoriales romaines à l'époque imperiale. Mythe et réalité* (Oxford: Unit of the prosopographical research, 2000), 412.

---

74 Barnes, "The Election," 49–50. See family tree in annex.
75 Michele R. Salzman, *The Codex-Calendar of 354 and the Rhythms of Urban Life in Late Antiquity* (Berkeley-Los Angeles-Oxford: University of California Press, 1990), 201.

3.3 Macrobius, Symmachus and Ambrose

Ambrose's name is highly unusual. His family's African background – perhaps on his mother's side – could be meaningful as Flavius Macrobius Ambrosius Theodosius, commonly called Macrobius, may have been of African descent and could very well be related to the Symmachi family.[76] David Kelly claims a link between the families of Macrobius and Ambrose does exist, without, once again, providing satisfactory evidence.[77] But the fact that he both bore the name *Ambrose* and was related to Symmachus underlines yet again the African familial link between Ambrose and Symmachus.

4 Conclusion

Ultimately, the familial kin that bounds Ambrose and Symmachus does not appear clearly in their correspondences, and remained hidden behind the practice of friendship and the exchange of letters. As an aristocrat, Symmachus expected Ambrose to lend him assistance if required, since recommendations and personal networks were the only means available to gain official positions. If Ambrose's episcopal network is based on the Greco-roman practice of *amicitia*, the vocabulary used traditionally has evolved since for Ambrose, the term of kinship cannot be used anymore for people who are not Christians.

The identity of Ambrose's parents remains unknown and the reasons behind the lack of information are different in both cases. Nothing can prove with any degree of certainty that Ambrose's father held the charge of Praetorian prefect of the Gauls. Moreover, we do not know exactly when Ambrose's mother left Trier for Rome. It was either after the death of Ambrose's father around 340 AD, or when Ambrose's sister took the veil between 352 and 355 AD. Elaborating on Timothy Barnes' theory, we have suggested that Ambrose and Symmachus were cousins, but they were in one way or another related, albeit not as *cliens* as stated by Neil McLynn. Somehow, they were blood relatives. I remain convinced that Ambrose's mother is their common parent. I am likewise convinced that Ambrose's mother had family ties in Africa, but originally came from Rome. We know that Ambrose considered himself a Roman living in Rome. I think that this is mostly due to the fact that his mother was a Roman woman. As for his

---

[76] Macrobius, *Commentaire au songe de Scipion*, t. 1, trans. Mireille Armisen-Marchetti (Paris: Les Belles Lettres, 2003): xi.
[77] Family tree elaborated by David Kelly, never published.

father's background? Obviously, his name sounds Greek, but the *Urania* family had a mausoleum in Rome. The *Uranii*, despite their Eastern background, would have spread the Western part of the Empire in Italy.

Bibliography

Primary Sources

Ambrose of Milan. *De Nabuthae*. Edited by Charles Schenkl, CSEL 32 (2), Prague-Vienna-Leipzig: F. Tempsky, 1897.

Ambrose of Milan. *De virginibus*. Edited by Ignazio Cazzaniga, Turin: In aedibus Io. Bapt. Paraviae, 1948.

Ambrose of Milan. *De Excessu Fratris*. Edited by Otto Faller, CSEL 73, Vienna: Hoelder-Pichler-Tempsky, 1955.

Ambrose of Milan. *Epistulae et acta*. Edited by Otto Faller and Michaela Zelzer, CSEL 82/ 1–3, Vienna: Hölder-Pichler-Tempsky, 1968–1990.

Ambrose of Milan. *De viduis. Exhortatio virginitatis*. Edited by Franco Gori, *Verginità*, Milan-Rome: Cità Noua Editrice, 1989.

Ramsey, Boniface. *Ambrose*. The Early Church Fathers. London-New York: Routledge, 1997.

Augustus Henry Eugene de Romestin, Eugene de Romestin and Henry Thomas Forbes Duckworth (trans.). *From Nicene and Post-Nicene Fathers, Second Series*, Vol. 10, edited by Philip Schaff and Henry Wace, Buffalo-New York: Christian Literature Publishing Co., 1896.

Codex Theodosianus. Edited by Theodor Mommsen and Paul Meyer, Berlin: Weidmannos, 1954.

Inscriptiones Latinae Christianae Veteres vol. 1. Edited by Ernestus Diehl, Berlin: Weidmannos, 1961.

Jerome of Stridon. *Lettres (Epistulae)*. Trans. Jérôme Labourt, Paris: Les Belles Lettres, 1951.

Macrobius, *Commentaire au songe de Scipion, t. 1*. Trans. Mireille Armisen-Marchetti, Paris: Les Belles Lettres, 2003.

Martyrologium Hieronymianum. Edited by Giovanni Battista de Rossi and Louis Duchesne, Brussels: Acta Sanctorum, 1894.

Paulinus of Milan *Vita Ambrosii*. Edited by Antoon A. R. Bastiaensen, *Vite de santi*, ed. Christine Mohrmann, Milan: Fondazione Lorenzo Valla: A. Mondadori, 1974.

Symmachus *Lettres, t. 1–4*. Trans. Jean-Pierre Callu, Paris: Les Belles Lettres, 1972–2002.

Secondary Literature

Adkin, Neil. "Is the Marcellina of Jerome Ep. 45.7 Ambrose's sister?" *Phoenix* 45 (1995): 68–70.

Barnes, Timothy, "The Election of Ambrose of Milan." In *Episcopal Elections in Late Antiquity*, edited by Johan Leemans, Peter Van Nuffelen, Shawn W. J. Keough and Carla Nicolaye, 39–59. Berlin/Boston: De Gruyter, 2011.

Baudrillart, Alfred (ed.). *Dictionnaire d'histoire et de géographie ecclésiastiques*, T. 9. Paris: Letouzey et Ané, 1949.
Brown, Peter. *Through the Eye of a Needle. Wealth, the Fall of Rome, and the Making of Christianity in the West, 350–550*. Oxford: Princeton University Press, 2012.
Bush, Archie, Steven Cerutti. "A Use of the Term *Frater* in Pro Caelio." *CJ* 82 (1) (1986): 37–39.
Cameron, Alan. "The Date and Identity of Macrobius." *JRS* 56 (1966): 25–38.
Corbier, Mireille. "Épigraphie et parenté." In *Épigraphie et histoire: acquis et problèmes. Actes du congrès de la Société des professeurs d'histoire ancienne, Lyon-Chambéry, 21–23 mai 1993*, edited by Yann Lebohec and Yves Roman, 101–152. Lyon: De Boccard, 1998.
de Rossi, Giovanni Battista. "Osservazioni sul nome gentilizio Aurelius di S. Ambrogio e di S. Agostino." *Bulletino di Archeologia Christiana* 3 (1865): 15–16.
Duval, Yves-Marie. *Ambroise de Milan, XVIe centenaire de son élection épiscopale : dix études*. Paris: Études augustiniennes, 1974.
Duval, Yves-Marie. "L'influence des écrivains africains du IIIe siècle sur les écrivains chrétiens de l'Italie du nord dans la seconde moitié du IVe siècle." In *Aquileia e l'Africa, Antichità altoadriatiche* 5, 191–225. Udine: Arti grafiche friulane, 1974.
Gioanni, Stéphane. "Augustin, Paulin, Ennode et les origines de la mémoire d'Ambroise." In *La mémoire d'Ambroise de Milan. Usages politiques d'une autorité patristique en Italie (Ve–XVIIIe siècle)*, edited by Patrick Boucheron and Stéphane Gioanni, 235–252. Rome: École française de Rome, 2015.
Humbert, Michel. *Le remariage à Rome: étude d'histoire juridique et sociale*. Milan: Giuffrè, 1972.
Jones, Arnold H. M., Martindale, John R. and Morris, John, eds. *The prosopography of the Later Roman Empire, T. I (260–395)*. Cambridge: Cambridge University Press, 1971.
Lanéry, Cécile. *Ambroise de Milan Hagiographe*. Paris: Collection des Études augustiniennes, 2008.
Lazzati, Guiseppe. *Ambrosius episcopus*. Milan: Vita e pensiero, 1976.
Lhuillier-Martinetti, Dominique. *L'individu dans la famille à Rome au IVe siècle d'après l'œuvre d'Ambroise de Milan*. Rennes: PUR, 2008.
Machado, Carlos. "Roman aristocrats and the Christianization of Rome." In *Pagans and Christians in the Roman Empire: The Breaking of a Dialogue*, edited by Rita Lizzi Testa and Peter Brown, 493–516. Münster: Lit-Verlag, 2011.
Mazzarino, Santo. *Storia Sociale del Vescovo Ambrosio*. Rome: "L'Erma di Bretschneider", 1989.
McLynn, Neil. *Ambrose of Milan: Church and Court in a Christian Capital*. Berkeley-Los Angeles: University of California Press, 1994.
Moorhead, John. *Ambrose. Church and Society in the Late Roman World*. London-New York: Longman, 1999.
Palanque, Jean-Rémy. *Saint Ambroise et l'empire romain. Contribution à l'histoire des rapports de l'Église et de l'État à la fin du quatrième siècle*. Paris: De Boccard, 1933.
Paredi, Angelo. *S. Ambrogio e la sua età*. Milan: Ampliata, 1960.
Pietri, Charles and Luce, eds. *Prosopographie chrétienne du Bas Empire, 2, Prosopographie de l'Italie chrétienne (314–604)*, vol. 1. Rome: École française de Rome, 1999.

Salzman, Michele R. *The Codex-Calendar of 354 and the Rhythms of Urban Life in Late Antiquity*. Berkeley-Los Angeles-Oxford: University of California Press, 1990.

Savon, Hervé. *Ambroise de Milan (340–397)*. Paris: Desclée, 1997.

Salomies, Ollies. "Réflexions sur le développement de l'onomastique de l'aristocratie romaine du Bas-Empire." In *Les stratégies familiales dans l'Antiquité tardive*, edited by Christophe Badel and Christian Settipani, 1–26. Paris: De Boccard, 2012.

Seeck, Otto. "Symmachos." In *Paulys Real-Encyclopädie der Classichen Altertumswissenschaft neue Bearbeitung*, IV (2), edited by Wilhelm Kroll and Karl Mittelhaus, 1135–1161. Stuttgart: J.B. Metzlersche Verlagsbuchhandlung, 1931.

Settipani, Christian. *Continuité gentilice et continuité familiale dans les familles sénatoriales romaines à l'époque impériale. Mythe et réalité*. Oxford: Unit of the prosopographical research, 2000.

Socii Bollandiani, ed. *Bibliotheca Hagiographica Latina Antiquae et Mediae Aetatis*. Brussels: Via dicta des "Ursulines", 1898–1899.

Wilson, Joseph P. "Three Non-Uses of Frater in *Pro Caelio* 32." *CJ* 83 (3) (1988): 207–211.

Gillian Clark
Influential Friends? Augustine's Episcopal Networks

Late in his life, Augustine told his congregation at Hippo how, unintentionally, he became a priest (*s.* 355). He was not looking for episcopal office, he said; indeed, he was so committed to establishing a monastic community that when he realised he was becoming known, he avoided any place which did not have a bishop. At Hippo there was a friend whom he hoped to win for his community, and he thought himself safe because there was already a bishop, but he was seized and made a priest. His friend and fellow-bishop Possidius, in his *Life of Augustine*, added to the story. It was a civil servant, one of the *agentes in rebus*, who wanted Augustine to come to Hippo and persuaded him to stay longer.[1] The then bishop of Hippo was overburdened and asked his people to provide him with a priest as helper; and Possidius heard from Augustine himself that when he wept at the forced ordination, some people thought it was from wounded pride, and assured him that though he was worthy of higher office, a presbyter was close in status to a bishop.[2] In recent years, sceptical historians have observed that "forced ordination" is a convention in stories of bishops, and have suggested that Augustine in fact sought office in the African church after being disappointed in his other hopes: a good marriage and a career in the imperial civil service (*conf.* 6.11.19); the patronage of Ambrose bishop of Milan, who baptized him; life as a cultivated Roman gentleman on his family property at Thagaste.[3] All these possibilities would require friends and supporters. Augustine would not be surprised to find widely different interpretations of what happens in a life (*conf.* 10.3.3), but, as is usually the case in writing about Augustine, these interpretations depend almost entirely on his own writings. The same applies to questions which are prompted by social network analysis. It is easy to suppose that Augustine had networks, and that they can be traced because his writings are so extensive. In practice, it is not so easy to trace his networks, or to answer the underlying questions: what is a network, and who is a friend?

---

1 *Agentes in rebus* were government inspectors; it is often, too readily, assumed that they were secret police. On their ranks and remits, see A.H.M. Jones, *The Later Roman Empire 286–602* (Oxford: Blackwell, 1964), 578–82.
2 Possidius, *vita Aug.* 3–4.
3 James J. O'Donnell, *Augustine: A New Biography* (Ecco: New York, 2005).

In 426/7, a year or two after he told the story of his ordination, Augustine reread all his books and made a chronological list, the *Retractationes*, adding occasional comments on anything which offended him or might mislead others (*ep.* 224.2).[4] Some of these books address or reply to a named person, or answer a request, or mention people Augustine knew.[5] *Confessions*, in particular, names some high-level contacts in capital cities, Carthage and Rome and Milan, from the time before Augustine was a bishop. But a contact at a particular time is not necessarily a friend or part of a network. Contacts may be made by chance or by strategy, through other connections or by personal initiative. People may have ties of personal affection, or they may be friends in the formal classical sense that they have a common cause and exchange favours, either as equals or because one is a patron of the other.[6] They may expect to share information as it reaches them, or they may do no more than exchange greetings in order to maintain the relationship. A network can consist of people who are constantly in touch with one another, or of people who can be invoked, individually or collectively, when a specific need arises. One person may belong to different networks, which overlap partially or not at all. Some people are seen as "networkers" because they have many contacts, use them on behalf of others, and willingly add to them; others are not so active. To add to the complexities, Christian friendship may have distinctive characteristics. In principle it is inclusive, because everyone is a child of the same father and a member of the same body, and social status or political rank are irrelevant; people may defer instead to their spiritual superiors.[7] But Christian friendship may exclude those who have different religious views, and may in practice maintain social expectations about who writes to whom.[8]

---

4 O'Donnell, *Augustine*, discusses this list as Augustine's attempt to control his reputation.
5 Names can be traced in the database of Augustine's letters at *www.scrinium.umk.pl*.
6 David Konstan, *Friendship in the Classical World* (Cambridge: Cambridge University Press, 1997).
7 On Augustine's letters to Christian officials, see Michael Stuart Williams, "Beloved Lord and Honorable Brother: The Negotiation of Status in Augustine, Letter 23," in *Unclassical Traditions II: Perspectives from East and West in Late Antiquity*, eds. Christopher Kelly, Richard Flower, Michael Stuart Williams (Cambridge: Cambridge Philological Society, 2011): 88–101; Robin Whelan, "Mirrors for Bureaucrats: Expectations of Christian Officials in the Theodosian Empire," *JRS* 108 (2018): 1–25.
8 Catherine Conybeare, *Paulinus Noster: Self and Symbols in the Letters of Paulinus of Nola* (Oxford: Oxford University Press, 2000); Stefan Rebenich, "Augustine on Friendship and Orthodoxy," in *A Companion to Augustine*, ed. Mark Vessey (Chichester: Wiley-Blackwell, 2012): 365–74. I thank Adrian Brändli and Conrad Leyser for discussion (February 2017) of Dr Brändli's

So there are many questions about friends and networks. Is there enough evidence to answer them? When Elizabeth Clark made pioneering use of social network theory in *The Origenist Controversy* (1992), she was reasonably confident that the range of available material made it possible to trace the relationships which she saw as important, even decisive, in theological choices; but she acknowledged the problem of letters which are now lost, or which were never received.[9] Letters are the obvious place to start the search for networks, because (as Augustine remarked, *retr.* 2.20) a letter says at the top who is writing to whom. Late antiquity is the great age of letter-collections.[10] Augustine's surviving letters are not among the largest collections, in comparison, for example, with the letters of Isidore of Pelusium.[11] But they are especially useful to historians, because Augustine did not have time to edit, select and arrange them for his own purposes. At the end of *Retractationes* (2.67) he observed that he had not yet started on his letters or sermons, and in a letter to the deacon Quodvultdeus (*ep.* 224) he wrote that most of the letters had been read to him, but he had not begun to dictate comments because of other urgent business. With more time, Augustine might have removed from his collection letters from other people, or letters which seemed unimportant, or which could be classed as memoranda (*commonitoria*). He did not do so, and the unedited collection includes an unusually large number of correspondents.[12] We know of 197, in comparison with a mere 32 in the letters which were carefully selected by Ambrose, and 73 for Jerome, who may have made some early selections.[13] Even in the collection of Symmachus, who holds the record for letters of recommendation in Latin, there are

---

Oxford doctoral thesis "*Inimica amicitia:* Friendship and the Notion of Exclusion in Early Christian Latin Literature".

9 Elizabeth A. Clark, *The Origenist Controversy: The Cultural Construction of an Early Christian Debate* (Princeton: Princeton University Press, 1992), 16–18.

10 Bronwen Neil and Pauline Allen, eds., *Collecting Early Christian Letters: From the Apostle Paul to Late Antiquity* (Cambridge: Cambridge University Press, 2015); Cristiana Sogno, Bradley Storin and Edward Watts, eds., *Late Antique Letter Collections: A Critical Introduction and Reference Guide* (Berkeley, Ca.: University of California Press, 2016).

11 See the contribution of Johan Leemans and Madalina Toca to this volume (pp. 83–100).

12 Claire Sotinel, "Augustine's Information Circuits," in *A Companion*, ed. Vessey, 125–37.

13 Andrew Cain, *The Letters of Jerome: Asceticism, Biblical Exegesis, and the Construction of Christian Authority in Late Antiquity* (Oxford: Oxford University Press, 2009), argues for two early collections of letters intended to present Jerome as an ascetic authority. On the correspondence of Ambrose, see Wolf Liebeschuetz, *Ambrose of Milan: Political Letters and Speeches* (Liverpool: Liverpool University Press, 2005), 27–46.

902 letters but a higher ratio of letters to correspondent, so only 129 correspondents in all.[14]

Some of Augustine's letters were long enough to count as a *libellus*, a short book.[15] For all the letters, as for the books, Augustine needed to correct errors or misleading statements, because he could not know who would read them. Unless he took special precautions, by entrusting a confidential message to a trusted carrier, he could assume that his letter was not a private document.[16] It would be read aloud to the recipient and to those present, and would be passed on, unpredictably, to other people. Augustine began a letter to his friend Evodius with the caution that the questions to which Evodius wanted answers were difficult even for intelligent people, and that Augustine's letters would be wanted by others who were less able to understand theology, but would still want to know "in a friendly or a hostile spirit" what he had said (*ep*. 162.1). One difficulty in tracing networks and connections is that a letter could reach many more people than its addressee. Another difficulty is the survival of letters. The earliest datable letters in Augustine's collection, like the earliest works listed in *Retractationes*, come from 386/7, the year in which he made his Christian commitment. It is unlikely that his archive ever held copies of all the letters he dictated or wrote in the next four decades. From those years, 35 of them as a very busy bishop, there now survive only 309 letters, 252 written by Augustine and the rest to him; 17 of the 252 have one or more co-authors.[17]

Augustine said that his letters had been read to him, but we do not know how he wanted them to be organised, or how they had been filed by Augustine himself or by his secretaries: in order of dictation, or by correspondent together with the correspondent's letter or letters, or in dossiers which might include documents and letters from other people?[18] Some of the complications are evi-

---

[14] Alan Cameron, "Were Pagans Afraid to Speak their Mind in a Christian World? The Correspondence of Symmachus," in *Pagans and Christians in Late Antique Rome*, eds. Michele Salzman, Marianne Sághy and Rita Lizzi Testa (Cambridge: Cambridge University Press, 2015): 64–111, discusses the editing of Symmachus' letters, with helpful comments on the conventions of letter-writing.

[15] For example, *ep*. 214.2 refers to *librum vel epistolam meam* to Sextus bishop of Rome, against the Pelagians.

[16] On letter-carriers, see Conybeare, *Paulinus*, 31–40; on confidential messages, see Sigrid Mratschek, "The Unwritten Letters of Augustine of Hippo," in *Scrinium Augustini: The World of Augustine's Letters*, eds. P. Nehring, M. Stróżyński and R. Toczko (Brepols 2017): 57–78.

[17] There are some debates on how to count the letters, see Jennifer Ebbeler, "The Letter Collection of Augustine of Hippo," in *Letter Collections*, eds. Sogno et al.: 239–53, at 242 and n. 19.

[18] On ways of organising letters, see Roy Gibson, "On the Nature of Ancient Letter Collections," *JRS* 102 (2012): 56–78.

dent in a letter (*ep.* 10*) to Augustine's longstanding friend and fellow-bishop Alypius, who had written that he hoped to return soon from a diplomatic mission to Italy. Augustine had already replied to acknowledge receipt of the books and memorandum sent by Alypius, but acknowledged them again in case the letter he was writing reached Alypius first. "Meanwhile I have found among some of my papers [*in quibusdam schedis*] a copy of the memorandum you made for your own use when you were first sent by the Council [of bishops] to the imperial court" (*ep.* 10*.1). He read the memorandum and found several important matters which Alypius had not then been able to settle, so he crossed out some points which were now achieved or did not seem urgent, and sent it to Alypius in case action was possible now. Then he added a further request for action. Slave-traders were shipping freeborn Romans overseas, where they could not be ransomed or vindicated. An earlier law of the emperor Honorius, directed to the then prefect of Africa, addressed this problem; but it imposed the probably lethal penalty of flogging with lead-tipped scourges. Augustine wanted the law reissued with a lesser penalty, and he added a copy to his own memorandum (*ep.* 10*.4). How was this sequence of letters, documents and memoranda to be filed? Was there the equivalent of a "pending" tray for letters awaiting a response from Augustine or a reply from his correspondent, or an "out" tray for letters awaiting a carrier?

In this case Augustine had copies of the relevant letters, but it cannot be assumed that a copy of an outgoing letter was always made, even when, according to the writer, the carrier was waiting.[19] Paulinus of Nola wrote (*ep.* 50.14) to Augustine:

> You replied to my second request for advice, while I was spending the winter at Carthage, with a letter – not extensive, but full of instruction in the faith – about the form of the resurrection. If you have a copy among your papers [*si habes relatam, sc. epistolam, in schedis*], please would you send it to me, or at least reconstruct it, which is easy for you? Even if the writing [*scriptura*] does not survive, since perhaps a short improvised letter was refused a place among your books, renew it for me with the same content, drawing on the treasure in your heart[20].

---

19 Cameron, "Symmachus," discusses the convention "the carrier is waiting". I owe to Mratschek, "Unwritten Letters" 60, references to Paulinus *ep.* 50.14 and to Aug. *ep.* 162.9.

20 Paulinus, *ep.* 50.14: *De resurrectionis forma non grandem sed plenam fidei instructione epistolam, qua secundae consultationi meae, dum Carthagini exhiemarem, rescripseras, si habes relatam in schedis, rogo ut mittas aut certe retexas eam mihi, quod tibi facile est. nam etsi scriptura non extat, quia forte brevis epistola ut tumultuaria tibi inter libros tuos haberi spreta sit, renova eam mihi eodem sensu promptam de thesauro cordis tuae...*

Paulinus no longer had the letter; Augustine, similarly, asked his friend Evodius for a copy of a letter which "has gone astray here and cannot be found" (*ep.* 162.9). Human error or chance is the most likely explanation why some letters were lost but others survived. It is puzzling that Augustine's letter-collection includes no letters from women, although Augustine corresponded with several women, including some of high social status: were their letters discarded?[21] Maximus of Madaura, writing an open letter to Augustine in defence of the traditional religion, suggested that an unwelcome letter might actually be destroyed: "I have no doubt that this letter will be stolen and will perish in flames or by some other means." In fact the letter survived in Augustine's correspondence (*ep.* 16), together with Augustine's reply, but without a clear indication of date.

After Augustine's death Possidius compiled, or added to, an *Indiculum* of his writings, including a list of the letters which were available at Hippo. About one third of them (89 out of 257) are lost, but the letter-collection which is now in print includes many more letters than Possidius listed. Some must have survived in collections made by others: that would help to explain why, in the letters transmitted in manuscripts, there are some standard groupings, but there is no canonical order.[22] Possidius chose in his *Life* of Augustine to present a series of confrontations with heretics, and the *Indiculum* classifies Augustine's writings, including his letters, by subject not by chronology.[23] This method has obvious disadvantages. Some letters range over several topics; many have to be classed as "Miscellaneous"; and the subject-classification gives a misleading impression that Augustine wrote systematically on (for example) Donatism.[24] Early print editions of the letters, in the fifteenth and sixteenth centuries, followed the available manuscripts in ordering the letters by correspondent, and grouping correspondents who were in some way related. But many letters have lost their initial *salutatio,* the formal or informal greeting from sender to recipient, which identifies the recipient and indicates the nature of the relationship.[25]

---

[21] Catherine Conybeare, "Spaces between Letters: Augustine's Correspondence with Women," in *Voices in Dialogue: Reading Women in the Middle Ages,* eds. Linda Olson and Kathryn Kerby-Fulton (Notre Dame, IN: University of Notre Dame Press, 2005): 55–72, with the response by Mark Vessey: 73–96.
[22] Ebbeler, "Letter Collection," 243–6.
[23] Erika Hermanowicz, *Possidius of Calama: A Study of the North African Episcopate* (Oxford: Oxford University Press, 2008).
[24] Éric Rebillard, "Augustine in Controversy with the Donatists before 411," in *The Donatist Schism: Controversy and Contexts,* ed. Richard Miles (Liverpool: Liverpool University Press, 2016): 297–316.
[25] Johannes Divjak, "Epistulae," in *Augustinus-Lexikon,* ed. C. Mayer, vol. 2 (Basel: Schwabe, 1996–2002): 893–1057, at 902–4.

The Maurist edition of 1688, using all the manuscript and print editions then available, re-ordered the letters by chronology, as far as the editors could reconstruct it. But many letters have no indication of date, and there have been challenges to the accepted dating, both absolute and relative.[26]

Survival, organisation, and dating of letters all present problems for reconstructing social networks, and the practicalities of letter-exchange show how difficult it is to answer basic questions about Augustine's relationship with any known correspondent: how often they were in contact, what topics they discussed, and how many other people were involved. Some letter-writers felt an obligation to keep in touch and reply promptly, even when they had nothing in particular to say.[27] But any exchange of letters depended on having a letter-carrier who could reach the recipient in reasonable time, despite bad weather or land and sea routes made dangerous by civil conflict. When Quodvultdeus (Aug. *ep.* 224) asked for a list of heresies, with explanations of why they are wrong, his letter remained unanswered until the arrival of a priest who had business in his region. Even then Augustine could not do as he asked, because another carrier had arrived from Alypius, who had an unexpected opportunity to send from Rome some books by Julian of Eclanum which needed an urgent response.

It is rarely possible to follow a conversation such as the early exchange with Augustine's friend Nebridius (*ep.* 3–14). Many correspondents are known only from one letter, which may be difficult to date, and even when there is information outside the correspondence, it is unlikely to resolve all the problems. One example is a letter from Longinianus (Aug. *ep.* 234), which is well known because it includes the earliest known self-identification as *paganus*. Augustine issued a brief philosophical challenge (*ep.* 233) which survives with the heading *Longiniano Augustinus*. The reply still has the *salutatio*: *Domino venerando et vere ac merito percolendo sancto patri Augustino*, "to the reverend lord, truly and deservedly to be cultivated, the holy father Augustine". This respectful greeting does not imply that Longinianus regarded Augustine as his spiritual father, that is, as his bishop; and if Augustine's lost *salutatio* addressed Longinianus as *filius*, this would not mean more than that Longinianus took at least a sympathetic interest in Christianity.[28] When and why did Augustine issue his philosophical

---

26 Especially by Pierre-Marie Hombert, *Nouvelles recherches de chronologie augustinienne* (Paris: Institut d'Études Augustiniennes, 2000).
27 An example is Symmachus *ep.* 1.15, discussed below.
28 Gillian Clark, "*Suscipiendus Filius:* Letters and the City of God," in *Scrinium Augustini: The World of Augustine's Letters*, eds. P. Nehring, M. Stróżyński and R. Toczko (Turnhout: Brepols 2017): 181–202.

challenge, and should we hear the elaborate self-deprecation of Longinianus as conventionally polite, or as ironic? Augustine returned another brief reply (*ep.* 235), which again has lost its *salutatio*, then Longinianus disappears from the correspondence. Was he the senior treasury official (*comes sacrarum largitionum*) in 399, prefect of the city of Rome in 401/2, and praetorian prefect of Italy in 406, who would have been a valuable contact for Augustine the bishop? There is no evidence beyond the coincidence of name.[29]

Similar questions arise if "episcopal networks" has the narrower sense of networks among bishops, rather than the networks of a particular bishop. Roman Africa had an unusually large number of bishops, over 600, because of its distinctive settlement patterns and because the rival churches wanted to have as many bishops as possible.[30] How many knew each other? The names of many bishops appear in the records of the Conference of Carthage (411), but we do not know how many had met before the conference, or met there, or kept in touch thereafter. Augustine's correspondents include only 29 bishops, and for 14 of the 29 their other contacts are not known.[31] His letters to bishops, formal and informal, show a range of contacts and concerns; they do not show how he invoked, or was invoked by, a network of like-minded colleagues.

With all these cautions in place, there follow some examples of Augustine's episcopal networks in the wider sense. The first dates from 395/6, the year in which Augustine became a bishop, and involves one of the great networkers, Paulinus of Nola, who was beginning a new ascetic life.[32] Augustine's letter-collection includes a reply by Paulinus to an approach from Alypius, Augustine's long-term friend, who had recently become bishop of their home town Thagaste.[33] Alypius was in Carthage when letters from Paulinus were brought to people Alypius knew (including Aurelius bishop of Carthage), and he saw an opportunity to make contact. The reply from Paulinus shows what Alypius wrote: he had first heard of Paulinus at Milan and knew one of his hymns; he sent five anti-Manichaean works by Augustine; and he asked Paulinus to lend the *Chronicle* of Eusebius for copying. Paulinus sent an encouraging reply. He found the *Chronicle* at Rome in the library of Domnio (a good place to look, because Domnio knew Jerome, who had translated the *Chronicle* into Latin with some addi-

---

29 Longinianus: *PLRE* 2.686–7.
30 Anna Leone, "Tracing the Donatist Presence in North Africa: An Archaeological Perspective," in *The Donatist Schism*, ed. Miles, 317–44.
31 Sotinel, "Circuits", 133–6.
32 Sigrid Mratschek, "*Multis enim notissima est sanctitas loci:* Paulinus and the Gradual Rise of Nola as a Center of Christian Hospitality," *JECS* 9 (2001): 511–53.
33 Paulinus *ep.* 3 = Aug. *ep.* 24.

tions³⁴); he asked for more about the Milan connection – was Alypius, like Paulinus, one of Ambrose's people, and which hymn did he know? – and he signed off with greetings to all at Carthage, Thagaste and Hippo. He also wrote (*ep.* 4) to Augustine, and followed up (*ep.* 6) when he heard nothing. Augustine was waiting for a carrier; eventually (Aug. *ep.* 27) his reply was brought by his patron Romanianus, whom he introduced as dedicatee of *De vera religione* (one of the books sent by Alypius). He also asked advice for Licentius son of Romanianus, who was too much absorbed by poetry. Paulinus continued this connection too. He wrote to Romanianus, enclosing a letter for Licentius, to say that long-awaited brothers had returned from Africa with letters from Aurelius, Alypius, Augustine, Profuturus, Severus – all the African bishops – and Romanianus would share his joy that Augustine was now co-bishop with Valerius.³⁵

Paulinus thereby extended his African networks to include Alypius, Augustine, and their friends, notably Romanianus and his son. But it cannot be assumed that some or all of these people corresponded regularly thereafter, or that information which reached one would reach the others, or that they agreed on theological questions. Augustine and Paulinus never met; from 25 years of friendship by letter there survive 4 letters of Paulinus to Augustine and 8 of Augustine to Paulinus.³⁶ Internal references suggest at least 26 missing letters, but the surviving letters also show long gaps and apologies for silence.³⁷ Augustine could invoke the help of Paulinus, but whether and when he did so, and what Paulinus did about it, would depend on circumstances. In their first exchange of letters, Paulinus said that he had received the books Alypius sent, not for his instruction alone but for the benefit of churches in many cities: was that an offer to have then copied and distributed? When Romanianus brought copies of Augustine's other books (*ep.* 27.5), did Paulinus have them further copied for his friends, or did he simply keep them at Nola until someone asked? Augustine told Secundinus the Manichaean that he could follow an argument further in *de libero arbitrio*, which he would find with Paulinus at Nola.³⁸ When Augustine

---

34 Mark Vessey, "Augustine among the Writers of the Church," in *A Companion*, ed. Vessey, 240–54, at p. 247; Dennis Trout, *Paulinus of Nola: Life, Letters, Poems* (Berkeley, Ca: University of California Press, 1999), at 114–15, on Paulinus making links at Rome; 202–6 on Africa.
35 Aug. *ep.* 32; see further Robin Lane Fox, *Augustine: Confessions and Conversions* (London: Allen Lane, 2016), 479–86.
36 Joseph Lienhard, "Paulinus of Nola," in *Augustine Through the Ages: An Encyclopedia*, ed. Allan D. Fitzgerald OSA (Grand Rapids: Eerdmans, 1999): 628–9.
37 Trout, *Paulinus*, 203.
38 *C.Sec.*11; Augustine sent *lib.arb.* to Paulinus, *ep.* 31.7.

wrote a long reply to questions from Paulinus about punishment (*ep.* 95), or about care for the dead (*de cura mortuorum*), did Paulinus share the letters with other friends? When Augustine and Alypius sent Paulinus (*ep.* 186) a long letter against Pelagius, noting that two councils of the African church had written to Rome, did they want Paulinus to reply with a declaration of support, to circulate the letter, to influence the bishop of Rome, or was it enough that they could circulate their own letter?[39]

A second example of networking illustrates a contact which would have been very useful to Augustine the bishop, if it had been maintained. Symmachus, another great networker, was proconsul of Africa in 373/4 and Prefect of the City when Augustine arrived in Rome a decade later. The governor of Africa had the high-ranking title of proconsul, but often the post occupied only one year in the life of a senator for whom Africa was marginal.[40] Symmachus, one of many Roman aristocrats who had property in Africa, continued to be helpful to Africans. Among them, perhaps, was Ponticianus, who was "making a notable career in the imperial civil service" (*praeclare in palatio militans, conf.* 8.6.14) when he visited, at Milan, his fellow-Africans Augustine and Alypius.[41] Augustine described this visit because Ponticianus, finding that they had a copy of the letters of Paul, told them about Antony of Egypt and others who had chosen the ascetic life. Symmachus recommended someone called Ponticianus to Syagrius (*ep.* 1.99), who may then have been proconsul of Africa (379) or praetorian prefect of Italy (380–2); he later mentioned *frater noster* Ponticianus (*ep.* 5.32). As Prefect of the City, Symmachus recommended Augustine when he was asked to suggest a Professor of Rhetoric for Milan (*conf.* 5.13.23), but in this case no letter of recommendation survives in his edited correspondence.[42] For all of Augustine's first career as a teacher of literature and rhetoric, all the evidence comes from *Confessions*. Augustine wrote that he met Vindicianus, the then proconsul of Africa, when he won a poetry competition at Carthage; he became *familiarior*, "rather friendly" with Vindicianus, and they discussed medicine and astrology.[43] Vindicianus had been a physician at the imperial court

---

[39] On Augustine's use of letters to invoke support against Pelagius, see Richard Miles, "Let's (Not) Talk About It: Augustine and the Control of Epistolary Dialogue," in *The End of Dialogue in Antiquity*, ed. Simon Goldhill (Cambridge: Cambridge University Press, 2008): 135–48.

[40] Brent Shaw, *Sacred Violence: African Christians and Sectarian Hatred in the Age of Augustine* (Cambridge: Cambridge University Press, 2011), 495–505.

[41] *PLRE* 1 p. 715.

[42] Jennifer Ebbeler and Cristiana Sogno, "Religious Identity and the Politics of Patronage: Symmachus and Augustine," *Hist.* 56 (2007): 230–42.

[43] *conf.* 4.3.5; Vindicianus (*PLRE* 1.967) is named at 7.6.8.

(*comes archiatrorum*), but Augustine did not say that they remained in contact, or that Vindicianus recommended him to the former proconsul Symmachus or to anyone else. When Augustine arrived in Rome a few years later, his contacts were Manichaeans (*conf.* 5.13.23), who gave him a place to stay and brought him to the attention of Symmachus.[44] In Milan he hoped for a *praesidatus* (*conf.* 6.11.19), the lowest rank of provincial governorship, and made formal calls on influential people, the "greater friends" whose support he needed (*conf.* 6.11.18). There is no sign that Symmachus (who died in 402) continued to be a "greater friend".

In contrast, five years before he encountered Augustine, Symmachus wrote on behalf of two Christians, one a teacher of rhetoric and the other a bishop. Palladius (Symm. *ep.* 1.15), taught rhetoric in Rome before he was summoned to the imperial court in 379.[45] Symmachus, writing to Ausonius, was pleased that he could add an enthusiastic report to a letter which would otherwise have been short; and in letters to Syagrius (*ep.* 1.94) and Eutropius (*ep.* 3.50), he regretted losing Palladius from Rome, but rejoiced in his prospects.[46] Palladius rose to be *comes sacrarum largitionum* and *magister officiorum*, a grander version of the career Augustine hoped to achieve. Clemens, bishop of Iol Caesarea in Mauretania, sought help when his town was unable to pay its taxes after suffering in the revolt of Firmus. He took the problem to the imperial court, achieved a rescript on tax concessions, and persuaded Symmachus to write to his brother who was *vicarius* of Africa. Symmachus (*ep.* 1.64) remarked that his brother might be surprised to find him recommending a bishop, but the bishop was acting rightly for his city.[47]

Augustine, returning from Italy to Africa, was aware (*s.* 355) that he was an obvious candidate for ordination. He had demonstrated personal holiness and renunciation of worldly goods, he was an excellent speaker and writer, and his earlier career gave him contacts in Rome and Milan which he could use for the benefit of his people.[48] But could he? There is a telling contrast with two of his contemporaries, who always knew someone to ask: Synesius, bishop

---

44 His host may have been Constantius (*Contra Faustum* 5.5) "who gathered many of you [Manichaeans] at his house in Rome".
45 Palladius 12, *PLRE* 1.660.
46 Syagrius 2, *PLRE* 1.862–3; Eutropius 2, *PLRE* 1.317.
47 Symmachus also wrote a letter commending two *decuriones* at Hippo (*ep.* 9.51, 399 AD), but see Ebbeler and Sogno, "Religious Identity," 237 against the view that this shows disregard of its bishop.
48 On the qualities expected of a bishop, see Claudia Rapp, *Holy Bishops in Late Antiquity: The Nature of Christian Leadership in an Age of Transition* (Berkeley Ca: University of California Press, 2005).

of Cyrene, and Libanius, teacher of rhetoric at Antioch, who wrote even more letters of recommendation than Symmachus.⁴⁹ For Libanius, as for Augustine, the letters which survive are a small proportion of those he must have written, but even with a 23-year gap there are 1545 letters over 15 years. Augustine had no comparable range of contacts, in his secular career or after his baptism. It is striking that he never names his teachers, or his fellow-students, or the students he taught in Carthage and Rome and Milan; the exceptions are Licentius, son of his patron, and Trygetius, formerly of the *militia*, who appear as his students in the early philosophical dialogue *de ordine*. From the time in Milan, the friends Augustine named in his early dialogues and in *Confessions* were aspiring civil servants or teachers and authors, many of them from Thagaste or nearby, and none of them is known to have reached the upper ranks of the civil service.⁵⁰ He did not become a protégé of Ambrose, who baptized him, nor does he appear in Ambrose's edited letters. Ambrose is respectfully mentioned in Augustine's early dialogues, then disappears from his writings for a decade until *Confessions*, written in the year of Ambrose's death (397).

Augustine's earliest known works are philosophical dialogues. His model was Cicero, but Cicero's participants are distinguished Romans gathering to relax in a fashionable villa, whereas Augustine's, in a borrowed house outside Milan, are family members and students, all from his home town Thagaste. Augustine may have chosen to make the dialogues socially inclusive, holding that everyone must be concerned about the blessed life, regardless of gender and educational level.⁵¹ But it is also possible that he did not know the Milanese philosophers and civil servants and clergy well enough to avoid offence if he took them as his characters. *Contra Academicos*, the first work listed in *Retractationes*, is dedicated to Augustine's long-term patron Romanianus; *De ordine* to the poet Zenobius, who is not otherwise known. The exceptional case is Manlius Theodorus, dedicatee of *De beata vita*, who at Milan was leading a life of philosophical *otium* after a distinguished career including the prefecture of Gaul; he was also a correspondent of Symmachus (*ep.* 5.4–16). Theodorus is not named in *Confessions*, but is often thought to be the man of "immense arrogance" who gave Augustine Platonist works (*conf.* 7.9.13). In this context, *typhus* connotes not social arrogance, but the intellectual arrogance characteristic of philosophers who rely on human reason.⁵² Augustine "ventures to name to your exceptional kindness"

---

49 The comparison with Synesius and Libanius is developed by Lane Fox, *Augustine*.
50 I owe to Neil McLynn (pers.comm.) the observation that Gregory Nazianzen also does not name his teachers, but does mention fellow-students at Athens.
51 Gillian Clark, *Monica: An Ordinary Saint* (Oxford: Oxford University Press, 2015), 80–115.
52 Augustine described his younger self as swollen with *typhus*, *conf.* 3.3.6.

(*beata v.* 1.6) the friends and family members who take part in the dialogue, and in *De ordine* he named Theodorus among those who do not judge by splendid appearance (1.11.31). But Theodorus, like Ambrose, vanishes from Augustine's writings, and in retrospect (*retr.* 1.2) Augustine thought he had said too much in the dedication of *De beata vita* to this man,"learned and Christian though he was." Theodorus emerged from retirement as consul 399, and became praetorian prefect of Italy in 408, but there is no sign that he was an influential friend of Augustine the bishop. His son, also Theodorus, was proconsul of Africa in 396, and Augustine later (in 405) mentioned a decision he made.[53] But no letter survives from Augustine to this proconsul hoping that his father is well; and there is no evidence that Augustine tried to resume contact with the elder Theodorus in 408, when Alaric and his war-band of Goths made it dangerous for four African bishops (including Possidius) to visit the bishop of Rome and go on to the imperial court at Ravenna.[54] Theodorus, as praetorian prefect, could have given them protection, if Augustine had felt able to ask.

Recent work on Augustine has revalued his status in his lifetime, as opposed to his status in later Western theology. Peter Brown started the process of putting Augustine in context, and James O'Donnell put him very firmly in his place.[55] Scholars now are inclined to believe Augustine's reminder to his congregation that when he took their concerns to a *potestas*, a powerful man, he was likely to be kept waiting at the door when others went in, and was often snubbed or refused when he was finally admitted to make his request (*s.* 302.17). Almost twenty years ago, Neil McLynn advanced the then subversive argument that Augustine rarely had social access to Roman aristocrats or imperial officials, and that his cordial relationships with the special envoy Marcellinus in 411/12, and with Macedonius the *vicarius Africae* in 413/14, were exceptional rather than typical.[56] In Augustine's first decade as bishop, from 395 to 404, there is no record of any contact with any of the 11 proconsuls, 5 of whom were correspondents of Symmachus; thereafter, evidence for contact often raises questions about date

---

[53] *Cresc.* 3.56.62; for the context, Shaw, *Sacred Violence:* 132–4.
[54] Hermanowicz, *Possidius*, 168–73. The Council of Carthage, in 407, ruled that bishops who wanted to lobby the imperial court must have written agreement from the bishop of Rome as well as the African bishops.
[55] Peter Brown, *Augustine of Hippo: A Biography* (London: Faber, 1967); a new edition with an Epilogue, 2000. O'Donnell, *Augustine*.
[56] Neil McLynn, "Augustine's Roman Empire," in *History, Apocalypse and the Secular Imagination: New Essays on Augustine's City of God*, eds. Mark Vessey, Karla Pollman and Allan D. Fitzgerald OSA (Bowling Green: Philosophy Documentation Center, 1999): 29–44.

or identity.⁵⁷ In 408, for example, Augustine sent the proconsul Donatus (*ep.* 100), most devoted to the name of Christ *Christi nominis amantissimus*, a respectful plea not to execute Donatists. Perhaps a year later (*ep.* 112) he wrote to a Donatus who was now free from business *negotia*, saying that he has heard praise for the administration of Donatus from people who did not know their *necessitudo*, their ties of friendship, and hoping they can meet, as they could not when Donatus was in office. The date of the letter is disputed, and in Africa there were many people called Donatus; Augustine himself confused two (*retr.* 1.21.3). But assuming that it is the same man, the *necessitudo* need not be closer than that Augustine, as bishop of Hippo, had written to the proconsul Donatus, who may have had property in Hippo. In another letter, Augustine seized a moment to write to his very old friend (*antiquissimo amico*) Marcianus, rejoicing that his friend in human concerns was now also a friend in divine concerns, and quoting Cicero, Terence and Virgil as well as the scriptures (*ep.* 258). Was this the Marcianus who was proconsul of Africa in 393/4, just before Augustine became a bishop?⁵⁸ It is not impossible: friends do advance in their careers. But it is impossible to prove.

Augustine could write a formal request to a proconsul, but it does not follow that they were, or soon became, part of a network of influential friends. Brent Shaw points out that only 20 of Augustine's extant letters are to imperial officials, and argues that Augustine did not previously know these people, but wrote, in his role as bishop, on a matter within their official remit.⁵⁹ It was part of his job to ask for remission of penalties, for enforcement of laws against pagans and heretics, and for reassurance that regime change in Italy had not changed the law. When Augustine wrote on behalf of the African bishops to Olympius (*ep.* 97), who became *magister officiorum* after the murder of Stilicho (408), this was not a case of invoking contacts from an earlier time in Italy. It was a formal letter, thanking Olympius for his reply to a first (lost) letter and urging him to reaffirm the laws against pagans and heretics. In general, there is no evidence that Augustine had Italian contacts, acquired during his few years in Milan and in Rome, who could give advance warnings about shifts in imperial policy or new appointments. Paulinus, at Nola, could easily be visited on the way to Rome for confidential discussions or exchange of information.⁶⁰ Augus-

---

57 I am much indebted to Sigrid Mratschek for discussion of Caecilianus: see her paper in this volume, p. 170 n. 107.
58 Marcianus, *PLRE* 1. 555.
59 Brent Shaw, "Augustine and Men of Imperial Power," *Journal of Late Antiquity* 8 (2015): 32–61.
60 Mratschek, this volume, p. 166 n. 89.

tine, at Hippo, was hospitable as befits a bishop (Possidius, *vita Aug.* 22), but was not on an obvious route. When it was "time to sail", to lobby at the imperial court or to seek support from the bishop of Rome, it was not Augustine who sailed from the seaport of Hippo. Alypius sailed; perhaps he had retained contacts from his time as a high-principled legal adviser at Rome (*conf.* 6.10.16), but he may simply have been a better traveller.[61]

There are two famous examples of Augustine's contacts with imperial officials. Flavius Marcellinus, *tribunus et notarius*, was the imperial special envoy in charge of the Conference of Carthage in 411, with the difficult remit of settling the century-long dispute between two churches, each of which claimed to be the true catholic church. Augustine is prominent in the official report of the Conference (the *Gesta*), with 70 interventions, 59 of them on the final day before the introduction of documents; he also wrote a summary of the papers, on the grounds that no one would ever read the whole (*ep.* 139.3). But this does not mean that Marcellinus, who had to show himself impartial, followed Augustine's script for the Conference.[62] He was impressed by Augustine's ability, and referred to him a range of theological questions, notably the difficulties raised by the former proconsul Volusianus (*ep.* 136, 143) who politely rebuffed Augustine's attempts to engage him in discussion of scripture. Augustine addressed *Marcelline carissime*, "dearest Marcellinus", on the question of infant baptism (*pecc. mer.* 1.1); *fili carissime Marcelline*, "dearest son Marcellinus", is the dedicatee of the opening books of *De civitate Dei*; and Augustine could write with unusual confidence to his brother Apringius, proconsul of Africa in 411/12, with his usual request for mercy (*ep.* 134.3). Marcellinus was executed in 413, probably before *City of God* books 1–3 began to be circulated.[63] Had he lived, would this intense correspondence have continued when the *tribunus et notarius* was posted elsewhere? The second famous example is Macedonius, vicar of Africa, who in 413/4 granted a request for mercy and encouraged further correspondence (Aug. *ep.* 153), questioning the principle of intercession in all cases and asking for some books Augustine had promised him, probably the first three books of *de civitate Dei*. Augustine sent a very long reply (*ep.* 153), and the books. Macedonius replied briefly but with enthusiastic praise (*ep.* 154), saying he would write from Italy if he lived and had leisure. There is no sign that he did, though Augustine wrote another long reply (*ep.* 155).

---

61 Diplomatic missions of Alypius in the 420s: *AugL* 1.260–5, s.v. "Alypius".
62 Neil McLynn, "The Conference of Carthage Reconsidered," in *The Donatist Schism*, ed. Miles, 220–48.
63 Gerard O'Daly, *Augustine's City of God: A Reader's Guide* (Oxford: Oxford University Press, 1999): 34.

Augustine was demonstrably a very active letter-writer, ready to use a connection and to sustain a correspondence in the service of his central tasks as a bishop: to intercede with power-holders, asking them to maintain the law but to temper justice with mercy; to resist beliefs which in his view endangered human relationship to God; and to move his hearers to respond to God's love. But it is not easy to trace networks of regular correspondents, and the expectation that Augustine had influential friends comes from reading back his later reputation; from assuming that when a correspondent shares a name with a known official, they are the same person; and from taking one encounter or letter-exchange to mean a lasting contact. The example of Augustine, who left so impressive a body of writings, illustrates the challenge of applying social network theory to the study of late antiquity. This theory has been useful in prompting historians to ask new questions and to consider why they do not have answers, but network analysis cannot supply the answers because it requires "big data", whereas the data available from late antiquity are few and almost always contested. "Information circuits", to use Claire Sotinel's term, depended on one person's decision to write or reply to another, and on having a trusted carrier who could make the journey. Networking was in practice difficult, and researchers now are trying to trace networks of communication from the tiny proportion of material which has survived. The techniques of network analysis and digital mapping may help to answer questions,[64] but probably they can do no more than redescribe in social-science language, and try to represent in diagrams, the information we already have. Researchers who use social network theory acknowledge that there are challenges on method, data, and interpretation.[65] Some people find it helpful to have visual depictions of nodes and connections, but others find it confusing, or even misleading when there is evidence only for one possible contact, but the lines on a map suggest a continuing connection. Nevertheless, social network theory has its uses, not only because funding bodies are interested in projects which link humanities to the social sciences, and such projects allow early-career researchers to become familiar with a range of evidence and to make their own academic networks. Social-science technical language needs translation into clear English, and that process prompts further thought about what is and what is not applicable to late antiquity. Redescribing in social-science language may even make social scientists realise that they have

---

64 Sotinel, "Circuits," 133; Ebbeler, "Letter Collection," 248 suggests that digital mapping might clarify what Augustine and a correspondent knew about a particular situation.
65 Tom Brughmans, Anna Collar and Fiona Coward, eds., *The Connected Past: Challenges to Network Studies in Archaeology and History* (Oxford: Oxford University Press, 2016); and see www.connectedpast.net for continuing discussion.

interests in common with historians of late antiquity, and may prompt them to think further about models and concepts which assume particular social structures and technologies of communication. All this is useful: but the challenge to social network theory remains.

Bibliography

Primary Sources

Augustine of Hippo. *Confessiones*, edited by L. Verheijen, CChr.SL 27. Turnhout: Brepols, 1981.
Augustine of Hippo, *Epistulae*, edited by A. Goldbacher, CSEL 34/1, 34/2, 44, 57, 58. Wien: Verlag der Österreichischen Akademie der Wissenschaften, 1895–1923.
Augustine of Hippo, *Retractationes*, edited by A. Mutzenbecher, CChr.SL 57. Turnhout: Brepols, 1984.
Augustine of Hippo, *Sermones*, edited by J.-P Migne, PL 38, 39. Paris, 1865.
Paulinus of Nola, *Epistulae*, edited by G. De Hartel, CSEL 29. Wien: Verlag der Österreichischen Akademie der Wissenschaften, 1999.

Secondary Literature

Brown, Peter. *Augustine of Hippo: A Biography*. London: Faber & Faber, 1967. New edition with an Epilogue, 2000.
Brughmans, Tom, Anna Collar and Fiona Coward, eds. *The Connected Past: Challenges to Network Studies in Archaeology and History*. Oxford: Oxford University Press, 2016.
Cameron, Alan. "Were Pagans Afraid to Speak their Mind in a Christian World? The Correspondence of Symmachus." In *Pagans and Christians in Late Antique Rome* edited by Michele Salzman, Marianne Sághy, and Rita Lizzi Testa, 64–111. Cambridge: Cambridge University Press, 2015.
Cain, Andrew. *The Letters of Jerome: Asceticism, Biblical Exegesis, and the Construction of Christian Authority in Late Antiquity*. Oxford: Oxford University Press, 2009.
Clark, Elizabeth A. *The Origenist Controversy: The Cultural Construction of an Early Christian Debate*. Princeton: Princeton University Press, 1992.
Clark, Gillian. *Monica: An Ordinary Saint*. Oxford: Oxford University Press, 2015.
Clark, Gillian. "*Suscipiendus Filius*: Letters and the City of God." In *Scrinium Augustini: The World of Augustine's Letters*, edited by P. Nehring, M. Stróżyński and R. Toczko, 181–202. Turnhout: Brepols, 2017.
Conybeare, Catherine. "Spaces between Letters: Augustine's Correspondence with Women." In *Voices in Dialogue: Reading Women in the Middle Ages*, edited by Linda Olson and Kathryn Kerby-Fulton, 55–72, with a response by Mark Vessey, 73–96. Notre Dame, IN: University of Notre Dame Press, 2005.
Conybeare, Catherine. *Paulinus Noster: Self and Symbols in the Letters of Paulinus of Nola*. Oxford: Oxford University Press, 2000.

Divjak, Johannes. "*Epistulae*." In *Augustinus-Lexikon*, edited by Christoph Mayer, vol. 2, 893–1057. Basel: Schwabe, 1996–2002.
Ebbeler, Jennifer, and Cristiana Sogno. "Religious Identity and the Politics of Patronage: Symmachus and Augustine." *Historia* 56 (2007): 230–42
Ebbeler, Jennifer. "The Letter Collection of Augustine of Hippo." In *Letter Collections*, eds. Sogno et al.: 239–53.
Gibson, Roy. "On the Nature of Ancient Letter Collections." *JRS* 102 (2012): 56–78
Hermanowicz, Erika. *Possidius of Calama: A Study of the North African Episcopate*. Oxford: Oxford University Press, 2008.
Hombert, Pierre-Marie. *Nouvelles recherches de chronologie augustinienne*. Paris: Institut d'Études Augustiniennes, 2000.
Jones, A.H.M. *The Later Roman Empire 286–602*. Oxford: Blackwell, 1964.
Konstan, David. *Friendship in the Classical World*. Cambridge: Cambridge University Press, 1997.
Lane Fox, Robin. *Augustine: Confessions and Conversions*. London: Allen Lane, 2016.
Leone, Anna. "Tracing the Donatist Presence in North Africa: An Archaeological Perspective." In *The Donatist Schism*, ed. Miles, 317–44.
Liebeschuetz, Wolf. *Ambrose of Milan: Political Letters and Speeches*. Liverpool: Liverpool University Press, 2005.
Lienhard, Joseph. "Paulinus of Nola." In *Augustine Through the Ages: An Encyclopedia*, edited by Allan D. Fitzgerald OSA, 628–9. Grand Rapids: Eerdmans, 1999.
McLynn, Neil. "Augustine's Roman Empire." In *History, Apocalypse and the Secular Imagination: New Essays on Augustine's City of God*, edited by Mark Vessey, Karla Pollman and Allan D. Fitzgerald OSA, 29–44. Bowling Green: Philosophy Documentation Center, 1999.
McLynn, Neil. "The Conference of Carthage Reconsidered." In *The Donatist Schism*, ed. Miles: 220–48.
Miles, Richard. "Let's (Not) Talk About It: Augustine and the Control of Epistolary Dialogue." In *The End of Dialogue in Antiquity*, ed. Simon Goldhill, 135–48. Cambridge: Cambridge University Press, 2008.
Miles, Richard, ed. *The Donatist Schism: Controversy and Contexts*. Liverpool: Liverpool University Press, 2016.
Mratschek, Sigrid. "*Multis enim notissima est sanctitas loci:* Paulinus and the Gradual Rise of Nola as a Center of Christian Hospitality." *JECS* 9 (2001): 511–53.
Mratschek, Sigrid. "The Unwritten Letters of Augustine of Hippo." In *Scrinium Augustini: The World of Augustine's Letters*, editd by P. Nehring, M. Stróżyński and R. Toczko, 57–78. Turnhout: Brepols, 2017.
Neil, Bronwen, and Pauline Allen, eds. *Collecting Early Christian Letters: From the Apostle Paul to Late Antiquity*. Cambridge: Cambridge University Press, 2015.
O'Daly, Gerard. *Augustine's City of God: a Reader's Guide*. Oxford: Oxford University Press, 1999.
O'Donnell, James. *Augustine: A New Biography*. New York: Ecco, 2005.
Rapp, Claudia. *Holy Bishops in Late Antiquity: The Nature of Christian Leadership in an Age of Transition*. Berkeley Ca: University of California Press, 2005.
Rebenich, Stefan. "Augustine on Friendship and Orthodoxy." In *A Companion*, ed. Vessey, 365–74.

Rebillard, Éric. "Augustine in Controversy with the Donatists Before 411." In *The Donatist Schism*, ed. Miles, 297–316.

Shaw, Brent. *Sacred Violence: African Christians and Sectarian Hatred in the Age of Augustine*. Cambridge: Cambridge University Press, 2011.

Shaw, Brent. "Augustine and Men of Imperial Power." *Journal of Late Antiquity* 8 (2015): 32–61.

Sogno, Cristiana, Bradley Storin and Edward Watts, eds. *Late Antique Letter Collections: A Critical Introduction and Reference Guide*. Berkeley, Ca.: University of California Press, 2016.

Sotinel, Claire. "Augustine's Information Circuits." In *A Companion*, ed. Vessey, 125–37.

Trout, Dennis. *Paulinus of Nola: Life, Letters, Poems*. Berkeley, Ca: University of California Press, 1999.

Vessey, Mark, ed. *A Companion to Augustine*. Chichester: Wiley-Blackwell, 2012.

Vessey, Mark. "Augustine among the Writers of the Church." In *A Companion*, ed. Vessey, 240–54.

Whelan, Robin. "Mirrors for Bureaucrats: Expectations of Christian Officials in the Theodosian Empire." *JRS* 108 (2018): 1–25.

Williams, Michael Stuart. "Beloved Lord and Honourable Brother: The Negotiation of Status in Augustine, *Letter* 23." In *Unclassical Traditions II: Perspectives from East and West in Late Antiquity*, edited by Christopher Kelly, Richard Flower, and Michael Stuart Williams, 88–101. Cambridge: Cambridge Philological Society, 2011.

Madalina Toca & Johan Leemans
The Authority of a 'Quasi-Bishop:' Patronage and Networks in the Letters of Isidore of Pelusium

1 Introduction

During the first decades of the fifth century, Pelusium was a middle-sized city in the North-Eastern Nile Delta. The city was the provincial capital of Augustamnica Prima and its easy access to the Mediterranean had provided a big harbour with the occasion to develop and flourish. With the metropolis and cultural centre Alexandria, as well as monastic centres in the desert not too far away, it was a place where talented people could start or develop a successful life, whether it be devoted to intellectual pursuits, an ecclesiastical career, the monastic life or a career in business, administration or politics.

In this article, we will focus on one of the best-known sons of this city: Isidore of Pelusium. His corpus of 2000 extant letters is a goldmine of information about late antique patronage and networking. We will first introduce Isidore and highlight some important points about his letters. The lions' share of the article will consist of an overview of the many types of networks and patronage Isidore was involved in, each of which will be made more concrete by examples taken from his letters. We conclude by evaluating what type of leadership Isidore's example bears testimony to and to what extent the term 'quasi-bishop' in the title may encapsulate this.

2 Isidore and his letters

Most of our knowledge about Isidore of Pelusium has to be derived from his extant letters. Isidore was a native from Pelusium and must have been born there ca. 360. After an extensive education in his native city and in Alexandria, he was appointed by the βουλή (city council) as σοφιστής (a tutor for advanced students). During his tenure of this position he came in contact with young people with high potential in Pelusium and with their parents. This was one of the foundations of his wide ever-expanding network: when they climbed the career ladder, Isidore kept in contact with them and they, in turn, asked for his advice and through their contacts helped him enlarge his network. Next, he changed his sec-

https://doi.org/10.1515/9783110553390-006

ular career for an ecclesiastical one and became a priest in Pelusium, under bishop Ammonius whom he greatly admired and who, in turn, trusted him. For many years Isidore served the church of Pelusium as one of its leading persons. No doubt this has deepened his identification with the city and the church of Pelusium and his determination to contribute to it as much as possible. Yet, everything changed dramatically with the appointment of Ammonius' successor, Eusebius, under whose leadership matters in the church of Pelusium went completely wrong. The situation must have been unpleasant, to say the least, as it made Isidore leave the city. For the last three decades of his life, Isidore lived as a monk in the Nitrian desert, in a monastery not too far from Pelusium. In these years the majority of his letters has been written. He died no later than 449 or 450.[1]

The corpus of about 2000 (mostly rather short) letters is Isidore's sole legacy.[2] These understudied letters document his dealings with bishops, priests, civil administrators, monks, and other inhabitants of Pelusium. Although a monk and living at a distance from his city, he clearly was well-informed about what went on. He entertained a wide network in and around Pelusium as well as in the monastic world of his region. He was held in high esteem and many contacted him

---

[1] This brief biographical sketch relies on the exhaustive discussion in the seminal monograph on Isidore by Pierre Évieux, *Isidore de Péluse*, ThH 99 (Paris: Beauchesne, 1995), 295–330. See also Johan Leemans, "Die Briefe des Isidor von Pelusium: Bildung, Glaube, Kommunikation," in *Von Rom nach Bagdad: Bildung und Religion in der späteren Antike bis zum Klassischen Islam*, eds. Peter Gemeinhardt and Sebastian Günther (Tübingen: Mohr Siebeck, 2012): 29–49; Ursula Treu, "Isidor II (von Pelusium)," *RAC* 18 (1998): 982–1002; Lillian Larsen, "The Letter Collection of Isidore of Pelusium," in *Late Antique Letter Collections: A Critical Introduction and Reference Guide*, eds. Cristiana Sogno, Bradley K. Storin and Edward J. Watts (Oakland, California: University of California Press, 2016): 286–308.

[2] The transmission of these letters is complicated. For a brief survey see Treu, "Isidor," 985–987. See also Cuthbert H. Turner, "The Letters of Saint Isidore of Pelusium," *JThS* 6 (1905): 70–86, Kirsopp Lake, "Further Notes on the Mss of Isidore of Pelusium," *JThS* 6 (1905): 270–282, Morton Smith, "Manuscript Tradition of Isidore of Pelusium," *HThR* 47 (1954): 205–210, Madalina Toca, "The Greek Manuscript Reception of Isidore of Pelusium's Epistolary Corpus," *BN* 175 (2017): 133–143. Until 2017, the letters 1214–1700 have been critically edited by P. Évieux, *Lettres 1214–1413*, and *Lettres 1414–1700* (in SC 422, and 454). He has changed the numbering adopted in the *Patrologia Graeca* 78, see Pierre Évieux, "Isidore de Péluse. La numérotation des lettres dans la tradition manuscrite," *Revue de recherches sur l'histoire des textes* 5 (1975): 45–72 and the concordance in Évieux, *Isidore de Péluse*, 411–418. Recently, letters 1701–2000 have also been published in SC 586 by Nicolas Vinel who prepared for publication the late Évieux' unfinished edition. In what follows we will consistently follow Évieux's numbering of the letters, and will refer to SC or PG (including page-numbers or column-numbers) when discussing a letter at length.

for advice or spiritual guidance. He also kept a close look at the affairs of the local church in Pelusium and he did not hesitate to intervene. For many people from his region, he was an unofficially recognised authority. According to a rough estimate, about 50% of Isidore's letters were written as response to queries from his correspondents in the form of letters,[3] and they were often a part of an on-going correspondence. This is reflected in a considerable number of addressees who received more than a few letters from Isidore.[4]

Unfortunately, the exploitation of this goldmine of information is hampered by at least three major factors. First, the letters are often short, and it has been thought that they were truncated by a compiler.[5] Content wise they are often not concrete, lacking precise historical information and making the identification of various episodes quite difficult. Moreover, much historical context, shared by writer and reader, is assumed and, hence, not explained. So, to continue the example, we can only guess whether there was a concrete reason to send out a friendly reminder, or a severe injunction[6] to do better (Isidore did not shy away from that either). The isolated character of this documentation makes it also hard to evaluate the historical reliability of what Isidore writes. In most cases we only hear his side of the story. At best, there is circumstantial evidence[7] that what is described is something one might expect or which is also on record for other regions or periods, but we seldom get further than this.

---

3 'Mehr als die Hälfte aller Briefe lässt deutlich erkennen dass sie eine Antwort auf eine Anfrage sind' (Treu, "Isidore," 989).
4 See Évieux, *Isidore de Péluse*, 91–241. There are actually quite some correspondents to whom he sends a couple of dozen letters: bishop Apollonius receives fourteen letters, priest Athanasius and *clarissimus* Dorotheus receive eighteen letters each, Ausonius the corrector receives seventeen, the soldier Isaiah receives at least fourteen letters, bishop Eusebius fifteen, deacon Eustathius receives about thirty six (some in common with other people), the sophist Harpocrates twenty eight, the *comes* Herminus forty one, bishop Hermogenes at least twenty four, bishop Isidore about thirty one, bishop Lampetius twenty seven, Paul (a monk or a clerk in Pelusium) receives forty three, Maron and Zosimus receive more than sixty letters, and deacon Eutonius receives seventy six. Thus, there is quite a wide range of variation among the people he is in constant contact with.
5 The most critical voice in this regard was that of Utto Riedinger, "Neue Hypotyposen-Fragmente bei Pseudo-Caesarius und Isidor von Pelusium," *ZNW* 51 (1960): 154–196, esp. 155.
6 For instance, in letter 1324 [5.75] to deacon Diogenes, Isidore blames him for losing his grace, and warns him that if he falls astray once more, he will not have anybody to help him recover. In letters 1478 [5.194] and 1776 [5.405] to deacon Palladius, Isidore exhorts him to abstain from lust, and reminds him that even if he escapes the judgment of people, he will not escape that of God.
7 For instance, for the events around the Council of Ephesus, the episcopal lists may help us spot the bishops from Isidore's entourage, etc.

A second factor that convolutes the examination of this corpus, is the difficulty of identifying the addressees of the letters. They are mentioned in the title of the letter but only by name, and often, but not always, function. As there are in the corpus some addressees with the same name, it is sometimes not even clear which letters have been sent to whom. Thus, it is not uncommon to have letters sent to one and the same person who appears within the corpus with up to four or five functions.

For instance, there are seventeen letters addressed to persons with the name 'Didymus:'[8] six of these letters sent to the 'priest Didymus'[9] (with the function attached), one letter addressed to 'Didymus and Heron,'[10] seven more to 'Didymus' without any title or function attached,[11] and finally there are also three letters to a 'Didymus *scholasticus*.'[12] When we exclude the letters addressed to Didymus *scholasticus* (for which the function attached makes it clear that we are dealing with a different character then the 'priest' Didymus), we are left with fourteen letters possibly addressed to one and the same person. On this basis, it has been rather common in scholarship to assume a connection between Isidore and Didymus the Blind. This is significant for the dating of the corpus: if this Didymus would indeed be proven to be the same person as Didymus the Blind, these letters must have been written before 395 when Didymus died, which would place them among the oldest of the whole corpus. Yet, a close examination of the fourteen letters shows that there are virtually no positive indicators to support the identification of Isidore's Didymus with Didymus the Blind and therefore the dating of the earliest letters based on the identification of Didymus as the addressee has a very weak basis.[13]

To give one more example, a Lampetius (without a function attached to his name) receives four letters, Lampetius the 'deacon' receives eight letters, the 'monk' two letters, and the 'bishop' twenty seven. In this case, it is not excluded that Lampetius the 'deacon' and 'monk' later became bishop of Casion.[14] However, there are also more unclear examples of letters sent to a name with several functions. For instance, (a) person(s) named 'John' receives six letters as 'dea-

---

[8] For a useful prosopographical list with all the addresses of Isidore's letters and their function, see Évieux, *Isidore de Péluse*, 387–410.
[9] Letters 681, 682, 1249 [5.28], 1448 [5.167], 1515 [4.20], 1949 [5.534].
[10] Letter 1818 [5.433].
[11] Letters 199, 201, 204, 205, 281, 330, 331.
[12] Letters 1492 [5.206], 1493 [5.207], and 1982 [4.152].
[13] For further discussion see Madalina Toca, "Isidore of Pelusium's Letters to Didymus the Blind," *StPatr* 96 (2017): 325–332.
[14] Évieux, *Isidore de Péluse*, 73.

con,' two letters as 'hermit,' one letter as 'monk,' four letters as '*scholasticus*,' and finally two as 'soldier.' This small dossier is a telling example of how difficult it is to identify the addressees with certainty.[15]

Finally, the brief and abstract character of many of the letters, together with the confusion given by several (seemingly unrelated) letters ascribed to the same addressee, bring up a third major struggle, namely the difficulty of dating the letters. While this problem cannot be solved on the level of each individual letter, the abovementioned hurdles can be partially overcome by the sheer size of the letter corpus, and the extensive knowledge we do have of the Later Roman Empire and Egypt in the fourth and early fifth centuries CE. This helps to contextualise the letters, make sense of them and place them at the end of the fourth and the first decades of the fifth century. Much effort has been put into the contextualisation of the material in the pioneering work of some scholars, most notably Pierre Évieux. Standing on the shoulders of his work, we are now able to offer in what follows a non-exhaustive bird's eye view of the breadth and variety of Isidore's activity as a patron and highlight with illustrations the role his network played therein.

3 Isidore's Patronage and Networks

3.1 Bonus, the ship-owner

Patronage and networks were especially valuable when in trouble. Then, an appeal to a high magistrate responsible for the issue under concern was crucial. This could occur directly or through an intermediary who put his network at the service of the person in trouble. Isidore clearly was willing to act as such an intermediary for individuals who approached him for help. The two letters related to the case of the ναύκληρος ('ship-owner') Bonus are a beautiful illustration. What had happened? Egypt was a major production centre for grain. Every year, many ships loaded to full capacity with grain left the harbours of Alexandria for Constantinople. This σιτοπομπία ('transport of corn') was an essential lifeline for the capital and, hence, a sensitive political issue. In 335 the probably slanderous accusation that Athanasius of Alexandria had the plan to prevent the grain fleet from sailing cost him the goodwill of Emperor Constantine. As it was

---

[15] According to Évieux, *Isidore de Péluse*, 74, it may be the case that John the 'hermit' and John the 'deacon' are one and the same person, and are both subsequently identified as the bishop of Hephaestus or bishop of Panephysis. However, this is quite difficult to prove.

so important, quite a few magistrates and a complete army of lower administrative personnel were involved in the practical organisation of this whole endeavour.

Bonus was a ναύκληρος who put his ship at disposal for this σιτοπομπία. Because of the bad weather, heavy winds and a storm on the Mediterranean, his boat with all the grain on board had sunk. This was a major financial loss for Bonus as he had to repay the value of the lost grain to the public treasury. Besides the financial burden on himself and his company, Bonus may also have feared repercussions from the government that put the future of his business in jeopardy. In this dire situation, Bonus asked Isidore for help. Isidore honoured Bonus' request and wrote two letters on his behalf: 299 and 300. The first letter was addressed to a certain Isidore, who is styled ἔπαρχος ('prefect'). This may indicate several very high functions.[16] Given that Bonus was clearly dependent on him and that he was in a position to help him in this regard, we may see with Évieux[17] this Isidore as the *praefectus augustalis* in Alexandria, who had the final responsibility for the ἄννωνα ('grain supply') and ultimately for 'the collection and shipment of the grain.'

In letter 299 Isidore asks his namesake, the ἔπαρχος, to acquit Bonus of having to pay back to the treasure the grain that went lost. After all, it was the bad weather and Bonus could not have done anything to prevent what had happened. This Isidore must have been a Christian because our Isidore casts his argument also in a theological vein: in situations on which we depend on God, we ask for his forgiveness when we have done something wrong. In a similar vein, Isidore should not let justice and the law prevail, but clemency.

Letter 300 has as its addressee Sozomenus, the δομέστικος ('assistant') of the ἔπαρχος. This letter served as a sort of introduction letter, delivered by Bonus himself to Sozomenus. Isidore informs him in one short sentence about Bonus' problems, about which he will already have heard from the prefect. Here too, explicit religious language is being used: Isidore points out that

---

[16] Terminologically it is also possible that the ἔπαρχος Isidore was *praefectus urbis* or *praefectus praetorio Orientis*, which would make him one of the highest officers in the central political structure of the Empire. We know of an Isidore who occupied such high-ranking positions and we know our Isidore had contact with this Isidore. It is probably the same person but given that Isidore can arrange a personal meeting between Bonus and this ἔπαρχος Isidore, it seems more likely that this took place when he was still holding a position in Egypt rather than in Constantinople. It is also more conceivable that the *praefectus augustalis* would be approached – to whose core-business this belonged – than the very powerful *praefectus urbis* or *praefectus praetorio* who had much more wide-ranging responsibilities, cf. Évieux, *Isidore de Péluse*, 101–102.
[17] Évieux, *Isidore de Péluse*, 102–103.

Bonus adheres to the 'orthodox religion' and that he is well-disposed in all regards towards Sozomenus. He requests Sozomenus to liberate Bonus from his miserable situation 'so that at the great day Christ may crown you with crowns of incorruptibility.' We do not know what the final outcome of Isidore's intervention was, but these letters are certainly a telling example of how Isidore put his contacts at work in favour of a fellow-Pelusian.

3.2 Complaints with the highest officials: The Gigantius-affair

But Isidore's contacts reached even much further into the highest circles of power. The issues he got involved with also went far beyond intervening on behalf of solving the plight of an individual Pelusian ναύκληρος. Isidore also acted as the spokesperson for the community of Pelusium, addressing very high placed magistrates with the request to rectify unjust situations with regard to the city. The Gigantius-affair is an interesting illustration of Isidore's commitment, well-documented in a dossier of 11 letters.[18] Gigantius, of Cappadocian origin, was making his way through the *cursus honorum* and had occupied an important ἀρχή ('function') in Pelusium. The testimony of the letters makes it clear that he was in a leading position in which he had much power over the inhabitants of Pelusium. He may well have been κορρήκτωρ ('provincial governor') of Augustamnica Prima and have resided in Pelusium, the capital of the province.

The letters describe in retrospect Gigantius' many wrongdoings and abuse of power in the past: fake accusations against landowners for not paying taxes; demanding more taxes; pressuring the small landowners into working as hired people on the large estates; confiscating the church funds that were collected to help the poor; false oaths; slander; theft and many more. The Pelusians, according to the exchange between his informants and Isidore, indeed suffered when Gigantius was governing them. But – still according to Isidore – Gigantius had crossed the line of what was deemed acceptable. He was put into chains, put on a boat to the court in Constantinople where he was taken into custody, tried, found guilty and robbed of his position.[19]

It is not clear how much of this is historical and how much were things wished for and hoped for at Pelusium. Nor is it sure how precise Isidore was informed

---

18 Letters 281, 351, 352, 430, 483–487, 489–490. We follow the analysis of Évieux, *Isidore de Péluse*, 48–56.
19 Letter 490.

about what happened exactly with Gigantius at the court in Constantinople. Even if his fate had been severe, the consequences were only temporary for the story takes an unexpected turn much later. We do not know when exactly this happened, how much later 'much later' exactly was, because Isidore is only using markers of relative chronology to situate Gigantius' tenure of his function in Pelusium: 'in the past,' 'at that time,' 'much earlier.' The unexpected turn is that, 'much later,' Gigantius is trying to be re-established in his position in Pelusium. When this rumour reaches Pelusium, Isidore (in his monastery) and his fellow-Pelusians are self-evidently upset at the idea that the terror of the past would come back. In this situation Isidore puts his network at the service of the city and the province in an attempt to prevent Gigantius' return.

He also writes to several very high-placed persons at the court in Constantinople with whom he was well-connected. Because the *tituli* of the letters only mention the addressees' names and not their function(s), it is hard to identify them with absolute certainty. The most conspicuous addressees[20] seem to be Rufinus, the *praefectus praetorio Orientis* (letters 178 and 489)[21] and Florentius, the *praefectus Urbis* (letter 486). For instance, in letter 178 Isidore reproaches Rufinus for having ignored the wrongdoings of the governor Cyrenius, and pleads him to take action or otherwise the Pelusians will be troubled.[22]

Three more letters (281 to Didymus, and 351 and 352 to Ammon) were addressed to other connections who were slightly lower in the hierarchy. In all these letters Isidore convincingly argues with reference to the atrocities of the past, that his addressees would use all their influence with the Emperor and within the highest-ranking political circles to avoid the return of Gigantius to Pelusium. Here one sees how far Isidore is willing to go to defend the interest of his compatriots. Even while in the monastery, he remains well-informed and in touch with what happened in the world and to his city and takes an active role in safeguarding the interests of the city and of the province.

---

[20] Isidore seems to contact quite some people in Constantinople about this episode: Seleucus (letter 484), Isidore (letter 485), Archonius (letter 487), Rufinus (letter 489), Catillianus (letter 490). See Évieux, *Isidore de Péluse*, 52.
[21] See Évieux, *Isidore de Péluse*, 59.
[22] This is not a singular case, as he also uses the very same discourse in letter 1328 [5.79] (SC 422, p. 370) to Cyril of Alexandria urging him to properly use his power and remove the οἰκονόμος ('administrator') Martinianus from his function. See section 3.4 below.

3.3 Letters to the emperor

When it comes to high-ranking addressees of Isidore, the crown-jewels in the correspondence are the letters he wrote to emperor Theodosius II himself. There are two items in the corpus whose *tituli* present them as letters addressed to this emperor. One is a petition about alleviating the taxes, the other a plea for the emperor's personal involvement in the council of Ephesus. In letter 35 Isidore demands a balanced exercise of power and the reduction of taxes (for the Pelusians, one presumes), as it should be expected from a noble leader who desires to attain the Kingdom of Christ.[23] He clearly uses religious language to give power to his argument, and perhaps to effectively impress Theodosius. As such, Isidore correlates the emperor's salvation with good and honest administration skills; he also pleads for mixing mildness with authority and for the fair distribution of wealth, while hinting at the danger of idolatry when one is inclined to keep too much for himself.

The request of letter 311 is of a different nature altogether. This letter is taken as one of the historical landmarks of the corpus as it directly refers to events around the council of Ephesus from 431. In it, Isidore asks for the emperor's presence no less ("If you would have the chance to be present at the deliberations in Ephesus")[24] and for his involvement in overseeing the council of Ephesus, as a strategic way to keep things from going astray. The implication here is that unless Theodosius supervises the voting and remedies the situation, the council is compromised. It is interesting that this letter has been understood to mean that Isidore was aiming to keep the emperor away from the council rather than in-

---

23 Letter 35 (PG 78, col. 204). On this letter see also G. Merianos and G. Gotsis, "Fifth-Century Patristic Conceptions of Savings and Capital: Isidore of Pelusium and Theodoret of Cyrrhus," in their *Managing Financial Resources in Late Antiquity* (London: Palgrave, 2017), at 121–122.

24 Letter 311 (PG 78, col. 361): Θεοδοσίῳ Βασιλεῖ. Εἰ μὲν αὐτὸς λαμβάνῃ καιροῦ παρεῖναι τοῖς κρινομένοις ἐν Ἐφέσῳ, προσέσται τούτοις εὖ οἶδα τὸ ἄμεμπτον. Εἰ δὲ ὀχλώδει ἀντιπαθείᾳ τὰς ψήφους ἐκδώσειας, τίς ἐξαιρήσεται τὴν σύνοδον σκωμμάτων: Παρέξεις δὲ τούτοις θεραπείαν, εἰ παύσειας τῶν δογματισμῶν τοὺς σοὺς διακόνους, πρὸς μέγα χάσμα διεστῶτας, βασιλεῖ ὑπηρετεῖσθαι καὶ Θεῷ διαφιλονεικεῖσθαι· μή πως τῷ κράτει σάλον ἐπενέγκωσι, τῇ πέτρᾳ τῆς Ἐκκλησίας προσρηγνύντες τὰ τῆς κακοπιστίας αὐτῶν μηχανήματα. Αὕτη γὰρ ἐρήρεισται, καὶ οὔτε ὑπὸ πυλῶν ᾅδου κυριεύεται, ὡς ὁ δράσας αὐτὴν Θεὸς ἐπηγγείλατο. "If you would have the chance to be present at the deliberations in Ephesus, I know that there will be no reproach for you on their part. But if you give up the elections to the turbulent anthypaty, who will set the synod free from the follies? You will do them a service, if you stop your servants from dogmatizing, [your servants] who are divided by a great hesitation whether to serve the emperor or contend against God; so that not to bring distemper to the sovereignty, dashing against the rock of the church the contrivances of their wrong belief. For this one stands firm and is not dominated by the gates of hell, as God, its doer, promised when He created it."

volve him in it.²⁵ However, according to Isidore, the emperor's presence as a guarantor of peace presents two advantages: on the one hand, his subordinates would not erroneously dogmatise, being torn between 'serving the emperor' and 'quarreling with God,' and on the other, the antipathies of the rival ecclesiastical parties (i.e. Cyril and Nestorius) would not escalate. One should differentiate here between the intervention of the emperor and that of his subordinates. Isidore only tries to prevent the latter, which is why he asks for the presence of the emperor at the council, to oversee the peace.²⁶ In any case, what we know from the conciliar proceedings is that Theodosius did not come in person, but entrusted his representative Candidianus with the practicalities,²⁷ who was later dismissed for possibly favouring Cyril's followers.²⁸

3.4 Letters to Cyril of Alexandria

Picking up from here, and standing in close relation with the Ephesus-event, Isidore's most high-ranking addressee from the ecclesiastical milieu is Cyril of Alexandria. Cyril is the recipient of no less than eleven letters, eight of which are addressed to 'bishop Cyril (of Alexandria)' – 310, 323, 324, 370, 627 [2.127], 1106 [3.306], 1328 [5.79], 1582 [5.268], and the remaining three to 'Cyril' without any title attached – 25, 393, 497.

The correspondence with Cyril develops along two main coordinates: one has to do with a local conflict, covering a number of complaints around the wrongdoings of the bishop of Pelusium, and the other, with a wider scope, is re-

---

25 See, for instance, Larsen, "The Letter Collection of Isidore of Pelusium," 301, footnote 26: "Ep. 311 ... critiques Theodosius II for imperial interference in conciliar proceedings."
26 Although not completely clear, Évieux distinguishes between the involvement of the emperor's subordinates and the emperor's own intervention: "... le Pélusiote demande à l'empereur de ne pas laisser ses subordonnés se mêler des affaires de l'Église à Éphèse. La tentation était grande, on le sait, pour l'empereur, si féru de théologie et si désireux de placer l'Église d'Orient sous le pouvoir impérial, de diriger selon son gré les sessions du concile afin d'éviter les affrontements entre les factions rivales" (Évieux, *Isidore de Péluse*, 47).
27 Norman Russell, *Cyril of Alexandria*, The Early Church Fathers (London, New York: Routledge, 2000), 46, 48–50; Susan Wessel, *Cyril of Alexandria and the Nestorian Controversy*, OECS (Oxford: Oxford University Press, 2004), 143, 167–169.
28 Russell, *Cyril of Alexandria*, 51. The documents exchanged between the parties (letters to and from Cyril, the reports of Nestorius, Candidianus, and John of Antioch) are preserved in the Proceedings of the Council in *Acta Conciliorum Oecumenicorum* (ACO), *tomus primus, volumus primus, pars prima – pars septima Concilium Universale Ephesinum*, ed. Eduard Schwartz (Berlin, Leipzig: Walter de Gruyter 1927–9).

lated to the council of Ephesus. Here we will mainly focus on the latter, as it sheds light on Isidore's ambitions on a larger scale than a home-grown quarrel. However, for the sake of comparison, it is useful to briefly present first the Pelusium affair as well.

The conflict erupts with the newly elected bishop Eusebius, accused by Isidore of having sold ordinations to unworthy candidates,[29] and having overlooked the abuses of the clerics,[30] among whom the priest Zosimus, and the οἰκονόμος ('administrator') Martinianus. Zosimus is central in this conflict, receiving the greatest number of letters from Isidore (eighty one!),[31] and together with Martinianus, they are depicted as two of the most detested people in Pelusium. Taking into account the large number of letters touching upon this conflict (at least two hundred letters) it is interesting to see how Isidore provides more often *ad hominem* attacks, and literary motifs (they are former slaves,[32] uneducated, vicious – letters 1035, 1048, 1902 [5.496] – and do not know the Scriptures), rather than concrete accusations (they misuse the church funds – letter 613, do not give alms – letters 544, 627).

It is in this conflict that Isidore draws Cyril by demanding him to step in and stop the abuses. To give one example, in letter 1328 [5.79][33] – adopting an extremely venomous tone – Isidore describes the greediness of the οἰκονόμοι,[34] who are only preoccupied with their own prosperity and are not distributing the funds fairly. Isidore also implies that unless Cyril takes responsibility for the church wealth's distribution, the poor will be continuously oppressed. Thus, it is interesting to see how Cyril is both suspected of having tacitly toler-

---

29 See for instance letters 26, 30, 119, 151, 215, 250, 341.
30 See letters 28, 119, 250, etc.
31 If one also counts the letters which are not only addressed to Zosimus and the letters which refer to him, without necessarily being addressed to him, there are no less than 178 letters related to this name, which – out of the 2000 letters – is quite an impressive number. See Évieux, *Isidore de Péluse*, 213.
32 It is interesting to see how they are both depicted as 'freed slaves,' or 'sons of slaves' (letters 890, 1822 [5.437], 1290 [5.59]), of uncertain origin (letter 627), a leitmotif for the unworthiness of a person for a higher position.
33 SC 422, p. 370.
34 The function of the οἰκονόμος was regulated only about the mid of the fifth century. They were mainly responsible with the financial aspects of the church, and were "ranked among a lesser and parallel group of clergy," as the financial and the liturgical aspects were quite separated, see Christopher Haas, *Alexandria in Late Antiquity. Topography and Social Conflict* (Baltimore, London: Johns Hopkins, 1997), 225. Ewa Wipszycka, *The Alexandrian Church: People and Institutions*, JJP.S 25 (Warsaw: The Raphael Taubenschlag Foundation, 2015), 256–7. Also ead., *Les ressources et les activités économiques des églises en Egypte du IVe – VIIIe siècle*, PapyBrux 10 (Brussels: Fondation Égyptologique Reine Élisabeth, 1972), 135–141.

ated the abuses of Eusebius and Martinianus, but is also considered the only one capable to end these wrongdoings. In any event, it is noteworthy how Isidore takes a stance against this unfortunate situation, and how he depicts himself as reacting to it through his letters. By the number of people involved, the claimed gravity of matters at stake, and the urgency of having things solved, Isidore manages to build up for himself the image of a passionate defender of the community and church in Pelusium, and of an old wise advisor of Cyril himself.

The second set of letters addressed to Cyril is related to the council of Ephesus, which reveals Isidore as playing on a different level. He surpasses the role of a local protagonist and gives amplitude to his image as a church figure engaged in greater ecclesiastical matters. To start with, in letter 310, Cyril is urged not to imitate the directions of his uncle (Theophilus of Alexandria),[35] but to show impartiality in his actions with regard to the Ephesus council. In doing so, he is rebuking two bishops of Alexandria at once. The letter preserves a strong criticism of Cyril, allegedly echoing not only Isidore's disappointment, but also the opinion of those gathered at Ephesus:

> Sympathy is not clear-sighted, and antipathy does not see at all. If you wish therefore to be clear of both eye-sores, do not come out with violent denials, and leave the accusations to a fair judgment. ... For many of those who have gathered at Ephesus are ridiculing you, that you are guarding your own enmity but you are not searching for the right belief of Jesus Christ. "He is the nephew of Theophilus," they say "and is imitating his judgment. For just as that one spread his clear mania upon the God-bearing and God-loved John, so this one longs to boast himself, though there is a great difference between those who are accused."[36]

The background of this letter should be understood in relation with Theophilus' attitude towards John Chrysostom whom Theophilus deposed in 403,[37] but also as referring to Cyril's rivalry towards Nestorius. Thus, comparing Cyril with Theophilus is meant to reveal an existing pattern which seems to be occurring again.

---

[35] On the relationship between Cyril and his uncle in the aftermath of the latter's dispute with John Chrysostom see Wessel, *Cyril of Alexandria*, 23–27, and 31–32.

[36] Letter 310 (PG 78, col. 361): Προσπάθεια μὲν οὐκ ὀξυδορκεῖ, ἀντιπάθεια δὲ ὅλως οὐχ ὁρᾷ. Εἰ τοίνυν ἑκατέρας λήμης βούλει καθαρεῦσαι, μὴ βιαίας ἀποφάσεις ἐκβίβαζε, ἀλλὰ κρίσει δικαίᾳ τὰς αἰτίας ἐπίτρεψον. ... Πολλοὶ γάρ σε κωμῳδοῦσι τῶν συνειλεγμένων εἰς Ἔφεσον, ὡς οἰκείαν ἀμυνόμενον ἔχθραν, ἀλλ' οὐ τὰ Ἰησοῦ Χριστοῦ ὀρθοδόξως ζητοῦντα. Ἀδελφιδοῦς ἐστι, φασί, Θεοφίλου, μιμούμενος ἐκείνου τὴν γνώμην. Ὥσπερ γὰρ ἐκεῖνος μανίαν σαφῆ κατεσκέδασε τοῦ θεοφόρου καὶ Θεοφιλοῦς Ἰωάννου, οὕτως ἐπιθυμεῖ καυχήσασθαι καὶ οὗτος, εἰ καὶ πολὺ τῶν κρινομένων ἐστὶ τὸ διάφορον.

[37] Évieux, *Isidore de Péluse*, 82; Norman Russell, *Theophilus of Alexandria* (London: Routledge, 2007), 31–34.

Though not specifically mentioned, Isidore probably also has in mind the fact that, at first, Cyril refused the rehabilitation of John Chrysostom.[38]

Taken together, letter 310 to Cyril and letter 311 to the emperor show Isidore rebuking the highest ecclesiastical authority and seeking to determine the involvement and, to some extent, the course of action, of an emperor in a church council. The rationale for his plan to involve the emperor, however, is explained in a different letter addressed to Cyril: in letter 1582 [5.268] Isidore complains that the priestly office was once strong enough to correct the flaws of the empire, but now it is under it. Distinguishing those who pretend to be priests (those who insult the priesthood through their wrong deeds) from true priesthood, Isidore notes that under the current circumstances it is reasonable that the imperial office corrects those who do not manage the church as they should. The rule of the emperor is therefore seen as absolutely necessary given the current state of the church, and Isidore writes letters to both leaders of his world to argue for the course of events which is most in accord with his view.[39]

Within this framework, letter 370 is particularly interesting for the way in which Isidore envisages his relationship to Cyril. In the same vein as in letter 310, Isidore does not hesitate to make demands from Cyril. Yet he does so through an interesting interplay of the 'father' – 'son' vocabulary: first, he adopts the tone of an older spiritual father who has to write to his son.[40] Then, modestly taking the persona of a son, he actually speaks as if impersonating the whole Egyptian Church, dependent upon Cyril's decisions.

> The examples of the holy Scripture frighten me, and I am compelled to write you that which is necessary. For if I am a father – as you are saying yourself – I fear the condemnation of Eli because he did not correct his sons who were erring. Or if I would happen to be your son, as I rather know [that I am], of you who are put in the posture of the great Mark, I am in distress about the penalties of Jonathan, which did not prevent his father for seeking the sorcerer. ... Therefore, in order for me not to be condemned, and for you not to be judged by God, bring the quarrels to an end. [...][41]

---

[38] See letter 75 of Atticus of Constantinople to Cyril concerning the reinstatement of John Chrysostom, and the unenthusiastic response of Cyril in letter 76. See John I. McEnerney, trans. *St. Cyril of Alexandria, Letters 51–110*, FaCh 77 (Washington, D.C.: The Catholic University of America Press, 2007), 83–85 and 86–91. Also Russell, *Cyril of Alexandria*, 206, n. 24.
[39] The same *topos* appears in letter 1346 [5.89] to Eusebius the priest in which Isidore underlines that "the piety of the rulers puts into light the impiety of the bishops" (SC 422, p. 394).
[40] See Larsen, "The Letter Collection of Isidore of Pelusium," 290.
[41] Letter 370 (PG 78, col. 392): Φοβεῖ με τὰ τῆς θείας Γραφῆς ὑποδείγματα, καὶ γράφειν τὰ χρεών ἀναγκάζομαι. Εἴτε γὰρ πατήρ εἰμι, ὡς ἔφης αὐτός, δέδια τοῦ Ἠλεὶ τὴν κατάκρισιν, ὅτι τοὺς υἱοὺς ἁμαρτόντας οὐκ ἐσωφρόνισεν · εἴτε υἱός σου τυγχάνω, ὡς μᾶλλον ἐπίσταμαι, τὸν μέγαν ἐκεῖνον σχηματίζοντος Μάρκον, ἀγωνιῶ τοῦ Ἰωνάθαν τὸ ἐπιτίμιον, ὅτι τὸν πατέρα ζητή-

Unfortunately, the letter remains obscure as to what the quarrels were actually about. While this might allude to Cyril's confrontations with Nestorius, with the Antiochenes, and so on, Évieux' suggestion that this letter refers to events that happened during the council of Ephesus, thus around June, or July 431, is not impossible.[42] In any event, this gives us a glimpse into the way Isidore envisages his interactions with Cyril, possibly around the Ephesus event.

Letter 324[43] then may hint to the aftermath of the council. There Isidore exhorts Cyril to persist in his teachings, without contradicting himself. For, when one is to compare his older with his newer writings, one shall not consider the changes and inconsistencies due to looseness, or vain glory. Given Isidore's aggravate tone, the letter was probably written immediately before the Formula of Union in 433, when the outcome was not yet clear.[44]

Finally, letter 323 is interesting because it contains Isidore's theological stance within the Christological debates of the day. He affirms that "the true God, over all things, became truly man neither having changed what he was or having taken what he was not, the only Son being from the beginning, of two natures (ἐκ φύσεων δυοῖν)[45] without beginning and without end, new and eternal."[46] Évieux dates it to either the period of the Nestorian quarrels or after the Council of Ephesus, during the quarrels with the Orientals (431–433).

To conclude: these letters show Isidore not only dealing with minor local conflicts and administrative matters, but interacting with, and trying to influence the highest exponents of power available – the bishop of Alexandria and the emperor, possibly even aiming at playing out one against the other.

σαντα ἐγγαστρίμυθον οὐκ ἐκώλυσε. ... Ἵνα τοίνυν κἀγὼ μὴ κατακριθῶ, καὶ αὐτὸς παρὰ Θεοῦ μὴ κριθῇς, παῦσον τὰς ἔριδας· [...].

42 Évieux, *Isidore de Péluse*, 83.
43 Letter 324 (PG 78, col. 369).
44 Évieux, *Isidore de Péluse*, 84.
45 According to Andreas Schmid, *Die Christologie Isidors von Pelusium*, Paradosis; Beiträge zur Geschichte der altchristlichen Literatur und Theologie 2 (Freiburg: Paulusverlag, 1948), 107, the ἐκ φύσεων δυοῖν formula is a later interpolation, and it does not seem customary before the synod of Constantinople (448). For a detailed analysis of the Christological *formulae* in letters 23, 303, 323 and 405, see Schmid, *Die Christologie*, 56–63.
46 Letter 323 (PG 78, col. 369): Ὅτι δὲ ὁ ἀληθινὸς καὶ ἐπὶ πάντων Θεὸς, ἄνθρωπος γέγονεν ἀληθῶς, οὔτε ὃ ἦν τραπείς, καὶ ὃ οὐκ ἦν προσλαβών, ἐκ φύσεων δυοῖν ὁ εἷς ὑπάρχων Υἱός, ἄναρχος καὶ ἀπέραντος, πρόσφατος καὶ ἀΐδιος...

3.5 Letters to monks

So far we have paid attention to Isidore's involvement with the higher echelons of politics and administration. These are interesting case-studies but they should not make us forget that Isidore was first and foremost a monk and a man of the church. A substantial part of his correspondence was addressed to monks and discusses issues that are pertinent to the concerns of that world.[47] The eleven letters he sent to the monk Strategius[48] may be seen as a master-example for many other letters to monks. One difference, though: Isidore and Strategius seem to have been friends. Not only does Isidore addresses him as "my friend" but in letter 1503, he announces a visit:

> If God so wills, you may expect to see me very soon in your monastery. For indeed, I will come to see your Piety (τὴν σὴν θεοσέβειαν), before everybody else. [I also come] to embrace the in all respects admirable Theodosius, as he is a friend already for a long time and as we hold him in high esteem."[49]

Apparently, Isidore and Strategius had been in close contact for some time. Strategius must have belonged to another monastery than Isidore. Between the two monasteries connections seem to have existed.

The other letters make clear that it was not really a friendship between two intimate friends but more that between two educated monks with Isidore taking on the role of spiritual guide. He gives Strategius advice about the virtuous life and sends him letters to congratulate him with the progress he is making on the path towards virtue. To Isidore, the virtue for the monk is, unsurprisingly, the mortification of the passions. In this regard, he also entertains a positive anthropology: thanks to the synergy between divine grace and human commitment, humans can achieve virtue. In this vein, in letter 572[50] Isidore offers some

---

[47] The announcement of a visit (letter 1503 [5.216]), praises of virtue (letter 1124), and concerns about battling passions (letter 1027), etc.
[48] Letters 572, 766, 898, 1025, 1027, 1028, 1124, 1303 [4.129], 1503 [5.216], 1901 [5.495], 1931 [5.519]. For a more extensive discussion of these letters, see Johan Leemans, "From Isidore to Strategius: An Example of Monastic Correspondence in Fifth-Century Egypt," in *Felici Curiositate. Studies in Latin Literature and Textual Criticism from Antiquity to the Twentieth Century, in Honour of Rita Beyers*, eds. Guy Guldentops, Christian Laes and Gert Partoens, IPM 72 (Turnhout: Brepols, 2017): 363–377.
[49] Letter 1503 (SC 454, pp. 170–171): Ἤδη με, σὺν Θεῷ δὲ εἰρήσθω, προσδόκησον ἐν τῷ μοναστηρίῳ · ἥξω γὰρ τὴν σὴν πρό γε πάντων ὀψόμενος θεοσέβειαν, καὶ τὸν διὰ πάντα θαυμάσιον Θεοδόσιον, διὰ μακροῦ φίλον ὄντα καὶ σφόδρα ἡμῖν τετιμημένον, περιπτυξόμενος.
[50] Letter 572 (PG 78, col. 513–516).

thoughts about the nature of evil in connection with Jer 13:23, where it is said: "Can the Ethiopian change his skin or the leopard his spots? Then also how could you do good who have been taught to do evil?" The text can be construed to mean that doing good is ultimately beyond human capacity. In Isidore's hands, however, the verse means exactly the opposite. Jer 13:23 says that, "you have been *taught* (μεμαθηκότες) evil." From this follows that evil does not belong to the nature or essence of the human being but that it is something that can be learned and, hence, also un-learned.

4 Conclusion: A Quasi-bishop?

Isidore assumed all kinds of pastoral and patronage duties, intervened for his city and church, tried to use his influence and put at work his best relations, supported specific causes in which he acted as benefactor (for instance the case of Bonus), but also intervened in mainstream clerical disputes. In all these cases, he can be rightly styled as a well-versed epistolographer, with the skills of a leading authority who projects himself as a leader watching over the flock. These examples, though rather different in nature, serve well to portray Isidore's decisional aspirations and the rhetorical devices he put at work to win his fights, and to depict himself the way he does. In this sense, while being a monk, he took on quite a few roles that were also adopted by bishops and he apparently did so with the same skills and success as many of his episcopal peers. Much of his successful attempts at networking must be ascribed to the network he built up in Pelusium during the years he was pursuing a secular career. When his pupils went on to higher offices they provided him ready access to a level of decision making inaccessible to the average Egyptian bishop. In this sense, Isidore was probably more influential than many local bishops were. But it would also be misleading to style him a quasi-bishop because he did not do some essential things a bishop should; *audientia episcopalis* and preaching are two obvious examples. But in a collective volume of studies on patronage and networks he is certainly not out of place. At least, he may serve us as a salutary reminder that also non-bishops with a substantial network could try to and succeeded in wielding power.

Bibliography

Primary Sources

Évieux, Pierre. *Isidore de Péluse. Lettres 1214–1413.* SC 422. Paris: Cerf, 1997.
Évieux, Pierre. *Isidore de Péluse. Lettres 1414–1700.* SC 454. Paris: Cerf, 2000.
Évieux, Pierre, Vinel, Nicolas. *Isidore de Péluse. Lettres 1701–2000.* SC 586. Paris: Cerf, 2017.
Migne, Jacques-Paul. *S. Isidori Pelusiotae epistolarum libri quinque post Jac. Billii, Cunr. Rittershusii et Andr. Schotti curas, ad codices Vaticanos exegit et plus bis mille locis emendauit, restituit, suppleuit P. Possinus, s.j. presb.* PG 78. Paris, 1860 and 1864.

Secondary Literature

Bayer, Leo. *Isidors von Pelusium klassische Bildung.* Paderborn: F. Schöningh, 1915.
Évieux, Pierre. *Isidore de Péluse.* ThH 99. Paris: Beauchesne, 1995.
Évieux, Pierre. "La numérotation des lettres dans la tradition manuscrite." *Revue d'histoire des textes* 5 (1975): 45–72.
Fouskas, Constantine. *Saint Isidore of Pelusium and the New Testament.* Athens, 1967.
Fouskas, Constantine. *Saint Isidore of Pelusium, His Life and His Works.* Athens, 1970 (publication of the thesis defended at Glasgow University in 1961).
Gemeinhardt, Peter and Günther, Sebastian. *Von Rom nach Bagdad. Bildung und Religion von der römischen Kaiserzeit bis zum klassischen Islam.* Tübingen: Mohr Siebeck, 2013.
Haas, Christopher. *Alexandria in Late Antiquity. Topography and Social Conflict.* Baltimore, London: Johns Hopkins, 1997.
Lake, Kirsopp. "Further Notes on the Mss of Isidore of Pelusium." *JThS* 6 (1905): 270–282.
Larsen, Lillian. "The Letter Collection of Isidore of Pelusium." In *Late Antique Letter Collections: A Critical Introduction and Reference Guide,* edited by Cristiana Sogno, Bradley K. Storin and Edward J. Watts, 286–308. Oakland, California: University of California Press, 2016.
Leemans, Johan. "From Isidore to Strategius: An Example of a Monastic Correspondence in Fifth-Century Egypt." In *Felici curiositate. Studies in Latin Literature and Textual Criticism from Antiquity to the Twentieth Century. In Honour of Rita Beyers,* edited by Guy Guldentops, Christian Laes and Gert Partoens, IPM 72, 363–375. Turnhout: Brepols, 2017.
Leemans, Johan. "Die Briefe des Isidor von Pelusium: Bildung, Glaube, Kommunikation." In *Von Rom nach Bagdad: Bildung und Religion in der späteren Antike bis zum Klassischen Islam,* edited by Peter Gemeinhardt and Sebastian Günther, 29–49. Tübingen: Mohr Siebeck, 2013.
McEnerney, John I., trans. *St. Cyril of Alexandria, Letters 51–110.* FaCh 77. Washington, D.C.: The Catholic University of America Press, 2007.
Merianos, Gerasimos and Gotsis, George. "Fifth-Century Patristic Conceptions of Savings and Capital: Isidore of Pelusium and Theodoret of Cyrrhus." In Gerasimos Merianos, George Gotsis, *Managing Financial Resources in Late Antiquity,* 117–158. London: Palgrave, 2017.

Riedinger, Utto. "Neue Hypotyposen-Fragmente bei Pseudo-Caesarius und Isidor von Pelusium." *ZNW* 51 (1960): 154–196.
Runia, David. "'Where, Tell Me, Is the Jew…?': Basil, Philo and Isidore of Pelusium." *VigChr* 46 (1992): 172–189.
Russell, Norman. *Cyril of Alexandria*. The Early Church Fathers. London: Routledge, 2000.
Russell, Norman. *Theophilus of Alexandria*. The Early Church Fathers. London: Routledge, 2007.
Schmid, Andreas. *Die Christologie Isidors von Pelusium*. Paradosis; Beiträge zur Geschichte der altchristlichen Literatur und Theologie 2. Freiburg: Paulusverlag, 1948.
Schwartz, Eduard. *Acta Conciliorum Oecumenicorum*. Berlin, Leipzig, 1914.
Smith, Morton. "Manuscript Tradition of Isidore of Pelusium." *HThR* 47 (1954): 205–210.
Toca, Madalina. "Isidore of Pelusium's Letters to Didymus the Blind." *StPatr* 96 (2017): 325–332.
Toca, Madalina. "The Greek Manuscript Reception of Isidore of Pelusium's Epistolary Corpus." *BN* 175 (2017): 133–143.
Treu, Ursula. "Isidor II (von Pelusium)." In *RAC* 18 (1998): 982–1002.
Turner, Cuthbert Hamilton. "The Letters of Saint Isidore of Pelusium." *JThS* 6 (1905): 70–86.
Wessel, Susan. *Cyril of Alexandria and the Nestorian Controversy*. Oxford: Oxford University Press, 2004.
Wipszycka, Ewa. *The Alexandrian Church: People and Institutions*. JJP.S 25. Warsaw: University of Warsaw, Faculty of Law and Admistration, Chair of Roman Law and the Law of Antiquity / Institute of Archeology, Department of Papyrology: The Raphael Taubenschlag Foundation, 2015.
Wipszycka, Ewa. *Les ressources et les activités économiques des églises en Egypte du IVe – VIIIe siècle*. PapyBrux 10. Brussels: Fondation Égyptologique Reine Élisabeth, 1972.

David M. Gwynn
Patronage Networks in the *Festal Letters* of Athanasius of Alexandria

Few fourth-century bishops had careers as long or as controversial as Athanasius of Alexandria.[1] And few bishops depended to such an extent on the network of relationships built up and maintained through episcopal patronage and mutual support. Athanasius held the see of Alexandria from 328 to 373, a period of dramatic transformation for Egyptian Christianity and the wider Church. He was exiled on five separate occasions by four different emperors, yet by his death Athanasius had strengthened Alexandrian authority within Egypt and was hailed as a hero of orthodoxy and champion of the emerging ascetic movement. As modern scholars seek to appreciate fully that remarkable achievement, the *Festal Letters* that delivered Athanasius' Easter message to the churches of Egypt and Libya offer an essential and often neglected resource. These annual letters reveal the evolving pressures that Athanasius faced during his long episcopate, and demonstrate the crucial role that patronage networks played in his eventual success.

> Let the ancient customs in Egypt, Libya and Pentapolis prevail, that the bishop of Alexandria has authority over all these places. For this is also customary for the bishop of Rome. Likewise in Antioch and the other provinces, let the churches retain their privileges.[2]

The see of Alexandria occupied a unique position within the early Christian Church.[3] The famous sixth canon of the Council of Nicaea in 325 upheld the au-

---

[1] For an overview of Athanasius' life and writings, see Timothy D. Barnes, *Athanasius and Constantius: Theology and Politics in the Constantinian Empire* (Cambridge, Mass. and London: Harvard University Press, 1993); David M. Gwynn, *Athanasius of Alexandria: Bishop, Theologian, Ascetic, Father* (Oxford: Oxford University Press, 2012); and the articles collected in Peter Gemeinhardt, ed., *Athanasius Handbuch* (Tübingen: Mohr Siebeck, 2011).
[2] Council of Nicaea (325), canon 6.
[3] The early history of the bishops of Alexandria is surveyed in Attila Jakab, *Ecclesia Alexandrina: Evolution sociale et institutionnelle du christianisme alexandrin (IIe et IIIe siècles)*, Christianismes anciens 1 (Bern and Oxford: Peter Lang, 2001) and Stephen J. Davis, *The Early Coptic Papacy: The Egyptian Church and its Leadership in Late Antiquity* (Cairo and New York: The American University in Cairo Press, 2004). For their status within the wider Egyptian Church, see also Annick Martin, *Athanase d'Alexandrie et l'Église d'Égypte au IVe siècle (328–373)*, CEFR 216 (Rome: École française de Rome, 1996), 17–214, and Ewa Wipszycka, *Études sur le christianisme dans l'Égypte de l'antiquité tardive*, SEAug 52 (Rome: Institutum Patristicum Augus-

thority of Alexandria, Rome and Antioch within their respective spheres of influence (with Jerusalem added in canon 7). But the control exerted by the Alexandrian bishops over their region was far greater than that of the bishops of Antioch, surrounded by other major cities, or even the bishops of Rome. There were no rival metropolitans in Egypt, only in Cyrenaica, and the Egyptian Church thus formed a natural hierarchical network with a single focal point. By the early fourth century, the bishop of Alexandria claimed the right to appoint or confirm all the bishops in his sphere, while those bishops in turn depended on Alexandrian approval to reinforce their own status. When he succeeded his mentor Alexander (312–28), Athanasius inherited leadership of that network together with the task of preserving ecclesiastical and theological unity across the diverse congregations that now looked to him for spiritual and pastoral guidance.

Inevitably, Alexandrian authority did not rest unchallenged. Theoretical control over clerical appointments was not always effective in practice. Even within the city of Alexandria itself the presbyter Arius gathered a sufficient following to oppose Alexander in the years preceding the Council of Nicaea.[4] Two Libyan bishops, Secundus of Ptolemais and Theonas of Marmarica, were exiled at Nicaea for their support of Arius against Alexander. Most significantly, the Melitian Schism which took shape in the aftermath of the Great Persecution created an alternative Egyptian clerical hierarchy that posed a direct threat to Alexandrian pre-eminence.[5] Melitius of Lycopolis denounced the relative mildness with which Peter of Alexandria (300–11) treated those who lapsed under persecution, and this rigorous attitude found adherents among the bishops of Upper Egypt, who also desired greater independence from Alexandrian hegemony. The *Breviarium Melitii*, the list of Melitian clergy including some 30 bishops that Melitius submitted to Alexander at Nicaea[6], records a Melitian presence all along the Nile Valley. Athanasius clashed repeatedly with the Melitians throughout his episcopate, and the speed with which such a rival and less centralised network spread highlighted the challenge Athanasius faced in joining Alexandrian Chris-

---

tinianum, 1996) and *The Alexandrian Church: People and Institutions*, JJP.S 25 (Warsaw: Journal of Juristic Papyrology, 2015).

[4] The standard introduction to Arius' controversial life remains Rowan D. Williams, *Arius: Heresy and Tradition*, 2nd edition (London: SCM Press, 2001).

[5] On the origins and nature of the schism, see further Martin, *Athanase d'Alexandrie*, 219–389, and Hans Hauben, "The Melitian 'Church of the Martyrs': Christian Dissenters in Ancient Egypt," in *Ancient History in a Modern University, Volume 2: Early Christianity, Late Antiquity and Beyond*, eds. T.W. Hillard, R.A. Kearsley, C.E.V. Nixon and A.M. Nobbs (Macquarie University: Ancient History Documentary Research Centre, 1998): 329–49.

[6] Cited in Athanasius, *Apologia contra Arianos* 71.

tianity more closely with the rest of Egypt. The situation was further confused when Athanasius' periods in exile saw competing bishops of Alexandria appointed, first Gregory (339–45) and then George (357–61), who promoted their own allies and hindered Athanasius' efforts to unify the Egyptian Church around himself.

Against this complex background, it is not difficult to grasp the weight that Athanasius placed on maintaining and expanding his episcopal network. Unfortunately, our knowledge of that network derives almost exclusively from Athanasius' perspective. Few writings survive from the Egyptian bishops on whose support Athanasius depended, with his close friend Serapion of Thmuis a partial exception,[7] and even less from Athanasius' Egyptian opponents.[8] What our evidence does make explicit, however, is Athanasius' commitment to preserving the personal relationships and bonds of communication and patronage on which his network was founded. Immediately after his accession to the episcopate, Athanasius travelled first to the Thebaid in 329–30 and then Pentapolis and Ammoniaca in 331–2.[9] It was the beginning of years of pastoral labours, and the loyal following that Athanasius inspired would prove priceless during his extended periods of persecution and exile. Athanasius' numerous writings, from theological treatises to individual correspondence, reinforced these ties and defined the ecclesiastical and spiritual principles of a Church united behind his leadership. Arguably the most important of those writings for understanding the evolving Athanasian network, although little studied until comparatively recently, are his Easter *Festal Letters*.

From at least the third century onwards, it was customary for the bishops of Alexandria to write two letters every year concerning the Easter celebration for circulation to the bishops subordinate to their see.[10] The first letter was a brief note, despatched shortly after each Easter, that announced the date of Easter for the following year. The *Festal Letter* proper was a longer work sent out in January or February of the year itself to confirm that date and to transmit the Alexandrian bishop's Easter message to his congregations. Athanasius originally

---

[7] For what is known of the life and writings of Serapion, see Klaus Fitschen, *Serapion von Thmuis: Echte und unechte Schriften sowie die Zeugnisse des Athanasius und Anderer*, PTS 37 (Berlin and New York: De Gruyter, 1992).
[8] *Papyrus London* 1914, the Melitian letter that complains of Athanasian violence before the Council of Tyre, might be interpreted as an attempt by Athanasius to break up a rival Melitian network.
[9] *Festal Index* 2 and 4.
[10] The earliest evidence comes from the episcopate of Dionysius (247–64), through Eusebius of Caesarea, *Historia Ecclesiastica* 7.20.

composed his *Festal Letters* in Greek, but the extant remnants have chiefly survived in Syriac and Coptic manuscripts.[11] The complex transmission process has allowed errors to creep into the traditional chronological order and numbering of Athanasius' letters,[12] yet their value makes them indispensable. No authentic Athanasian sermons survive, and the *Festal Letters* represent both our key source for his pastoral teachings and our best indication for how Athanasius' thought changed over time. Through those letters we still hear the voice of Athanasius speaking to his supporters, bringing to life the network that he fought so hard to sustain.

The very act of writing and circulating the annual *Festal Letter* was a statement of Alexandrian authority over Egypt and Libya and of the legitimacy of the sender as the bishop of Alexandria. It is probable that Athanasius' rivals Gregory and George distributed their own *Festal Letters* during their years in Egypt, although if they did so then no trace has remained,[13] and Athanasius always attempted to circulate a letter or just a brief notification of the Easter date even in his numerous periods of exile.[14] For Athanasius, however, the *Festal Letters* were far more than mere statements of legitimate authority. His Easter epistles expressed in a pastoral context Athanasius' vision of Christianity for a united Egyptian Church. The anti-'Arian' rhetoric so prominent in his polemical writings is largely absent, except for *Festal Letter* 10 for 338 which was composed in the tense period between his first and second exiles.[15] Instead, Athanasius calls on

---

11 The crucial Syriac manuscript was edited by William Cureton, *The Festal Letters of Athanasius* (London: Society for the Publication of Oriental Texts, 1848) and then revised and translated into English by Henry Burgess, *The Festal Letters of Saint Athanasius* (Oxford: John Henry Parker, 1854). It is Burgess' revised translation that is reprinted in Athanasius' volume in the *Nicene and Post-Nicene Fathers* series. The scattered Coptic fragments all originate from three manuscripts from the White Monastery of Shenoute, and were edited by Louis T. Lefort, *Saint Athanase: Lettres festales et pastorales en Copte*, *Scriptores Coptici* 19 (1955): 1–72 and 20 (1955): 1–55. The only complete modern translation of the extant fragments is into Italian by Alberto Camplani, *Atanasio di Alessandria. Lettere festali. Anonimo. Indice delle Lettere festali* (Milan: Paoline, 2003), although an English translation is currently under preparation for the *Liverpool Translated Texts* series by David Brakke and David M. Gwynn.
12 The difficulties are conveniently summarised in Barnes, *Athanasius and Constantius*, 183–91, and discussed in detail in Alberto Camplani, *Le Lettere Festali di Atanasio di Alexandria* (Rome: C.I.M., 1989), 17–196, and Camplani, *Atanasio di Alessandria*.
13 *Festal Index* 12 refers to an occasion when the 'Arians' were ridiculed for proclaiming the wrong Easter date (the entry is listed under 339–40, but appears to relate to Easter 346).
14 *Festal Letter* 13, written for the Easter of 341, opens by emphasising that despite oppression by the enemies of Christ, he has written "even from Rome".
15 *Festal Letter* 10 is analysed in detail by Rudolf Lorenz, *Der zehnte Osterfestbrief des Athanasius von Alexandrien* (Berlin and New York: De Gruyter, 1986). On Athanasius' polemic more

the faithful to praise God and give thanks for the gift of salvation. The Incarnation of the fully divine Son that dominates Athanasius' theological teachings was a natural theme for the Easter celebration,[16] and underlay the doctrinal orthodoxy that he required his churches to embrace.[17] For Athanasius, correct belief was in turn inseparably intertwined with a correct lifestyle, and so his *Festal Letters* place equivalent emphasis on a model of Christian behaviour that may be described as an 'asceticism of everyday life'.[18] Lay men and women were urged to adopt for Lent the principles of abstinence, fasting and prayer practiced by monks and virgins, sharing their commitment and bridging the gulf that threatened to separate ordinary Christians from the expanding ascetic movement.[19]

Every Athanasian *Festal Letter* must therefore be set within Athanasius' wider campaign to unify Egyptian Christianity. Each letter reinforced the theological and ascetic values that Athanasius sought to define as normative, while circulating the annual Easter message reaffirmed Athanasius' place at the head of the episcopal network and his relationship with the letters' recipients across Egypt and Libya. Three passages in particular merit more detailed attention. They come from different decades, and reflect the shifting challenges to his authority that Athanasius faced. Most importantly, all three passages make explicit the significance of the *Festal Letters* as an expression of patronage, a means not

---

widely, see David M. Gwynn, *The Eusebians: The Polemic of Athanasius of Alexandria and the Construction of the "Arian Controversy"* (Oxford: Oxford University Press, 2007).

16 "The Lord died in those days, that we should no longer do the deeds of death. He gave His life, that we might preserve our own from the snares of the Devil. And, what is most wonderful, the Word became flesh, that we should no longer live in the flesh, but in spirit should worship God, who is Spirit" (*Festal Letter* 6.1).

17 On Athanasius' theology and the *Festal Letters*, see Rosario P. Merendino, *Paschale Sacramentum. Eine Untersuchung über die Osterkatechese des Hl. Athanasius von Alexandrien in ihrer Beziehung zu den frühchristlichen exegetisch-theologischen Überlieferungen* (Münster, Westfalen: Aschendorff, 1965); Khaled Anatolios, *Athanasius: The Coherence of His Thought*, Routledge early church monographs (London and New York: Routledge, 1998); Nathan K.-K. Ng, *The Spirituality of Athanasius: A Key for Proper Understanding of This Important Church Father*, EHS.T 733 (Bern: Peter Lang, 2001).

18 Thus David Brakke, *Athanasius and the Politics of Asceticism*, OECS (Oxford: Clarendon Press, 1995), 198–200.

19 Athanasius envisaged ascetic commitment not as the sole preserve of a spiritual elite but as a path open to every Christian man and woman according to their potential: see his exegesis of the Parable of the Sower in *Festal Letter* 10.4.

only to communicate with the other Egyptian bishops but to determine who should be members of the episcopal network itself.[20]

> I have also thought it necessary to inform you of the bishops that have succeeded those who have fallen asleep. In Tanis, instead of Elias is Theodorus. In Arsenoitis, Silvanus instead of Calosiris. In Paralus, Nemesion instead of Nonnus. In Bucolia is Heraclius. In Tentyra, Andronicus instead of Saprion, his father. In Thebais, Philon instead of Philon. In Maximianopolis, Herminus instead of Atras. In the lower Apollon, Sarapion instead of Plution. In Aphrodito, Serenus is in the place of Theodorus. In Rhinocoruron, Salomon. In Stathma, Arabion. And in Marmarica, in the eastern Garyathis, Andragathus in the place of Hierax, in the southern Garyathis, Quintus instead of Nicon. So that to these you may write, and from these receive the canonical letters.[21]

> I have also thought it necessary to inform you of the appointment of bishops, which has taken place in the stead of our blessed fellow-ministers, that you may know to whom to write and from whom you should receive letters. In Syene, therefore, Nilammon instead of Nilammon of the same name. In Laton, Masis instead of Ammonius. In Coptos, Psenosiris instead of Theodorus. In Panos, because Artemidorus desired it on account of his old age and weakness of body, Arius is appointed coadjutor. In Hypsele, Arsenius, having become reconciled to the Church. In Lycopolis, Eudaemon instead of Plusianus. In Antinoopolis, Arion instead of Ammonius and Tyrannus. In Oxyrynchus, Theodorus instead of Pelagius. In Nilopolis, instead of Theon, Amanthius and Isaac, who are reconciled to each other. In Arsenoitis, Andreas instead of Silvanus. In Prosopitis, Triadelphus instead of Sarapammon. In Diospolis, on the river side, Theodorus instead of Sarapammon. In Saiton, Paphnutius instead of Nemesion. In Xois, Theodorus instead of Anubion, and there is also with him Isidorus, who is reconciled to the Church. In Sethroitis, Orion instead of Potammon. In Clysma, Tithonas instead of Jacob, and there is with him Paulus, who has been reconciled to the Church.[22]

> I have been eager to inform you of this as well: that in place of Sun [...] Isidorus has been established in place of Dracontius, Isaac in place of Agathos, Ammon in place of Didymus, Epiphanius in place of Agathos-Daimon, Sarapion in place of Leonites, Isaiah in place of Mark, and in Marmarica of Libya Loucius – and all these men are ascetics, being in the life of monasticism – and Sarapammon in place of Nammon, and in place of [...] Write to them and receive from them writings of peace as is customary.[23]

---

20 The first two passages are translated from Syriac by Burgess, *Festal Letters*, reproduced here with slight revisions. The third passage is translated from Coptic by Brakke, *Politics of Asceticism*. There is a detailed analysis of the two Syriac lists in Martin, *Athanase d'Alexandrie*, 62–74.
21 *Letter to Serapion* ("*Festal Letter* 12") 2; c.337 or c.339/40.
22 *Festal Letter* 19.10; Easter 347.
23 *Festal Letter* 40; Easter 368.

For modern scholars, these passages are a wellspring of information concerning the episcopal lists for fourth-century Egypt.[24] The Egyptian Church, incorporating Libya and the Pentapolis of Cyrenaica, possessed approximately 60 bishops in 324 and 90–100 bishops from the 340s to the early 400s. Of the bishoprics which can be located with a fair degree of certainty, there were some 44 in the Delta (which was denser in population than the outer regions), 29 in the Nile Valley, and the rest in Libya and the Pentapolis.[25] Although *Festal Letter* 40 provides only names without accompanying sees (the sole exception being Libyan Marmarica), the other two passages cover a sizeable proportion of the Egyptian episcopate. *Festal Letter* 19 alone identifies the holders of 16 sees, several of whom can be cross-referenced through surviving papyri such as Ammonius and Arion of Antinoopolis (from the Hermopolite records) and Theodorus of Oxyrhynchus.[26]

For Athanasius, on the other hand, each of these *Festal Letters* asserted his right to confirm appointments to the Egyptian episcopacy. By acting as a patron in this manner, he upheld the authority of Alexandria while also (at least in theory) securing the loyalty of those whose appointments he approved. Significantly, a number of the departed ministers who passed on between 336 and 347 had previously appeared in the signature list of the Egyptian bishops who defended Athanasius against his condemnation at the Council of Tyre in 335.[27] And the repeated insistence that letters should be exchanged only with the bishops whom he named strongly implies the existence of rival claimants whose legitimacy Athanasius wished to deny. Several of the sees at stake are known to have had Melitian bishops as well, including Eudaemon of Tanis and Lucius of Antinoopolis (both of whom signed the *Encyclical Letter* of the Eastern Council of Serdica in 343 which repeated Athanasius' condemnation).[28]

All three passages therefore share a common purpose to strengthen the Egyptian Church behind Athanasius' leadership. Yet each passage also has its own particular nuances and must be placed within its proper setting. The text

---

24 The register compiled by Klaas A. Worp, "A Checklist of Bishops in Byzantine Egypt (A.D. 325–c.750)," *ZPE* 100 (1994): 283–318 remains an indispensable resource, although inevitably now slightly outdated due to new discoveries.
25 The data is reconstructed in Martin, *Athanase d'Alexandrie*, 17–115.
26 Worp, "Checklist", 296 and 303. On the complex evidence for Theodorus, see Lincoln H. Blumell, *Lettered Christians: Christians, Letters, and Late Antique Oxyrhynchus*, NTTSD 39 (Leiden: Brill, 2012), 149–54.
27 Quoted in Athanasius, *Apologia contra Arianos* 78.
28 The documentation is preserved in Latin by Hilary of Poitiers, *Against Valens and Ursacius* 1.2.1–29.

preserved with the Syriac *Festal Index* as *Festal Letter* 12 is actually a personal letter that Athanasius wrote from exile in the west in either *c.*337 or *c.*339/40 to his friend Serapion of Thmuis.[29] Athanasius asked Serapion to circulate to the Egyptian churches the Easter message that he enclosed with its list of appointments. If we accept the earlier date of *c.*337, during Athanasius' first period of exile after the Council of Tyre, then he remained titular bishop of Alexandria as emperor Constantine refused to allow a replacement to be elected. If we take the later date, which falls within Athanasius' second exile, then the official bishop of Alexandria in *c.*339/40 was Gregory and Athanasius' assertion of his Alexandrian legitimacy would have a stronger edge. Whichever date is preferred, Athanasius' concern was to secure his position despite his distance from Egypt, and in doing so to lay foundations for his return.

A still more striking example is provided by *Festal Letter* 19, written for Easter 347. Athanasius' second exile lasted from 339 to 346, while Gregory of Cappadocia occupied the Alexandrian see. Gregory died in 345, and Athanasius returned to Alexandria the next year to a rapturous reception which Gregory of Nazianzus later compared to Christ's Entry to Jerusalem.[30] Athanasius' long absence in the west, however, meant that considerable work was required to re-establish his authority, not only in Alexandria but across Egypt and Libya. Clergy appointed by Gregory must have occupied a number of local churches and had to be integrated or expelled, while at the same time the Melitian movement with its rival hierarchy continued to persist.

The entire text of *Festal Letter* 19, one of the longer *Letters* in Athanasius' corpus, was a response to the challenges he faced. The letter opens by giving thanks to God that "He has brought us from a distance and granted us again to send openly to you, as customary, the Festal Letters"[31]. The main body of the letter then proclaims at length that only the true Christian can celebrate the Easter festival, denouncing the Jews, pagans and heretics who misunderstand the scriptures and the nature of sacrifice. This warning to those who may have fallen away during Athanasius' absence is combined with a rallying call for unity, before the letter concludes with the postscript listing the bishops appointed to the 16 sees. The previous occupants of these sees had died during Athanasius' years in exile (with the exception of Artemidorus of Panos who had

---

29 "Having, according to custom, written the Letter respecting the festival, I have sent it to you, my beloved; that through you all the brethren may be able to know the day of rejoicing" (*Letter to Serapion* 1).
30 Gregory of Nazianzus, *Oration* 21.29.
31 *Festal Letter* 19.1.

requested a coadjutor due to his age and infirmity) and their successors are now confirmed in office.

Athanasius' list of appointments included three men who are said to have "reconciled to the Church" – Arsenius of Hypsele, Isidorus of Xois and Paulus of Clysma – as well as Amanthius and Isaac of Nilopolis who have reconciled with each other. Arsenius, who is recognised in the letter as the sole bishop of Hypsele, is almost certainly the same Melitian cleric who had been involved in the charges against Athanasius that led to his original condemnation at the Council of Tyre.[32] Isidorus and Paulus are named as colleagues of the bishops in their respective sees, just as Isaac has reconciled with Amanthius in Nilopolis. It is entirely plausible that Isidorus, Paulus and Isaac were also Melitians who had acknowledged Athanasius' authority.[33] These defections would suggest that the schism was losing momentum by the 340s, although Athanasius would come into conflict with the Melitians again in the 360s.

Alternatively, Isidorus and Paulus could be appointments by Gregory now accepted by Athanasius.[34] Their sees do not appear in the original *Breviarium Melitii*, and there is no definitive evidence for the later creation of Melitian bishops after 325, which casts doubt on their Melitian identity. The issue at stake which required reconciliation in the letter would thus need a different cause, with the obvious possibility being that these men were appointed by Gregory and had subsequently been approved by Athanasius (perhaps after the submission of some proof of orthodoxy). There is no indication of any purge of the Egyptian clergy after Athanasius' return in 346, so this may explain how Gregorian appointments were absorbed under Athanasius' leadership. Over the course of the decade that followed, Athanasius secured the loyal support of the vast majority of the Egyptian Church. So great was that loyalty, that when he was driven into exile once more in 356 Athanasius was able to remain safe within Egypt, protected by his Alexandrian congregations and by the ascetics of the desert.

Both the *Letter to Serapion* and the *Festal Letter* of 347 also reveal one further crucial element in Athanasius' drive to unite Egyptian Christianity. This concerns the celebration of Lent. During Athanasius' episcopate, the Egyptian practice of Lent changed from a 6-day fast before Holy Week to a longer 40-day fast.[35] *Festal*

---

[32] Arsenius was the Melitian priest whom Athanasius was accused of having had killed, a charge that was convincingly disproved when Athanasius' supporters produced Arsenius alive.
[33] Barnes, *Athanasius and Constantius*, 95; Gwynn, *Athanasius of Alexandria*, 39.
[34] Martin, *Athanase d'Alexandrie*, 73; Camplani, *Atanasio di Alessandria*, 430.
[35] The exact date of this change is debated. For the arguments in favour of 334, see David Brakke, "Jewish Flesh and Christian Spirit in Athanasius of Alexandria," *JECS* 9 (2001): 457–61 and Camplani, *Atanasio di Alessandria*, 178–81.

Letter 6, which was most probably written for Easter 334, includes a scriptural justification for the 40-day fast that appears to mark the introduction of the new practice. This need for a scriptural justification reflects the novelty of Athanasius' reform, and clearly he did face resistance. The *Letter to Serapion* upheld the 40-day fast while Athanasius was in exile, and emphasised the need for Egypt to share the customs of the wider Church. "For it is a disgrace that when all the world does this, those alone who are in Egypt, instead of fasting, should find their pleasure".[36] After his glorious return in 346, Athanasius felt it necessary to repeat that message once more, reminding his audience that "he who neglects to observe the fast of forty days, as one who rashly and impurely treads on holy things, cannot celebrate the Easter festival"[37]. Acceptance of the 40-day fast had become one more marker of the true Christian and of those who recognised Athanasius' authority, while the extended fast served Athanasius' pastoral mission by promoting ascetic practices among the lay congregation and encouraging a greater focus of prayer on the Easter celebration.

Several decades separate the first two passages we have considered, both preserved in the Syriac manuscript of the *Festal Letters*, from the third passage which comes from the fragmentary *Festal Letter* 40 for Easter 368 and survives in Coptic. The intervening years had seen Athanasius exiled three more times, commencing with his prolonged desert sojourn 356–62, but by 368 Athanasius' position in Egypt was relatively secure. Yet tensions remained. The old threat of the Melitians still endured, and new divisions were emerging due to the rapid growth of the ascetic movement inspired by the examples of Antony and Pachomius.

The episcopal list provided in the fragments from *Festal Letter* 40 differs from the Syriac passages in omitting the sees of the bishops named, which inevitably raises problems for identification. But most significant is the emphasis that "all these men are ascetics, being in the life of monasticism"[38]. The ascetic movement was arguably the greatest potential challenge to episcopal authority over the late-antique Church.[39] There had always been those within early Christianity

---

36 *Letter to Serapion* ("*Festal Letter* 12") 1. The *Letter to Serapion* has occasionally been cited as evidence that Athanasius was inspired to impose the 40-day fast in Egypt by his experiences in exile in the west. But this letter does not introduce the extended fast, but rather urges Serapion to enforce a practice that has already been imposed.
37 *Festal Letter* 19.9.
38 *Festal Letter* 40.
39 On this vast subject, see particularly Andrea Sterk, *Renouncing the World yet Leading the Church: The Monk-Bishop in Late Antiquity* (Cambridge, Mass.: Harvard University Press, 2004); Claudia Rapp, *Holy Bishops in Late Antiquity: The Nature of Christian Leadership in an Age of Transition* (Berkeley, Los Angeles and London: University of California Press, 2005), 137–52; and the articles of Martin and others collected in Alberto Camplani and Giovanni Filor-

who had questioned whether the worldly concerns required of the clergy were truly compatible with Christian moral and spiritual commitment. The rise of ascetic holy men and women brought those tensions into renewed focus. The ascetic renunciation of society in order to follow a life in Christ threatened to create an alternative Christian elite, one that might undermine or supersede the bishop in offering guidance to the Christian community.

Through his promotion of ascetics to the episcopate, Athanasius played a fundamental role in integrating monks and clergy and defining the ascetic qualities expected of late-antique bishops.[40] This was a policy that he had begun long before 368 when *Festal Letter* 40 was written. In *c*.354, a few years after *Festal Letter* 19, Athanasius wrote his well-known letter to the monk Dracontius who had fled back to his monastery to avoid episcopal office.[41] After rebuking Dracontius that he would have to defend himself before Christ for neglecting his flock, Athanasius insisted that monastic values and clerical duties were not incompatible and recalled other monks like Serapion who had followed the clerical path. These monk-bishops brought renewed energy and ascetic virtue to the episcopate, and their loyalty to Athanasius strengthened his bond with the wider ascetic community. Certainly, his appeal to Dracontius succeeded. As bishop of Hermopolis Parva, Dracontius supported Athanasius at the Council of Alexandria in 362, and *Festal Letter* 40 records his death in office and his succession by Isidorus.

The second underlying theme behind the episcopal list in *Festal Letter* 40 concerns the revival of the schismatic Melitians. Having featured prominently in Athanasius' polemical writings of the 330s and 340s, the Melitians appear to have declined and there are only limited references in Athanasius' numerous writings of the 350s. The *Festal Letters* of the late 360s, however, contain a series of anti-Melitian passages, which may indicate a Melitian resurgence in Upper Egypt around this time.[42] One such passage occurs in *Festal Letter* 39 for Easter 367, the famous letter that defined the canon of scripture.[43] Athanasius condemned the Melitians for their use of apocryphal books, stamping his authority once again over the beliefs and practices of the Egyptian Church. The extant frag-

---

amo, eds., *Foundations of Power and Conflicts of Authority in Late-Antique Monasticism*, OLA 157 (Leuven: Uitgeverij Peeters en Departement Oosterse Studies, 2007).
40 Brakke, *Politics of Asceticism*, 80–110.
41 Sterk, *Renouncing the World*, 16–18; Gwynn, *Athanasius of Alexandria*, 125–7. See also the contribution of Peter Gemeinhardt to the present volume pp. 138–142.
42 *Festal Letters* 37 (364), 39 (367), 41 (369); see further Camplani, *Le Lettere Festali*, 262–82.
43 For the text of this letter, see now David Brakke, "A New Fragment of Athanasius's Thirty-Ninth *Festal Letter:* Heresy, Apocrypha and the Canon," *HThR* 103 (2010): 47–66.

ments of *Festal Letter* 40 do not identify the Melitians by name, but do include a specific attack upon the disorder caused by irregular ordinations and people "electing clergy for other dioceses that are not theirs". The disorder created is said to have affected monasteries as well as churches, suggesting that those responsible were recruiting clergy from monks just as Athanasius had. Even as late as 368, therefore, the theoretical Alexandrian control over clerical ordination was not as absolute as might be thought (although the Melitians do not appear to have ordained bishops, only lesser clergy). Both Athanasius' definition of the scriptural canon and his emphasis on proper ordination were intended, at least in part, to reinforce his overall vision of a united Church with himself at the head.

The *Festal Letters* provided an ideal vehicle for announcements to the entire Egyptian Church. Indeed, after considering the three bishop lists that survive from Athanasius' letters, one might reasonably ask why there are not more from his long and controversial episcopate. Possibly other notes have disappeared in transmission. Many of his letters are highly fragmentary, and the appointment lists that we have from *Letters* 19 and 40 were added as an appendix after the concluding salutation which may have made it easier for them to be lost (the more personal *Letter to Serapion* follows a slightly different structure).[44] Nevertheless, whether they contained a list or not, every *Festal Letter* was a statement of patronage and authority. The bishop of Alexandria upheld his privileges by addressing his congregations and laying down guidelines for the bishops within his sphere. When Athanasius wrote *Festal Letter* 39 on the scriptural canon, the most renowned of his Easter messages, he claimed the right not only to oversee the interpretation of scripture but also to define what *was* scripture. *Festal Letter* 39 is in fact the only Athanasian *Festal Letter* for which we have explicit testimony of its reception, when the letter was read out and then posted in Pachomian monasteries.[45] It has even been suggested that the collection of 'Gnostic' codices discovered at Nag Hammadi were buried by nearby Pachomian monks after Athanasius condemned the reading of such non-canonical works.[46]

---

[44] One example of a lost episcopal list may be provided by *Festal Letter* 39, where the extant fragments break off after the salutation with the words: "when the blessed Lampon, bishop of Darnei, died ... was appointed ...".
[45] Bohairic *Life of Pachomius* 189.
[46] E.g. James M. Robinson, ed., *The Nag Hammadi Library in English*, 4th revised edition (Leiden: Brill, 1996), 19–20, although see the thoughtful comments of Hugo Lundhaug and Lance Jenott, *The Monastic Origins of the Nag Hammadi Codices* (Tübingen: Mohr Siebeck, 2015), 146–51.

Yet patronage, a theme that connects a number of the articles in this volume, is always a two-way process. It is Athanasius' words and vision which have survived, and his career bears testimony to the loyalty earned through his unceasing pastoral efforts. But the audiences for Athanasius' *Festal Letters* also benefited. Those who were named in the episcopal lists were strengthened within their sees, particularly in communities divided by the Melitian Schism. And for every recipient, the annual arrival of the *Festal Letter* renewed their bond with Alexandria and no less importantly their bond with their fellow bishops across Egypt. All the churches received the same message and shared the same Easter practices, including the 40-day Lenten fast. Thus they were joined in a network whose strands ran not only towards Alexandria but throughout Egyptian Christianity. Athanasius urged his congregations to exchange letters as was customary in each episcopal list, and the traditional formula with which he closed the majority of his extant *Festal Letters* reaffirmed that sense of collective identity. "All the brethren who are with me salute you. Salute one another with a holy kiss".

Ultimately, Athanasius succeeded in forging a unified Egyptian Church of laity, clergy and ascetics alike. That unity receives vivid (if somewhat problematic) expression in the *Epistula ad Afros*, an encyclical letter composed by Athanasius on behalf of the Egyptian bishops in 367 for despatch to the west:

> It is not only ourselves that write, but all the bishops of Egypt and the Libyas, some ninety in number. For we all are of one mind in this, and we always sign for one another if any chance not to be present.[47]

It was this success, in which the *Festal Letters* were just one albeit vital component, that provides the key to resolving the greatest puzzle Athanasius' career raises for modern scholarship. Despite years in exile and rivals in Alexandria and beyond, Athanasius not only maintained but strengthened his position in the Church, and laid the foundations on which his two greatest Alexandrian successors Theophilus (385–412) and Cyril (412–44) would build.[48]

---

[47] Athanasius, *Epistula Ad Afros* 10.
[48] It is not a coincidence that these two bishops are the authors of the only other major collections of *Festal Letters* to survive from late-antique Egypt. The *Festal Letters* of Theophilus are translated in Norman Russell, *Theophilus of Alexandria* (London: Routledge, 2007), and receive detailed analysis in Krastu Banev, *Theophilus of Alexandria and the First Origenist Controversy: Rhetoric and Power*, OECS (Oxford: Oxford University Press, 2015). For an introduction to Cyril's *Festal Letters*, see Pauline Allen, "Cyril of Alexandria's *Festal Letters:* The Politics of Religion," in *Studies of Religion and Politics in the Early Christian Centuries*, eds. David Luckensmeyer and Pauline Allen, Early Christian studies 13 (Banyo, Qld.: Centre for Early Christian Studies, 2010): 195–210, and the translation and notes by Philip R. Amidon and John J. O'Keefe, *Saint Cyril of*

Bibliography

Primary Sources

Amidon, Philip R. and John J. O'Keefe. *Saint Cyril of Alexandria, Festal Letters*, 2 volumes. Washington, D.C.: Catholic University of America Press, 2009–2013.

Brakke, David. "A New Fragment of Athanasius's Thirty-Ninth *Festal Letter:* Heresy, Apocrypha and the Canon." *HThR* 103 (2010): 47–66.

Burgess, Henry. *The Festal Letters of Saint Athanasius*. Oxford: John Henry Parker, 1854.

Camplani, Alberto. *Le Lettere Festali di Atanasio di Alexandria*. Rome: C.I.M., 1989.

Camplani, Alberto. *Atanasio di Alessandria. Lettere festali. Anonimo. Indice delle Lettere festali*. Milan: Paoline, 2003.

Cureton, William. *The Festal Letters of Athanasius*. London: Society for the Publication of Oriental Texts, 1848.

Fitschen, Klaus. *Serapion von Thmuis: Echte und unechte Schriften sowie die Zeugnisse des Athanasius und Anderer*. Berlin and New York: De Gruyter, 1992.

Lefort, Louis T. *Saint Athanase: Lettres festales et pastorales en Copte. Scriptores Coptici* 19 (1955):1–72 and 20 (1955): 1–55.

Lorenz, Rudolf. *Der zehnte Osterfestbrief des Athanasius von Alexandrien*. Berlin and New York: De Gruyter, 1986.

Robinson, James M., ed. *The Nag Hammadi Library in English*, 4th revised edition. Leiden: Brill, 1996.

Russell, Norman. *Theophilus of Alexandria*. London: Routledge, 2007.

Secondary Literature

Allen, Pauline. "Cyril of Alexandria's *Festal Letters:* The Politics of Religion." In *Studies of Religion and Politics in the Early Christian Centuries*, edited by David Luckensmeyer and Pauline Allen, Early Christian studies 13, 195–210. Banyo, Qld.: Centre for Early Christian Studies, 2010.

Anatolios, Khaled. *Athanasius: The Coherence of His Thought*. Routledge early church monographs. London and New York: Routledge, 1998.

Banev, Krastu. *Theophilus of Alexandria and the First Origenist Controversy: Rhetoric and Power*. OECS. Oxford: Oxford University Press, 2015.

Barnes, Timothy D. *Athanasius and Constantius: Theology and Politics in the Constantinian Empire*. Cambridge, Mass. and London: Harvard University Press, 1993.

Blumell, Lincoln H. *Lettered Christians: Christians, Letters, and Late Antique Oxyrhynchus*. NTTSD 39. Leiden: Brill, 2012.

Brakke, David. *Athanasius and the Politics of Asceticism*. OECS. Oxford: Clarendon Press, 1995.

Alexandria, Festal Letters, 2 volumes, FaCh (Washington, D.C.: Catholic University of America Press, 2009–2013).

Brakke, David. "Jewish Flesh and Christian Spirit in Athanasius of Alexandria." *JECS* 9 (2001): 453–81.

Camplani, Alberto, and Giovanni Filoramo, eds. *Foundations of Power and Conflicts of Authority in Late-Antique Monasticism*. OLA 157. Leuven: Uitgeverij Peeters en Departement Oosterse Studies, 2007.

Davis, Stephen J. *The Early Coptic Papacy: The Egyptian Church and its Leadership in Late Antiquity*. Cairo and New York: The American University in Cairo Press, 2004.

Gemeinhardt, Peter, ed. *Athanasius Handbuch*. Tübingen: Mohr Siebeck, 2011.

Gwynn, David M. *The Eusebians: The Polemic of Athanasius of Alexandria and the Construction of the "Arian Controversy"*. Oxford theological monographs, Oxford: Oxford University Press, 2007.

Gwynn, David M. *Athanasius of Alexandria: Bishop, Theologian, Ascetic, Father*. CThC. Oxford: Oxford University Press, 2012.

Hauben, Hans. "The Melitian 'Church of the Martyrs': Christian Dissenters in Ancient Egypt." In *Ancient History in a Modern University, Volume 2: Early Christianity, Late Antiquity and Beyond* edited by T.W. Hillard, R.A. Kearsley, C.E.V. Nixon and A.M. Nobbs, 329–49. Macquarie University: Ancient History Documentary Research Centre, 1998.

Jakab, Attila. *Ecclesia Alexandrina: Evolution sociale et institutionnelle du christianisme alexandrin (IIe et IIIe siècles)*. Christianismes anciens 1. Bern and Oxford: Peter Lang, 2001.

Lundhaug, Hugo and Lance Jenott. *The Monastic Origins of the Nag Hammadi Codices*. STAC 97. Tübingen: Mohr Siebeck, 2015.

Martin, Annick. *Athanase d'Alexandrie et L'Église d'Égypte au IVe siècle (328–373)*. CEFR 216. Rome: École française de Rome, 1996.

Merendino, Rosario P. *Paschale Sacramentum. Eine Untersuchung über die Osterkatechese des Hl. Athanasius von Alexandrien in ihrer Beziehung zu den frühchristlichen exegetisch-theologischen Überlieferungen*. Münster: Aschendorff, 1965.

Ng, Nathan K.-K. *The Spirituality of Athanasius: A Key for Proper Understanding of This Important Church Father*. EHS.T 733. Bern: Peter Lang, 2001.

Rapp, Claudia. *Holy Bishops in Late Antiquity: The Nature of Christian Leadership in an Age of Transition*. The transformation of the classical heritage 37. Berkeley, Los Angeles and London: University of California Press, 2005.

Sterk, Andrea. *Renouncing the World yet Leading the Church: The Monk-Bishop in Late Antiquity*. Cambridge, Mass.: Harvard University Press, 2004.

Williams, Rowan D. *Arius: Heresy and Tradition*, 2nd edition. London: SCM Press, 2001.

Wipszycka, Ewa. *Études sur le christianisme dans l'Égypte de l'antiquité tardive*. SEAug 52. Rome: Institutum Patristicum Augustinianum, 1996.

Wipszycka, Ewa. *The Alexandrian Church: People and Institutions*. JJP.S 25. Warsaw: Journal of Juristic Papyrology, 2015.

Worp, Klaas A. "A Checklist of Bishops in Byzantine Egypt (A.D. 325–c.750)." *ZPE* 100 (1994): 283–318.

Peter Gemeinhardt
Bishops as Religious Mentors: Spiritual Education and Pastoral Care

1 Episcopal mentorship in Late Antiquity: A heuristic framework

Late antique bishops often were assiduous letter-writers. It thus does not come as a surprise that the present conference builds, among others, on such epistolary exchanges when analyzing episcopal networks. Accordingly, my paper will also start with episcopal letter-writers. In the year 413, Paulinus of Nola sent a letter to Augustine and asked him to explain the meaning of several biblical passages. He approached his fellow bishop in North Africa as teacher, more precisely, as "blessed *doctor* of Israel"[1], and asked for instruction, e. g., about Ephesians 4:11, according to which the Holy Spirit made "some (of the Christians) apostles, some prophets, some evangelists, some pastors and teachers". Paulinus asked for the particularity of each of these appointments, since all these notions seemed to indicate "a similar, almost identical duty of teaching".[2] More specifically, he questioned Augustine about the difference between *pastor* and *doctor*, since "both these names are normally applied to those with a position of authority in the Church".[3] Paulinus closed his letter with an invocation of God's mercy and a praise of his friend and colleague:

This paper has been written in connection to my work within the DFG-funded Collaborative Research Centre 1136 "Education and Religion in Cultures of the Mediterranean and Its Environment from Ancient to Medieval Times and to the Classical Islam" at the University of Göttingen, sub-project C 04 "Communication of Education in Late Antique Christianity: Teachers' Roles in Parish, Family and Ascetical Community".

1 Paulinus of Nola, *ep.* 50.2 (CSEL 29, 404.17 von Hartel): *benedicte doctor Israel*. The translations are partly taken from P.G. Walsh, *Letters of St. Paulinus of Nola*, vol. 2, ACW 36 (London: Paulist Press, 1967), pp. 276–95, without marking minor amendments. Walsh translates "learned doctor of Israel" without further explanation.
2 Paulinus of Nola, *ep.* 50.9 (CSEL 29, 412.1–2 von Hartel): *in omnibus enim his nominibus simile et prope unum doctrinae officium video fuisse tractatum.*
3 Paulinus of Nola, *ep.* 50.9 (CSEL 29, 412.9–11 von Hartel): *Inter pastores specialiter et doctores quid intersit, dinoscere uolo, quia praepositis ecclesiae utrumque nomen adscribi solet.*

> May God through your prayers have mercy on me and cause His countenance to shine on me (Ps 66:2 Vulg.; cf. Ps 4:7) through the lamp of your word (Ps 118:105 Vulg.), holy lord and most blessed and loving brother in Christ the Lord. You are my master in the faith of the truth and my patron in the bowels of Christ's love.[4]

This letter documents a relationship which might be termed 'mentorship': a person asks for guidance by a more experienced person who is able and willing to impart knowledge and wisdom to the mentee. It is a personal and enduring relationship, not an encounter which takes place once only. At the same time, the letter is evidence of an episcopal network: both partners are bishops, and the mentor – Augustine – is asked to fulfill an episcopal duty, that is, to interpret the Scriptures and thus to function as mediator between God and man. It goes without saying that Paulinus' humility is itself a rhetorical device which was frequently employed in late antique epistolography. But I would argue that there is more at stake than rhetoric: Christian letter-writers like these two bishops witness to exegetical discussion as new content of epistolary exchange.[5] While both of them undoubtedly were aware that their letters would be collected, published, and spread over the Mediterranean, there is no reason to deny that Paulinus was really asking for hermeneutical advice and that Augustine was willing to provide what Paulinus requested, be it 'spiritual education' in exegetical matters or, in his *On the Care of the Dead*, directed to the same addressee, 'pastoral care', to introduce the two modern notions mentioned in the title of my paper. Using these terms as heuristic tools, I will argue that episcopal mentorship unfolded itself as a combination of care of texts and care of souls, that is, as spiritual education and pastoral care, intrinsically intertwined and as a whole applied by an episcopal mentor to a mentee.

A few preliminary remarks should be made. First, 'mentor' is, to be sure, an analytical notion which does not occur in the sources. Although one could refer to the Odyssey where the goddess Athena in the guise of 'Mentor'[6] accompanies young Telemachus on his journey to Pylos, this story apparently did not inspire a notion of 'mentorship' in Greek or Latin. In modern research, the term is sometimes used without defining it explicitly: to mention just one example, George

---

[4] Paulinus of Nola, *ep.* 50.18 (CSEL 29, 423.9–13 von Hartel): *Deus misereatur mei per orationes tuas et inluminet uultum suum super me per lucernam uerbi tui, sancte domine, beatissime frater in domino Christo unanime, magister meus in fide ueritatis et susceptor meus in uisceribus caritatis Christi.*

[5] For the Christian transformation of the traditional epistolographical genre, see Peter Gemeinhardt, *Das lateinische Christentum und die antike pagane Bildung*, STAC 41 (Tübingen: Mohr Siebeck, 2007), 214–222.

[6] Homer, *Od.* 2.268: Μέντορι εἰδομένη ἠμὲν δέμας ἠδὲ καὶ αὐδήν.

Demacopoulos' volume on spiritual direction in the Early Church employs this notion casually and also as sub-heading[7], but uses it interchangeably with 'spiritual direction' or 'guidance' and 'leadership'. For the sake of the present volume, I should like to stress that I understand 'mentorship' as a relationship which can be related to 'spiritual' matters (but it is not necessarily confined to them), which is based on a certain hierarchy (though this authority can undergo changes) and in which the mentor acts intentionally, that is, he knows what he (or she) is doing, and what is the aim of his (or her) educating for the mentee.

Second, employing the notion of 'pastoral care' does not imply that I will be looking for the patristic background of a pastoral theology for today. In turn, I intend to use a modern expression to classify and compare phenomena which can be observed in late antique sources. There is however no unanimous definition of 'pastoral care' with respect to patristic sources yet. One and a half decades ago, in an instructive series of papers, Pauline Allen and Wendy Mayer have reflected upon 'pastoral care' as it can be observed in patristic sources, with particular attention to episcopal agency.[8] Among the aspects which they identified as 'pastoral care' (teaching, direction for daily life, mission, administration, intercession, application of ritualized forms of care, social welfare)[9], teaching figures prominently when it comes to interaction between a mentor and a mentee. I will thus focus on episcopal teaching which comprises an exegetical as well as a spiritual dimension and which, moreover, includes catechesis and private instruction as well as public preaching (a topic to which Gillian Clark has devoted an inspiring paper).[10] As we have seen, Augustine was awarded the title *magister* by Paulinus, and Jerome wrote to him: "You are a bishop, the teacher of the

---

[7] George Demacopoulos, *Five Models of Spiritual Direction in the Early Church* (Notre Dame IN: University of Notre Dame Press, 2007), 35–42 ("Spiritual mentoring and the ascetic community", on Athanasius' guidance for male and female ascetics) and 89–92 (on Augustine's "Mentoring Subordinate Clergy").

[8] See esp. the more theoretical passages of Pauline Allen and Wendy Mayer, "Through a Bishop's Eyes: Towards a Definition of Pastoral Care in Late Antiquity," *Aug.* 40 (2000): 345–397, 346–61, and ibid. 361–78 as well as Wendy Mayer, "Constantinopolitan Women in Chrysostom's Circle," *VigChr* 53 (1999): 265–288 and ead., "Patronage, Pastoral Care and the Role of the Bishop at Antioch," *VigChr* 55 (2001): 58–70, 60, on John Chrysostom as primordial example.

[9] See the list in Mayer, *Patronage*, 60.

[10] Gillian Clark, "Pastoral Care: Town and Country in Late-Antique Preaching," in *Urban Centers and Rural Context in Late Antiquity*, eds. Thomas S. Burns and John W. Eadie (East Lansing MI: Michigan State University Press, 2001): 265–284. Though this paper has 'pastoral care' in the title (and is highly informative in many respects), it provides no definition of the precise meaning of this notion.

churches of Christ."¹¹ How did bishops live up to this expectation, and how did they build and use networks in order to fulfill their duty?

Third, one might ask whether such a mentorship is peculiar to episcopal networks. In some sense, the answer is no: of course there are similar relationships in which no bishop was involved, to mention only the monastic fathers of the desert and their disciples.[12] Above all, the *Sayings of the Desert Fathers* reveal a standard model of a mentor-like relationship, namely, the unquestioned authority of the elder and the obedience of the disciple – although there we can observe a certain dynamic within this structure, since the disciple often became an elder who instructed other would-be anchorites himself.[13] What is characteristic of the bishop in Late Antiquity, compared to the hermits, is the variety of different kinds of mentorships which could be exercised by one and the same person: e.g., the epistolary corpus of Augustine illustrates that not only fellow bishops like Paulinus but also laymen, be they pagans or recent converts, state officials or philosophers, and moreover male and female ascetics, appear as mentees of bishops.[14] Notably, a bishop was entitled and obliged to exercise another kind of authority than a desert elder, an authority of a more formalized kind, but it is clear that, in Late Antiquity, a certain ascetic background was reckoned important to support the authority of the office-holder.[15] Thus there is indeed overlap with other kind of mentorships, and I certainly do not claim that such mentorships define the bishop's office completely. The present paper will nonetheless argue that mentorship relations are part and parcel of the late antique bishop's privileges and duties, and that investigating their shape and con-

---

11 Jerome, *ep.* 112.15 (CSEL 55, 384.21 Hilberg): *episcopus es, ecclesiarum Christi magister.*
12 See, e.g., Demacopoulos, *Models*, 107–126 on John Cassian.
13 For the role of the *abba* in the *Apophthegmata Patrum*, see William Harmless, *Desert Christians: An Introduction to the Literature of Early Monasticism* (Oxford: Oxford University Press, 2004), 169–71.
14 See Frank Morgenstern, *Die Briefpartner des Augustinus von Hippo. Prosopographische, sozial- und ideologiegeschichtliche Untersuchungen*, Bochumer Historische Studien. Alte Geschichte 11 (Bochum: Brockmeyer, 1993) and the list of corresponding persons in Augustine's epistolary corpus in Johannes Divjak et al., "Art. Epistulae," in *AugL* 2 (2002): 893–1057, 1037–1046.
15 For this see Andrea Sterk, *Renouncing the World Yet Leading the Church. The Monk-Bishop in Late Antiquity* (Cambridge MA/London: Harvard University Press, 2004), Marcella Forlin Patrucco, "Bishops and Monks in Late Antique Society," *ZAC* 8 (2004): 332–345 and Demacopoulos, *Models*, 15–16.

tent might shed new light on the specific challenges of this ecclesiastical role and office in Late Antiquity.[16]

In what follows, I will briefly highlight three constellations of mentorships from different regions, all from the first hundred years after the emergence of the so-called *Reichskirche*. I will thereby resist the temptation to tell the whole story simply by referring to Augustine's life and writings, although my paper will – for good reason – start with a glimpse into his letters, that is, into his correspondence with the pagan senator Volusianus (chapter 2.1.). I will then turn to Zeno of Verona and his sermons to neophytes (chapter 2.2.) in order to illustrate how mentorship after the conversion could be exercised within a highly pluralized religious world. Both sub-chapters will contribute to our understanding of bishops as mentors of non-Christians and neophytes. In chapter 3, I move to Constantinople where we will meet bishops and virgins in interaction, namely John Chrysostom and Olympias. Chapter 4 will tackle a related question, that is, of bishops as mentors of male ascetics, referring to Athanasius' letter to Dracontius. Although, as I am well aware of, there might be other and perhaps even more illuminating examples of episcopal mentorship, my protagonists should enable us to highlight different types of episcopal mentors and situate them within their respective networks in the late antique Mediterranean.

2 Bishops and (possible) converts

2.1 Augustin and Volusianus

There may have been many bishops who acted as religious mentors, but without doubt, Augustine has left the most extensive documentation. In his letters and treatises, he gave spiritual advice to bishops and laymen, virgins and functionaries: one might even regard the monumental *City of God* as an exercise of mentorship, insofar this *magnum opus et arduum*[17] was initially dedicated to Marcellinus, a Roman tribune, who asked for consolation and explanation after the sack of Rome by the Goths in 410.[18] The most instructive textual witness with re-

---

[16] On this, see more extensively Claudia Rapp, *Holy Bishops in Late Antiquity. The Nature of Leadership in an Age of Transition*, The Transformation of the Classical Heritage 37 (Berkeley CA et al.: The University of California Press, 2005).
[17] Augustine, *civ.* 1 praef. (CChr.SL 47, 1.8 Dombart/Kalb).
[18] After having formulated this assertion, I discovered that Alfred Schindler had claimed more than two decades ago that *De civitate dei* had, besides its apologetic aim, a pastoral function (Alfred Schindler, "Augustin," in *Geschichte der Seelsorge in Einzelporträts*, ed. Christian Möller,

spect to mentorship is however Augustine's epistolary corpus. Accordingly, it is a crucial (if limited) set of letters which I will examine here: Augustine's letters to and from Volusianus.

With Rufius Antonius Agrypnius Volusianus, we encounter a prominent Roman senator, holder of eminent offices, and a friend of the tribune Marcellinus. Volusianus wrote to Augustine in 411 or 412 while he was himself present in Carthage.[19] In his family, some people had decided to conduct an ascetic life: e.g., Volusianus' mother had already converted to Christianity, and his niece Melania the Younger would eventually become one of the most popular female saints of the Roman aristocracy.[20] Volusianus himself still adhered to the traditional cults when he received letters from Augustine and posed himself questions about the incarnation and the miracles of Christ; he became Christian just before his death in 437. He is thus a representative of circles in the Roman society within which religious and philosophical questions were debated, and elaborate answers were expected from prominent spokesmen of Christianity, which had only recently become the one and only religion which was supported by imperial legislation. It is thus of interest how Augustine approached an educated pagan in order to exercise religious mentorship in written form.[21]

As it is clear from Augustine's first letter, Volusianus had sent him greetings, and Augustine responded by inviting the senator "to apply yourself to the truly and surely Sacred Letters", that is, to studying the Bible, "a sound and substantial study... which does not allure the mind with fanciful language, nor strike a flat or wavering note by means of any deceit of the tongue"[22]. The last phrase is

---

vol. I (Göttingen: Vandenhoeck & Ruprecht, 1994): 189–207, 193: "So hat die Thematik des 'Gottesstaats' (civitas dei) ziemlich direkt mit der Frage zu tun, weshalb Gott uns Glück und Unglück im Leben schickt, auch dann, wenn wir weder das eine noch das andere verdient zu haben glauben."

[19] For biographical data and career, see PLRE 2.1184–1185 (Volusianus 6).

[20] See Wilhelm Geerlings, "Die Belehrung eines Heiden: Augustins Brief über Christus an Volusianus," in *Collectanea Augustiniana. Mélanges Tarsicius Jan van Bavel*, éd. par Bernard Bruning, vol. II = *Aug(L)* 41 (Leuven: Peeters, 1991): 451–468, 452.

[21] For an analysis of Augustine's letters 132 and 137 (to Volusianus) and 135 (written by the latter to Augustine himself), see Christian Tornau, *Zwischen Rhetorik und Philosophie. Augustins Argumentationstechnik in De ciuitate Dei und ihr bildungsgeschichtlicher Hintergrund*, UaLG 82 (Berlin/New York: Walter de Gruyter, 2006), 57–71. The translations follow Wilfrid Parsons (tr.), *Saint Augustine: Letters*, vol. 3 (131–164). FaCh 20 (Washington D.C.: The Catholic University of America Press, 1953).

[22] Augustine, *ep.* 132 (CSEL 44, 79.12–16 Goldbacher): *unde meritis tuis reddens salutationis obsequium hortor, ut ualeo, ut litterarum uere certe que sanctarum te curam non pigeat inpendere. sincera enim et solida res est nec fucatis eloquiis ambit ad animum nec ullo linguae tectorio inane aliquid ac pendulum crepitat.*

revealing: it alludes to Persius' *Satires*[23] and thus testifies to the thorough learning of the writer which would without doubt be recognized by the reader who had received an equal schooling. Augustine's letter thus employed a cultural code in order to establish a social relationship among men of letters. To introduce a spiritual dimension into this well-known mode of communication, Augustine exhorted Volusianus to be "more desirous of reality (*res*) than of words (*verba*)".[24] It is not polished speech which is important, but spiritual content: thus, Volusianus should not mistakenly disregard the supposed rude language of the biblical writings:

> The very kind of speech, by which the Holy Scripture is composed, is accessible for all, although only few will penetrate it! She contains certain things in an obvious manner which speaks to the heart of the unlearned and the learned like an intimate friend, without any polish; but she hides other things in mysteries and does not elevate them herself by virtue of haughty speech, so that an intellect which is slow in the uptake and without erudition would not dare to come to her like a poor man to wealth, but by her modest way of speaking, she invites everyone.[25]

Clearly, Augustine had his own spiritual biography in mind, which was accessible in the *Confessions*, where he narrated his own premature repudiation of the Bible.[26] Spiritual education thus includes rendering the mentee sensible to the specific literary form of the Christian message. It is telling that this approach is paralleled in Augustine's treatise *On the First Catechetical Instruction* according to which the introductory catechetical lecture is to be adjusted to the schooling and the literary taste of the would-be convert, and where Augustine goes to great lengths to explain how to dissipate the prejudices of those "who come from the schools of the teachers of grammar and oratory – people who you would neither count among the idiots nor among the erudite" and who are in danger to miss the point of the instruction in the Bible due to their mistaken literary 'haut goût'.[27]

---

23 Persius, *Sat.* 5.24–5: *Dinoscere cautus, quid solidum crepet et pictae tectoria linguae.*
24 Augustine, *ep.* 132 (CSEL 44, 79.16–17 Goldbacher): *multum mouet non uerborum sed rerum auidum.*
25 Augustine, *ep.* 137.5.18 (CSEL 44, 122.10–123.2 Goldbacher): *modus autem ipse dicendi, quo sancta scriptura contexitur, quam omnibus accessibilis, quamuis paucissimis penetrabilis! ea, quae aperta continet, quasi amicus familiaris sine fuco ad cor loquitur indoctorum atque doctorum; ea uero, quae in mysteriis occultat, nec ipsa eloquio superbo erigit, quo non audeat accedere mens tardiuscula et inerudita quasi pauper ad diuitem, sed inuitat omnes humili sermone.*
26 See Augustine, *conf.* 3.5.9 (CChr.SL 27, 31.5–10 Verheijen).
27 Augustine, *cat. rud.* 9.13.1, 3 (CChr.SL 46, 135.1–4, 11–16 Bauer): *sunt item quidam de scholis usitatissimis grammaticorum oratorum que uenientes, quos neque inter idiotas numerare audeas,*

In accordance with his critique of contemporary public teaching, Augustine recommended Volusianus urgently to keep away from persons "who take more pleasure in the sword-play of words than in the enlightenment of knowledge"[28]. He should better write to the bishop himself if "in your reading or meditation some difficulty arises"[29]. Augustine thus presented himself as a competent guide to the biblical *verba* and, more importantly, to the *res* which lay hidden behind these words. Accordingly, he exhorted Volusianus not to estimate his own schooling too much, because this would prevent him from discovering the deeper spiritual meaning of the divine Scriptures. As mentioned above, Augustine himself had experienced this, and this story was publicly known from his *Confessions* which Volusianus even might have read.

Volusianus however refused to become a humble disciple of the bishop and, in his response, addressed Augustine not as a teacher and a bishop but as a peer, that is, as a graduate of the same school system. Volusianus who belonged to the upper Roman society did not wish to accept without further explanation the instruction of Augustine who came from a lower social stratum. While Volusianus readily acknowledged the superior intellect of Augustine[30], he wished to enter into a debate with the former teacher which should make use of classical grammar, rhetoric, and philosophy as basis of the dialogue instead of the Bible. If Volusianus was prepared to accept Augustine's mentorship, it was on grounds of his authority as former public teacher, not as Christian bishop.[31] Undoubtedly, he did not reckon it a given that a Christian bishop should act as mentor of a pagan senator.

While the letters of Augustine to and from high-ranking contemporaries are, generally speaking, important sources of late antique debates between traditionalist Roman pagans and Christians on education and religion[32], the bishop de-

---

neque inter illos doctissimos, quorum mens magnarum rerum est exercitata quaestionibus... maxime autem isti docendi sunt scripturas audire diuinas, ne sordeat eis solidum eloquium, quia non est inflatum, neque arbitrentur carnalibus integumentis inuoluta atque operta dicta uel facta hominum, quae in illis libris leguntur, non euoluenda atque aperienda ut intelligantur, sed sic accipienda ut litterae sonant.

28 Augustine, *ep.* 132 (CSEL 44, 80.9–10 Goldbacher): *magisque linguae certaminibus quam scientiae luminibus delectantur.*

29 Augustine, *ep.* 132 (CSEL 44, 80.2–4 Goldbacher): *si quid autem, uel cum legis uel cum cogitas, tibi oritur quaestionis, in quo dissoluendo uidear necessarius, scribe, ut rescribam.*

30 Augustine, *ep.* 135.2 (CSEL 44, 92.7–8 Goldbacher): *accepisti, uir totius gloriae capax, inperitiae confessionem.*

31 See the references in the *exordium* of the letter: Augustine, *ep.* 135.1 (CSEL 44, 89.13–91.6 Goldbacher); cf. Tornau, *Rhetorik*, 62–3.

32 See Gemeinhardt, *Christentum*, 204–5.

cidedly did not wish to enter this arena with Volusianus: although he followed the epistolary conventions of his time when addressing Volusianus[33], in the following letter, he praised the latter's intellect which seemed to him markedly different from "these proud little minds who make no account of grace, who make a great show of their ability, but can do nothing either to cure their own faults or even to check them."[34] Although Augustine quoted Sallustius and Virgil two times each in his letter, he did so solely in order to recommend a conscious Christian appropriation of the classics.[35] "In a world approaching its end"[36], the role-model would be no longer the orator but the ordinary Christian believer:

> Though once the most ignorant, the most lowly, the fewest in number, they become learned, they are ennobled, their numbers are multiplied. The most famous minds, the most cultured speech, the admirable skill of the brilliant, the eloquent and the learned are brought under the yoke of Christ, and turned to preaching the way of love of God and salvation.[37]

Accordingly, at the end of his letter, Augustine repeated his exhortation to read the Bible as the corpus of what Christian Tornau has termed "the new classics of Augustine".[38] In this way, he aimed at winning back his role as mentor of a forthcoming Christian who had still to get rid of his erudite ballast. Augustine, however did not achieve his goal and did not live to see Volusianus' conversion: After a splendid career in the service of the Empire, Volusianus was taught the faith, and at the end of the day, he indeed got baptized, but only in 437, that is, seven years after Augustine's death. And it was not the bishop but his relative, the

---

[33] Augustine, *ep.* 138.1.1 (CSEL 44, 126.5–6 Goldbacher): *inlustris uir et eloquentissimus nobisque dilectissimus Volusianus.*
[34] Augustine, *ep.* 137.1.1 (CSEL 44, 97.13–98.2 Goldbacher): *ingenium quippe et eloquium tuum tam excellens tam que luculentum prodesse debet etiam ceteris, contra quorum tarditatem seu peruersitatem conuenientissime defendenda est tantae gratiae dispensatio, quam superbae animulae nihili pendunt, quae nimis affectant plurimum posse et ad sua uitia sananda uel etiam frenanda nihil possunt.*
[35] See Tornau, *Rhetorik*, 66, referring to Christian Gnilka, *Chrêsis. Die Methode der Kirchenväter im Umgang mit der antiken Kultur, vol. I: Der Begriff des "rechten Gebrauchs"* (Basel/Stuttgart: Schwabe, 1984), 177–86.
[36] Augustine, *ep.* 137.4.16 (CSEL 44, 120.4 Goldbacher): *mundo declinante in extrema.*
[37] Augustine, *ep.* 137.4.16 (CSEL 44, 119.15–120.2 Goldbacher): *ex inperitissimis, ex abiectissimis, ex paucissimis inluminantur, nobilitantur, multiplicantur. praeclarissima ingenia, cultissima eloquia mirabiles que peritias acutorum, facundorum atque doctorum subiugant christo et ad praedicandam uiam pietatis salutis que conuertunt.*
[38] Tornau, *Rhetorik*, 71.

saint-like younger Melania who convinced Volusianus to receive baptism on his deathbed.[39]

Notwithstanding this delay, the letters are outstanding examples of episcopal pastoral care which was based on spiritual and theological instruction. This educational enterprise aimed not only at instructing the mentee how to conduct a Christian life but also how to reach out for salvation beyond one's own death.[40] Augustine did not threaten Volusianus but expressed a deep pastoral concern: in the turmoil of the barbarian invasions, classical erudition could no longer provide orientation and had to give way to a spiritual education, authoritatively represented by a Christian bishop. Ideally, Volusianus was not only supposed to convert to Christianity but, moreover, to become a herald of the Christian faith himself among his peers, employing his rhetorical abilities as well as his network of relatives, friends, and colleagues in the Roman senate.[41] If he was successful, Volusianus – once himself a cultured despiser of Christianity – could be even more effective in spreading the faith than the bishops themselves. Augustine's letters are therefore fine examples of how a bishop attempted to build networks with educated pagans in order to impart to them spiritual knowledge, raised from the Bible.[42]

2.2 Zeno and the neophytes

But what if high-ranking and ordinary people actually accepted baptism? Did episcopal mentorship end – or continue? Without doubt, lasting relationships were also established (or, if there had been previous contacts, stabilized) during the catechumenate which was also a place of intensified mentorship, albeit of a more formalized kind. We have already hinted at Augustine's treatise *On the First Catechetical Instruction*, which was aimed at catechizing an individual; here, the

---

39 Gerontius, *v. Melan.* 50, 53, 55 (SC 90, 224, 230–232, 236 Gorce).
40 See Augustine, *ep.* 137.1.1 (CSEL 44, 97.6–12 Goldbacher): *quis autem nostrum, qui Christi, ut possumus, gratiam ministramus, cum tua uerba legerit, ita te uelit doctrina instrui christiana, ut tibi tantum sufficiat ad salutem non huius uitae, quam uaporis esse simillimam tantillum apparentis et ilico uanescentis atque pereuntis sermo diuinus admonere curauit, sed illam salutem, propter quam adipiscendam et in aeternum obtinendam christiani sumus?*
41 This is expressed in Augustine, *ep.* 137.1.1 (CSEL 44, 97.12–16 Goldbacher): *parum est ergo nobis sic te instrui, ut tibi sit liberando satis. ingenium quippe et eloquium tuum tam excellens tamque luculentum prodesse debet etiam ceteris, contra quorum tarditatem seu peruersitatem conuenientissime defendenda est tantae gratiae dispensatio.*
42 For this, see also Paul R. Kolbet, *Augustine and the Cure of Souls. Revising a Classical Ideal* (Notre Dame IN: Notre Dame Press, 2010), 139–53.

experienced bishop strongly recommended to develop personal ties between catechist and catechumen. But then we should add the collection of *Pre-Baptismal Catecheses* of Cyril of Jerusalem: they provide an example of another kind of catechizing, namely, of a whole bunch of people who had enrolled for baptism and now received their spiritual formation during the lenten period but were not in every case personally acquainted with the bishop[43] – the same is true for the instruction which Augustine himself received before being baptized: there is no hint of a personal relationship to bishop Ambrose. Therefore, the institutionalized catechumenate seems to reveal other dimensions of episcopal agency: in the *Apostolic Constitutions*, roughly contemporary to Augustine's early episcopal career, the bishop is named "your ruler and governor, your king and potentate; he is, next after God, your earthly god, who has a right to be honoured by you."[44]

At first glance, this seems quite different from pastoral care, and there is indeed a tension between the bishop who takes care of souls by virtue of interpersonal communication and the bishop as representative of the ecclesiastical hierarchy who is entitled to teach with unquestioned authority what the faithful have to believe and how they should act according to Christian standards of orthodoxy and ethics. But one must not forget that privileges always include responsibilities; in other words, a bishop was obliged to live up himself to the reverence and obedience he could expect from his flock. Not everyone could expect a long treatise on Christology, as Volusianus requested (and received) from Augustine, but every convert would be assured that the bishop felt responsible for his or her earthly welfare and eternal salvation.

Mentorship did therefore not end with the conversion of a pagan like Volusianus. It remained an episcopal obligation to the neophytes: they needed to be taught continually the faith as well as the Christian way of life, and if they were many, this was most effectively done by preaching. That is, the catechetical instruction before receiving baptism at Easter was followed by the regular Sunday worships where bishops gave speeches on biblical texts, on questions of moral

---

[43] For a comparison of these different circumstances of Christian teaching, see Peter Gemeinhardt, "Teaching Religion in Late Antiquity: Divine and Human Agency," *StPatr* 92 (2017): 271–277. For Cyril, see moreover Olga Lorgeoux, "Cyril of Jerusalem as Catechetical Teacher: Religious Education in Fourth-Century Jerusalem," in *Teachers in Late Antique Christianity*, eds. Peter Gemeinhardt, Olga Lorgeoux and Maria Munkholt Christensen, SERAPHIM 3 (Tübingen: Mohr Siebeck, 2018): 76–91; for the fourth-century catechumenate in general and Augustine in particular, William Harmless, *Augustine and the Catechumenate* (Collegeville MN: Liturgical Press, ²2014) 35–87 and *passim*.

[44] *Const. App.* 2.26.4 (SC 320, 238.30–32 Metzger): οὗτος ἄρχων καὶ ἡγούμενος ὑμῶν, οὗτος ὑμῶν βασιλεὺς καὶ δυνάστης, οὗτος ὑμῶν ἐπίγειος θεὸς μετὰ Θεόν, ὃς ὀφείλει τῆς παρ' ὑμῶν τιμῆς ἀπολαύειν. Tr. ANF 7, 410.

conduct, and on the martyrs' sufferings and redemption. Besides well-known sources like the homilies of Augustine and John Chrysostom and other more or less prominent bishops, the very first Latin corpus of sermons deserves special attention.[45] It was composed in the decades between 360 and 380 by the North Italian bishop Zeno of Verona. Zeno's audience was apparently a mixture of Christians of long standing and of newly baptized converts, and it is the latter group which is addressed by the bishop in a way which I would like to refer to as representing a particular kind of episcopal mentorship.

Zeno, like Augustine, pointed out that "made-up speech" (*sermo fucatus*) is not appropriate for the faithful within the Church of God who rightly expect truth, not polished words. He himself was prepared to endure people laughing at him, a humble man without eloquence and formal erudition, as he depicted himself.[46] To be sure, Zeno used the stylistic devices of the Second Sophistic and employed what is known as the 'neo-asianic style' which he might have learned from Apuleius' writings[47], and he was well aware that already Plato and Virgil witnessed to the presentiment among pagan philosophers and poets against the Christian teaching of the resurrection.[48] But he also drew a sharp distinction:

> But we, brothers, have received our instruction not from an ingenious presentiment but from God the teacher himself, and for our sake he proved by himself what he taught –

---

[45] For an analysis of this hitherto little tapped corpus of sermons see now Bärbel Dümler, *Zeno von Verona zu heidnischer Kultur und christlicher Bildung*, STAC 75 (Tübingen: Mohr Siebeck, 2013), esp. pp. 418–42 for the Christian education of the converts. Her study is instructive in many ways as well as problematic in some respect, because the analysis applies Varro's scheme of a "tripartite theology" to the sermons, while it is not employed by Zeno himself (as Dümler, *Zeno von Verona*, 10 acknowledges herself). See my review of Dümler's book in *ZAC* 17 (2013): 640–642. Cf. also the recent study of Robert McEachnie, "Zeno, Chromatius, and Gaudentius. Italian Preachers Amid Transition," in *Preaching in the Patristic Era. Sermons, Preachers, and Audiences in the Latin West*, eds. Anthony Dupont et al. (Leiden / Boston: Brill, 2018): 454–476.
[46] Zeno, *tract.* 2.1.1 (CChr.SL 22, 145.6–9 Löfstedt): *Sed ego non curem, de me quemadmodum quis iocetur. Non enim in ecclesia dei fucatus quaeritur sermo, sed ueritas pura, a qua longe omnes illi non immerito aberrauerunt, qui iustitiam dei manere in eloquentiae uiribus aestimabant.* Translations of Zeno's sermons are mine.
[47] Dümler, *Zeno von Verona*, 40.
[48] Zeno, *tract.* 1.2.2, 4 (CChr.SL 22, 15.11–15, 15.30–16.35 Löfstedt): *... praesertim cum eorundem ille sapientissimus dicat hanc esse mortem, cum corpore animus tamquam carcere clausus tenetur, illam esse ueram uitam, cum idem animus custodia carceris liberatus ad eum locum, unde uenerit, reuertatur... Poetae autem melius, qui duplicem uiam apud inferos ponunt: impiorum unam, quae ducit in tartarum, piorum aliam, quae ducit ad elisium, eo fortius addentes, quod defunctorum ibidem non tam formae quam facta noscantur ac necessario recipiant secundum quod mundanae administrationis suis in actibus portant, recte dicentes: 'quisque suos patimur manes'* (Virgil, *Aen.* 6.743). See Gemeinhardt, *Christentum*, 414–15.

we are able not only to claim that the souls of the deceased live on but to demonstrate it by conspicuous facts.⁴⁹

Zeno took the scepticism of the former pagans serious and tried to transform their thinking by pointing out the biblical proofs for what they knew from the school-texts. As bishop, he acted as educator in a Christian sense, that is, as a second, or more precisely, spiritual educator for the new-born Christians, and he did so on behalf of God the teacher and of the Church "who – as our mother – nourishes you at the limits of the holy altar, full of pleasant scent".⁵⁰ A true follower of Christ would thus be "educated by his doctrine"⁵¹ which was exclusively offered by the bishop as Christ's deputy on earth.

But like Augustine, Zeno also combines care of texts (or doctrines) and care of souls. In one of his sermons, he initially addressed his "most beloved brothers" in general but then turned to the neophytes in particular, the "newborn Christians" (*nouelli Christiani*), and exhorted them, his "sweetest blossoms" (*dulcissimi flores*), to learn to discern and of course avoid different kinds of pagan sacrifices and prepare sacrifices for themselves "which the Holy Spirit freely offers, the Father accepts, and by which the Son – who is our teacher – is glorified".⁵² Zeno presented himself as the earthly agent of this *magisterium diuinae sapientiae*⁵³ whose primordial aim was religious instruction and ethical erudition.⁵⁴ But this is only possible on ground of a fundamental pastoral concern which is necessitated by the intellectual but also emotional ambiguity of the new-born Christians,

> who are wavering and uncertain; they stand in the middle between the pious and the impious people because they cannot stop to adhere to both parties. They are not faithful, be-

---

49 Zeno, *tract.* 1.2.5 (CChr.SL 22, 16.36–9 Löfstedt): *Nos uero, fratres, quos non ingeniosa suspicio, sed deus magister instruxit, propter nos in semet ipso probando quod docuit, uiuere animas mortuorum non tam dicere quam oculatis rebus sufficimus approbare.*
50 Zeno, *tract.* 1.32 (CChr.SL 22, 83.9–10 Löfstedt): *suaue redolentibus sacri altaris feliciter enutrit a cancellis.* See also *tract.* 1.59.5 (ibid. 135.42–3) where Zeno hinted at Isaac, the son of Abraham and Sarah, whoo had been fed with an accelerated education (*festinata educatione nutritus*).
51 Zeno, *tract.* 1.3.16 (CChr.SL 22, 27.137–28.138 Löfstedt): *sua doctrina formatos.*
52 Zeno, *tract.* 1.25.1 (CChr.SL 22, 73.2 Löfstedt): *fratres dilectissimi*; *tract.* 1.25.3 (ibid. 73.19): *Primo omnium sacrificiorum tria esse genera, nouelle, disce, Christiane, ne quo seducaris errore*; *tract.* 1.25.13 (ibid. 76.114–17): *Itaque, dulcissimi flores mei, talia sacrificia procurate, quae sanctus spiritus libenter offerat, pater probet, filius, qui magister est noster, probata glorietur per eundem.*
53 Zeno, *tract.* 2.1.2 (CChr.SL 22, 145.11 Löfstedt). See Dümler, *Zeno von Verona,* 434–36.
54 For this, see Dümler, *Zeno von Verona,* 425–34.

cause they still have the touch of infidelity; they are no unbelievers, because they display the imprint of the faith: their confession obeys to God, their deeds to the world.[55]

Religious mentorship in Zeno thus meant to navigate such former pagans through the shallows of the world which they had willingly renounced but which remained to be a concern and a threat to them. Acting as mentor, Zeno time and again pointed out how to defeat the temptation of participating in pagan cults and Christian worship at the same time.[56] The bishop – as loving pastor and substitute of the divine teacher – imparted knowledge of the Christian way of life on his flock, and this would remain a focal point of episcopal agency as long as pagans converted to Christianity "with the speed of a spinning wheel", as Gaudentius of Brescia put it.[57] Zeno's sermons are thus a highly interesting source for fleshing out what was demanded from a Christian bishop as mentor, teacher, and pastor, beyond the hierarchical images of the episcopate in the *Apostolic Constitutions* and related treatises of that time.

3 Bishops and virgins: John Chrysostom and Olympias

But there was, at least, a third group which afforded religious mentorship: ascetics, more precisely, hermits, monks, and virgins who formed an expanding and attractive segment of the Christian population. Their loyalty and indebtedness to the clergy, especially in the case of virgins, was however often regarded as precarious. Situations where female ascetics accepted bishops as mentors are not in many cases well documented. All the more, John Chrysostom's relationship to

---

[55] Zeno, *tract.* 1.35.4–5 (CChr.SL 22, 90.36–41 Löfstedt): ... *ambiguos utique christianos ac lubricos, qui inter pios impios que sint medii nullam partem tenentes ad plenum, cum utramque tenere non desinunt. Fideles non sunt, quia habent aliquid infidelitatis insertum; infideles non sunt, quia habent imaginem fidei, professione deo, factis saeculo seruientes.* For such *incerti*, see Maijastina Kahlos, *Debate and Dialogue. Christian and Pagan Cultures c. 360–430* (Aldershot: Ashgate, 2007), 30–4 and ead., "Incerti in Between – Moments of Transition and Dialogue in Christian Apologetics," *Parola del Passato* 59 (2004): 5–24.
[56] See Peter Gemeinhardt, *Die Kirche und ihre Heiligen. Studien zu Ekklesiologie und Hagiographie in der Spätantike*, STAC 90 (Tübingen: Mohr Siebeck, 2014), 55–60.
[57] Gaudentius, *serm.* 8.25 (CSEL 68, 67.189–92 Glück): *Constat autem populum gentium ex errore idolatriae, ubi olim fuerat devolutus, nunc ad Christianae veritatis cultum celeritate rotae cuiusdam properare currentis.*

the wealthy widow and deaconess Olympias is a significant case in point and deserves our interest.[58]

Due to the instigations of patriarch Theophilus of Alexandria and because of an unexpected loss of support by emperor Arcadius, John Chrysostom was dethroned as bishop of Constantinople by the so-called 'Synod of the Oak' in 403.[59] In the following year, he was exiled to the city of Cucusus and, in 407, ordered to move to Arabissus and to Pityus on the eastern coast of the Black Sea, but he died during the journey. From Cucusus, between late 404 and early 407, John wrote 17 letters to Olympias which are part of a wide-ranging correspondence of the bishop with fellow bishops and other people who were sympathetic to his cause.[60] The addressee was a prominent woman in Constantinople who, after her husband, the city prefect Nebridius, had passed away in 386, had refused to marry again and instead founded and directed a community of virgins.[61] Palladius, in his *Dialogue on the Life of John Chrysostom*, and the anonymous but contemporaneous *Life of Olympias* report that God's generosity had saved her virginity during the short time of her marriage[62], and in his *Lausiac History*, Pal-

---

[58] For John Chrysostom exercising pastoral care, see the studies of Allen and Mayer mentioned above; for Olympias in general and her relationship to the bishop in particular, see Katharina Greschat, *Gelehrte Frauen des frühen Christentums. Zwölf Porträts*, Standorte in Antike und Christentum 6 (Stuttgart: Hiersemann, 2015), 79–90; for the friendship between both, see Carolinne White, *Christian Friendship in the Fourth Century* (Cambridge: Cambridge University Press, 1992), 94–97. The deeds and speeches of John Chrysostom after he had become bishop of the Eastern capital need not bother us here in detail; for an accurate account of this period of his life, see Claudia Tiersch, *Johannes Chrysostomus in Konstantinopel (398–404). Weltsicht und Wirken eines Bischofs in der Hauptstadt des Oströmischen Reiches*, STAC 6 (Tübingen: Mohr Siebeck, 2002).
[59] For the pre-history of this dramatic event see Tiersch, *Johannes Chrysostomus*, 327–53.
[60] See Tiersch, *Johannes Chrysostomus*, 397. Altogether 235 letters have been preserved, most of which are awaiting a critical edition. Only letters from Chrysostom to Olympias are extant, not vice versa.
[61] Besides shorter notices in Palladius, *h. Laus.* 56 (FC 67, 296 Hübner) and Sozomen, *h. e.* 8.24.4–7 (FC 73/4, 1034–7 Hansen), the main sources are Palladius, *dial.* 16–17 (SC 341, 318–320, 342–350 Malingrey) and the anonymous *Life of Olympias* (SC 13bis, 406–449 Malingrey) which draws heavily on the *Dialogue*'s biographical information but might still have been written by a contemporary, even if not by an eyewitness (Anne-Marie Malingrey, "Introduction," in Jean Chrysostome, *Lettres à Olympias. Seconde édition augmentée de la Vie anonyme d'Olympias*, introduction, texte critique, traduction et notes par Anne-Marie Malingrey, SC 13bis (Paris: Les Éditions du Cerf, 1968): 393–404, 396). Except for the *Lausiac History*, translations are mine.
[62] Palladius, *dial.* 17 (SC 341, 342.139 Malingrey); *V. Olymp.* 2 (SC 13bis, 410.15–16 Malingrey), however with the qualification "as the rumour says" (ὡς ἡ φήμη διδάσκει), since the author knew well that 1 Tim. 5:14 ordered explicitly that young widows should marry again (quoted ibid. 342.141–2).

ladius even insists that she had only been the bride of Nebridius; according to this account, Olympias died without having been married except to the "word of truth", that is, Christ.[63] This is most probably an hagiographical exaggeration of her virginity: it was not unusual that widows from the upper classes began to conduct an ascetic life after their husbands and / or children had died. Palladius underlines that Olympias would have been an attractive bride, "adorned by descent and wealth, by erudition in all sorts of knowledge, by good disposition of nature and by the blossoms of youth."[64]

It is however unusual that Olympias was interested in theological and exegetical matters: she asked Gregory of Nyssa for a commentary to the *Song of Songs* which he was happy to provide.[65] Apparently, Olympias was well connected to the Cappadocian theologians, and it has even been suggested that, before founding the communities of virgins, her house might have served as a hub for erudite discussion about Christian life and doctrine among clerics and laymen.[66] This leads us to a notice in the *Lausiac History* which must interest us here:

> [Olympias] took part in no small contests on behalf of the truth, instructed many women, addressed priests with reverence, paid honor to bishops, and was deemed worthy to be a confessor on behalf of the truth.[67]

Olympias, according to Palladius, acted as catechist of other women (πολλάς τε κατηχήσασα γυναῖκας), and this is recalled in her *Life*: "she catechized many women who did not believe and supported them with everything necessary for living"[68]. In doing so, she complemented and enlarged the teaching which the whole convent received from the bishop (see below). Of course, Olympias was not entitled to teach publicly, but it is nonetheless clear that she played an important role within the episcopal network in Constantinople and beyond in Cap-

---

[63] Palladius, *h. Laus.* 56.1 (FC 67, 296.9–11 Hübner).
[64] Palladius, *dial.* 17 (SC 341, 342.142–344.144 Malingrey): καὶ γένει καὶ πλούτῳ καὶ παιδείᾳ μαθημάτων πολυτελῶν καὶ εὐφυΐᾳ φύσεως καὶ ἄνθους ὥρᾳ κεκοσμημένη.
[65] Gregory of Nyssa, *hom. in Cant.* prol. (GNO 6, 3.1–4.10 Langerbeck).
[66] Greschat, *Frauen*, 80.
[67] Palladius, *h. Laus.* 56.2 (FC 67, 296.12–15 Hübner): οὐ μικροὺς ἀγῶνας ἀγωνισαμένη ὑπὲρ ἀληθείας, πολλάς τε κατηχήσασα γυναῖκας, καὶ σεμνολογήσασα πρεσβυτέρους, καὶ τιμήσασα ἐπισκόπους, καὶ ὁμολογίας κατηξιώθη τῆς ὑπὲρ ἀληθείας. Tr.: Palladius, *The Lausiac History*, trans and ann. Robert T. Meyer, ACW 34 (Westminster MD: The Newman Press / London: Longmans, Green & Co., 1965), 137.
[68] *V. Olymp.* 15 (SC 13bis, 442.12–13 Malingrey): πολλάς τε τῶν ἀπίστων κατηχήσασα γυναῖκας καὶ τὰ πρὸς τὸ ζῆν ἐπικουρήσασα.

padocia, and it can be inferred from the lines quoted above that she had the possibility to approach clergymen and even bishops.[69]

Moreover, Olympias was regarded as a 'confessor', that is, as a martyr-like woman who actually did not die due to a persecution but was ready to suffer for her belief in Christ and her loyalty to the legitimate bishop. The last words of the quotation refer to an accusation of arson: the church of Hagia Sophia had fallen victim to the flames just after John Chrysostom had left the city, and his followers were blamed for setting the church on fire.[70] Olympias was also called to trial. Instead of entering into community with John Chrysostom's successor Arsacius, she accepted an immense fine and left Constantinople; most probably she went to Cyzicus into exile.[71] In the Johannite camp, Olympias was renowned for her perseverance, and John himself wrote to her from Cucusus in order to strengthen her against the attacks of her opponents: While she is going to see her enemies tormented and in deep distress, "they will see you (among the deceased) in the blessed part with the martyr's crown, chanting with the angels, reigning together with Christ".[72] Here, the bishop employed martyrological terminology to describe Olympias' behaviour, and so did Palladius by referring to her "fighting fights on behalf of the truth" (as quoted above).

In the latter's *Dialogue*, she received even more praise: when the "deacon" asks for the reasons of the fame of this woman, he is rebuked by the "bishop":

> What kind of woman is she? – Do not say 'woman', but 'what kind of human being'. Because notwithstanding the constitution of the body, she is a man. – In which respect? – Regarding the conduct of life and pains and knowledge and obedience in sufferings.[73]

---

69 See Palladius, *dial.* 17 (SC 13bis, 348.195–205 Malingrey). While in his *Dialogue*, written shortly after Olympias' death in 408, Palladius elaborates upon the relationship of Olympias to John Chrysostom, a dozen years later, in his *Lausiac History*, he omits this occurrence. This might be due to the circumstance – as Greschat, *Frauen*, 87 hypothesizes – that the treatise was dedicated to Lausus, an influential office-holder (*praepositus sacri cubiculi*) at the emperor's court who would not have appreciated to be reminded of the affairs of 403–4.
70 In fact, already the ancient sources contradict each other in naming who was guilty; see Tiersch, *Johannes Chrysostomus*, 379–80.
71 Sozomen, *h. e.* 8.24.7 (FC 73/4, 1036.5–7 Hansen); see Tiersch, *Johannes Chrysostomus*, 390–1.
72 John Chrysostom, *ep. Olymp.* 8.10d (SC 13bis, 202.62–65): Ὄψονταί σε καὶ οὗτοι πάλιν ἐν τῇ μακαρίᾳ λήξει ἐκείνῃ στεφανηφοροῦσαν, μετὰ τῶν ἀγγέλων χορεύουσαν, τῷ Χριστῷ συμβασιλεύουσαν.
73 Palladius, *dial.* 16 (SC 341, 318.185–320.190 Malingrey): Ποταπὴ γυνὴ τυγχάνει οὖσα; Μὴ λέγε "γυνή," ἀλλ' "οἷος ἄνθρωπος"· ἀνὴρ γάρ ἐστι παρὰ τὸ τοῦ σώματος σχῆμα. Ἐν τίνι; Ἔν τε βίῳ καὶ πόνοις καὶ γνώσει καὶ τῇ τῶν περιστάσεων ὑπομονῇ. See also Pseudo-Martyrius, *Oratio funebris in laudem Sancti Iohannis Chrysostomi* 130 (ed. by Martin Wallraff, tr. by Cristina

Among many interesting features of Olympias' life, it is significant that she as a woman was reckoned leader of the Johannite movement (but then she was, as Palladius repeats a few lines below, "a woman of male character", ἀνδρεία γυνή).⁷⁴ Such a suspicion did however not come out of thin air: According to the anonymous *Life of Olympias*, the future "holy imitator of God"⁷⁵ had been a follower of John Chrysostom from early on and "followed his divinely inspired teachings with intelligence and purity".⁷⁶ After John had decided that the bishop's palace should no longer be used for banquets but serve as place of his own quasi-monastic dwelling⁷⁷, the community of virgins which she had founded in immediate neighbourhood to the Hagia Sophia⁷⁸ took care of John's modest needs. Olympias herself spent part of her money on his household in order to spare the episcopal budget for caritative purposes.⁷⁹ But their relationship was not only about food and finances. According to the *Life*, the famous bishop of the imperial city also functioned as spiritual mentor of a small circle of women who had "chosen the heavenly kingdom"⁸⁰:

> Never any other man or woman from outside was allowed to visit them, with the only exception of the most holy patriarch John who came continually and supported them by his very wise teaching.⁸¹

Obviously, John Chrysostom felt responsible for the religious instruction of Olympias and her fellow virgins and for hearing their confession – successfully so: the devil did not succeed in distracting the members of this "saintly choir and angel-

---

Ricci, Quaderni della Rivista di Bizantinistica 12 (Spoleto: Fondazione Centro italiano di studi sull'alto medioevo, 2007), 186.11–12): ἀνδρίαν δὲ εἰσδεξαμένην, πᾶσαν ἀνθρωπίνην ἔννοιαν ὑπερβαίνουσαν, ἐν γυναικείῳ τε ὁμοῦ καὶ ἁπαλῷ τῷ σώματι.

74 Palladius, *dial.* 17 (SC 341, 342.123 Malingrey).
75 *V. Olymp.* 14 (SC 13bis, 436.9 Malingrey): ἡ ὁσία καὶ θεομίμητος Ὀλυμπιάς. Cf. Palladius, *dial.* 16 (SC 341, 328.293–4 Malingrey): Τί οὖν; Κακὸν πεποίηκεν Ὀλυμπιάς, τὸν ἑαυτῆς Κύριον μιμησαμένη; The praise is repeated at the end of ch. 16 (ibid. 328.312–15).
76 *V. Olymp.* 5 (SC 13bis, 416.15–17 Malingrey): πάνυ συνετῶς καὶ εἰλικρινῶς ἐπομένη τοῖς θεοπνεύστοις διδάγμασι τοῦ ἁγιωτάτου τῆς αὐτῆς ἁγίας ἐκκλησίας ἀρχιεπισκόπου Ἰωάννου.
77 This ascetic life-style was, on the one hand, characteristic of monk-bishops around 400 CE (see Forlin Patrucco, *Bishops*, 334, 339–40), on the other hand it seems to have been offending for many people in Constantinople who had estimated the former prefect Nectarius as patriarch.
78 *V. Olymp.* 6 (SC 13bis, 418.1–5 Malingrey).
79 See Tiersch, *Johannes Chrysostomus*, 160.
80 *V. Olymp.* 6 (SC 13bis, 418.20–1 Malingrey): τὴν ἐπουράνιον ἐπελέξαντο βασιλείαν.
81 *V. Olymp.* 8 (SC 13bis, 422.5–9 Malingrey): οὐδὲ γὰρ ἦν τινα ἐκ τῶν ἔξωθεν ἢ ἄνδρα ἢ γυναῖκα εἰσελθεῖν πρὸς αὐτάς, εἰ μὴ μόνον τὸν ἁγιώτατον πατριάρχην Ἰωάννην, συνεχῶς εἰσερχόμενον καὶ ὑποστηρίζοντα αὐτὰς διὰ τῆς πανσόφου αὐτοῦ διδασκαλίας.

like institution"[82] from their ascetic practice. Their community was "directed, first, by God's grace, and second, by the uninterrupted teaching of the most holy patriarch".[83] I only mention in passing that, just here, we encounter a crucial aspect of mentorship, namely, the problem of sexes among ascetics. One of the charges brought forward against John Chrysostom by his opponents at the "Synod of the Oak" in 403 concerned his "meeting with women in private without any chaperon person"[84]. Apparently, the former would-be hermit John who had renounced sexuality did not reckon this a danger for himself or the virgins. His opponents however did, thus highlighting a peculiar problem of bishops as mentors of women. The bishop himself, "the herald of truth and teacher" endured these calumnies "like a noble athlete"[85], that is, like a martyr, and Olympias would imitate him in this respect, as we have seen.

But there is still another dimension of mentorship. While Olympias was known to conduct an ascetic, obedient, and frugal life, she also acted as a door-opener and even, so to speak, as a female patron, for the new bishop into society and politics of Constantinople.[86] John, already famous as preacher in Antioch, did not really have a clue about how to handle ecclesiastical affairs in the presence of the emperor's family and the members of the urban society of Constantinople, and Olympias, formerly wedded to a high-ranking office-holder, introduced him to people and procedures (although with little success, because John performed badly as bishop of the capital, as the long lists of complaints brought forward against him at the 'Synod of the Oak' illustrate). Based on the letters to Olympias and the *Life of Olympias*, we thus observe a kind of reciprocal mentorship between the bishop and the virgin. It is telling that, after his deposition, John gave not only a farewell speech to the bishops who were assembled in the bishop's palace (ἐπισκοπεῖον) but also to Olympias "who had never left the church" (that is, when John came under pressure) and other female vir-

---

[82] *V. Olymp.* 8 (SC 13bis, 422.1–2 Malingrey): ἡ ἁγία χορεία καὶ ἀγγελικὴ κατάστασις τῶν ἁγίων γυναικῶν ἐκείνων.
[83] *V. Olymp.* 9 (SC 13bis, 424.2–4 Malingrey): τὴν κατὰ πρῶτον μὲν λόγον τῇ χάριτι τοῦ θεοῦ, δεύτερον δὲ καὶ τῇ ἀδιαλείπτῳ διδασκαλίᾳ τοῦ ἁγιωτάτου πατριάρχου κατορθωθεῖσαν..
[84] Mayer, "Patronage", 65, referring to the 15th accusation quoted by Photius, *bibl. cod.* 59 (SC 342, 104,36–7 Malingrey): Ὅτι δέχεται γυναῖκας μονοπρόσωπα πάντας ἐκβάλλων ἔξω..
[85] *V. Olymp.* 8 (SC 13bis, 424.12–14 Malingrey): ἀλλ' ὁ τῆς ἀληθείας κῆρυξ καὶ διδάσκαλον ὥσπερ γενναῖος ἀθλητὴς τῶν ἀντιπάλων τὰς προσβολὰς δεχάμενος.
[86] See Mayer, *Women*, 284: "In the late fourth century wealthy senatorial women provided an entrée into Constantinopolitan politics and an avenue for the emperor that was otherwise denied to the usually lesser-ranked clergy." As mentioned above, Olympias devoted a considerable share of her immense wealth to caritative projects of the bishop; see Tiersch, *Johannes Chrysostomus*, 153–4 and 160–1.

gins who were waiting for him in the baptism chapel (βαπτιστήριον).[87] He exhorted them to pray for him, but also to keep their devotion to the church and accept anyone who would happen to be elected as successor, "because the church cannot be without a bishop."[88] Obviously, although John reckoned himself legitimate patriarch, he foresaw that there would be a replacement soon; and if the new bishop would be chosen "involuntarily and without having intrigued against John and with the consent of the whole people"[89], he should succeed him as mentor of the virgins. Episcopal mentorship was inevitably tied to personal relationships, but could also, as this incident shows, be connected to the office itself in order to secure continuous mentorship under difficult circumstances.

The *Dialogue* also testifies to the fact that these women were "intimately associated with the bishop in the mind of the population", as Wendy Mayer put it[90], and this was certainly due to his teaching them and exercising pastoral care for their community. John continued to counsel Olympias, as mentioned above, by writing consolatory letters from his exile and tried to soften her grief when she complained that "I do no longer hear your voice and enjoy the instruction to which I am accustomed."[91] The mutual longing of both the patriarch and the virgin is however framed by traditional epistolary *topoi* (as mentioned above)[92] which were well known to the experienced orator and the high-ranking woman who shared the curriculum of ancient education. But John adds another dimension to this exchange of amiabilities when, in another letter, he narrates his deep concern when he had learnt about Olympias'severe illness and his relief when he was told that she had recovered.[93] Then he continues with praise of her indulgence:

---

[87] Palladius, *dial.* 10 (SC 341, 206.34–36, 50–1 Malingrey).
[88] Palladius, *dial.* 10 (SC 341, 208.61 Malingrey): οὐ δύναται γὰρ ἡ ἐκκλησία ἄνευ ἐπισκόπου εἶναι.
[89] Palladius, *dial.* 10 (SC 341, 208.58–9 Malingrey): καὶ ὃς ἂν ἄκων ἀχθῇ ἐπὶ τὴν χειροτονίαν, μὴ ἀμβιτεύσας τὸ πρᾶγμα, κατὰ συναίνησιν τῶν πάντων.
[90] Mayer, *Women*, 273.
[91] John Chrysostom, *ep. Olymp.* 8.11a (SC 13bis, 202.8–9 Malingrey): Οὐκ ἀκούομεν τῆς γλώττης ἐκείνης, οὐδὲ ἀπολαύομεν τῆς συνήθους διδασκαλίας. See Greschat, *Frauen*, 82–3.
[92] Cf., e.g., John Chrysostom, *ep. Olymp.* 7.5e (SC 13bis, 216.48–52 Malingrey): Τοιούτων γὰρ τῶν γραμμάτων τούτων τὸ φάρμακον ὡς καὶ εὐθυμίαν σοι ἐμποιῆσαι πολλήν. See also (more elaborate) *ep. Olymp.* 8.13c (ibid. 216.48–52): Ἐπιθυμοῦμεν δὲ ἐν τῇ αὐτῇ εὐφροσύνῃ εἶναί σε νῦν ἐν ᾗ καὶ αὐτόθι διατρίβοντες ἑωρῶμεν. Κἂν τοῦτο μάθωμεν, οὐ μικρὰν καὶ αὐτοὶ τῆς ἐρημίας ἐν ᾗ νῦν ἐσμεν καρπωσόμεθα τὴν παράκλησιν
[93] John Chrysostom, *ep. Olymp.* 12.1b (SC 13bis, 318.27–32 Malingrey).

For not only to bear misfortunes bravely but to be actually insensible to them, to overlook them, and with such little exertion to wreathe your brows with the garland prize of patience, neither labouring, nor toiling, neither feeling distress nor causing it to others, but as it were leaping and dancing for joy all the while, this is indeed a proof of the most finished philosophy.[94]

Olympias, who had been instructed by the bishop, performs like a Christian philosopher, and one gets the impression that the mentor is deeply impressed by his mentee's steadfastness:

> Therefore I rejoice, and leap for joy, I am in a flutter of delight, I am insensible to my present loneliness and the other troubles which surround me, being cheered, and brightened, and not a little proud on account of your greatness of soul, and the repeated victories which you have won, and this not only for your own sake, but also for the sake of this large and populous city, where you are like a tower, a haven, a wall of defense, speaking in the eloquent voice of example, and through your sufferings instructing either sex to strip readily for this contest....[95]

Again, we observe a mutual relation of mentorship: John comforts the martyr-like woman who had remained in Constantinople but takes comfort himself from her victories. Instead of the exiled bishop, a woman functions as substitute regarding the education of loyal and faithful Christians. In his last letter to Olympias, written at the beginning of 407, John Chrysostom refers to his treatise "That no one can harm the man who does not injure himself"[96], and it can safely be guessed that the latter was supposed to circulate this text and his message among the friends and sympathizers of the bishop. Without presenting herself in public, Olympias is recognized as intermediate spokesperson and, moreover, true imitator of the bishop – and that means, of Christ. This is the core of her

---

[94] John Chrysostom, *ep. Olymp.* 12.1b (SC 13bis, 318.38–44 Malingrey): Τὸ γὰρ μὴ μόνον φέρειν γενναίως τὰ δυσχερῆ, ἀλλὰ μηδὲ παρόντων αὐτῶν αἰσθάνεσθαι, ἀλλ' ὑπερορᾶν καὶ μετὰ πολλῆς τῆς ἀπραγμοσύνης τὸν τῆς ὑπομονῆς ἀναδήσασθαι στέφανον, οὐ κάμνουσαν, οὐδὲ ἱδροῦσαν, οὐδὲ πράγματα ἔχουσαν, οὐδὲ ἑτέροις παρέχουσαν, ἀλλ' ὥσπερ σκιρτῶσαν καὶ χορεύουσαν, τοῦτο τῆς ἀκριβεστάτης φιλοσοφίας ἐστὶν ἀπόδειξις. Tr. Stephens, 297.
[95] John Chrysostom, *ep. Olymp.* 12.1b (SC 13bis, 318.44–320.52 Malingrey): Διὰ ταῦτα χαίρω καὶ σκιρτῶ, πέτομαι ὑπὸ τῆς ἡδονῆς, οὐκ αἰσθάνομαι τῆς παρούσης ἐρημίας οὐδὲ τῶν λοιπῶν περιστάσεων, εὐφραινόμενος καὶ γαννύμενος καὶ σφόδρα καλλωπιζόμενος ἐπὶ τῇ σῇ μεγαλοφροσύνῃ καὶ ταῖς ἐπαλλήλοις νίκαις, οὐ διὰ σὲ μόνον, ἀλλὰ καὶ διὰ τὴν μεγάλην καὶ πολυάνθρωπον πόλιν ἐκείνην ᾗ καὶ ἀντὶ πύργου καὶ λιμένος γέγονας καὶ τείχους, λαμπρὰν τὴν διὰ τῶν πραγμάτων ἀφιεῖσα φωνὴν καὶ ἑκάτερον τὸ γένος ἐν τοῖς παθήμασί σου παιδεύουσα καὶ ἀποδύεσθαι ῥᾳδίως πρὸς τοὺς τοιούτους ἀγῶνας. Tr. Stephens, 297.
[96] John Chrysostom, *ep. Olymp.* 17.4c (SC 13 bis, 384.32–35 Malingrey), referring to the treatise *Quod nemo laedatur nisi a seipso* (SC 103, Malingrey).

comprehensive philosophy, that is, of her ascetic life-style in which John Chrysostom had instructed his female mentee. Whereas most people, like, e.g., pilots (κυβερνῆται) are versed in a single kind of knowledge or ability (ἐπιστήμη), Olympias displays "the power of a philosophical soul which is superior to every kind of storm"[97], and one might even say that the exiled bishop saw himself mirrored in the exemplary behaviour of a woman who, as we have seen, should be reckoned a man.

To sum up: if mentorship unfolds as combination of spiritual education and pastoral care, the relationship between John Chrysostom and Olympias is an important case in point. This does however not rule out other ties which bound the bishop to the virgin: the contemporaries were well aware that John could endure his exile only because of the continuous financial support by Olympias.[98] The learned and well-connected woman herself acted as his patroness, and after he had been forced to resign and leave Constantinople, she stepped in as exemplary Christian and loyal mentee who now instructed others by her life, even if not by preaching.

4 Bishops and monks: Athanasius and Dracontius

Another intricate relationship comes finally to the fore in the writings of Athanasius, namely, between bishops and monks. The Alexandrian bishop may duly be seen as expert in networking, regarding his fellow bishops as well as state officials but also male and female ascetics[99], and has left an extensive documentation of his thoughts, deeds, and passions, although it must be admitted that in most cases we only have his own (certainly not impartial) point of view. While, in the present volume, David Gwynn deals with Athanasius' *Festal Letters* as a source of patronage networks between the patriarch and the faithful as well

---

[97] John Chrysostom, *ep. Olymp.* 12.1d (SC 13bis, 322.82–3 Malingrey): Σοὶ δέ ἐστιν ἐπιστήμη παντὸς ἀνωτέρα χειμῶνος, τῆς φιλοσόφου ψυχῆς ἡ δύναμις. Tr. Stephens, 298. Cf. ibid. (p. 322.96): Τοιαύτη σου τῆς τέχνης ἡ σοφία...
[98] See, e.g., Sozomen, *h. e.* 8.27.8 (FC 73.4, 1048.25–1050.2 Hansen).
[99] A comprehensive and illuminating survey is provided by David Brakke, *Athanasius and the Politics of Asceticism* (Oxford: Clarendon Press, 1995) (for the *Letter to Dracontius* see pp. 99–110); see also Demacopoulos, *Models*, 27–8. Like John Chrysostom, Athanasius would qualify for a study of episcopal mentorship with regard to virgins' communities, but the documentation, in this case, is difficult because the respective texts survive mainly in Coptic and Syriac and bear less traits of their original setting than Chrysostom's letters to Olympias.

as his fellow bishops[100], I will focus here on the 'Letter to Dracontius' (written in 354) which is important for the relationship of the Egyptian episcopate to the monastic movement; Annick Martin has termed this letter "[un] véritable manifeste athanasien sur la place du moine dans l'Eglise".[101] Dracontius was no simple monk but, in the 350s[102], Athanasius had appointed him bishop of Hermopolis parva near Nitria where he had presumable lived before in a monastery. Eventually, he had returned to his cell, due to the insinuations of fellow monks: being a bishop would not earn him an eternal reward; he had once sworn never to accept an episcopal office; it was simply impossible for a bishop to avoid sin continually.[103] Apparently, Dracontius obeyed them.

We are thus witness to a highly interesting conflict between two kinds of "advisers" (συμβουλεύοντες)[104], the first being the members of the monastic community, the second the patriarch of Egypt, acting as representative of the faithful. The question was a crucial one: Should one regard monasticism and ecclesiastical life within a civic environment as opposites or as mutually enriching? Did monks have a duty to serve the Christian community, and how could such a service be harmonized with their spiritual aims which they had motivated them to leave the world behind? In short, who was right: the "compatibilists", so to speak, or the "incompatibilists"?

---

100 See pp. 101-117 in the present volume, and David M. Gwynn, "Athanasius of Alexandria as a pastoral father," StPatr 72 (2014): 123–132, esp. 126: "Athanasius' role as a pastoral father draws together the more widely studied ecclesiastical, theological and ascetic elements of his career."
101 Annick Martin, "Les relations entre le monachisme égyptien et l'institution ecclésiastique au IVème siècle," in Foundations of Power and Conflicts of Authority in Late-Antique Monasticism, eds. Alberto Camplani and Giovanni Filoramo, OLA 157 (Leuven et al.: Peeters, 2007): 13–46, 23. I use the critical edition in vol. II, fascicle 8 of the Athanasius Werke. The translations are taken from Archibald Robertson (tr.), St. Athanasius: Select Works and Letters, NPNF 4 (repr. Grand Rapids MI: Eerdmans, 1987), 557–60 (without marking minor modifications). – It would be interesting to investigate whether the Life of Antony also displays forms of mentorship. At least on the text surface, one will find instead ascetical mentorship of bishops in dangerous situations or even exile, but the purpose of the Life is certainly also episcopal oversight over the anchorites; see Peter Gemeinhardt, "Einleitung," in Athanasius von Alexandrien, Vita Antonii. Leben des Antonius, übers. und eingel. von Peter Gemeinhardt, FC 69 (Freiburg et al. 2018): 16–21.
102 The date can only be fixed between 346/7 (when Dracontius' predecessor Agathammon was still alive) and 356/7 (when Dracontius was exiled by the emperor Constantius II, see below p. 141). It seems probable to me that Dracontius withdrew quite soon after having been ordained and that Athanasius did not wait too long with his letter after this retirement, so that the ordination would have taken place after 350 (cf. Brakke, Athanasius, 108–9).
103 Athanasius, ep. Drac. 3.3; 5.1; 9.1 (AW II, 316.11–12; 317.16–17; 320.18–20 Brennecke et al.).
104 Eleven times, Athanasius speaks of anonymous συμβουλεύοντές σοι (which he reckons hostile to himself and dangerous to Dracontius), once (with the same expression) of himself.

In order to disentangle this dilemma, Athanasius aims at establishing himself as mentor in a twofold way: as bishop, on the one hand, he is in charge of the monks because there remain, first of all, members of the church (a claim that was not easily accepted by the Pachomian monks who were skeptical about a too close interconnection with the episcopal hierarchy[105]); as metropolitan, on the other hand, he is the superior of every single bishop and, moreover, responsible for the orthodox belief, ecclesiastical administration, and spiritual guidance of the Church of Egypt. Thus he admonishes Dracontius to "take thought of the church"[106] – that is, of the church as a whole and as his local church – and to think of the importance of his office: "If there had been no bishops, how would you yourself have become a Christian?"[107] Since the duty of every Christian is to imitate the Saints (in Athanasius' terminology: the prophets, apostles, and first members of the Christian community in Jerusalem[108]), Dracontius is exhorted to imitate the apostle Paul who, "in teaching and preaching the Gospel, had his converts as his 'joy and crown'".[109] Athanasius mocks Dracontius' monastic advisors who reject the apostolic fundation of ecclesiastical offices:

> If, as they say, teaching and government is an occasion of sin, let them not be taught themselves, nor have presbyters, lest they deteriorate, both they and those who teach them![110]

In contrast, the bishop has to imitate the saints and teach his flock how to appropriate biblical role-models themselves, and this is what Dracontius needs to be taught himself. As Athanasius puts it: "the crown is given not according to position, but according to action"[111], and such action has its criterion in its use for the community of the faithful. Thus, "withdrawal" (ἀναχώρησις) which

---

105 See Brakke, *Athanasius*, 103.
106 Athanasius, *ep. Drac.* 3.1 (AW II, 316.5 Brennecke et al.): φρόντιζε τῆς ἐκκλησίας.
107 Athanasius, *ep. Drac.* 4.1 (AW II, 316.18 Brennecke et al.): πῶς ἂν ἐγένου σὺ Χριστιανὸς ἐπισκόπων μὴ ὄντων;
108 Athanasius, *v. Anton.* 2.2–4 (SC 400, 132.7–134.24 Bartelink); see Brakke, *Athanasius*, 105.
109 Athanasius, *ep. Drac.* 4.4 (AW II, 317.8–10 Brennecke et al.): ὥσπερ δὲ τὸ "οὐαί μοι οὐκ εὐαγγελιζόμενος" (1 Cor 9:16) οὕτως διδάσκων καὶ κηρύσσων τὸ εὐαγγέλιον "χαρὰν καὶ στέφανον" (Phil 4:1; 1 Thess 2:19) εἶχε τοὺς μαθητευομένους.
110 Athanasius, *ep. Drac.* 10.3 (AW II, 321.15–18 Brennecke et al.): εἰ γὰρ τὸ διδάσκειν καὶ προΐστασθαι πρόφασίς ἐστιν ἁμαρτίας κατ' ἐκείνους, μὴ διδασκέσθωσαν αὐτοὶ μηδὲ πρεσβυτέρους ἐχέτωσαν, ἵνα μὴ χείρους ἑαυτῶν γένωνται αὐτοί τε καὶ οἱ διδάσκοντες αὐτούς.
111 Athanasius, *ep. Drac.* 9.2 (AW II, 321.4–5 Brennecke et al.): καὶ γὰρ ὁ στέφανος οὐ κατὰ τόπον, ἀλλὰ κατὰ τὴν πρᾶξιν ἀποδίδοται.

was fundamental to the ascetic movement (and to Athanasius' *Life of Antony*)[112], could be dangerous if it is a withdrawal not only *to* the desert or a monastery but *from* the church's life.[113] From this point of view, dwelling single-handedly in the desert and taking on the episcopal office are perfectly compatible yet not of the same value: acting as bishop is more important, for it is of greater use for more people. In any case, participating in "ordinance of the church" (τῇ ἐκκλησιαστικῇ διατάξει)[114] should not be regarded as one option among many others; in contrast, it lies at the very core of any Christian life.

Athanasius thus exercises mentorship by instructing Dracontius about his office (which he had taken over long before!) and by dissipating his anxiety that he would lose his holiness through the entanglement into secular affairs. Athanasius replies: "Come to us who love you and who give you scriptural advice"[115] – here, Athanasius speaks of himself as συμβουλεύων, so to speak as a counter-advisor. The many biblical quotations (mostly referring to Paul's self-understanding as apostle) are supported by the names of seven bishops who were formerly monks.[116] Hence no reason for Dracontius to lament "as though you alone had been elected from among monks"[117] and to gainsay the validity of his ordination.

In the end, Athanasius was successful: Dracontius returned to his bishopric and remained henceforth faithful to his metropolitan. In 357 he was exiled by the emperor Constantius[118], but returned to his seat and participated in the synod of Alexandria in 362.[119] Athanasius had managed to convince him to accept his spiritual education about the imitation of the saints – a topic which was, of course, even more prominent in the contemporaneous *Life of Antony*, written shortly

---

112 The *Life of Antony* illustrates the ambiguity of ἀναχώρησις and ἀναχωρεῖν which became only with Athanasius' writings technical terms of early monasticism; on the general question of the emergent monastic terminology, see Gemeinhardt, Einleitung, 99.
113 In *ep. Drac.* 1.3 (AW II, 315.4–6 Brennecke et al.), Athanasius warns Dracontius that such an ἀναχώρησις could cause schisms within this region's episcopate; moreover, it could be taken as pretext for others to flee the office (*ep. Drac.* 3.1; ibid. 316.4–6). See Brakke, *Athanasius*, 106–7.
114 Athanasius, *ep. Drac.* 10.5 (AW II, 321.24 Brennecke et al.).
115 Athanasius, *ep. Drac.* 7.1 (AW II, 318.24–5 Brennecke et al.): καὶ δεῦρο πρὸς ἡμᾶς τοὺς ἀγαπῶντάς σε τοὺς συμβουλεύοντάς σοι τὰ τῶν γραφῶν.
116 Cf. Athanasius, *ep. Drac.* 7.2 (AW II, 318.27–319.5 Brennecke et al.).
117 Athanasius, *ep. Drac.* 8.1 (AW II, 320.8 Brennecke et al.): Μὴ τοίνυν κωλυέτωσάν σε μοναχοὶ ὡς μόνον ἐκ μοναχῶν κατασταθέντα.
118 Athanasius, *h. Ar.* 72.4 (AW II, 223.1 Opitz): Δρακόντιον μὲν ἐπίσκοπον εἰς τὰ ἔρημα περὶ τὸ Κλύσμα ἐξώρισαν. Cf. also Athanasius, *fug.* 7.4 (ibid. 73.9–13); *Epistula Ammonis* 32 (SHG 19, 119.1–2 Halkin); Jerome, *v. Hilar.* 20.9–10 (SC 508, 268.31–4 Leclerc/Morales).
119 Athanasius, *tom.* 10.2 (AW II, 350.1 Brennecke et al.).

after 356.¹²⁰ Thus, religious mentorship appears as a kind of triangulation of the mentee, the mentor, and the model to be imitated, and Athanasius is at pains to make clear that his mentorship is appropriate by proving that his interpretation of the biblical narrative is correct. Episcopal mentorship thus competes with other ways and goals of spiritual guidance, and it goes without saying that there were often other issues of more secular nature involved.¹²¹

5 Conclusion: Teaching religion in a transforming world

My explorations cover roughly the first hundred years after the persecutions of Christians by the Roman authorities ceased. This does not mean that the topic has now been told exhaustively – quite the contrary. It would be interesting, to name only one prominent example, to include Gregory the Great whose *Pastoral Rule* might be reckoned the first pastoral theology proper (and has much to do with spiritual education).¹²² But also his letters to other bishops might serve as source for the exercise of mentorship under difficult circumstances. At the end of the 6th century, in Rome and beyond, many things had however changed, regarding the bishop's office and duties as well as his audiences and individual partners and counterparts, so that I must refrain from including Gregory in this survey.

Let us draw some conclusions. We have investigated three types of mentor-mentee relationships. Addressees of mentorship by bishops were a lettered pagan and a group of recent converts (ch. 2), a senatorial virgin and her fellow ascetics (ch. 3) and a former monk who now (reluctantly) himself acted as bishop (ch. 4). And we have met four different bishops from four different regions, from North Africa and Italy (ch. 2) to Constantinople (ch. 3) and Lower Egypt (ch. 4), faced with different challenges within an expanding church and a transforming society, both highly pluralized and longing for counsel and orientation. The emerging picture cannot be but selective. There are however some common fea-

---

120 Athanasius, *v. Anton.* 2.4 (SC 400, 132.18–19 Bartelink); but see already id., *inc.* 57.2 (SC 199, 466.6–8 Kannengiesser).
121 For other aspects of Athanasius' activities and literary self-fashioning as a teacher, see now Uta Heil, "Athanasius of Alexandria. Teacher and Martyr of the Christian Church," in *Paul as Homo Novus. Authorial Strategies of Self-Fashioning in Light of a Ciceronian Term*, eds. Eve-Marie Becker/Jacob Mortensen (Göttingen: Vandenhoeck & Ruprecht, 2018): 177–196, 181–188.
122 See George E. Demacopoulos, *Gregory the Great. Ascetic, Pastor, and First Man of Rome* (Notre Dame IN: University of Notre Dame Press, 2015), 53–81.

tures which enable us to compare the miniatures which I have presented. These similarities may by summarized as follows:

1. Mentorship presupposes hierarchy, but it also bridges hierarchical patterns. Spiritual education affords clearly defined roles (who is the teacher and who is taught?), but one also needs experience to guide the addressee to a higher goal – conversion, Christian life, being a faithful bishop –, and it appears crucial that the mentor has already achieved such experience (in ascetic as well as in exegetical or pastoral matters). We therefore have to discern mentorship from leadership and patronage, although there is overlap.
2. Mentorship involves responsibility for the spiritual welfare of the mentee – it may thus be viewed as a variant of pastoral care in the late antique understanding of this notion, located within an eschatological horizon. It does however include the dimension of direction, not only of counselling (this might well be viewed differently under modern auspices).
3. Mentorship is about teaching. That bishops are called *magister* indicates that the relationships which we have scrutinized should be viewed as processes of teaching and learning. Otherwise than in the catechumenate or in public schools, such teaching requires personal relationships, but it also requires knowledge of what is to be taught (doctrine and ethics) and didactic skills (based on ancient rhetoric). In this respect, episcopal mentorship is not fundamentally different from what we observe in the desert monks or pagan philosophical teachers (including, in previous times, the school of Origen at Alexandria and Caesarea).
4. Mentorship regularly refers to the Scriptures, and that however renders it different from other contexts of guidance, leadership, or teaching. What I have named a triangulation with regard to Athanasius and Dracontius but what was at stake from the outset of this paper (see initially Paulinus' request to Augustine!) can be generalized: the relationship of mentor and mentee is viewed in the light of the biblical texts which offer stories, models, and precepts for a Christian life. That means that God who speaks through the Scriptures (and whose agency is visible in the narrations of martyrs and contemporary saints) is, so to speak, the 'final mentor' who oversees the deeds and words of his earthly representatives.
5. Mentorship aims at building networks by creating strong personal ties between mentor and mentee, be it prominent pagans, newly converted laymen, ascetic women or fellow bishops (occasionally former monks). Whether we term the result obedience, loyalty, or reciprocal support, the outcome is a strengthened and (ideally) reliable relationship between mentor and mentee. But again, this stability was based on certain criteria, among which

the ability to interpret the Scriptures and to teach Christian behaviour stands out.

Thus, the notion of mentorship might be helpful in describing and classifying episcopal agency as far as bishops endeavored to teach single persons or small groups a Christian way of life and, if necessary, to support the mentor's case. Augustine expected this from Paulinus, Zeno from his flock, John Chrysostom from Olympias, and Athanasius from Dracontius. Mentors could offer their experience with down-to-earth struggles and with the staircase to heaven. Networking with the divine mentor was beyond the powers of late antique bishops, even of successful networkers like Athanasius and Augustine. One might however suggest that such networks between heaven and earth were actually knit in the liturgy (and this would add a special dynamic to the bishop's position as mediator between human beings and Christ, as mentor of his flock and mentee of the Lord). But this is another story.

Bibliography

Primary Sources

Ammon. *Epistula*. In *Sancti Pachomii vitae graecae*. Éd. par François Halkin. SHG 19, 97–121. Bruxelles: Société des Bollandistes, 1932.

Athanasius. *Apologia de fuga sua*. In Athanasius Werke, vol. 2. Ed. by Hans-Georg Opitz, 68–86. Berlin: de Gruyter, 1934–1941.

Athanasius, *De incarnatione verbi*. Introduction, texte critique, traduction et notes par Charles Kannengiesser. SC 199. Paris: Les Éditions du Cerf, 1973.

Athanasius. *Epistula ad Dracontium*. In *Athanasius Werke*, vol. 2. Ed. by Hanns Christof Brennecke / Uta Heil / Annette von Stockhausen, 314–321. Berlin / New York: de Gruyter, 2006. – St. Athanasius. *Select Works and Letters*. Tr. by Archibald Robertson. NPNF 4, 557–560. Repr. Grand Rapids MI: Eerdmans, 1987.

Athanasius, *Historia Arianorum*. Athanasius Werke, vol. 2. Ed. by Hans-Georg Opitz, 183–230. Berlin: de Gruyter, 1934–1941.

Athanasius. *Tomus ad Antiochenos*. In *Athanasius Werke*, vol. 2. Ed. by Hanns Christof Brennecke / Uta Heil / Annette von Stockhausen, 340–351. Berlin / New York: de Gruyter, 2006.

Athanasius. *Vita Antonii*. Introduction, texte critique, traduction et notes par G.J.M. Bartelink. SC 400. Paris: Les Éditions du Cerf, ²2004. – Athanasius von Alexandrien. *Vita Antonii. Leben des Antonius*. Übers. und eingel. von Peter Gemeinhardt. FC 69. Freiburg: Herder, 2018.

Augustinus. *Confessionum libri XIII*. Curante Lucas Verheijen. CChr.SL 27. Turnhout: Brepols, 1990.

Augustinus. *De catechizandis rudibus*. Curante Johannes B. Bauer. CChr.SL 46, 121–178. Turnhout: Brepols, 1969.

Augustinus. *De civitate Dei*. Curante Bernard Dombart / Alfons Kalb. CChr.SL 47 / 48. Turnhout: Brepols, 1955.

Augustinus. *Epistulae*. Curante Alois Goldbacher. Vol. 3: *Epistulae 124–184 A*. CSEL 44. Wien: Hoelder-Pichler-Tempsky, 1904. – Saint Augustine: *Letters*. Tr. by Wilfrid Parsons. Vol. 3: *Letters 131–164*. FaCh 20. Washington D.C.: The Catholic University of America Press, 1953.

Les Constitutions Apostoliques. Introduction, texte critique, traduction et notes par Marcel Metzger. Vol. 1. SC 320. Paris: Les Éditions du Cerf, 1985. – *Apostolic Constitutions*. Tr. by A. Roberts / J. Donaldson. In *The Ante-Nicene Fathers*. Vol. 7, 391–505. Repr. Grand Rapids MI: Eerdmans, 1989.

Gaudentius of Brixen. *Tractatus*. Ed. by Ambrosius Glück. CSEL 68. Wien: Hoelder-Pichler-Tempsky, 1936.

Gerontius. *Vie de sainte Mélanie*. Texte grec, introduction, traduction et notes par Denys Gorce. SC 90. Paris: Les Éditions du Cerf, 1962.

Gregory of Nyssa. *Homiliae in Canticum Canticorum*. Curante Hermann Langerbeck. GNO 6. Leiden: Brill, 1960.

Jean Chrysostome. *Lettres à Olympias*. Introduction, texte critique, traduction et notes par Anne-Marie Malingrey. SC 13bis. Paris: Les Éditions du Cerf, 1968.

Jerome. *Epistulae*. Curante Isidor Hilberg. 3 vols. CSEL 54–56. Wien: Hoelder-Pichler-Tempsky, 1910–1918.

Jerome. *Vita Hilarionis*. In Jérôme. *Trois vies de moines (Paul, Malchus, Hilarion)*. Texte grec, introduction, traduction et notes par Paul Leclerc / Edgar M. Morales. SC 508, 212–299. Paris: Les Éditions du Cerf, 2007.

Pseudo-Martyrius. *Oratio funebris in laudem Sancti Iohannis Chrysostomi*. Ed. by Martin Wallraff. Tr. by Cristina Ricci. Quaderni della Rivista di Bizantinistica 12. Spoleto: Fondazione Centro italiano di studi sull'alto medioevo, 2007.

Palladius. *Historia Lausiaca. Geschichten aus dem frühen Mönchtum*. Hg. und übers. von Adelheid Hübner. FC 67. Freiburg 2016. – Palladius. *The Lausiac History*. Tr. by Robert T. Meyer. ACW 34. Westminster MD: The Newman Press / London: Longmans, Green & Co., 1965.

Palladius. *Dialogue sur la vie de Jean Chrysostome*. 2 vols. Introduction, texte critique, traduction et notes par Anne-Marie Malingrey. SC 341/342. Paris: Les Éditions du Cerf, 1988.

Paulinus of Nola. *Epistulae*. Curante Wilhelm von Hartel. CSEL 29. Wien: Hoelder-Pichler-Tempsky, 1894. – *Letters of St. Paulinus of Nola*. Tr. by P.G. Walsh. Vol. 2. ACW 36. London: Paulist Press, 1967.

Sozomenus. *Historia Ecclesiastica. Kirchengeschichte*. 4 vols. Hg. und übers. von Günter Christian Hansen. FC 73/1–4. Turnhout: Brepols, 2004.

Vie d'Olympias. In Jean Chrysostome. *Lettres à Olympias. Seconde édition augmentée de la Vie anonyme d'Olympias*. Introduction, texte critique, traduction et notes par Anne-Marie Malingrey. SC 13bis, 406–449. Paris: Les Éditions du Cerf, 1968.

Zeno of Verona. *Tractatus libri duo*. Curante Bengt Löfstedt. CChr.SL 22. Turnhout: Brepols, 1971.

Secondary Literature

Allen, Pauline and Wendy Mayer. "Through a Bishop's Eyes: Towards a Definition of Pastoral Care in Late Antiquity." *Aug.* 40 (2000): 345–397.

Brakke, David. *Athanasius and the Politics of Asceticism*. Oxford: Clarendon Press, 1995.

Clark, Gillian. "Pastoral Care: Town and Country in Late-Antique Preaching." In *Urban Centers and Rural Context in Late Antiquity*, edited by Thomas S. Burns and John W. Eadie, 265–284. East Lansing MI: Michigan State University Press, 2001.

Demacopoulos, George. *Five Models of Spiritual Direction in the Early Church*. Notre Dame IN: University of Notre Dame Press, 2007.

Demacopoulos, George E. *Gregory the Great. Ascetic, Pastor, and First Man of Rome*. Notre Dame IN: University of Notre Dame Press, 2015.

Divjak, Johannes et al. "Art. Epistulae." In *AugL* 2 (2002): 893–1057.

Dümler, Bärbel. *Zeno von Verona zu heidnischer Kultur und christlicher Bildung*. STAC 75. Tübingen: Mohr Siebeck, 2013.

Forlin Patrucco, Marcella. "Marcella, Bishops and Monks in Late Antique Society." *ZAC* 8 (2004): 332–345.

Geerlings, Wilhelm. "Die Belehrung eines Heiden: Augustins Brief über Christus an Volusianus." In *Collectanea Augustiniana. Mélanges Tarsicius Jan van Bavel, éd. par Bernard Bruning*, vol. II = Aug(L) 41, 451–468. Leuven: Peeters, 1991.

Gemeinhardt, Peter. *Das lateinische Christentum und die antike pagane Bildung*. STAC 41. Tübingen: Mohr Siebeck, 2007.

Gemeinhardt, Peter. *Die Kirche und ihre Heiligen. Studien zu Ekklesiologie und Hagiographie in der Spätantike*. STAC 90. Tübingen: Mohr Siebeck, 2014.

Gemeinhardt, Peter. "Teaching Religion in Late Antiquity: Divine and Human Agency." *StPatr*, 92 (2017): 271–277.

Gemeinhardt, Peter. "Einleitung." In *Athanasius von Alexandrien, Vita Antonii. Leben des Antonius, übers. und eingel. von Peter Gemeinhardt*, 7–100. FC 69. Freiburg et al.: Herder, 2018.

Gnilka, Christian. *Chrêsis. Die Methode der Kirchenväter im Umgang mit der antiken Kultur*, vol. I: *Der Begriff des "rechten Gebrauchs"*. Basel/Stuttgart: Schwabe, 1984.

Greschat, Katharina. *Gelehrte Frauen des frühen Christentums. Zwölf Porträts*. Standorte in Antike und Christentum 6. Stuttgart: Hiersemann, 2015.

Gwynn, David M. "Athanasius of Alexandria as a Pastoral Father." *StPatr* 72 (2014): 123–132.

Harmless, William. *Desert Christians: An Introduction to the Literature of Early Monasticism*. Oxford: Oxford University Press, 2004.

Harmless, William. *Augustine and the Catechumenate*. Collegeville MN: Liturgical Press, ²2014.

Heil, Uta. "Athanasius of Alexandria. Teacher and Martyr of the Christian Church" In *Paul as Homo Novus. Authorial Strategies of Self-Fashioning in Light of a Ciceronian Term*, edited by Eve-Marie Becker/Jacob Mortensen, 177–196. Göttingen: Vandenhoeck & Ruprecht, 2018.

Kahlos, Maijastina. "Incerti in Between – Moments of Transition and Dialogue in Christian Apologetics." *Parola del Passato* 59 (2004): 5–24.

Kahlos, Maijastina. *Debate and Dialogue. Christian and Pagan Cultures c. 360–430*. Aldershot: Ashgate, 2007.

Kolbet, Paul R. *Augustine and the Cure of Souls. Revising a Classical Ideal*. Notre Dame IN: Notre Dame Press 2010.

Lorgeoux, Olga. "Cyril of Jerusalem as Catechetical Teacher: Religious Education in Fourth-Century Jerusalem." In *Teachers in Late Antique Christianity*, edited by Peter Gemeinhardt, Olga Lorgeoux and Maria Munkholt Christensen, SERAPHIM 3, 76–91. Tübingen: Mohr Siebeck, 2018.

Malingrey, Anne-Marie. "Introduction." In Jean Chrysostome. *Lettres à Olympias. Seconde édition augmentée de la Vie anonyme d'Olympias*. Introduction, texte critique, traduction et notes par Anne-Marie Malingrey. SC 13bis, 393–404. Paris: Les Éditions du Cerf, 1968.

Martin, Annick. "Les relations entre le monachisme égyptien et l'institution ecclésiastique au IVème siècle." In *Foundations of Power and Conflicts of Authority in Late-Antique Monasticism*, edited by Alberto Camplani and Giovanni Filoramo, OLA 157, 13–46. Leuven et al.: Peeters, 2007.

Mayer, Wendy. "Constantinopolitan Women in Chrysostom's Circle." *VigChr* 53 (1999): 265–288.

Mayer, Wendy. "Patronage, Pastoral Care and the Role of the Bishop at Antioch." *VigChr* 55 (2001): 58–70.

McEachnie, Robert. "Zeno, Chromatius, and Gaudentius. Italian Preachers Amid Transition." In *Preaching in the Patristic Era. Sermons, Preachers, and Audiences in the Latin West*, edited by Anthony Dupont et al., 454–476. Leiden / Boston: Brill, 2018.

Morgenstern, Frank. *Die Briefpartner des Augustinus von Hippo. Prosopographische, sozial- und ideologiegeschichtliche Untersuchungen*. Bochumer Historische Studien. Alte Geschichte 11. Bochum: Brockmeyer, 1993.

Rapp, Claudia. *Holy Bishops in Late Antiquity. The Nature of Leadership in an Age of Transition*. The Transformation of the Classical Heritage 37. Berkeley CA et al.: The University of California Press, 2005.

Schindler, Alfred. "Augustin." In *Geschichte der Seelsorge in Einzelporträts*, edited by Christian Möller, vol. I, 189–207. Göttingen: Vandenhoeck & Ruprecht, 1994.

Sterk, Andrea. *Renouncing the World Yet Leading the Church. The Monk-Bishop in Late Antiquity*. Cambridge MA/London: Harvard University Press, 2004.

Tiersch, Claudia. *Johannes Chrysostomus in Konstantinopel (398–404). Weltsicht und Wirken eines Bischofs in der Hauptstadt des Oströmischen Reiches*. STAC 6. Tübingen: Mohr Siebeck, 2002.

Tornau, Christian. *Zwischen Rhetorik und Philosophie. Augustins Argumentationstechnik in De ciuitate Dei und ihr bildungsgeschichtlicher Hintergrund*. UaLG 82. Berlin/New York: Walter de Gruyter, 2006.

White, Carolinne. *Christian Friendship in the Fourth Century*. Cambridge: Cambridge University Press, 1992.

Sigrid Mratschek
Crossing the Boundaries: Networks and Manifestations of Christian Hospitality

1 Hospitality and globalisation

Hospitality, irrespective of its religious value, was for Ambrose of Milan a globally recognised *publica species humanitatis*.[1] It was a duty for every bishop,[2] but was also practised among those running monastic centres, and in cooperation with patrons from high society. Ambrose – who at home entertained consuls and prefects – had advised clergy specifically that they should decline invitations to go out, as that would render them unavailable at home to prospective guests; and Augustine had followed his example.[3] Augustine for his part consid-

---

This paper has benefited from comments and lively discussion at the "Episcopal Networks" Conference in September 2016. I am most grateful to the convenors, Peter Gemeinhardt and Carmen Cvetković, for their generous hospitality, to Theresia Hainthaler (St. Georgen) and Gregor Emmenegger (Fribourg) for their valuable advice and their unstinting support through their libraries, and to my Polish colleagues Rafał Toczko (Toruń) and Stanisław Adamiak (Warsaw) for use of the *Scrinium Augustini* database and of unpublished manuscripts of the homonymous conference volume edited by Przemysław Nehring *et al.* (Turnhout: Brepols, 2017). Special thanks are due to Gillian Clark (Bristol), Neil McLynn (Oxford) and Brent D. Shaw (Princeton) for their stimulating ideas on the interaction between Augustine and the protean Caecilianus.

1 Ambrose (*off.* 2.21.103) picks up Cicero's definition (*off.* 1.139; 2.64): *Commendat plerosque etiam hospitalitas. Est enim publica species humanitatis, ut peregrinus hospitio non egeat, suscipiatur officiose, pateat advenienti ianua. Valde id decorum totius est orbis existimationi, peregrinos cum honore suscipi, non desse hospitalis gratia, occurrere officiis liberalitatis, explorari adventus hospitum.*
2 For bishops specifically 1 *Tim* 3:2; Herm. *mand.* 8.10; *Sim.* 9.27.2; Aug. *s.* 355.2; Hier. *in Tit.*; Isid. *eccl. off.* 2.5.17, and in canon 9 of the Council of Aachen in 814. See Michaela Puzicha, *Christus peregrinus. Die Fremdenaufnahme (Mt 25,35) als Werk der privaten Wohltätigkeit im Urteil der Alten Kirche* (Münster: Aschendorff, 1990), 38–39 and Andrew Arterbury, *Entertaining Angels. Early Christian Hospitality in its Mediterranean Setting* (Sheffield: Phoenix Press, 2005), 129.
3 Ambr. *off.* 1.20.86: *Unde prudenter facitis convenire ecclesiasticis, et maxime ministrorum officiis arbitror, declinare extraneorum convivia vel ut ipsi hospitales sitis peregrinantibus* ... Sulp. Sev. *dial.* 1.25.6: *exemplum beati Ambrosi episcopi ..., qui eo tempore consules et praefectos subinde pascere ferebatur.* See Neil B. McLynn, *Ambrose of Milan. Church and Court in a Christian Capital* (Berkeley et al.: University of California Press, 1994), 257. Cf. Possid. *vita Aug.* 27.2 on visiting: *Servandum quoque in vita et moribus hominis dei referebat, quo instituto sanctae memoriae Ambrosii compererat ...*

https://doi.org/10.1515/9783110553390-009

ered it a mark of high favour to enjoy unrestricted access to the bishop of Milan.[4] Sozomenus praised Acacius, bishop of Beroea (present-day Aleppo), for his *philoxenia*, as he "let his episcopal quarters stand open at all hours so that strangers and citizens might see him without misgivings, even at the times for eating and sleeping".[5]

Much-cited models were Abraham, Lot and the widow of Sarepta,[6] but a theory of Christian hospitality is nowhere in evidence. All that can be said is that Greek hospitality (ξενία), whose behavioural code, in Homer, upheld even for enemies, was replaced by religiously and ethically motivated Christian hospitality.[7] The constitutive quality for the Christian centres was neither a vow nor obedience but spiritual unity (*unanimitas*); and the preferred medium for generating and demonstrating solidarity was the letter.[8] A remarkably large number of pagan and Christian discourses reflect differing perspectives, values and expectations, while the tangible living realities of guests known by their name, their visits and their interactions with the host have hitherto been almost totally disregarded.[9]

---

4 Aug. *conf.* 6.3.3: *Saepe cum adessemus – non enim vetabatur quisquam ingredi aut ei venientem nuntiari mos est – sic eum* (sc. *Ambrosium*) *legentem vidimus tacite* ...
5 Soz. *h.e.* 7.28.2: τεκμήριον δὲ μεγίστης ἔδωκεν ἀρετῆς παρὰ πάντα τὸν χρόνον τὸ ἐπισκοπικὸν καταγώγιον ἠνεῳγμένον ἔχων, ὡς καὶ τροφῆς ὥρᾳ καὶ ὕπνου ἀδεῶς οἷς ἐδόκει ξένοις τε καὶ ἀστοῖς αὐτὸν ὁρᾶν.
6 See Gard Granerød and Andrew Arterbury, "Hospitality", *EBR* 12 (Berlin/Boston: de Gruyter, 2016), 449 and 453–54; Otto Hiltbrunner, Denys Gorce and Hans Wehr, "Gastfreundschaft", *RAC* 8 (Stuttgart: Anton Hiersemann, 1972), 1071–73.
7 David Konstan, *Friendship in the Classical World* (Cambridge: Cambrige University Press, 1997), 33–37, Arterbury, *Entertaining Angels*, 130–31, and Paul Viard, "Hospitalité", *DSp* 7 (Paris: Bauchesne, 1969), 808–31.– In the real Christian world, friendship contacts in practice extended, as with Augustine, from intense juvenile friendships to Christian philosophy circles to meetings with fellow bishops and politicians.
8 On visions of cooperation between all the members of a unified church cf. e. g. the appeal at Paul. Nol. *ep.* 2.3 (*unitas spiritus*); 13.1: *per ipsum* [sc.*Christum*] *ut unius corporis membra conectimur*. On this and on the "literary networks" see Sigrid Mratschek, *Der Briefwechsel des Paulinus von Nola. Kommunikation und soziale Kontakte zwischen christlichen Intellektuellen* (Göttingen: Vandenhoeck & Ruprecht, 2002), 600, passim and Peter Gemeinhardt, *Das lateinische Christentum und die antike pagane Bildung* (Tübingen: Mohr Siebeck, 2007), esp. 230. In *Did.* 11.13 Christian faith was a criterion for acceptability of guests, but reference to targeted denial of hospitality to "heretical" groups is found only in the polemics of Jerome (*adv. Ruf.* 3.17).
9 Networks in the Holy Land have been systematically researched by David Hunt, *Holy Land Pilgrimage in the Later Roman Empire* (Oxford: OUP, 1982), church networks by Claire Sotinel, "La circulation de l'information dans les Églises," in *La circulation de l'information dans les États antiques*, eds. Laurent Capdetrey and Jocelyne Nelis-Clément (Bordeaux: Ausonius, 2006): 177–94, literary and social networks by Sigrid Mratschek, *Briefwechsel* and "Paulinus

Members of the educated Christian elite, whose hospitality networks progressively ramified across the whole Mediterranean area, were innovative in that they remade the past.¹⁰ As so often happens with processes of cultural change, the reception of spatial concepts saw the new added to the old but not replacing it: the transformation of topography and the creation of sacred spaces was additive, not substitutive.¹¹ Travellers' contrasting accounts of pilgrimages to the Holy Land – now increasingly undertaken – bring the Mediterranean geography of the sacred into sharp focus. While the Bordeaux pilgrim setting out from his home in 333 as a private citizen journeyed for some 14 months and 2200 Roman miles along the Roman Empire's highways to reach Constantinople, yielding precedence in overnight lodgings to privileged senators on imperial business, Egeria's pilgrimage of 381–84 from the Atlantic to the Euphrates would have been impossible, for all her curiosity and enthusiasm for the holy places, without the hospitality and local knowledge of monks and bishops along the way.¹²

Spatial concepts are considered today to reflect power relationships, social practices, and attributions by others and self. For Egeria, Paula and Melania the Younger – who was said never to have put her copy down – the new Christian travel guide was the Bible.¹³ During the fourth century, as David Hunt has shown, an alternative to the established system of privileged government mail and transportation (*cursus publicus*) was introduced in the form of a Christian hospitality system and incorporated into the church's organisational structures.¹⁴ Outwardly it amounted to a meticulous reproduction of the contempo-

---

and the Gradual Rise of Nola as a Center of Hospitality", *JECS* 9 (2001) 511–553, travel and hospitality by Denys Gorce, *Les voyages, l'hospitalité et le port du lettre dans le monde chrétien des IV et V siècles* (Paris: Auguste Picard, 1925).

10 Averil Cameron, "Remaking the Past," in *Late Antiquity. A Guide to the Postclassical World*, eds. Glen W. Bowersock, Peter Brown and Oleg Grabar (Cambridge [Mass.] and London: The Belknap Press of Harvard UP, 1999): 1–20; Averil Cameron, "Education and Literary Culture. Conclusion," in *The Late Empire A.D. 337–425*, eds. Averil Cameron and Peter Garnsey, CAH 13 (Cambridge: Cambridge University Press, 1998): 706–7.

11 Cf. Peter Burke: *Die Renaissance in Italien. Sozialgeschichte einer Kultur zwischen Tradition und Erfindung* (London: B.T. Batsford, 1972, trans. Rainhard Kaiser, Berlin: Klaus Wagenbach, 1996), 29 in a different context.

12 *It. Eg.* 19.5 (*de extremis porro terris venires*); Valerius, *ep.* 5: SC 296, 346 (*extremo occidui maris oceani litore*).

13 *It. Eg.* 4.3; 10.7; Hier. *ep.* 108.8.1 and *v. Mel.* 21.

14 Hunt, *Holy Land Pilgrimage*, 56–63. Cf. Anne Kolb, *Transport und Nachrichtentransfer im Römischen Reich*, (Berlin: Akademie Verlag, 2000), 206–26 on the infrastructure of the *cursus publicus*, Sotinel, "Circulation", 194, which focuses on the circulation of information among councils and churches, and Mratschek, *Briefwechsel*, 274–394 on communication and mail systems.

rary secular communications system and its hostels (*mansiones*). Sulpicius Severus describes the widely observed hospitality ritual, found even among the desert-dwelling monks, with which Martin of Tours had welcomed him in Marmoutier: "He honoured me by inviting me to his table, poured water himself over my hands, and in the evening washed my feet".[15] To choose to stay more than two or three days was to violate the most basic rules of politeness, and those who did so would be swiftly enrolled in the roster of daily tasks (*opera manuum*) required by the hostel.[16] By 394/96 the social practice of Christian hospitality had gained recognition to the point that a canon promulgated by the council of the *Septem Provinciae* in Gaul probibited as an abuse the soliciting of food and drink "on the pretext of a pilgrimage" (*sub specie peregrinationis*).[17] By about the 6th century the network of Christians was so extensive that hostels for men and for women (*xenodochia*) lined the most important sites along the pilgrim routes, offering "to strangers acceptance, many well-laden tables, and beds for more than 3000 sick".[18]

It was bishops and the leaders of ascetic movements that developed and promoted spatial concepts of this kind and created transregional structural spaces. Egeria tells of *ospitia* at the Church of the Holy Sepulchre (*Anastasis*), where she lodged alongside Jerusalem pilgrims following their blessing by the bishop.[19] She reports on the monks of the ascetic community Der-el-Arbein situated in Wadi-el-Leja, who allowed her to lodge there before her ascent of Jebel Musa (Mount Sinai), and indulged her party with every possible form of hospitality (*omnem humanitatem*).[20] The bishop of Carrhae (Haran) advised her that the Per-

---

[15] Sulp. Sev. *Mart.* 25.3: *cum me sancto convivio suo dignatus esset adhibere, aquam manibus nostris ipse obtulit. Ad vesperum autem pedes nobis ipse abluit.* See Jacques Fontaine's commentary in SC 135, 1052–56.

[16] *Did.* 12.1–5 with Hiltbrunner, "Gastfreundschaft," 1107. Up to one week with the monks of Nitria, cf. Pall. *h. Laus.* 7.4. On services rendered by monks from elsewhere in garden or bakery work or in kitchens as cook, see above and Mratschek, *Briefwechsel*, 308, 580.

[17] Conc. Galliae, *Conc. Nemausense a. 394*, can. 5: *Additum aetiam est ut, quia multi, sub specie peregrinationis, de ecclesiarum conlatione luxoriant, victura non omnibus detur ...*

[18] *It. Anton. Placent.* 23: *xenodochia virorum ac mulierum, susceptio peregrinorum, mensas innumerabiles, lecta aegrotorum amplius tria milia.* See Hunt, *Holy Land Pilgrimage*, 64.

[19] *It. Eg.* 25.7 (Jerusalem, at the Holy Sepulchre): *Recepit se episcopus et vadent se unusquisque ad ospitium suum ut se resumant.*

[20] *It. Eg.* 3.1: *ingressi sumus montem, et pervenientes ad monasteria quedam susceperunt nos ibi satis humane monachi, qui ibi commorabantur, perbentes nobis omnem humanitatem.* According to Egeria *terras Saracenorum*, Saracene country (*It. Eg.* 7.6), see David Caner, "Sinai Pilgrimage and the Ascetic Romance: Pseudo-Nilus' *Narrationes* in Context", in *Travel, Communication and Geography in Late Antiquity. Sacred and Profane*, ed. Linda Ellis and Frank L. Kidner (Aldershot and Burlington: Ashgate, 2004): 135–47, esp. 142–43.

sian frontier was only 5 *mansiones* journey beyond Nisibis, and that Abraham's homeland in Ur, being on Persian territory, was now out of reach for Roman travellers.[21]

According to Martina Löw's spatial sociology, spaces are constituted in perception, memory and imagination by the linking of places (*spacing*) and the actors and social assets located at such places (*synthesising*).[22] And the formation of the sacred in the Christian cultures of Late Antiquity and the linking up of Christian centres in the Roman Empire were indeed both associated with the emergence of a new form of hospitality: Peter Brown[23] has pointed out that late antique society was held together by "intense networks of reciprocal gifts", while unreciprocated beneficence to the poor was considered provocative behaviour. Contrary to the view upheld by earlier scholarship from Gorce to Hiltbrunner and Pohl, however, which insisted on a dichotomy between the pagan tradition of reciprocity and the non-reciprocated Christian act of altruism,[24] the socio-anthropological hospitality concept specific to Classical Antiquity (*philoxenia, hospitalitas*), with its obligation to reciprocity, lived on in Late Antiquity.

The seminal text was Mt 25:35. Here the guest is the incarnation of Christ: "For when I was hungry, you gave me food; when thirsty, you gave me drink; when I was a stranger, you took me into your home ... Anything you did for one of my brothers here, however humble, you did for me."[25] Christian intellectuals such as Ambrose, Paulinus of Nola, Augustine and John Chrysostom made this the basis of a competing model that transcended the pagan tradition of gift exchange with the anticipated everlasting "treasure in Heaven", and accorded to

---

21 *It. Eg.* 20.12. Hunt, *Holy Land Pilgrimage*, 62, n.55 accordingly infers the *terminus post quem* of her journey as being 363, after the armistice between Jovian and Sassanides.
22 Martina Löw, *Raumsoziologie* (Frankfurt a. Main: Suhrkamp, 2001).
23 Peter Brown, *Through the Eyes of the Needle. Wealth, the Fall of Rome, and the Making of Christianity in the West, 350–550 AD* (Princeton and Oxford: Princeton University Press, 2012), 76–77.
24 Christine Dorothy Pohl, *Making Room: Recovering Hospitality as a Christian Tradition* (Grand Rapids: Eerdmans, 1999) and Otto Hiltbrunner, *Gastfreundschaft in der Antike und im frühen Christentum* (Darmstadt: Wissenschaftliche Buchgesellschaft, 2005), 175: "Christen erwarten keine Gegenleistung". Different readings only in Arterbury, *Entertaining Angels*, 132, Granerød, Arterbury et al., "Hospitality," 449–59, and Brown, *Eyes of the Needle*, 232, as "fruitful reciprocity" in Paulinus of Nola.
25 Gorce, "Gastfreundschaft," 1103–4, and on the Incarnation of Christ, Catherine Conybeare, *Paulinus Noster. Self and Symbols in the Letters of Paulinus of Nola* (Oxford: Oxford University Press, 2000), 127–28.

the poor, as owners of spiritual wealth, their own role in Christian discourse:[26] reciprocation of beneficence might take place later and in non-material form, as has been persuasively demonstrated by Marcel Mauss and Pierre Bourdieu.[27] Even a Christian author like Lactantius, who would shudder when speaking of "one-sided" hospitality to beggars, confirmed that the deed's reward would be conferred by God.[28]

Innovative ideas such as these could claim to be integrating not the elites only but all of human society (including seemingly "useless people" like the poor), up to its furthest, darkest margins of the earth, into the "global" network of Christians; the social practices of Christian hospitality launched the "communications revolution" of the fourth century. Exchange of letters was the medium that implemented and expanded it into a worldwide web of Christian intellectuals, of exemplary value for the Latin-speaking West in the form of the social and personal relationships linking Augustine, Paulinus, Jerome, Sulpicius Severus

---

[26] Paul. Nol. *ep.* 13.11: *Itaque patronos animarum nostrarum pauperes ...* See Mratschek, *Briefwechsel*, 129–30; "Geben und Nehmen in den Briefen des Paulinus von Nola: der himmlische Bankier und der Wohltäter der Armen," in *Zwischen Alltagskommunikation und literarischer Identitätsbildung: Studien zur lateinischen Epistolographie in Spätantike und Frühmittelalter*, ed. Gernot M. Müller (Stuttgart: Franz Steiner, 2018): 109–129, Richard Finn, *Almsgiving in the Later Roman Empire. Christian Promotion and Practice 313–450* (Oxford: Oxford University Press, 2006) 182–88, 205 on "The Redescription of the Poor", and Lucy Grig, "Throwing Parties for the Poor: Poverty and Splendour in the Late Antique Church," in *Poverty in the Roman World*, eds. Margaret Atkins and Robert Osborne (Cambridge: Cambridge University Press, 2006): 154. On "recompense for hospitality" cf. Ambr. *Abr.* 1.5.34: *Bona est hospitalitas, habet mercedem suam, primum humanae gratiae, deinde quod maius est remunerationis divinae.* Paul. Nol. *ep.* 1.1: *fragilis substantiae pretio caelum Christumque mercatus.* Aug. *s.* 173.3–4 (etc.). See Brown, *Eyes of the Needle*, 230–232, and Jill Harries, "Treasure in Heaven: Property and Inheritance among Senators in Late Rome," in *Marriage and Property – Women and Marital Customs in History*, ed. Elizabeth M. Craik (Aberdeen: Aberdeen University Press, 1984): 54–70.

[27] Marcel Mauss, *Essai sur le don* (Paris: Presses Universitaires de France, 1950), trans. Eva Moldenhauer, *Die Gabe. Form und Funktion des Austauschs in archaischen Gesellschaften* (Frankfurt a. M.: Suhrkamp, 2009), 157; Pierre Bourdieu, *Le sense pratique* (Paris: Les éditions de Minuit, 1980), trans. Günter Seib, *Sozialer Sinn. Kritik der theoretischen Vernunft* (Frankfurt a. M.: Suhrkamp, 2009), 180–81, 192–93, cf. Michael L. Satlow's "Introduction" in *The Gift in Antiquity*, ed. Michael L. Satlow (Malden, MA and Oxford: Wiley-Blackwell, 2013): 4–11.

[28] Lact. *inst.* 6.12.2: *tenendum est igitur omni modo, ut ab officio misericordiae spes recipiendi absit omnino; huius enim operis et officii merces a deo est expectanda solo ...* (Hope of return must be absolutely missing). Cf. 6.11.28: *unum igitur certum et verum liberalitatis officium est egentes atque inutiles alere.* (The only true and certain obligation is to feed the needy and useless); 6.11.18: *inutiles sunt hominibus, sed utiles deo* (Men have no use for them, but God has). The apodosis is ignored in Hiltbrunner, *Gastfreundschaft*, 175 and Brown, *Eyes of the Needle*, 76.

and Rufinus, for the Greek East between the Cappadocians.[29] As Umberto Eco has pointed out, "The distinguishing characteristic of a network is that each point can be linked to any other such point, and where the connections have not yet been created they can still be envisaged and created. A network is a territory without limits."[30] It is in this sense that the fourth-century world described here was a networked world, criss-crossed as it was by visitors, ambassadors, messengers, refugees and guests. Social science theory and network and globalisation analysis can be used to show that peer-polity interaction[31] in the form of vigorous competition for primacy and prominence among Christian centres of mutually distinct character – episcopal sees, monasteries, pilgrimage places – and intercultural impacts played a key role not only in the formation of religious groups, but also in the rise of Christianity itself.[32]

2 Mobility: Sites of memory in the Holy Land and the Orient

Drive, faith in human perfectibility and an advanced state of competitiveness among the new religious and intellectual centres were the distinctive features characterising the creative Christian elite. Aristocratic women from Rome and

---

29 Mratschek, *Briefwechsel* (2002) for the west, Raymond Van Dam, *Becoming Christian. The Conversion of Roman Cappadocia* (Philadelphia: University of Pennsylvania Press, 2003) for the east.
30 Translated from Umberto Eco, "Die Enzyklopädie als Labyrinth", in *Kulturwissenschaft*, ed. Uwe Wirth (Frankfurt a.M.: Suhrkamp, 2008): 263.
31 Peer-polity interaction, a concept first used in modern archaeology, is defined by Colin Renfrew, "Introduction" in *Peer Polity Interaction and Socio-Political Change*, eds. Colin Renfrew and John F. Cherry (Cambridge: Cambridge University Press, 1986: 1–18) as embracing the entire spectrum of forms of interaction. For the Graeco-Roman world, see e.g. Irad Malkin, *A Small Greek World: Networks in the Ancient Mediterranean* (Oxford: Oxford University Press, 2011) and Martin Pitts and Miguel J. Versluys, eds. *Globalisation and the Roman World. World, Connectivity and Material Culture* (Cambridge: Cambridge University Press, 2015).
32 Sotinel, "Circulation", 194, points out "que la transmission des nouvelles occupe une place stratégique dans l'histoire du christianisme", but the interaction is not confined to the institutional level. On the competition between pilgrim groups and the multiplicity of sites in the Holy Land, see Jaś Elsner, "Piety and Passion: Contest and Consensus in the Audiences for Early Christian Pilgrimage in Pilgrimage", in *Pilgrimage in Graeco-Roman & Early Christian Antiquity*, eds. Jaś Elsner and Ian Rutherford (Oxford: Oxford University Press, 2005): 411–434; on diversity and the dynamics of religious groups also Éric Rebillard, "Late Antique Limits of Christianness," in *Group Identity and Religious Individuality in Late Antiquity*, eds. Éric Rebillard and Jörg Rüpke (Washington: The Catholic University of America Press, 2015): 293–317.

Constantinople, wealthy and prestigious, established themselves in the Holy Land by founding monasteries and running households in their own right: Melania the Elder in Jerusalem, Olympias in Constantinople, and Paula in Bethlehem. The hospitality offered by Melania the Elder and Rufinus, lent worldwide fame by jeering allusions in Jerome to *exempla* of extravagance like Croesus and Sardanapalus,[33] made the Mount of Olives the focal point of Theodosian Jerusalem. For 23 years, Melania ran a convent for 50 nuns and supported bishops, monks and pilgrims throughout the Roman world by means of regular cash payments.[34] Her dispute with Proculus, governor of Palestine, over her activism in the cause of expelled monks,[35] had not prevented her from opening her monasteries on the Mount of Olives: visitors from the imperial court, Silvia, sister-in-law of the praetorian prefect Fl. Rufinus, and his wife and daughter, were welcome, and shared in East-West exchanges of relics of martyrs.[36] The hospitality networks leading from Olympias, the widow of the urban prefect Nebridius, far from a mere palace system in Constantinople, were "omnipresent on land and at sea", as John Chrysostom was to comment in retrospect.[37] He himself may well have benefited from them when the bishop suffered a bout of fever on his journey into exile and was given temporary shelter in Seleucia's country villa in Caesarea in spite of the hostility of the local bishop, and again when he had reached his place of exile in Cucusus (modern Göksun), where Dioscorus placed a country abode at his disposal, to spare him the worst rigours of winter.[38]

The episode in Jerome dealing with the arrival in Palestine in 385 of his patroness Paula clearly illustrates how competing pagan and Christian perceptions

---

[33] Hier. *ep.* 57.12.5: *inter Croesi opes et Sardanapalli delicias.* Palladius (*h. Laus.* 54.2; 46) offers a more sympathetic assessment of Melania's 37 years providing hospitality.

[34] Pall. *h. Laus.* 46.5–6 c.377–400 AD. See Peter Brown: *The Body and Society. Men, Women and Sexual Renunciation in Early Christianity* (New York: Columbia University Press, 1988, London: Faber and Faber, 1991), 280.

[35] Sigrid Mratschek, "Melania and the Unknown Governor of Palestine," *Journal of Late Antiquity* 5 (2012): 250–68.

[36] On Silvia's pilgrimage (Pall. *h. Laus.* 55), see Paul Devos, "Silvie la sainte pèlerine", *AB* 91 (1973): 105–20, on taking in wife and daughter after Rufinus was murdered 395 (Zos. 5.8.2–3), see *PLRE* I. 778–91 s.v. Flavius Rufinus 18, on the members of the Theodosian court Mratschek, *Briefwechsel*, 438–43. Sulpicius Severus in Primuliacum und Gaudentius in Brixia enjoyed the use of Silvia's relics, cf. Paul. Nol. *ep.* 31.1 (*multorum ex Oriente martyrum reliquiis*) and Gaud. *Tract.* 17.14 on the 40 martyrs of Sebaste.

[37] Joh. Chrys. *ep.* 8.10a: Οὐ γὰρ ἡ οἰκία σου παντὶ ἐλθόντι ἀνέῳκτο μόνον, ἀλλὰ καὶ πανταχοῦ γῆς καὶ θαλάσσης πολλοὶ ταύτης ἀπήλαυσαν τῆς φιλοτιμίας διὰ τῆς φιλοξενίας. For John Chrysostom's letters to Olympias see also the contribution of Peter Gemeinhardt to the present volume (pp. 117–147).

[38] On Seleucia's hospitality see Joh. Chrys. *ep.* 9.2a–3b, on that of Dioscorus *ep.* 9.4a.

of hospitality might meet head-on. Flavius Florentius, the proconsul, sent *apparitores* to offer her a lodging in the praetorium of Caesarea Maritima, but Paula preferred a *humilis cellula* and *angustum hospitium* in Bethlehem to the governor's palace.[39] For a retreat to Bethlehem, the Bible provided the narrative framework in which Christians of Late Antiquity interpreted the world and represented their identity as a collective drama and continuation within the context of the salvation story.[40] In practice the new foundation in Bethehem competed against its counterpart in Jerusalem.[41] Whereas Jerusalem owed its paradigmatic status to Golgotha and the Mount of Olives as the historic sites associated with the Passion and Resurrection, Bethlehem as the *villula Christi* acquired a status of its own as an appropriate memorial site sufficiently remote from the seat of the governor and also not in Jerusalem's shadow. Jerome's allusions to the Nativity enable him to stylise his patroness in the mould of Mary while simultaneously justifying the religious foundations and roadside pilgrim hostel that she was funding: if the Holy Family had sought lodging in Bethlehem and been turned away, now Paula's foundations would guarantee a brisk turnover of pilgrims from East and West sojourning a while at the birthplace of Christ and finding a welcome and shelter in this *diversorium peregrinorum*.[42] Jerome himself became a "lover of the inn at Bethlehem and of the Crib of Our Lord".[43]

---

39 Hier. *ep.* 108.9.2: *proconsule Palaestinae qui familiam eius optime noverat, praemissis apparitoribus iussisset parari praetorium, elegit humilem cellulam*. See *PLRE* II. 396 s.v. Fl. Florentius 11 and Joseph Patrich, *Studies in the Archaeology and History of Caesarea Maritima. Caput Judaeae, Metropolis Palaestinae* (Leiden, 2011: Brill) 105–6, 211–18 on the governor's residence. In view of the large accompanying group of clients and slaves it is questionable whether Paula spent the first three years in "cramped accommodation". See Stefan Rebenich, *Hieronymus und sein Kreis. Prosopographische und sozialgeschichtliche Untersuchungen*, Hist.E 72 (Stuttgart: Franz Steiner), 193–95; dissenting, Hunt, *Holy Land Pilgrimage*, 22, 172, who points to the monastic cells alongside the Sepulchre.
40 1 *Cor* 15:23–28, cf. Paul M. Blowers, "Interpreting Scripture," in *The Cambridge History of Christianity*, vol. 2: *Constantine to c. 600*, eds. Augustine Casiday and Frederick W. Norris (Cambridge: Cambridge University Press, 2007): 633–34.
41 Both were western foundations, with twin monasteries for men and women. See Hunt, *Holy Land Pilgrimage*, 174.
42 Hier. *ep.* 14.4: *nec multo post in sancta Betleem mansura perpetuo angusto per triennium mansit hospitio, donec extrueret cellulas ac monasteria et diversorium peregrinorum iuxta viam conderet, quia Maria et Ioseph hospitium non invenerant.* Cf. Jerome's laments (*ep.* 71.5) over the flood of visitors: *frequentia commeantium et peregrinorum turbis.* See Andrew Cain, *The Letters of Jerome. Asceticism, Biblical Exegesis, and the Construction of Christian Authority in Late Antiquity* (Oxford: Oxford University Press, 2009), 173, n. 31.

Under Theodosius too, the Mount of Olives monastery in Jerusalem proved to be a counterpart in terms of visitor reception to Jerome's institution in Bethlehem, which was developing into a "pivot in the religious and intellectual relations of Christendom".[44] The visitor profile in Bethlehem, where Jerome's personality and epistolary contacts dominated, proved to be more disparate socially than the relatively homogeneous body of pilgrims from Theodosius' entourage in Jerusalem. Jerome's invitations crossed the Mediterranean on their way to aristocrats such as the senator Paulinus of Nola, Fabiola or Eusebius of Cremona, to provincials like the wealthy Spaniard Lucinus or a soldier Exsuperantius, to whom Jerome wrote: "I have knocked at the door of friendship; if you open it, you will find ready hosts".[45] A Gaul, Postumianus, who fled the Egyptian church's dissents c. 400 and sought refuge in Bethlehem's hospitality, remained there for six months.[46]

The hospitality networks of Central Asia Minor were further boosted by the influence and example of Bishop Basil in Caesarea, both of which found imitators among the bishops of Sasima, Podanos and Ancyra.[47] The most conspicuous sign of the bishops' growing prestige in the cities was the new skyline of churches and hostels. Gregory of Nazianzus is full of admiration as he describes the large complex of buildings constructed by Basil outside Caesarea, a church, a residence for the bishop and clergy, a hostel for travellers, a hospital for the sick, and a poorhouse: "A good thing is the love for man, the feeding of the poor, and help rendered to human weakness," he wrote. "Go out of the city a little way and contemplate the new city, the administration of piety, the stores com-

---

[43] Hier. *ep.* 77.2.3: *diversorii Bethlehemitici et praesepis dominici amator* ... See *Jerome's Epitaph on Paula: A Commentary on the Epitaphium Sanctae Paulae*, ed. and trans. Andrew Cain (Oxford: Oxford University Press, 2013) 17–18.

[44] On "holy Bethlehem" as the Christian *omphalos* (Greg. Naz. *or.* 18.17), see *Jerome's Epitaph*, ed. Cain, 18–19, and Yves-Marie Duval, "Les premiers rapports de Paulin avec Jérôme: Moine et philosophe", *Studi tardoantichi* 7 (1989): 216.

[45] Hier. *ep.* 71.4.1–2 (Lucinus' *abundantia*); *ep.* 64.8, 77.7–9 (Fabiola's return from Palestine); 53.10–11 (Paulinus of Nola); 57.2.2 (Eusebius Cremonensis, *vir apud suos haut ignobilis*); *ep.* 145.5 (Exuperantius): *pulsavi amicitiarum fores; ... non crebro habebis hospites*. On contacts to Rome *ep.* 47.3.1 (to Desiderius): *quodsi exemplaria libuerit mutari, vel a sancta Marcella, quae manet in Aventino, vel a Loth temporis nostri, Domnione, viro sanctissimo accipere poteris*. The Roman circle kept in close touch with ascetic circles in Upper Italy and Aquitania, see Rebenich, *Hieronymus*, 195–97 and Mratschek, *Briefwechsel*, 468–72.

[46] Sulp. Sev. *dial.* 1.8–9, esp. 1.7.6: *non fuit animus ibi consistere, ubi recens fraternae cladis fervebat invidia*. 1.8.1: *Igitur inde digressus Betleem oppidum petii, quod ab Hierosolymis sex milibus separatur, ab Alexandria autem sedecim mansionibus abest*. See Hunt, *Holy Land Pilgrimage*, 179.

[47] On hospitality in Caesarea, Sasima and Podanos see Hunt, *Holy Land Pilgrimage*, 66, on the hospitality of the deaconess Magna at Ancyra Pall. *h. Laus.* 66–68 also.

munally gathered together by the owners where the surfeit of wealth is piled high."⁴⁸ No wonder this "new city" was called *Basileias* after its founder.

3 Overcoming social barriers: Xenodochia in Italy

In the Roman West, affluent senators would indicate their Christian sympathies by establishing a *xenodochium* in *Portus Traiani*, the port of Rome and first landfall for foreigners arriving from every part of the world, and a *nosocomium* in the city proper.⁴⁹ In the "performative space" of letter exchange and in the dialogue between preacher and audience, those who practised hospitality metamorphosed into heroes and heroines in the eschatologically advancing history of salvation.⁵⁰ An exhilarated Jerome writes that Pammachius had "transplanted a twig from Abraham's tree to the Ausonian shore", at the point where Aeneas had landed after his odysseys.⁵¹ Jerome differed from Vergil and Gregory of Nazianzus in entertaining no dream of a newly founded city; fusing pagan imagery from Rome's mythical past – depictions of the Trojans devouring their "tables" – with diminutives expressive of Christian humility, he sketches his own personal imagining of Pammachius' hostel for strangers: "a small village such as his", Bethlehem, a new "House of Bread".⁵² Given appropriate conduct, he holds out to the new ascetic, Pammachius, (and to himself) the prospect of a similar destiny to that of their shared role model Abraham: "After dispensing hospitality

---

48 Greg. Naz. *or.* 43.63: Καλὸν φιλανθρωπία καὶ πτωχοτροφία καὶ τὸ τῆς ἀνθρωπίνης ἀσθενείας βοήθημα. Μικρὸν ἀπὸ τῆς πόλεως πόελθε καὶ θέασαι τὴν καινὴν πόλιν, τὸ τῆς εὐσεβείας ταμεῖον, τὸ κοινὸν τῶν ἐχόντων θησαύρισμα, εἰς ὃ τὰ περιττὰ τοῦ πλούτου ... Cf. Basil *ep.* 94, on the name Soz. *h.e.* 6.34.9. See Van Dam, *Becoming Christians*, 95.
49 Hier. *ep.* 66.11 (to Pammachius), and *ep.* 77.6 (to Fabiola). See Cain's suggestion (*Letters of Jerome*, 177) that the two letters should be read "in tandem".
50 Jennifer V. Ebbeler, *Pedants in the Apparel of Heroes? Cultures of Latin Letter-Writing from Cicero to Ennodius*. (Ph.D. diss. University of Pennsylvania, 2001), 163–68 on strategies of letter exchange through which the writer of a letter can manipulate his own identity and that of his correspondent.
51 Hier. *ep.* 66.11.1: *Audio te xenodochium in portu fecisse Romae et virgam de arbore Abraham in Ausonio plantasse litore, quasi Aeneas nova castra metaris et super undam Thybridis, ubi ille cogente quondam penuria crustis fatalibus et quadris patulis non pepercit* ... On Abraham Ambr. Gen. 18.8, cf. Verg. Aen. 7.115.
52 Hier. *ep.* 66.11.1: ... *tu viculum nostrum, id est domum panis, aedificas et diuturnam famem repentina saturitate conpensas*. "House of Bread" is the translation of Bethlehem, see *Eusebius Hieronymus*, trans. Ludwig Schade, BKV 1 (Kempten, München: Josef Kösel, 1914), 161, n. 4.

on so many occasions ..., he was deemed worthy to offer it to God as his guest".[53] All the world had heard about Pammachius' hostel for foreigners in the port of Rome, Jerome affirms;[54] but his charity competed with that of Fabiola, whose endowments reached far beyond the imperial capital to the islands and monastic communities of the Tyrrhenian Sea: "Rome was too small for her charity", Jerome declared with reference to the high point of her life:[55] "Her pilgrimage to Jerusalem, where she was received by a great crowd of people and had briefly enjoyed *his* hospitality".[56]

In Nola, at the centre of the crisis-hit Roman empire, by the tomb of Felix the martyr, Paulinus erected heavenly dwellings, *caelestes mansiones* (*Ep.* 32.18), the *Basilica Nova,* a poorhouse, a monastery and pilgrim hostel. Paulinus and his monks lived in close contact with the destitute, whose physical presence and prayers constituted "the foundations" in the lower storey,[57] while he himself, Therasia, the monks and favoured guests (*boni*) occupied cells in the monastery's upper storey.[58] As with Basil, the ascetic centre was by c. 400 coming to look increasingly like a "large city", in the end outstripping Nola's old city centre, Cimitile.[59] The hospitality concept dominated Paulinus' thinking to the point where he felt himself to be the guest of the saint whose bones he revered here: Felix was the master of the house where he lived, the *dominaedius* of Nola.[60]

---

[53] Hier. *ep.* 66.11: *Et tamen, postquam crebro hospitalitatis officio, dum homines non refutat, suscipere meruit deum* (sc. Abraham).
[54] Hier. *ep.* 77.10.3: *xenodochium in portu Romano situm totus pariter mundus audivit.*
[55] Hier. *ep.* 77.6.5: *Angusta misericordiae Roma fuit.* A catalogue of innumerable sufferings combined with a Virgilian litotes (*Aen.* 6.625 – 27) enhances the statement's impact.
[56] Hier. *ep.* 77.7.1: *Unde repente et contra opinionem Hierosolymam navigavit, ubi multorum excepta concursu nostro parumper usa est hospitio.*
[57] Paul. Nol. *carm.* 21.389 – 94: *Subdita pauperibus famulatur porticus aegris / ... hospitiis inopumque salubria praestat / vulneribus nostris consortia sede sub una, / commoda praestemus nobis ut amica vicissim, /* fundamenta *illi confirment* nostra *precantes, / nos fraterna inopum foveamus corpora tecto.*
[58] Paul. Nol. *carm.* 21.386 – 87 (in the annexe of the Basilica Vetus): *Post haec geminato tegmine crevit / structa domus, nostris quae nunc manet hospita cellis. carm.* 27.397 (Lodgings for the *boni* in the upper storey); *ep.* 29.13 (*celluli hospitales*). See Tomas Lehmann, *Paulinus Nolanus und die Basilica Nova in Cimitile/Nola* (Wiesbaden: Reichert, 2004), 205 – 7 and Mratschek, *Briefwechsel*, 60, 550 – 52.
[59] Paul. Nol. *carm.* 18.180: *magna ... urbs.* See Mratschek, *Briefwechsel*, 250 – 52.
[60] On concepts of *amicitia* and *hospitium*, see Paulinus' (*ep. 13.21* to Pammachius) appeal for hospitality: *Aperiamus et nos domicilia nostra fratribus ..., dum omnis advenae transitum prompta humanitate suscipimus.* Felix as *communis patronus dominaedius meus/noster* (*ep.* 5.15; 32.10); *dilectissimus dominaedius noster* (*ep.* 18.3); *dominaedius meus/noster* (*ep.* 28.6; 29.13; *carm.* 23.109);

It was a great boost for the reputation of the shrine and its guardian – on this Paulinus and Cicero[61] agree – when Melania the Elder, grand-daughter of the consul Antonius Marcellinus,[62] chose Paulinus' monastery for her first night's rest in Italy upon returning home to Rome from her twenty-seven-year pilgrimage to the Orient.[63] The presence of prominent visitors from Theodosian court circles such as Flora, related to the proconsul Aemilius Florus Paternus, and the wife of the ex-consul Baebianus illustrates the extent to which court establishment had found its way into the most fashionable resort of ascetic Christianity in Italy.[64] Paulinus, who saw his own life as a journey (*peregrinatio*) in quest of Felix, recorded their respective *adventus* in his letters and poems. He described the seven aristocrats (*proceres*) from the clan of Melania the Younger, who sat among his audience in 407, on the feast day of Felix, to listen to their host's poetic autobiography, as *munera*, gifts prepared for him by the saint.[65] He hoped that they would settle as permanent guests (*sempiterni hospites*) in Nola.[66] Thanks to the network of Christian hospitality created by Paulinus, the monastery, after initial set-

---

Clarus as Sulpicius Severus' permanent guest (*perpetuus hospes*) thanks to the relics at Primuliacum (*ep. 32.6*). See Mratschek, "Hospitality," 512–14 and "Friendship," 724.
[61] Cic. *off.* 2.64: *Est enim ... valde decorum patere domos hominum inlustrium hospitibus inlustribus ...*
[62] Paul. Nol. *ep.* 29.8: *Marcellino consule avo.* He was cos. 341, see *PLRE* I. 548–49 s.v. Marcellinus 16.
[63] Paul. Nol. *ep.* 29.9 on Melania's reception by the *magna et potentissimorum et carorum propinquorum Romae copia* early in the year 400.
[64] Aug. *cura mort.* 1.1: *scripsisti per homines filiae nostrae religiosissimae* Florae ... She had settled in Nola with her household. See John Matthews, *Western Aristocracies and Imperial Court A.D. 364–425* (Oxford: Oxford Clarendon Press, 1990), 144, and Dennis E. Trout, *Paulinus of Nola. Life, Letters, and Poems* (Berkeley, Los Angeles, London: University of California Press, 1999), 42.
[65] Paul. Nol. *carm.* 21.203–6: *videtis omnes munera hoc anno data / vobis in uno iuncta Felicis sinu, / mancipia Christi, nobiles terrae prius / nunc vero caelo destinatos incolas.* See Anika L. Kleinschmidt: *Ich-Entwürfe in spätantiker Dichtung. Ausonius, Paulinus von Nola und Paulinus von Pella* (Heidelberg: Winter, 2013), 205–7. On Paulinus' *peregrinatio(nes)* to Nola, cf. Paul. Nol. *ep.* 5.4: *... denique ut a calumniis et peregrinationibus requiem capere visus sum ...*; *carm.* 21.398–99: *Inde propinquos trans iuga Pyrenes adii peregrinus Hiberos.* Paulinus' perception of *peregrinus* as one coming home to God (or Felix) and pilgrim does not in my view conflict with Augustine's perception, cf. Mratschek, *Briefwechsel*, 210–11, 569, different view in Gillian Clark, "Pilgrims and Foreigners: Augustine on Travelling Home," in *Travel, Communication and Geography in Late Antiquity. Sacred and Profane*, eds. Linda Ellis and Frank L. Kidner (Aldershot and Burlington: Ashgate, 2004): 155.
[66] Paul. Nol. *carm.* 21. 266–69: *Hos ergo Felix in suo sinu abditos / mandante Christo condidit tectis suis / mecum sumpsit sempiternos hospites.*

backs,[67] was transformed into a meeting-place for rich and poor and an interface of communication between church and state. In addition to streams of pilgrims from southern and central Italy year after year coming to the tomb of Felix, the shrine at Nola received more than 40 named individual guests and journeying groups from Palestine, Egypt, Asia Minor, North Africa, Dacia and Gaul.[68]

4 Hospitality culture and global connectivity

Networks of hospitality and cooperation linking places far apart brought the Christian world of Late Antiquity closer together. An exchange agreement (*foedus*) would be sealed with guest gifts, eulogies and relics, or through the ritual of the joined hands.[69] The means of implementation were the organisation and transfer of knowledge, which turned the Mediterranean into a circulating library.[70] Recited at Nola before Melania the Elder and Nicetas of Remesiana, Sulpicius Severus' *Life of Martin* had made its way from Gaul to Italy, Egypt and Illyricum,[71] and his *Dialogues* had been transmitted as far as Palestine, where they were read by Jerome in Bethlehem in 412.[72] After Nicetas, in 403, had come directly from Dacia for a second time to see Paulinus, who gave him a guided tour of his monastery and a *Natalicium* (9), the ascetic centres of Augustine in

---

67 Instead of Sulpicius Severus, the *pueri* of Severus came to Nola in early summer 396 and Victor c. 400, and, instead of Victricius, his deacon Paschasius and the latter's travel companion Ursus in July 397/98.
68 See the list of visitors and guests, Mratschek, *Briefwechsel*, 640–42 and "Hospitality," 552–53.
69 On exchanges of eulogies and relics, see Mratschek, *Briefwechsel*, 427–43. On the gesture between Nicetas of Remesiana and Paulinus of Nola, cf. Paul. Nol. *carm.* 27.346–48: *Nodemus socias in vincula mutua palmas / inque vicem nexis alterno foedere dextris / sermones varios gressu spatiante seramus.*
70 On the desire for "worldwide dissemination" see Uran. *ep. de obitu* 3: *Martinus ... cuius vita ab omnibus legitur.* Likewise Sulpicius Severus on Jerome's works (*dial.* 1.8.4): *cum per totum orbem legatur* (sc. *Hieronymus*). See Mratschek, *Briefwechsel*, 463–64, and "Zirkulierende Bibliotheken. Medien der Wissensvermittlung & christliche Netzwerke," in *L'étude des correspondances dans le monde romain*, ed. Jean-Christophe Jolivet et al. (Lille: Halma, 2011): 325–50.
71 Sulp. Sev. *dial.* 2 (3).17.4: *... ut mox per illum nostrum libellum non per Italiam tantum, sed per totum etiam diffudit Illyricum. dial.* 2 (3) 17.5–7: *Ad Africam ... Carthagini* (5), *ad laevam Achaiae sinum ... Corinthus, ... Athenae* (6), *ad Aegyptum ... universae Asiae* (7).
72 Hier. *in Ezech.* 11.36.1.5: *... et nuper Severus noster in dialogo cui 'Gallo' nomen imposuit ...*

Africa, of Severus in Gaul, and in Dacia also knew about the new buildings at Nola.[73]

It is the points where the boundaries between East and West were overcome through the practice of hospitality that best illustrate the closely-knit nature of the networks already linking the Christian centres in the fourth century. Hospitality shown by the aristocrat Paula at Rome in her urban palace to two bishops, Epiphanius of Salamis (Constantia), and Paulinus of Antioch, during the synod of 382 under Pope Damasus, provided the impetus for her pilgrimage – and her hospitality was duly returned on Cyprus and at Antioch in compliance with the established norms.[74] Friendships made in the Holy Land would be renewed in the West. Palladius and Melania the Elder were neighbours on the Mount of Olives; Melania the Younger and Pinianus generously hosted Palladius and his companions in their palace in 405, when he came to Rome, following the deposition of John Chrysostom as bishop of Constantinople, with a mission to seek diplomatic backing. "They entertained us with hospitality and abundant provisions for the journey", the bishop of Helenopolis recalled, "gaining for themselves with great joy only the fruit of eternal life by their god-given works of the best way of life".[75]

We encounter the younger Melania's senatorial relations again after the fall of Rome, in Africa, staying with Paulinus' correspondents Augustine and Alypius. Augustine accompanies his apology for not having immediately visited those "who have fled (Alaric) across the sea and have come from a great distance

---

[73] On the second visit to Italy see Paul. Nol. *carm.* 27.233–34: ... *longinqua tellure mihi modo missus* (sc. *Nicetas*) *ad istum / ecce diem venit* ... Augustine quotes Paul. Nol. *carm.* 23 (*nat.* 7), *carm.* 18 (*nat.* 6); Nicetas receives Paul. Nol. *carm.* 27 (*nat.* 9), Severus a *natalicium*, see Mratschek, *Briefwechsel*, 224, 413–14.

[74] Hier. *ep.* 108.6.1: ... *quorum Epiphanium etiam hospitem habuit, Paulinum in aliena manentem domo, quasi proprium, humanitate possedit.* 108.7.2–3: ... *tandem vidit Cyprum, ubi sancti et venerabilis Epiphanii pedibus provoluta decem ab diebus retenta est... Inde brevi cursu transfretavit Seleuciam, de qua ascendens Antiochiam, sancti confessoris Paulini modicum caritate detenta* ... See Cain, *Letters of Jerome*, 131–32.

[75] Pall. *h. Laus.* 61.7: ... ἀναπαύσαντες ἡμᾶς καὶ ξενδοχείᾳ καὶ ἐφοδίοις δαψιλεστάτοις, μετὰ πολλῆς χαρᾶς καρπούμενοι τὴν αἰώνιον ζωὴν τοῖς θεοδωρήτοις ἔργοις τῆς ἀρίστης πολιτείας. On Palladius and Melania the Elder see Hunt, *Holy Land Pilgrimage* 184–85, on support for John Chrysostom Peter Brown, "The Patrons of Pelagius", in *Religion and Society in the Age of Saint Augustine*, ed. Peter Brown (London: Wipf and Stock, 1972): 210–15 and Wolfgang Liebeschuetz, *Barbarians and Bishops. Army, Church and State in the Age of Arcadius and Chrysostom* (Oxford: Clarendon Press, 1992), 225–26.

to see him" with an indirect invitation to Hippo.⁷⁶ Putting an embarrassing episode during the visit there behind them – Augustine had difficulty in rescuing the enormously rich Pinianus from enforced ordination as a priest⁷⁷ – the family lived for seven years on their extensive estates near Thagaste and built two autonomous monasteries before deciding about 417 to move permanently to Palestine.⁷⁸ In the East, Melania's itineraries crossed with those of members from the Theodosian court.

Lausus, formerly *praepositus sacri cubiculi* to Theodosius II, dedicatee of Palladius' *Historia Lausiaca*, received Melania in 436 at his palace, which was renowned for its unique collection of pagan statues in fifth-century Constantinople.⁷⁹ The Empress Aelia Eudocia, meeting Melania three years later on her way to Palestine, honoured her by attending in person at the consecration of the martyr's shrine for Stephen in Jerusalem, which she had had constructed alongside the Church of the Ascension on the Mount of Olives.⁸⁰ Such encounters and rituals contributed to the transformation of Palestine into a "Utopian" sacred world,⁸¹ now defined anew by its visitors – for whom it boosted perceived prestige and thus influence more powerfully than anything they could achieve in the real world.

Africa, "suffering under its notorious dryness" and by "the spiritual aridity of its nobility", is thirsting for men like Paulinus:⁸² it was with such emotive appeals that Augustine implored the champion of the ascetic movement, barely ar-

---

76 Aug. *ep.* 124.1–2: ... *ad quos volatu maria transeunda fuerant, tam in proximo constitutos, tam de longinquo visendi nos gratia venientes* ... (2) ... *si haec civitas, in qua laboramus, digna non est, quia nec ego audeo dignam putare, quae nobiscum de vestra praesentia conlaetatur.*
77 Aug. *ep.* 125–26.
78 Aug. *ep.* 124–26; *v. Mel.* 34–35, esp. 22: Ἔκτισαν δὲ καὶ μοναστήρια μεγάλα δύο ἐκεῖσε, παρασχόντες αὐτοῖς αὐτάρκη πρόσοδον. See Elizabeth A. Clark, "Piety, Propaganda, and Politics in the Life of Melania the Younger", *StudPatr* 18.2 (1989): 167 and 175.
79 Pall. *h. Laus.* Praef. (*ad Lausum bonae memoriae*) and 61 (Melania the Younger); *v. Mel.* 53: Καὶ ὑπεδέξατο ὁ κύριος Λαῦσος ὁ πρεπόσιτος ... See Cyril Mango, Michael Vickers, and E.D. Francis, "The Palace of Lausus at Constantinople and its Collection of Ancient Statues", *Journal of the History of Collections* 4 (1992): 89–98.
80 *v. Mel.* 57–58, esp. 58, where the Empress requested that the ceremony be held in her presence. See Hunt, *Holy Land Pilgrimage* 232–33 and Noel Lenski, "Empresses in the Holy Land: The Creation of a Christian Utopia in Late Antique Palestine", in *Travel*, ed. Ellis and Kidner: 117.
81 Brilliantly observed by Lenski, "Empresses," 122.
82 Aug. *ep.* 31.4 to Paulinus and Therasia: *Qua re non inpudenter rogo vos et flagito, ut in Africam maiore talium hominum siti quam siccitatis nobilitate laborantem venire dignemini.* This metaphor was an echo of an earlier Paulinus letter (Aug. *ep.* 25.2 = Paul. Nol. *ep.* 4.2): *Cuius desiderio sitivit in te anima mea, et ubertate tui fluminis inebriari terra mea concupivit.* On the invitations, see also Aug. *ep.* 27.6 and Mratschek, *Briefwechsel* 95–96.

rived in Nola (395/96), to come to Hippo in person. In March 405, reacting to news of the first invasion of northern Italy by Goths under Alaric, Augustine renewed his invitation to his friend to consider evacuating his monastery at Nola and bring his entire monastic community over to join him in Africa.[83] Both appeals failed. For readers trained in philosophy like Augustine and Cicero, all human beings were foreigners (*peregrinantes*) in their own earthly city wandering around like visitors (*hospites*) and seeking for their true home.[84] Paulinus for his part was firmly resolved "to stand fast at the place (i.e. Nola) where he was happier (*felicior*, i.e. closer to Felix)".[85] He believed the bones of the saint to be the best protection against the barbarians, and on the eve of the battle of Pollentia had reaffirmed his heroic stance in a poem to Felix.[86] Augustine's word-play on the name Felix can be seen to respond subtly to Paulinus' style and argumentation.[87]

The return of hospitality offered by Paulinus to the envoys from the African synods and from Augustine reminds us of the importance that Cicero ascribed to interactions with eminent guests from abroad in his treaty *On Obligations* (*off.* 2.64): "For those wishing to achieve a great deal in an honourable way it is exceedingly useful to have high standing among foreign peoples through one's guests by means of wealth and favour".[88] During the decade between

---

[83] Aug. *Ep.* 80 with the new interpretation by Sigrid Mratschek, "Augustine, Paulinus, and the question of moving the monastery," in *Inter cives necnon peregrinos. Essays in honour of Boudewijn Sirks*, eds. Jan Hallebeek et al. (Göttingen: Vandenhoeck & Ruprecht, 2014): 545–61.

[84] Clark, "Pilgrims and Foreigners", 149–58, esp. 156, compares Aug. *civ.* 1.1 with reference to *civitas peregrina*, seeking its home in the *stabilitas sedis aeternae*, with Cic. *acad.* 1.3.9: *Nam nos in nostra urbe peregrinantis errantisque tamquam hospites* ... Ambrose too (*Abr.* 1.5.34) asserts that as temporary sojourners on earth we are strangers, with only limited-duration hospitality rights, and will shortly depart hence: *omnes in hoc incolatu hospites sumus; ad tempus enim habitandi habemus hospitium: emigremus propere*. On the metaphor of life as a journey, see Marion Giebel, *Reisen in der Antike* (Darmstadt: Wissenschaftliche Buchgesellschaft, 1999), 207–11, with different examples.

[85] See discussion of the little question (*quaestiuncula*) in Aug. *ep.* 80.2: ... *cum dixisses ita de illo, quo **felicior** uteris, loco perseverare decrevisse, ut, si quid de te aliud domino placuerit, eius voluntatem praeferas tuae*.

[86] Paulinus had reaffirmed his heroic stance on 14 January 402, the eve of the battle of Pollentia, in a festal poem to Felix (*carm.* 26.22–25): *Hunc (sc. Felicis sanctum diem) ego, si Getis agerem male subditus armis, / inter et inmites celebrarem laetus Alanos, / et si multiiugae premerent mea colla catenae, / captivis animum membris non iungeret hostis* ...

[87] On the wordplay with the name, e.g. Paul. Nol. *carm.* 21.414–15: *tu Felix semper felix mihi ... / perpetua pater et custos pietate fuisti*.

[88] Cic. *off.* 2.64 (on *hospites inlustres* and *homines externi*): *Est enim vehementer utile iis, qui honeste posse multum volunt, per hospites apud externos populos valere opibus et gratia*.

398 and 408, with Nola already recognised as Italy's prime hub for church politics, and before Paulinus was ordained bishop, diplomatic activity increased rapidly. Augustine noted with mixed feelings that sojourns at Nola by delegations of African bishops were becoming a permanent phenomenon: "When the brethren, our most intimate friends, see you constantly", he wrote to Paulinus, "and you frequently return their greetings, mutually desirous of each other's company, it is not so much an enhancement of my happiness as an assuagement of misfortune".[89]

Analysis of Augustine's "unwritten letters", salutations and allusions together with minutes of African synods and imperial constitutions permits us to infer how many delegations travelling on secret business and led by bishops and other clergy (including Theasius, Evodius of Uzalis, Possidius of Calama, Fortunatianus, Severus of Mileve, Restitutus and Florentius) stopped over at the Nola monastery in order to seek advice from Paulinus before continuing their journey to the imperial court or to meet the bishop in Rome.[90] Networking beyond the confines of the Mediterranean proved a successful strategy for interventions against circumcellions and pagans in North Africa, for agitation against the usurper Gildo or against the rehabilitation of the monk Pelagius – and also for the transfer of knowledge. Effects and counter-effects stemming from the hospitality it afforded led to Nola becoming involved in internal church conflicts and gaining fresh political influence, while the human mix of the monastic community varied constantly in the ever-changing stream of visitors.[91]

5 Conflicts and hospitality: Asylum

No subject is as explosive as asylum for victims of political persecution, and nothing more illuminating with regard to the ethics of hospitality. During Late Antiquity, asylum was granted in cases of barbarian invasion, ecclesiastical dis-

---

[89] Aug. *ep*. 95.1: *Cum vos* (i.e. *Paulinum*) *fratres nostri coniunctissimi nobis, quos nobiscum desiderati desiderare et salutati resalutare consuestis, assidue vident, non tam augentur bona nostra quam consolantur mala.*
[90] Sigrid Mratschek, "The unwritten Letters of Augustine of Hippo", in *Scrinium Augustini. The World of Augustine's Letters,* eds. Przemysław Nehring et al., IPM 76 (Turnhout: Brepols, 2017): 57–77 = expanded English version of "Die ungeschriebenen Briefe des Augustinus von Hippo," in *'In Search of Truth': Augustine, Manichaeism and other Gnosticism. Studies for Johannes van Oort at Sixty,* eds. Jacob A. van den Berg et al. (Leiden and Boston: Brill, 2011): 109–22.
[91] E.g. during the papal election of 419, see Mratschek, *Briefwechsel*, 512–17, 643, for aristocrats see "Hospitality," 539–45.

pute, and of the state exceeding its power encroachment on individual rights. The German Republic's Basic Law (Art. 16a) provides that there must be intentional violation of human rights on the part of the state, calculated by its intensity to exclude the victim from the community, and grave enough to violate the victim's human dignity. But what is the nature of the "hospitality" appropriate to those seeking asylum? Ambrose answers: "Such is the grace inherent in hospitality that we joyfully accept all associated perils along with it".[92] In his first sermon as a young priest in Antioch, John Chrysostom had praised Bishop Flavianus with an allusion to Cicero, because "he opened" the house of his forefathers "at all times to those from any part of the world who were suffering persecution for the sake of the truth", so that it seemed less "his house" than a "house of strangers".[93] As a combative bishop of Constantinople he granted asylum ("a place to rest") to the monks banished from Egypt by Bishop Theophilus, while his own fellow-bishop Acacius of Beroea complained bitterly of having failed to find any comfortable lodging[94] – and so made enemies of Acacius and Theophilus, who both urged that John be deposed and sent into exile.[95]

Anecdotes that stylise John, the court bishop, as the bishop of the poor and oppressed,[96] the bishop who breached traditional norms of church law and Christian hospitality, tend to conceal deeper political motivations and disappointed expectations. Support for the Egyptian monks had to do with the power struggle that smouldered for years between Alexandria and Constantinople, and the right of appeal direct to the bishop attached to the imperial court.[97]

---

[92] Ambr. *in Luc.* 5.35: *Tanta hospitalitatis gratia, ut libenter in nos aliena pericula transferam.*
[93] Joh. Chrys. *serm. 8 in Gen.* 1.4. Cf. Cic. *off.* 1.139: *nec domo dominus, sed domino domus honestanda est, et, ut in ceteris habenda ratio non sua solum, sed etiam aliorum* ... Sidon. *ep.* 4.1.1 (on Consentius' villa): *qui ... hospites epulis, te pascit hospitibus ...*
[94] On the expulsion of the Egyptian monks and and asylum for them in the Anastasis in Constantinople, see Pall. *dial.* 6–7, esp. 7,87–89: καὶ δοὺς αὐτοῖς ἐν τῇ Ἀναστασίᾳ καλουμένῃ ἐκκλησίᾳ μονὰς τὴν ἀνάπαυσιν ... On Acacius' guest-room Pall. *dial.* 6,8–10: Συνέβη δὲ κατ' ἐκεῖνο καιροῦ ἐπιστάντα Ἀκάκιον, τὸν ἐπίσκοπον Βεροίας, ἀστοχῆσαι, ὥς ἔλεγεν, καταγωγίου καλοῦ.
[95] Arrian in Photius, *Bibl.* 59 (ed. Henri, vol. 1, 52) on the accusers at the Synod of the Oak in July 403: ἐν ᾗ ὑπῆρχον κατάρχοντες Θεόφιλός τε ὁ Ἀλεξανδρείας, Ἀκάκιος ὁ Βεροίας ...
[96] On his way into exile, John Chrysostom wrote to his rich patroness Olympias, perhaps inspired by personal experience, that "it was the peasants and manual workers who took in and in every way supported those who had been driven from their homes by the mighty" (*ep.* 7.5b,18–20): τοὺς δὲ ἀγοραῖοι καὶ χειροτέχναι ὑποδεχόμενοι παρὰ τῶν ἐν δυναστείαις ἐλαυνομένους πάντα ἐθεράπευον τρόπον ...
[97] But cf. the ordinance forbidding bishops any involvement in the affairs of other dioceses, Conc. Nicaenum a. 325, *can.* 5: *Conciliengeschichte. Nach den Quellen bearbeitet von* Carl Joseph Hefele, vol. I² (Freiburg i.Br.: Herder, 1873), 386–88; Conc. Constantinopolitanum a. 381, *can.* 2,

The inferior quality of Acacius' guest suite takes on new meaning when seen in its political context. From an early date (381) Acacius had been one of the most forceful advocates of the election of Flavianus, and had been placed by John in 398 at the head of a delegation sent to the bishop of Rome to plead for the readmission of Flavianus to the church and to end the Antiochene schism. The issue, therefore, was not simply a breach of etiquette arising because the ascetic John Chrysostom (in contrast to Ambrose) had done away with the practice of holding guest banquets in the episcopal palace,[98] but John's failure, as a bishop of Constantinople, to bestow on Acacius the privileged treatment and the supportive patronage that his loyalty merited.

In addition to Greek temple asylum, a further possibility in Classical Antiquity was to flee to the sacrosanct statues of the emperor or seek asylum in churches – alternatives that were taken up as early as 343 and were enshrined in the laws of the Theodosian Code (9.45.1–4) from 392 to 431.[99] Where John Chrysostom by hosting Egyptian monks breached the church's traditional legal norms forbidding the export of a diocesan matter beyond that diocese's frontiers, Augustine exploited every possible legal remedy whenever state security forces, by breaching church asylum rights, trespassed literally on church ground. As bishop of Hippo he sent off three terse and forceful protest letters to the competent authorities (*ep.* 114–16) – to Florentinus, an officer of Boniface, Count (*comes*) of Africa, to the bishop of Cirta Fortunatus, and to Generosus, governor (*consularis*) of Numidia – in which he intervened against the arrest, by the commander of the coastguards, of a tenant farmer named Faventius whom fear of his rich landlord had driven to seek refuge in the church at Hippo. In the letters, the bishop argued in favour of applying the exceptional law (*CTh* 9.2.6)[100] conceding to any detained person, on request, the right to moderate mu-

---

vol. II² (Freiburg i.Br.: Herder, 1875), 15–17. Claudia Tiersch, *Johannes Chrysostomus in Konstantinopel (398–404)* (Tübingen: J.C.B. Mohr Siebeck, 2002), 331–34.
98 Guests were rare at his episcopal table, cf. Pall. *dial.* 12.17: Ὁμολόγηται μὲν ὅτι μόνος ἤσθιεν. But cf. the praise of Theodoret in Photius, *Bibl.* 508a (ed. Henry, vol. 8, 108): Καὶ τίς Ἰωάννου φιλοξενώτερος; on this, see Tiersch, *Johannes Chrysostomus*, 165–66, and on the difference between Ambrose and John entertaining guests at meals, cf. McLynn, *Ambrose*, 247.
99 On how the canonical legislation was being applied in practice in 343, see Conc. Serdicense, *can.* 5, ed. Cuthbert H. Turner, *Ecclesiae occidentalis monumenta iuris antiquissima*, vol. 1 (Oxford: Clarendon Press, 1899), 462: ... *saepe contigit ut ad misericordiam ecclesiae confugiant* ... See Harald Siems, "Asyl in der Kirche? Wechsellagen des Kirchenasyls im Mittelalter", in *Das antike Asyl. Kultische Grundlagen, rechtliche Ausgestaltung und politische Funktion*, ed. Martin Dreher (Cologne, Weimar, Vienna, 2003: Böhlau): 266–68.
100 Aug. *ep.* 113 (CSEL 34/2 659): ... *non solum eximietas tua sed etiam ipse, quisquis ille est, in cuius causa Faventius sic raptus est, merito me culpabit et recte reprehendet iudicans utique, si*

nicipal custody for 30 days in the town of his arrest, to enable him to put his affairs in order. When a tax evader, Fascius, was unable to pay off his tax debt of 17 *solidi* in a single sum and fled to church refuge rather than be handed over to the tax-collectors,[101] the bishop personally borrowed the requisite sum from a certain Macedonicus and paid it over.[102] On expiry of the asylum right and the loan term with no solution yet in sight, Augustine directed that the necessary sum should be raised from a collection and if necessary the church funds.[103]

The notably broad interpretation of Christian right-of-asylum, without regard to rank, religious denomination or political sympathies of the individuals concerned, is reflected by the cases of two top officials – Eutropius, consul and grand chamberlain at the imperial court in Constantinople, and Marinus, *comes rei militaris* of Italy and Africa.[104] Eutropius who had stripped the churches of their right to grant asylum, after his fall from favour in 399, sought asylum himself at the altar of the first church of St. Sophia;[105] and John Chrysostom, in his celebrated sermon on the "vanity of earthly glory", seized the opportunity to

---

etiam ipse <u>ad auxilium ecclesiae confugisset</u>, ... rogo itaque benignitatem ... hoc interim apud apparitorem, qui eum tenet, petitionem meam adiuvare digneris ut faciat, quod imperatoris lege praecipitur (CTh 9.2.6), ut eum apud acta municipalia interrogari faciat, utrum sibi velit dies triginta concedi, quibus agat sub moderata custodia in ea civitate, in qua detentus est, ut sua ordinet sumptusque provideat. See Stanisław Adamiak, "Asking für Human Mercy. Augustine's Intercession with the Men in Power", in *Scrinium Augustini. The World of Augustine's Letters*, eds. Przemysław Nehring et al., IPM 76 (Turnhout: Brepols, 2017): 19–40, esp. 35–36.– CTh 9.2.6 was promulgated by Caecilianus on 21 Jan. 409, PPO Italiae et Illyrici (PLRE II. 244–46, s.v. Caecilianus 1) under Honorius and Theodosius.

101 Aug. ep. 268.1–3, esp. ep. 268.1: *Cum enim frater noster Fascius debito decem et septem solidorum ab opinatoribus urgeretur, ut redderet, quod ad praesens, unde explicaret se, non inveniebat, ne corporalem pateretur iniuriam, <u>ad auxilium sanctae ecclesiae convolavit.</u>*

102 Aug. ep. 268.1: *Illi enim exactores ... gravissimis me querelis oneraverunt ita, ut eis illum traderem ... Ita ergo maiore necessitate coartatus a fratre nostro Macedonio decem et septem solidos accepi, quos in causam eius continuo dedi ...*

103 Aug. ep. 268.3 to plebs and presbyters of Hippo: *Scripsi etiam presbyteris, ut, si quid minus fuerit post conlationem sanctitatis vestrae, compleant ex eo, quod habet ecclesia ...*

104 PLRE II. 440–44 s.v. Eutropius 1 and PCBE de l'Afrique 704 s.v. Marinus 4; PLRE II. 724 s.v. Marinus 1.

105 Joh. Chrys. *Eutrop*. 1 (PG 52, 392): Καὶ ἡ μὲν πολημηθεῖσα Ἐκκλησία παρὰ σοῦ τοὺς κόλπους ἥπλωσε καὶ ἐπεδέξατο ("The church that you had wronged opened her arms and took you in"). Cf. *Eutrop.* 3 (PG 52, 593): Ὅτι, φησίν, εἰς ἐκκλησίαν κατέφυγεν ὁ πολεμήσας αὐτήν διηνεκῶς. The *Great Church* at Constantinople, which according to Socrates (*h.e.* 2.16) was renamed at the end of the fourth century, in his lifetime, as the church *of the sacred Wisdom (Sophia)*, was the predecessor of the famed *Hagia Sophia* of Justininian; see Gilbert Dagron, *Naissance d'une capitale. Constantinople et ses institutions de 330 à 451* (Paris: Presses Universitaires de France, 1974), 399, 500.

defend his enemy's life, initially against the populace, then the military and finally the emperor himself.[106]

Marinus, during the persecution of supporters of Heraclianus, had on 13 September 413 ordered the execution of two of Augustine's friends – Fl. Marcellinus, who had presided over the Carthage conference of 411, and his brother Apringius, proconsul of Africa;[107] yet Marinus too enjoyed the protection of the church. There were more than 14 chapters to the report with which Augustine complained about Marinus to His Excellency Caecilianus,[108] former praetorian prefect of the West, currently successor to the executed Apringius empowered by the court to deal with the 'rebellion of Heraclian';[109] "He who had cruelly thrown the entire Church into mourning", after his own fall from power, "took refuge under the Church's right of asylum (sc. at Carthage) after offending his pa-

---

106 See the sermon on "Ματαιότης ματαιοτήτων, καὶ πάντα ματαιότης" (Joh. Chrys. *Eutrop*. 1: PG 52, 391), in which the bishop characterised Eutropius – alluding to *Eccl*. 1.2. – as an example of the "transience of earthly glory". Joh. Chrys. *Eutrop*. 2 (PG 52, 393): Τῇ γὰρ προτεραίᾳ, ὅτε ἐπ' αὐτὸν ἦλθον ἐκ τῶν βασιλικῶν αὐλῶν πρὸς βίαν ἀφελκύσαι βουλόμενοι, καὶ τοῖς σκεύεσι προσέδραμε τοῖς ἱεροῖς (The day before, when soldiers came from the imperial palace to take him by force, he fled into the sanctuary and to the altar). *Eutr*. 5 (PG 52, 396): ἐξαρπάσωμεν τοῦ κινδύνου τὸν αἰχμάλωτον, τὸν φυγάδα, τὸν ἱκέτην, ἵνα καὶ αὐτοὶ τῶν μελλόντων ἀγαθῶν ἐπιτύχωμεν … (Let us therefore save the captive, the refugee, the supplicant from peril, that we may ourselves be rewarded in Heaven). Cf. Socr. *h.e.* 6.5 und Soz. *h.e.* 8.7.4. Eutropius initially got off lightly with confiscation of his possessions and exile on Cyprus, but then in 399 was executed for high treason (*CTh* 9.40.17). See Alan Cameron and Jacqueline Long: *Barbarians and Politics at the Court of Arcadius* (Berkeley and Los Angeles: University of California Press, 1993), 318 and 325, and Dagron, *Constantinople*, 500.
107 *PLRE* II. 711–12 s.v. Fl. Marcellinus 10 and *PLRE* II. 123 s.v. Apringius 1. See Adamiak, "Asking für Human Mercy," 39 on Augustine's ambiguous stance, and Neil McLynn, "Augustine's Roman Empire," in *Christian Politics and Religious Culture in Late Antiquity*, ed. N. McLynn (Farnham and Burlington: Ashgate Variorum, 2009): 40–43 on "the shock of Marcellinus's execution".
108 Cf. the contribution of Gillian Clark to the present volume (61–83).
109 "The most convenient hypothesis" to account for Caecilianus' presence at Carthage, see recently Brent D. Shaw, "Augustine and Men of Imperial Power," *Journal of Late Antiquity* 8 (2015): 46–47, who dates both Augustinian letters (*ep*. 86 and 151) to the year 413, after rejecting all of the long series of earlier reconstructions. In my view, however, an earlier dating for *ep*. 86 in 405 with Caecilianus as a vicar of Africa, probably promoted to proconsul (McLynn, "Augustine's Roman Empire," 37–38 and *PLRE* II. 245–46 s.v. Caecilianus 1, on the problems cf. *PCBE de l'Afrique* 178–79 s.v. Caecilianus 6) cannot be excluded, as "the proconsul of Africa received appeals from the other provinces of the African diocese, thus having in them a jurisdiction concurrent with that of the vicar." See Arnold H.M. Jones, *The Later Roman Empire (LRE) 284–602* (Oxford: Blackwell, 1990), 481, based on *CTh* 11.30.62 (A.D. 405) to Diotimus, the predecessor of Apringius, and Val. III, *Nov*. 13.12 (A.D. 445).

tron (the emperor Honorius). He could not be denied it".¹¹⁰ Church asylum and the current power-political networks linking Marinus and Caecilianus had here prevailed over older ecclesiastical networks. Augustine, who had praised his old friend (*vetus amicum*) Caecilianus for his "diligence in Christian piety" (*pietatis Christianae diligentia*), who had claimed him as "a spiritual son" (*suscipiendus filius*) and who in 409 had invoked the law of the praetorian prefect, now denounced the passivity of the selfsame *vir illustris* in the matter of the Marinus case as the conduct "of a catechumen" rather than that of a believer and dutiful official of his seniority, his past record and his righteousness:¹¹¹ "If you fail to exert yourself on behalf of the common good," thundered the culminating passage of Augustine's letter, before it broke off, "it would be better to spend your nights and days in sleep than to keep watch in labours of the state that bring no benefit to people".¹¹²

---

110 Aug. *ep.* 151.11: *Gratuita igitur crudelitate nulla necessitate … atrociter contristavit ecclesiam* (sc. Marinus), … <u>cuius ecclesiae</u> etiam ipse cum patronum offendisset, <u>petivit auxilium</u> nec ei potuit denegari. Marinus, zelo stimulatus an auro corruptus, was recalled from Africa and dismissed (Oros. *hist.* 7.42.17).

111 Aug. *ep.* 151.1: *Nam <u>veterem amicum</u> et … talem ac tantum virum in peregrinis positum curisque publicis laborantem … ep.* 86: *Administrationis tuae castitas et fama virtutum, <u>pietatis quoque Christianae</u> laudanda diligentia et fida sinceritas … ep.* 86: *… dolemus regionem Hipponensem-Regiorum et ei vicinas partes confines Numidiae praesidiali edicti tui vigore nondum adiuvari meruisse, domine eximie et in Christi caritate vere meritoque honorabilis ac <u>suscipiende fili</u>.* Despite Shaw's reservations ("Augustine and Men of Imperial Power," 44–46) based on the common name and the wording of the edict, Caecilianus, the addressee of *ep.* 86 and 151, seems to be the same person as the high-ranking official who is styled *excellentia tua* (86; 151.14); on the appellate jurisdiction cf. Jones above, *LRE* 481 (n. 109). Yet it remains uncertain whether Caecilianus was a baptized Christian or a catechumen, as the address "suscipiende fili," spiritual son, can mean either one. See Gillian Clark, "Letters and the City of God," in *Scrinium Augustini. The World of Augustine's Letters*, eds. Przemysław Nehring et al., IPM 76 (Turnhout: Brepols, 2017): 192–94 citing Aug. *ep.* 1 A* to Firmus.

112 Aug. *ep.* 151.14: *Unum est autem …, quod in te molestissime fero, <u>quod</u>, cum sis aetatis et huius vitae atque probitatis, <u>adhuc vis esse catechumenus</u>, quasi fideles non possint …, tanto fidelius ac melius administrare rem publicam. … Si enim hoc (i.e. quod bene sit hominibus) <u>non agitis</u>, vel dormire satius est noctes diesque quam vigilare in laboribus publicis nulli utilitate hominum profuturis.* Augustine's wording "You still **wish** to be a catechumen" is to be understood as a reproach of passivity in "a beginner in Christian faith," who should show greater commitment to receiving baptism. See Clark's illuminating distinction, "Letters and the City of God," esp. 202: A committed Christian, as opposed to a catechumen, "needed to act, not to discuss" Christian topics. Augustine alludes here to the broken promises to await the emperor's reply, and to Caecilianus' oath, likewise broken; cf. 151.5 (*falsae promissiones* resp. *nobis ita iurasti*). It must be doubted whether Augustine ever received a response to his "hard demands," see Shaw, "Augustine and Men of Imperial Power," 47. For a different view see McLynn, "Augustine's Roman Em-

Bibliography

Primary Sources

Ambrose, *Opera, pars I–IV*, ed. Karl Schenkl, CSEL 32, Prague–Vienna–Leipzig: F. Tempsky and G. Freytag, 1897–1902.
Ambrose, *Les Devoirs livres I–III*, ed. and trans. Maurice Testard; Introduction et livre I, Paris: Les Belles Lettres, 1984; livres II–III, Paris: Les Belles Lettres, 1992.
Antonius Placentinus, *Itinerarium*, ed. Paul Geyer, Itineraria et alia geographica, CChr.SL 175, Turnhout: Brepols, 1965, 127–53.
Augustine, *Epistulae*, ed. Alois Goldbacher, CSEL 34, 44, 57, 58, Prague–Vienna–Leipzig: Hölder, Pichler, F. Tempsky and G. Freytag, 1895, 1904, 1911, 1923.
Augustine, *De civitate Dei libri XXII*, ed. Bernhard Dombart, Alfons Kalb and Johannes Divjak, 5th ed., Stuttgart and Leipzig: Teubner, 1993.
Augustine, *De cura pro mortibus gerenda*, ed. Josef Zycha, CSEL 41, Prague–Vienna–Leipzig: F. Tempsky and G. Freytag, 1900, 621–60.
Basil of Caesarea, *The Letters*, 4 vols., ed. Roy J. Deferrari, LCL, London: Heinemann, Cambridge, Mass.: Harvard University Press, 1926–34.
Cicero, *De officiis*, ed. Michael Winterbottom, Oxford: Clarendon Press, 1994.
Cicero, *Academica*, ed. and comm. James S. Reid, repr. 2nd ed. London: Macmillan, 1885; Hildesheim: Georg Olms, 1984.
Concilia Galliae 314–506, vol. 1: *Concilium Nemausense a. 394 vel 396*, ed. Charles Munier (de Clerk = ed. Concilia Galliae a. 511–695), CChr.SL 148, Turnhout: Brepols, 1963, p. 50–51.
Conciliengeschichte. Nach den Quellen bearbeitet von Carl J. Hefele, vol. 1–2, 2nd ed., Freiburg i. Br: Herder, 1873 and 1875.
Ecclesiae occidentalis monumenta iuris antiquissima canonum et conciliorum Graecorum interpretationes Latinae, ed. Cuthbert H. Turner, vol. 1, Oxford: Clarendon Press, 1899.
Didache. Traditio Apostolica. Zwölf-Apostel-Lehre. Apostolische Überlieferung, FC 1, trans. Georg Schöllgen, FC 1, Freiburg i.Br.: Herder, 1991.
Gaudentius of Brescia, *Tractatus XXI*, ed. Ambrosius Glück, *CSEL* 68, Vienna–Leipzig: F. Tempsky and G. Freytag, 1936.
Gregory of Nazianzus, *Discours 42–43*, ed. and trans. Jean Bernardi, SC 384, Paris: Les Éditions du Cerf, 1992.
Itinerarium Burdigalense, ed. Paul Geyer and Otto Cuntz, Itineraria et alia geographica, CChr.SL 175, Turnhout: Brepols, 1965, 1–26.
Itinerarium Egeriae, ed. Aet. Franceschini and Robert Weber, Itineraria et alia geographica, CChr.SL 175, Turnhout: Brepols, 1965, 35–90.
Jerome, *Epistulae*, ed. Isidor A. Hilberg, CSEL 54–56, Vienna–Leipzig: F. Tempsky and G. Freytag, 1910–18.

---

pire," 42–43, who dates Aug. *ep.* 151 too late "in the aftermath of Marcellinus' rehabilitation" of 30 Aug. 414 (*CTh* 16.5.55 to Julianus, proconsul of Africa) and conjectures that Caecilianus needs Augustine's endorsement.

Jerome, *Chronicon*. Eusebius' Werke VII, ed. Rudolf Helm and Ursula Treu, GCS 47, 3rd ed. Berlin: Walter de Gruyter, 1984.

Jerome, *Opera exegetica IV: Commentariorum in Hiezechielem libri XIV*, ed. F. Glorie, CChr.SL 75, Turnhout: Brepols, 1964.

Jerome, *Tractatus sive homiliae in psalmos. In Marci evangelium aliaque varia argumenta*, ed. Germain Morin, CChr.SL 78, 2nd ed. Turnhout: Brepols, 1958.

John Chrysostom, *In Eutropium homiliae*, ed. Jacques Paul Migne, PG 52, Paris: Migne, Petit-Montrouge, 1859, col. 389–414.

John Chrysostom, *Lettres à Olympias*. 2nd ed. augmentée de la *Vie anonyme d'Olympias*, ed. and trans. Anne-Marie Malingrey, SC 13bis, Paris: Les Éditions du Cerf, 1968.

John Chrysostom, *Sermons sur la Genèse*, ed. and trans. Laurence Brottier, SC 433, Paris: Les Éditions du Cerf, 1998.

Lactantius, L. Caecilius Firmianus, *Divinarum institutionum libri septem*, ed. Eberhard Heck, BT, libri I–II Munich: Saur, 2005; III–VI Berlin: Walter de Gruyter, 2009.

Orosius, *Historiae adversum paganos libri VII, accedit eiusdem liber apologeticus*, ed. Karl Zangemeister, CSEL 5, Vienna: Karl Gerold d.J., 1882.

Palladius, *Historia Lausiaca*, ed. Cuthbert Butler, vol. II, Cambridge: Cambridge University Press 1904, repr. Hildesheim: Georg Olms, 1967.

Palladius, *Dialogue sur la Vie de Jean-Chrysostome*, vol. I–II, ed. and trans. Anne-Marie Malingrey and Philippe Leclercq, SC 341–42, Paris: Les Éditions du Cerf, 1988.

Paulinus Nolanus, *Epistulae. Carmina*, ed. Wilhelm von Hartel, CSEL 29–30, Vienna 1894. Editio altera supplementis aucta curante Margit Kamptner, Vienna: Österreichische Akademie der Wissenschaften, 1999.

Photius, *Bibliothèque*, ed. and trans. René Henry, Index par Jacques Schamp, vol. 1–9, Paris: Les Belles Lettres, 1959–91.

Possidius, *Vita Augustini*, ed. Anton A.R. Bastiaensen, in *Vita dei santi III*, Turnhout: Brepols, 1974, 130–240.

Sidoine Apollinaire, *Lettres*, ed. and trans. André Loyen, vol. II–III, Paris: Les Belles Lettres, 1970.

Sokrates, *Kirchengeschichte*, ed. and trans. Günther Christian Hansen, GCS N.F. 1, Berlin: Akademie-Verlag, 1995.

Sozomenus, *Historia ecclesiastica. Kirchengeschichte*, ed. Joseph Bidez and Günther Christian Hansen (GCS N.F. 4), trans. Günther Christian Hansen, FC 73/1–4, Turnhout: Brepols, 2004.

Sulpicius Severus, *Libri qui supersunt*, ed. Karl Halm, CSEL 1, Vienna: Karl Gerold d.J., 1866.

Sulpicius Severus, *Vie de Saint Martin I–III*, ed. and trans. Jacques Fontaine, SC 133–35, Paris: Les Éditions du Cerf, 1967–69.

Uranius, *Epistula de obitu*, ed. Jacques Paul Migne, PL 53, Paris: Migne, Petit-Montrouge, 1847, col. 859–66.

Valerius of Bierzo, *Lettre sur la bienheureuse Égérie*, ed. and trans. Manuel C. Díaz y Díaz. In *Égérie. Journal de voyage (Itinéraire)*, ed. and trans. Pierre Maraval, SC 296, Paris: Les Éditions du Cerf, 1982, 321–49.

Vergilius, P. Maro, *Aeneis*, ed. Gian Biago Conte, BT, Berlin: Walter de Gruyter, 2009.

Vie de Sainte Mélanie, ed. and trans. Denys Gorce, SC 90, Paris: Les Éditions du Cerf, 1962.

Zosimus, *Histoire nouvelle*, livres 1–6, ed. and trans. François Paschoud, Paris: Les Belles Lettres: 1971, 1979, 1986, 1989.

Secondary Literature

Adamiak, Stanisław. "Asking for Human Mercy. Augustine's Intercession with the Men in Power". In *Scrinium Augustini. The World of Augustine's Letters*, edited by Przemysław Nehring, M. Strozynski & R. Toczko, IPM 76, 19–40. Turnhout: Brepols, 2017.

Arterbury, Andrew E.. *Entertaining Angels: Early Christian Hospitality in its Mediterranean Setting*. New Testament Monographs 8. Sheffield: Sheffield Phoenix Press, 2005.

Blowers, Paul M. "Interpreting Scripture." In *The Cambridge History of Christianity*, vol. 2: *Constantine to c. 600*, edited by Augustine Casiday and Frederick W. Norris, 618–636. Cambridge: Cambridge University Press, 2007.

Bourdieu, Pierre: *Le sense pratique*. Paris: Les éditions de Minuit, 1980; trans. Günter Seib: *Sozialer Sinn. Kritik der theoretischen Vernunft*. Frankfurt a. M.: Suhrkamp Verlag, 2009.

Brown, Peter. *Through the Eye of a Needle. Wealth, the Fall of Rome, and the Making of Christianity in the West, 350–550 AD*. Princeton and Oxford: Princeton University Press, 2012.

Brown, Peter. *The Body and Society. Men, Women and Sexual Renunciation in Early Christianity*. New York: Columbia University Press, 1988, repr. London: Faber and Faber, 1991.

Brown, Peter. 1968. "The Patrons of Pelagius: The Roman Aristocracy between East and West". *JThS* n.s. 19: 93–114 = In *Religion and Society in the Age of Saint Augustine*, 208–26. London: Wipf and Stock Publishers, 1972.

Cain, Andrew. *The Letters of Jerome. Asceticism, Biblical Exegesis, and the Construction of Christian Authority in Late Antiquity*. Oxford: Oxford University Press, 2009.

Cain, Andrew, ed. and trans. *Jerome's Epitaph on Paula: A Commentary on the Epitaphium Sanctae Paulae*. Oxford: Oxford University Press, 2013.

Cameron, Averil. "Education and Literary Culture. Conclusion". In *The Late Empire A.D. 337–425*, edited by Averil Cameron and Peter Garnsey, CAH 13, 704–7. Cambridge: Cambridge University Press, 1998.

Cameron, Averil. "Remaking the Past." In *Late Antiquity. A Guide to the Postclassical World*, edited by Glen W. Bowersock, Peter Brown, and Oleg Grabar, 1–20. Cambridge [Mass.] and London: The Belknap Press of Harvard University Press, 1999.

Clark, Elizabeth A. "Piety, Propaganda, and Politics in the Life of Melania the Younger," *StPatr* 18.2 (1989): 167–83.

Clark, Gillian. "Letters and the City of God". In *Scrinium Augustini. The World of Augustine's Letters*, edited by Przemysław Nehring, M. Strozynski and R. Toczko, IPM 76, 181–202. Turnhout: Brepols, 2017.

Clark, Gillian. "Pilgrims and Foreigners: Augustine on Travelling Home". In *Travel, Communication and Geography in Late Antiquity. Sacred and Profane*, edited by Linda Ellis and Frank L. Kidner, 149–58. Aldershot: Ashgate, 2004.

Conybeare, Catherine. *Paulinus Noster. Self and Symbols in the Letters of Paulinus of Nola*. Oxford: Oxford University Press, 2000.

Dagron, Gilbert. *Naissance d'une capitale. Constantinople et ses institutions de 330 à 451*. Paris: Presses Universitaires de France, 1974.

Dam, Raymond Van. *Becoming Christian. The Conversion of Roman Cappadocia*. Philadelphia: University of Pennsylvania Press, 2003.

Ebbeler, Jennifer V.. *Pedants in the Apparel of Heroes? Cultures of Latin Letter-Writing from Cicero to Ennodius*. Ph.D. diss. University of Pennsylvania, 2001.

Eco, Umberto. "Die Enzyklopädie als Labyrinth". In *Kulturwissenschaft*, edited by Uwe Wirth, 262–67. Frankfurt am Main: Suhrkamp, 2008.
Elsner, Jaś. "Piety and Passion: Contest and Consensus in the Audiences for Early Christian Pilgrimage". In *Pilgrimage in Graeco-Roman & Early Christian Antiquity*, edited by Jaś Elsner and Ian Rutherford, 411–34. Oxford: Oxford University Press, 2005.
Gemeinhardt, Peter. *Das lateinische Christentum und die antike pagane Bildung*. Tübingen: J.C.B. Mohr Siebeck, 2007.
Gorce, Denys. *Les voyages, l'hospitalité et le port des lettres dans le monde chrétien des IV et V siècles*. Paris: Librairie Auguste Picard, 1925.
Granerød, G., Arterbury, Andrew E. et al.. "Hospitality". In *EBR* 12: 449–59. Berlin: Walter de Gruyter, 2016.
Grig, Lucy. "Throwing Parties for the Poor: Poverty and Splendour in the Late Antique Church". In *Poverty in the Roman World*, edited by Margaret Atkins and Robin Osborne, 145–61. Cambridge: Cambridge University Press.
Harries, Jill. "'Treasure in Heaven': Property and Inheritance among Senators of Late Rome". In *Marriage and Property*, edited by Elizabeth M. Craik, 54–70. Aberdeen: Aberdeen University Press, 1984.
Hiltbrunner, Otto. *Gastfreundschaft in der Antike und im frühen Christentum*, Darmstadt: Wissenschaftliche Buchgesellschaft, 2005.
Hiltbrunner, Otto, Gorce, Denys and Wehr, Hans. "Gastfreundschaft". In *RAC* 8: 1061–1123. Stuttgart: Anton Hiersemann, 1972.
Hunt, David. *Holy Land Pilgrimage in the Later Roman Empire 312–460*. Oxford: Oxford University Press, 1982.
Jones, Arnold H.M.. *The Later Roman Empire 284–602. A Social, Economic, and Administratice Survey (LRE)*, vol. 1–2. Oxford: Blackwell, repr. 1990.
Kolb, Anne. *Transport und Nachrichtentransfer im Römischen Reich*. Berlin: Akademie Verlag, 2000.
Konstan, David. *Friendship in the Classical World*. Cambridge: Cambridge University Press, 1997.
Lehmann, Tomas. *Paulinus Nolanus und die Basilica Nova in Cimitile/Nola*, Wiesbaden: Reichert, 2004.
Lenski, Noel. "Empresses in the Holy Land: The Creation of a Christian Utopia in Late Antique Palestine." In *Travel, Communication and Geography in Late Antiquity. Sacred and Profane*, edited by Linda Ellis and Frank L. Kidner, 113–24. Aldershot: Ashgate, 2004.
Liebeschuetz, John Hugo Wolfgang Gideon. *Barbarians and Bishops: Army, Church and State in the Age of Arcadius and Chrysostom*. Oxford: Clarendon Press, 1992.
Löw, Martina. *Raumsoziologie*. Frankfurt am Main: Suhrkamp, 2001.
Malkin, Irad. *A Small Greek World: Networks in the Ancient Mediterranean*. Oxford: Oxford University Press, 2011.
Mango, Cyril, Vickers, Michael, and Francis, E.D.. "The Palace of Lausus at Constantinople and its Collection of Ancient Statues", *Journal of the History of Collections* 4 (1992): 89–98.
Matthews, John. *Western Aristocracies and Imperial Court AD 364–425*. Oxford 1975: Oxford University Press, repr. 1990: Oxford Clarendon Press, 1990.

Mauss, Marcel. *Essai sur le don*. Paris: Presses Universitaires de France, 1950; trans. Eva Moldenhauer, *Die Gabe. Form und Funktion des Austauschs in archaischen Gesellschaften*. Frankfurt am Main: Suhrkamp, 2009.

McLynn, Neil B. *Ambrose of Milan. Church and Court in a Christian Capital*. Berkeley, Los Angeles, London: University of California Press, 1994.

McLynn, Neil B. "Augustine's Roman Empire". In *Christian Politics and Religious Culture in Late Antiquity*, edited by N.B. McLynn, 29–44. Farnham and Burlington: Ashgate Variorum, 2009.

Mratschek, Sigrid. *Der Briefwechsel des Paulinus von Nola. Kommunikation und soziale Kontakte zwischen christlichen Intellektuellen*. Göttingen: Vandenhoeck & Ruprecht, 2002.

Mratschek, Sigrid. "*Multis enim notissima est sanctitas loci:* Paulinus and the Gradual Rise of Nola as a Center of Hospitality," *JECS* 9 (2001): 511–53.

Mratschek, Sigrid. "Zirkulierende Bibliotheken. Medien der Wissensvermittlung & christliche Netzwerke." In *L'étude des correspondances dans le monde romain*, edited by Jean-Christophe Jolivet et al., 325–50. Lille: HALMA, 2011.

Mratschek, Sigrid. "Augustine, Paulinus, and the Question of Moving the Monastery." In *Inter cives necnon peregrinos. Essays in Honour of Boudewijn Sirks*, edited by Jan Hallebeek et al., 545–61. Göttingen: Vandenhoeck & Ruprecht, 2014.

Mratschek, Sigrid. "The Unwritten Letters of Augustine of Hippo." In *Scrinium Augustini. The World of Augustine's Letters*, edited by Przemysław Nehring, M. Strozynski and R. Toczko, IPM 76, 57–77. Turnhout: Brepols, 2017 (revised and extended English version of "Die ungeschriebenen Briefe des Augustinus von Hippo." In *In Search of Truth': Augustine, Manichaeism and other Gnosticism. Studies for Johannes van Oort at Sixty*, edited by Jacob A. van den Berg et al., 109–22. Leiden and Boston: Brill, 2011.

Mratschek, Sigrid. "Geben und Nehmen in den Briefen des Paulinus von Nola: der himmlische Bankier und der Wohltäter der Armen." In *Zwischen Alltagskommunikation und literarischer Identitätsbildung: Studien zur lateinischen Epistolographie in Spätantike und Frühmittelalter*, editd by Gernot M. Müller, 109–129. Stuttgart: Franz Steiner, 2018.

Pitts, Martin and Versluys, Miguel J., eds. *Globalisation and the Roman World. World, Connectivity and Material Culture*. Cambridge: Cambridge University Press, 2015.

Patrich, Joseph. *Studies in the Archaeology and History of Caesarea Maritima. Caput Judaeae, Metropolis Palaestinae*. Leiden: Brill, 2011.

Pohl, Christine Dorothy. *Making Room: Recovering Hospitality as a Christian Tradition*. Grand Rapids: Eerdmans, 1999.

Puzicha, Michaela. *Christus peregrinus. Die Fremdenaufnahme (Mt 25,35) als Werk der privaten Wohltätigkeit im Urteil der Alten Kirche*. Münster: Aschendorff, 1990.

Rebenich, Stefan. *Hieronymus und sein Kreis. Prosopographische und sozialgeschichtliche Untersuchungen*. Stuttgart: Franz Steiner, 1992.

Rebillard, Éric. "Late Antique Limits of Christianess." In *Group Identity and Religious Individuality in Late Antiquity*, edited by Éric Rebillard and Jörg Rüpke, 293–317. Washington: The Catholic University of America Press, 2015.

Renfrew, Colin, and Cherry, John F., eds. *Peer Polity Interaction and Socio-Political Change*. Cambridge: Cambridge University Press, 1986.

Satlow, Michael L., ed. *The Gift in Antiquity*, Malden, MA and Oxford: Wiley-Blackwell, 2013.

Shaw, Brent D., "Augustine and Men of Imperial Power," *JLA* 8 (2015): 32–59.
Siems, Harald. "Asyl in der Kirche? Wechsellagen des Kirchenasyls im Mittelalter," in *Das antike Asyl. Kultische Grundlagen, rechtliche Ausgestaltung und politische Funktion*, edited by Martin Dreher, 261–99. Cologne, Weimar, Vienna: Böhlau, 2003.
Sotinel, Claire. "La circulation de l'information dans les Églises." In *La circulation de l'information dans les États antiques*, edited by Laurent Capdetrey and Jocelyne Nelis-Clément, 177–94. Bordeaux, Ausonius. Diffusion Paris: de Boccard, 2006.
Tiersch, Claudia. *Johannes Chrysostomus in Konstantinopel (398–404). Weltsicht und Wirken eines Bischofs in der Hauptstadt des Oströmischen Reiches*. Tübingen: J.C.B. Mohr Siebeck, 2002.
Trout, Dennis E. *Paulinus of Nola. Life, Letters, and Poems*. Berkeley, Los Angeles, London: University of California Press, 1999.
Viard, Paul, "Hospitalité." In *DSp* 7: 808–31. Paris: Bauchesne, 1969.

Carmen Angela Cvetković
Niceta of Remesiana's Visits to Nola: Between Sacred Travel and Political Mission

At the very dawn of the fifth century, Paulinus of Nola received on at least two occasions the visits of Niceta, the bishop of Remesiana, a town from the Roman province of Dacia Mediterranea situated on the important road *Via Militaris*. This road traversed the centre of the Illyrian peninsula and constituted the main overland connection between Western Europe and Constantinople. Niceta's first visit to Nola took place in the winter of 400 on the occasion of the feast of St Felix, Paulinus' patron saint celebrated on January 14. According to Paulinus, he returned to Nola a few years later during the winter of 403 taking part again in St Felix's annual celebration. Paulinus seems to have been so touched by Niceta's gesture, that he expressed his high regard for the Dacian bishop in *Epistula 29*, a letter addressed to Sulpicius Severus in the spring of 400 and then went on to dedicate not one but two poems to his newly acquired Illyrian friend: *Carmen 17*, a *propemticon*[1] or farewell poem composed by Paulinus upon Niceta's departure from Nola in January 400 and *Carmen 27*, a *natalicium*,[2] usually written in honor of St Felix but dedicated this time partially also to Niceta's second visit to Nola.[3] Paulinus' testimony about Niceta represents the most extensive and substantial ancient evidence about the Illyrian bishop who is mentioned only briefly in a handful of other ancient sources. There is no information about the early part of Niceta's life, although a certain Nicha figures as one of the addressees of a letter sent by bishop Germinius of Sirmium in 365/366 to a number of Illyrian bishops.[4] It has been argued that Nicha might be a corruption for Ni-

---

[1] For a discussion of the genre of this poem see, Robert Kirstein, *Paulinus Nolanus* (Basel: Schwabe & Co, 2000), 74–86 and André Basson, "A Transformation of Genres in Late Latin Literature: Classical Literary Tradition and Ascetic Ideals in Paulinus of Nola," in *Shifting Frontiers in Late Antiquity*, eds. R.W. Mathisen and Hagith Sivan (Aldershot: Variorum, 1996): 267–276.
[2] The bulk of Paulinus' poems are written in this genre. They commemorate "the day when Felix, by dying, was 'born' from earth to Heaven," see Peter Brown, *The Cult of the Saints: Its Rise and Function in Latin Christianity* (Chicago: Chicago University Press, 1981), 57.
[3] Paulinus' account of Niceta includes *Epistula* 29.14 (CSEL ²29, 261.19–262.6 Hartel), *Carmen* 17 (CSEL ²30, 81–96 Hartel) and *Carmen* 27 (CSEL ²30, 262–291 Hartel).
[4] This letter of the bishop Germinius of Sirmium has been preserved in Hilary of Poitiers, *Fragmenta* B 12 (CSEL 65, 160.22–24 Feder). An additional contemporary source for Niceta is Innocentius I of Rome who mentions the Illyrian bishop in *Epistula* 16 and *Epistula* 17 (PL 20,

ceta as it would have been easy to mistake *et* for *h* in reading the Dacian wax tablets.⁵ If this is the case then Niceta ought to have been at the beginning of his episcopal career and at least thirty years of age according to the canons of an ancient council.⁶ The only certain dates in his life are his visits to Nola in Italy, in the years 400 and 403, recorded by Paulinus of Nola and the mention of his name in two letters of the bishop of Rome Innocent I (402–417) from 412 and 414 addressed to Illyrian bishops.⁷ Based on this patchy evidence it has been conjectured that Niceta lived most likely between 335 and 414.⁸

At first glance this kind of fragmentary material seems totally inadequate for a study of networks which requires more abundant information about social contacts. And yet, as Paulinus' account about Niceta contains some evidence about small-scale social interaction among church elites from different Roman provinces, it may provide valuable insights regarding the formation and development of trans-regional ecclesiastical networks in an age when Christianity spread at a rapid pace across the Late Roman Empire. Therefore, the aim of this paper is confined to exploring only a segment of Paulinus' extensive ecclesiastical network, namely his ties with his far distant visitor, the Illyrian bishop Niceta.⁹ In exam-

---

520 A–521 A; 526D–527 A, published also as *Epistula* 9 and *Epistula* 14 in *Vetustissimae epistulae romanorum pontificum*, ed. Hermann-Josef Sieben, FC 58/2, Freiburg: Herder, 2014, 429–431 and 462–465). Other ancient sources that mention Niceta are: Gennadius of Marseille, *De viris illustribus* 22 (TU 14/1a, 70.13–24 Richardson); Cassiodorus, *Institutiones divinarum et saecularium litterarum* 1.16.3 (FC 39/1 216.24–217.6 Bürsgens); an *Ordo de catechizandis rudibus* to be found in *Codex Monacensis lat.* 6325 [Fris. 125], saec. IX, fol. 139v in A.E. Burn, "Neue Texte zur Geschichte des apostolischen Symbols", *Zeitschrift für Kirchengeschichte* 25 (1904) 152 which mentions Niceta in a list of Latin ecclesiastical authors between Hilary and Jerome. The Catholic Church remembers Niceta every year on June 22: *Eodem die sancti Nicetae, Romatianae civitatis episcopi, doctrina, sanctisque moribus clari*. See Caesarius Baronius (ed.), *Martyrologium Romanum. Ad Novam Kalendarii rationem, & Ecclesiasticae historiae veritatem restitutum*, Gregorii XIII. Pont. Max. Iussu Editum, Coloniae Aggrippinae 1603, 117.

5 Andrew E. Burn, *Niceta of Remesiana: His Life and Works* (Cambridge: Cambridge University Press, 1905), xxxvii–xxxviii.
6 According to Canon 11 of the Council of Neocaesarea (c. 315) a presbyter should be at least thirty years of age when ordained regardless of his merit, see P. Schaff and H. Wace, eds. *Nicene & Post-Nicene Fathers,* Second series, Vol.14 (Edinburgh: T&T Clark), 244.
7 On the dating of Innocent's *Epistula* 16 and 17 to Illyrian bishops, see Geoffrey Dunn, "The Letter of Innocent I to Marcian of Niš" in *Saint Emperor Constantine and Christianity*, ed. Dragiša Bojović (Niš: Centre of Church Studies, 2013): 319–339.
8 Burn, *Niceta of Remesiana*, xxxv, first made this suggestion, which has been accepted by subsequent scholars.
9 The relationship between Paulinus and Niceta has received some scholarly attention. A lengthier treatment is offered by Pierre Fabre, *Saint Paulin de Nole et l'amitié chrétienne* (Paris: Boccard, 1949) 221–231. More recently, other scholars have incidentally touched upon

ining the social ties that bind Paulinus and Niceta, I will rely on a set of guiding questions inspired by the work of earlier social anthropologists on networks whose methodology has shown some advantages when applied to ancient material.[10] Although such a methodology has been mainly used in the study of person's total network,[11] it also allows for an examination of partial networks isolated from the total network on the basis of some criterion such as friendship, patronage, religious affiliation etc.[12] Thus, attention will be first paid to the nature of Paulinus' and Niceta's relationship. We will seek to detect its type, to identify the roles that Niceta and Paulinus occupy in relation to each other and in their own networks, and to understand the norms and expectations that govern their relationship and influence their behavior. The question of intimacy will also be addressed as an indicator of the qualitative nature of their relationship. Subsequently, we will examine how the two clergymen put to work their newly established relationship in order to achieve their respective ends. It is expected that by dealing with these questions some new light will be shed on issues pertaining to ecclesiastical communication which extended beyond the local.

Before turning our attention to these aspects however, it is necessary to verify the soundness of Paulinus' dossier about Niceta when undertaking a study of their relationship because, apart from a short paragraph mentioning the Illyrian bishop in a letter addressed by Paulinus to Sulpicius Severus, the rest consists of two literary poems regarded usually as fictional works and therefore as highly unreliable.

---

some aspects of this relationship, see Denis Trout, *Paulinus of Nola: Life, Letters, and Poems* (Berkeley: University of California Press, 1999), 198–199; 214–215; Sigrid Mratschek, *Der Briefwechsel des Paulinus von Nola: Kommunikation und Soziale Kontakte zwischen christlichen Intellektuellen* (Göttingen: Vandenhoek & Ruprecht, 2002) 544–546 and Sigrid Mratschek, "*Multis enim notissima est sanctitas loci:* Paulinus and the Gradual Rise of Nola as a Center of Christian Hospitality," *JECS* 9 (2001): 541–542.

10 Jeremy Boissevain, *Friends of Friends: Networks, Manipulators and Coalitions* (Oxford: Basil Blackwell, 1974).

11 Margaret Mullet, *Theophylact of Ochrid: Reading the Letters of a Byzantine Archbishop* (Aldershot: Variorum, 1997).

12 Boissevain, *Friends*, 28.

1 Paulinus' literary testimony about Niceta and its historical value

From Paulinus' testimony about Niceta it is possible to gather some valuable information about the episcopal activities of this Illyrian bishop at the turn of the fifth century. In a short passage from *Epistula* 29, Paulinus informs Sulpicius Severus about the 'revered' (*venerabilis*) and 'most learned' (*doctissimus*) bishop Niceta, from Dacia who came to visit him in Nola after he had previously been in Rome where he was much admired, presumably for his learning.[13] In the same passage, it is mentioned that Niceta arrived in Nola after the visit of Melania the Elder and that Paulinus seized the opportunity to read to both of them from the *Vita Martini* authored by his friend Sulpicius Severus. This letter written in the spring of 400 records what is usually regarded as Niceta's first visit to Nola.[14]

Remembering the same first visit, *Carmen* 17 speaks about Niceta's hasty departure from Nola immediately after the feast of St Felix on January 14, despite the dangerous navigation conditions in midwinter. A large part of this poem presents a fairly detailed description of the route Niceta was about to travel on his return voyage from Nola to Dacia. As indications of itineraries in the surviving evidence of this age are extremely rare,[15] the information provided by Paulinus, if accurate, is immensely valuable. He pictures Niceta travelling on a *via spatiosa*[16] through the regions of Southern Italy to Hydruntum and Lupiae (the modern Italian cities of Otranto and Lecce), crossing the Adriatic Sea to Epirus and, avoiding the overland route *Via Egnatia*, continuing his journey by sea around the Greek peninsula to Thessalonike. Paulinus adds several more stations to Niceta's journey: Philippi in Macedonia, Tomi in Scythia Minor, and Scupi in Dardania, the neighboring province of Niceta's Dacia Mediterranea. In addition, Niceta is presented as being fond of hymn singing, a habit imported

---

13 *Epistula* 29.14: *quo genere te et venerabili episcopo atque doctissimo Nicetae, qui ex Dacia Romanis merito admirandus advenerat, et plurimus dei sanctis in veritate non magis tui praedicator quam mei iactans revelavi.*
14 For the dating of this letter and for the dating of Paulinus' works in general see, J. T. Lienhard, *Paulinus of Nola and Early Western Monasticism* (Köln: Hanstein, 1970) 190.
15 Claire Sotinel, "How were Bishops Informed? Information Transmission across the Adriatic Sea in Late Antiquity" in *Travel, Communication and Geography in Late Antiquity: Sacred and Profane*, eds. Linda Ellis and Frank L. Kidner (Aldershot: Ashgate, 2004): 65.
16 Kirstein, *Paulinus Nolanus*, 113 identifies this *via spatiosa* mentioned by Paulinus with *via Traiana*.

by Latin Christians from the East, as an ascetic figure, as a teacher, and as a missionary bishop involved in the conversion to the Roman Christian faith of the tribes of Bessi, Getae, Dacians and of the people of Scythia. Finally, the poem offers also information about how Paulinus viewed his own relationship with the bishop Niceta.

Carmen 27 contains almost no references to contemporary events, but it informs about the second visit of Niceta to Nola who returned to his friend Paulinus during the course of the fourth year since his first travel.[17] This piece of information enabled modern scholars to locate Niceta's second visit to Nola in the winter of 403. A large portion of the poem presents Paulinus leading Niceta on a virtual tour of the monumental architectural complex at Cimitile in order to show to his guest the renovations and the new buildings which have been achieved during their three years of separation. The numerous references to Niceta, Paulinus' main interlocutor in the second half of the poem, divulge little factual information about the Illyrian bishop. We learn only that Niceta had to travel a long way to reach Nola, to cross again the sea during wintertime without being afraid of the Goths.[18]

Among all Paulinus' sources regarding Niceta, it is mainly *Carmen 17* that has been regarded as problematic and in particular the description of Niceta's meandering journey back to his homeland. Scholarly views on this subject vary widely: from those who reject Paulinus' description of Niceta's itinerary as inauthentic and the result of interpolations,[19] to those who claim that Paulinus' text should be accepted but with a major emendation that should read *per Stobitanam urbem* instead of *per Tomitanam urbem*. As Stobi was a town located on the direct route connecting Thessalonike with Remesiana, they argue that it would make more sense to have Niceta travel back home through Stobi rather than through Tomi, the Scythian town on the coast of the Black Sea.[20] There

---

17 *Carmen* 27.333: *venisti tandem quarto mihi redditus anno*
18 *Carmen* 27.338–340.
19 Kirstein, *Paulinus Nolanus*, claims that 52 out of 340 verses need to be considered the result of later interpolations. Among these verses are those which record the cities through which Niceta travelled on his journey back home. Kirstein's arguments have been called into question by Hermann Tränkle, "Vermeintliche Interpolationen bei Paulinus von Nola," *Hermes* 130:3 (2002): 338–361.
20 This emendation has been first suggested in the eighteenth century in *Critica historico- Chronologica in...annales ecclesiasticos...C. Baroni*, ed. F. Pagi (Antwerpen, 1727) 2.13. A.E. Burn, Niceta's first editor, accepts it as uncontroversial. Supporters of this view are mentioned in Y.-M. Duval, "Nicéta d'Aquilée. Histoire, Légende et conjectures anciennes," in *Grado nella storia e nell' arte*, BD 1 (Udine, 1980): 169. Kirstein, *Paulinus Nolanus*, 187–188 dismisses conveniently the entire strophe as interpolation. More recently, the idea of Niceta's journey to Tomi has

are also a few scholars who, despite Paulinus' clear description of Niceta's travel by sea from Italy to Thessalonike circumnavigating the Peloponnese penisula,[21] consider that, after crossing the Adriatic, Niceta must have followed the overland route, the Via Egnatia, either from the harbor of Aulona or Durrachium on the Dalmatian coast to Thessalonike.[22] Finally, there are a couple of isolated voices, including myself, who accept Paulinus' description of Niceta's itinerary as accurate. Hagith Sivan has been the first to observe that Niceta's stop at Philippi in Macedonia does not follow the direct route connecting Thessalonike with Remesiana and that the poem contains also references to Niceta's missionary activity in Scythia, which appear to confirm his voyage as far as Tomi.[23] She defends Paulinus' familiarity with the geography of the eastern provinces reminding of his connections with his mentor, Ausonius, whose close family members held eminent positions in the province of Illyricum and whose works present frequent references to the cities of the Greek world.

To these arguments adduced by Sivan, I would like to add some of my own. A fifth century source, namely Palladius, reports that in 406, only a few years after Niceta's second journey to Italy, an ecclesiastical embassy dispatched to Constantinople in order to carry letters of support for John Chrysostom from Milan, Aquileia and Rome travelled at public expense following the route of the imperial courier.[24] However, after crossing the Adriatic, instead of disembarking from their ship at Durrachium or Aulona in order to follow the Via Egnatia, the shortest route to Constantinople,[25] the envoys continued their maritime travel and coasted Greece to Athens from where they tried to reach first Thessalonike and subsequently Constantinople. The itinerary presented by Palladius coincides with Paulinus' description of the first half of Niceta's journey. This indicates that at the beginning of the fifth century to travel by sea from Italy to Thessalonike

---

been rejected by Alina Soroceanu who conjectures that Niceta's hasty departure from Nola has to do with the bishop's catechetic activity which required him to be present at the beginning of the Lent period in his homeland, see Alina Soroceanu, *Niceta von Remesiana: Seelsorge und Kirchenpolitik im spätantiken unteren Donauraum* (Frankfurt: Peter Lang 2013), 143–144.

21 *Carmen* 17.17–20: *Arctoos procul usque Dacos/ ibis Epiro gemina videndus/ et per Aegeos penetrabis aestus/ Thessalonicem.*

22 P.G. Walsh, *The Poems of Paulinus of Nola* (New York, 1975) 374, n. 21 and Soroceanu, *Niceta von Remesiana*, 138–139.

23 Hagith Sivan, "Nicetas' (of Remesiana) Mission and Stilicho's Illyrican Ambition: Notes on Paulinus of Nola *Carmen* XVII (*propemticon*)," *REAug* 41 (1995): 80.

24 Palladius, *Dialogus* 4.1–3, 4.38. For a detailed discussion of how the embassy of western bishops travelled from Italy to Constantinople see, Sotinel, "How were Bishops Informed?," 65–68.

25 Sotinel, "How were Bishops Informed?," 67.

was not unusual even when there were urgent matters to be communicated. However, the question arises as to why in both situations the ecclesiastical envoys chose another route than the Via Egnatia. A possible reason why travelers of this period were avoiding the overland route between Durrachium and Thessalonike might have been because at the end of the fourth century the road became "a free way for plunder and its security was seriously threatened…Alaric's spree along the Via Egnatia in 395 was a notable example of Gothic disruption of the region".[26] This disruption, which lasted for two decades, may well explain the preference of travelers for maritime, circuitous, yet safer routes between Rome and the eastern provinces of the Roman Empire.

Another argument in favor of Paulinus' accurate geographical information in this poem is to be made in connection with Niceta's missionary work among the tribes of the Bessi, Getae, Dacians and Scythians. If Niceta was busy with converting to Christianity these barbarian people, this would have taken him through northern Macedonia, southern and northern Thrace, to the Danubian provinces of Illyricum on the road indicated by Paulinus. Although the strophes illustrating Niceta's missionary work display a plethora of traditional rhetorical 'othering' techniques,[27] references to 'Scythia' and the 'Scythians' have been too easily dismissed as mere literary *topoi* used as derogatory labels *par excellence* in order to indicate the backwardness and primitivism of these regions and their people.[28] In fact, when trying to gaze beyond the heavy rhetoric of this paragraph, the information provided by Paulinus about some of the people encountered by Niceta on his journey is absolutely factual. For example, Paulinus' description of the Bessi as warriors and gold-seekers corresponds to the account of numerous ancient sources about these people. They locate the Bessi in the region from the Haemus and Rhodope Mountains to the Aegean Sea and refer to them as 'brigands among brigands' and as the best gold-miners of the gold and silver deposits of the Pangaion Mountain. This mountain was situated in the vicinity of Phillipi, the city mentioned by Paulinus as a station in Niceta's journey. The mention to 'both Dacians' (*uterque Dacus*) and the distinction between those who live in the hinterland and those who dwell on the banks of

---

[26] Elizabeth Key Fowden, "Macedonia", in *Late Antiquity: A Guide to the Postclassical World*, eds. Glenn Bowersock, Peter Brown, Oleg Grabar (Cambridge, Mass: Belknap Press, 1999): 549.
[27] For Paulinus' representation of the otherness of the barbarians in this poem, see Carmen Cvetković, "Christianity, *Romanitas* and the Politics of Otherness," in *La naissance de l'autrui: De l'Antiquité à la Renaissance*, ed. Jérôme Lagouanère (Paris: Classiques Garnier 2019): 154–157.
[28] Kirstein, *Paulinus Nolanus*, 214: "Scythe steht hier nicht für ein bestimmtes Volk, sondern wie öfters, generalisierend für verschiedene im Nordosten beheimatete Barbarenvölker."

the Danube,²⁹ is no doubt a correct reference to the inhabitants of the Illyrian province of Dacia which at the end of the fourth century was divided between Dacia Mediterranea and Dacia Ripensis. Paulinus does not say much about the Getae, but it is clear that he does not identify them with the Goths as some interpreters claim.³⁰ The ancient geographer Strabo was the first to describe the Getae as Thracian tribes who lived close to the Black Sea on both sides of the Danube and who spoke the same language as the Dacians.³¹

Finally, by mentioning and describing Niceta's sea journeys across the Adriatic in midwinter, Paulinus brings evidence for the possibility of maritime travel during the winter season when it has long been assumed in modern scholarship that the sea was officially closed for navigation between November and March. Only recently, studies have challenged this traditional view about non-winter sailing, showing that maritime travel during winter months was possible and fairly common albeit more dangerous and not so frequent as in the summer months.³²

I hope that enough has been said in order to safely conclude that when stripped from rhetorical embellishments and exaggerations, far from being a mere figment of his imagination, Paulinus' factual information about Niceta and his journey appears to be surprisingly accurate.

2 Paulinus' relationship with Niceta

Similar difficulties related the nature of the sources need to be borne in mind also when paying attention to the way in which Paulinus represented his ties with Niceta. First, Paulinus's account is one-sided and there is no possibility to know Niceta's view about their relationship. Second, the fact that Paulinus speaks about Niceta in verses rather than prose may give rise to suspicions regarding the sincerity of his enthusiasm for his Illyrian guest, which may be attributed rather to conventions of genre, than to the existence of authentic affection between the two. It has already been observed that when writing to his intimates Paulinus always relies on prose and that the use of verse for his acquaintances may indicate that there is some distance and reserve between Paulinus and his addressees.³³ Despite these reservations however, it is worth exam-

---

29 *Carmen* 17.249–252.
30 Kirstein, *Paulinus Nolanus*, 215.
31 Strabo, *Geographica* 7.3.14.
32 James Beresford, *The Ancient Sailing Season* (Leiden: Brill, 2013), 269.
33 Fabre, *Saint Paulin*, 178.

ining Paulinus' texts as they do not only foreground his personal ties with Niceta but they also offer revealing information about the norms and expectations governing the social conduct of Christian elites. The starting point for this investigation is the forms of address used by Paulinus in relation with Niceta which may enable us to deduce something about the nature and quality of their relationship.

In all sources mentioned, Paulinus speaks of Niceta in highly praising terms. In *Epistula* 29 Niceta is introduced to Sulpicius as a 'revered and most learned bishop'.[34] In the poems, Paulinus refers often to Niceta using the term *sacerdos*, which until the beginning of the fifth century designated habitually the bishop, being only rarely used for presbyters.[35] The titles *pater* or *parens* commonly applied to bishops[36] and employed time and again by Paulinus to address Niceta,[37] indicate that, as a bishop, Niceta occupied a higher position in the ecclesiastical hierarchy than Paulinus, who at the time of Niceta's visit was a simple presbyter. As the same terms are used in order to refer to spiritual guidance, it is certain that Paulinus regarded Niceta not only as a superior in the ecclesiastical ranks, but also as a spiritual mentor[38]. One passage is particularly explicit about Niceta's role as Paulinus' spiritual father and deserves to be quoted: 'He exercises twin rights as teacher and father, both to approve our good achievements and to condemn our bad, to correct our mistakes and kindly organize our future course of action.'[39] In addition, such appellatives may also indicate the fact that Niceta was considerably older than Paulinus. This was an argument used by A.E. Burn, Niceta's first editor, in his attempt to estimate Niceta's age when visiting Nola and in general.[40]

---

34 *Epistula* 29.14: *venerabili episcopo atque doctissimo Nicetae.*
35 *Carmen* 17.43: *sacerdotem domino canentem*; *Carmen* 17.191–192: *usque felices quibus es sacredos/praestitus oras*; *Carmen* 27.154: *sacerdotis redditus*; *Carmen* 27.231: *Nicetes, domini puer atque sacerdos.* For the usage of the term *sacerdos*, see Roger Gryson, *Le prêtre selon Saint Ambroise* (Louvain: Université Catholique de Louvain, 1967) 134–136.
36 See Ernst Jerg, *Vir venerabilis: Untersuchungen zur Titulatur der Bischöfe in den ausserkirchlichen Texten der Spätantike als Beitrag zur Deutung ihrer öffentlichen Stellung* (Wien: Herder, 1970) 149.
37 *Carmen* 17.65: *unde nos iustis precibus tuorum/ qui suum recte repetunt parentem*; *Carmen* 17.245: *Te patrem dicit plaga totae Borrae*; *Carmen* 27.345: *nunc age sancte parens*; *Carmen* 27.360: *ergo, veni pater.*
38 On bishops and mentorship ties, see in this volume the contribution of Peter Gemeinhardt on bishops as religious mentors, pp. 117–149.
39 *Carmen* 27.353–355: *gemino qui iure magistri/ et patris ut bene gesta probet, sic improba damnet,/ corrigat errata et placidus disponat agenda.*
40 Burn, *Niceta of Remesiana*, xxxv.

Often the titles *pater* and *parens* are accompanied by the qualificative 'holy' (*sanctus*).[41] While *sanctus* is another term commonly applied to bishops, in Paulinus' description of Niceta, more than simply an apostrophe, *sanctus* is used in order to illustrate a new idea of a bishop who, at the end of the fourth century, under the influence of popular writings on ecclesiastical leadership, was increasingly expected to set an example through his moral and virtuous conduct.[42]

Niceta is not only acknowledged as a most learned individual (*doctissimus*) but he is also invoked repeatedly throughout Paulinus' poems as a *magister* ('teacher' or 'master') being praised in addition for his wisdom and for his gift of discernment.[43] In Paulinus' works it is only the Apostle Paul and sporadically Augustine who are referred to as *magister*.[44] Since he bestowed this title relatively often on his Illyrian guest, Paulinus must have been genuinely impressed with Niceta's learning and educational activities.

Finally, Niceta is also addressed as a patron (*patronus*), although this title is usually reserved by Paulinus to Felix.[45] Moreover, like Felix, he is considered to be a saint proper[46] and the friend (*amicus*) of Paulinus' heavenly patron.[47] By considering Niceta the friend of Felix, Paulinus bestows upon his Illyrian guest an honor that he never dared to claim for himself, for he never uses the terms *amicitia* or *amicus* in connection with his relationship with Felix.[48] Surprisingly, nowhere in these poems does Paulinus refer directly to Niceta using the word *amicus*, although on several occasions the context allows us to deduce that he considered Niceta to be a friend. For example in *Carmen 27*, he points out that, to Nola, Niceta returned 'in the company of friends', and he suggests that the reason for Niceta's return to Nola is that the latter has been 'conquered

---

[41] *Carmen* 17.8: *sancte Niceta*; *Carmen* 27.324–325: *Tu sancte, paterno / sucipe me Niceta sinu*; *Carmen* 27. 345: *sancte parens*; *Carmen* 27. 360: *nun age sancte parens*.

[42] Claudia Rapp, *Holy Bishops in Late Antiquity: The Nature of Christian Leadership in an Age of Transition* (Berkeley: University of California Press, 2005), 41–55; Rita Lizzi Testa, "The Late Antique Bishop: Image and Reality," in *A Companion to Late Antiquity*, ed. Philip Rousseau (Malden, MA: Wiley-Blackwell, 2009): 535.

[43] *Carmen* 17.247: *et sui discors fera te magistro / pectora...*; *Carmen* 17.321: *non unius populi magistrum*; *Carmen* 27. 233: *ecce deim venit, vir tam bonus ore magistro*; *Carmen* 27.243: *sed quoniam lateri meus assidet ipse magister*; *Carmen* 27. 269: *attentusque diu pascentis in ora magistri*; *Carmen* 27.353: *gemino qui iure magistri/ et patris ut bene gesta probet*.

[44] Fabre, *Saint Paulin*, 226.

[45] *Carmen* 17.306. See Kirstein, *Paulinus Nolanus*, 240.

[46] *Carmen* 27.151.

[47] *Carmen* 27.199.

[48] Catherine Conybeare, *Paulinus Noster: Self and Symbols in the Letters of Paulinus of Nola* (Oxford: Oxford University Press, 2000), 89.

by friendship.'⁴⁹ The fact that Paulinus does not call Niceta directly *amicus* may have various reasons. In general, Paulinus preferred to use the term 'brother' (*frater*) in addressing Christian friends, in accordance with the way in which Christians usually called each other using terms that belonged to the sacred bonds of kinship in order to indicate that their relationships are more intense and special than the secular ones.[50] Only occasionally does Paulinus designate intimate friends such as Severus as *amicus*.[51] Another reason why the term *amicus* is not applied to Niceta might be that, just as *frater*, *amicus* gives the impression that the relationship is based on equality. Niceta, however, is never called a 'brother', but a 'father', clearly indicating that he occupies a superior position in relation with Paulinus.

All the reverential forms of address used by Paulinus in connection with Niceta convey chiefly inequality and reveal a hierarchical or asymmetrical relationship between the two. That Paulinus regarded Niceta as being superior to him is eloquently illustrated by one of the last paragraphs of *Carmen* 17, where Paulinus pictures his Illyrian guest and himself continuing their relationship in the afterlife. Due to his great virtue Niceta is imagined as occupying an elevated position, on the top of a mountain, in the company of other saints and in the proximity of God. In contrast, Paulinus, describes himself humbly as dwelling in a lower station, far distant from the privileged place earned by Niceta[52]. Moreover, as Niceta is considered to be Paulinus' superior both in 'position and in merit', undoubtedly because of his episcopal office as well as his virtuous life, he is required to intercede through his prayers on Paulinus's behalf before God in the same way in which in the social reality of Late Antiquity a patron would be required to intervene on behalf of his client. To imagine that there existed a social hierarchical system in the invisible realm as there existed one in the real world was not something unusual in Late Antiquity.[53] Obviously there are marked differences be-

---

49 *Carmen* 27.163: *Comitatus amicis*; *Carmen* 27.343: *victus amicitia, victus felicis amore*.
50 Stefan Rebenich, "Augustine on Friendship and Orthodoxy," in *A Companion to Augustine*, ed. Mark Vessey (Malden, MA: Wiley Blackwell, 2012): 369. On how Augustine addressed in his letters baptised Christians as *frater* and on other titles used by Christians for their epistles' addressees, see Peter Gemeinhardt, *Das lateinische Christentum und die antike pagane Bildung* (Tübingen: Mohr Siebeck, 2007), 236–240.
51 *Epistula* 11.5.
52 *Carmen* 17.299–318.
53 For how the social web of interpersonal relationships was transferred to the description of spiritual relationships in the invisible realm in Late Antiquity, see Rebenich, "Augustine," 366. Analogies between this world and the next abounded in fourth century Christian literature. See Christopher Kelly, *Ruling the Later Roman Empire* (Cambridge, Mass: Belknap Press, 2004),

tween the two. The earthly hierarchy usually has the emperor positioned at the top, followed by mighty aristocrats who acted as intermediaries for people situated in inferior positions who sought the emperor's help. In the heavenly realm it is God or Christ who occupies the highest spot, while saints, martyrs or bishops (such as Niceta) intercede by means of prayer on behalf of simple believers. One hierarchy is temporal, confined exclusively to the visible world; the other one is spiritual and is present both in this life and in the next. The only hierarchy that matters for Paulinus is that of the invisible and spiritual realm in which he, a simple presbyter, occupies a distinctly lower position than Niceta, a bishop.

When taking into account only the evidence discussed so far the relationship between Paulinus and Niceta appears principally as one of patronage due to its distinct asymmetrical nature. Such impression is strengthened by the fact that it requires a set of obligations on both sides: it is a relationship in which Paulinus owed respect and gratitude in return for Niceta's spiritual and doctrinal guidance and for his intercession as a bishop on Paulinus' behalf both in this world and in the next. And yet, despite depicting a strikingly hierarchical relationship, Paulinus is keen to make extensive use of the language of Christian friendship and to shower Niceta with affection. Thus, although Niceta is not called directly a friend,[54] he is the father for whom above all others Paulinus' love prevails.[55] They are united in unsurpassing love.[56] God has bound them with the hidden bonds of so deep a love, claims Paulinus, that no power can break this inner link. Deriving from Christ's love, their own love transcends space and time and will continue to exist even when their life will come to an end. Therefore, Paulinus does not need to feel sadness over Niceta's hasty departure from Nola, because unity of heart and mind overcomes physical separation. [57]

Several main tenets of Paulinus' theory of Christian friendship are present in the account of his relationship with Niceta: the belief that God creates friendship and that the love of Christian friends for each other derives from the love of Christ; the idea that true friendship cannot exist without a shared devotion to Christ; the claim that no matter how great a separation exists between friends they remain in unity of heart and mind and their bond is eternal.[58] What

---

243–244 for an illustration of how John Chrysostom's vision about the end of the world corresponded to an administrative apocalypse.
54 See above, pp. 188–189.
55 *Carmen* 27.180.
56 *Carmen* 17.69.
57 *Carmen* 17.295–299.
58 Carolinne White, *Christian Friendship in the Fourth Century* (Cambridge: Cambridge University Press, 1992) 153.

seems to be clear from this analysis of Paulinus and Niceta's relationship is that Christian friendship[59] may be established between individuals of unequal status without necessarily the need to abolish this inequality as we might be tempted to expect in light of our own modern ideas about friendship. Describing such unequal or asymmetrical friendships seems not to be something unusual for Paulinus. According to Carolinne White, many of Paulinus' friendships "though very affectionate on both sides, contain more than a hint of the traditional forms of Roman patronage with its formal obligations on either side."[60] Despite the fact that she has not looked at Paulinus' account about Niceta, White has observed that Paulinus' "relationships with such men as Augustine and Jerome are colored by his sense of these men's superiority."[61] The same may be said about the way in which he viewed his relationship with Niceta.

Such conclusion contradicts Catherine Conybeare's claims that Paulinus considered Christian friendship as subsisting only between those who were equals in God's eyes.[62] Moreover, her assertions that Paulinus never uses hierarchical language in addressing those whom he considers to be his friends, as this runs counter to every precept of friendship he espouses, are also at variance with the evidence discussed above concerning Paulinus' description of his relationship with Niceta which is pervaded by his consistent use of indisputable hierarchical terms.

If, based exclusively on its asymmetrical nature, we were to consider the relationship between Niceta and Paulinus as simply a patronage type relationship, then Paulinus' excessive display of affection for Niceta, a guest whom he meets only briefly for the first time and whom he sees again shortly three years later, would appear highly dubious, more dependent on literary conventions than indicative of genuine fondness between the two churchmen. It is only when read in the context of Paulinus' theory of Christian friendship that we may comprehend how it is possible to exhibit such unbridled enthusiasm for a new acquaintance. Elsewhere in his writings, Paulinus claims that Christian friendships are perfect from the very beginning and that they do not need to develop over time in the

---

[59] The literature on Christian friendship is vast. Apart from White, *Christian Friendship*, for a concise view of the topic and further bibliography, see also Sigrid Mratschek, "Friends, Friendship," *Encyclopedia of the Bible and its Reception* 9 (2014): 723–727.
[60] White, *Christian Friendship*, 149.
[61] White, *Christian Friendship*, 149.
[62] Conybeare, *Paulinus Noster* 90. She accepts that Paulinus makes use of the language of patronage only in relationship with Felix, his patron saint.

manner of secular friendships.⁶³ Therefore, Paulinus does not need to restrain his affection for his newly acquired friend on account of not having spent much time together. Related to this belief is the striking idea that all Christians who lead a life devoted to Christ are already friends whether they have met in person or not.⁶⁴ They are members of one body, sharing one head who is Christ, living off one bread and sharing one house.⁶⁵ Furthermore, as God is the one who creates friendship, he is also deemed responsible for predestining certain men to become friends from the beginning of time.⁶⁶

Paulinus' ideas about Christian friendship coupled with the belief that salvation cannot be achieved without the intercession of others need to be borne in mind when attempting to understand his conduct towards his Christian fellow believers. What at first glance might seem incomprehensible or dubious becomes understandable in light of his principles about Christian friendship and his religious beliefs. In fact, many of Paulinus' friendships, including his relationship with Niceta, provide a clear illustration of how religious ideology influences social behavior. Apart from encouraging the rapid formation of new social connections between members of the Christian elite from various parts of the Roman Empire, religious ideology also influences their mode of operation, which differs significantly from that of secular relationships.

3 Ecclesiastical networks in action

While it is important to understand the way in which Paulinus perceived his relationship with his Illyrian guest as this enables us to better comprehend their social behavior, focusing exclusively on the nature of their relationship will offer us only a partial picture about what was exchanged between these two churchmen on the occasion of Niceta's visits in Nola. So far, it has been shown that in this asymmetrical friendship, Paulinus offered unrestrained affection and praise in exchange for spiritual guidance, perhaps also for theological knowledge given the fact that Niceta is recognized as a *magister* and, above all, for Niceta's intercession on his friend's behalf in the spiritual realm. However, their friendship cannot have been limited to an exchange of affection, pleasan-

---

63 See *Epistula* 13.2 to Pammachius and *Epistula* 42.1 to Florentius, the bishop of Cahors. For a discussion of this aspect of Paulinus' theory of friendship see White, *Christian Friendship*, 153–154.
64 *Epistula* 3.1.
65 *Epistula* 13.3.
66 *Epistula* 11.5.

tries, requests and favors. In order to understand more about how both Paulinus and Niceta put their relationship to work, we need to examine their connection in the broader context of Niceta's travels to Italy. Paulinus' fragmentary account will serve as a springboard for the following discussion which will develop rather around Paulinus' silences than around his concrete answers about particular aspects of Niceta's visits.

As a matter of fact, the account about Niceta neglects to answer a simple yet essential question, namely, what could have determined the Illyrian bishop to travel to Italy twice within a relatively short span of time, on each occasion during the winter, and to face in addition to the difficult weather conditions also the threat posed by the Goths, as Paulinus himself reports? Although the reasons behind Niceta's travels may only be conjectured, by delving into a discussion of the possible causes for his long-distance journeys, we hope to gain new insights about episcopal connectivity and communication between the Illyrian and the Italian churches in this obscure period.

An indirect clue for Niceta's travels may be provided by *Epistula* 29 which reveals that prior to visiting Paulinus in Nola, Niceta was in Rome.[67] This led many scholars to suppose that far from being merely a pilgrim at the shrine of St Felix as Paulinus would have us believe, Niceta's visits to Italy, in particular to Rome, might have had also a political purpose. Thus, Burn was the first to suggest that Niceta had business to transact in Rome concerning matters of ecclesiastical discipline in the Illyrian churches affected by the political transfer of *Illyricum orientale* to the eastern empire in 379.[68] As a tentative context for Niceta's visit, Burn hints at the competition between the see of Rome and the see of Constantinople over Eastern Illyricum, based on the assumption that in order to counteract the influence of the Constantinopolitan counterpart, the bishop of Rome, Damasus (366–384) gave vicarial powers to Acholius, the bishop of Thessalonike, making him metropolitan bishop over Eastern Illyricum, as early as 384. Burn assumes that on his return home, Niceta went to inform his metropolitan, the bishop of Thessalonike, and his neighboring fellow bishops from Stobi and Scupi about the results of his journey.

Building her argument along similar lines, more recently, Hagith Sivan sees Niceta's journey as throwing new light on the attempts of the Roman church to extend its jurisdiction over the eastern provinces of the empire.[69] In her view, Niceta's journey as far as Tomi coupled with his missionary work among the people

---

67 *Epistula* 29.14.
68 Burn, *Niceta of Remesiana*, l–lii.
69 Sivan, "Niceta's Mission".

of Scythia, the Bessi, the Getae and the Dacians, have been ordered from Rome with the aim of preparing the way for a Western intervention in these territories. Like Burn, she also claims that Niceta's visits to Italy should be interpreted in the context of the rivalry between the Roman and Constantinopolitan sees generated by their attempts to secure ecclesiastical control over the Eastern Illyricum. Whereas Burn saw the competition between the two main episcopal sees reflected in the creation of the vicariate of Thessalonike, Sivan adduces as main evidence the missionary work organized by John Chrysostom, during his first tenure as bishop of Constantinople, among the Goths settled along the Danube and his correspondence with a number of Macedonian and Illyrian bishops, which, in her view "was meant to drive a wedge between the pope and the Illyrican church."[70]

Without any doubt both Burn and Sivan were correct to point out the 'political' dimension of Niceta's visits to Italy. However, their claim that these travels need to be interpreted in the context of the tensions between Rome and Constantinople is debatable as there is no substantial evidence in the sources of this time to support the existence of such frictions. The vicariate of Thessalonike considered the main source of discord between the two major episcopal sees seems to have been established later than Burn assumed.[71] As for John Chrysostom, the bishop of Constantinople seems to have had a much better relationship with the bishops of Rome and the bishops of Italy than his predecessors and he enjoyed the support of his Western episcopal counterparts throughout his episcopacy and, especially, after his deposition and final exile in 404 when both the bishop of Rome, Innocent I and the emperor Honorius intervened on his behalf.[72]

---

[70] Sivan, "Niceta's Mission", 86.

[71] The claim that the vicariate of Thessalonike was established during Damasus' episcopacy has been rejected by S.L Greenslade, "The Illyrian Churches and the Vicariate of Thessalonica", *JThS* 46 (1945) 17–30 and Charles Pietri, *Roma Christiana: recherches sur l'Église de Rome, son organisation, sa politique, son idéologie de Miltiade à Sixte III (311–430)* (Paris: Éditions du Seuil), 1077–1093. More recently, Geoffrey Dunn argues for the creation of the vicariate of Thessalonike during Siricius' episcopacy (384–399) with the aim to counter the influence of Ambrose of Milan in the region. However, he also observes that at the beginning of the fifth century the authority exercised by Innocent I in regard with the Eastern Illyricum was not all-encompassing, but reduced to judicial matters. The ecclesiastical control over Eastern Illyricum will become a source of increasing animosity between Constantinople and Rome much later in the decades after Innocent I's death, see Geoffrey Dunn, "The Church of Rome as a Court of Appeal in the Early Fifth Century: The Evidence of Innocent I and the Illyrian Churches," *JEH* 64 (2013a) 684 and 679.

[72] See above Palladius' testimony about the embassy of Italian bishops travelling to Constantinople and carrying letters of support for John Chrysostom, pp. 184–185.

Instead of seeing Niceta as an agent of Rome sent on a mission to counter the growing influence of the see of Constantinople over Eastern Illyricum, I propose to search first for the reasons behind Niceta's travels to Italy in Illyricum itself.

Niceta was a pro-Nicene[73] bishop and at the end of the fourth century the links that pro-Nicene Illyrian churches established especially with the church of Milan and other North Italian churches had been drastically disturbed by the Gothic invasions which affected the provinces of Pannonia, Noricum and Dalmatia, thus isolating Eastern Illyricum from their traditional pro-Nicene allies.[74] Moreover, after the death of Ambrose in 397, the authority of the metropolitan see of Milan weakened considerably. In such circumstances deprived of the support that usually came from Milan in matters of doctrinal affairs, one may assume that a pro-Nicene bishop such as Niceta, who belonged to the Latin-speaking area of Illyricum turned most naturally to Rome in his attempt to secure new allies for his active promoting of pro-Nicene Christianity in an area where he most likely still faced opposition from active heterodox churches.[75]

All stops mentioned by Paulinus when describing Niceta's journey are episcopal sees, and, moreover, pro-Nicene episcopal sees. If on his journey back

---

[73] I use the term 'pro-Nicene' in order to designate a form of Christianity whose supporters adopted firmly the Nicene Creed, describing the Son as equal and *homoousious* ('of the same substance') with the Father. This is the type of Christianity that was promoted by the bishops of Rome and Milan in the last decades of the fourth century and which became mainstream and dominant in the following decades. While modern scholars refer to this form of Christianity in various ways (e.g. 'Catholic', 'Orthodox','Nicene', 'neo-Nicene'), by opting for the term 'pro-Nicene', I follow Lewis Ayres who used this term in order to distinguish between theologies that emerge in the second half of the fourth century and which are not identical with the Nicene theology developed in the 320s and 330s, see Lewis Ayres, *Nicaea and Its Legacy: An Approach to Fourth Century Trinitarian Theology* (Oxford: Oxford University Press, 2004), 236.
[74] Pietri, *Roma Christiana*, 1085–1086.
[75] Homoian Arianism was widespread in Illyricum and modern scholars regard it as the predominant form of Christianity in this region at the end of the fourth century. The Homoians described the Son as being 'like' the Father without further qualification and they subordinated the Son to the Father. The label 'Homoian Arianism' has been famously coined by R.P.C. Hanson, *The Search for the Christian Doctrine of God: The Arian Controversy 318–381* (Edinburgh: Clark, 1988). In addition, there is also evidence for the existence of followers of Photinus and Bonosus. The latter seems to have been a bishop of Naissus (and not of Serdica as it has been long assumed) hence a close neighbour of Niceta. He was condemned for rejecting the perpetual virginity of Mary by a council of bishops convened at Capua in Italy in ca. 392. The letters of Innocent I from 412 and 414 where the name of Niceta is mentioned among the addressees deal with the problem of Bonosus' uncanonical ordinations in Illyricum. For the existence of heterodox churches in Illyricum at the end of the fourth century, see Pietri, *Roma Christiana*, 1086.

home, Niceta stopped to visit and report to his fellow bishops from Thessalonike, Phillipi, Tomi and Scupi, in accordance with the directives of canons 11 and 12 from the council of Serdica which stipulated that travelling bishops should show their official papers to the bishops whose episcopal sees were located on the main road,[76] then he had more opportunities to find episcopal allies for his pro-Nicene cause. The bishop of Thessalonike at the time of Niceta's visit was Anysius. He was a supporter of pro-Nicene Christianity and an ally and correspondent both of John Chrysostom and of the bishops of Rome, Siricius and Innocent I. Bishop of Phillipi might have been a certain Briso, mentioned by the historian Socrates as having attended the council summoned in 403 at the orders of the empress Eudoxia to condemn John Chrysostom.[77] Tomi was another important centre for pro-Nicene Christianity. At the time of Niceta's visit, the bishop of the city was Theotimus, a friend of John Chrysostom and an ecclesiastical writer to whom Jerome dedicated a few lines in his work *De viris illustribus*: "Theothimus, bishop of Tomi, in Scythia, has published brief and epigrammatical treatises in the form of dialogues and in olden style. I heard that he is now writing other works."[78] The historian Socrates mentions that Theotimus came to Constantinople to defend John Chrysostom against the attack of Epiphanius.[79] This means that he was still a bishop in 403. Like Niceta, Theotimus was also known as a missionary bishop who attempted to win barbarians, especially Huns and Goths, settled along the Danube from Homoian Arianism or paganism to pro-Nicene Christianity.[80] Finally, there is no information available about the bishop of Scupi, Niceta's last stop mentioned by Paulinus, however, as the see of Scupi became a metropolitanate already during Niceta's life, it is highly likely

---

[76] Canon 11 has been suggested by Gaudentius, the bishop of Naissus, a city located in the immediate vicinity of Niceta's Remesiana, in an attempt to reduce the large number of travelling bishops with petitions to the imperial court. The bishops who travelled by invitation were allowed to proceed, but if a bishop was suspected of travelling by ambition, his papers were not signed and he was not admitted to community, see Hamilton Hess, *The Early Development of Canon Law and the Council of Serdica* (Oxford: Oxford University Press, 2002), 208–209. Soroceanu, *Niceta von Remesiana*, 143 also supports the view that Niceta had, most likely in accordance with these canons, visited the bishops of the cities located on the highway.

[77] Socrates, *Historia Ecclesiastica* 6.18.

[78] Jerome, *De viris illustribus* 131: *Theotimus Scythiae Tomorum episcopus, in morem dialogorum et veteris eloquentiae breves commaticosque tractatus edidit. Audio eum et alia scribere.*

[79] Socrates, *Historia Ecclesiastica* 6.12.

[80] Sozomenus, *Historia ecclesiastica* 7.28. For a brief discussion of Theotimus' activities as a bishop of Tomi, see Jacques, Zeiller, *Les origines chrétiennes dans les provinces danubiennes de l'Empire Romain* (Paris: Boccard, 1918) 547–549.

that it also promoted pro-Nicene Christianity.⁸¹ If, on his return journey from Rome, Niceta visited fellow bishops supporters of pro-Nicene Christianity, it may be argued that among his reasons for doing so was either to expand his episcopal network or to strengthen already existing ties with bishops who could have provided the support he needed in his struggle with the adversaries of the pro-Nicene faith. While it is a demonstrated fact that Niceta promoted and defended pro-Nicene faith through his preaching in front of his congregation and through his writings,⁸² Paulinus' testimony about his travels around the Mediterranean sheds light on alternative ways in which Niceta championed this form of Christianity. Niceta's activities as a bishop seem to confirm Daniel H. Williams's observation that "the conflict between pro-Nicenes and anti-Nicenes was not purely a debate between intellectuals and cannot therefore be fully understood by evaluating the conflict in terms of *dogmengeschichte* alone. The controversy was waged in an arena much wider than that of theological exchange."⁸³

However, apart from searching for ecclesiastical pro-Nicene allies, Niceta could have had another important reason to travel to Italy and subsequently to return to Illyricum during wintertime stopping in the episcopal sees recorded by Paulinus on his return journey home. The dates of Niceta's both visits to Italy coincide with episcopal elections for the see of Rome.⁸⁴ On November 26, 399 the bishop Siricius died and the episcopal see of Rome became vacant for twenty days until the election of Anastasius.⁸⁵ According to Geoffrey Dunn,⁸⁶ there is the possibility to have had two different dates, one for the election and another

---

81 Burn, *Niceta of Remesiana*, liii, considers that Scupi must have become a metropolitanate between 386 and 412.
82 Niceta's activity as a pro-Nicene bishop is confirmed by the contemporary testimony of Paulinus and the bishop of Rome Innocent I. His writings were recommended together with those of Ambrose already by Cassiodorus as a most useful compendium to matters of faith, see Cassiodorus, *Institutiones* 1.16.3. Modern scholarship acknowledges Niceta's contribution to fourth century theological developments, see Burn, *Niceta*, and Soroceanu, *Niceta von Remesiana*. More recently, it has been claimed that Niceta's catechetical writings belong most likely to an earlier stage in the development of Latin pro-Nicene theology, see Carmen Angela Cvetković, "Episcopal Literary Networks in the Late Antique West: Niceta of Remesiana and Ambrose of Milan", StPatr 85 (2017) 177–185.
83 Daniel, H. Williams, *Ambrose of Milan and the End of the Nicene-Arian Controversies* (Oxford: Clarendon Press), 85.
84 For dating the start of Anastasius and Innocent I's episcopate, see Geoffrey Dunn, "Canonical Legislation on the Ordination of Bishops: Innocent I's Letter to Victricius of Rouen," in *Episcopal Elections in Late Antiquity*, eds. Johan Leemans et al. (Berlin: De Gruyter, 2011): 145–146, n. 2.
85 *Liber pontificalis* 41.1.
86 Dunn, "Canonical Legislation," 146–147.

for the ordination of the future bishop, which suggests that the ceremony of Anastasius' ordination as bishop of Rome must have taken place in the second half of December when based on Paulinus' *Epistula* 29, Niceta was most likely in Rome. Anastasius held the see of Rome for three years and ten days and after his death on December 402 he was followed by Innocent I who was elected to the episcopate in the same month. We find again Niceta in Nola just a few weeks later for the celebration of the feast of St Felix, although this time there is no evidence about a previous trip to Rome.

We search in vain for any information about how either Anastasius or Innocent had been elected to the episcopate. What may be deduced from the available sources is rather vague. Writing to Anysius of Thessalonike after his ordination, Innocent I notes that he had been elected as bishop of Rome 'with the consent of the holy priests and all the clergy and people', where *sacerdotes* (translated here as holy priests) designates the bishops.[87] However, he says nothing about what bishops had been eligible to be involved in this process. And in one of Innocent I's letters sent to Victricius of Rouen who asked for advice with episcopal elections, referring to the number of bishops required to attend an ordination Innocent states only that a single bishop does not ordain.[88] While there is no indication that Niceta was present at the ordination of the bishop of Rome, it may be argued nevertheless that he must have been fully aware of who the newly elected Roman bishop was and he had a good reason to stop on his journey back home in all the episcopal sees mentioned by Paulinus in order to inform his fellow bishops who were perhaps absent from the event about the results of the episcopal elections. This spontaneous way of disseminating ecclesiastical news would correspond with what Claire Sotinel has observed about the transmission of information on ecclesiastical questions at this time which she describes as "neither centralized nor even organized."[89] Yet she has noticed that the names of the holders of great episcopal sees were efficiently communicated despite the fact that the churches did not seem to use the official channels of communication, namely the *cursus publicus*.[90] These were transmitted most likely by participating bishops, which used alternative channels of communication and Niceta would perfectly match this description. In addition, another argument that Niceta was not a total stranger to the bishop of Rome comes from the letters written by Innocent I in 412 and 414 which mention Niceta

---

[87] Innocent I, *Epistula* 1 (PL 20, 464; FC 58/2, 368–371 Sieben).
[88] Innocent I, *Epistula* 2 (PL 20, 468–485; FC 58/2, 372–389 Sieben).
[89] Claire Sotinel, "Augustine's Information Circuits," in *A Companion to Augustine*, ed. Mark Vessey (Maldon, MA: Wiley-Blackwell, 2012): 127–128.
[90] Sotinel, "How were Bishops Informed?".

by name. In particular, the letter sent to Marcianus, Niceta's neighbor and the bishop of Naissus, singles out Niceta among other bishops as "our brother Niceta"[91] suggesting that Innocent might have known him better, presumably because of the latter's visits to Rome.

Finally, Niceta's role as an ecclesiastical messenger appears to be confirmed by additional evidence deriving from another ancient source. Sulpicius Severus in his *Dialogi* composed around 404 mentions to his friend Postumianus how important was Paulinus in spreading "that first little book of ours (i.e. *Vita Martini*) not only through Italy, but even through the whole Illyricum."[92] Although he does not mention Niceta as responsible for disseminating the news about his book about St Martin in Illyrian ecclesiastical circles, it is highly likely that his book became known in this region through the intermediary of Niceta. At the beginning of the fifth century, Niceta was Paulinus' main, if not sole, connection in this region and Paulinus' *Epistula* 29 makes it clear that during his first stay in Nola, Niceta was informed about Sulpicius and his *Vita Martini*.

In light of this discussion, it is the exchange of news which emerges as a major aspect of the relationship between Niceta and Paulinus. There is no doubt that Niceta informed Paulinus about his homeland and about his travels around the Mediterranean, which Paulinus described later accurately in his poems in Niceta's honor. Most likely, Niceta informed both Paulinus and later the bishops from Illyricum about the episcopal elections in Rome which took place at the time when he was present in the city. In return, Paulinus has seized this opportunity to inform Niceta about the literary activity of his friend Sulpicius Severus, probably encouraging him to carry the news about this book to his fellow Illyrian bishops. Peter Brown's observation that in the world of late antiquity friendship meant, first and foremost, information[93] seems to be eloquently illustrated by Niceta's and Paulinus' friendship.

4 Conclusion

As literary works, Paulinus' poems are usually approached with much suspicion by modern scholars, however when read cautiously they constitute a major

---

91 Innocent I, *Epistula* 16 (PL 20:520B): *et fratrem nostrum Nicetam*.
92 Sulpicius Severus, *Dialogi* 3.17.4: *sicut primum illum nostrum labellum non per Italiam tantum, sed per totum etiam diffudit Illyricum*. On this passage see Mratschek, *Briefwechsel* 463 and 546 and also her contribution to this volume, p. 162.
93 Peter Brown, *Power and Persuasion in Late Antiquity: Towards a Christian Empire* (Madison: University of Wisconsin Press, 1992), 47.

source of information for a variety of topics. Thus, we owe to Paulinus a great deal of our knowledge about the obscure figure of the Illyrian bishop Niceta of Remesiana. Although Paulinus' primary concern in his poems was to praise in Niceta a set of spiritual qualities that at the end of the fourth century were expected to belong to the episcopal ideal, delving into a discussion about their relationship and about the reasons behind Niceta's travels to Nola brings to the fore important aspects regarding the connectivity of Christian elites in late antiquity and regarding trans-regional ecclesiastical communication. This paper has identified the relationship between Paulinus and Niceta as one of Christian friendship despite its distinct hierarchical nature and has highlighted the role of religious ideology in shaping social behavior and in contributing to the rapid formation of ecclesiastical networks between Christian elites coming from different Roman provinces. Based on Paulinus' testimony, a whole new dimension has been added to Niceta's promotion of pro-Nicene Christianity, which was not simply confined to producing theological treatises and pastoral work within his own community, but included missionary activities and a sustained effort to build ecclesiastical ties with other episcopal sees from other regions than Illyricum. Last but not least, it is almost certain that Niceta adopted the role of messenger of ecclesiastical news to his fellow bishops, informing them as Sulpicius reports, about what influential Christian works had been produced in the regions he just visited or communicating to them the results of important events such as the outcome of Roman episcopal elections. Thanks to Paulinus' texts Niceta emerges as an able church leader who was part of a trans-regional network of pro-Nicene bishops that extended from Rome and Nola in Italy to Tomi on the shores of the Black Sea.

Bibliography

Primary Sources

Cassiodorus, *Institutiones divinarum et saecularium litterarum*, edited by Wolfgang Bürsgens FC 39/1. Freiburg: Herder, 2003.
Jerome, *De viris illustribus*, edited by Claudia Barthold. Mülheim: Carthusianus Verlag, 2011.
Palladius, *Dialogues sur la vie de Jean Chrysostome*, edited by Anne-Marie Malingrey, SC 342. Paris: Les Editions du Cerf, 1988.
Paulinus Nolanus, *Carmina* edited by G. de Hartel CSEL 30. Wien: Verlag der Österreichischen Akademie der Wissenschaften, 1999.
Paulinus Nolanus, *Epistulae* edited by G. de Hartel, CSEL 29. Wien: Verlag der Österreichischen Akademie der Wissenschaften, 1999.

Socrates Scholasticus, *Kirchengeschichte*, edited by Günther Christian Hansen. Berlin: De Gruyter, 1995.
Strabo, *Geographika*, edited by Stefan Radt. Göttingen: Vandenhoeck & Ruprecht, 2002–2011.
Sulpicius Severus, *Gallus: Dialogues sur les vertus de Saint Martin*, edited by Jacques Fontaine, SC 510. Paris: Les Éditions du Cerf, 2006.
Vetustissimae Epistulae Romanorum Pontificum edited by Hermann-Josef Sieben, FC 58/2. Freiburg: Herder 2014.

Secondary Literature

Basson, André. "A Transformation of Genres in Late Latin Literature: Classical Literary Tradition and Ascetic Ideals in Paulinus of Nola." In *Shifting Frontiers in Late Antiquity*, edited by R.W. Mathisen and Hagith Sivan, 267–276. Aldershot: Variorum,1996.
Beresford, James. *The Ancient Sailing Season*. Leiden: Brill, 2013.
Boissevain, Jeremy. *Friends of Friends: Networks, Manipulators and Coalitions*. Oxford: Basil Blackwell, 1974.
Brown, Peter. *The Cult of the Saints: Its Rise and Function in Latin Christianity*. Chicago: Chicago University Press, 1981.
Brown, Peter. *Power and Persuasion in Late Antiquity: Towards a Christian Empire*. Madison: University of Wisconsin Press, 1992.
Burn, Andrew. E. *Niceta of Remesiana: His Life and Works*. Cambridge: Cambridge University Press, 1905.
Conybeare, Catherine. *Paulinus Noster: Self and Symbols in the Letters of Paulinus of Nola*. Oxford: Oxford University Press, 2000.
Cvetković, Carmen Angela. "Christianity, *Romanitas* and the Politics of Otherness in the Late Ancient West." In *La naissance de l'autrui: De l'Antiquité à la Renaissance* , edited by Jérôme Lagouanère, 149–160. Paris: Classiques Garnier, 2019.
Cvetković, Carmen Angela, "Episcopal Literary Networks in the Late Antique West: Niceta of Remesiana and Ambrose of Milan," *StPatr* 85 (2017) 177–185.
Dunn, Geoffrey. "Canonical Legislation on the Ordination of Bishops: Innocent I's Letter to Victricius of Rouen." In *Episcopal Elections in Late Antiquity*, edited by Johan Leemans, Peter van Nuffelen, Shawn W. J. Keough and Carla Nicolaye, 127–145. Berlin: De Gruyter, 2011.
Dunn, Geoffrey. "The Church of Rome as a Church of Appeal in the Early Fifth Century: The Evidence of Innocent I and the Illyrian Churches," *JEH* 64 (2013a): 679–699.
Dunn, Geoffrey. "The Letter of Innocent I to Marcian of Niš." In *Saint Emperor Constantine and Christianity*, edited by Dragiša Bojović, 319–339. Niš: Centre of Church Studies, 2013b.
Duval, Yves-Marie. "Nicéta d'Aquilée. Histoire, légende et conjectures anciennes." In *Grado nella storia e nell'arte*, vol. 1, 161–206. Udine 1980.
Fabre, Pierre. *Saint Paulin de Nole et l'amitié chrétienne*. Paris: Boccard, 1949.
Gemeinhardt, Peter. *Das lateinische Christentum und die antike pagane Bildung*. Tübingen: Mohr Siebeck, 2007.

Greenslade, S.L. "The Illyrian Churches and the Vicariate of Thessalonica" *JThs* 46 (1945): 17–30.
Gryson, Roger. *Le prêtre selon Saint Ambroise*. Louvain: Université Catholique de Louvain, 1968.
Hess, Hamilton. *The Early Development of Canon Law and the Council of Serdica*. Oxford: Oxford University Press, 2002.
Jerg, Ernst. *Vir venerabilis: Untersuchungen zur Titulatur der Bischöfe in den ausserkirchlichen Texten der Spätantike als Beitrag zur Deutung ihrer öffentlichen Stellung*. Wien: Herder, 1970.
Kelly, Christopher. *Ruling the Later Roman Empire*. Cambridge, Mass: Belknap Press, 2004.
Key Fowden, Elizabeth. "Macedonia." In *Late Antiquity: A Guide to the Postclassical World*, edited by Glenn Bowersock, Peter Brown and Oleg Grabar, 549–550. Cambridge, Mass: Belknap Press, 1999.
Kirstein, Robert. *Paulinus Nolanus*. Basel: Schwabe & Co, 2000.
Lizzi Testa, Rita. "The Late Antique Bishop: Image and Reality." In *A Companion to Late Antiquity*, edited by Philip Rousseau, 525–539. Malden, MA: Wiley-Blackwell, 2009.
Mratschek, Sigrid, *Der Briefwechsel des Paulinus von Nola: Kommunikation und Soziale Kontakte zwischen christlichen Intellektuellen*. Göttingen: Vandenhoeck & Ruprecht, 2002.
Mratschek, Sigrid, "*Multis enim notissima est sanctitas loci:* Paulinus of Nola as a Center of Christian Hospitality," *JECS* 9 (2001) 511–553.
Mratschek, Sigrid, "Friends and Friendship." In *Encyclopedia of the Bible and its Reception* 9 (2014) 723–727.
Mullet, Margaret. *Theophylact of Ochrid: Reading the Letters of a Byzantine Archbishop*. Aldershot: Variorum, 1997.
Pietri, Charles. *Roma Christiana: Recherches sur l'Église de Rome, son organisation, sa politique et son idéologie de Miltiade à Sixte III (311–440)*, 2 vols. Paris: Boccard, 1976.
Rapp, Claudia. *Holy Bishops in Late Antiquity: The Nature of Christian Leadership in an Age of Transition*. Berkeley: University of California Press, 2005.
Rebenich, Stefan. "Augustine on Friendship and Orthodoxy." In *A Companion to Augustine*, edited by Mark Vessey. 365–374. Maldon, MA: Wiley-Blackwell, 2012.
Sivan, Hagith. "Nicetas' (of Remesiana) Mission and Stilicho's Illyrican Ambition: Notes on Paulinus of Nola *Carmen XVII (propemticon)*. *Revue des Études Augustiniennes* 41(1995): 79–91.
Soroceanu, Alina. *Niceta von Remesiana: Seelsorge und Kirchenpolitik im spätantiken unteren Donauraum*. Frankfurt: Peter Lang, 2013.
Sotinel, Claire. "How were Bishops Informed? Information Transmission across the Adriatic Sea in Late Antiquity." In *Travel, Communication and Geography in Late Antiquity. Sacred and Profane*, edited by Linda Ellis and Frank L. Kidner. Aldershot: Ashgate, 2004.
Sotinel, Claire. "Augustine's Information Circuits." In *A Companion to Augustine*, edited by Mark Vessey, 125–137. Maldon, MA: Wiley-Blackwell, 2012.
Tränkle, Hermann."Vermeintliche Interpolationen bei Paulinus von Nola." *Hermes* 130/3 (2002): 338–361.
Walsh, P.G. *The Poems of St Paulinus of Nola*. New York: Newmann Press, 1975.
White, Carolinne. *Christian Friendship in the Fourth Century*. Cambridge: Cambridge University Press, 1992.

Williams, Daniel, H. *Ambrose of Milan and the End of Nicene-Arian Controversies*. Oxford: Clarendon Press, 1995.

Zeiller, Jacques. *Les origines chrétiennes dans les provinces danubiennes de l'Empire Romain*. Paris: Boccard, 1918.

Part 2: **Episcopal Networks in Context**

Daniel K. Knox
The Impact of the Laurentian Schism on Ennodius of Pavia's Participation in Episcopal Networks

In the middle ages, a child became a member of a number of different communities and groups the moment he was born. He was not only born into his own kindred, he was also born into his father's network of associations, including friends, lords and vassals. These connections were inherited as if they were property. He was also able to enter new groups himself; in fact, it was almost compulsory for him to do so. He could bind himself to new lords, or bind to himself new vassals, and he could form new political allegiances and new friendships.[1]

Gerd Althoff's summary of social opportunities in the early middle-ages describes well the situation that a sixth-century elite might find themselves in. However, while such an individual might need to seek out new networks and groups their ability to forge connections was not solely decided by their innate social ability or resources. While we often like to think that we make choices, the reality is that choices are often made for us in advance. Events and our participation in them frequently limit and determine our options. Such was the case for Ennodius (fl. c. 473–521), a sixth-century deacon in Pavia and Milan who rose to be the Bishop of Pavia in 514. Ennodius participated in the Events of the Laurentian Schism that divided the Roman Church in the early sixth century as an intellectual asset in the support of Pope Symmachus' cause. Ennodius' participation in these events opened up social opportunities and facilitated his participation in the networks of Symmachus' supporters; but it also limited his ability to participate in the networks of those individuals who supported Symmachus' rival Laurentius.[2] While Ennodius' status as a regional aristocrat compelled him to seek out social opportunities, not all doors were fully open to him. One way in which we can measure and detect Ennodius' participation in these networks is by examining the letters of his literary corpus and measuring the epistolary actions that are visible. In this analysis I am interested in two epistolary actions in particular: the sending of letters to individuals and the men-

---

[1] Gerd Althoff, *Family, Friends and Followers: Political and Social Bonds in Early Medieval Europe* (Cambridge: Cambridge University Press, 2004), 2.
[2] Laurentius 15, in *Prosopographie chrétienne du Bas-Empire 2: Prosopographie de l'Italie chrétienne, 313–604*, eds. Charles Piétri, Luce Piétri and Janine Desmulliez (Rome: École française de Rome, 1999), 1239–1242. Henceforth *PCBE*.

tioning of third parties in letters that they are not the recipient of. By analysing a network model of these actions, we can compare Ennodius' ties to other participants in the Laurentian Schism and the extent to which he participated in their broader networks.

1 Ennodius and his corpus

Ennodius was a regional aristocrat of Northern Italy who had emigrated from Arles in his youth following the death of his parents to live with an aunt in Pavia.[3] Traditionally Ennodius has been thought to have originated from a cadet branch of the Anicii clan, particularly due to his kinship with Anicius Probus Faustus,[4] however as Alan Cameron noted there is not much solid evidence for ascribing the Ennodii Anician status.[5] Ennodius was a talented writer whose extensive knowledge of style at times verges towards pedantry. Although a *parvenu* in Italian society, Ennodius was able to advance his position through both his literary talents and church office. The Church offered regional elites such as Ennodius an excellent path for social advancement.[6] Ennodius began his career in the Church of Pavia under the episcopate of Epifanius, who he would later compose a hagiography of. Subsequently he became a deacon in the Church of Milan under the bishop Laurentius, and it was at Milan that he would be employed as an intellectual asset during the opening decade of the sixth century. Following his career as a deacon Ennodius would go on to become the bishop of Pavia (Ticinum) and lead two papal embassies in 515 and 517 before his death in 521.[7]

Ennodius' surviving works are made up of an extensive cache of letters, poetry, and prose written between the beginning of the sixth century and his election as Bishop of Pavia in 513. It seems that when Ennodius died in 521 his documents were collated and circulated by an unknown third party who left no clues

---

[3] For an extensive discussion of Ennodius' early life see: Stefanie A.H. Kennell, *Magnus Felix Ennodius: A Gentleman of the Church* (Ann Arbor: The University of Michigan Press, 2000), 4–42.
[4] Sometimes referred to as Faustus Niger, henceforth referred to in this chapter as Faustus Probus; see J.R. Martindale, *The Prosopography of the Later Roman Empire Volume 2* (Cambridge: Cambridge University Press, 1980), 454–456: Henceforth *PLRE* 2; Anicius Probus Faustus 4, *PCBE* 2/1, 140.756–759.
[5] Alan Cameron, "Anician Myths," *JRS* 102 (2012), 168.
[6] See, Patrick Amory, *People and Identity in Ostrogothic Italy, 489–554* (Cambridge: Cambridge University Press, 1997), xvi – xvii.
[7] Kennell, *Magnus Felix Ennodius*, 4.

as to their motives. Ennodius' role in preserving the documents is unclear, however there is a consensus that the documents were drawn from Ennodius' archives and that at some point they had been arranged into four folios for later editing – probably by Ennodius himself.[8] We have to then be very careful in drawing conclusions from the collection as a whole – particularly regarding Ennodius' involvement in its assembly. These issues have been compounded by the approaches of modern editors to the texts. Stefanie Kennell notes that most approaches to Ennodius's works have been guided by the modern arrangement of his collection by the seventeenth century editor Jacques Sirmond. Sirmond sought to tidy up the chaotic structure of the manuscript as if it were a wild meadow in need of landscaping.[9] Sirmond's 1611 edition organized Ennodius's works into nine books of letters (297 in total), two of poems, four classes of *dictiones*, and ten *opuscula miscella*.[10] While this organization has made navigating Ennodius' works easier and much more thematic, it has taken away any semblance of shared chronology between the works.[11] Kennell prefers Friedrich Vogel's *Monumenta Germaniae Historica* edition which follows the ordering of the manuscripts.[12] Kennell argues that the chronological archiving of the original documents is partly preserved in the manuscript order – representing an initial gathering and collation of the texts.[13] While agreeing that a general chronology is apparent, Richard Bartlett has critiqued the ordering of some items in the collection, particularly the poems which seem to have been inserted out of order between chronological groups of letters.[14] My analysis will only deal with the chronology of Ennodius' letters in broad terms. The initial model that I will consider collates all of Ennodius' epistolary actions into a single synchronous network graph. Further discussion will rely on placing these actions in their chronological context but only in the broadest sense.

---

8 Stefanie A. H. Kennell, "Ennodius and His Editors," *CM* 51 (2000), 268; Richard Bartlett, "The Dating of Ennodius' Writings," in *Atti Della Seconda Giornata Ennodiana*, ed. Edoardo D'Angel (Naples: Dipartimento di Filogia Classica dell Universita degli studi di Napoli Federico II., 2003), 55–74; Pauline Allen, "Rationale for Episcopal Letter Collections in Late Antiquity," in *Collecting Early Christian Letters from the Apostle Paul to Late Antiquity*, eds. Bronwen Neil and Pauline Allen (Cambridge: Cambridge University Press, 2015): 18–34.
9 Kennell, "Ennodius and His Editors," 257–259.
10 Kennell, *Magnus Felix Ennodius*, 2–3.
11 Kennell, "Ennodius and His Editors," 268–270.
12 Kennell, *Magnus Felix Ennodius*, 3; *Magni Felicis Ennodii Opera*, ed. Friedrich Vogel. MGH AA 7 (Berlin, 1885). Throughout the chapter I will use Vogel's numbering of Ennodius' works.
13 Kennell, "Ennodius and His Editors," 266–270; Kennell, *Magnus Felix Ennodius*. 3.
14 Bartlett, "The Dating of Ennodius' Writings," 53–74.

The first part of this analysis reconstructs a network model from Ennodius' preserved epistolary actions. It is impossible to reconstruct a complete image of Ennodius' social network from the fossilized remains of his literary production – in this case 297 letters, although it is tempting to try. Even though the corpus is quite extensive, it represents a fraction of the literary output that we might expect from a sixth-century ecclesiastic official such as Ennodius. We can only hope to reconstruct a *mimesis* of Ennodius' social world and only then as Ennodius leaves it to us. We should not make the mistake of conflating Ennodius' remaining communication as a network in itself. Rather, what we can find is the traces of the networks that he participated in and analyse the broad trends that remain visible.

The second part of the analysis looks more closely at individual letter exchanges and is therefore on firmer ground. Still the ground is only *slightly* firmer, as in these cases we will only be able to examine the exchanges from the perspective of Ennodius, who did not preserve any of the responses to his letters. Many failed social actions are preserved, and it is often impossible to judge the extent to which Ennodius' social endeavours were reciprocated. Despite this, Ennodius' letters have long been used as a source of information regarding the social and political life of Ostrogothic Italy. This is due both to Ennodius's many ties to prominent members of Rome's senatorial aristocracy and the sheer volume of his corpus.[15] I will use these exemplars to contextualize the broad trends exhibited in the initial analysis.

2 Locating episcopal networks

My network model of Ennodius' epistolary patterns is based on two social actions: the sending of letters and the mentioning of third parties in letters that they are not the addressee of.[16] In modelling and analysing these two actions I want to stress that I am not trying to recreate "Ennodius' network" – rather the model will be used to detect evidence for Ennodius' participation in the networks of the individuals that he corresponded with. Even a partial model of Ennodius' communication will be able to provide evidence of this by showing which individuals and groups he was most tied to, both in terms of volume of correspondence and the structural position of the letter recipients within the

---

15 See, for instance, John Moorhead, *Theoderic In Italy* (Oxford: Clarendon Press Oxford, 1993).
16 The models and measures quoted in this study were prepared using: S.P. Borgatti, M.G. Everett, and L.C. Freeman, Ucinet 6 for Windows: Software for Social Network Analysis (Harvard, MA: Analytic Technologies, 2002).

model. Recipients (or network actors) to whom Ennodius was well connected are more likely to feature in his letters to other individuals or have individuals mentioned to them. On the other hand, actors whom Ennodius was not well connected to should be more structurally isolated in the model as well as receiving a lower volume of epistolary actions overall.

My focus in this paper is to identify the position of episcopal networks within Ennodius' wider social world. Locating episcopal networks in the literary corpus of Ennodius of Pavia is not as straightforward as in the works of other contemporary writers. The corpus of Ennodius differs significantly from those of his Gallo-Roman near contemporaries Sidonius Apollinaris, Ruricius of Limoges, and Avitus of Vienne in that it is not dominated by the conversations of bishops to other bishops. Rather a large proportion of Ennodius preserved writing is addressed and dedicated to important senators and holders of curial office in the Ostrogothic court. That said, episcopal business and politics are a major theme throughout the collection. The Ennodius that we see in his letters and poems is, as Kennell rightly asserts, first and foremost a deacon of the churches of Pavia and Milan, no matter the subject that he addresses in any one case.[17] Ennodius was therefore a participant in the episcopal networks of others. Ennodius was a crucial intellectual asset for the churches of Pavia, Milan, and Rome. His literary skills were put to use promoting the agenda of Pope Symmachus during the Laurentian schism and celebrating the episcopates of the bishops Epifanius of Pavia and Laurentius of Milan. However, the communication patterns of Ennodius only give us a partial picture of these episcopal networks. For instance, while we have letters that show him conducting official business on behalf of Bishop Laurentius, we don't have any preserved letters to Laurentius himself. This is understandable as Ennodius had little need to write to Laurentius, rather Ennodius dedicated several poems to his bishop. As my network model was focused on epistolary communication, this relationship was not captured. This means that rather than attempt to recreate the episcopal networks of Symmachus and Laurentius, my task is to identify where these networks intersect with that of Ennodius.

Before discussing Ennodius' episcopal activity in more detail I will outline the broad network trends present across his surviving correspondence.[18] **Figure 1** is a graph that represents the two epistolary actions visible in Ennodius' letters: the sending of letters and the mentioning of third parties. Of the 133 actors in the

---

[17] Kennell, *Magnus Felix Ennodius*, 16.
[18] A fuller discussion of these trends can be found in Daniel K. Knox, "Measuring the Correspondence of Ennodius of Pavia: An Initial Social Network Analysis," *Annual of Medieval Studies at CEU* 23 (2017): 20–34.

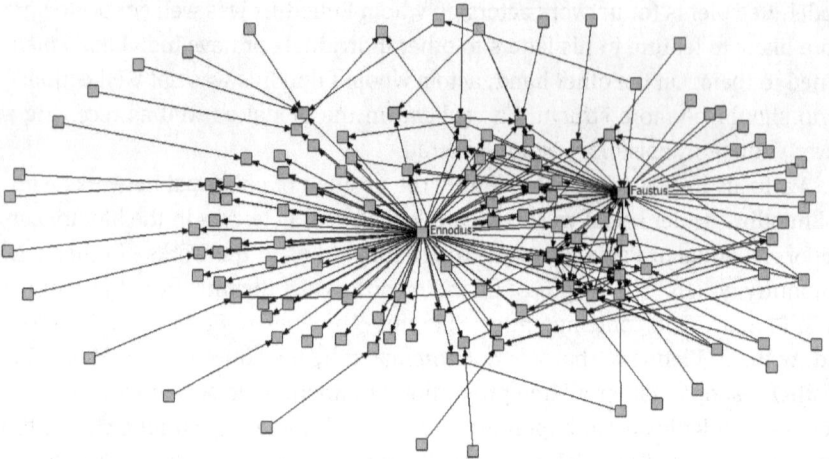

Figure 1: Broad Trends

network 87 are the recipients of letters from Ennodius. The remaining 46 actors are individuals who are only represented by third party mentions.[19] Two trends are apparent in **Figure 1**. There is a large ring of pendent actors who are only connected to the rest of the network either through Ennodius or one other actor. Largely the graph resembles a star pattern with a lack of horizontal connectivity and is dominated by structural holes: areas of the graph with limited connections between actors.[20] The exception to this pattern is the highly connected area that lies between Ennodius and Faustus Probus. This section of the graph is dominated by actors who have multiple ties beyond Ennodius – that is, they are either mentioned in letters to others or they have others mentioned to them. Compared to the large area of pendants, this section of the graph is denser in connections and the actors are less reliant on Ennodius for connections to the rest of the graph. Rather than structural holes, this part of the graph is characterized by triadic-closure. Not only are the actors in this part of the graph connected to Ennodius but they are connected to each other, knitting the graph together in triangular patterns. This can be an indicator of the networks that Ennodius was an active participant in. This is because active

---

[19] The two epistolary actions are not mutually exclusive, and many actors are the recipients of both.
[20] For a general introduction to the concepts discussed, see John Scott, *Social Network Analysis* (Los Angeles: Sage, 2013).

Table 1: Undirected and Directed Network Centrality

Actor	Undirected	In-degree	Out-degree
Faustus	0.37	0.28	0.098
Eugenes	0.1	0.038	0.068
Liberius	0.1	0.038	0.068
Albinus	0.09	0.038	0.053
Agapitus	0.09	0.038	0.053
Senarius	0.7	0.03	0.053
Symmachus Papa	0.6	0.023	0.038
Florus	0.06	0.023	0.045
Avienus	0.06	0.045	0.015
Beatus	0.045	0.015	0.03
Parthenius	0.045	0.03	0.015
Euprepria	0.04	0.015	0.023

participation in networks tends to increase triadic closure.[21] As an individual builds a relationship with another, they are introduced to other members of the network and build relationships with them – our friends' friends become our friends.

Examining the broad patterns in the network graph can tell us a lot about Ennodius' network activity but it also helps to confirm our observations by measuring the structural importance of the actors more precisely. We can examine this by comparing two network measures: *centrality* and *betweenness*. Centrality considers the extent to which an actor is connected to other actors within a network by comparing the sum of an actor's ties to the total possible number of ties in the network. Betweenness measures the extent to which the actors function as bridges between other actors and therefore the importance of their structural position in the network.[22] These measures help us to understand an actor's importance in relationship to other actors in a network. In **Tables 1** and **2** we see a considerable amount of overlap in the individuals with the highest scores of cen-

---

21 Mark S. Granovetter, "The Strength of Weak Ties," *AJS* (1973): 1361–1363.
22 Scott, *Social Network Analysis*, 84–89.

Table 2: Network 'Betweenness'

Actor	Degree of Betweenness
Faustus	7.674
Beatus	1.238
Symmachus Papa	1.110
Eugenes	1.042
Liberius	0.912
Florus	0.815
Parthenius	0.734
Agapitus	0.574
Albinus	0.525
Hormisdas	0.379

trality and betweenness. In both measures Faustus Probus has the highest score by a large margin when compared to other network actors. As we saw in **Figure 1** Faustus dominates the network of Ennodius. It is also worth noting the relatively high betweenness scores of Pope Symmachus, the senator Liberius,[23] and the deacon Hormisdas[24] – all of whom were contacts of Ennodius during the Laurentian Schism.

We see a similar situation emerge when we compare **Tables 1** and **2** with the raw number of epistolary actions received by each actor. **Table 3** shows the actors that received the highest number of letters, and **Table 4** shows the actors that are mentioned as third parties most frequently. Again, in both measures Faustus leads by a large margin. There is also a great deal of overlap between the individuals in **Tables 3** and **4** and those in the previous tables. However, some individuals who were not so structurally significant appear as significant recipients of letters: the senator and philosopher Boethius, whose relationship with Ennodius will be considered later in this paper, stands out in this regard.[25] As a broad rule, what we can see is that those actors who are the most structur-

---

23 Liberius 3, *PLRE* 2, 677–681; Liberius 4, *PCBE* 2/2, 1298–1301.
24 Hormisdas, *PCBE* 2/1, 1015–1016.
25 Boethius 5, *PLRE* 2, 233–237; *PCBE* 2/1, 312–316.

Table 3: Actors – Received Letters

Actor	Number of Letters
Faustus	52
Avienus	23
Senarius	11
Eugenes	9
Euprepria	8
Adeodatus Presbyterus	7
Avitus	7
Boethius	7
Florus	7
Hormisdas	7
Symmachus Papa	6
Agapitus	6
Agnellus	6

Table 4: Actors with Highest Mentions

Actors	Mentions
Faustus	16
Avienus	9
Parthenius	5
Cynegia	4
Sabinus	4
Atticus	3
Faustinus	3
Laurentius	3
Lupicinus	3

ally significant in the network graph are also significant in terms of the volume of correspondence that they received.

With the broad trends established I can begin to contextualize them with a specific example: Ennodius' participation in the Laurentian Schism and the episcopal network of Pope Symmachus.

3 The Laurentian Schism

One event looms large in the episcopal communication of Ennodius: the Laurentian Schism. The turn of the sixth century was a tumultuous time in Italy with factions competing over the Roman See during the episcopates of both Anastasius and Symmachus.[26] It was the election of 498 that would prove most divisive, with two candidates being elected on the same day: Symmachus and Laurentius. The underlying causes of the Laurentian schism are unclear but certainly the relationship between the Bishop of Rome and the Emperor in Constantinople played a part. The Roman Church was a benefactor of the political transformation in the late fifth century and it exploited the political space created by the change in power in Italy to create for itself the foundations of an independent powerbase.[27] This was spurred on by a major break with the Emperor and the Eastern churches – the Acacian Schism. While all Roman bishops of this period attempted to assert and increase their authority, there was by no means a coherent papal doctrine that defined the period. Rather, each sought to improve their own situations, often coming into conflict with the positions of their predecessors, the Ostrogothic kings, emperors, and the senatorial elite.[28] The argument that set the tone for this increasing papal independence was Pope Gelasius's statement that the world was ruled by two powers: "There are two powers, Augustus Emperor, which primarily rule this world: the sacred authority of the Church, and the power of the Emperor."[29] Gelasius's division of the world into a sacred sphere overseen by papal *auctoritas* and a civil world controlled by *imperium* was symptomatic of the increasing political fragmentation of the Mediter-

---

26 Moorhead, *Theoderic*, 58–60.
27 John Meyendorff, *Imperial Unity and Christian Division: The Church 450–680* (New York NY: St Vladimir's Seminary Press, 1989), 158.
28 Amory, *People and Identity*, 195.
29 Gelasius *Ep. 12: Duo quippe sunt, imperator Auguste, quibus principaliter mundus hic regitur: auctoritas sacra pontificum, et regalis potestas.* In *Epistolae Romanorum pontificum genuinae et quae ad eos scriptae sunt a S. Hilaro usque ad Pelagium II.*, ed. Andreas Thiel, vol. 1 (Brunsberg: Eduard Peter, 1867). Trans. John S. Ott, Portland State University.

ranean in the late fifth and early sixth centuries. Symmachus certainly followed Gelasius in carving out a more independent powerbase. Pope Symmachus' was not a supporter of the Emperor Anastasius' policies, while his competitor Laurentius seems to have had a more pro-Anastasian position.[30] A position that many senators supported ensuring the contested election was a drawn out.

The impact of the Laurentian Schism for the senatorial elite has been well noted.[31] However, as Alan Cameron argued, the long-standing assumption that the Laurentian schism fell within the wider factional dispute between the Anicii and the Decii has been often over emphasised.[32] While individuals did choose sides, there is no clear evidence that this was due to any sense of coherent clan politics. Support for Symmachus was spearheaded by Faustus Probus and was strong in Northern Italy with regional aristocrats such as Ennodius. Ennodius, following the lead of his bishop in Milan, Laurentius,[33] was a staunch supporter of Pope Symmachus throughout the Laurentian Schism and Symmachus had made use of Ennodius as an intellectual asset. Ennodius composed the *Libellus adversus eos qui contra synodum scribere praesumpserunt*,[34] a polemic against those senators who wished to hold Symmachus to account during the contested papal election. The Laurentian faction held much more sway among members of the senatorial elite. Two decorated senators were at the forefront: Festus and Probinus.[35] These two were joined by other prominent senators including: Faustus Albus,[36] Symmachus, and Boethius.[37]

Ennodius maintained strong connections with Symmachus and several of his supporters, in particular: Hormisdas, one of Symmachus' deacons and his successor as pope; Liberius, a leading figure in Ostrogothic politics; and Symmachus's chief ally Faustus Probus. For the most part these actors rank highly in letters received, mentions, centrality, and betweenness. In **Figure 2** we can see that they all lie in the hyper connected section of the network graph. To this

---

30 Moorhead, *Theoderic*, 134–135.
31 See John Moorhead, "The Laurentian Schism: East and West in the Roman Church," *ChH* 47/2 (1978): 125–136; Moorhead, *Theoderic*, 114–139; P.A.B. Llewellyn, "The Roman Church During the Laurentian Schism: Priests and Senators" *ChH* 45/4 (1976), 417–427.
32 Alan Cameron, "Anician Myths," 169.
33 Not to be confused with the deacon Laurentius who contested the papacy.
34 Ennodius, *Opera*, 49.
35 Festus 5, *PLRE* 2, 467–469; Festus 2, *PCBE* 2/1, 812–814; Probinus 2, *PLRE* 2, 910; Probinus 1, *PCBE* 2/2, 1836–1837.
36 Faustus 4, *PLRE* 2, 451–452; Faustus 5, *PCBE* 2/1, 759; Symmachus 9, *PLRE* 2, 1044–1046; Symmachus 6, *PCBE* 2/2, 2146.
37 Moorhead, *Theoderic*, 129–133.

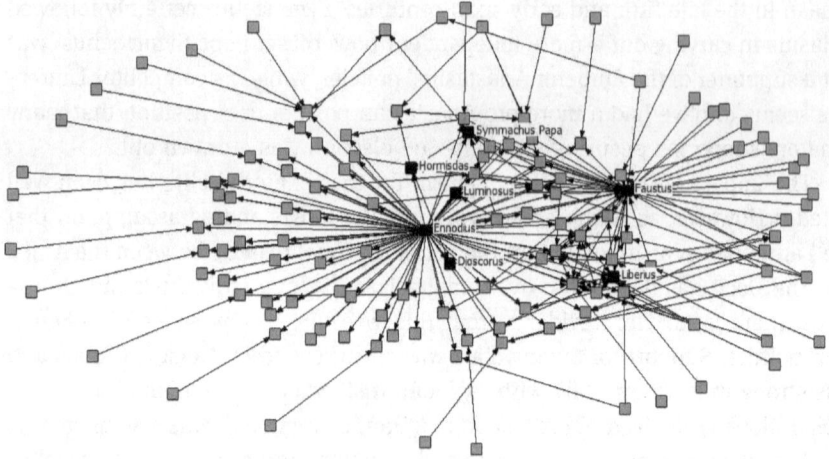

Figure 2: Supporters of Pope Symmachus

group we can add the layman Luminosus[38] and the deacon Dioscorus, who Ennodius' wrote to in the course of official duties. Faustus Probus' position in this group is problematic in that he ranks so highly throughout the entire corpus of letters that his significance cannot be solely tied to his role in the schism. However, overall Ennodius was not only closely tied to this group, but they were tied to each other. That is Ennodius' interacted with them as a group, both by writing to them directly and mentioning them in letters to other members of the group. In his interactions with individuals aligned with Pope Symmachus we can see the trace of an episcopal network which Ennodius participated both officially as a deacon and personally as an individual.

Ennodius' official participation in the network that surrounded Symmachus stemmed from his duties as a deacon in the church of Milan. As has been mentioned above, during the schism the Milanese church, led by its bishop Laurentius, was a strong supporter of Symmachus' cause. Indeed, Ennodius' official involvement in the schism is directly tied to Laurentius' support for Symmachus. Bishop Laurentius of Milan attended the synods of 501 and 502 which debated the core issues of the schism, and the Milanese church loaned a large sum of money (over 400 solidi of gold) to support Symmachus. As a deacon of the Milanese church Ennodius was entrusted with the task of recovering the expendi-

---

38 Luminosus, *PLRE* 2, 692–693; Luminosus 1, *PCBE* 2/2, 1336–1337.

ture.³⁹ Ennodius wrote to three individuals repeatedly to try and retrieve the funds: the layman Luminosus, and the deacons Hormisdas and Dioscorus. Ennodius wrote three letters to Luminosus in various attempts to recover the funds and stressed that the burden of repaying the money would fall on him if the papacy defaulted.⁴⁰ Failing to get a resolution from Luminosus, Ennodius appealed to Hormisdas and Discorus, but again seems to have been rebuffed. This was not Ennodius' first exchange with Hormisdas and throughout the letter he seems concerned with minimizing the request to the relationship that the request might have posed with deferential language.⁴¹ In all of the exchanges Kennell notes that Ennodius had to strike a careful balance between politeness and firmness in making the request to get the funds returned to him.⁴² In these exchanges Ennodius was participating in his role as a deacon of the Milanese church – but the very real possibility of damage to his personal standing existed. In these instances, the business of episcopal networks overlapped and conflicted with personal relationships. Ennodius had to represent the interests of his own church, but if he pursued those interests too vigorously then he threatened his own ability to benefit from those networks by alienating important members.

While his official duties came with the possible of risk of harm to his personal relationships, they also presented opportunities for social advancement for Ennodius and his relatives. In *Op.* 226 Ennodius wrote to Pope Symmachus and from the outset explicitly states that the pope owed him a favor:

> While the care of your crown governs the apostolic throne and you rule the summit of the heavenly empire, it is favorable for the profit of a relative. He holds the promise for my duties, he holds hope without blemish, ... such that what one earns repays many.⁴³

The duties that Ennodius refers to in his opening statement is his composition of the *Libellus* three years earlier that had helped to secure the papal throne for Symmachus.⁴⁴ The relative that Ennodius hoped would profit from his endeavors was his nephew Parthenius.⁴⁵ Ennodius makes it clear that Symmachus should

---

39 Kennell, *Magnus Felix Ennodius*, 41–42.
40 To Luminosus: Ennod. *Op.* 77, 139, 283; to Hormisdas and Discorus: Ennod. *Op.* 300.
41 Kennell, *Magnus Felix Ennodius*, 42.
42 Kennell, *Magnus Felix Ennodius*, 41–42.
43 Ennod. *Ep.* 5.10: *Dum sedem apostolicam coronae vestrae cura moderator et caelestis imperii apicem regitis, blanditur profectibus parentum quod meis promissum tenetur officiis. Spem sine labe obtinet apud constantem virum fideliter obsecutus. Grandis est pompa praestantis, quotiens quod unus meruit plurimis repensatur.*
44 Kennell, *Magnus Felix Ennodius*, 47.
45 Parthenius 2/3: *PLRE* 2, 832–834; Parthenius 2, *PCBE* 2/2, 1589.

favor Parthenius because he was a relative – *consanguinitate* – of Ennodius.[46] Parthenius was traveling to Rome in order to further his studies and Ennodius furnished him with letters of recommendation to Pope Symmachus and three other addressees: Luminosus, Faustus, and Faustus Iunior.[47] In addition to advancing Parthenius' prospects, Ennodius hoped that introducing his nephew to his important contacts would strengthen his own ties to them. In the recommendation of his nephew Ennodius declared to Pope Symmachus that Parthenius would act as if he were a hostage and help to secure the good relations between the two, connecting them through his travels.[48] Of course the reception that Parthenius received on his arrival was crucial – a rejection of Parthenius would be a rejection of Ennodius. Therefore, who Ennodius recommended him too was an important decision.

The identification of the two Fausti addressed in the letters is a matter of debate. *The Prosopography of the Later Roman Empire* argues that the two individuals are Faustus Albus (*Op.* 227) and Faustus Probus (*Op.* 228).[49] Kennell agrees with this argument and adds that the letter to Faustus Albus contains none of the familiarity seen in other letters to Faustus Probus and that the briefer final letter of the four is clearly addressed to Ennodius' favourite contact. The *Prosopographie chrétienne du Bas-Empire* however disagrees with this position entirely, arguing that the letters are "*sans doute*" addressed to Faustus Probus and his son Avienus (addressed as Faustus Iunior).[50] Assigning Faustus Albus as an addressee of one of these four letters certainly would seem at odds both with the other addressees having been supporters of Pope Symmachus as well as the fact that Faustus Albus is otherwise not well represented in Ennodius' letters – only receiving two other letters throughout the collection. Symmachus and Faustus Probus were, as we have seen, frequent recipients of Ennodius' letters; and Ennodius had a pre-existing relationship with Luminosus. Faustus Albus however stands out among this group as being an individual to whom Ennodius was not particularly closely connected with. Perhaps Ennodius sought to provide his nephew with recommendations to a broader group of individuals than just those connected closely to Symmachus and his network. This type of action would support Kennell's interpretation of the stiffness of the letter supposedly addressed to Faustus Albus. However, the interpretation presented in the PCBE

---

[46] Ennod. *Op.* 226: *Fovete ergo cuius veniendi causas patefacta consanguinitate didicistis.*
[47] Ennod. *Op.* 225, 226, 227, 228.
[48] Ennod. *Ep.* 226: *habetis obsidem, in quo dilucide meritorum apud uos meorum qualitas innotescat*; Kennell, *Magnus Felix Ennodius*, 45.
[49] PLRE 2, 832–834.
[50] Kennell, *Magnus Felix Ennodius*, 44–47; PCBE 2/1, 227–228.

which assigns *Op.* 228 to Avienus fits the overall patterns of Ennodius' preserved correspondence. Avienus was Ennodius' second most important correspondent (after his father) and he had likely studied under Ennodius in Pavia. Given that the act of making a recommendation carried great personal risk it makes sense that Ennodius would target those who he could be sure would support his request.

Indeed, from further letters, it is clear that Faustus Probus provided the support that Ennodius had requested.[51] Faustus's willingness to assist is evident in the easy expectation that Ennodius displays in his recommendation of Parthenius: "Parthenius, the son of my sister, wishes to seem a gentleman through the discipline of liberal studies, he hopes, if I am not mistaken, to have evidence of your support."[52] Ennodius's confidence of Faustus's willingness and ability to help his nephew is clear – Parthenius need only show up with the letter in hand and Faustus will provide him with a stipend. Ennodius's connection to Faustus is so prominent in the letter collection in part because of the value of the relationship to Ennodius – he knew that he could count on Faustus' support.

What is clear from this episode is that Ennodius hoped to exploit the episcopal networks that he participated in as a functionary for his own and his family's social benefit. His clerical and intellectual duties helped him to build the social capital required in order to exploit Symmachus and his allies for personal gain. In some respects, this is a chicken and egg scenario: were Ennodius actions in support of Symmachus driven by the fact that he was closely connected to Symmachan supporters such as Faustus Probus and a member of the Milanese church? Or did his actions lead to greater prestige and involvement in these episcopal networks? Most likely these were reinforcing principals. Ennodius' position as a deacon in a Symmachian aligned church and his social ties to key individuals such as Faustus determined that he would participate in networks tied to Symmachus. In turn, his participation in these networks reinforced his social position and opened up further opportunities. Of course, the reverse was also true, and it seems that Ennodius' support of Symmachus limited the opportunities for him to participate in other networks.

Senators who were tied to the Laurentian faction are underrepresented in Ennodius' letters with some only receiving letters after the end of the schism in 506. Faustus Albus was the recipient of one letter in the collection – *Op.* 301 in 508.[53] Similarly the senator Symmachus,[54] Boethius' father-in-law, re-

---

51 Ennod. *Op.* 368.
52 Ennod. *Op.* 228: *Partenius sororis meae filius per liberalis studii disciplinas ingenuus uult uideri: optat, ni fallor, peculii uestri habere testimonium.*
53 Moorhead, *Theoderic*, 132.

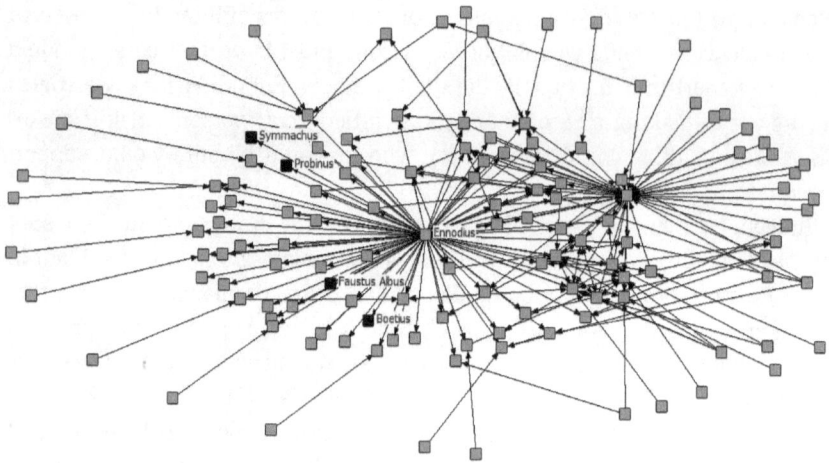

Figure 3: Supporters of Laurentius

ceived three letters starting with *Op.* 358 dated to 509, while Probinus is only the recipient of a single letter in the collection – *Op.* 426 written in 511.[55] Festus, Laurentius's chief supporter, does not feature in the collection at all. Only Boethius received a significant number of letters from Ennodius. Both Moorhead and Kennell note that Ennodius' preserved communication with this group of senators dates to after the resolution of the schism in Pope Symmachus' favor.[56] In addition to this observation we can add that even when Ennodius did contact these individuals it appears that he did not have much success in penetrating their networks. Structurally, as is clear in **Figure 3**, the chief supporters of Laurentius lie in the isolated area of the network which is dominated by structural holes. They lack ties to actors other than Ennodius as they were not mentioned by Ennodius in letters to other correspondents. Ennodius' relationship with Boethius illustrates this issue well.

---

[54] Not to be confused with the Bishop of Rome.
[55] Moorhead, *Theoderic*, 132.
[56] Moorhead, *Theoderic*, 132–133; Kennell, *Magnus Felix Ennodius*, 108.

4 Boethius

Boethius presents an interesting situation. The recipient of seven letters beginning in 507, Boethius otherwise seems to be a relatively important correspondent of Ennodius. The two writers shared a tumultuous relationship, with Ennodius penning some particularly venomous versus that attacked Boethius's sexual appetite.[57] Still, after the settlement of the schism Ennodius appeared to make an attempt to kindle a relationship – and was seemingly pleased with the arrival of letters from Boethius in *Op.* 271: "Regarding the letters, for the first I admit that I owe a debt, for the other I proffer affection."[58] Overall Bartlett argues that the tone of the letters suggests that Ennodius was still weary of Boethius but was interested in taking advantage of Boethius' rising status in the Ostrogothic court.[59] A particular group of letters: *Op.* 370, 408, 413, and 415, date to the period of Boethius's consulship in 510 and deal with Ennodius's attempts to profit from Boethius's new appointment. Consuls celebrated their appointments with displays of largess and Ennodius hoped to gain the gift of one of Boethius's unused houses in Milan.[60] Ennodius was unsuccessful in his attempt, but the episode shows that Ennodius was willing to put aside past differences if the possible returns were worth it. Ennodius had also sought to enroll himself as a client of Boethius' father-in-law Symmachus (*Op.* 426).[61] Still, in spite of these letters, Boethius remains a contradiction within Ennodius's network. While he received a significant number of letters from Ennodius, structurally Boethius is a non-factor. He lacks the centrality and betweenness of other more prestigious actors such as Faustus Probus, Liberius, and Pope Symmachus. Ennodius did not bind himself to Boethius through third parties – either by mentioning them in his letters to him or mentioning him in letters to others. Ennodius does not even invoke Boethius's relatives even though he contacts them elsewhere in the collection.

Ennodius' efforts to seek the support of Boethius and his father could be seen as an example of robust action. Robust actions are "non-comital actions that keep future lines of action open".[62] In this case seeking to establish better relations with Boethius and his father-in-law Symmachus provided Ennodius

---

[57] Bartlett, "The Dating of Ennodius' Writings," 61.
[58] Ennod. *Op.* 271: *de utrisque enim epistulis una obsequitur debito, altera praestatur affectui.*
[59] Bartlett, "The Dating of Ennodius' Writings," 61.
[60] Bartlett, "The Dating of Ennodius' Writings," 61.; Kennell, *Magnus Felix Ennodius*, 108–109.
[61] Bartlett, "The Dating of Ennodius' Writings," 62.
[62] John F. Padgett and Walter W. Powell, *The Emergence of Organizations and Markets* (Princeton NJ: Princeton University Press, 2012), 24. See also John F. Padgett and Christopher K. Ansell, "Robust Action and the Rise of the Medici," *AJS* 98/6 (1993): 1259–1319.

with the possibility of access to broader social relations in the future even though neither party was committed to this outcome by taking part in the exchange. This could be very beneficial to Ennodius, who as we have seen was very reliant on his relationship with Faustus Probus and several other prominent individuals. From the evidence of his preserved communication we cannot know for sure what his motives were in seeking out these relationships (beyond his immediate requests) with Boethius and his father-in-law, however broadening his social horizons would have been a prudent move for a regional aristocrat such as Ennodius.

A key issue in measuring the impact of the schism is that the loyalties of many individuals fluctuated or are not known. But crucially the biggest impact of the schism seems to be that Ennodius lacked alternative paths which could have supported his overtures to individuals who had supported Laurentius. This is particularly clear in the case of Boethius who responded to Ennodius's letters despite the defamatory efforts of Ennodius during the Schism. Still Ennodius does not mention Boethius to others or others to Boethius, nor did he make any recommendations of students or relatives to him. Structurally he was unable to tie Boethius more closely to him, and this is reflected in his lack of success in gaining from Boethius's position – he never did get the house that he wanted! While Boethius was politically a match for Faustus, he counts as a weak connection for Ennodius. This is perhaps a result of Ennodius having no one to tie him more closely to Boethius. So, while Ennodius communicated with Boethius, it seems that he did not participate in the same networks.

5 Conclusions

The network analysis of epistolary actions provides us with an additional lens through which to judge the participation of individuals such as Ennodius in networks which we do not have a large amount of evidence for. The prominence of supporters of Pope Symmachus in Ennodius' preserved correspondence can be seen not only in the volume of epistolary actions that they received but also in their relation to other supporters among Ennodius' correspondents. Supporters of Pope Symmachus were a part of a dense web of correspondents with whom Ennodius corresponded frequently and who were frequently mentioned in his letters to others. As we have seen, there are fewer preserved conversations with supporters of Laurentius. The glaring exception to this was Boethius who was the recipient of seven letters. Even so Boethius was not well connected to the rest of Ennodius' contacts through letter mentions – he does not feature in any shared conversations. So, while Ennodius may have been willing to seek out an improved relationship with Boethius, it seems that he found it difficult to build up the relationship by bringing others into the conversation. In this sense the Laurentian Schism and Ennodius' actions in it helped to determine which networks he was able to participate in successfully. By and large these were the episcopal networks that he navigated as a deacon, and the networks of Pope Symmachus and his supporters – particularly that of Faustus Probus. Whereas he lacked the ability to participate significantly in the networks of those who had opposed the pope, even if he did occasionally write to these individuals.

Bibliography

Primary Sources

Gelasius. *Epistle 12*, "*Duo Quippe Sunt*". Trans. John S. Ott, Portland State University, from Andreas Thiel, ed., *Epistolae Romanorum pontificum genuinae et quae ad eos scriptae sunt a S. Hilaro usque ad Pelagium* II., vol. 1, Brunsberg: Eduard Peter, 1867.
Magni Felicis Ennodii Opera, ed. Friedrich Vogel. *MGH AA 7*. Berlin: 1885.

Secondary Literature

Allen, Pauline. "Rationale for Episcopal Letter Collections in Late Antiquity." In *Collecting Early Christian Letters from the Apostle Paul to Late Antiquity*, edited by Bronwen Neil and Pauline Allen, 18–34. Cambridge: Cambridge University Press, 2015.
Althoff, Gerd. *Family, Friends and Followers, Political and Social Bonds in Early Medieval Europe*. Cambridge: Cambridge University Press, 2004.
Amory, Patrick. *People and Identity in Ostrogothic Italy, 489–554*. Cambridge: Cambridge University Press, 1997.
Bartlett, Richard. "The Dating of Ennodius' Writings." In *Atti Della Seconda Giornata Ennodiana*, edited by Edoardo D'Angelo, 53–74. Naples: Dipartimento di Filogia Classica dell Universita degli studi di Napoli Federico II., 2003.
Borgatti, S.P., Everett, M.G. and Freeman, L.C. *Ucinet 6 for Windows: Software for Social Network Analysis*. Harvard, MA: Analytic Technologies, 2002.
Cameron, Alan. "Anician Myths." *JRS* 102 (2012): 134–171.
Granovetter, Mark S. "The Strength of Weak Ties." *AJS* 78 (1973): 1360–1380.
Kennell, Stefanie A.H. *Magnus Felix Ennodius: A Gentleman of the Church*. Ann Arbor: The University of Michigan Press, 2000.
Kennell, Stefanie A.H. "Ennodius and His Editors." *CM* 51 (2000): 251–270.
Knox, Daniel K. "Measuring the Correspondence of Ennodius of Pavia: An Initial Social Network Analysis." *Annual of Medieval Studies at CEU* 23 (2017): 20–34.
Llewellyn, P.A.B. "The Roman Church During the Laurentian Schism: Priests and Senators." *ChH* 45/4 (1976): 417–427.

Martindale, J.R. *The Prosopography of the Later Roman Empire Volume 2*. Cambridge: Cambridge University Press, 1980.

Meyendorff, John. *Imperial Unity and Christian Divisions, The Church 450–680*. New York NY: St Vladimir's Seminary Press, 1989.

Moorhead, John. "The Laurentian Schism: East and West in the Roman Church." *ChH* 47/2 (1978): 125–136.

Moorhead, John. *Theoderic In Italy*. Oxford: Clarendon Press Oxford, 1993.

Padgett, John F. and Christopher K. Ansell. "Robust Action and the Rise of the Medici." *AJS* 98/6 (1993): 1259–1319.

Padgett, John F. and Walter W. Powell. *The Emergence of Organizations and Markets*. Princeton NJ: Princeton University Press, 2012.

Piétri, Charles, Luce Piétri and Janine Desmulliez, eds. *Prosopographie chrétienne du Bas-Empire 2: Prosopographie de l'Italie chrétienne, 313–604*. Rome: École française de Rome, 1999.

Scott, John. *Social Network Analysis*. Los Angeles CA: Sage, 2013.

Jamie Wood
Building and Breaking Episcopal Networks in Late Antique *Hispania*

1 Approaching episcopal networks in late antique Iberia

Like other Mediterranean regions, during late antiquity there was a steady growth of episcopal power in *Hispania* (roughly, the Iberia Peninsula) and the office of bishop frequently became a source of conflict within and between Christian communities.[1] As key figures within their cities and members of regional aristocracies, bishops have often been seen as playing a pivotal role in managing the transition from Roman to post-Roman *Hispania*.[2] Considerable efforts have been made to unravel how the office of bishop was theorised and institutionalised at church councils, in particular in the work of Isidore of Seville, who in turn drew extensively on the earlier writings of Augustine and Gregory the Great.[3] However, the mechanics by which a bishop's power was established, maintained, and sometimes challenged and overthrown within his city have not been explored systematically, nor has their relationship to the extensive processes of rule-making engaged in by the episcopate of the Visigothic kingdom during the sixth and seventh centuries.[4]

---

[1] Andrew Fear, José Fernández Urbiña, Mar Marcos Sanchez, eds., *The Role of the Bishop in Late Antiquity: Conflict and Compromise* (London: Bloomsbury, 2013). On bishops more generally, see Claudia Rapp, *Holy Bishops in Late Antiquity: The Nature of Christian Leadership in an Age of Transition*, The Transformation of the Classical Heritage 37 (Berkeley: University of California Press, 2005.)

[2] For general studies, see: R. L. Stocking, *Bishops, Councils and Consensus in the Visigothic Kingdom, 589–633* (Ann Arbor: University of Michigan Press, 2000); Céline Martin, *La géographie du pouvoir dans l'Espagne visigothique* (Paris: Septentrion, 2003); Michael Kulikowski, *Late Roman Spain and Its Cities* (Baltimore: Johns Hopkins University Press, 2004).

[3] Pierre Cazier, *Isidore de Séville et la Naissance de l'Espagne Catholique*, ThH 96 (Paris: Beauchesne, 1994).

[4] David Natal and Jamie Wood, "Playing with Fire: Conflicting Bishops in Late Roman Spain and Gaul," in *Making Early Medieval Societies: Conflict and Belonging in the Latin West, 300–1200*, eds. Conrad Leyser and Kate Cooper (Cambridge: Cambridge University Press, 2016): 33–57.

There have been a number of recent studies of episcopal elections in late antiquity and the middle ages.[5] However, the situation in the Iberian Peninsula has received minimal attention despite the fact that there is considerable evidence for disputing bishops (or disputes about bishops) from the period.[6] Episcopal elections were often potential moments at which consensus broke down, and the subsequent resolution of disputes was an opportunity to reassert communal solidarity. Scholars have generally focused their energies on unpicking the relationship between normative statements about how elections *should* work and evidence for their functioning in practice. In the process, they have revealed a great deal about the functioning of religious authority on the ground, demonstrating that rules were not followed blindly, but often moulded in response to shifting social or political contexts at a local level.

This chapter examines the cultivation and operation of networks of *groups* of bishops within *Hispania*, rather than the networks of an individual bishop, although this latter element is significant in some of the cases that are examined. If they were to succeed, the bishops of late antique *Hispania* had to negotiate a wide range of networks at local, regional, and international levels. Conflicts over episcopal office often seem to have been caused by and/or led to interference by bishops from elsewhere in *Hispania* and further afield, while the regulations that were laid down by church councils for the resolution of such disputes required the consent (and thus encouraged the interference) of neighbouring bishops. Yet episcopal power was deeply embedded in local and regional communities: subordinate clergy and local and regional elites were vital to establishing (or challenging) a new bishop's power in his city. Likewise, royal and imperial power often had a decisive impact on the outcome of disputes over episcopal office. Clergy, people, and monarchy were, at various times, directly incorporated into the formal processes that were laid down for the making of bishops at councils and in pastoral or theological texts. Procedure thus reflected the pragmatic experience of balancing potentially conflicting interest groups and agreeing on a mutually acceptable candidate.

The first written evidence for Christianity in the Peninsula is a letter of Cyprian, written in the middle of the third century to intervene in a debate over how to deal with bishops who had compromised with the Roman authorities during

---

5 Johan Leemans, Peter Van Nuffelen, Shawn W. J. Keough and Carla Nicolaye, eds., *Episcopal Elections in Late Antiquity*, AKG 119 (Berlin: Walter De Gruyter, 2011); Jörg Peltzer, *Canon Law, Careers and Conquest: Episcopal Elections in Normandy and Greater Anjou, c 1140–c 1230* (Cambridge: Cambridge University Press, 2012).
6 On the Iberian Peninsula, see: Peter Norton, *Episcopal Elections 250–600: Hierarchy and Popular Will in Late Antiquity* (Oxford: Oxford University Press, 2007), 114–115; 130; 154–156.

an episode of persecution.[7] From the late fourth century to the end of the seventh century, letters, histories, hagiographies, theological and pastoral texts, and normative legal sources and, especially, church council rulings provide sometimes quite detailed insights into processes of episcopal disputing and network building. These disputes occured across late antiquity and throughout the Peninsula and occurred during a period in which the politico-religious context was changing constantly. Under Roman emperors and Visigothic kings, amid shifting confessional allegiances under Homoian and Nicene rulers, conflict over the episcopal office took place consistently. Despite the wide range of sources, the evidence for the majority of these disputes is incomplete and limited. In most instances the outcome is unknown and, with the exception of the Priscillianist controversy, one-sided and limited to the perspective of the victors. Despite these limitations, considering disputes as snapshots of the formation, operation and occasional disintegration of networks offers further insights into the social and political processes underpinning episcopal power in late antique Iberia.

Exploration of conflicts over episcopal office in late antique Iberia can develop understandings of how episcopal power was established and sometimes challenged in specific contexts. This chapter does not contend that the cases that it mentions are typical of episcopal elections more generally, because the fact that a conflict took place increased the likelihood that sources would be generated and later preserved. However, it does suggest that such sources, when viewed collectively, present a consistent image of disputes over episcopal office. They reveal social dynamics that are usually obscured from view. By unpicking cycles of dispute and resolution, it is possible to observe the important role that social, political, and ecclesiastical networks played in the establishment and maintenance of the bishop's position in his city and in relation to his peers at the provincial level. The chapter explores four key themes relating to disputes over episcopal office in late antique Iberia: first, episcopal vacancies as moments at which conflict was liable to occur; second, the reactive attempts to disputants to build networks during conflicts, especially their use of church councils as venues for the resolution of conflict; third, the social and political contexts in which episcopal networks operated during conflicts, including the role of family in disputes over episcopal office; and fourth, the concern to safeguard and monitor church property at moments of transition between episcopates. Each of these themes is related to the numerous disputes that are outlined in the *Vitas Sanctorum Patrum Emeritensium*, a seventh-century hagiographical source that focus-

---

[7] For more on this episode, with bibliography, see: Geoffrey D. Dunn "Cyprian of Carthage and the Episcopal Synod of Late 254," *REAugP* 48 (2002): 229–247.

es most of its narrative on the development of the bishopric of Mérida in the sixth century. The *Vitas Sanctorum Patrum Emeritensium* provides some detailed information about conflicts over the episcopate in Mérida, former capital of late Roman *Hispania* and often considered the most powerful bishopric of the post-Roman period in the Iberian Peninsula.

2 Episcopal vacancies as moments of conflict

The procedures for episcopal election that are laid down in normative sources such as church councils and theological texts mask the complexity of the situations in which elections and depositions actually took place. In theory, comprovincial bishops, including the metropolitan of the province, were required to ensure that a bishop was elected. This is emphasised repeatedly in the council canons, in texts that define the episcopal office, like Isidore's *De ecclesiasticis officiis*, a kind of guidebook on church offices written in the early seventh century, and in accounts of disputes, where it is a point of complaint against opponents, as in the case of Priscillian at the end of the fourth century.[8] A mid-third century letter of Cyprian of Carthage to the Spanish bishops makes clear that other constituencies were required to ensure that a bishop's election was legitimate: the local clergy and people (i.e. congregation). The aim seems to have been to achieve consensus at the level of the city and province around the choice of the new bishop. The different scale levels of the church structure were supposed to be brought into alignment in order to ensure consensus about the chosen candidate.[9] However, the theoretical neatness of procedures for episcopal elections was sometimes not matched in practice and episcopal vacancies often led to 'succession crises' as various interested parties sought to influence the election process. For example, throughout the period, bishops often interfered across provincial boundaries.

The *Vitas Sanctorum Patrum Emeritensium* was redacted in two stages, in 633 or shortly thereafter and then sometime between 666 and 681.[10] It provides a great deal of information about conflicts over the bishopric: there were disputed elections, irregular procedures for ensuring the selection of favoured candidates, and attempts by the Visigothic king and local elites to influence the choice of

---

[8] Isidore of Seville, *De ecclesiasticis officiis* 2.5. On Priscillian, see Anthony R. Birley, "Magnus Maximus and the Persecution of Heresy," *BJRL* 66 (1983): 21–22.
[9] Natal and Wood, "Playing with Fire."
[10] On the date of the text, see Isabel Velázquez, *Vidas de los santos Padres de Mérida* (Madrid: Editorial Trotta, 2008), 11–15.

bishops. The hagiographer situates the origin of conflicts in the malign intentions of heretics, jealousy over the wealth of the bishopric, or personal rivalries. These narratives are undoubtedly designed primarily to establish the sanctity of favoured bishops, as the author makes plain when he refers to the overt modelling of the text on Gregory the Great's *Dialogues*.[11] Santiago Castellanos has argued that the text carries a powerful message about the need for social unity within a community that had for decades been riven by conflict over the episcopal office.[12] In Mérida, conflict over the bishopric thus seems to have been endemic, although such episodes were later downplayed as communities strove for coherence or victorious disputants sought to demonstrate that they ruled legitimately.

The bishopric of Mérida used to be viewed as highly exceptional within Iberia due to its wealth and status. Increasingly, however, this interpretation is being nuanced. It is clear that while Mérida was perhaps the most prosperous bishopric in late antique *Hispania*, it stood at one end of a spectrum and that many other cities, especially on the southern and eastern coasts were, according to a seminal work by Roger Collins, "self-reliant and economically self-sufficient, with nothing to gain from their kings, only tolerating their occasional exactions [...] But what is important to note is that Mérida and towns like it, at least in Baetica and Lusitania, had the resources and more importantly the self-consciousness and self-reliance to live in practice independent of royal authority."[13] It is hardly suprising, therefore, that in Mérida and elsewhere there was considerable conflict at the local level over the office of bishop, due to its access to resources and connections to broader ecclesiastical and political networks. Unfortunately, however, the acts of the bishops of other cities are not recorded in the beguiling detail of the *Vitas Sanctorum Patrum Emeritensium*, nor do their conflicts receive extended narrative treatment; usually only snippets remain.

As was noted in the introduction, disputed elections (and depositions) tended to lead to the production of written sources. Orderly elections, by contrast, do not seem to have generated as much comment or documentation, or at least there does not seem to have been a need to preserve and refer back to them at a later date. There are few references to consensual elections, although some sources do emphasise the unproblematic nature of episcopal succession in their favoured bishopric. For example, in his mid-seventh century *De viris il-*

---

[11] *Vitas Sanctorum Patrum Emeritensium*, Praefatio, 1.
[12] Santiago Castellanos, "The Significance of Social Unanimity in a Visigothic Hagiography: Keys to an Ideological Screen," *JECS* 11 (2003): 387–419.
[13] Roger Collins, "Mérida and Toledo: 550–585," in *Visigothic Spain: New Approaches*, ed. Edward James (Oxford: Clarendon Press, 1980): 198–199.

lustribus Bishop Ildefonsus of Toledo catalogued a series of orderly transitions from one bishop of his see to the next.[14] Ildefonsus's story of uninterrupted and peaceful succession was part of a broader narrative that sought to emphasise the historical status of his bishopric by stressing continuity of episcopal office there.[15] The author of the *Vitas Sanctorum Patrum Emeritensium* sought to achieve a similar balance, although in his case the strategy was to emphasise communal solidarity in the aftermath of conflict over the bishopric.[16] More generally, as a collective, the bishops of Visigothic Iberia consistently expressed the opinion that consensus decision-making was the best means of governing society.[17] The ecclesiastical imaginary thus stressed the need for all members of the community to unify behind their leader, although the detailed accounts of elections that we possess suggest that these were moments of potential strife and that the completion of the election did not necessarily lead to the resolution of attendant conflict.

3 Church councils and the reactive resolution and generation of conflict

Church councils were envisaged as an effective means of resolving disputes and legislated regularly on the matter of episcopal office, often in response to cases where the rules had not been followed. Councils were supposed to take place regularly within each ecclesiastical province and their minutes record a number of disputes over the episopal office. Councils were also meant to be convened at the level of the individual bishopric and were meant to function as venues for communication between the bishop and his subordinates, as well as providing an opportunity for bishops to monitor their clergy.[18] The meetings that would have been held to fill a vacant see must also have functioned as a form of quasi-council, as they were supposed to canvass the opinions of the clergy within the bishopric over candidates. However, far from serving to resolve disputes as

---

[14] Ildefonsus of Toledo, *De viris illustribus* Praefatio, 1, 2, 4, 6, 7, 12, 13, (all Toledo), 5, 11 (both Zaragoza), 8 (Seville), 9 (Gerona), 10 (Palencia).
[15] Jamie Wood, "Playing the Fame Game: Bibliography, Celebrity and Primacy in Late Antique Spain," *JECS* 20 (2012): 613–640.
[16] Castellanos, "The Significance of Social Unanimity."
[17] In general, see Stocking, *Bishops, Councils and Consensus*.
[18] Stocking, *Bishops, Councils and Consensus*, 100–111.

the normative sources envisaged, councils often contributed to the generation, continuation, and escalation of conflict.

Alongside their stated roles as venues for the resolution of conflict and ecclesiastical governance, councils were moments at which Nicene episcopal and clerical networks came together. Although there was only one recorded synod of the Arian church in Visigothic Spain, called by King Leovigild at Toledo in 580, mentioned briefly in hostile Nicene sources, the Arian bishops represented a potential competing network.[19] Leovigild seems to have supported the Arian episcopate by promoting its activities collectively in council and, as we shall see in the case of Mérida, individually at the level of the city. This was probably part of a broader campaign in which attempted – and failed – to reconcile the Nicene and Arian elements of the population of *Hispania*, at the same time asserting his power over peripheral regions of the Peninsula, actions that were depicted as part of a persecution by later Nicene historians.

Rachel Stocking has unpicked the efforts of Isidore to cover up the various failures of councils to resolve the case of Bishop Martianus of Écija, who was mistakenly deposed at the Third Council of Seville (presided over by Isidore), following an investigation in Écija. The records of the Third Council of Seville are not extant, but it probably took place in 624.[20] Subsequent investigations at the Fourth Council of Toledo in 633, again chaired by Isidore, revealed that Martianus had been "framed" by Aventius, who had succeeded him as bishop of Écija. The Fourth Council of Toledo, held in 633, downplayed what had happened at Seville and, although Martianus had his episcopal rank reinstated, Aventius remained bishop of Écija.[21] The records of the original council at Seville seem to have been deliberately excluded from the recension of the *Hispana*, a collection of church council canons that may have been compiled by Isidore in Seville in 633, nor are the full records of the council found in any other version of the *Hispana*.[22] This meant that the bishops who were tasked with reviewing the case at the sixth Council of Toledo, held in 638, two years after Isidore's death, struggled to find any written record of what had gone on at the Third Council of Seville fourteen years earlier. In the course of their investigation

---

19 John of Biclarum, *Chronica* 58.
20 Rachel L. Stocking, "Martianus, Aventius, and Isidore: Provincial Councils in Seventh-Century Spain," *EMEu* 6 (1997): 169–188.
21 Martianus was blamed for putting himself in a position that left him open to false accusations. Écija therefore had two bishops from 633–638.
22 Even in 625 the records seem to have been hard to get hold of because Braulio of Zaragoza (*Ep.* 3) wrote to Isidore asking for a copy; E. A. Thompson, *The Goths in Spain* (Oxford: Clarendon, 1969), 171.

they generated a document known as the *Exemplar iudicii inter Martianum et Aventium Episcopos*. This document reveals that the charges against Martianus included: speaking against the king; consulting a female diviner about the life of the king and his own future; having a female slave look after his wardrobe; and having illicit sexual relations. The Sixth Council of Toledo also unravelled what had happened at Écjia in order to generate these accusations. Aventius had forced clerical clients to give false testimony, had used an under-age witness, and had illiterate witnesses of low status sign a false statement that they could not read. Once this testimony was discounted there was only one witness against Martianus, which was insufficient to 'convict' him. Seventeen further witnesses were questioned and the case finally decided in Martianus' favour. Although Aventius was sentenced to penance, he was allowed to retain his episcopal rank.[23]

Stocking argued that the dispute was not resolved for so long because to have done so would have called into question the entire programme of conciliar governance that Isidore saw as fundamental to governing church and society.[24] The failure of the bishops at the Third Council of Seville – including Isidore himself – to recognize that they were being duped potentially undermined faith in the efficacy of the legal procedure and the rituals that gave it divine sanction. Ultimately, this had the potential to call into question the efforts of the bishops to evangelise the population of Hispania. If the bishops could not take care of their own business, how could they be trusted to take care of everyone else's? Their efficacy and their authority would be called into question. Ultimately, it seems that the ideal of a spiritually-inspired episcopal network in council was more important to Isidore than securing the correct outcome in any one individual dispute over episcopal office.

Those who sought to resolve disputes were clearly reactive rather than proactive, seeking to activate latent networks or to generate new connections to potentially powerful sponsors. But so too were disputants, several of whom seem to have played a waiting game – once the circumstances were in their favour, appeals were made against former judgements, calling on their connections and referring back to records generated in earlier conflicts. For example, Martianus waited until Isidore had died before bringing his case before yet another council, having been fobbed off on at least two previous occasions. Two bishops in *Spania*, the Byzantine province in the south west, who had been deposed in the early 590s, seem to have waited until a change in imperial regime (i.e. until the em-

---

23 Thompson, *The Goths*, 287–289 for an overview of the case.
24 Stocking, "Martianus, Aventius, and Isidore," 185–188.

peror Maurice had been killed) before taking up their case with Pope Gregory the Great in the early 600s, who sent a dossier of imperial laws with his agent to Spain to argue the case.[25] Throughout late antiquity, disputants were willing to call in support from elsewhere in their conflicts, either from ecclesiastics outside *Hispania*, such as Cyprian of Carthage, Ambrose of Milan, and Gregory, or from imperial, royal or aristocratic backers, as in the case of Priscillian.[26] Their letters were appealed to during later efforts to resolve conflict; for example, when a letter of Ambrose was cited in the canons of the first council of Toledo around 400.[27]

4 Contextualising episcopal networks

It is clear, therefore, that the bishops of *Hispania* did not operate in a socio-political vacuum. Rather than sitting apart from elites, they were almost without exception members of aristocracies. Any attempt to unravel how they were appointed and then exercised their authority must therefore take account of the social, political, and even economic contexts in which they operated. Although appointment as a bishop provided the office holder with opportunities to cultivate connections to their peers within and beyond Hispania, both the normative and the narrative sources reveal that they also had to balance a range of cross-cutting relationships at various scale levels, from the city to the province and beyond.

Non-ecclesiastics often interfered in episcopal disputes throughout late antiquity. For instance, much of Priscillian's support seems to have come from aristocrats in Gaul. Imperial authorities often involved themselves in disputes over episcopal office, both at the start of the period and in the Byzantine province at the end of the sixth century. Over time, Visigothic kings played an increasingly prominent role in appointing bishops and by the early seventh century they had the final decision.[28] This is made plain in an exchange of letters between Isidore of Seville and Braulio of Zaragoza in 632, which shows that they were colluding to get their candidate selected by the king to take over the vacant see of Tarragona:

---

[25] R. González Fernández, "Las cartas de Gregorio Magno al defensor Juan: La aplicación del derecho de Justiniano en la Hispania Bizantina en el siglo VII," *AnCr*14 (1997): 287–298.
[26] Natal and Wood, "Playing with Fire," 39–46.
[27] This is recorded in the *Exemplar definitivae sententiae translate de gestis*, which was appended to the records of the First Council of Toledo, for the text of which see: José Vives, ed., *Concilios Visigóticos e Hispano-Romanos* (Barcelona-Madrid: CSIC, Instituto Enrique Flórez, 1963): 30–33.
[28] Norton, *Episcopal Elections*, 156.

I suggest that, since Eusebius, our metropolitan [i.e. Eusebius of Tarragona, the chief bishop of Tarraconensis], has died, you might have compassion and that you might suggest to your son, our lord [King Sisenand], that he appoint someone to this position whose teaching and holiness might be a model of life for the others. I commend this present son in all matters to your most blessed power [...] may I be deemed worthy to be enlightened by your eloquence on his account.²⁹

Elite bishops could still hope to influence the king's choice, even across putative provincial boundaries in the case of Isidore (who was from Baetica, not Tarraconensis). By the early seventh century, therefore, a more top-down approach to episcopal appointments had been adopted, although it is unclear whether kings oversaw the selection of all bishops or focused on the more powerful sees. It is also likely that, as the Braulio-Isidore correspondence indicates, the king may have either chosen from a shortlist or ratified choices that had been made by ecclesiastics at the local or provincial level.³⁰

While the populations of cities were often less than enthusiastic in supporting their bishop, they did not necessarily respond positively to outside interference, royal or otherwise. The case of Priscillian and its aftermath at the end of the fourth century brought numerous accusations of factional division in the cities, including between clerical groups. Such support clearly continued in the aftermath of the various ecclesiastical rulings and imperial edicts that were made against Priscillian and his supporters. After the Council of Zaragoza, which, despite not naming him, was probably intended to end Priscillian's activities, the Priscillianists sought to mobilise support in Mérida against one of their leading opponents, Hydatius, who was bishop there. They were attacked and beaten back by a crowd of Hydatius' supporters.³¹ After the execution of its leader at the hands of the imperial government of Magnus Maximus sometime between

---

29 Braulio of Zaragoza, *Ep.* 5: *suggero ut, quia Eusebius metropolitanus noster decessit, habeas misericordiae curam et hoc filio tuo, nostro domno, suggeras ut illum illi loco preficiat, cuius doctrina et sanctitas ceteris sit uitae forma. Hunc autem filium presentem beatissimae potestati uestre per omnia commendo et tam de his que bic suggessimus quam etiam de his que supra questi fuimus eloquio uestro per eum inlustrari mereamur.*
30 From 646 there is an exchange of letters between Braulio of Zaragoza (*Ep.* 31–32) and King Chindaswinth, in which the former unsuccessfully petitions the latter to refrain from appointing his favorite deacon as Bishop of Toledo.
31 For an overview of these events, see Birley, "Magnus Maximus," 19–23; Victoria Escribano, "Heresy and Orthodoxy in Fourth-century Hispania: Arianism and Priscillianism," in *Hispania in Late Antiquity: Current Perspectives*, eds. Kim Bowes and Michael Kulikowski (Leiden: Brill, 2005): 121–149. On Priscillian more generally, see Henry Chadwick, *Priscillian of Avila: The Occult and the Charismatic in the Early Church* (Oxford: Clarendon, 1976).

385 and 387, the Priscillianist network did not disintegrate but its members sought to entrench their position in the north west of *Hispania* and it was not until 400 that a council was held at Toledo (in the province of Carthaginiensis, not Gallaecia, where the 'movement' was probably centred) that sought to bring them to order.

Several other sources suggest that clerical factionalism was an issue at the level of the bishopric. As in the case of the attempt of Priscillian's supporters to stir up trouble for their enemies at Mérida, records of the depositions of bishops within the Byzantine territories in the 590s and of Martianus of Écjia in Baetica in the 620s stress that their opponents had mobilised clients – including among the local clergy – against them.[32] Diocesan councils provided venues for the investigation of episcopal conduct (or misconduct), but, as was noted earlier, were also envisaged an opportunity for bishops to monitor their clergy. The clergy at the level of the bishopric were thus subject to regulation, just like the bishops within the province. Their inclusion in the procedures that were laid down for electing bishops was a pragmatic recognition of their active investment in seeing preferred, or at least acceptable, candidates appointed.

The early 580s witnessed a particularly tumultuous period of conflict over the episcopal office at Mérida. This seems to have been caused by the attempts of Leovigild, the Arian King of the Visigoths, to exert more direct control over the city, as part of his largely successful efforts to assert royal authority over parts of the Peninsula that had previously been only tied loosely to the Visigothic state. There were additional reasons why Mérida would have been a target for Leovigild: it was head of the ecclesiastical and civil province of Lusitania; it had a tradition of independence from and resistance to central control by the Visigothic kings; it had strong trading connections to the eastern Mediterranean; and, as was noted in the introduction to this chapter, it was perhaps the wealthiest bishopric in *Hispania*.[33] Leovigild's interest in the bishopric may also have been connected to his religious policy, ill-understood due to the hostile accounts of later Nicene historians, to reconcile Arian and Nicene populations.

Irrespective of his actual motivation, the *Vitas Sanctorum Patrum Emeritensium* describes Leovigild's actions as a persecution against the Nicene population of the city. According to the hagiographer, the hero of Mérida 's resistance to Leovigild's attempts to assert his authority was Masona, the Nicene bishop. The 'persecution' involved various measures, including: calling on Masona to

---

[32] Stocking, "Martianus, Aventius, and Isidore," 172; Margarita Vallejo Girvés, "Bizancio ante la conversión de los visigodos: los obispos Jenaro y Esteban," in *XIV Centenario Concilio III de Toledo (589–1989)* (Toledo: Arzobispado de Toledo, 1991): 477–483.
[33] Collins, "Mérida and Toledo," 194–196.

convert to Arianism (and thus securing him for a competing episcopal network); attempting to gain control of the key basilica of Saint Eulalia; requiring Masona to leave Mérida and travel to the king in Toledo, the capital; staging debates between the Arians and Nicenes; and exiling Masona from the city.

Most significantly for the purposes of this chapter, however, Leovigild tried to manipulate episcopal appointments as a way of undermining Masona. For instance, after failing to persuade Masona to convert to Arianism, one of Leovigild's first actions was to appoint an Arian bishop called Sunna, who incited disorder within the city.[34] Sunna and Leovigild were unable to dislodge Masona who, together with "all the people" (*universus populus*) vigorously resisted the "false bishop" (*pseudoepiscopus*) in defence of their bishop.[35] Later, Leovigild exiled Masona to a monastery and replaced him with Nepopis, a Catholic bishop from another city:

> After this a false priest (*pseudosacerdos*) called Nepopis was set up in his place and made the man of God's replacement in the city of Mérida. He was a profane man, a true servant of the Devil, and angel of Satan, a harbinger of the Antichrist, and a bishop of another town.[36]

After Masona had been in exile for three years, Leovigild apparently realised his error and reinstated Masona. Nepopis was forced to return to his own city in disgrace.[37]

Kings were clearly able to make and break bishops, should they wish, but it is clear that the failure of Sunna and Nepopis was due, at least partially, to their lack of local support. Although, the hagiographer emphasises that some of Nepopis's followers accompanied him to Mérida, the struggles of outsiders to secure their position in Mérida in the early 580s is reminiscent of the failed efforts of Priscillian's supporters to intervene in the city against their opponent Hyda-

---

[34] *Vitas Sanctorum Patrum Emeritensium* 5.5, l. 8–12: *Quendam scilicet uirum pestiferum Arriane hereseos prauitatem per omnia uindicantem, cui nomen erat Sunna, pro seditiosis simultatibus excitandis et pro conturbationem sanctissimi uiri uel tonus populi in eadem ciuitatem episcopum Arriane partis instituit* [...].

[35] *Vitas Sanctorum Patrum Emeritensium* 5.5, l. 36–37.

[36] *Vitas Sanctorum Patrum Emeritensium* 5.6, l. 135–138: *Post hec subrogatur ei pseudosacerdos Nepopis quidam nomine atque in locum uiri Dei in Emeretensem urbem substituitur, homo namque profanus, seruus sane diaboli, angelus Satane, prenuntius Antixpi et hic erat aliene ciuitatis episcopus*.

[37] *Vitas Sanctorum Patrum Emeritensium* 5.8.

tius two hundred years beforehand.[38] Bishops were thus able to resist the efforts of their peers and of kings to intervene in their bishoprics and in Mérida there are several examples of how they tried to do this. The hagiographer notes repeatedly that Masona mobilised the local population in shows of loyalty, for example through processions, and emphasises in a more general sense the size and cohesion of his support base in comparison to those of his opponents.[39] Scholarship has demonstrated that in late antiquity processions served, among other things, as fora for the display of consensus behind community leaders.[40] At Mérida they functioned, at least in the mind of the hagiographer, as ritualised manifestations of the associations that bonded the bishop to his city and, potentially, as a means of signalling resistance to outside interference. Cultivating connection to local populations was vital if the bishop was to establish his power in the first place and later to resist outside interference or challenges from within the bishopric. Election thus depended on more than the will of the monarch; local support was also necessary if an elected candidate was to remain in office.

---

38 *Vitas Sanctorum Patrum Emeritensium* 5.8, l. 54–56: "he fled, leaving the city in disgrace with a few helpers, who all belonged to his household and followed behind him" (*Quumque prior ipse cum paucis fugeret, post ipsum cuncti ad eum pertinentes urbem ignominiose egressi*).
39 *Vitas Sanctorum Patrum Emeritensium* 5.6, l. 21–24: "When the most holy bishop Masona was suddenly snatched away and carried off from the bosom of his holy church and, though innocent, taken into exile like a condemned man, the voice of all the citizens of Mérida cried out moaning in unbearable grief" (*Hincquum subito sanctissimus uir Masona episcopus e gremio raptus eclesie sancte tolleretur et indemnis quasi reus ad exilium duceretur, omnium uox ciuium Emeretensium eiulato magno cum intolerabilibus lacrimis prestrepebant*); 5.8, l. 42–43: "accompanied by an enormous retinue he returned from his place of exile to the city of Mérida" (*cum maximo comitatu de loco quo religatus fuerat ad urbem Emeretensem reuersus est*); 5.8, l. 59–60: "holy Masona was returning to the city of Mérida with a great host on the self-same road" (*sanctum Masonam cum infinita multitudine per ipsam uiam regredi ad Aemeritam ciuitatem*); 5.8, l. 75–76: "he came to the city with all rejoicing in great joy" (*quum inmenso gaudio gaudentibus cunctis ad urbem peruenit*); 5.8, l. 79–81: "he entered the city exulting in the Lord and with all his people rejoicing" (*exultans in Domino, exultantibus uniuersis, urbem ingressus est*).
40 On Spain, see Michael McCormick, *Eternal Victory: Triumphal Rulership in Late Antiquity, Byzantium, and the Early Medieval West* (Cambridge: Cambridge University Press, 1986), 297–327; Hendrick W. Dey, *The Afterlife of the Roman City: Architecture and Ceremony in Late Antiquity and the Early Middle Ages* (Cambridge: Cambridge University Press, 2015), 140–160; Jocelyn N. Hillgarth, "Popular Religion in Visigothic Spain," in *Visigothic Spain: New Approaches* ed. Edward James (Oxford: Clarendon Press, 1980): 51–52. See also: Jacob A. Latham, "From Literal to Spiritual Soldiers of Christ: Disputed Episcopal Elections and the Advent of Christian Processions in Late Antique Rome," *ChH* 81 (2012): 298–327; Ine Jacobs, "Domination ecclésiastique et espaces urbains. La rue à colonnade comme toile de fond de l'affirmation chrétienne," *Antiquité Tardive* 22 (2014): 263–286.

Leovigild's intervention disrupted Masona's position, creating space and providing resources for challenges to emerge. When viewed in the context of the rest of the text and the author's consistent effort to show that there had always been consensus in the city, it seems more likely that royal actions simply catalysed latent opposition within the population of the city (and perhaps further afield in the case of Nepopis and his supporters), at the same time encouraging elements of the Nicene population to unite behind Masona. In addition, both Masona and his Arian opponents sought to control the basilica and relics of the city's holy patron, Santa Eulalia, and the *Vitas Sanctorum Patrum Emeritensium* stresses that her support was responsible for his ultimate victory. A range of cross-cutting networks, from the worldly to the holy, had to be cultivated if the bishop was to establish his power within the city and resist challenges from within and without.

The council rulings and, especially, some of the theoretical works make clear that election processes had been developed in response to episodes of misconduct and faulty election procedures. Royal and imperial authorities involved themselves consistently in episcopal elections and/or depositions, as did aristocratic sponsors, often due to their pre-existing ties to (or enmities with) specific candidates. In giving the 'people' a role in the election of bishops, the rulebooks thus recognised the tendency of elites to intervene at local and supra-local levels. Rules were thus documents of practice as much as normative statements and provide insight into processes of disputing and network-making, as well as into the pragmatic attitudes of those bishops who made such normative pronouncements in the context of conflict resolution. Practices of episcopal election thus evolved in dialogue with a pre-existing tradition that was very clear on how bishops *should* be selected *in theory* at the same time drawing on the bitter experience of trying to make an election or a deposition 'stick' in a real social world.

5 Property and episcopal disputing

The formation of episcopal dynasties in a number of important cities further demonstrates the importance of local power bases for the establishment of the bishop's power. Notably, Isidore succeeded his brother, Leander, as bishop of Seville around the year 600, while their brother became bishop of nearby Écjia. Justinian of Valencia's three brothers became bishops at some point in the mid-sixth century.⁴¹ The emergence of such dynasties suggests that, as elsewhere in the post-Roman Mediterranean, control of the episcopal office was a key means by which elites consolidated power.⁴²

The embeddedness of the episcopacy in local and regional power networks, alongside the considerable economic interests of the church contributed to a focus on property within disputes. Several councils made rulings to ensure that episcopal property was secured after the death of the incumbent and there were consistent efforts to regulate the relationship between the bishop's personal patrimony and that of the church. The property of the bishop and his church appears to have been particularly vulnerable to the clergy when a see was vacant and various procedures were put in place to prevent its misappropriation. For example, church councils repeatedly state that neighbouring bishops should keep careful watch over the goods of the church when it became evident that an incumbent was dying and should continue monitoring it after his death, at which point an inventory was to be sent to the metropolitan, who appointed an overseerer for the property.⁴³

Accounts of disputes also address economic factors and underline the point that during the transition from one episcopate to the next church property was at risk. For example, when Nepopis, the Nicene bishop who was apppointed in Mérida by King Leovigild in the 580s as part of his conflict with Masona, was forced to return to his own city in disgrace, he sought to take with him, using a large number of wagons and men of the church of Mérida, "a great amount of silver, ornaments, and anything else he saw of beauty in the churches in Mérida", only to be foiled by Masona.⁴⁴ Gregory the Great argued that if it was judged that the bishops who had been deposed in the Byzantine province in the early 590s had been treated unjustly, they should be compensated for any losses by those responsible, or their successors.⁴⁵

One of the disputes at Mérida from the mid-sixth century focused largely on the fate of the considerable wealth that Bishop Paul had accrued as a reward for

---

41 Isidore of Seville, *De viris illustribus* 21–22: Justinian of Valencia, Justus of Urgell, Nebridius of Egara and Elpidius of Huesca; Thompson, *The Goths*, 43.
42 For family traditions of clerical service and their possibly influence on episcopal elections see Rapp, *Holy Bishops*, 195–199. For clerical dynasties see the contribution of Volker Menze to the present volume.
43 Thompson, *The Goths*, 31, 47–50; P. D. King, *Law and Society in the Visigothic Kingdom* (Cambridge: Cambridge University Press, 1972), 60, 67, 128, 154–157, 160, 179.
44 *Vitas Sanctorum Patrum Emeritensium* 5.8, l. 46–50: *argentum copiosum et ornamentum insignia et quicquid meliora uidit in Emeritensem eclesiam plaustris plurimis perhoneratis per homines Emeritensis eclesie clam nocturno tempore ad suam ciuitatem fraudulenter misit.*
45 For this case, see González Fernández, "Las cartas de Gregorio Magno."

saving the life of a wealthy citizen's wife. This episode underlines the fact that episcopal power had to be exercised within a matrix of intersecting networks. The *Vitas Sanctorum Patrum Emeritensium* notes that Paul was a Greek and came from the East to Mérida.[46] Connections to the eastern Mediterranean were clearly maintained under Paul's leadership because Greek traders from his home region came to Mérida and "according to the custom they presented themselves on arrival to the bishop".[47] Masona soon realised that Fidelis, his nephew, was with the merchants and pressured them into leaving him in Mérida, mentoring him as a successor. Paul's connections to the East reflect the broader integration of many of the cities of the south into international trading networks, while his attempts to secure the succession for his nephew provides us with an insight into how other bishops may have sought to establish episcopal dynasties.[48]

In effect, Paul held the church to ransom – if Fidelis was not elected in his place during his lifetime, then he would not bequeath his fortune to the church of Mérida.[49] Paul's actions were unpopular with at least some of the population of Mérida. The hagiographer reports that after Paul's death some "poisonous men" persistently murmured "with wicked words against the most blessed bishop Fidel in order to drive him from the place where he had been set".[50] In response, Fidelis had to threaten to withdraw from the episcopal office and to remove his personal wealth from the service of the church in order to persuade his opponents to back down and accept his rule.[51] In theory, bishops were supposed to relinquish their personal property before taking up office, nor, according to the rules, were bishops meant to name their successors.[52] The actions of Paul and Fidelis in relation to the succession and their property were thus highly dubious in at least two respects. The hagiographer stresses that this was perfectly acceptable behaviour, which suggests that, in fact, there was some nervousness

---

[46] *Vitas Sanctorum Patrum Emeritensium* 4.1.
[47] *Vitas Sanctorum Patrum Emeritensium* 4.3, l. 6–7: *ex more episcopo prebuerunt occursum.*
[48] Paul Reynolds, *Hispania and the Roman Mediterranean, AD 100–700: Ceramics and Trade* (London: Duckworth, 2010), 120.
[49] *Vitas Sanctorum Patrum Emeritensium*, 4.4.
[50] *Vitas Sanctorum Patrum Emeritensium* 4.5.1: *Post cuius discessum quidam pestiferi homines iuxta id quod uir Dei predixerat uerbis malignis contra beatissimum Fidelem episcopum musitare ceperunt, ut eum de loco quo constitutus fuerat per quaquumque occasione pellerent.*
[51] *Vitas Sanctorum Patrum Emeritensium* 4.5.
[52] Rapp, *Holy Bishops*, 212–213.

about its legality and that it was a continued point of contention in the city into the seventh century.⁵³

Access to economic power and family relationships, rather than legal procedures, often seem to have been the determining factors in contested succesions, enabling a well-connected patron to overcome competing factions and to decide who held the episcopacy and how their power was exercised. The property of bishops was a concern for the church in the province of Lusitania, of which Mérida was the capital, into the second half of the seventh century. The provincial council of Mérida, held in 666, dealt with various matters pertaining to the management of church property, including the manumission of slaves, the relationship between the property of the church and of the bishop, and how a bishop's property might be treated upon his death.⁵⁴ Family relationships and property holding were thus intimately intertwined and reflect the fact that conflict over the episcopal office was inseparable from the material conditions of the locality.

6 Conclusions

Bishops are perhaps the most visible element of the broader networks that sometimes cooperated and sometimes conflicted, both within the locality and with other ecclesiastical, imperial or royal systems of power. Indeed, in parts of the Iberian Peninsula, it was the potential of bishops – and the local elites to which they were connected – to generate and sustain connections across political boundaries that brought them into conflict with Visigothic kings and Byzantine governors in the late sixth and seventh centuries. Yet while episcopal networks within provinces, within Iberia and outside – for example with Rome – clearly played a significant role in processes of conflict generation and resolution, as well as in attempts to regulate away future disputes, other factors were equally important. Subordinate clergy and the local population – i.e. local and regional elites – were vital to establishing and/or challenging a new bishop's power in his city. Likewise, royal (and sometimes imperial) power had a significant impact – usually decisive – on the outcome of disputes over episcopal office. The involvement of clergy, people, and monarchy was, at various times, directly incorporated into the processes by which bishops were made. Rules thus seem to have been modeled actively on the practical experiences of

---

53 *Vitas Sanctorum Patrum Emeritensium* 4.5, l. 6–7: "as was his right under church law" (*quod ille sublatis de iure eclesie prediis suis se ab eis separaret*).
54 *Council of Mérida* 13–14, 16, 18, 20–21, in *Concilios Visigóticos e Hispano-Romanos*, ed. Vives: 334–341.

episcopal elections. We need to look beyond episcopal networks, therefore, if we are to fully understand the making of bishops in late antique *Hispania* and elsewhere.

Analysis of the contested episcopal elections of late antique *Hispania* demonstrates that the neat networks of bishops described by the normative sources were rather more ephemeral in practice. The rhetoric of the bishops and their focus on consensus decision making at councils masks the insecurity of their position on a local level and in relation to other sources of power. Disputes over episcopal office reveal a range of interpenetrating and overlapping social relationships that were responsible for establishing and challenging episcopal power at local, regional, and trans-regional levels. Bishops were key hingemen, balancing a range of interest groups and conflicts over their position encouraged the formation of yet further networks in efforts to solve problems.[55] Networks thus generated conflicts over the episcopal office in late antique Iberia, both at the individual and collective level, at the same time as contributing to their resolution, and generating yet further associations. In the long term, this process assisted the development of a well-developed pastoral vision of the episcopacy and of conciliar governance, but also laid the groundwork for future disputing.

Episcopal networks – of individual bishops and of groups of bishops – were important, but bishops (individually and collectively) operated within a nexus of cross-cutting relationships: with fellow members of the regional nobility, with clients within their bishopric, and with contacts further afield, for example in other provinces. Such relationships were not necessarily fixed but required cultivation, their tendency to shift and to generate conflict with other networks meaning that the ethos of cooperation and consensus among the episcopal elite laid down by church councils was not often realised in practice. What is more, the generation and resolution of disputes seems in many cases to have been constitutive of episcopal networks – coalitions were formed in order to influence and to confirm elections, and sometimes to try to depose unwanted candidates. Bishops came together in efforts to resolve disputes and forestall future conflict. Rather than breaking up networks, then, conflict over episcopal office therefore often helped to generate them.

---

[55] On the concept of social, political and cultural brokers in late antiquity and the early middle ages more generally, see Helmut Reimitz, *History, Frankish Identity and the Framing of Western Ethnicity, 550–850* (Cambridge: Cambridge University Press, 2015): 282–291; Helmut Reimitz, "Cultural Brokers of a Common Past: History, Identity and Ethnicity in Gregory of Tours and the Chronicles of Fredegar," in *Strategies of Identification: Ethnicity and Religion in Early Medieval Europe*, eds. Walter Pohl and Gerda Heydemann (Turnhout: Brepols, 2013): 257–301.

Bibliography

Primary sources

Braulio of Zaragoza, *Epistolae:* Luis Riesco Terrero, ed., *Epistolario de San Braulio: introducción, edición crítica y traducción.* Sevilla: Universidad de Sevilla, 1975. [English translation: Claude W. Barlow, *Iberian Fathers*, vol. 2: *Braulio of Saragossa, Fructuosus of Braga*. Washington: Catholic University of America Press, 1969, 15–112]
Conciliar Acta: José Vives, ed., *Concilios Visigóticos e Hispano-Romanos.* Barcelona, Madrid: CSIC, Instituto Enrique Flórez, 1963.
Ildefonsus of Toledo, *De viris illustribus:* Carmen Codoñer Merino, *El "De viris illustribus" de Ildefonso de Toledo: Estudio y edición crítica.* Salamanca: Universidad de Salamanca, 1972. [English translation: A. T. Fear, *Lives of the Visigothic fathers.* Liverpool: Liverpool University Press, 1997, 107–122]
Isidore of Seville, *De ecclesiasticis officiis:* Christopher M. Lawson, ed., *Sancti Isidori Episcopi Hispalensis. De Ecclesiasticis Officiis.* CChr.SL 113. Turnhout: Brepols, 1989. [English translation: Thomas L. Knoebel, Isidore of Seville: De ecclesiasticis officiis. New York, Mahwah, N.J.: The Newman Press, 2008]
Isidore of Seville, *De viris illustribus:* Carmen Codoñer Merino, ed., *El "De viris illustribus" de Isidoro de Sevilla.* Salamanca: CSIC, Instituto "Antonio de Nebrija", Colegio Trilingüe de la Universidad, 1964.
John of Biclarum, *Chronica:* Carmen Cardelle de Hartmann, ed., *Victoris Tunnunensis Chronicon: cum reliquiis ex Consularibus Caesaraugustanis et Iohannis Biclarensis Chronicon.* CChrSL 173 A. Turnhout: Brepols, 2001, 59–83. [English translation: Kenneth Baxter Wolf, *Conquerors and Chroniclers of Early Medieval Spain.* Liverpool: Liverpool University Press, 1990, 57–77]
Vitas Sanctorum Patrum Emeritensium: Antonio Maya Sánchez, ed., *Vitas sanctorum patrum emeretensium.* CChrSL 116. Turnhout: Brepols, 1992. [English translation: A. T. Fear, *Lives of the Visigothic fathers.* Liverpool: Liverpool University Press, 1997, 45–105]

Secondary sources

Birley, Anthony R. "Magnus Maximus and the Persecution of Heresy." *BJRL* 66 (1983): 13–43.
Castellanos, Santiago. "The Significance of Social Unanimity in a Visigothic Hagiography: Keys to an Ideological Screen." *JECS* 11 (2003): 387–419.
Cazier, Pierre. *Isidore de Séville et la Naissance de l'Espagne Catholique.* ThH 96. Paris: Beauchesne, 1994.
Chadwick, Henry. *Priscillian of Avila: The Occult and the Charismatic in the Early Church.* Oxford: Clarendon, 1976.
Collins, Roger. "Mérida and Toledo: 550–585." In *Visigothic Spain: New Approaches*, edited by Edward James, 189–219. Oxford: Clarendon Press, 1980.
Dey, Hendrick W. *The Afterlife of the Roman City: Architecture and Ceremony in Late Antiquity and the Early Middle Ages.* Cambridge: Cambridge University Press, 2015.

Dunn, Geoffrey D. "Cyprian of Carthage and the Episcopal Synod of Late 254." *REAugP* 48 (2002): 229–247.

Escribano, Victoria. "Heresy and Orthodoxy in Fourth-century Hispania: Arianism and Priscillianism." In *Hispania in Late Antiquity: Current Perspectives*, edited by Kim Bowes and Michael Kulikowski, 121–149. Leiden: Brill, 2005.

Fear, Andrew, José Fernández Urbiña, and Mar Marcos Sanchez, eds. *The Role of the Bishop in Late Antiquity: Conflict and Compromise*. London: Bloomsbury, 2013.

González Fernández, R. "Las cartas de Gregorio Magno al defensor Juan: La aplicación del derecho de Justiniano en la Hispania Bizantina en el siglo VII." *AnCr* 14 (1997): 287–298.

Hillgarth, Jocelyn N. "Popular Religion in Visigothic Spain." In *Visigothic Spain: New Approaches*, edited by Edward James, 3–60. Oxford: Clarendon Press, 1980.

Jacobs, Ine. "Domination ecclésiastique et espaces urbains. La rue à colonnade comme toile de fond de l'affirmation chrétienne." *Antiquité Tardive* 22 (2014): 263–286.

King, P. D. *Law and Society in the Visigothic Kingdom*. Cambridge: Cambridge University Press, 1972.

Kulikowski, Michael. *Late Roman Spain and Its Cities*. Baltimore: Johns Hopkins University Press, 2004.

Latham, Jacob A. "From Literal to Spiritual Soldiers of Christ: Disputed Episcopal Elections and the Advent of Christian Processions in Late Antique Rome." *ChH* 81 (2012): 298–327.

Leemans, Johan, Peter Van Nuffelen, Shawn W. J. Keough, and Carla Nicolaye, eds. *Episcopal Elections in Late Antiquity*. AKG 119. Berlin: Walter De Gruyter, 2011.

Martin, Céline. *La géographie du pouvoir dan l'Espagne visigothique*. Paris: Septentrion, 2003.

McCormick, Michael. *Eternal Victory. Triumphal Rulership in Late Antiquity, Byzantium, and the Early Medieval West*. Cambridge: Cambridge University Press, 1986.

Natal, David and Jamie Wood. "Playing with Fire: Conflicting Bishops in Late Roman Spain and Gaul." In *Making Early Medieval Societies: Conflict and Belonging in the Latin West, 300–1200*, edited by Conrad Leyser and Kate Cooper, 33–57. Cambridge: Cambridge University Press, 2016.

Norton, Peter. *Episcopal Elections, 250–600: Hierarchy and Popular Will in Late Antiquity*. Oxford: Oxford University Press, 2007.

Peltzer, Jörg. *Canon Law, Careers and Conquest: Episcopal Elections in Normandy and Greater Anjou, c 1140–c 1230*. Cambridge: Cambridge University Press, 2012.

Rapp, Claudia. *Holy Bishops in Late Antiquity: The Nature of Christian Leadership in an Age of Transition*. The Transformation of the Classical Heritage 37. Berkeley: University of California Press, 2005.

Reimitz, Helmut, *History, Frankish Identity and the Framing of Western Ethnicity, 550–850*. Cambridge: Cambridge University Press, 2015.

Reimitz, Helmut. "Cultural Brokers of a Common Past: History, Identity and Ethnicity in Gregory of Tours and the Chronicles of Fredegar." In *Strategies of Identification: Ethnicity and Religion in Early Medieval Europe*, edited by Walter Pohl and Gerda Heydemann, 257–301. Turnhout: Brepols, 2013.

Reynolds, Paul. *Hispania and the Roman Mediterranean, AD 100–700: Ceramics and Trade*. London: Duckworth, 2010.

Stocking, Rachel L. *Bishops, Councils and Consensus in the Visigothic Kingdom, 589–633*. Ann Arbor: University of Michigan Press, 2000.
Stocking, Rachel L. "Martianus, Aventius, and Isidore: Provincial Councils in Seventh-Century Spain." *EMEu* 6 (1997): 169–188.
Thompson, E. A. *The Goths in Spain*. Oxford: Clarendon Press, 1969.
Vallejo Girvés, M. "Bizancio ante la conversión de los visigodos: los obispos Jenaro y Esteban." In *XIV Centenario Concilio III de Toledo (589–1989)*, 477–483. Toledo: Arzobispado de Toledo, 1991.
Velázquez, Isabel. *Vidas de los santos Padres de Mérida*. Madrid: Editorial Trotta, 2008.
Wood, Jamie. "Playing the Fame Game: Bibliography, Celebrity and Primacy in Late Antique Spain." *JECS* 20 (2012): 613–640.

Erika Manders
Macedonius, Constantius and the Changing Dynamics of Power

In the first three centuries AD the Roman emperor incontestably possessed supreme religious authority within the Empire.[1] One clear institutional reflection of this was the title *pontifex maximus*, which became linked to emperorship already from the Julio-Claudian dynasty onward.[2] How the emperor's position as head of the religious organization of the Roman state was played out is visible on coins, frequently bearing references to the title *pontifex maximus* or images of the emperor sacrificing, and also in letters in which subjects consulted the emperor on religious matters.[3] Pliny, for instance, when governor of Bithynia-Pontus, wrote a letter to Trajan in which he asked the emperor for advice on moving tombs:

> Having been petitioned by some persons to grant them the liberty (agreeably to the practice of Proconsuls) of removing the relics of their deceased relations, upon the suggestion, that either their monuments were decayed by age, or ruined by the inundations of the river, or for other reasons of the same kind; I thought proper, Sir, knowing that it is usual at Rome to consult the pontifical college on such matters, to ask you, as the sovereign of that sacred order, what course you would have me follow.[4]

I would like to thank Daniëlle Slootjes and Olivier Hekster for commenting on an earlier draft of this article and Hans Teitler for many helpful bibliographical suggestions.

[1] Fergus Millar, *The Emperor in the Roman World (31 BC – AD 337)* (Ithaca, NY: Cornell University Press, 1992), 355; Mary Beard, John North and Simon Price, *Religions of Rome. Volume I: A History* (Cambridge: Cambridge University Press, 1998), 186; Ruth Stepper, *Augustus et Sacerdos. Untersuchungen zum römischen Kaiser als Priester* (Stuttgart: Franz Steiner Verlag, 2003), 12; Erika Manders, *Coining Images of Power. Patterns in the Representation of Roman Emperors on Imperial Coinage, A.D. 193–284* (Leiden and Boston: Brill, 2012), 134, 139–140.
[2] On the title *pontifex maximus*, see most recently Alan Cameron, "*Pontifex Maximus*: From Augustus to Gratian – and Beyond," in *Emperors and the Divine – Rome and its Influence*, ed. Maijastina Kahlos (Helsinki: Helsinki Collegium for Advanced Studies, 2016): 139–159; Roald Dijkstra and Dorine van Espelo, "Anchoring Pontifical Authority. A Reconsideration of the Papal Employment of the Title *Pontifex Maximus*," *JRH* 41.3 (2017): 312–325.
[3] On coins referring to the emperor's priestly role, see Manders, *Coining Images of Power*, 133–145. On the letters: Millar, *The Emperor in the Roman World*, 361.
[4] Pliny, *Ep.* 10.68 (translation: *LCL*): *Petentibus quibusdam, ut sibi reliquias suorum aut propter iniuriam vetustatis aut propter fluminis incursum aliaque his similia quocumque secundum exemplum proconsulum transferre permitterem, quia sciebam in urbe nostra ex eius modi causa colle-*

Although Trajan answered that Pliny should follow the precedent created by earlier governors in the province, the correspondence clearly illustrates the emperor's dominant influence on public aspects of Roman religious life.[5]

The Christianization of both Empire and emperorship had, however, severe consequences for the emperor's power in religious matters; with the change of the religious basis underlying imperial power and the increase in importance and influence of the bishop, both parties, emperor and bishop, now claimed religious authority.[6] Constantine was the first emperor who had to deal with this new situation and the fact that he convoked as well as presided over ecclesiastical councils reflects "his claim to play the major role in church affairs" and thus his attempt to secure an important position for the emperor within ecclesiastical structures.[7]

In this article, the focus lies on one of Constantine's successors, Constantius II, and on how he dealt with the new dynamics of religious power. Much has been written on this son of Constantine and church politics. Constantius' attitude towards the bishops has often been placed in the context of imperial attempts to establish unity within the Church and thus within the Empire, after his father.[8] Some even claim that Constantius can be seen as the first caesaropapistic emperor.[9] A clear balance of power between church and state under

---

gium pontificum adiri solere, te, domine, maximum pontificem consulendum putavi, quid observare me velis.
5 Manders, *Coining Images of Power*, 140.
6 On the (shifting) balance of power between emperor and bishop in the fourth century, see Johannes Hahn, "The Challenge of Religious Violence. Imperial ideology and Policy in the Fourth Century AD," in *Contested Monarchy. Integrating the Roman Empire in the Fourth Century AD*, ed. Johannes Wienand (Oxford: Oxford University Press, 2015): 379–403; Patricia Just, *Imperator et Episcopus. Zum Verhältnis von Staatsgewalt und christlicher Kirche zwischen dem 1. Konzil von Nicaea (325) und dem 1. Konzil von Konstantinopel* (Stuttgart: Franz Steiner Verlag, 2003).
7 Cameron, *"Pontifex Maximus,"* 157. See also Glen Bowersock, "From Emperor to Bishop: The Self-Conscious Transformation of Political Power in the Fourth Century A.D.," *CP* 81.4 (1986): 298–307, 303. On Constantine's relationship with the bishops see Harold Drake, *Constantine and the Bishops: The Politics of Intolerance* (Baltimore: The John Hopkins University Press, 2000).
8 See for instance Steffen Diefenbach, "A Vain Quest for Unity: Creeds and Political (Dis)Integration in the Reign of Constantius II," in *Contested Monarchy*, ed. Wienand, 353–378; Susanna Elm, *Sons of Hellenism, Fathers of the Church* (Berkeley, Los Angeles and London: University of California Press, 2012), 28–53; Wolfgang Hagl, "Die Religionspolitik der Kaiser Constantin und Constantius II. im Spiegel kirchlicher Autoren," in *Christen und Heiden in Staat und Gesellschaft des zweiten bis vierten Jahrhunderts. Gedanken und Thesen zu einem schwierigen Verhältnis*, eds. Gunther Gottlieb and Pedro Barceló (Munich: Verlag Ernst Vögel, 1992): 103–129, 109.
9 On the image of Constantius as the founder of Caesaropapism in modern literature, see Klaus Girardet, "Kaiser Konstantius II. als "Episcopus Episcoporum" und das Herrscherbild des kir-

this particular emperor underlies both opinions. I will argue, however, that the latter was not the case; the interaction between Constantius and bishop Macedonius of Constantinople reveals the emperor's struggle in coming to terms with a new powerful religious authority. At least in this case, Constantius' attitude towards the bishop seems to reflect practical dilemmas (new dynamics of power) rather than theoretical ideals (a policy aimed at religious and political unity).[10]

Remarkably, Macedonius has not received much attention in modern literature; a comprehensive study of this controversial bishop is still lacking.[11] The latter is obviously not my aim here. Nevertheless, by focusing on this particular bishop I hope to offer some counterweight to the emphasis on the role of the See of Alexandria in studies on Constantius, and thus on his relationship with the bishop Athanasius.[12] Although Alexandria was, together with Constantinople, Antioch and Jerusalem, one of the most important Sees within the Empire, Constantinople had a unique position. In comparison with especially Alexandria which was "rooted in an illustrious pagan past", this particular city was Christian from the outset.[13] As the new capital of the Empire it had a different status, and in Constantinople bishop and emperor stood in close contact with one another.[14]

---

chlichen Widerstandes (Ossius von Corduba und Lucifer von Calaris)," *Hist.* 26.1 (1977): 95–128, 96; Just, *Imperator et Episcopus*, 159 with n. 149.

10 See also Stevenson on Constantius' exile policy: "(…) Constantius appears more as a capable administrator attacking practical imperial concerns than as a fanatic refereeing abstruse theological disputes", Walt Stevenson, "Exiling Bishops: The Policy of Constantius II," *DOP* 68 (2014): 7–27, 7–8. In addition, Just, *Imperator et Episcopus*, 204, states the following: "Was den jeweiligen Kaiser bewog, verschiedene Bischöfe unterschiedlich zu behandeln, waren also keine persönlichen Glaubensüberzeugungen, sondern tagespolitische Erfordernisse und Überlegungen der Realpolitik."

11 According to Gwynn "Macedonius still awaits proper scholarly investigation," see David Gwynn, "Christian Controversy and the Transformation of Fourth-Century Constantinople," in *Religious Practices and Christianization of the Late Antique City (4th–7th cent.)*, ed. Aude Busine (Leiden: Brill, 2015): 206–220, 212 n. 22.

12 See for instance David Gwynn, *Athanasius of Alexandria: Bishop, Theologian, Ascetic, Father* (Oxford: Oxford University Press, 2012); Timothy Barnes, *Athanasius and Constantius: Theology and Politics in the Constantinian Empire* (Cambridge, MA and London: Harvard University Press, 1993).

13 Gwynn, "Christian Controversy," 206.

14 Emperors resided permanently in Constantinople only from the Theodosian dynasty onward. Constantius resided in Antioch during a large part of his reign. See Bernd Isele, *Kampf um Kirchen. Religiöse Gewalt, Heiliger Raum und Christliche Topographie in Alexandria und Konstantinopel (4. Jh.)* (Münster: Aschendorff Verlag, 2010), 18.

Macedonius' prominence on the Constantinopolitan stage of power covered almost Constantius' whole reign. He presented himself as a candidate for the episcopal throne after the death of Alexander in 337, the year in which Constantius rose to power. In 342, after the death of Eusebius, Macedonius gained the See, which he held, with some interruptions, until his deposition in 360, one year before Constantius' death. The following analysis distinguishes three moments or phases within Macedonius' episcopate: his election and installation (337–349), his persecution of dissidents after the final ejection of Paul in 349, and the removal of Constantine's tomb (359). These were the moments in which direct imperial involvement in episcopal affairs can be attested and in which the emperor's struggle with the new power dynamics becomes clearly visible.

2 A contested run-up

Shortly after the death of Constantine in 337, the first bishop of Constantinople, Alexander, died and two candidates, Paul and Macedonius, competed for the bishopric.[15] The pro-Nicene candidate Paul gained the See, but through an accusation of Macedonius, who served as a presbyter under Paul and belonged to the Arian party, he was expelled by the emperor who had been "highly incensed" at his consecration.[16] Eusebius of Nicomedia was appointed in his stead.[17] After the death of Eusebius in 341, however, the rivalry between Paul and Macedonius flared up again; Paul tried to regain the bishopric, whereas Macedonius was elected by Paul's opponents. This resulted in bloody strife between the supporters of Paul and those of Macedonius and, eventually, in the killing of Constantius' *magister equitum* by an angry mob.[18] This general, Hermogenes, had attempted to restore order in Constantinople by violently executing an imperial order that commanded the expulsion of Paul, but he met with resistance from the populace and was murdered. Upon the news of Hermogenes' death Constantius hastily traveled, on horseback in mid-winter, from Antioch to Constantino-

---

15 Regarding the chronology of Macedonius' and Paul's episcopates, I follow Barnes, *Athanasius and Constantius*, 212–217.
16 Socrates, *h.e.* 2.7.1. See also Sozomen, *h.e.* 3.4.2. On Macedonius' accusation, see Athanasius, *Hist. Ar.* 1.7. All translations from Socrates and Sozomen in this article are adapted from Zenos and Hartranft respectively.
17 Gwynn, "Christian Controversy," 212.
18 Sozomen, *h.e.* 3.7.4–6; Socrates, *h.e.* 2.13.1–3; Amm. Marc. 14.10.2.

ple.¹⁹ As a reaction to the general's murder, the emperor halved the city's grain supply, according to Sozomen "probably from the idea that luxury and excess made the populace idle and disposed to sedition".²⁰ That this punishment provoked comment can be discerned from a passage in a speech of Libanius, a panegyric to Constantius and Constans composed between 344 and 349 in Nicomedia:

> For while this great war was being prosecuted through to its end, sedition broke out unexpectedly from within against the emperor, and a very considerable disturbance seized the greatest of the cities in this part of the world, second only to the greatest of them all. ... So now what must I say first or last? ... How he [Constantius] departed from Persia without taking account of the Persians on the grounds that they would nowhere put in an appearance, or the speed of his march in which he outran the Spartans, or the excess of the winter weather or the snowstorms or the continuous rain? ... How he sailed across the strait as if concealed in a divine mist?...How he executed no one but chastened the malefactors? How, when he had provided the opportunity for discussion within the senate, he was the most powerful speaker there? But is it right to omit all this and recall the exchange of dialogue, in which he swiftly overthrew the cleverest part of the senate?²¹

Taking into account that the speech aimed at praising both rulers before a Nicomedian audience, this particular passage seems to hint at discussions in the Senate about Constantius' clemency.²² The emperor's *clementia* in this case did not stand on its own, as it characterized Constantius' dealing with the important cit-

---

19 Sozomen, *h.e.* 3.7.7; Socrates, *h.e.* 2.13.5.
20 Sozomen, *h.e.* 3.7.7. See also Socrates, *h.e.* 2.13.5.
21 Lib. *or.* 59.94, 96–7 (translation: Skinner, see n. 22): τοσούτου γὰρ πολέμου διαντλουμένου τῷ βασιλεῖ στάσις ἔνδοθεν ἐξ ἀπροσδοκήτων ἐκινήθη καὶ κατεῖχε ταραχή τις οὐ μετρία τὴν μεγίστην μὲν τῶν τῇδε πόλεων, τῆς δὲ ἁπασῶν μεγίστης δευτέραν. ... ἐνταῦθα δὴ τί πρῶτον ἢ τί τελευταῖον χρὴ λέγειν; ... πότερον ὡς ἀπανέστη τῆς Περσίδος ὑπεριδὼν ἐκείνων ὡς οὐδαμοῦ φανησομένων, ἢ τῆς πορείας τὸ τάχος ᾧ τοὺς Λακεδαιμονίους παρέδραμεν, ἢ τοῦ χειμῶνος τὰς ὑπερβολὰς ἢ τῶν νιφάδων τὰς ἐμβολὰς ἢ τῶν ὄμβρων τὴν συνέχειαν; ... ἀλλ' ὡς τὸν πορθμὸν διέπλευσεν ὥσπερ θείᾳ νεφέλῃ κεκαλυμμένος; ... ἀλλ' ὡς οὐδένα μὲν διέφθειρε, τοὺς δὲ κακουργοῦντας ἐσωφρόνισεν; ἀλλ' ὡς ἐξουσίαν εἰς λόγον τῇ βουλῇ παρασχὼν πλεῖστον ἐκράτει λέγων; ἀλλὰ πάντα ταῦτα ἀφέντα τῶν ἀμοιβαίων λόγων μνημονεῦσαι δίκαιον, οἷς τὸ δεινότατον τῆς βουλῆς κατεπάλαισεν ὀξέως;
22 Alexander Skinner, "Violence at Constantinople in A.D. 341–2 and Themistius, *Oration* 1," *JRS* 105 (2015): 234–249, 235. Probably, this measure had not affected the urban poor, at least when the supply of free grain was linked to the distribution of *tesserae*. Then, only the "well-to-do citizens" were targeted and the punishment could indeed be labeled "a cosmetic cut", as Neil Mc Lynn does. See Neil McLynn, "Christian Controversy and Violence in the Fourth Century," *Kodai* 3 (1992): 15–44, 25.

ies within his empire.²³ Also the emperor's attitude towards Macedonius seems to have been characterized by *clementia*. Although he held Macedonius responsible for the many killings (amongst which numbered the murder of Hermogenes) and was irritated because Macedonius was ordained without his consent, he allowed Macedonius to carry on with his pastoral work in the city.²⁴ Yet, the emperor left Constantinople without confirming his ordination.²⁵

---

23 See Henck's article on Constantius' interaction with the urban citizenry, Nick Henck, "Constantius II and the cities," in *Wolf Liebeschuetz Reflected: Essays Presented by Colleagues, Friends and Pupils*, eds. John Drinkwater and Benet Salway (London: Institute of Classical Studies, School of Advanced Study, University of London, 2007): 147–156. On Hermogenes and Macedonius, see esp. 153–156. Norton argues that this relatively mild reaction can be explained through the fact that Constantinople was the new capital. See Peter Norton, *Episcopal Elections 250–600. Hierarchy and Popular Will in Late Antiquity* (Oxford: Oxford University Press, 2007), 56.

24 Socrates, *h.e.* 2.13.6–7: ὠργίζετο γὰρ καὶ κατ' αὐτοῦ, οὐ μόνον ὅτι παρὰ γνώμην αὐτοῦ κεχειροτόνητο, ἀλλ' ὅτι καὶ διὰ τὰς μεταξὺ αὐτοῦ τε καὶ Παύλου γενομένας στάσεις πολλοί τε ἄλλοι καὶ ὁ στρατηλάτης ἀνῄρητο. Ἐάσας οὖν αὐτὸν ἐν ᾗ ἐχειροτονήθη ἐκκλησίᾳ συνάγειν, αὖθις ἐπὶ τὴν Ἀντιόχειαν ἀνεχώρησεν. Translation: "... being irritated against him not only because he had been ordained without his own consent; but also because on account of the contests in which he had been engaged with Paul, Hermogenes, his general, and many other persons had been slain. But having given him permission to minister in the church in which he had been consecrated, he returned to Antioch." Sozomen, *h.e.* 3.7.8: οὐ μὴν ἀλλὰ καὶ πρὸς Μακεδόνιον ἐχαλέπαινεν ὡς τῆς ἀναιρέσεως τοῦ στρατηγοῦ καὶ ἄλλων πολλῶν αἴτιον, καὶ ὅτι, πρὶν αὐτὸν ἐπιτρέψαι, ἐχειροτονήθη. Translation: "He manifested great displeasure against Macedonius also, because he was the occasion of the murder of the general and of other individuals and also, because he had been ordained without first obtaining his sanction." In contrast with Socrates Sozomen does not explicitly mention that Macedonius could continue his work.

25 Socrates says that Constantius "hesitated ... to ratify the appointment of Macedonius to the bishopric of that city" (2.13.6) and Sozomen reports that the emperor "returned to Antioch, without having either confirmed or dissolved his ordination" (3.7.8). Barnes, *Athanasius and Constantius*, 68, does not mention the emperor's refusal to confirm Macedonius' ordination. Whether or not Paul was exiled by Constantius after the murder on Hermogenes still forms a subject of debate in scholarly literature, see for instance McLynn, "Christian Controversy," 25 with n. 70, who rejects a possible exile. He bases his claim on the letter of the eastern bishops from Serdica, in which no measure against Paul is mentioned and from which it can be deduced that only one exile of Paul (that of 337–340) was known to them. In addition, he follows Dagron's statement that the life of Paul in Socrates and Sozomen was modeled on that of Athanasius. See Gilbert Dagron, *Naissance d'une capitale: Constantinople et ses institutions de 330 à 451* (Paris: Presses universitaires de France, 1974), 431. However, it is hard to imagine, as McLynn argues, that Paul was permitted to stay in the city and that he could continue his pastoral work (evidence for this is lacking), especially because, initially, Hermogenes was sent to Constantinople by Constantius in order to expel Paul. That Constantius would have abandoned this intention after the murder on his general seems unlikely to me. Barnes, *Athanasius and Constantius*, 213–214, on the other

Unsurprisingly, this "non-solution" of Constantius did not put an end to the rivalry for the episcopal throne and in 343, at the council of Serdica, the western bishops reinstated Paul.²⁶ Shortly thereafter, in 344, Constantius commanded the praetorian prefect, Philip, to expel Paul again and to install Macedonius as the bishop of Constantinople.²⁷ After Paul was ejected, the prefect and Macedonius went to the St Eirene Church, accompanied by soldiers.²⁸ The soldiers thought that the multitude that had gathered around the church resisted their order to give way, so they killed thousands of people.²⁹ Although both Socrates and Sozomen describe this event as an accident, Socrates seems to hold the bishop responsible for the killings:

> After such distinguished achievements, Macedonius, as if he had not been the author of any calamity, but was altogether guiltless of what had been perpetrated, was seated in the episcopal chair by the prefect, rather than by the ecclesiastical canon. Thus, then, by means of so many murders in the church, Macedonius and the Arians grasped the supremacy in the churches.³⁰

Paul and Athanasius travelled to Trier to the court of Constans who, in the spring of 345, wrote to Constantius and asked for the restoration of both bishops.³¹ Paul was re-installed and Macedonius deposed. However, the struggle for the bishopric continued and in 349 Paul was ejected again. This expulsion turned out to be the last, however, as he was eventually killed in 350. According to Socrates he was strangled by those who conducted him to his place of banishment, Cucusus in Cappadocia. The author initially mentions that the emperor Constantius gave

---

hand, states that Paul was expelled and immediately ran off to the imperial court at Trier (based on CSEL 65.67.2/3).
26 Non-solution: McLynn, "Christian Controversy," 25.
27 Socrates, *h.e.* 2.16 and Sozomen, *h.e.* 3.9. The western bishops at Serdica did not mention Paul's name. According to Barnes, "Constantius was very slow to restore the bishops deposed from eastern sees who were in exile in the West, and Paul made a premature attempt to return to his see". Barnes, *Athanasius and Constantius*, 214.
28 Both Socrates and Sozomen do not specify which church is meant here.
29 According to Socrates, *h.e.* 2.16.13, 3150 people were killed.
30 Socrates, *h.e.* 2.16.14–15: Ἐπὶ τοιούτοις δὴ τοῖς κατορθώμασιν ὁ Μακεδόνιος ὡς οὐδὲν φαῦλον πεπραχώς, ἀλλὰ καθαρὸς καὶ ἀθῷος τῶν γενομένων τυγχάνων, ὑπὸ τοῦ ἐπάρχου μᾶλλον ἢ ἀθῷος τῶν γενομένων τυγχάνων, ὑπὸ τοῦ ἐπάρχου μᾶλλον ἢ ὑπὸ ἐκκλησιαστικοῦ κανόνος ἐνθρονίζεται. Οὕτως μὲν οὖν Μακεδόνιος καὶ Ἀρειανοὶ διὰ τοσούτων φόνων τῆς ἐκκλησίας ἐκράτησαν.
31 Socrates, *h.e.* 2.22.4. See also Barnes, *Athanasius and Constantius*, 214. According to Barnes, *Athanasius and Constantius*, 69, "the western emperor had become the champion of all the eastern bishops who were in exile in the west, convinced that their deposition imperiled Christian orthodoxy."

the order to send him into exile, later he says that he was banished at the instigation of Macedonius.[32] Sozomen is unsure about whether Paul died a natural death or not, yet he writes the following: "it is still reported that he was strangled by the adherents of Macedonius".[33] Macedonius regained the See, which he held until 360, when he was permanently deposed by Constantius.[34]

Twelve years passed between the moment in which Macedonius made his first bid for episcopal power and the beginning of an eleven-year period in which he held the See without interruption. In these years, from 337 to 349, the emperor frequently interfered in matters regarding the occupation of the episcopal See in the capital. To a certain extent the contest over the election of the bishop of Constantinople reflected the struggle for power between the two imperial brothers Constans and Constantius who supported different candidates. But when looking at the power balance between emperor and bishop, the dominance of Constantius in ecclesiastical affairs is clear. The emperor was pulling the strings: he decided who would gain the See of Constantinople and who would not, and did not shy away from using military force.[35] We should take into account, however, that Constantinople was the Eastern capital and was thus of special importance to the emperor, and the same applies to other key cities within the Empire, such as Alexandria. In the latter city Constantius also decided who sat on the episcopal throne.[36] In a smaller provincial town the emperor would probably have been less inclined to intervene in episcopal elections.[37] Be that as it may, regarding the struggle for the bishopric in Constantinople in the years 337–349, the influence of the emperor was the decisive factor.[38]

However, the way in which Constantius dealt with Macedonius after the sedition that resulted in the killing of Hermogenes probably reflects the beginning of a slow shift in the dynamics of power. If Libanius' rhetorical questions reflect what actually happened, they show that the emperor's reaction to the whole situation was well thought through; in the debate with the senate he "swiftly overthrew the cleverest part of the senate".[39] It is therefore hardly conceivable that

---

32 Socrates, *h.e.* 2.26.6 and 5.9.1.
33 Sozomen, *h.e.* 4.2.2. See also 3.3.5.
34 Barnes, *Athanasius and Constantius*, 148–149.
35 See also Norton, *Episcopal Elections*, 84.
36 See for instance Constantius' influence on the election of Gregory and George.
37 Norton, *Episcopal Elections*, 82.
38 Imperial intervention was only one of the factors that played a role in episcopal elections in Constantinople, see Peter Van Nuffelen, "Episcopal Succession in Constantinople (381–450 C.E.): The Local Dynamics of Power," *JECS* 18 (2010): 425–451, 445.
39 See n. 21.

his approach regarding Macedonius resulted from a laissez-faire policy, not least because it was the Eastern capital he was dealing with.[40] But why then did the emperor only refrain from officially ordaining Macedonius (he allowed him to remain in Constantinople and to continue his pastoral work), when he held him responsible for the killing of Hermogenes? In 337, after the death of Alexander and the first bloody confrontation between supporters of Paul and Macedonius, Constantius simply translated a bishop from another See.[41] In 341 it looks as if the emperor could no longer ignore Macedonius. Therefore, it seems that Constantius' "non-solution" does not reflect the emperor's "dominance in ecclesiastical affairs", as McLynn argues, but an increasing influence of Macedonius and thus changes in the balance of power between emperor and bishop.[42]

3 The persecutions

Both Socrates and Sozomen report that after the final removal of Paul, Macedonius started persecuting those who opposed his views (pro-Nicene Christians and Novatians).[43] They hold the bishop responsible for various atrocities: torture, confiscation of property, exile, and murder. Socrates describes in detail the tortures that were inflicted upon the Novatians:[44]

> Many persons eminent for their piety were seized and tortured, because they refused to communicate with him: and after the torture, they forcibly constrained the men to be partakers of the holy mysteries, their mouths being forced open with a piece of wood, and then the consecrated elements thrust into them. Those who were so treated regarded this as a punishment far more grievous than all others. Moreover they laid hold of women and children, and compelled them to be initiated [by baptism]; and if any one resisted or otherwise spoke against it, stripes immediately followed, and after the stripes, bonds and imprisonment, and other violent measures. I shall here relate an instance or two whereby the reader may form some idea of the extent of the harshness and cruelty exercised by Macedonius

---

40 See Norton's remark in n. 23.
41 Isele, *Kampf um Kirchen*, 45. On the relationship between Constantius and Eusebius, see Just, *Imperator et Episcopus*, 160–164. According to Just, Constantius appointed Eusebius in order to show his brothers that he decided on ecclesiastical matters in the East, see p. 228.
42 McLynn, "Christian Controversy," 25.
43 Socrates, *h.e.* 2.27 and 2.38; Sozomen, *h.e.* 4.2 and 4.20–21.
44 On Socrates' relationship with the Novatians, see Martin Wallraff, *Der Kirchenhistoriker Sokrates. Untersuchungen zu Geschichtsdarstellung, Methode und Person* (Göttingen: Vandenhoeck & Ruprecht, 1997), 253. See also Isele, *Kampf um Kirchen*, 93 with n. 302. On the Novatians, see Vera Hirschmann, *Die Kirche der Reinen. Kirchen- und sozialhistorische Studie zu den Novatianern im 3. bis 5. Jahrhundert* (Tübingen: Mohr Siebeck, 2015).

and those who were then in power. They first pressed in a box, and then sawed off, the breasts of such women as were unwilling to communicate with them. The same parts of the persons of other women they burnt partly with iron, and partly with eggs intensely heated in the fire.⁴⁵

Although, in Gaddis' words, Socrates tried to "rework the story into a classic tale of persecution" and "some hyperbole" is thus undoubtedly present in this bloody account, the passage demonstrates that Macedonius used force and coercion in his dealings with members of other religious sects.⁴⁶ In Socrates' and Sozomen's discussion of Macedonius' acts of persecution emphasis is put on two particular events. First, attention is paid to the destruction of churches, with special focus on the near-demolition of the Novatian church in Pelargus.⁴⁷ When the demolition by Macedonius' agents was about to begin, the Novatians are said to have removed their church, brick by brick, to another part of the city. Second, the persecution of followers of Novatus in Mantinium is described.⁴⁸ Four military cohorts were sent against them, resulting in the deaths of many Paphlagonians and nearly all the soldiers.

Socrates and Sozomen seem to have different opinions on the role of the emperor in these acts of religious violence. Socrates reports that, after the removal of Paul, the bishop gained "very great ascendancy over the emperor" and that Macedonius used imperial power to carry out his persecution of dissidents:⁴⁹

---

45 Socrates, *h.e.* 2.38.6 – 10: (…) πολλοὶ δὲ τῶν ἐπισήμων ἐπ' εὐλαβείᾳ <ἀνδρῶν> συλληφθέντες ᾐκίζοντο, ἐπεὶ μὴ ἐβούλοντο μετασχεῖν τῆς κοινωνίας αὐτοῦ. Μετὰ δὲ τοὺς αἰκισμοὺς βίᾳ τῶν μυστηρίων μετέχειν τοὺς ἄνδρας ἠνάγκαζον· ξύλῳ γὰρ διαιροῦντες τὰ στόματα τῶν ἀνθρώπων τὰ μυστήρια ἐνετίθεσαν· οἱ δὲ ὑπομένοντες τοῦτο μείζονα τῶν ἄλλων τιμωριῶν κόλασιν ταύτην ἐνόμιζον. Γύναιά τε καὶ παιδία συναρπάζοντες μυεῖσθαι ἠνάγκαζον· εἰ δέ τις παρῃτεῖτο ἢ ἄλλως ἀντέλεγεν, εὐθὺς ἐπηκολούθουν πληγαὶ καὶ μετὰ τὰς πληγὰς δεσμοί τε καὶ στρεβλώσεις καὶ τἆλλα δεινά. Ὧν ἑνὸς ἢ δυοῖν καὶ στρεβλώσεις καὶ τἆλλα δεινά. Ὧν ἑνὸς ἢ δυοῖν ἐπιμνησθεὶς φανερὰν τὴν ἀπήνειαν καὶ ὠμότητα Μακεδονίου καὶ τῶν ἀκμασάντων τότε ἀνθρώπων τοῖς ἀκούουσιν καταστήσω. Γυναικῶν γὰρ τῶν μὴ ἀνασχομένων μετασχεῖν τῶν μυστηρίων τοὺς μαζοὺς ἐν κιβωτῷ βαλόντες ἀπέπριον, ἄλλων τε γυναικῶν τὰ αὐτὰ μόρια τοῦτο μὲν σιδήρῳ, τοῦτο δὲ ᾠὰ εἰς ἄκρον ἐν πυρὶ θερμανθέντα προσφέροντες ἔκαιον.
46 Michael Gaddis, *There is No Crime for Those Who Have Christ. Religious Violence in the Christian Roman Empire* (Berkeley, Los Angeles and London: University of California Press, 2005), 78, n. 30.
47 Socrates, *h.e.* 2.38.14 – 25; Sozomen, *h.e.* 4.20.4 – 7. Isele places the destruction of the Novatian church at Pelargus in the context of Macedonius' "Eroberung des urbanen Raums" (*Kampf um Kirchen*, 95).
48 Socrates, *h.e.* 2.38.29 – 32; Sozomen, *h.e* 4.21.1 – 2.
49 Socrates, *h.e* 2.27.1.

For having prevailed on his sovereign to co-operate with him in devastating the churches, he procured that whatever pernicious measures he determined to pursue should be ratified by law. And on this account throughout the several cities an edict was proclaimed, and a military force appointed to carry the imperial decrees into effect.⁵⁰

Later, in his description of the events regarding the church at Pelargus, he again mentions an imperial edict aimed at the demolition of churches:

> The emperor's edict and the violence of Macedonius had doomed to destruction the churches of those who maintained the doctrine of consubstantiality; the decree and violence reached this church [at Pelargus], and those also who were charged with the execution of the mandate were at hand to carry it into effect.⁵¹

In addition, in Socrates' account of the bishop's measures against the followers of Novatus at Mantinium the author portrays Macedonius as having access to the military in order to execute his violent acts; with the emperor's permission four companies of soldiers were sent into Paphlagonia.⁵² Socrates thus portrays Macedonius as having influence on Constantius, who facilitated the bishop's persecutions.

In Sozomen's account the emperor plays a less prominent role in the violent acts that Macedonius committed in Constantinople and the neighboring cities after the expulsion of Paul. Whereas Socrates records active imperial support through edicts, Sozomen does not mention any decree. Instead, he reports that Macedonius was assisted by monks and by alliances with neighboring bishops and that the emperor, in the end, was "displeased when he heard of these transactions [the persecution of the followers of Paul], and imputed the blame of them to Macedonius and his adherents".⁵³ Later, Sozomen even states that Macedonius destroyed churches, such as the Novatian church at Pelargus,

---

50 Socrates, h.e. 2.27.2–3: Πείσας γὰρ τὸν βασιλέα συλλαμβάνεσθαι αὐτῷ πορθοῦντι τὰς ἐκκλησίας παρασκευάζει νόμῳ κυροῦσθαι, ὅσα κακῶς πράττειν ἠβούλετο. Καὶ τὸ ἐντεῦθεν κατὰ πόλεις μὲν νόμος προυτίθετο, στρατιωτικὴ δὲ χεὶρ ὑπουργεῖν ἐκεκέλευστο τοῖς τοῦ βασιλέως θεσπίσμασιν (...). One of the dominant themes in Socrates' description of Constantius is his influenceability, see Hartmut Leppin, *Von Constantin dem Großen zu Theodosius II. Das christliche Kaisertum bei den Kirchenhistorikern Socrates, Sozomenus und Theodoret* (Göttingen: Vandenhoeck & Ruprecht, 1996), 64.
51 Socrates, h.e. 2.38.16: Ὁ βασιλέως νόμος καὶ ἡ Μακεδονίου βία καθαιρεῖσθαι τῶν τὸ ὁμοούσιον φρονούντων τὰς ἐκκλησίας ἐκέλευον. Ἥκει δὴ τὸ θέσπισμα καὶ ἡ βία καὶ κατὰ τῆσδε τῆς ἐκκλησίας, καὶ ἤπειγον οἱ προστεταγμένοι τοῦτο ποιεῖν.
52 Socrates 2.38.29. On the appearance of soldiers and the army in Socrates' work, see Wallraff, *Der Kirchenhistoriker Socrates*, 126–127.
53 Sozomen, h.e. 4.2.4.

"*under the pretext* [italics are mine] that the emperor had commanded the demolition of all houses of prayer in which the Son was recognized to be of the same substance of the Father".[54] This seems to imply that, according to Sozomen, an imperial edict which commanded the destruction of churches had not been issued.[55] As described above, however, Socrates was not at all skeptical about the existence of an imperial decree legitimizing violent acts against religious dissidents.[56]

Regarding the military actions against the Novatians at Mantinium, Socrates testifies that Macedonius sent four cohorts of soldiers into Paphlagonia by the *permission of the emperor*, whereas Sozomen relates that the bishop *persuaded the emperor* to send four cohorts.[57] The military intervention ended up in the slaughter of the soldiers, which caused the anger of the emperor.[58] Thus, in the work of the latter, the emperor is portrayed as more reluctant to help Macedonius.

Socrates' and Sozomen's description of the persecutions under Macedonius and the involvement of Constantius clearly reveals the complex relationship between emperor and bishop. It is evident that Macedonius needed the emperor in his persecution of dissidents; he was dependent on secular instruments of power, such as soldiers and edicts. Even when Constantius did not issue an edict that commanded the destruction of churches of fellow-Christians, the fact that both authors refer to imperial law in this context might hint at common practice: without imperial power bishops could not carry out their acts of violence.[59] This dependence on the emperor should however not be understood

---

54 Sozomen, *h.e.* 4.20.3.
55 See Leppin, *Von Constantin dem Großen zu Theodosius II*, 66 with n. 51: "Sozomenus ... sagt lediglich, daß Makedonios sich auf einen entsprechenden Erlaß des Kaisers berufen habe, erklärt aber nicht, daß es ihn wirklich gegeben habe. Seine Wortwahl (προϊσχόμενος) suggeriert eher das Gegenteil."
56 Most likely such an edict had not been issued. See n. 50 and Rudolf Lorenz, *Die Kirche in ihrer Geschichte. Das vierte Jahrhundert (Osten)* (Göttingen: Vandenhoeck & Ruprecht, 1992), 170: "Es fehlt an *Häretikergesetzen* des Konstantius, da es erst seit der Annahme der Formel v. Konstantinopel (360) wieder eine reichskirchliche 'Orthodoxie' gab. Es ist hier von den ihn umgebenden Bischöfen abhängig."
57 Socrates, *h.e.* 2.38.29 and Sozomen, *h.e.* 4.21.1.
58 Sozomen, *h.e.* 4.21.3.
59 Ramsay MacMullen, "The Historical Role of the Masses in Late Antiquity," in *Changes in the Roman Empire: Essays in the Ordinary*, ed. Ramsey MacMullen (Princeton: Princeton University Press, 1990): 250–276, 266. On the limits of episcopal power in interreligious conflicts, see Maijastina Kahlos, "Pacifiers and Instigators – Bishops and Interreligious Conflicts in Late Antiquity," in *The Role of the Bishop in Late Antiquity. Conflict and Compromise*, eds. Andrew Fear, José Fernández Ubiña and Mar Marcos (London e.a.: Bloomsbury, 2013): 63–82.

as a sign of the bishop's weakness. To a certain extent the bishop determined religious policy. Moreover, as Fowden has argued already in relation to bishop George of Alexandria (356–361), the bishop disposed of troops, which points to "an exceptional degree of influence over the emperor himself".[60] So the difference in the role that Socrates and Sozomen attribute to Constantius might reflect the emperor's struggle with an increasing episcopal influence.

4 The end of Macedonius' episcopate

What happened in Mantinium seems to have been the beginning of Macedonius' downfall; Sozomen relates that "many of the friends of Macedonius blamed him for having occasioned so great a disaster, and the emperor was displeased, and regarded him with less favor than before".[61] His declining reputation only grew worse when Macedonius started to tamper with the remains of Constantius' father. In 359, when the emperor was absent from Constantinople, Macedonius removed the coffin of Constantine from his mausoleum in the Holy Apostles to the church of St. Acacius. This caused a bloodbath in the latter church, as a fight between two groups of people, one approving and the other condemning the removal, broke out.[62]

Socrates explicitly mentions that the bishop removed the tomb without consulting the emperor on this matter and both Socrates and Sozomen present the state of the building, which was apparently falling into ruin, as the bishop's motive for this remarkable deed.[63] Mango supports this point of view as "many of Constantine's buildings were unsound and had to be strengthened by his successor".[64] He bases his claim on Julian's Oration 1 and Zosimus. Julian says only generally that Constantius restored unsound buildings and Zosimus mentions that some of Constantine's buildings were erected hastily and could not stand

---

[60] Garth Fowden, "Bishops and Temples in the Eastern Roman Empire A.D. 320–435," *JThS* n.s. 29 (1978): 53–78, 60. See also Isele, *Kampf um Kirchen*, 57.
[61] Sozomen, *h.e.* 4.21.2–3.
[62] Socrates, *h.e.* 2.38.35–44; Sozomen, *h.e.* 4.21.3–6.
[63] Socrates, *h.e.* 2.38.35 and Sozomen, *h.e.* 4.21.3.
[64] Cyril Mango, "Constantine's Mausoleum and the Translation of Relics," *ByZ* 83 (1990): 51–62, 60. Striking is that Mango labels Macedonius "a dedicated and energetic leader, who was later to be tarred with the brush of heresy" ("Constantine's Mausoleum," 59). Mango seems to ignore the fact that during this bishop's episcopate many people were killed or violently persecuted. Yet, Macedonius did support the urban poor (he founded an institution that cared for the sick, see e.g. Susanna Elm, *'Virgins of God'. The Making of Asceticism in Late Antiquity* (Oxford: Oxford University Press, 1994), 112). See also Gwynn, "Christian Controversy," 215.

long. No explicit reference to the Holy Apostles is made.⁶⁵ Therefore, it is debatable that Macedonius' motive for moving Constantine's remains was the deplorable state of the Holy Apostles.

McLynn presents another hypothesis for Macedonius' removal of the tomb of Constantius' father.⁶⁶ According to him, Macedonius wanted to cut the "imperial cult" that was developing there in order to strengthen episcopal preeminence. McLynn refers here to the relics of apostles and saints which were brought to the Holy Apostles on the emperor's orders and were "received with great ceremony".⁶⁷ Yet, the relics of the apostle Luke and the evangelist Andrew, the first human relics that came to Constantinople, probably did not arrive in 357, as is commonly assumed. On the basis of a chronology constructed from the events mentioned in the *Passio Artemii* of John of Rhodes, Woods argues that the relics were translated to the Holy Apostles in March 360, *after* the deposition of Macedonius.⁶⁸ The translation of the relics of the apostle Timothy furthermore occurred in July 360, instead of 356/357, according to this author.⁶⁹ Burgess, however, argues against Woods and thinks that the relics of Luke and Andrew were transferred to Constantinople in 336, during the reign of Constantine.⁷⁰ Be that as it may, what we can nevertheless distill from these different opinions is that the translation of Luke's and Andrew's relics, and perhaps also those of Timothy, presumably did *not* take place when Macedonius was sitting on the episcopal throne: either the relics were not yet present or Constantine had translated them. This also makes Constantius' supposed advancement of the imperial cult under Macedonius' episcopate less probable as a direct cause for the removal of Constantine's tomb.

---

65 Julian, *or.* 1.33 and Zosimus 2.32.1. Downey links the state of the Holy Apostles to an earthquake mentioned by Ammianus Marcellinus (17.7.1–8) which destroyed Nicomedia in 358. See Glanville Downey, "The Builder of the Original Church of the Apostles at Constantinople: A Contribution to the Criticism of the 'Vita Constantini' Attributed to Eusebius," *DOP* 6 (1951): 53–80, 74. However, Downey mentions that Macedonius used the state of the Apostles as a pretext to remove Constantine's tomb. Moreover, it seems more likely that Constantius (instead of Constantine) had built this particular church: Downey, "The Builder of the Original Church of the Apostles at Constantinople," 53. See also Isele, *Kampf um Kirchen*, 76.
66 Isele places Macedonius' removal of Constantine's tomb in the context of destruction of "innerstädtischen Identifikationsmechanismen" and thus within the framework of the bishop's struggle for control of the urban space (see n. 45), *Kampf um Kirchen*, 51–69; 204–205.
67 McLynn, "Christian Controversy," 28.
68 David Woods, "The Date of the Translation of the Relics of Ss. Luke and Andrew to Constantinople," *VigChr* 45 (1991): 286–292.
69 Woods, "The Date of the Translation," 290.
70 Richard Burgess, "The Passio S. Artemii, Philostorgius, and the dates of the invention and translations of the relics of Sts Andrew and Luke," *AnBoll* 121 (2003): 5–36.

It is thus difficult to prove that the removal of Constantine's tomb had a link with either the state of the Holy Apostles or the translation of relics. Yet, although the direct cause for the event is hard to determine, McLynn may well be right in placing the removal in the broader context of the power struggle between emperor and bishop, which fits within the framework that is outlined in this article. After all, what it clearly demonstrates is that, at least concerning this matter, the bishop no longer considered the emperor's authority as self-evident. The difference with the time of Trajan in which the emperor was consulted on the removal of tombs which were not even his father's, as discussed in the introduction, is telling. Constantius' reaction to Macedonius' claim of superiority therefore does not come as a surprise: he immediately deposed Macedonius and thus showed *his* superiority.

Bibliography

Primary sources

Ammianus Marcellinus. Translated by J.C. Rolfe. Cambridge: Harvard University Press, 1950.
Athanasius, *Arian History*. Translated by A. Robertson, in: P. Schaff (ed.), *Nicene and post-Nicene Fathers* 2.2. New York: The Christian Literature Company, 1891.
Julian, *Orationes*. Translated by W.C. Wright. 1913. Cambridge: Harvard University Press.
Pliny, *Epistulae*. Translated by B. Radice. 1969. Cambridge: Harvard University Press.
The Ecclesiastical History of Socrates Scholasticus. Translated by A.C. Zenos, in: P. Schaff (ed.), *Nicene and post-Nicene Fathers* 2.2. New York: The Christian Literature Company, 1890.
Socrate de Constantinople, *Histoire Ecclésiastique*, Livres II–V. Translated by P. Périchon and P. Maraval. SC 505. Paris: Les Éditions du Cerf, 2005–2006.
The Ecclesiastical History of Sozomen. Translated by C.D. Hartranft, in: P. Schaff (ed.), *Nicene and post Nicene Fathers* 2.2. New York: The Christian Literature Company, 1890.
Sozomène, *Histoire Ecclésiastique*, Livres III–IV. Translated by A.-J. Festugière and G. Sabbah. SC 418. Paris: Les Éditions du Cerf, 1996.
Zosimus, *New History*. Translated by R.T. Ridley. Canberra: Australian Association for Byzantine Studies, 1982.

Secondary sources

Barnes, Timothy. *Athanasius and Constantius: Theology and Politics in the Constantinian Empire*. Cambridge, MA and London: Harvard University Press, 1993.
Beard, Mary, North, John, and Price, Simon. *Religions of Rome. Volume I: A History*. Cambridge: Cambridge University Press, 1998.

Bowersock, Glen. "From Emperor to Bishop: The Self-Conscious Transformation of Political Power in the Fourth Century A.D." *CP* 81 (1986): 298–307.

Burgess, Richard. "The Passio S. Artemii, Philostorgius, and the Dates of the Invention and Translations of the Relics of Sts Andrew and Luke." *AnBoll* 121 (2003): 5–36.

Cameron, Alan. "*Pontifex Maximus:* From Augustus to Gratian – and Beyond." In Maijastina Kahlos (ed.). *Emperors and the Divine – Rome and its Influence*, 139–159. Helsinki: Helsinki Collegium for Advanced Studies, 2016.

Dagron, Gilbert. *Naissance d'une capitale: Constantinople et ses institutions de 330 à 451*. Paris: Presses universitaires de France, 1974.

Diefenbach, Steffen. "A Vain Quest for Unity: Creeds and Political (Dis)Integration in the Reign of Constantius II." In *Contested Monarchy. Integrating the Roman Empire in the Fourth Century AD*, 353–378, edited by Johannes Wienand, Oxford: Oxford University Press, 2015.

Dijkstra, Roald, and Dorine van Espelo. "Anchoring Pontifical Authority. A Reconsideration of the Papal Employment of the Title *Pontifex Maximus*." *JRH* 41 (2017): 312–325.

Downey, Glanville. "The Builder of the Original Church of the Apostles at Constantinople: A Contribution to the Criticism of the "Vita Constantini" Attributed to Eusebius." *DOP* 6 (1951): 53–80.

Drake, Harold. *Constantine and the Bishops: The Politics of Intolerance*. Baltimore: The Johns Hopkins University Press, 2000.

Elm, Susanna. *'Virgins of God'. The Making of Asceticism in Late Antiquity*. Oxford: Oxford University Press 1994.

Elm, Susanna. *Sons of Hellenism, Fathers of the Church*. Berkeley Los Angeles and London: University of California Press, 2012.

Fowden, Garth. "Bishops and Temples in the Eastern Roman Empire A.D. 320–435." *JThS* n.s. 29 (1978): 53–78.

Gaddis, Michael. *There is No Crime for Those Who Have Christ. Religious Violence in the Christian Roman Empire*. Berkeley, Los Angeles and London: University of California Press, 2005.

Girardet, Klaus. "Kaiser Konstantius II. als 'Episcopus Episcoporum' und das Herrscherbild des kirchlichen Widerstandes (Ossius von Corduba und Lucifer von Calaris)." *Hist.* 26 (1977): 95–128.

Gwynn, David. *Athanasius of Alexandria: Bishop, Theologian, Ascetic, Father*. Oxford: Oxford University Press, 2012.

Gwynn, David. "Christian Controversy and the Transformation of Fourth-Century Constantinople." In *Religious Practices and Christianization of the Late Antique City (4th-7th cent.)*, edited by Aude Busine, 206–220. Leiden: Brill, 2015.

Hagl, Wolfgang. "Die Religionspolitik der Kaiser Constantin und Constantius II. im Spiegel kirchlicher Autoren." In *Christen und Heiden in Staat und Gesellschaft des zweiten bis vierten Jahrhunderts. Gedanken und Thesen zu einem schwierigen Verhältnis*, edited by Gunther Gottlieb and Pedro Barceló, 103–129. Munich: Verlag Ernst Vögel, 1992.

Hahn, Johannes. "The Challenge of Religious Violence. Imperial ideology and Policy in the Fourth Century AD." In *Contested Monarchy. Integrating the Roman Empire in the Fourth Century AD*, edited by Johannes Wienand, 379–403. Oxford: Oxford University Press, 2015.

Henck, Nick. "Constantius II and the cities." In *Wolf Liebeschuetz reflected: essays presented by colleagues, friends and pupils*, edited by John Drinkwater and Benet Salway, 147–156. London: Institute of Classical Studies, School of Advanced Study, University of London, 2007.

Hirschmann, Vera. *Die Kirche der Reinen. Kirchen- und Sozialhistorische Studie zu den Novatianern im 3. Bis 5. Jahrhundert*. Tübingen: Mohr Siebeck, 2015.

Isele, Bernd. *Kampf um Kirchen. Religiöse Gewalt, Heiliger Raum und Christliche Topographie in Alexandria und Konstantinopel (4. Jh.)*. Münster: Aschendorf Verlag, 2010.

Just, Patricia. *Imperator et Episcopus. Zum Verhältnis von Staatsgewalt und christlicher Kirche zwischen dem 1. Konzil von Nicaea (325) und dem 1. Konzil von Konstantinopel*. Stuttgart: Franz Steiner Verlag, 2003.

Kahlos, Maijastina. "Pacifiers and Instigators – Bishops and Interreligious Conflicts in Late Antiquity." In *The Role of the Bishop in Late Antiquity. Conflict and Compromise*, edited by Andrew Fear, José Fernández Ubiña and Mar Marcos, 63–82. London et al.: Bloomsbury, 2013.

Leppin, Hartmut. *Von Constantin dem Großen zu Theodosius II. Das christliche Kaisertum bei den Kirchenhistorikern Socrates, Sozomenus und Theodoret*. Göttingen: Vandenhoeck & Ruprecht, 1996.

Lorenz, R. *Die Kirche in ihrer Geschichte. Das vierte Jahrhundert (Osten)*. Göttingen: Vandenhoeck & Ruprecht, 1992.

MacMullen, Ramsay. "The Historical Role of the Masses in Late Antiquity." In *Changes in the Roman Empire: Essays in the Ordinary*, edited by Ramsey MacMullen, 250–276. Princeton: Princeton University Press, 1990.

Manders, Erika. *Coining Images of Power. Patterns in the Representation of Roman Emperors on Imperial Coinage, A.D. 193–284*. Leiden and Boston: Brill, 2012.

Mango, Cyril. "Constantine's Mausoleum and the Translation of Relics." *ByZ* 83 (1990): 51–62.

McLynn, Neil. "Christian Controversy and Violence in the Fourth Century," *Kodai* 3 (1992): 15–44.

Norton, Peter. *Episcopal Elections 250–600. Hierarchy and Popular Will in Late Antiquity*. Oxford: Oxford University Press, 2007.

Millar, Fergus. *The Emperor in the Roman World (31 BC – AD 337)*. Ithaca, NY: Cornell University Press, 1992.

Nuffelen, Peter van. "Episcopal Succession in Constantinople (381–450 C.E.): The Local Dynamics of Power." *JECS* 18 (2010): 425–451.

Skinner, Alexander, "Violence at Constantinople in A.D. 341–2 and Themistius, *Oration* 1." *JRS* 105 (2015): 234–249.

Stepper, Ruth. *Augustus et Sacerdos. Untersuchungen zum römischen Kaiser als Priester*. Stuttgart: Franz Steiner Verlag, 2003.

Stevenson, Walt. "Exiling Bishops: The Policy of Constantius II." *DOP* 68 (2014): 7–27.

Wallraff, Martin. *Der Kirchenhistoriker Sokrates. Untersuchungen zu Geschichtsdarstellung, Methode und Person*. Göttingen: Vandenhoeck & Ruprecht, 1997.

Woods, David. "The Date of the Translation of the Relics of Ss. Luke and Andrew to Constantinople." *VigChr* 45 (1991): 286–292.

Jakob Engberg
Caring for African Confessors in Exile: The Ministry of Numeria and Candida during the Decian Persecution (Cyprian, *Epistulae* 21–22)

In the summer of 249 the experienced Roman senator, Decius, was dispatched by the emperor Philip the Arab to Moesia Superior to suppress the revolt of the governor of that province, Pacatianus. Decius accomplished this quite easily, since Pacatianus was murdered by his own troops upon Decius' arrival. Subsequently however, the troops proclaimed Decius emperor. Philip marched against him, but was killed at Verona in September 249. Decius inherited or possibly provoked one-three other revolts and these revolts (and his own) made it possible for the Quadi to raid Pannonia and the Goths to raid Moesia and Thrace. In this situation, it was prudent to solicit divine help and to seek to reform or punish those who in their neglect of the gods, could be blamed for jeopardizing the pax deorum and thus causing the present strenuous situation. Around the New Year Decius issued an edict calling on all the inhabitants of the empire, excluding the Jews, to make sacrifices to the gods and setting up local commissions to monitor the compliance with the edict.[1]

---

[1] Cyprian, *Epistulae* 19.31 (henceforth quoted *ep.*), *Oracula Sibyllina* 13.87–88, Eusebius of Caesarea, *Historia ecclesiastica* (henceforth quoted *h.e.*) 6.39–41 (including the contemporary evidence of Dionysios), *Acta Maximi* 1, *Martyrium Pionii* 3.2, *Acta Carpi, Papyli et Agathonicae* 4, Aurelius Victor, *Liber de Caesaribus* 28, Zosimus 1.21.23, Gregory of Nyssa, *Vita Gregorii Thaumaturgi*, Lactantius, *De mortibus persecutorum* 4 and John R. Knipfing, "The Libelli of the Decian Persecution," *HThR* 16 (1923): 345–390. See also Fik Meijer, *Kaiser sterben nicht im Bett. Die etwas andere Geschichte der römischen Kaiserzeit. Von Caesar bis Romulus Augustulus (44 v. Chr.–476 n. Chr.)* (Darmstadt: Wissenschaftlicher Buchgesellschaft, 2003), 98–102, Michael Grant, *The Collapse and Recovery of the Roman Empire* (London: Routledge, 1999), 7–10, Joachim Molthagen, *Der römische Staat und die Christen im zweiten und dritten Jahrhundert* (Göttingen: Vandenhoeck und Ruprecht, 1970), 81–82, Fergus Millar, *The Emperor in the Roman World (31 BC – AD 337)* (London: Duckworth, 1992), 567–568, J. Patout Burns Jr. and Robin M. Jensen, *Christianity in Roman Africa – The Development of Its Practices and Beliefs* (Cambridge: Eerdmans, 2014), 12–20 and 521–522. For the past fifty years it has been the dominant position in scholarship that the purpose of the edict was not the persecution of Christians but the performance of sacrifice (cf. Graeme W. Clarke, "Double-trials in the Persecution of Decius," *Hist.* 22 (1973): 650: "It is no longer controversial that the 'Persecution of Decius' began as a general call to sacrifice to the gods and became a persecution of Christians only as a result of non-com-

In the first quarter of 250 three African siblings, Numeria, Candida and Celerinus were caught up in the resultant Decian persecution of Christians. The reactions of the three siblings, when confronted with the authorities, differed, and together they reflect a range of the reactions of other Christians of their time. Celerinus confessed, likely both before a commission of lower magistrates and before higher magistrates, was tortured and imprisoned under severe conditions for nineteen days but then released.² Numeria bribed the magistrates in order to avoid the sacrifice, whereas Candida sacrificed.³ We know of their fates because one of them, Celerinus, around July 250 wrote a letter to his fellow Christian confessor, Lucian, who was in prison in Carthage, because Lucian responded, because both letters ended up in the preserved corpus of Cyprian's letters and because there are further references to Celerinus in other letters written by Cyprian.⁴

---

pliance to this call by some Christians."). 25 years ago Ittai Gradel convincingly argued that this position is untenable: Decius was, given his experience as a governor, full aware that its implementation would bring the Christians in focus (Ittai Gradel, "De moribus persecutorum. Om baggrunden for de romerske kristenforfølgelser," Religionsvidenskabeligt Tidsskrift 22 (1993): 21–40). Gradel's article was published in Danish and has been little noticed. Similar arguments are however now made. Decius' edict was without precedence, was designed to mark a break with his predecessors' policy. The measures stipulated for the monitoring of the compliance with the edict can be designated "totalitarian" and demonstrate that Decius expected that Christians would be unwilling to comply, cf. Ulrich Huttner, "Zwischen Traditionalismus und Totalitarismus. Zur Ideologie und Praxis der Regierung des Kaisers Decius," in ibid.: 37–56 and Bruno Bleckmann, "Zu den Motiven der Christenverfolgung des Decius," in Deleto paene imperio Romano. Transformationsprozesse des Römischen Reiches im 3. Jahrhundert und ihre Rezeption in der Neuzeit, eds. Klaus Peter Johne, Udo Hartmann and Thomas Gerhardt (Stuttgart: Franz Steiner Verlag, 2006): 57–72. See further Cyprian, ep. 19.2, 55.4, 55.7 and 55.16, Cyprian, De lapsis 3, 13, 28 (henceforth quoted laps.) and Cyprian, De unitate ecclesiae 19: confession of being Christian is, like under earlier persecutions, reason enough for punishment, and those who complied with the edict and sacrificed were still punished when they later confessed to be Christians (cf. also Clarke, "Double-trials in the Persecution of Decius," 650 and 655). In all likelihood, Decius motives were intertwined. Decius was likely interested both in the restoration of the pax deorum and in marking a break with his predecessor. He issued his edict knowing well that this would either force the compliance of Christians, who had hitherto neglected to worship the deities in their superstitious devotion to Christ (and thus putting the pax deorum in jeopardy), or bring about their just punishment. If thus motivated, his motives resonate very well with the motives of earlier persecutors and opponents of Christians, his measures are then unique in the history of persecutions, but his motives are typical, cf. Jakob Engberg, Impulsore Chresto. Opposition to Christianity in the Roman Empire c. 50–250 AD (Frankfurt: Peter Lang, 2007).

2 Cyprian, ep. 21, 22.1 and 39.1–4.

3 Cyprian, ep. 21.3.

4 Cyprian forwarded the two letters (ep. 21 and 22) along with a letter (ep. 27) which he later in the year 250 addressed to the priests and deacons in Rome (ep. 27.3). On the dating of the letters, see Graeme W. Clarke, The Letters of St. Cyprian of Carthage. Translated and Annotated, vol. 1–4

When Celerinus writes his letter, both he and the sisters are in Rome. They are however clearly from Africa originally and connected to Africa by ties of family and friendship.[5]

In Celerinus' letter, he described how the two sisters in Rome cared for 65 exiles or refugees from Africa – exiles or refugees who are also called confessors.[6] If the brother's account is to be trusted, we gain a rare glimpse into an example of the "logistics" of exile or flight from persecution and into some practical issues such as how exiles or refugees were supported financially and how they traveled.

It is the purpose of this article to raise and discuss the following series of questions: Can we trust the main outline of Celerinus' letter, in particular his claim about his sisters caring for as many as 65 other African Christians arriving in Rome as a result of the persecutions? If so, where did the two sisters apostatize and where did Celerinus confess? How, when and why did the three siblings arrive in Rome, and did they travel together or in order to meet each other? Further, how did the 65 other Christians arrive in Rome? Were some or even all of the 65 African Christians formally exiled from Africa or were some or even all of them "just" fleeing in order to avoid further persecution? If some were banished, were they banished to Rome or simply banished from Africa? Related to this is the question why they ended up in Rome and not in another place of exile. Finally, where did the sisters get the means from to support the 65 other African Christians?

Celerinus' account is far from detailed, and it does not address all these issues, nor does the three other letters that mentions him or his sisters. So the questions will be raised and a number of possible answers will be pointed out.

(New York: Newman Press, 1984), 1:313–314 and Henneke Gülzow, *Cyprian und Novatian. Der Briefwechsel zwischen den Gemeinden in Rom und Karthago zur Zeit der Verfolgung des Kaisers Decius* (Tübingen: Mohr Siebeck, 1975), 52–57. For other letters referring to Celerinus see *ep.* 37 and 39. It is possible to identify the Celerinus mentioned in these letters with the Celerinus mentioned by Cornelius in a letter to Fabius (Eusebius, *h.e.* 6.43.6).

5 Cyprian, *ep.* 21, 22, 37 and 39.

6 Cyprian, *ep.* 21.2 and 21.4. In this article, "an exile" is a person who has been formally banned from her or his province, while "a refugee" designates a person, who have fled from persecution. As we will see below, such a distinction is seldom made in texts from antiquity including in the texts discussed here.

1 Is Celerinus' account to be trusted?

The purpose of Celerinus' letter is to obtain forgiveness from Lucian and other confessors for his two sisters.[7] The idea that a Christian who suffered at the hands of persecutors might in prayer intercede with God and thereby and through the suffering obtain forgiveness for or even atone for the sins of this Christian and of her or his fellow Christians had by the mid-third century been developing for decades, if not centuries. Variously early Christian authors had promoted, acknowledged, modified, toned down (or even discouraged the more extreme versions of) such ideas.[8] By the time of Cyprian many Christians believed that martyrs could obtain pardon for lapsed Christians from God, and that those thus forgiven were also entitled to full reinstating in the community of the Church. The major purpose of several of Cyrian's letters and one of his tracts was to curb such ideas and maintain that only established ecclesiastical authorities (bishops and bishops in council) had the power to rule in favor of full reinstating.[9] Celerinus writes in this context in a time, where Cyprian's view had yet to be fully articulated, and it is likely the relevance of Celerinus' letter for this discussion, that has resulted in its inclusion in the corpus of Cyprian's letters and in its preservation.

Celerinus does not expect to be martyred himself, since he is no longer imprisoned. Celerinus therefore lack the status to intercede with the Lord for forgiveness for the sisters. He informs Lucian that the presbyters in the Church of Rome have also given the sisters a hearing. The presbyters have ruled that the sisters should continue in their work and await the decision when a new bishop is appointed.[10] He thus solicits intercession from Lucian and other imprisoned confessors back in Carthage, in the expectation that Lucian and the other confessors will soon die as martyrs.[11] With such a purpose, one could suspect that Celerinus would exaggerate his sisters' help for the refuges or exiles from Africa. Indeed Celerinus' base his hope on Lucian's willingness and ability to solicit divine forgiveness for his sisters on a number of "pillars". Firstly, he points to his own grief and his friendship with Lucian. Secondly, he points to Lucian's

---

7 Cyprian, *ep.* 21.2–4.
8 Col 1:24–2:5, *Pastor Hermae, Similitudines* 9.28, *Martyrium Polycarpi* 7.3–8.1, Tertullian, *De pudicitia* 22.4–6, Tertullian, *De baptismo* 16, Clement of Alexandria, *Stromateis* 4.9.75, *Passio Perpetuae et Felicitatis* 7–8, 18.3 and 21.1, Origen, *Exhortatio ad Martyrium* 30, Origen, *In Leviticum homiliae* 9.9 and Cyprian, *laps.* 17–20 and 36.
9 Cyprian, *ep.* 18, 19 and 37, Cyprian, *laps.*
10 Cyprian, *ep.* 21.3.
11 Cyprian, *ep.* 21.1.

personal knowledge of his sisters and the compassion he expects from Lucian out of this personal relationship. Further Celerinus points to the impending martyr-status of Lucian and the other imprisoned confessors. Finally, and most relevant for this article, he describes the repentance and charitable work done by Numeria and Candida:

> For I do believe that Christ, in accordance with their repentance and the works they have rendered to our exiled colleagues who came to us from you, from whom you will learn of their works, that Christ, I believe, will now pardon them if you, His martyrs, intercede.[12]

Celerinus is brief in his description of his two sister's services, but the wording seems very deliberate. I quote the next passage from Graeme Clarke's translation since it remarkably well captures the clear emphasis, which Celerinus puts on his sisters' personal involvement and physical presence. With reference to the 65 Africans, Celerinus writes:

> To meet them my sisters have gone down to the harbor in person and have escorted them up to the city; they have seen to the needs of the sixty-five and have looked after them in every way right up to the present time. All of them are in their care.[13]

It is emphasized that it is the sisters personally who went down to the harbor, that they escorted the Africans, that they have supported, protected and cared for all of them and that they continue to do so.[14]

The two sisters' eagerness to greet their fellow African's at the harbor and their subsequent diligent care for them would not only be testimony to their love, but also to courage. The arrival of 65 Christian exiles or refugees on a ship from Africa in the harbor and their subsequent walk with them would hardly have been an occasion that would have gathered a crowd. On the other hand, it was an occasion that would hardly go unnoticed. There would be some risk that some official or that some potential *delator* might have noticed or even known of the arrival and thus some risk that the two sisters greeting and escorting the African Christians would be noticed. The sisters' subsequent care for the 65 could have brought the same kind of attention to their persons.[15] In a near-contemporary letter by Rome's bishop, Cornelius, he describes how his rival No-

---

12 Cyprian, *ep.* 21.2.
13 Cyprian, *ep.* 21.4, translated by Clarke, *The Letters of St. Cyprian of Carthage*, 1:106.
14 Cyprian, *ep.* 21.4. On the value of fasting, penance, charity and the giving of alms for apostates see Cyprian, *laps.* 29–32 and 35–36, see further Burns and Jensen, *Christianity in Roman Africa*, 313–330.
15 Cyprian, *ep.* 21.4.

vatian out of love for his own life cowardly refused to care for his fellow Christians during the persecution.[16] Given Cornelius' conflict with Novatian it is impossible to know whether he is accurately depicting Novatian's actions and motives. For our purpose, however, the description is evidence that it was considered to involve a certain potential risk (but not necessarily hazard) to be seen to help persecuted Christians.[17] Celerinus thus has a clear interest in highlighting the courage and love of his sisters in their repentance and care for the confessors.

His account is nevertheless to be trusted in its main outline. It is a contemporary letter written to a contemporary audience and he sends in his letter greetings from the 65 African Christians, six of whom are presented as known to Lucius and mentioned by name, Macarius, Cornelia, Emerita, Saturninus, Calpurnius and Maria.[18] Further, as we have seen, Celerinus expects that some of these confessors will themselves inform Lucius about the works of Numeria and Candida.[19] The communication between the imprisoned Christians in Carthage and the exiled African Christians in Rome was maintained both through letters and through the travelling back and forth of Christians.[20] In conclusion, Celerinus' outline of events represents the truth: his sisters had apostatized, but they had repented. Living in Rome (either for a long time or having just arrived) they went out to greet 65 African Christians arriving by ship, escorted them, cared for them and continued to care for them.

---

[16] Cornelius in Eusebius, *h.e.* 6.43.16.

[17] Cyprian *ep.* 5.2, and 8.3, Eusebius, *h.e.* 7.11.25. There is however ample testimony that Christians were nevertheless expected to care for their persecuted or even imprisoned sisters and brothers in the Lord – and testimony that many Christians lived up to such expectations. Lucian, *De morte Peregrini* 11–16, *Passio Perpetuae et Felicitatis* 3.5–8, 4.1, 4.10, Tertullian, *Ad uxorem* 1.4, Cyprian, *ep.* 8.3, 14.2, 40.1, 55.9, Eusebius, *h.e.* 7.11.25 – some examples also from the Decian persecution and some concerns lapsed Christians (like Numeria and Candida), who cared for and sheltered Christian refugees. See further Clarke, "Double-trials in the Persecution of Decius," 657–658 and Daniel D. Sullivan, *The Life of the North Africans as Revealed in the Works of Saint Cyprian* (Washington: The Catholic University of America, 1933), 69–70.

[18] Cyprian, *ep.* 21.4.

[19] Cyprian, *ep.* 21.2, see the quotation above.

[20] Cyprian, *ep.* 21, 22 and 39. There was a similar correspondence and communication through travelers between African Christians and confessors in Rome, see for example ep. 37.1, where Celerinus in early 251 has traveled (back) from Rome to Africa, brought news about and from Roman confessors to Cyprian and where Cyprian responds with a letter to these confessors. See further examples in Cyprian, *ep.* 8.3.

2 Numeria, Candida and Celerinus: The location of their "falls" and confession and their arrivals in Rome

Where did the two sisters apostatize and where did the brother confess? Did they travel to Rome together or separately, were their arrival there connected to the persecution or not? The preserved letters are not clear on this, so likely it is presumed to be known by the readers or irrelevant information.

It is likely that Numeria apostatized (through bribing the magistrates) in Rome. Celerinus refers in his letter to Numeria approaching the status of the *Three Fates* before she bribed herself out of sacrificing, and these statues were located close to the Rostra at Forum Romanum.[21]

Regarding the two other siblings, it is unclear whether Celerinus confessed in Africa or in Rome and whether Candida sacrificed in Africa or in Rome. Graeme Clarke argues that Celerinus confessed in Rome finally before Decius himself, and that Lucian had been to Rome to visit Celerinus, before the persecution broke out. Clarke is so confident about this theory, that he calls an earlier scholar's statement about Celerinus being tried in Carthage "a slip".[22] Clarke's argument builds on two passages, one in letter 21 (written by Celerinus), where Celerinus recalls how he had seen Lucian off, and one in letter 22 (written by Lucian), where Lucian praises Celerinus for having scarred away the great serpent himself with his confession. We will look at the two passages in chronological order.[23]

Had Lucian visited Celerinus in Rome shortly before the outbreak of the persecution? The passage used to support the hypothesis that Lucian had visited Rome mentions that Celerinus saw Lucian off and laments that he has since then not heard from him.[24] Lucian is partly blamed for his lack of communication – Celerinus had himself not forgotten to write letters while he was in prison –, partly excused, since imprisoned confessors frequently forget the affairs of

---

[21] Pliny the Elder, *Naturalis historia* 34.11.22. See Clarke, *The Letters of St. Cyprian of Carthage*, 1:327 note 26. Could there however had been similar statues, similarly located, in the Roman colony of Carthage? Concerning city topography, Roman colonies, including Carthage were often modeled after Rome, cf. Cyprian, *laps.* 8 and 24 where Cyprian mentions buildings and places in Carthage modeled after Rome.

[22] Clarke, *The Letters of St. Cyprian of Carthage*, 1:316 note 1, his reference is to Hippolyte Delehaye, *Les passions des martyrs et les genres littéraires* (Brussels, 1921), 355.

[23] Clarke, *The Letters of St. Cyprian of Carthage*, 2:188–189, note 8.

[24] Cyprian, *ep.* 21.1, and Clarke, *The Letters of St. Cyprian of Carthage*, 1:319–320, note 5.

this world.²⁵ The passage is however totally unspecific about where, how or when Lucian was seen off. There is no mention of Rome, no maritime setting and no hint as to whether this happened before or during the persecution. The passage can just as easily be understood in a way where Celerinus in some way saw Lucian off in Carthage upon Lucian's arrest, imprisonment or even more likely on another less dramatic occasion situated in Africa and known by both of them.

Was Celerinus tried by Decius himself? This was first proposed by Edward Benson in 1897.²⁶ This proposal has been followed by both W.H.C. Frend with reference to Cyprians letter 37.1 and by Clarke with reference to a statement made by Lucian in letter 22.1 and a statement by Cyprian in letter 39.2. Frend does not explain his position and fails to state how he finds support for it in letter 37.1.²⁷ I find no hint in this passage that would place Celerinus' trial in Rome, and no hint that it should have been conducted in front of Decius. Clarke on the other hand provides an argument he writes "it is argued that here *ipso infestationis principe et auctore*, on the accumulated evidence, refers in all likelihood rather to the Emperor Decius than to the arch-enemy Satan."²⁸ It follows from what Clarke writes that he is well aware that Satan and/or Demons were in contemporary Christian texts presented as the true instigators of persecutions, and that he thus needs to state that it is not a demon, nor Satan that is being referred to here.²⁹

Against such a firm conclusion based on ambiguous evidence, we may advance an argument from silence and an argument from what Cyprian and Lucian does write. Firstly, if Celerinus confessed before Decius, this would have made him clearly outstanding.³⁰ Both Celerinus, in his letter to Lucian, and Cyprian,

---

25 Cyprian, *ep.* 21.1.
26 Edward White Benson, *Cyprian. His Life, His Times, His Work* (London: Macmillan, 1897), 70. See also Robin Lane Fox, *Pagans and Christians in the Mediterranean world from the second century AD to the conversion of Constantine* (London: Viking, 1986), 454.
27 W.H.C. Frend, *The Rise of Christianity* (Philadelphia: Fortress Press, 1984), 322 and 334, note 77.
28 Clarke, *The Letters of St. Cyprian of Carthage*, 2:188–189 note 8. See also Graeme W. Clarke, "Some Observations on the Persecution of Decius", *Antichthon* 3 (1969): 66–67.
29 Tertullian, *Apologeticum, Passio Perpetuae et Felicitatis*, Cyprian, *ep.* 25.1, 38.1, 39.2, 60.2, 66.4, Cyprian, *laps.* 2 and 13. See further Hans von Campenhausen, *Die Idee des Martyriums in der alten Kirche* (Göttingen: Vandenhoeck & Ruprecht 1964), 155–158.
30 Clarke acknowledges that this would make Celerinus exceptional and writes, "Celerinus was thus, most unusually, tried before the Emperor himself", Clarke, *The Letters of St. Cyprian of Carthage*, 2:189 note 8. There is however, as Fergus Millar observes (commenting on Celerinus

in his letters to the presbyters and deacons have a clear interest in emphasizing the status of Celerinus. Cyprian is in his letter 39 written to the presbyters, deacons and the congregation in Carthage justifying that he has appointed Celerinus as lector without prior consultation with them.[31] His main justification is Celerinus' brave confession, so why would he fail to clearly state it if Celerinus had been tried by Decius? It would have made a comparison with even Peter and Paul possible. In Celerinus' letter Celerinus' need to draw on his own status as confessor is couched by a need for Celerinus to appear modest about himself, but even so why would he also fail to even hint at such an exceptional trial? While Cyprian does want to present Celerinus as modest in accepting his appointment as lector, there is no reason for Cyprian to be modest on Celerinus' behalf.[32] Secondly, while Cyprian writes in the singular about the "leader and author" of the persecution and of the "serpent", who with Celerinus bound feets was both "crushed and conqured", these two references in the singular frame a passage that talks in the plural about Celerinus' judges and persecutors. This would indicate what Lucian also seems to be hinting at, that Celerinus during his nineteen day trial had faced multiple magistrates, some of whom were of higher rank, than those Lucian had faced.[33]

Having concluded that we have no evidence for situating Celerinus in Rome before and at the outbreak of the persecution of Decius and of proposing that he was tried by Decius himself, we will now look at some circumstantial evidence that might provide us with hints about Celerinus' usual place of residence. From letter 37 it is evident that Celerinus traveled (back?) to Africa in late 250 or early 251 and from letter 39 that he intends to stay there for good, as a lector

---

and Clarke's theory), "no reason in principal why some Christian should not have been accused before the emperor" (Millar, *The Emperor in the Roman World*, 568).

31 To do so on his own, without prior approval of the presbyters and the congregation was against practice, cf. Hans von Campenhausen, *Ecclesiastical Authority and Spiritual Power in the Church of the First Three Centuries* (London: A. and C. Black, 1969), 274–275 and Charles A. Bobertz, *Cyprian of Carthage as Patron: A Social Historical Study of the Role of Bishop in the Ancient Christian Community of North Africa* (Yale (unpublished dissertation), 1988), 190–201. Bobertz shows how Cyprian in letters 38 and 39 argued with stronger confidence compared to earlier in his exile, but Bobertz' analysis also shows how carefully and skillfully Cyprian justifies his ordination of Celerinus.

32 Clarke argues similarly but with the opposite conclusion. Writing about the uniqueness of a trial before the emperor Clarke continues "to emphasize this unusual feature being germane to Cyprian's present purpose" (Clarke, *The Letters of St. Cyprian of Carthage*, 2:189 note 8). I find no evidence of any "emphasis", and since such an emphasis would have been "germane" I conclude that Cyprian would have emphasized it clearly if Celerinus had been tried before Decius.

33 Cyprian, *ep.* 39.2 and *ep.* 22.1.

in the Church of Carthage. His willingness to make the journey from Rome to Africa during the winter and his resolve to remain there would indicate that Africa was his residence prior to the persecution and his usual place of residence.[34] Towards the end of letter 39, in which Cyprian has justified that he has installed Celerinus as a Lector, Cyprian seems concerned with the financial situation of Celerinus.[35] He and another confessor, Aurelius, who has also been made lector, are both marked out for the rank of presbyter and further they will both as of now receive the same gifts (*sportulae*) and allowances (*divisiones mensurnas*) as a presbyter. Does this concern for the financial situation of the two confessors, perhaps especially for Celerinus, since no mention of any need for financial support was made in the previous letter that Cyprian wrote concerning Aurelius appointment, indicate that they, or perhaps only Celerinus, were financially pressed?[36] Had they (or just Celerinus) lost part of (most of) their (his) patrimony during the persecution? Had some of their (Celerinus') fortune been confiscated? Had Celerinus' flight or exile to Rome and his subsequent (home-) journey to Africa strained the transferable part of his fortune?[37] Had he supported his sisters in supporting the 65 Africans in Rome?

Culprits condemned formally to exile (*in perpetuum* or *ad tempus*) would often have their fortunes confiscated; and from Cyprian's letters we learn that this also happened during the Decian and Valerian persecutions to exiled Christian confessors.[38] More generally, there is evidence in the corpus of Cyprian's letters that African Christian confessors were exiled, and some of them at least formally, during the Decian and Valerian persecutions.[39] We will take a closer look at two of these references, since they are of particular relevance to establish the location of Celerinus' trial and/or the status of the 65 African Christians mentioned in Celerinus' letter (whether they were formally exiled or whether they were refugees).

In a letter written by Cyprian to imprisoned confessors in Carthage and dated to April, Cyprian refers to recent cases where other (African?) confessors

---

[34] For the dating of letter 37 see Clarke, *The Letters of St. Cyprian of Carthage*, 2:171–172 and 174–175, notes 10–11.
[35] This and the following, Cyprian, *ep.* 39.4–5. For Aurelian being made lector see Cyprian, *ep.* 38.
[36] Cyprian, *ep.* 38.
[37] Apuleius, *Metamorphoses* 11.28.1. The "hero" in this passage of Apuleius' novel complain that the cost of his travels has strained his modest patrimony severely.
[38] Cyprian, *ep.* 19.2 *omnibus spoliati* and 24.1 *possessiones quas nunc fiscus tenet*, Cyprian, *laps.* 2, 11–12 and 36.
[39] Cyprian *ep.* 13.4, 19.2, 24.1, 38.1, 59.6, 66.4, 66.7 and Cyprian, *laps.* 2.

were punished and driven into exile.⁴⁰ Legal technical terms are not used but the context here is clearly suggesting that we are dealing with formal banishment after trial and confession, and not "just" flight in order to avoid further persecution. Could Cyprian here be referring to Celerinus and/or (some of) the 65 African (confessors in exile) mentioned in Celerinus' letter? The same applies to a passage in Cyprians letter 19 written to the presbyters and deacons in Carthage. Here Cyprian argues that penitent apostates should not be prematurely reinstated. One of his arguments is that those who have been exiled, driven from their homeland and have had their possessions plundered have not yet returned to their own Church – why should the apostates then be allowed to?⁴¹ For our purpose, it is significant that Cyprian links confession, banishment and confiscation of property.

On balance, the discussion above will put the three siblings in each their own category. On Candida we have absolutely no indication of whether she was living in Rome or in Africa prior to the persecution. Given that a majority of people in the Roman Empire as in most agrarian societies would live for most of their lives relatively close to the place of residence of the family, the balance of probability would point to Africa. On Celerinus the little information we do have adds to this probability and points (albeit inconclusively) to Africa. On Numeria, the reference to the three statues would point to Rome. Perhaps the persecution prompted Celerinus and/or Candida to travel to Rome. Perhaps in Celerinus' case to avoid further persecution after confession or perhaps because of an exile sentence for a stipulated period.⁴² In Candida's case perhaps to avoid local *delatores*, who might notice her penance and could bring a second case before the magistrates.⁴³ If either Candida or Celerinus or both of them were prompted by the persecutions to leave Africa, then it would have been attractive to go to Numeria's place of residence – this explaining why all three of them ended up in Rome, where we in any case find them in mid-250, when Celerinus wrote his letter.

---

40 Cyprian, *ep.* 10.1: *suscepta poena est quae confessors Christi fecit extorres*.
41 Cyprian, *ep.* 19.2.
42 For a discussion of this see below.
43 Cf. Cyprian, *laps*. 13: apostates, who had sacrificed were not immune to further persecution if they demonstrated renewed allegiance to Christ.

3 The 65 African Christians, their status and itinerary

In his letter, Celerinus informed Lucian that his sisters went down to the harbor to greet the 65 African Christians, when they arrived.[44] It is unclear whether he means the river-harbor of Rome, Ostia or Portus. Since the harbor is not named, it would be logical to presume that he is referring simply to the river-harbor of Rome. The context would however suggest otherwise. As we have seen, Celerinus is trying to present his sisters in a positive light. Having the sisters out to greet the confessors in Ostia or Portus would emphasize their eagerness to serve and their courage.[45] To picture them awaiting leisurely for their fellow Africans to be transferred to riverboats in Ostia or Portus and then to greet them only at Rome's river harbor would seem much less heroic and welcoming – and further there would be a likelihood that the arrivals would be scattered with the two sisters being unable to greet all of them. The number of travelers arriving, presumably on the same ship, points to an ocean-harbor rather than the river-harbor of Rome.[46] 65 travelers could easily be billeted aboard a grain ship along with its main bulk of cargo.[47] The lack of specificity in Celerinus' description would point to Ostia rather than Portus, as the more famous of the two locations. The distance from both Portus and Ostia to Rome is finally a walking distance and was considered as such in antiquity, a factor which would in itself make the alternative hypothesis of a transfer in Ostia from an ocean-going vessel to a number of riverboats less likely.[48]

In a number of places, Celerinus refers to the 65 African Christians collectively as confessors. He designates their status both by using the term confessor and by referring them as colleagues of Lucian and himself.[49] A number of the African confessors are named and sends their greetings from Rome to Lucian and his fellow prisoners. One of them is called Saturninus and his courage when confess-

---

[44] Cyprian, *ep.* 21.4.
[45] Compare Acts 20:15–17 and 28:11–15.
[46] Cf. below, p. 46–47.
[47] Cf. below, p. 46–47.
[48] Minucius Felix, *Octavius* 2,3–4 and Acts 28:11–16. Lionel Casson, *The Ancient Mariners: Seafarers and Sea Fighters of the Mediterranean in Ancient Times* (Princeton: Princeton University Press, 1991), 288 and idem, *Travel in the Ancient World* (London: John Hopkins University Press, 1994), 126–128.
[49] Cyprian, *ep.* 21.4: *omnes confessors qui inde huc a vobis venerunt*; *ep.* 21.2: *collegas nostros... qui a vobis venerunt.*

ing Christ under torture in Carthage is praised.[50] Does Celerinus' reference to the 65 as confessors mean that they were all confessors, or that some of them were, while others were simply other Christian accompanying the confessors in their flight or banishment? From later sources, there is ample evidence that banished Christians could be accompanied in exile by followers, as could of course other traveling Christians.[51] Equally, Acts describes how Paul en route for his trial in Rome was accompanied by the author (and others). The "authenticity" of the we-passages in Acts are disputed, but even if they are not "authentic", then the evidence is even stronger that it was conceivable for a prisoner or exile to have followers. It would serve the purpose of the letter to refer to all the 65 exiles as confessors, since having the sisters caring for 65 confessors would seem more glorious, than having them care for 65 ordinary African Christians or a mixed group of some confessors and some followers. However, given again that we are dealing with a contemporary letter, given that some of the confessors are named in the letter and send their greetings and given that direct communication between these confessors and the recipients of the letter is presumed, it would be counterproductive for Celerinus to blatantly misrepresent the status of the 65 African Christians.[52] Finally, Lucian's letter acknowledges the status of both Celerinus and those greeting Lucian in Celerinus' letter as confessors. Specifically, Saturninus, who was particularly praised for courage in Celerinus' letter is again drawn forward, but specifically as one among many confessors, who are with Celerinus.[53] Celerinus' own status as confessor is equally acknowledged by Lucian, even in a way, where it is praised that Celerinus has confessed before higher magistrates than has been the case with Lucian himself.[54] It follows from this that we are either dealing with a group of 65 confessors or that we are dealing with a mixed group, where a significant number of the 65 were confessors.

Celerinus clearly states that the 65 have come to Rome from Africa and that some level of coercion was involved.[55] It is however difficult to decide whether he implies that they have been legally banished from Africa or whether they have simply decided to flee from persecution. The phrasing of the letter is of little

---

50 Cyprian, *ep.* 21.4.
51 Margarita Vallejo Girvés, "Banished Bishops Were Not Alone: The Two Cases of Theodoros Anagnostes, Guardian and Assistant," in *Clerical Exile in Late Antiquity*, eds. Julia Hillner, Jörg Ulrich and Jakob Engberg (Frankfurt: Peter Lang, 2016): 193–212.
52 Cyprian, *ep.* 21.4.
53 Cyprian, *ep.* 22.3.
54 Cyprian, *ep.* 22.1.
55 Cyprian, *ep.* 21.2: *collegas nostros... extorres qui a vobis venerunt*; *ep.* 21.4: *omnes confessors qui inde huc a vobis venerunt*.

help here. As so often in cases of exile the terminology employed is unspecific and not legally technical.[56] We have to turn to the context in order to pursue an answer. Here the contemporary status of the letter does not preclude that Celerinus could have referred to 65 refugees as exiles – he would not thereby have been creating an excessive status claim. There are many examples in our sources of refugees being referred to or referring to themselves as exiles – so no firm distinction in terminology was being made between those formally relegated and refuges.[57]

Some legal sources from earlier imperial times would however seem to indicate that we are hardly dealing with formal exile, and indeed this has, in the case of one of the confessors, been argued in scholarship. With reference to one of the confessors, the particularly brave Saturninus, Clarke writes that he "cannot be in Rome, legally relegated to the City. Relegation specifically excluded Rome, being the *communis patria*, as a place of residence for *relegati*."[58]

This stipulation goes back to Claudius, but at the time of Decius it was not just an archaic and obsolete First Century norm, its content had been repeated by the influential jurists Callistratus and Ulpian, both of whom were active in the early Third Century – and their opinions found there ways into the Justinian Code.[59] Specifically Ulpian states that those whom a magistrate has banished from a province should also be barred from Rome and Italy.[60] Callistratus makes no mention of any ban on Italy, but like Ulpian, he mentions that a provincial, who is exiled from his home province, cannot remain in Rome. He adds the explanation to this alluded to by Clarke above, and states that Rome is the common fatherland of all.[61]

On one level, the evidence from Suetonius and more importantly Ulpian and Callistratus would seem to clinch the matter, the 65 confessors (or the confessors among them) were not formally banished from Africa – equally (cf. above), Celerinus could not have been formally banished from Africa to Rome. If so it would be illegal for them to take up residence in Rome (or following Ulpian even Italy),

---

56 See also Clarke, *The Letters of St. Cyprian of Carthage*, 1:230 note 5.
57 Jakob Engberg, "Exile and the Dissemination of Donatist Congregations," in *Clerical Exile in Late Antiquity*, eds. Hillner, Ulrich, and Engberg, 146–147; Julia Hillner, "Approaches to Clerical Exile in Late Antiquity: Strategies, Experiences, Memories and Social Networks," in *ibid.*, 14, 21–24, 34 and David Reis, "Tracing the Imaginary in Imperial Rome," in *ibid.*, 227–228.
58 Clarke, "Double-trials in the Persecution of Decius," 660.
59 Suetonius, *Claudius* 23.2, *Digestae* 48.22.7.15 (Ulpian) and 48.22.18 (19) (Callistratus).
60 *Digestae* 48.22.7.15: *quibus a magistratibus provinciae interdicerentur, urbe quoque et Italia summoverentur.*
61 *Digestae* 48.22.18.1 (Callistratus)

ipso facto they must be Christians who fled from persecution. When taking a closer look however the case is less clear. With Ulpian and Callistratus we are dealing with normative sources. Ulpian issued his statement in his now lost work *On the Office of Governors*. His need in such a work to inform (would be) governors that those banished from their own province are also banished from Rome would indicate that we are not dealing with common knowledge (even among those most likely to know). Further, in the same passage he provided an example of the wording whereby governors would customarily pronounce sentence on banished criminals. Significantly, the customary statement makes no mention of Rome or Italy saying simply: "I banish him from this province and its islands" and then adding, according to Ulpian, a date by which the culprit must leave.⁶² When Ulpian assumes that not all (would be) governors know of the tradition for barring provincial exiles from Rome and Italy and when verdicts are according to Ulpian normally passed in this way without the mentioning of such a barring, could we assume that the 65 African Christians would have known that they were barred from entering Rome and Italy? This more open interpretation is supported when we examine Callistratus. He stated that a relegated person cannot remain or take up residence in Rome "even if this is not included in the verdict"⁶³ Callistratus thereby confirms that a sentence was not always specific about the ban on entering Rome. Further, the discrepancy between Ulpian and Callistratus, where Ulpian mentions both Rome and Italy, whereas Callistratus mentions only Rome, would indicate that the stipulation was actually less well known or well-established in the minds of even two of the sharpest legal minds of their age. There remains even further the possibility that the African governor had been specific about this ban, or that some of the 65 exiled would have independent knowledge about such a ban, but that they had simply chosen to ignore it counting on them going undetected among the number of (African) travelers regularly arriving in Rome. Turning from normative to descriptive sources there is evidence that does show that at least in the fourth Century and later (times where the stipulation would still be applying according to the inclusion in the *Digest*) exiles did arrive in Rome (and Italy).⁶⁴

The existence of the stipulations banning exiled provincials from entering Rome will tend to decrease slightly the likelihood that we are dealing with a case where the governor of Africa banished several Christians from Africa, but

---

62 *Digestae* 48.22.7.17 (Ulpian).
63 *Digestae* 48.22.18.1 (Callistratus): *etsi id sententia comprehensum non est*.
64 *Passio Maximini et Isaac*. See further Engberg, "Exile and the Dissemination of Donatist Congregations," 145–164 and https://www.clericalexile.org/location/9 (8 exile cases arriving and taking up residence in Rome), accessed February 3, 2018.

only very slightly. It will significantly decrease the likelihood however that the governor specifically relegated the Africans *to* Rome. There is at least one later exile case related to Carthage, that indicates that governors could arrange for the transportation of a significant number of condemned Christians to their place of exile aboard a single ship.⁶⁵ The existence of the ban of entering Rome for exiled provincials would however make it unlikely that the transport *to* Ostia/Portus or Rome was organized by the governor. In the end though, the discussion above shows that the arrival of the exiles in Rome cannot be used to argue with any certainty that we are dealing just with a group of refuges. The possibility remains that we are dealing with a group of Christians that included a significant portion of people who were formally banished from Africa. The possibility also remains that Cyprian was referring to these confessors and exiles when he in April 250 wrote his letter 10 mentioning confessors recently punished with exile.⁶⁶ Both flight from persecution and formal banishment are attested in contemporary sources in connection to the Decian and the subsequent Valerian persecutions. From Cyprian's *De lapsis*, we know that other African Christians were formally banished during the Decian persecution, just as some African Christians fled to avoid persecution.⁶⁷ Cyprian himself fled from Carthage during the Decian persecution and was formally exiled during the Valerian persecution.⁶⁸ Dionysius of Alexandria had similar experiences.⁶⁹ Flight in order to avoid persecution, but more particularly formal exile after confiscation of property (a practice attested during the Decian persecution, see above) would put the 65 in need of financial support.⁷⁰

Regardless of whether the 65 were refuges, exiles formally banished or both we still need to answer why they, given that they were likely not compelled by

---

65 *Passio Maximini et Isaac* 12.
66 Cf. above and Cyprian, *ep.* 10.1.
67 Cyprian, *laps.* 2.
68 Cyprian, *laps.* and *ep.* 8.1. Gregory of Nyssa, *Vita Gregorii Thaumaturgi* (PG 46.949 A) also reports that Gregory fled at the outbreak of Decius' persecution.
69 Dionysius' letter to Dometius and Didymus in Eusebius, *h.e.* 7.11.20–23 is related to the flight and exile under the Decian persecution, although Eusebius mistakenly places it under Valerian. Dionysius also refers to the flight under Decius in his letter to Germanus (Eusebius, *h.e.* 6.40.1), a letter written during the formal exile under Valerian (Eusebius, *h.e.* 6.40). On Dionysius' exile see Jörg Ulrich, "Dionysius of Alexandria in Exile", in Hillner, Ulrich and Engberg (eds.), *Clerical Exile in Late Antiquity*, 115–128. See further on confiscation during the Decian persecution Millar, *The Emperor in the Roman World*, 568–571.
70 Clarke has convincingly argued, that Cyprian is expressing special concern for confessors, who have had their possessions confiscated in his letter 5. See Clarke, *The Letters of St. Cyprian of Carthage*, 1:185 note 8.

the governor of Africa to go to Rome specifically, let alone conveyed there in a transport organized by the governor, made the choice of travelling to Rome. One primary and a number of derived or secondary factors would have contributed to this choice.

First and foremost, for an African who needed to leave his home province in the spring of 250 it would have been easiest, cheapest and safest to travel to the area of Ostia, Portus and Rome. The ties of transport, trade and culture between Africa and Rome would expedite a transit of the 65 African Christians to Rome.[71] There was a lively trade between Africa and Rome. The most important commodity traded was grain and the trade in this commodity alone ensured a lively transit of vessels. During the principate the province of Africa was considered to be the most important area in supplying grain for Rome, more important than Egypt and Sicily combined.[72] If two ancient sources are combined we find that Rome's population required approximately 400,000 tons of grain annually. Some modern estimates would half this figure. If we follow Josephus and estimate that half of Rome's need for grain would have been supplied from Africa, this would have required the transportation of 100,000–200,000 tons of grain from Africa to Rome annually. Traditionally the Romans would only sail during eight months of the year. In respect to the all-important grain supply of Rome, the emperor Claudius instituted a system of insurance that prompted traders to sail throughout most of the winter.[73] If we estimate the intensity of this winter travel optimistically as half that of the other months then this means that 10,000–20,000 tons of grain would have been transported from Africa to Rome each month during the eight months of the sailing season with 5,000–10,000 being carried in each of the four months from mid-November to mid-March. A typical Roman trading vessel was able to carry 100–150 tons of cargo, while the largest could carry up to 600 tons.[74] The largest vessels were the grain-vessels. If we optimistically estimate that the average vessel engaged in the grain-trade would have been able to carry 500 tons this means that twenty to forty of these large sailing vessels from Africa would have been arriving in Ostia or Portus every month during spring, summer and fall – effectively one

---

71 Casson, *The Ancient Mariners*, 198–212 and idem, *Travel in the Ancient World*, 149–162.
72 This and the following Josephus, *De bello iudaico* 2.382–386 and *Epitome de Caesaribus* 1.6, interpreted by Fik Meijer and Onno van Nijf, *Trade, Transport and Society in the Ancient World* (London: Routledge, 1992), 98–99. The grain from Africa was also considered premium quality, cf. Pliny the Elder, *Naturalis Historia* 18.66–68 and 89.
73 Suetonius, *Claudius* 18–19.
74 According to Meijer and Nijf, *Trade, Transport and Society*, 152, extreme cases are also known of vessels holding as much as 1000 tons.

ship every day. Ships of these sizes are known to have carried along with their bulk cargo upwards of 100 passengers each.⁷⁵ The passengers would in most cases negotiate the prize for the transport with the skipper, the owner or the owner's representative. Most passengers were expected on such travels to have slept on deck, either in their own tents or in open air, and most travelers were expected to care for their own provisions of food and drink. A letter from 404 describing a travel from Alexandria to Ptolemais mentions that a Jewish skipper carrying more than 50 passengers including about 15 young and pretty females had, out of consideration for their modesty and to the annoyance of the man writing the letter, taken the unusual provision of separating the male and female passengers on the deck by using an old torn sail as a curtain.⁷⁶ Only the most wealthy of passengers would have stayed in cabins at the stern. Likely, then the 65 African Christians would have negotiated for themselves a transit from Africa to Ostia in one of the grain-ships that during the spring of 250 would have been leaving on a more or less daily basis. Most if not all would have slept on deck and would have cared for their won provisions during a 3–8 days transit.⁷⁷

Secondly, and tied to these strong links of trade and culture, the established community of Africans living in Rome, Portus and Ostia would have increased the likelihood that some of the travelers could find support from networks, either of other African Christians or just of other Africans.⁷⁸

Thirdly, the significant Christian community in Rome could have been expected to offer support for Christian refugees from Africa even if the pressure from the persecution and the influx of refugees from other parts of the empire would have diminished the resources available for this.⁷⁹

---

75 Meijer and Nijf, *Trade, Transport and Society*, 158 and 170–176. Josephus has described how he traveled on a grain-ship with as many as 600 people aboard, crew and passengers, the ship was wrecked in the Adriatic and only about eighty were saved, Josephus, *Vita* 15.
76 Synesius, *Epistula* 4.
77 North- and West-bound voyages were longer in duration, than South- or West-bound. The course from Carthage to Ostia was Northeasterly.
78 Minucius Felix, *Octavius* presupposes African's in Rome being tied to each other in bonds of friendship Christian to Christian and pagan to Christian. After 410 the stream of refugees was reversed, and Roman refugees would find or (in the case of the rich) offer networks and support in Africa, Clarke, *The Letters of St. Cyprian of Carthage*, 1:315 and Peter Brown, *Through the Eye of a Needle. Wealth, the Fall of Rome, and the Making of Christianity in the West, 350–550 AD* (Princeton: Princeton University Press, 2012), 300–303 and 323–325.
79 Cornelius in Eusebius, *h.e.* 6.43.11 testifies to the ability of the Roman congregation in the mid-third century to support a large number of people financially.

Fourthly, the relative anonymity that was possible in this the largest city of the empire would be an advantage if some of the exiles or refugees wanted to avoid further confrontations with the authorities.

4 How did Numeria and Candida finance their support for the 65 Africans?

Celerinus informs Lucian that his sisters have cared for and continue to care for the 65 African Christians.[80] He is quite specific that they have been and are caring for all of them, for all their needs and that they are all with them, but he is not specific about the length of time during which they have offered this elaborate support. Chances are that Lucian would have had an idea about this from his knowledge of the (named) confessors mentioned in Celerinus' letter, his knowledge of their trails and his knowledge of the time of the year in which he received the letter.[81] We are less privileged. Scholars have however laboured to date the letters included in the Cyprianic corpus and the events described in them. Following such studies, Celerinus' letter is dated to July 250. We know from the letter that Numeria and Candida apostatized well before Easter (i.e. April 7, 250) and that Celerinus had spend Easter mourning them.[82] Their apostasy and Celerinus' confession and nineteen days trail must therefore be placed between January and mid-March. If we are right in presuming that Celerinus and Candida traveled to Rome after their confession and "fall" and arriving of course before the 65 confessors, then that narrows the arrival of the confessors down to February to June 250. If Cyprian is referring to the 65 in his letter 10 from April, their exile must have occurred by the latest in April. We are therefore dealing with a length of support of anything from two to twelve weeks, but not much beyond this. What would it have required to support 65 people in Rome for even two weeks? This would have depended most significantly on the status and expectancy of the exiles. Given these uncertainties we are left with the sense, which is also conveyed by Celerinus' letter, namely that the sisters have rendered and are rendering a significant ministry that may contribute to motivate Lucian and his colleagues to pray for the forgiveness for their grievous sin. Rome was con-

---

[80] Cyprian, *ep.* 21.4.
[81] Cyprian, *ep.* 21.4.
[82] Cyprian, *ep.* 21.4.

sidered a notoriously expensive place to live, in terms of accommodation, food and other necessities.⁸³

Where did Numeria and Candida have the means from? Cyprian informs us of Celerinus, Numeria and Candida's family background in his letter 39.⁸⁴ His grandmother Celerina had been martyred in an earlier persecution in Carthage, and so had his paternal and maternal uncles Laurentinus and Egnatius.⁸⁵ Significantly, in our context we learn that these uncles had been soldiers.⁸⁶ Graeme Clarke has argued that allusions in the letter, where Cyprian justifies his ordination of Celerinus indicates that Celerinus himself had done army service.⁸⁷ If Clarke is right in assuming that the military language and the military metaphors (used however also elsewhere, when Cyprian refers to martyrs or confessors)⁸⁸ are meant to also resonate with Celerinus' past then a passage in letter 39.2 could indicate that Celerinus, in spite of his youth, had already risen beyond the rank of an ordinary soldier.⁸⁹ Could some of the wealth spent by Numeria and Candida on their ministry for the 65 African Christians in their care come from wealth accumulated in a family, which on both sides had a tradition for doing military service?

Commenting on the role of the army and municipal elites in third century Roman society the historians Naphtali Lewis and Meyer Reinhold wrote:

> Beginning with Septimius Severus the imperial power was openly based upon the armed forces, and this marked the start of the social revolution of the third century. The state

---

83 Wolfgang Szaivert and Reinhard Wolters, *Löhne, Preise, Werte. Quellen zur römischen Geldwirtschaft* (Darmstadt: Wissenschaftliche Buchgesellschaft, 2005), 30 and 89–90 and Christiane Kunst, *Leben und Wohnen in der römischen Stadt* (Darmstadt: Wissenschaftliche Buchgesellschaft, 2006), 114–117. See for example Apuleius, *Metamorphoses* 11.28.1 and Iuvenal 3.180.
84 Cyprian, *ep.* 39.3.
85 Augustine delivered at least two sermons in a basilica in Carthage dedicated to Celerina (*Sermo* 48 and *Enarratio in Psalmos* 99). See Benson, *Cyprian*, 70 and Clarke, *The Letters of St. Cyprian of Carthage*, 2:190–191 note 14.
86 For other examples of third Century Christian soldiers being prosecuted and executed for being Christians see Eusebius, *h.e.* 6.41.16–17 and 7.15.
87 Cyprian, *ep.* 39.4, Clarke, *The Letters of St. Cyprian of Carthage*, 2:188–189, note 8 and Cyprian, *ep.* 22.1, Clarke, *The Letters of St. Cyprian of Carthage*, 1:319–320, note 5.
88 Cyprian, *De unitate ecclesiae* 1.
89 Celerinus is said to be *inter Christi milites antesignanus*, i.e. he is either seen as a leader or one of the picked legionaries assigned to protect the standard of the legion. Given the religious devotion to standards, it would seem more productive for Cyprian to use the term in a sense where he is alluding to a past, where Celerinus had some kind of command. Clarke offers another interpretation, "skirmishers", but the references provided actually give examples of either junior noncommissioned officers or crack troops assigned to the protection of the standard.

was rapidly militarized, and the soldiery, enriched by large emoluments and illegal extortions, became the new privileged class, supplanting the civilian, propertied class.[90]

It may be exaggerated to follow Lewis and Reinhold in stating that the wealth of ordinary soldiers grew in the third century to rival that of local municipal elites. Their perception was typical of their generation of scholarship, which to some degree followed the rhetoric and the moralizing tone of the second to third century historians Herodian and Dio Cassius. Later scholarship has toned down the scale of the third-century crisis and emphasized points of continuity from the second into the fourth centuries.[91] There is little doubt however that while the Roman imperial army had traditionally provided its soldiers with above average incomes and chances for social mobility the third century witnessed for soldiers a considerable increase in levels of pays, and more significantly increased frequencies and levels of special donations and chances for irregular forms of income.[92]

The emperors of the Severan dynasty had been famous for caring for soldiers and neglecting others. The contemporary historians Dio Cassius and Herodian both report about increased annual pay, the granting of new privileges, the rise in different rations and not least "large donations".[93] The donations were given to celebrate victories over other pretenders to the throne, the rise to office of new members of the imperial dynasty, their anniversaries in office and similar events. Both authors saw a moral decline and an excessive burden for the state

---

[90] Naphtali Lewis and Meyer Reinhold, *Roman Civilization. Sourcebook II: The Empire* (New York: Harper, 1966), 419.
[91] Anthony King and Martin Henig, eds. *The Roman West in the Third Century: Contributions from Archaeology and History*, vols. 1–2, International Series 109 (Oxford: British Archeological Reports, 1981), Averil Cameron, *The Later Roman Empire* (London: Fontana, 1993), 1–12 and Erik Christiansen, *A History of Rome: From Town to Empire and from Empire to Town* (Aarhus: Aarhus University Press, 1995), 150–157.
[92] Lawrence Keppie, *The Making of the Roman Army. From Republic to Empire* (London: BT Batsford, 1984), 147–148 and 182, Graham Webster, *The Roman Imperial Army* (London: Adam and Charles Black, 1974), 256–260, Peter A. Brunt, "Pay and Superannuation in the Roman Army," *PBSR* 18 (1950): 50–71, George R. Watson, *The Roman Soldier* (New York: Cornell University Press, 1969), 75–117, 137–138 and 188 notes 231–233, Alfred von Domaszewski, *Der Truppensold der Kaiserzeit*, NHJ X (1900), 225–241, Marcus Junkelmann, *Die Legionen des Augustus. Der römische Soldat im archäologischen Experiment* (Mainz: Philipp von Zabern, 1994), 120–127, H.M.D. Parker, *The Roman Legions* (Cambridge: Heffer and Sons, 1958), 214–224 and Michał Duch, *Economic Role of the Roman Army in the Province of Lower Moesia (Moesia Inferior)* (Poznan: ACTA HUMANISTICA GNESNENSIA XVI, 2017), 77–83.
[93] This and the following see for example Herodian, *Historiae* 3.8.4–5, Dio Cassius, *Historiae* 75.2.3–6 and 78.36.1–3, the quotations are from Herodian.

in all this, and in the words of Herodian the soldiers were taught "to covet money" and they were turned "to luxurious living." While we need not trust their picture of a decline in moral and while the increase in pay may be ascribed to gradual inflation, there is little doubt that the Severan emperors and Julia Domna and Julia Menease acting behind the throne were prompted on several occasions to consolidate their power through donations to the army. This policy was accelerated during the following turbulent years up to and including the rise to power of Decius.

It is thus safe to conclude, that a family that may have included soldiers on both the mothers and the fathers side, would have been able over time and given sensible investments to accumulate a considerable wealth. The execution of three members of the family and the possible exile of a fourth could have interfered with this, but not necessarily significantly, if the "martyrs" and the exile had succeeded, as it was customary, in passing on major parts of their patrimony to their heirs prior to their condemnation. Given such practices it is even possible (yet unsupported by any evidence) to imagine that Celerinus could have passed on some of his patrimony to either one or both of his sisters prior to his own confession and possible exile verdict.

Such a scenario would help, but would not be required, to explain how the sisters could afford to support the 65 Africans. According to Roman law and Roman customs as they had developed daughters were expected from late republican and throughout imperial times to receive a significant part of the inheritance after their fathers.[94] Different scenarios would have placed Numeria and Candida in control of their parts of the patrimony. The firmest control was possible if one or both of them had given birth to three children and if one or both of them were widows or divorced. The birth of three children, according to the reforms of Augustus, made a women legally independent and left her in control of her own property. In practice the likelihood that a husband could interfere remained. If Numeria was living in Rome with a husband this would likely have been in his estate and she would not have been free to use that place as a basis for her help to the 65 Africans. It would have required the consent or

---

94 This and the following Suzanne Dixon, *The Roman Family* (Baltimore: Johns Hopkins University Press, 1992), 41–53 and 71–83, John P.V.D. Balsdon, *Roman Women. Their History and Habits* (London: Cox and Wyman, 1962), 45–47, Gillian Clark, *Women in Late Antiquity. Pagan and Christian Lifestyles* (Oxford: Oxford University Press, 1993), 15–17, Paul Veyne, *A History of Private Life. From Pagan Rome to Byzantium* (Harvard: Harvard University Press, 1992), 33–50 and 139–160. See also Tertullian, *Ad uxorem* 2.5, where Tertullian envisages that some pagan husbands marriage to Christian wives, put hands on their dowry and get away with it because they threaten to denounce the wives to the authorities as Christians.

even the collaboration of her husband. Such a consent would have been more likely, but not secured given the potential danger and apparent expenses involved, if the husband was also a Cristian. Tertullian advises that a Christian women in marriage with a pagan husband may be forced to tone down her charitable work so as not to enrage her husband.⁹⁵ Without the birth of three children, a male member of a women's family would be in some position to interfere with the control of such a women's dowry and with her part of the patrimony even if this women was divorced or widowed. The trend from the first century BC to the third century AD was that this level of male control was lessened, but it remained. In our case, the guardian could easily have been Celerinus, and for all we can tell he would not have disapproved of the use his sisters made of their patrimony in supporting the 65 Africans and atoning for their "fall".

5 Conclusion

Celerinus' letter to Lucian with his descriptions of his two sisters support for a number of exiled African Christians, Lucian's reply and Cyprian's references to Celerinus has given us insight into some of the involuntary displacement that resulted from the Decian persecution. Further, it has provided us with an opportunity to discuss the practical and financial logistics involved in this and an example of how ties of common origin, prior acquaintance and networks were employed, solicited and capitalized to cushion the physical, material and mental/spiritual blows of the Decian persecution.

The following conclusion will present a sample of the most likely scenarios that have been discussed and arrived at above. In January to March three Christian siblings of African stock were confronted by the emperor Decius' edict requiring sacrifice to the Roman deities. They reacted differently, and their reactions represent a spectrum of the ways in which other Christians reacted to the harsh realities of the Decian persecution. Two of the siblings, Celerinus and Candida, likely lived in Africa at the outbreak of the persecution, one of them, Numeria, likely lived in Rome. Celerinus refused to sacrifice, he confessed that he was Christian, was imprisoned, tortured for nineteen days, but then released either with an exile sentence or with an impulse that led him to flee to Rome. Earlier theories advanced in scholarship according to which the trial of Celerinus took place in Rome and before the Emperor Decius himself have

---

95 Tertullian, *Ad uxorem* 2.3–5.

been shown to be unsupported by the evidence and unlikely. Candida sacrificed, but accompanied her brother to Rome, perhaps prompted by a desire to avoid further delating and further demands for sacrifice. Numeria in Rome bribed her way out of the requirement to offer sacrifice. Both sisters regretted their fall and together and with the help of their brother, they sought ways to atone for their fall and obtain forgiveness on earth and in heaven. They celebrated Easter in morning, they prayed and they petitioned the presbyters in Rome who instructed them to await the appointment of a new bishop. In this context it was somehow brought to their attention that 65 African Christians, a significant number of whom would have been confessors, prompted by the persecution and likely including in their group people who had been formally exiled, were about to arrive at Ostia. The sisters went out to greet them, they escorted them to Rome and over the next weeks or even months up until the summer of 250, they cared for the needs of these 65 Africans. They did so out of their own patrimony, with at least moral support from their brother and apparently without any interference from any concerned, unwilling or hostile husbands. The family fortune might have its origin in a family tradition for service in the army. Access to (parts) of the patrimony would have been easier and a base for the support and the siblings own sojourn in Rome provided, if we are right in assuming that Numeria was living in Rome prior to the persecution. The 65 Africans likely arrived to Ostia on the same ship, likely a ship involved in the grain trade. They likely arranged and financed their own transportation, it is unlikely even if they were formally banished, that the governor of Africa would have arranged the transport. If some, most or all of them were formally exiled it is unlikely that they were specifically banished to *Rome* (or Ostia or Portus), since this conflicts with normative third century ideas about conditions of exile.

After Candida and Numeria had cared for these African Christians for an unspecified time lasting anything from two weeks to three months, Celerinus wrote a letter to his friend Lucian, who was imprisoned back in Carthage. Celerinus petitioned Lucian and his fellow confessors for forgiveness for the sisters. The support of the sisters for the 65 African Christians was emphasized, the 65 were described as exiles and as confessors and some of them forwarded their greetings to Lucian and added their own pleading on behalf of Candida and Numeria to that of Celerinus. Lucianus duly granted the forgiveness in the name of a martyr, who had already died, in his own name and in the name of further imprisoned African confessors, who expected soon to die. In early 251 Celerinus traveled back to Africa. There is some indication that he found himself without much funding, which could indicate that the persecution had resulted in his patrimony being either confiscated (as part of an exile verdict), transferred (to the sisters) or largely liquidated under unfavorable conditions to provide means for the travel to and from Rome. On the more positive side, he found himself there with all the status of a confessor and this prompted Cyprian to instate him in the office as lector in the church of Carthage and to assign him financial support on the level of a presbyter.

Bibliography

Primary Sources

Clarke, Graeme W. *The Letters of St. Cyprian of Carthage. Translated and Annotated*, vol. 1–4. New York: Newman Press, 1984.
Diercks, G.F. *Sancti Cypriani Episcopi Epistularium* (CChr.SL III, C, B, and D). Turnhout: Brepols, 1994, 1996 and 1999.

Secondary Literature

Balsdon, John P.V.D. *Roman Women. Their History and Habits.* London: Cox and Wyman, 1962.
Benson, Edward White. *Cyprian. His Life, His Times, His Work.* London: Macmillan, 1897.
Bleckmann, Bruno. "Zu den Motiven der Christenverfolgung des Decius." In *Deleto paene imperio Romano. Transformationsprozesse des Römischen Reiches im 3. Jahrhundert und ihre Rezeption in der Neuzeit*, edited by Klaus Peter Johne, Udo Hartmann and Thomas Gerhardt, 57–72. Stuttgart: Franz Steiner Verlag, 2006.
Bobertz, Charles A. *Cyprian of Carthage as Patron: A Social Historical Study of the Role of Bishop in the Ancient Christian Community of North Africa.* Yale (unpublished dissertation) 1988.
Brown, Peter. *Through the Eye of a Needle. Wealth, the Fall of Rome, and the Making of Christianity in the West, 350–550 AD.* Princeton: Princeton University Press, 2012.
Brunt, Peter A. "Pay and Superannuation in the Roman Army." *PBSR* 18 (1950): 50–71.
Burns, J. Patout Jr. and Jensen, Robin M., eds. *Christianity in Roman Africa: The Development of Its Practices and Beliefs.* Cambridge: Eerdmans, 2014.
Cameron, Averil. *The Later Roman Empire.* London: Fontana, 1993.
Campenhausen, Hans von. *Die Idee des Martyriums in der alten Kirche.* Göttingen: Vandenhoeck & Ruprecht 1964.
Campenhausen, Hans von. *Ecclesiastical Authority and Spiritual Power in the Church of the First Three Centuries.* London: A. and C. Black, 1969.
Casson, Lionel. *The Ancient Mariners: Seafarers and Sea Fighters of the Mediterranean in Ancient Times.* 2nd edition. Princeton: Princeton University Press, 1991.
Casson, Lionel. *Travel in the Ancient World.* London: John Hopkins University Press, 1994.
Christiansen, Erik. *A History of Rome: From Town to Empire and from Empire to Town.* Aarhus: Aarhus University Press, 1995.
Clark, Gillian. *Women in Late Antiquity. Pagan and Christian Lifestyles.* Oxford: Oxford University Press, 1993.

Clarke, Graeme W. "Some Observations on the Persecution of Decius." *Antichthon* 3 (1969), 68–73.
Clarke, Graeme W. "Double-Trials in the Persecution of Decius." *Hist.* 22 (1973), 650–663.
Delehaye, H. *Les passions des martyrs et les genres littéraires.* Brussels: Bureaux de la Société des Bollandistes, 1921.
Dixon, Suzanne. *The Roman Family.* Baltimore: Johns Hopkins University Press, 1992.
Domaszewski, Alfred von. *Der Truppensold der Kaiserzeit.* NHJ X, 1900, 225–241
Duch, Michał. *Economic Role of the Roman Army in the Province of Lower Moesia (Moesia Inferior).* Poznan: ACTA HUMANISTICA GNESNENSIA XVI, 2017.
Engberg, Jakob. *Impulsore Chresto. Opposition to Christianity in the Roman Empire c. 50–250 AD.* Frankfurt: Peter Lang, 2007.
Engberg, Jakob. "Exile and the Dissemination of Donatist Congregations." In *Clerical Exile in Late Antiquity*, edited by Julia Hillner, Jörg Ulrich, Jörg and Jakob Engberg, 145–164. Frankfurt: Peter Lang 2016.
Fox, Robin Lane. *Pagans and Christians in the Mediterranean world from the second century AD to the conversion of Constantine.* London: Viking, 1986.
Frend, W.H.C. *The Rise of Christianity.* Philadelphia: Fortress Press, 1984.
Gradel, Ittai. "*De moribus persecutorum.* Om baggrunden for de romerske kristenforfølgelser." *Religionsvidenskabeligt Tidsskrift* 22, 1993, 21–40.
Grant, Michael. *The Collapse and Recovery of the Roman Empire.* London: Routledge, 1999.
Gülzow, Henneke. *Cyprian und Novatian. Der Briefwechsel zwischen den Gemeinden in Rom und Karthago zur Zeit der Verfolgung des Kaisers Decius.* Tübingen: Mohr Siebeck, 1975.
Hillner, Julia, Jörg Ulrich, Jörg and Jakob Engberg, eds. *Clerical Exile in Late Antiquity*, Frankfurt: Peter Lang, 2016.
Hillner, Julia. "Approaches to Clerical Exile in Late Antiquity: Strategies, Experiences, Memories and Social Networks." In *Clerical Exile in Late Antiquity*, edited by Julia Hillner, Jörg Ulrich, Jörg and Jakob Engberg, 11–43. Frankfurt: Peter Lang, 2016,
Huttner, Ulrich. "Zwischen Traditionalismus und Totalitarismus. Zur Ideologie und Praxis der Regierung des Kaisers Decius." In *Deleto paene imperio Romano. Transformationsprozesse des Römischen Reiches im 3. Jahrhundert und ihre Rezeption in der Neuzeit*, edited by Klaus Peter Johne, Udo Hartmann and Thomas Gerhardt, 37–56.Stuttgart: Franz Steiner Verlag, 2006.
Johne, Klaus Peter, Udo Hartmann and Thomas Gerhardt, eds. *Deleto paene imperio Romano. Transformationsprozesse des Römischen Reiches im 3. Jahrhundert und ihre Rezeption in der Neuzeit.* Stuttgart: Franz Steiner Verlag, 2006.
Junkelmann, Marcus. *Die Legionen des Augustus. Der römische Soldat im archäologischen Experiment.* Mainz: Philipp von Zabern, 1994.
Keppie, Lawrence. *The Making of the Roman Army. From Republic to Empire.* London: BT Batsford, 1984.
King, Anthony and Martin Henig, eds. *The Roman West in the Third Century: Contributions from Archaeology and History*, vols. 1–2. Oxford: British Archeological Reports, International Series 109, 1981.
Knipfing, John R. "The Libelli of the Decian Persecution." *HThR* 16 (1923): 345–390.
Kunst, Christiane, *Leben und Wohnen in der römischen Stadt.* Darmstadt: Wissenschaftliche Buchgesellschaft, 2006.

Lewis, Naphtali and Meyer Reinhold. *Roman Civilization. Sourcebook II: The Empire*. New York: Harper, 1966.
Meijer, Fik. *Kaiser sterben nicht im Bett. Die etwas andere Geschichte der römischen Kaiserzeit. Von Caesar bis Romulus Augustulus (44 v. Chr.–476 n. Chr.)*. Darmstadt: Wissenschaftliche Buchgesellschaft, 2003.
Meijer, Fik and Onno van Nijf. *Trade, Transport and Society in the Ancient World*. London: Routledge, 1992.
Millar, Fergus. *The Emperor in the Roman World (31 BC – AD 337)*. London: Duckworth, 1992.
Molthagen, Joachim. *Der römische Staat und die Christen im zweiten und dritten Jahrhundert*, Göttingen: Vandenhoeck und Ruprecht, 1970.
Parker, H.M.D. *The Roman Legions*, Cambridge: Heffer and Sons, 1958.
Reis, David. "Tracing the Imaginary in Imperial Rome." In *Clerical Exile in Late Antiquity*, edited by Julia Hillner, Jörg Ulrich, and Jakob Engberg, 213–231. Frankfurt: Peter Lang, 2016.
Sullivan, Daniel D. *The Life of the North Africans as Revealed in the Works of Saint Cyprian*. Washington: the Catholic University of America, 1933.
Szaivert, Wolfgang and Reinhard Wolters. *Löhne, Preise, Werte. Quellen zur römischen Geldwirtschaft*. Darmstadt: Wissenschaftliche Buchgesellschaft, 2005.
Ulrich, Jörg. "Dionysius of Alexandria in Exile." In *Clerical Exile in Late Antiquity*, edited by Julia Hillner, Jörg Ulrich and Jakob Engberg, 115–128. Frankfurt: Peter Lang, 2016.
Vallejo Girvés, Margarita. "Banished Bishops Were Not Alone: The Two Cases of Theodoros Anagnostes, Guardian and Assistant." In *Clerical Exile in Late Antiquity*, edited by Julia Hillner, Jörg Ulrich and Jakob Engberg, 193–212. Frankfurt: Peter Lang, 2016.
Veyne, Paul. *A History of Private Life. From Pagan Rome to Byzantium*. Harvard: Harvard University Press, 1992.
Watson, George R. *The Roman Soldier*. New York: Cornell University Press, 1969.
Webster, Graham. *The Roman Imperial Army*. London: Adam and Charles Black, 1974.

Daniëlle Slootjes
The Impact of Geographical and Administrative Boundaries on Late Antique Bishops

1 Introduction

The acceptance of the Christian religion by Constantine the Great, and the subsequent growth and increasing visibility of this religion throughout the communities of the empire coincided with extensive changes in the administrative structures of the empire in the fourth century. The almost doubling of the number of provinces, the emergence of dioceses as well as prefectures led to a more complex and multi-layered administrative system. As scholars now agree, these far-reaching changes did not occur over night, but took several decades, if not the better part of the fourth century, to be implemented.[1] Cities and provinces

---

[1] Arnold H.M. Jones, *The Later Roman Empire* (Oxford: Oxford University Press, 1964, reprinted Baltimore 1992), 42–47, 373–377; Timothy D. Barnes, *The New Empire of Diocletian and Constantine* (Cambridge MA: Harvard University Press, 1982); Karl L. Noethlichs, "Zur Entstehung der Diözesen als Mittelinstanz des spätrömischen Verwaltungssystems," *Hist.* 31 (1982): 70–81; Timothy D. Barnes, "Praetorian Prefects 337–361," *ZPE* 94 (1992): 249–260; Joachim Migl, *Die Ordnung der Ämter. Prätorianerpräfektur und Vikariat in der Regionalverwaltung des Römischen Reiches von Konstantin bis zur Valentinianischen Dynastie* (Frankfurt am Main: Peter Lang, 1994); Bernhard Palme, "Die *Officia* der Statthalter in der Spätantike. Forschungsstand und Perspektiven," *Antiquité Tardive* 7 (1999): 95–98; Constantin Zuckerman, "Sur la Liste de Vérone et la province de Grande Arménie, la division de l'Empire et la date de création des dioceses," in *Mélanges Gilbert Dagron = Travaux et Mémoires* 14, (Paris: Association des Amis du Centre d'Histoire et Civilisation de Byzance, 2002), 617–637; Michael Kulikowski, *Late Roman Spain and its Cities* (Baltimore: Johns Hopkins University Press, 2004), 69–71; Denis Feissel, "L'empereur et l'administration impériale," in *Le Monde Byzantin I. L'Empire romain d'Orient (330–641)*, ed. Cecile Morrison (Paris: Presses Universitaires de France, 2004), 108–110; Daniëlle Slootjes, "Late Antique Administrative Structures: On the Meaning of Dioceses and their Borders in the Fourth Century," in *Aspects of Ancient Institutions and Geography. Studies in Honor of Richard J.A. Talbert*, eds. Lee Brice and Daniëlle Slootjes (Leiden: Brill, 2014): 177–195; Daniëlle Slootjes, "The Effects of the Diocletianic and Constantinian Provincial Reforms on Provinces, Governors and Dioceses in the Age of Constantine's Sons," in *In the Shadows of Constantine and Julian: The Roman Empire AD 337–361*, eds. Nicholas Brian-Baker and Shaun Tougher (Cambridge: Cambridge University Press, forthcoming 2019); Daniëlle Slootjes, "The Decision-making Process behind the Anchoring of Provinces and Dioceses into a New Late Roman Administrative System: A Case Study of the Diocese of Hispaniae," in *Land, Labour and Power: Governing Ancient Empires*.

had of course already been in place for many centuries, but especially the dioceses and prefectures appeared as new units within the system. Moreover, these changes led to a significant increase in the number of imperial officials that were needed: governors, *vicarii*, prefects, military duces and a staff for each of these officials.[2] From the perspective of the imperial government, the growth in the number of officials led to an increasing visibility of imperial control and authority throughout the various regions of the empire. Although to modern standards the size of the Late Roman bureaucracy would still be considered fairly small, in comparison to previous centuries in Roman history the intensification of the bureaucracy would have been considerable. Although we are almost completely left in the dark about the decision making process of this large scale administrative operation that extended over a longer period in the fourth century covering the reign of several emperors, the administrative transformation can be considered effective in that it remained in place and operational for an extended period of time. Of course, the fifth century saw a substantial breakdown in administrative structures in the western half of the Roman Empire, while they continued to function in the eastern half of the Empire.

While the empire underwent these administrative (and also geographical) changes a further transformation took place of the traditional religious landscape in which the Christian communities were now allowed to exist openly and started to create an empire wide and unified Christian community. The acceptance of Christianity within the Empire's religious landscape and its subsequent growth and increasing influence in Roman society at large had major consequences for the social position of its religious leadership, in particular for bishops.[3] Although the second and third centuries had seen an establishment of a hierarchy of officials within the early Christian communities, from the early fourth century onwards this process intensified, leading to a rapid increase of the number of church officials.[4] Remarkably, thus, both the imperial government as well as the growing number of Christian churches were in need of more

---

Proceedings of the 3rd to 5th International Conferences of the Research Network Imperium and Officium, eds. Michael Jursa, Bernhard Palme and Sven Tost (Vienna, forthcoming 2019). The formation of prefectures as territorial units was part of a development that followed over the course of the fourth century. See Barnes, *New Empire*; Migl, *Ordnung*, 161–208.

2 Cf. Palme, *Officia*.

3 J. H.Wolfgang G. Liebeschuetz, *The Decline and Fall of the Roman City* (Oxford: Oxford University Press, 2001), 138–139; Peter Kritzinger, *Ursprung und Ausgestaltung bischöflicher Repräsentation* (Stuttgart: Franz Steiner Verlag, 2016).

4 Elisabeth Herrmann-Otto, *Ecclesia in Re Publica. Die Entwicklung der Kirche von pseudostaatlicher zu staatlich inkorporierter Existenz* (Frankfurt am Main: Peter Lang, 1980); Liebeschuetz, *Decline*, 137–168.

officials to run their organizational system. Bishops functioned mostly at the level of their Christian communities, thus at the civic level of cities, although they would also cooperate with other bishops at a regional or provincial level, and even at an empire wide level at the church councils. Notably, for the Christian churches and for the imperial government comparable or even parallel local, provincial and empire wide structures and arrangements played an important role for their internal institutions.

This contribution examines the relation between the office of the late antique bishop and the imperial geographical and administrative structures. The question will be raised if, and to what extent the wide-ranging changes of the administrative structures in the fourth century had an effect on the functioning of church institutions and leadership. In other words, were the institutions of provinces, dioceses and prefectures accommodating to bishops for instance in their functioning? One of the leading notions in the analysis will be the concept of 'boundaries', both geographically and administratively. Were boundaries primarily used as physical and administrative markers that expressed where and when bishops could exercise power or were they also seen as limiting to a bishop's position? Insights into these issues will enhance our understanding of the position of bishops in relation to their own church communities, to fourth century developments in the Christian churches at large as well as to the imperial administrative structures.

2 Bishops and geographical boundaries: Their location of appointment

Various decisions taken at the ecumenical and provincial church councils dealt with geographical boundaries related to bishops. First of all, bishops – once appointed to a certain community – were not allowed to move freely to a different location and community, as for instance canon fifteen of the Council of Nicaea in 325 regulated:

> On account of the great disturbance and discords that occur, it is decreed that the custom prevailing in certain places contrary to the Canon, must wholly be done away; so that neither bishop, presbyter, nor deacon shall pass from city to city. And if any one, after this decree of the holy and great Synod, shall attempt any such thing, or continue in any such course, his proceedings shall be utterly void, and he shall be restored to the Church for which he was ordained bishop or presbyter.[5]

---

5 COGD 1, 27.299–28.312; Council of Nicaea, Canon fifteen: *Propter multam perturbationem, et*

This issue of 'Ortsgebundenheit' seems to have been a recurring theme, as it had been on the agenda earlier at the Council of Arles of 314 and was repeated again at the Council of Serdica in 343.[6] At the councils the sentiment seems to have been strong that it was not for the individual bishop to decide to move elsewhere, as it was considered wrong and inappropriate for a bishop to have the ambition to move, for instance, to other larger or more 'important' church communities. Furthermore, from the churches' point of view, they wanted a bishop building a long term and solid relationship with the members of his community. A local bishop should be able to present his community with a level of stability and confidence, especially in a time when the accepted presence of Christian communities within the cities of the Roman Empire was a relatively young phenomenon. It would be particularly damaging and destabilizing for local communities if bishops then spontaneously started to move from location to location. It was not only in the best interest of local communities to have a bishop who would stay for a long period of time, it was also in the interest of regional and empire wide church leadership, as it would help them to keep a certain level of control over their local appointments. Thus, at the church councils, canons were issued that ordered bishops who were appointed for life to a certain community to stay there to develop a lasting relationship with their community. In practice, many bishops were appointed in the region where they had their origins which means that they often already had strong familial and/or economic ties to the region in which they ended up administering a Christian community.[7] Furthermore, during the election process of a bishop who would be appointed by the other bishops in his provinces, local communities could show their consent by way of acclamations thereby thus already indicating some type of connection with him even if they did not know him well.[8]

Remarkably, the Church's encouragement of stable, life-long and regional appointments of bishops stands in sharp contrast with the Roman Republican

---

seditiones, quae fiunt: placuit consuetudinem omnimodis amputari, quae, praeter regulam, in quibusdam partibus videtur admissa: ita ut de civitate ad civitatem, non episcopus, non presbyter, non diaconus transferatur. Si quis autem, post definitionem sancti et magni concilii, tale quid agere tentaverit, et se hujuscemodi negotio manciparit, hoc factum prorsus in irritum ducatur, et restituatur Ecclesiae cui fuit episcopus, aut presbyter, aut diaconus ordinatus.

6 Council of Arles, Canon 2; Council of Serdica, Canon 1. See also Herrmann-Otto, *Ecclesia*, 297.
7 For instance, Synesius who became bishop of Ptolemais in 410, was born in nearby Cyrene, and Augustine, bishop of Hippo in 395, was born in Thagaste which was in the same region. Cf. also Claire Sotinel, "Le recrutement des évêques en Italie aux IVe et Ve siècles: essai d'enquête prosopographique," in *Church and Society in Late Antique Italy and Beyond*, ed. Claire Sotinel (Farnham: Ashgate, 2010): 193–204.
8 Liebeschuetz, *Decline*, 141. Herrmann-Otto, *Ecclesia*, 298–302.

and Imperial government's practice of appointment of officials. The length of the term for the offices of the *cursus honorum*, of governors or other administrative officials had traditionally been limited to a year or at most a few years. Moreover, officials – in particular provincial governors – would be sent throughout the empire to provinces where – in principle – they had no origins or connections. To the Roman government this would be of the utmost importance and an advantage, as both the short term of office and the supposed lack of previous connections should prevent officials to build a strong local network with which they could rebel against the government. At the same time, this is not to say that local relationships were not important to governors; on the contrary, they were crucial for their survival.[9] However, after their term of office they were supposed to – and would want to – return home to their families.

The contrast between the policy regarding the geography of appointment of officials by the church and by the imperial government reveals a fundamental difference between the way in which the state and the church positioned their officials within Roman society. The Roman state, on the one hand, was primarily focused on keeping the various territories of its empire together and at peace. Its officials were instrumental in this process, but these men should never gain prominent individual positions of power and influence as ultimately this might endanger the stability of the Roman state, as many examples of ambitious individuals in the last century of the Roman Republic and in the third century had demonstrated. The church, on the other hand, seems to have deliberately sought that close connection between individual bishops and their communities. Indeed, the ideals and beliefs of Christianity called for officials that would be able to establish close and life-long relations with the members of the Christian communities.[10] A bishop who functioned exceptionally well might be offered the position of metropolitan bishop, although that would probably result in a move to a different city, which would not be the regular course of events. Personal career ambitions for promotion were not part of the Christian ideals, although of course in practice church officials were human and thus sometimes quite ambi-

---

[9] Peter Brown, *Power and Persuasion in Late Antiquity* (Madison: University of Wisconsin Press, 1992), 23 and 29; Daniëlle Slootjes, *The Governor and his Subjects in the Later Roman Empire* (Leiden: Brill, 2006a), 179–184.
[10] Frank D. Gilliard, "Senatorial Bishops in the Fourth Century," *HThR* 77 (1984): 153–175; Liebeschuetz, *Decline*, 137–168; Peter Brown, *Poverty and Leadership in the Later Roman Empire* (Hanover NH: Brandeis University Press, 2002); Claudia Rapp, *Holy Bishops in Late Antiquity. The Nature of Christian Leadership in an Age of Transition* (Berkeley – Los Angeles – London: University of California Press, 2005); Andrea Sterk, *Renouncing the World Yet Leading the Church* (Cambridge MA: Harvard University Press, 2004).

tious. The fact that several church councils, as mentioned, re-emphasized the rule that bishops should remain in their community with their appointment for life might be an indication of such personal aspirations.

Notably, one might argue that the often local or regional origins of bishops combined with a geographical restriction on the locations where bishops were allowed to perform their duties simultaneously led to an increase of personal power and influence at local level. In contrast, high status imperial officials, such as governors, would not come from the area where they were appointed, and could never compete with the type of personal contacts that bishops could acquire. Though, of course, with an appointment for life, it might have been more valuable to a bishop to cultivate local relationships, whereas a governor would leave after a short term of office. As a consequence, once bishops had become permanent and prominent members in the cities and smaller communities of the Roman Empire, they started – as I have demonstrated elsewhere – to take over some of the duties of provincial governors such as his role as judge in local cases.[11] Indeed, bishops' local long term presence made them well positioned as mediators between the local and imperial levels, more so perhaps than governors.[12] In other words, bishops thereby crossed the boundaries of the imperial administration. To a large extent, this shift or even take over of administrative duties was caused by a clear difference in level of representation, visibility and accessibility. In absolute numbers, there were many more church officials present within one province compared to one provincial governor who had to travel around to meet the inhabitants of his province. If a provincial needed help, church officials were more likely to be present as well as able to assist.

---

[11] Daniëlle Slootjes, "Governor Trumped by Bishop: Shifting Boundaries in Roman Religious and Public Life," in *The Impact of Imperial Rome on Religions, Ritual and Religious Life in the Roman Empire. Proceedings of the fifth workshop of the international network Impact of Empire (Roman Empire, c. 200 B.C. – A.D. 476), Münster, 2004*, eds. Lukas de Blois, Peter Funke and Johannes Hahn (Leiden: Brill, 2006b): 219–231; Michael E. Moore, *A Sacred Kingdom: Bishops and the Rise of Frankish Kingship, 300–850* (Washington D.C.: The Catholic University of America Press, 2011), 22.

[12] Moore, *Sacred Kingdom*, 21.

3 Bishops and the geographical boundaries of the imperial administration

This section focuses on the question if, and how the physical geographical and administrative boundaries of the late empire, consisting of the boundaries of cities, provinces, dioceses and prefectures had an effect on the way in which bishops could run their religious communities' affairs. Most modern scholarship seems to accept the idea that the organization of the late roman churches and its leadership, at an empire wide level, adopted the imperial administrative structures for their church structures as well, assuming that the administrative organization represented a convenient and adoptable arrangement for the hierarchy of church officials. Remarkably little research has been done on this adoption, which seems to be taken for granted. In this section I will argue that at the level of cities and provinces the Christian churches matched the organization of the imperial government, but at the level of the administrative dioceses and prefectures it did not correspond to these administrative structures.

3.1 Cities and provinces

Once Constantine had accepted the Christian religion empire wide, the bishops as representatives of the increasing number of Christian churches throughout the empire set in motion a process to develop a more unified church structure as has become clear from the acts of the various church councils of the fourth and fifth centuries. Throughout the centuries of the Roman Empire the system of cities and provinces, as the essential administrative units of the imperial government, had proven their effectiveness, and it was only natural to integrate the church communities into this system as well. The city and its territory became therefore also the basic unit of the church organization with its own bishop and clergy.[13] As the cities were part of a larger network that made up a province, the bishoprics also fell within the boundaries of a province.[14]

In the canons of the first ecumenical council of Nicaea in 325 we get a glimpse of the adoption of secular structures of the existing provinces into those of the church. Canon four that deals with the appointment of new bishops

---

13 Moore, *Sacred Kingdom*, 38–39.
14 David Hunt, "The Church as a Public Institution," in *Cambridge Ancient History*[2] XIII, 238–276 (Cambridge: Cambridge University Press, 1998), 242.

mentions that all the bishops within one province should be involved with that appointment that furthermore needed to be ratified by the metropolitan bishop.[15] In canon five it was stated that in every province a provincial synod should be held twice a year.[16] In other words, the existing administrative and geographical units of the provinces were seen by the church as practical or logical units as well.

With this type of overlapping structure of cities and provinces a bishop might be comparable to a secular official as Liebeschuetz argued: "the urban bishop was as it were an official of a second Empire-wide administration, with comparable access to the head of state".[17] Of course, this 'second Empire-wide administration' had not emerged overnight, but had developed slowly over a period of decades if not centuries. Besides, bishops were certainly not treated as secular officials by the emperors and would in principal not have regarded themselves as secular leaders either, even though eventually they might have taken over duties such as court cases that had been part of the responsibilities of provincial governors.[18]

---

15 COGD I, 21.89 – 22.101; Council of Nicaea, Canon four: *Episcopum convenit maxime quidem ab omnibus qui sunt in provincia episcopis ordinari. Si autem hoc difficile fuerit, aut propter instantem necessitatem, aut propter itineris longitudinem, tribus tamen omnimodis in idipsum convenientibus, et absentibus quoque pari modo decernentibus, et per scripta consentientibus, tunc ordinatio celebretur. Firmitas autem eorum quae geruntur per unamquamque provinciam, metropolitano tribuatur episcopo.*
16 COGD I, 22.107 – 31; Council of Nicaea, Canon five: *De his qui communione privantur, seu ex clero, seu ex laico ordine, ab episcopis per unamquamque provinciam, sententia regularis obtineat: ut hi qui abjiciuntur ab aliis, ab aliis non recipiantur. Requiratur autem, ne pusillanimitate, aut contentione, vel alio quolibet episcopi vitio videatur a congregatione seclusus. Ut hoc ergo decentius inquiratur, bene placuit, annis singulis, per unamquamque provinciam bis in anno concilia celebrari: ut communiter omnibus simul episcopis provinciae congregatis, discutiantur hujusmodi quaestiones. Et sic, qui suo peccaverunt evidenter episcopo, excommunicati rationabiliter ab omnibus aestimentur: usquequo, vel in communi, vel eidem episcopo placeat humaniorem pro talibus ferre sententiam. Concilia vero celebrentur, unum quidem ante Quadragesimam Paschae: ut omni dissensione sublata munus offeratur Deo purissimum: secundum vero, circa tempus autumni.*
17 Liebeschuetz, *Decline*, 139. Cf. Herrmann-Otto, *Ecclesia*.
18 There were, of course, bishops who conducted themselves as secular officials, as, for instance, Paul of Samosata who was heavily criticized for behaving like a worldly leader. Daniëlle Slootjes, "Bishops and Their Position of Power in the Late Third Century CE: The Cases of Gregory Thaumaturgus and Paul of Samosata," *Journal of Late Antiquity* 4 (2011): 100 – 15. See Fergus Millar, "Paul of Samosata, Zenobia and Aurelian: the church, local culture and political allegiance in third-century Syria," *JRS* 61 (1971): 1 – 17, and Rudolf Haensch, "Römische Amtsinhaber als Vorbilder für die Bischöfe des 4. Jahrhunderts?," in *The Representation and Perception of Roman Imperial Power. Proceedings of the third workshop of the international network Impact of Empire (Roman Empire, c. 200 B.C. – A.D. 476), Netherlands Institute in Rome, March*

In general, in regard to cities and provinces we can conclude that most bishops were held by the traditional urban limits and provincial boundaries for exercising power and influence at the basic level of their local church community and administration. These were the natural civic boundaries that were considered equally suitable for the structure of the church. However, one development in the early church should be treated as an exception to the limitation of bishop's power within cities and provinces, and that is the emergence of the patriarchates, i.e. Rome, Alexandria, Antioch, Jerusalem and Constantinople. The patriarchs of these cities possessed authority that went beyond the level of cities and provinces.

We find an early glimpse of discussions regarding the boundaries of the powers of the patriarchs in the famous though difficult to interpret first half of canon six of the Council of Nicaea (325)[19]:

> Let the ancient customs in Egypt, Libya and Pentapolis prevail, that the Bishop of Alexandria have jurisdiction in all these, since the like is customary for the Bishop of Rome also. Likewise in Antioch and the other provinces, let the Churches retain their privileges.[20]

This canon mentions the bishops of Rome, Alexandria and Antioch as a reference to their positions as important episcopal sees. The authority of the bishop of Alexandria is being discussed most explicitly in that it is stated that his ecclesiastical jurisdiction should be accepted in Egypt, Libya and Pentapolis, thus including the territory of several provinces. Similar supra-provincial prerogatives seem to be implied for Rome and Antioch as well, though they are not mentioned specifically. How are we to understand this part of the canon? If the bishop of Alexandria would have jurisdiction in the provinces Egypt, Libya and Pentapolis, he would thereby thus supersede the jurisdiction of metropolitan bishops who would have been appointed there. Would he make their position in those

---

20–23, 2002, eds. Lukas de Blois, Paul Erdkamp, Olivier Hekster, Gerda de Kleijn and Stephan Mols (Amsterdam: Gieben, 2003), 117–136; Slootjes, "Governor Trumped"; Moore, *Sacred Kingdom*, 40–44 on the episcopal courts.

19 Henry Chadwick, "Faith and Order at the Council of Nicaea: A Note on the Background of the Sixth Canon," *HThR* 53 (1960): 171–195; David M. Gwynn, *The Eusebians. The Polemic of Athanasius of Alexandria and the Construction of the 'Arian Controversy'* (Oxford: Oxford University Press, 2007); Christopher A. Beeley, *The Unity of Christ: Continuity and Conflict in Patristic Tradition* (New Haven: Yale University Press, 2012), 105–170.

20 COGD I, 23.140–7; Council of Nicaea, canon six: *Antiqua consuetudo servetur per Aegyptum, Libyam, et Pentapolim, ita ut Alexandrinus episcopus horum omnium habeat potestatem. Quia et urbis Romae episcopo parilis mos est. Similiter autem et apud Antiochiam, caeterasque provincias, suis privilegia serventur Ecclesiis.*

provinces thus superfluous? I would argue that in this canon a first glimpse becomes visible of the emergence of a part of the ecclesiastical hierarchy and subsequent administration that would deviate from the structures of the civic administrative boundaries of the empire and that would grow out of the internal developments of the church and especially its leadership in several cities of the Empire that were considered prominent in Christian traditions. In one way or other these cities, i.e. Rome, Alexandria, Antioch, Jerusalem and eventually Constantinople as well considered themselves to have played a crucial role in the history of Christianity. These cities and their bishops presented themselves as principal and outstanding locations that should be regarded as leading for the direction in which an empire wide church would head. Consequently, they almost naturally regarded their power and privileges to extend beyond the traditional civic institutions and boundaries of cities or provinces. In other words, next to the church hierarchy of bishops and metropolitan bishops who functioned mostly at the level of cities and provinces, another system of patriarchates emerged that had its own geographical boundaries expressing their power and influence.

3.2 Dioceses in the ecclesiastical organization

Whereas cities and provinces had been part of the Roman administrative structures, dioceses and prefectures were newly created units. Were bishops and their functioning affected by the emergence of the administrative dioceses and prefectures? The following analysis focuses only on dioceses, since the prefectures seem to have been purely civic units that do not appear in Christian sources as meaningful for the organization of the Christian churches. Dioceses, on the other hand, would become part of the church organization, though in a different way than scholarship has assumed for the past century. The word 'diocese' was not being mentioned in the canons of the first ecumenical council of Nicaea, although that is not surprising, as the term diocese did not emerge in many other sources of the early fourth century either. Most references to dioceses are to be dated to the later fourth century, specifically in legal texts from the 370s onwards.[21] Whereas this can be seen as an indication of the dioceses being well

---

[21] *CTh* 2.26.1 of 330 seems exceptional in its reference to Asiana, one of the dioceses. *CTh* 1.5.13 (of 389); 1.15.12 (of 386); 6.13.1 (of 413); 7.6.3 (of 377); 7.10.1 (of 405); 10.19.7 (of 370–3); 10.19.12 (of 392); 12.1.97 (of 383); 12.12.9 (of 382); 16.1.3 (of 381); *Const. Sirm.* 3.12 (of 384). John B. Bury, "The Provincial List of Verona," *JRS* 13 (1923): 127–151; Arnold H.M. Jones, "The Date and Value of the Verona List," *JRS* 44 (1954): 21–29; Barnes, *New Empire*, 201–208; Migl, *Ordnung*, 55; 63–64;

established within the administrative structures by the mid-to-late fourth century, simultaneously it could also point to a 'slow start' of the incorporation of the dioceses into the official administrative hierarchy. Consequently, dioceses not being mentioned in the canons of the council of Nicaea in 325 would certainly fit that notion.

When we turn to the canons of the council of Constantinople in 381, a shift in terminology can be observed. By that time, dioceses had become a more established unit within the imperial administrative structures which might be reflected in the text of the canons as well. The text of canon two is of particular interest here as 'dioceses' appear several times:

> The bishops are not to go beyond their dioceses to churches lying outside of their bounds, nor bring confusion on the churches; but let the Bishop of Alexandria, according to the canons, alone administer the affairs of Egypt; and let the bishops of the East manage the East alone, the privileges of the Church in Antioch, which are mentioned in the canons of Nicaea, being preserved; and let the bishops of the Asian Diocese administer the Asian affairs only; and the Pontic bishops only Pontic matters; and the Thracian bishops only Thracian affairs. And let not bishops go beyond their dioceses for ordination or any other ecclesiastical ministrations, unless they be invited. And the aforesaid canon concerning dioceses being observed, it is evident that the synod of every province will administer the affairs of that particular province as was decreed at Nicaea. But the Churches of God in heathen nations must be governed according to the custom which has prevailed from the times of the Fathers.[22]

In general, this canon prescribed that bishops in the administering of their duties should stay within the boundaries of the dioceses and it re-emphasized that the

---

Zuckerman, *La Liste*, 628. As for the fourth century administrative sources on dioceses, the *Laterculus Veronensis* seems to give the first official attestation of dioceses. Apart from some references in literary sources (such as Eusebius of Caesarea, *Vit. Const.* 3.19 and 3.36), legal texts and in particular the *Codex Theodosianus* represent the most important sources for the situation of the dioceses in the fourth century.

22 COGD I, 65,317–43; Council of Constantinople, canon two: *Qui sunt super dioecesim episcopi, ad ecclesias extra suos terminus sitas ne accedant, neque confundant ecclesias: sed secundum canones, Alexandriae quidem episcopus, quae sunt in Aegypto tantum administret. Orientis autem episcopie Orientem solum gubernent: servatis privilegiis, quae Antiochena ecclesiae Nicaenis canonibus tribute sunt. Et Asianae dioceseos episcopi, Asianam diocesim ea tantum quae ad Ponticam dioecesim pertinent, et Thraciae quae sunt in Thracia gubernent. Non vocati autem episcopi super dioecesim, non accedant propter ordinationem, vel alias dispensations faciendas. Servato autem suprascripto de dioecesibus canone, manifestum est quod ea quae ad unamquamque provinciam pertinent, synodus provinciae administret, secundum ea quae in Nicaea definite sunt. Ecclesias autem Dei quae sunt in barbaricis gentibus, gubernari oportet secundum eam quae obtinuit partum consuetudinem.*

provincial councils of bishops should only deal with provincial ecclesiastical matters. Furthermore, it seems to re-affirm the privileges of the bishop of Alexandria and of Antioch, as had been expressed previously in canon six of the Council of Nicaea, as discussed in the previous section. How are 'dioceses' to be understood in the four instances in which it was used in this canon? Were the 'dioceses' referring to the already existing administrative units of the imperial government and were they used here in the canons to clarify the geographical position and powers of bishops within the church hierarchy?[23] Or, were the church provinces indeed grouped together into some sort of church diocese? Most modern scholarship seems to have accepted the idea that 'diocese' in Christian sources of the fourth and fifth centuries would geographically refer to the territory of the civic dioceses but then used for the church's organization, as if the church would have taken over that structure for its own purposes. This interpretation assumed that beyond the level of the local Christian communities and the province the following larger unit that united groups of bishops was the diocese.[24] The notion of a 'church diocese' as early as the late fourth century that would match the geographical territory of the civic diocese seems untenable in terms of church leadership for such a church diocese at this early stage. Whereas we could argue that the metropolitan bishops had their counterpart in civic governors, there existed not a church official as counterpart of the civic *vicarius*. I want to argue that it is time for a serious re-assessment, as a close reading of the ancient sources leads to a different conclusion, that 'diocese' had another meaning within the church structures than it had within the imperial government's administration.

Recent scholarship, especially by the French scholar Florian Mazel, has tried to convince us to abandon our traditional idea of continuity through dioceses in the church structures. Even more, he has argued that in the fourth through the sixth centuries the church tried to step away from some of the old Roman territorial and administrative units and legal distinctions.[25] Based on a broad range of especially Christian sources, Mazel has claimed that 'diocese' was most often used to indicate a group of baptismal churches headed by a bishop and geographically situated close together.[26] In this definition, dioceses would have rep-

---

23 Cf. Florian Mazel, *L'Évêque et le Territoire. L'Invention Médiévale de l'Espace (Ve–XIIIe siècle)* (Paris: Editions du Seuil, 2016), 98.
24 Hunt, *Public Institution*, 244. Also, Herrmann-Otto, *Ecclesia*, 54–57.
25 Mazel, *L'Évêque*, 97; 160. Mazel's point being that dioceses change especially in the tenth century and then they get the meaning they continue to have in the church nowadays.
26 Mazel, *L'Évêque*, 95–95; 'un groupe d'églises baptismales que réunissent une certaine proximité topographique'. Michel Lauwers, "*Territorium non facere diocesim*. Conflits, limites et rep-

resented smaller units within the larger units of provinces, quite different and opposite from the Roman administrative dioceses that grouped together several provinces.

Mazel's interpretation has the following consequence for the interpretation of the second canon of Constantinople. In the first, third and fourth instance of the use of the term 'diocese' in this canon, it would refer to dioceses as smaller units within provinces, as it urged bishops 'not to go beyond their *dioceses* to churches lying outside of their bounds, nor bring confusion on the churches' (first instance of 'diocese' in canon two). The bishops that are being admonished here would be the regular bishops in the cities and not the metropolitan bishops that headed an entire province. In the council of Épaone of the year 517 this type of use of dioceses as smaller church territories was confirmed.[27]

The second instance of 'diocese' in the canon, which mentioned the 'Asian Diocese', and indirectly referred to the Pontic and Thracian diocese as well, I would interpret not as alluding to dioceses as smaller units within one province, but because of their geographical and civic markers 'Asiana', 'Pontica' and 'Thracia' as references to the civic dioceses which in these particular instances might have been suitable for the church organization as well. Again, here we might catch a glimpse of both a match and mismatch of civic and church institutions. Where suitable, the church would accept the existing civic structures, such as in the case of Asiana, Pontica, and Thrace (though this canon makes not yet clear what the position would be of the bishop of Constantinople whose authority was confirmed during this Council of 381), but the church would apply other structures if needed, such as in the case of the bishop of Alexandria and Egypt, thereby not employing existing civic institutions such as the diocese of Orientis.

Although much more research is needed on this topic of the use of the meaning of the terminology of 'dioceses' in the Christian sources, a closer reading of this second canon of the Council of Constantinople has demonstrated that by the end of the fourth century there seem to have been two types of dioceses: Roman imperial administrative dioceses and ecclesiastical dioceses, functioning within two separate and different hierarchies and organizations. In the subsequent fifth

---

resentations territorials du diocèse (*Ve–XIIIe siècle*)," in *L'Espace du Diocèse. Genèse d'un Territoire dans l'Occident médiéval (Ve–XIIIe siècle)*, ed. Florian Mazel (Rennes: Presses Universitaire Rennes, 2008), 23–24. Cf. also Florian Mazel, *De la cité au diocèse. Église, pouvoir et territoire dans l'Occident médiéval* (Rennes: Presses Universitaire Rennes, 2009).

27 Mazel, *L'Évêque*, 97. Council of Épaone of 517: canon five and eight, making a distinction of categories of churches being situated in cities and their territories: (1) *monasteria*; (2) *basilicae*; (3) *dioceses*, which was confirmed in the councils of Orléans of 538 (canon 21) and of 541 (canon 33).

century, the civic dioceses ended up in an unclear and most likely declining state, and perhaps simply disappeared. Dioceses within the ecclesiastical structures just started to emerge, perhaps as small units within the provinces, but clearly not as units comparable in size to the civic ones. Michel Lauwers has argued that within Christian sources of the fourth through the eight centuries we come across the word *dioceses*, but only in rare instances, especially compared to the use of words such as *civitas*, *territorium*, or *provincia* in discussions on the territorial powers and structures of the church.[28] According to both Mazel and Lauwers it took another few centuries before the church changed the use of 'diocese' into the type of ecclesiastical unit that we now know from the Middle Ages and later.

4 Conclusion

This contribution has presented an examination of the way in which existing civic structures and institutions might have had an impact on the way in which late antique bishops could exercise their position of power and influence within their Christian communities. Especially cities and provinces proved a fruitful framework within which bishops could fulfill their duties. However, developments within the Christian churches and their leadership in the fourth century called for other types of organization as well which were further created by the church. The second half of this contribution has offered a first step towards a reconsideration of our notion of the meaning of dioceses, both as civic and ecclesiastical organizations. It has become clear that civic dioceses were not units that were simply taken over by the church for its own purposes, but we should be much more careful in our analyses of the instances in which dioceses are mentioned in the late antique ancient Christian sources.

---

[28] Lauwers, *Territorium*, 33–34.

Bibliography

Primary sources

Alberigo, Giuseppe (†) and Melloni, Alberto (eds.). *Conciliorum Oecumenicorum Generaliumque Decreta Vol. I. The Ecumenical Councils. From Nicaea I to Nicaea II (325–787)*. Turnhout: Brepols, 2006 (= COGD).
Cameron, Averil, and Hall, Stuart G. *Eusebius, Life of Constantine. Introduction, Translation and Commentary*. Oxford: Clarendon Press, 1999.
Migne, J.P. *Patrologiae Cursus Completus Series Latina*. Paris: Garnier, 1841–.
Mommsen, Theodor; Meyer, Paul M.; Krueger, Paul. *Theodosiani libri xvi cum Constitutionibus Sirmondianis et Leges Novellae ad Theodosianum pertinentes*. Dublin: Weidmann, 1970–1971.
Pharr, Clyde. *The Theodosian Code and Novels, and the Sirmondian Constitutions*. New York: Greenwood Press, 1952.
Tanner, Norman. *Decrees of the Ecumenical Councils*. Two vols. London: Sheed & Ward, 1990.
Winkelmann, Friedhelm. *Eusebius von Caesarea. Über das Leben des Kaisers Konstantin*. Berlin: Akademie Verlag, 1975.

Secondary literature

Barnes, Timothy D. *The New Empire of Diocletian and Constantine*. Cambridge MA: Harvard University Press, 1982.
Barnes, Timothy D. "Praetorian Prefects 337–361." *ZPE* 94 (1992): 249–260.
Beeley, Christopher A. *The Unity of Christ: Continuity and Conflict in Patristic Tradition*. New Haven: Yale University Press, 2012.
Brown, Peter. *Power and Persuasion in Late Antiquity*. Madison: University of Wisconsin Press, 1992.
Brown, Peter. *Poverty and Leadership in the Later Roman Empire*. Hanover (NH): Brandeis University Press, 2002.
Bury, John B. "The Provincial List of Verona." *JRS* 13 (1923): 127–151.
Destephen, Sylvain. *Prosopographie Chrétienne du Bas-Empire*. Vols. 3. Diocèse d'Asie (325–641). Paris: Association des amis du Centre d'histoire et civilisation de Byzance, 2008.
Chadwick, Henry. "Faith and Order at the Council of Nicaea: A Note on the Background of the Sixth Canon." *HThR* 53 (1960): 171–195.
Feissel, Denis. "L'Empereur et l'Administration Impériale." In *Le Monde Byzantin I. L'Empire romain d'Orient (330–641)*, edited by Cecile Morrison, 79–110. Paris: Presses Universitaires de France, 2004.
Gilliard, Frank D. "Senatorial Bishops in the Fourth Century." *HThR* 77 (1984): 153–175.
Gwynn, David M. *The Eusebians. The Polemic of Athanasius of Alexandria and the Construction of the 'Arian Controversy'*. Oxford: Oxford University Press, 2007.
Haensch, Rudolf. "Römische Amtsinhaber als Vorbilder für die Bischöfe des 4. Jahrhunderts?" In *The Representation and Perception of Roman Imperial Power. Proceedings of the third

workshop of the international network Impact of Empire (Roman Empire, c. 200 B.C. – A.D. 476), Netherlands Institute in Rome, March 20–23, 2002, edited by Lukas de Blois, Paul Erdkamp, Olivier Hekster, Gerda de Kleijn and Stephan Mols, 117–136. Amsterdam: Gieben, 2003.

Herrmann-Otto, Elisabeth. *Ecclesia in Re Publica. Die Entwicklung der Kirche von pseudostaatlicher zu staatlich inkorporierter Existenz*. Frankfurt am Main: Peter Lang, 1980.

Hunt, David. "The Church as a Public Institution." In *Cambridge Ancient History*[2] XIII, 238–276. Cambridge: Cambridge University Press, 1998.

Jones, Arnold H.M. "The Date and Value of the Verona List." *JRS* 44 (1954): 21–29.

Jones, Arnold H.M. *The Later Roman Empire*. Oxford: Oxford University Press, 1964 (reprinted Baltimore 1992).

Kritzinger, Peter. *Ursprung und Ausgestaltung bischöflicher Repräsentation*. Stuttgart: Franz Steiner Verlag, 2016.

Kulikowski, Michael. *Late Roman Spain and its Cities*. Baltimore: John Hopkins University Press, 2004.

Liebeschuetz, J. H. Wolfgang G. *The Decline and Fall of the Roman City*. Oxford: Oxford University Press, 2001.

Lauwers, Michel. "*Territorium non facere diocesim*. Conflits, limites et representations territorials du diocèse (Ve–XIIIe siècle)." In *L'Espace du Diocèse. Genèse d'un Territoire dans l'Occident médiéval (Ve–XIIIe siècle)*, edited by Florian Mazel, 23–65. Rennes: Presses Universitaire Rennes, 2008.

Mazel, Florian, ed. *L'Espace du Diocèse. Genèse d'un Territoire dans l'Occident médiéval (Ve–XIIIe siècle)*. Rennes: Presses Universitaire Rennes, 2008.

Mazel, Florian. *De la cité au diocèse. Église, pouvoir et territoire dans l'Occident médiéval*. Rennes: Presses Universitaire Rennes, 2009.

Mazel, Florian. *L'Évêque et le Territoire. L'Invention Médiévale de l'Espace (Ve–XIIIe siècle)*. Paris: Editions du Seuil, 2016.

Migl, Joachim. *Die Ordnung der Ämter. Prätorianerpräfektur und Vikariat in der Regionalverwaltung des Römischen Reiches von Konstantin bis zur Valentinianischen Dynastie*. Frankfurt am Main: Peter Lang, 1994.

Millar, Fergus. "Paul of Samosata, Zenobia and Aurelian: the church, local culture and political allegiance in third-century Syria." *JRS* 61 (1971): 1–17.

Moore, Michael E. *A Sacred Kingdom: Bishops and the Rise of Frankish Kingship, 300–850*. Washington D.C.: *Catholic* University of America Press, 2011.

Noethlichs, Karl L. "Zur Entstehung der Diözesen als Mittelinstanz des spätrömischen Verwaltungssytems." *Hist.* 31 (1982): 70–81.

Palme, Bernhard. "Die *Officia* der Statthalter in der Spätantike. Forschungsstand und Perspektiven." *Antiquité Tardive* 7 (1999): 85–133.

Rapp, Claudia. *Holy Bishops in Late Antiquity. The Nature of Christian Leadership in an Age of Transition*. Berkeley – Los Angeles – London: University of California Press, 2005.

Rebillard, É. *Christians and Their Many Identities in the Late Antiquity, North Africa, 200–450 CE*. Ithaca: Cornell University Press, 2012.

Slootjes, Daniëlle. *The Governor and His Subjects in the Later Roman Empire*. Leiden: Brill, 2006a.

Slootjes, Daniëlle. "Governor Trumped by Bishop: Shifting Boundaries in Roman Religious and Public Life." In *The Impact of Imperial Rome on Religions, Ritual and Religious Life in the Roman Empire. Proceedings of the fifth workshop of the international network Impact of Empire (Roman Empire, c. 200 B.C. – A.D. 476)*, Münster, 2004, edited by Lukas de Blois, Peter Funke and Johannes Hahn, 219–231. Leiden: Brill, 2006b.

Slootjes, Daniëlle. "Bishops and Their Position of Power in the Late Third Century CE: The Cases of Gregory Thaumaturgus and Paul of Samosata." *Journal of Late Antiquity* 4 (2011): 100–15.

Slootjes, Daniëlle. "Late Antique Administrative Structures: On the Meaning of Dioceses and Their Borders in the Fourth Century." In *Aspects of Ancient Institutions and Geography. Studies in Honor of Richard J.A. Talbert*, edited by Lee Brice and Daniëlle Slootjes, 177–195. Leiden: Brill, 2014.

Slootjes, Daniëlle. "The Decision-making Process behind the Anchoring of Provinces and Dioceses into a New Late Roman Administrative System: A Case Study of the Diocese of Hispaniae." In *Land, Labour and Power: Governing Ancient Empires. Proceedings of the 3rd to 5th International Conferences of the Research Network Imperium and Officium*, edited by Michael Jursa, Bernhard Palme and Sven Tost. Vienna, forthcoming 2019.

Slootjes, Daniëlle. "The Effects of the Diocletianic and Constantinian Provincial Reforms on Provinces, Governors and Dioceses in the Age of Constantine's Sons." In *In the Shadows of Constantine and Julian: The Roman Empire AD 337–361*, edited by Nicholas Brian-Baker and Shaun Tougher. Cambridge: Cambridge University Press, forthcoming 2019.

Sotinel, Claire. "Le recrutement des évêques en Italie aux IVe et Ve siècles: essai d'enquête prosopographique." In *Church and Society in Late Antique Italy and Beyond*, edited by Claire Sotinel, 193–204. Farnham: Ashgate, 2010.

Sterk, Andrea. *Renouncing the World Yet Leading the Church*. Cambridge MA: Harvard University Press, 2004.

Zuckerman, Constantin. "Sur la Liste de Vérone et la province de Grande Arménie, la division de l'Empire et la date de création des diocèses." In *Mélanges Gilbert Dagron*. Travaux et Mémoires 14, 617–637. Paris: Association des Amis du Centre d'Histoire et Civilisation de Byzance, 2002.

Andrea Sterk
Bishops and Mission Beyond the Frontiers: From Gothia to Nubia

Entertaining a company of bishops in the hearing of Eusebius of Caesarea, Constantine once famously affirmed: "You are bishops of those within the church, but I am a bishop... over those outside."[1] Precisely what Constantine meant by this statement is much debated, but it reflected the way subsequent Roman emperors viewed Christianity and Christian mission both within and beyond their borders. It also shaped the way Eusebius's fifth-century continuators – whether Nicene or non-Nicene historians – constructed their narratives of Christianization. Whatever role bishops may have played, these historians presented mission as the domain of the Christian emperor – initiated, sponsored, or overseen by him. Though hagiography, letters, and archeology significantly complicate this picture of leadership in mission, an emphasis on top-down conversion dominates both the sources and their modern interpreters. This approach has tended to obscure the role of less prominent christianizers, often dubbed "accidental" or "incidental" missionaries.[2]

A focus on imperially-sponsored mission has also distorted our view of the agency of bishops and their networks in evangelizing non-Christian peoples. The independent role of bishops, and even their concern for pagan peoples beyond their borders, has been questioned. As E.A. Thompson argued, "If there was no Christian community beyond the relevant frontier, then no bishop was sent there."[3] In a recent monograph Sergey Ivanov has taken this argument even further. Not only were the Byzantines unconcerned with evangelizing barbarians, but they viewed the idea with disdain.[4] Despite abundant evidence of "Greek cultural snobbery," an analysis of episodes from the East Roman frontiers suggests that there was actually more episcopal initiative in missionary work than has sometimes been assumed. To be sure, most late antique bishops believed

---

The author would like to thank the Institute for Advanced Study in Princeton, N.J., where she conducted much of the research for this essay.

1 Eusebius, *Vita Contantini* 4.24.
2 For further discussion of these tendencies see Andrea Sterk, "'Representing' Mission from Below: Historians as Interpreters and Agents of Christianization," *ChH* 79:2 (2010): 271–304.
3 E.A. Thompson, *The Visigoths at the Time of Ulfila* (Oxford: Clarendon, 1966), xvii.
4 His title gives an apt representation of his main argument: Sergey Ivanov, "*Pearls Before Swine*": *Missionary Work in Byzantium* (Paris: ACHCByz, 2015).

that Jesus' command to make disciples of "all nations" (Matthew 28:19) had already been fulfilled by the original apostles.[5] Yet others took seriously their apostolic calling to continue the work of evangelizing pagans, and some cultivated networks to collaborate in this endeavor.

In an important article on bishops and churches in barbarian lands, Ralph Mathisen nuanced Thompson's characterization of Roman missions to barbarian peoples and made two important distinctions.[6] First, he distinguished between east and west, noting that in the west, with one exception, no known bishops or clerics were sent to barbarian regions while in the east, Roman emperors and some bishops felt responsible for churches and Christianization in barbarian territories. Second, he distinguished approaches toward more "civilized" peoples, where Roman ecclesiastical models largely prevailed (for example, in Armenia and Persia), from the approach toward "less cosmopolitan" peoples, where single bishops were appointed for entire ethnic groups.[7] I will be primarily concerned with episcopal involvement in mission to these "less cosmopolitan" peoples on the Roman frontiers, particularly the Goths and the Nubians. Three principal issues will concern me: the initiative in mission, the selection and oversight of missionaries, and the nature of missionary activity.[8]

1 Gothia: From Ulfila to Chrysostom

Prior to John Chrysostom's engagement with the Goths, we have evidence of at least three sets of missionary initiatives involving bishops in mid-fourth-century Gothia.[9] Best known is the work of Ulfila. An assimilated Gothic descendant of Cappadocian Christians abducted two generations earlier, Ulfila became a leader of the faithful in exile. The four main sources on his life – the letter of his disciple, Auxentius, and the ecclesiastical histories of Philostorgius, Socrates, and Sozomen – represent competing Nicene and non-Nicene perspectives; all

---

[5] Ivanov, *"Pearls Before Swine,"* 16–17, 36–37.
[6] Ralph W. Mathisen, "Barbarian Bishops and the Churches 'in barbaricis gentibus' during Late Antiquity," *Speculum* 72 (1997): 664–697.
[7] Mathisen, "Barbarian Bishops," 665–670.
[8] On the terms conversion, Christianization, and mission, see Ian Wood, *The Missionary Life: Saints and the Evangelisation of Europe, 400–1050* (Harlow: Longman, 2001), 3–5. Like Wood, I will be using "mission" primarily to refer to the evangelization of pagans across cultural or geographic boundaries.
[9] On the complexity of these sources, see Noel Lenski, "The Gothic Civil War and the Date of the Gothic Conversion," *Greek, Roman and Byzantine Studies* 36/1 (1996): 51–87.

are incomplete, and they differ on the details of his episcopal consecration, his conversion to Homoianism, and the chronology of events in Gothic history. Yet they all put a positive spin on Ulfila's career.[10] Though precise dates are impossible to reconstruct from the conflicting narratives, piecing together parts of each account gives us an overview of his missionary activity. Ordained bishop of the Goths, or bishop of the Christians in Gothia, by Eusebius of Nicomedia, Ulfila "began to preach the Gospel" among them. He taught them "to live by the rule of evangelic, apostolic, and prophetic truth," Auxentius writes, "and he showed the Christians (among them) to be truly Christians, and multiplied their numbers."[11] He not only evangelized pagan Goths north of the Danube, but he led a large group of Gothic Christians from persecution in barbarian lands to the safety of Roman soil, a feat for which he is compared with Moses.[12]

Both before and after crossing the Danube, Ulfila's linguistic abilities were foundational to his evangelism and teaching. All the historians mention his translation of the Scriptures into the Gothic language, a task which may well have involved a team working under the bishop's supervision.[13] From his location in Moesia, just over the Roman frontier, Ulfila continued to lead the church, teach the Scriptures, and preach and write in Greek, Latin, and Gothic.[14] He also continued to oversee missionary efforts among the pagan Goths under Athanaric, which provoked persecution and martyrdom.[15] Yet despite trials and opposition, Ulfila's followers continued his work. Selenas, his "secretary" [ὑπογραφεύς]

---

[10] On the contradictory sources on Ulfila see Neil McLynn, "Little Wolf in the Big City: Ulfila and his Interpreters," in *Wolf Liebeschuetz Reflected: Essays Presented by Colleagues, Friends, and Pupils*, eds. John Drinkwater and Benet Salway (London: Institute of Classical Studies, 2007), 125–135 and Hagith Sivan, "Ulfila's Own Conversion," HThR 89 (1996): 373–86. On Ulfila and missionary work see also Herwig Wolfram, "Vulfila, Bishop and Secular Leader of His People but not Their Apostle," in Guido M. Berndt and Roland Steinacher (eds.), *Arianism: Roman Heresy and Barbarian Creed* (Burlington, VT: Ashgate, 2014): 131–144.

[11] Auxentius, *Vita Ulfilae* 35[56] in Peter Heather and John Matthews, *The Goths in the Fourth Century* (Liverpool: Liverpool University Press, 1991), 141. Philostorgius, *h.e.* 2.5, places Ulfila's consecration during the reign of Constantine; Auxentius places it under Constantius.

[12] Auxentius, 37[59]: Heather and Matthews, 142. Similarly Philostorgius, *h.e.* 2.5, praises him as "the Moses of our time."

[13] Carla Falluomini, *The Gothic Version of the Gospels and Pauline Epistles. Cultural Background, Transmission and Character* (Berlin/Boston: de Gruyter, 2015), 8, notes that divergences in the Greek text suggest collaboration. Translation work may have begun before the Danube crossing and continued in the politically more stable context of Moesia.

[14] Auxentius, 33[53–54]: Heather and Matthews, *The Goths*, 140.

[15] Socrates, *h.e.* 4.33.7; Sozomen, *h.e.* 6.37. On Ulfila's continued evangelistic work from his base in the Roman Empire see also Lenski, "Gothic Civil War," 79–80, 81–82, and Herwig Wolfram, *History of the Goths* (Berkeley: University of California Press, 1998), 80–82.

and episcopal "successor" [διάδοχος], was of mixed Gothic and Phrygian descent, and like Ulfila, the bishop taught both in Gothic and in Greek.[16] Jordanes, the sixth-century historian of the Goths, emphasized both their continued evangelistic zeal after the Danube crossing and their use of the Gothic language: "They preached the Gospel [*evangelizantes*] both to the Ostrogoths and to their kinsmen the Gepidae...and they invited all people of their speech everywhere to attach themselves to this sect."[17]

Besides Ulfila, a group known as the Audians also engaged in evangelistic activity in Gothia from the 340s through the 360s. Originally from Mesopotamia, their founder, Audius, was known for the "purity of his life, godly zeal, and faith" and for renouncing "luxury and wantonness," especially "money-loving" among the clergy and bishops of his homeland.[18] His reproach of certain leaders caused them to expel Audius and his companions, after which he was consecrated bishop by another rebelling bishop. Epiphanius of Salamis initially praises Audius's manner of life explaining that "he earned his living with his own hands," as did the bishops and presbyters with with him.[19] He then responds in detail to the Audians' two doctrinal deviations but concludes by again lauding their admirable way of life.[20]

Toward the end of his account Epiphanius returns to Audius himself explaining that in old age the bishop was exiled to Scythia by the emperor for promoting rebelliousness among the laity. However, Audius went further still, "even to the interior of Gothia," where he instructed the Goths, promoted monastic life, and ordained Gothic clergy and bishops.[21] After his death, other bishops were ordained who continued the ministry Audius had begun, spreading their version of Christian faith and life beyond their land of origin. Epiphanius mentions Uranius of Mesopotamia and Silvanus of Gothia, among others. Indeed, several times he connects Audius with other bishops and clergy who collaborated

---

16 Socrates, *h.e.* 5.23; Sozomen *h.e.* 7.17. See also Falluomini, *Gothic Gospels*, 8 and 10–11 on the multilingual context of the Goths' conversion and Selenas, who may have been one of Ulfila's helpers.
17 Jordanes, *Get.* 25.133; *The Gothic History of Jordanes*, trans. Charles C. Mierow (Princeton: Princeton University Press, 1915), 88.
18 Epiphanius, *Adversus haereses* [=*Panarion*] 70.1.2–3 in *The Panarion of Epiphanius of Salamis*, Books II and III, trans. Frank Williams, 2nd revd. ed., NHS 63 (Leiden: Brill, 2013), 413.
19 Epiphanius, *Panarion*, 70.2.1.
20 Epiphanius, *Panarion* 70.14.6. He lauds Audius's "completely orthodox observance" of the Trinity but devotes much of his account to a refutation of the Audians' two errors: anthropomorphism (70.2,3–8,11) and refusal to celebrate the Paschal Feast on Sunday (70.9,1–14,4). Cf. Theodoret, *h.e.* 4.9.
21 Epiphanius, *Panarion*, 70.14.5.

with him. After the death of Bishops Uranius and Silvanus, the Audians' numbers dwindled, yet small communities remained in Chalcis and the Euphrates region. "Audian refugees" had also reached Palestine, Arabia, and Cyprus, where they lived for several years in Epiphanius's own day. Though they effectively evangelized in Gothia, the Audians were eventually driven out by the persecution of a pagan Gothic king, and "not only they," Epiphanius adds, "but also the Christians of *our kind* who were there."[22]

This comment of Epiphanius brings us to a third set of missionary initiatives among the fourth-century Danubian Goths, those assumed to be Nicene in orientation and known primarily through *The Passion of St. Saba the Goth* and several letters of Basil of Caesarea. Set during Athanaric's persecution in the early 370s, the *Passion* introduces a "church of God dwelling in Gothia," a small Christian community facing persecution at the hands of ruling pagan elites.[23] Saba himself is described as a Goth by race, "orthodox in faith," devout and ascetic in behavior. Yet he is also a bold, if not provocative, witness reproaching idolaters and even spurning the efforts of pagan villagers to rescue him from persecution.[24] No bishops are mentioned in Gothia, though Saba himself may have served as a lector, and the non-Gothic presbyter Sansalas, who was persecuted together with Saba, seems to have moved back and forth with relative ease across the Gothic-Roman frontier.[25] After Saba's martyrdom, the *dux Scythiae*, Junius Soranus, had his remains transported to Cappadocia in keeping with "the wishes of

---

22 Epiphanius, *Panarion*, 70.15.2–3. [my emphasis]
23 *Passio S. Sabae Gothi*, ed. Hippolyte Delehaye, *Analecta Bollandiana* 31 (1912): 216–224; English translation: Heather and Matthews, *The Goths*, 104–110. See also Johann Leemans, "The Martyrdom of Sabas the Goth: History, Hagiography, and Identity," in *Christian Martyrdom in Late Antiquity (300–450 AD): History and Discourse, Tradition and Religious Identity*, eds. Peter Gemeinhardt and Johan Leemans (Berlin/Boston: de Gruyter, 2012), 201–223. Though full of hagiographic topoi, the *Passio* has been widely recognized as a valuable historical source on fourth-century Gothia. This particular Gothic community was occupied in the fourth century by the Tervingi confederation.
24 *Passio* 2.1–2; for Saba's refusal of pagan attempts to abet him, see *Passio* 3.1–4 and 7.4. On the ambiguity of Saba's confession see Paul Purvis, "Sabas: 'Orthodox' or 'Arian'?," in *Arianism*, eds. Berndt and Steinacher, 67–85.
25 *Passio* 4.1–6. On bishops and their absence among the Danubian Goths, see Ralph W. Mathisen, "Barbarian 'Arian' Clergy, Church Organization, and Church Practices," in *Arianism*, eds. Berndt and Steinacher, 150–154. On the likelihood that Saba was among the lower clergy, see Leemans, "Martyrdom of Sabas," 205. On Sansalas see Wolfram, *History of the Goths*, 106 and Heathers and Matthews, *The Goths* 106, n.27. On the fluidity of the borders, Constantine Zuckerman, "Cappadocian Fathers and the Goths," *Travaux et Mémoires* 11 (1992): 479.

the college of presbyters."²⁶ In a letter to the same *dux* Soranus, Basil encouraged the evangelistic work in Gothia reminding his correspondent that his church prays "for those who speak boldly for the name of the Lord."²⁷

In Basil's letters to Ascholius, a Cappadocian priest involved in mission to the "barbarians beyond the Danube," we learn more about Nicene efforts in Gothia.²⁸ In Letter 164 Basil refers to Ascholius as "the trainer" of the athlete Saba who has also strengthened many others in the struggle for the faith. His ministry reminds Basil of the Cappadocian missionary Eutyches, who "tamed the barbarians by the power of the Spirit."²⁹ Basil describes the cruel persecution of Gothic Christians in his own day in terms that parallel the *Passion of St. Saba*.³⁰ Letter 165 focuses on the recent martyrdom of Saba and his relics, which the *dux* Soranus had arranged to have transported to Cappadocia. Basil rejoices in this gift for Ascholius's homeland and refers to Saba as "a martyr, who recently finished his struggle in the barbarian land neighboring your own."³¹ Such phrases strongly suggest that missionary work in Gothia was conducted by Roman Christians based just over the frontier. While it strains the imagination to see this arrangement as an elaborately organized "centre missionaire" for training, sending, and checking the progress of missionaries throughout the lower Danube,³² the *Passion of St. Saba* and related letters of Basil suggest a network of Christians involved in missionary outreach to pagan Goths. From these sources we know that at least one bishop (Basil) encouraged the work while traveling priests (Sansalas, Gouththikas, Ascholius), a military official (the *dux* Soranus), and native Gothic Christians (Saba and other villagers) all played a role in spreading the faith.

---

26 *Passio* 8.2: Heather and Matthews, *The Goths*, 110. On the πρεσβυτέριον and the significant autonomy of presbyters in this region see Zuckerman, "Cappadocian Fathers," 476–477 and Mathisen, "Barbarian, 'Arian' Clergy," 151–152.
27 *Ep.* 155 in *Saint Basile: Lettres 2* (Paris: Les Belles Lettres, 1961), ed. Yves Courtonne, 80.
28 *Ep.* 164.1: Courtonne 2, 98. On the interconnection of Basil's letters with the *Passio* of St. Saba and the debated identity of the recipient, Ascholius, see Zuckerman, "Cappadocian Fathers," 473–479, and Lenski, "Gothic Conversion," 77–78. *Ep.* 154 makes it clear that the recipient is a Nicene Christian, for Basil praises his devotion to Athanasius as evidence of sound faith.
29 Ibid. Eutyches' identity is uncertain, but Zuckerman, "Cappadocian Fathers," 478 and n. 22 argues that he was most likely the recent martyr Euticus, from Scythia Minor.
30 Zuckerman, "Cappadocian Fathers," 478–479, argues strongly for Ascholius's authorship of the *Passion*.
31 *Ep.* 165: Courtonne 2, 101.
32 J. Coman, "Saint Basile le Grand et L'Église de Gothie: Sur les missionnaires cappadociens en Scythie Mineure et en Dacie," *The Patristic and Byzantine Review* 3 (1984): 64.

As these episodes reveal, Gothic Christianity comprised a combination of Homoian, Audian, and Nicene communities by the mid-fourth century and a corresponding mixture of missionary efforts.³³ The texts are much less detailed and more ambiguous than we might wish, but they throw some light on the involvement of bishops. Though Philostorgius connected Ulfila's mission with the emperor, and Audius's missionary work has been deemed "accidental" due to his exile,³⁴ the bishops themselves clearly initiated missionary activity. Ulfila's most obvious accomplishment was the creation of Gothic letters and translation of the Bible, though he also taught and evangelized as did his successors. He continued to oversee missionary efforts in Gothia after finding refuge for his people in Roman territory. Audius taught and promoted monastic life, both before and after his episcopal ordination, and his ascetic lifestyle and renunciation of wealth suggest that care for the poor was a prominent feature of his ministry. Unofficial evangelists like Saba spoke out boldly to the pagans of their village, while priests like Ascholius, "the trainer," may have functioned as more intentional missionaries. There is no mention of a bishop in Saba's village, but references in both the *Passio* and Basil's correspondence suggest a base of missionary activity in the empire; and bishops like Basil encouraged the work.³⁵ In each case we see a broad network of personnel involved in mission to the Goths, yet bishops were often central figures in these efforts.

John Chrysostom's involvement with the Goths in Constantinople and his multifaceted strategy of Christianization has received renewed attention in recent years. Wendy Mayer has highlighted his missionary activity outside Constantinople making the intriguing connection between bishops and presbyters in Antioch and mission to Phoenicia.³⁶ Chrysostom's letters from exile throw light on his

---

33 Wolfram, "Vulfila, Bishop and Secular Leader," 135 refers to "three different denominations" of Christians north of the Danube.
34 On Philostorgius's representation of the missions of both Ulfila and Theophilus see Anna Lankina, "Reassessing Historiography in Late Antiquity: Philostorgius on Religion and Empire" (PhD diss., University of Florida, 2014), 88–123. Lenski, 77, describes Audius's mission as "entirely accidental."
35 There is no evidence of Basil sending out missionaries, but his preaching, social engagement, and supervision of chorbishops suggest he consistently had pagans in view. See Uwe Walter Knorr, *Basilius der Grosse. Sein Beitrag zur christlichen Durchdringung Kleinasiens* (Dissertation, Tübingen, 1968). Though cautious about using the term "mission" in any modern sense, Knorr describes his contribution "zu einer künftigen Missionsgeschichte der Spätantike." (4)
36 Wendy Mayer, "Patronage, Pastoral Care, and the Role of the Bishop in Antioch," *VigChr* 55 (2001): 58–70. Mayer includes mission as one of seven categories of pastoral care in late antiquity. See also Jonathan Peter Stanfill, "Embracing the Barbarian: John Chrysostom's Pastoral Care of the Goths" (Ph.D. Diss., Fordham University, 2015). On mission to the Goths in Constan-

ideal of mission and his guidance of missionary activity both in Phoenicia (roughly modern-day Lebanon) and among the Goths beyond Roman frontiers. According to Theodoret, when John led the church in Constantinople he recruited zealous monks, "armed them with imperial edicts," and sent them to destroy the pagan shrines of Phoenicia.[37] John's correspondence provides a fuller and rather different picture of this mission, which was of great personal concern to him. He had likely played an administrative role in the Phoenician mission as a presbyter in Antioch and Bishop Flavian's right-hand man before moving to Constantinople, and he had maintained relations with a cluster of Antiochene presbyters and wealthy laity from the capital.[38] On his way to exile in Cucusus in summer 404, John writes to the presbyter Constantius, who had replaced him as Flavian's adjutant in Antioch and was expected to succeed him as bishop. He encourages Constantius amid the current tumult not to neglect his responsibilities to oversee "the destruction of paganism, the construction of churches, and the care of souls."[39] John also reminds him of his duty to care for the churches of Phoenicia, Arabia, and the East, areas that traditionally fell under Antiochene jurisdiction.[40] Urging Constantius to write often, he inquires about the number of churches built each year, the holy men who had joined the Phoenician mission, and the progress they have made; and he mentions that he has personally persuaded a hermit from Nicaea to join the mission work there.

Following his arrival in Cucusus, a cluster of John's letters reflect his continued preoccupation with missionary activity in Phoenicia.[41] He first writes to two priests in Zeugma in an effort to recruit more missionaries. He asks the monk-presbyter Nicholas, who was particularly involved with the Phoenician mission,

---

tinople see Chris De Wet, "John Chrysostom and the Mission to the Goths: Rhetorical and Ethical Perspectives," *HTS Teologiese Studies/Theological Studies* 68/1 (2012): 1–10.

37 Theodoret, *h.e.* 5.29; GCS NF 5, 329–330.

38 See Mayer, "Bishop in Antioch," 67–70 and John Norman Davidson Kelly, *Golden Mouth: The Story of John Chrysostom: Ascetic, Preacher, Bishop* (Ithaca: Cornell University Press, 1996), 142–144.

39 *Ep.* 221; PG 52.732–33. On the date and circumstances see Roland Delmaire, "Les 'lettres d'exil' de Jean Chrysostome. Études de chronologie et de prosopographie," *RechAug* 25 (1991), 120–121. Though expected to become Flavian's successor, Constantius was supplanted by the ordination of Porphyrius, the candidate of John's enemies in Constantinople. See Palladius, *dial.* 16; SC 341, 64–109.

40 On Antioch's jurisdiction over Phoenicia, see Delmaire, "Les 'lettres d'exil'," 120; on ecclesiastical jurisdiction beyond imperial frontiers see Mathisen, "Barbarian Bishops," 667–670.

41 These letters are discussed in Wendy Mayer, "The Bishop as a Crisis Manager. An Exploration of Early Fifth-Century Episcopal Strategy," in *Studies of Religion and Politics in the Early Christian Centuries*, eds. David Luckensmeyer and Pauline Allen (Strathfield, Australia: St. Paul's, 2010), 169–171.

to send the presbyters John and Gerontius there.⁴² He also writes to Gerontius, urging him to go to Phoenicia before winter and noting that he has asked Constantius to furnish whatever is necessary, "whether for building or for the needs of the brethren."⁴³ At the same time he writes to encourage those directly involved with the mission, "the presbyters and monks instructing the pagans in Phoenicia"; he not only lauds their evangelizing work but assures them that the requisite practical provisions, "whether garments, shoes, or food," would be amply supplied.⁴⁴ During the same period, John praises the presbyter Basilius for his "zeal toward the pagans, overturning their error and leading them by the hand toward the truth."⁴⁵ Similarly, writing to his friend Agapetus, he commends the presbyter Elpidius, who was evangelizing the pagans of the Amanos mountains between Cilicia and Syria. Elpidius has already delivered many from impiety, built churches, and established monasteries, John explains, urging Agapetus to support him generously.⁴⁶ In the summer of 405 Chrysostom was still guiding the mission to Phoenicia, where pagan violence had recently resulted in injuries and the death of several monks. He urges the presbyter Rufinus to hurry there to restore order.⁴⁷ Other letters address wealthy lay patrons informing them of the progress and needs of the mission and thanking them for their financial support.⁴⁸ At least ten of John's letters from 404 to 405 concern the Phoenician mission revealing not only his own continued oversight from exile but a remarkable network of presbyters, monks, and wealthy laypeople engaged with different aspects of the ministry.

The Phoenician mission is the best documented in Chrysostom's correspondence, but it does not represent the full scope of his missionary involvement. Besides his letter to Constantius reminding him of his extensive supervisory responsibilities, Letter 9 to Olympia shows John's concern for evangelization beyond Roman frontiers, specifically efforts in Persia. He urges Olympia not to abandon Maruthas, bishop of the frontier town of Martyropolis in Mesopotamia, who had served as an ambassador to Yazdegard I and had been instrumental in the evangelization of Persia, the building of churches, and eventually the estab-

---

42 *Ep.* 53; PG 52, 637–638, dated to early September 404. In *ep.* 69 he thanks Nicholas for his oversight of the work in Phoenicia. On the recipients and circumstances of these letters see Delmaire, "Les 'lettres d'exil'," 99, 121, 129–130, 135–136, and 145.
43 *Ep.* 54; PG 52, 638–639.20–21.
44 *Ep.* 123; PG 52, 676–78; quote at 677.25–27.
45 *Ep.* 28; PG 52, 627.24–25
46 *Ep.* 175; PG 52, 711–712.
47 *Ep.* 126; PG 52, 685–687
48 *Ep.* 51 to Diogenes (PG 52, 636–37) and *ep.* 21 to Alphius (PG 52, 624).

lishment of a Sasanian church in Iran.⁴⁹ Though Maruthas had been involved in Chrysostom's deposition at the Synod of the Oak, John had written to him twice in exile, eager to learn of the progress he had made in Persia and what he hoped to accomplish on his next trip.⁵⁰ The tone and content of this passage suggest that John had been personally involved in initiating a mission to the Sasanians and show that he continued to encourage missionary activity in Persia while in exile. Theodoret affirms that Chrysostom's vision of mission, and hence his own ecclesiastical jurisdiction, extended beyond his see to include the provinces of Thrace, Asia, and Pontus as well as Phoenicia and Scythia.⁵¹ In a panegyric included in Photius's *Bibliotheca*, Theodoret went further still, placing John "in the same rank as the apostles" [πρὸς τοὺς ἀποστόλους συγγένειαν] because of his evangelistic outreach among the Scythians, Persians, and Babylonians.⁵²

Yet John was most directly involved with the Goths. Alongside his pastoral care of Goths in Constantinople, his oversight of missions in Gothia had two geographical foci, the Crimea and the Lower Danube. Involvement with the Crimean Goths began while John still occupied the Constantinopolitan see, but it continued in exile, as revealed in three letters from late November 404.⁵³ Following his appeal for information from Maruthas about missionary work in Persia, in Letter 9 to Olympias he turns to the subject of the Goths. He explains that Unila, whom he had consecrated bishop for the Crimean Gothic community, had recently died, and the deacon Moduarius had brought John a letter from the king of the Goths requesting a bishop to replace him.⁵⁴ Judging from his name, Unila himself was probably a Goth, most likely recruited from the Gothic monastery Promotus in the suburbs of Constantinople. Another letter about the dilemma of Unila's replacement addresses the monks of this monastery, which has been described

---

49 *Ep.* 9.5a; Anne-Marie Malingrey, *Lettres à Olympias*, 2nd ed., SC 13bis (Paris: Éditions du Cerf, 1968), 236. On Maruthas's involvement with Yazdegard and the spread of Christianity in Persia, see Socrates, *h.e.* 7.8. See also Walt Stevenson, "John Chrysostom, Maruthas and Christian Evangelism in Sasanian Iran," *StPatr* 47 (2010): 301–07.
50 *Ep.* 9.5a; Malingrey, 236, 3–10. He asks Olympia to let him know whether she has delivered the two letters he had sent to Maruthas requesting such information. Regarding Maruthas at the Synod of the Oak, see Sozomen, *h.e.* 8.16; regarding this letter, see Kelly, *Golden Mouth*, 144 and 264–265.
51 Theodoret, *h.e.* 5.28–31; GCS NF 5, 329–331.
52 Photius, *Bibliotheca*, 273 in *Photius. Bibliothèque*, ed. René Henry (Paris: Belles Lettres, 1977), 8, 109.19–21.
53 *Ep.* 9.5.18–20; *ep.* 206; *ep.* 207. On the dating and addressees of these letters see Delmaire, "Les 'lettres d'exil'," 147 and 149.
54 *Ep.* 9.5b.18–20. On Unila's identity, the probable circumstances of his consecration, and the nature of his mission, see Stanfill, "Embracing the Barbarian," 208–219.

as a "seminary" for Gothic clergy.⁵⁵ As we have seen in the Phoenician context, it was from monasteries that John most often recruited missionaries and leaders for the church. Though Christianity had been brought to the Crimean Goths already in the third century, a significant pagan population remained. Indeed the "great works" for which John praised Unila probably involved the conversion of pagans.⁵⁶ Like his letter to Olympia, his letters to the deacon Theodolus and the monks of the Gothic monastery urged them to stall for time to prevent his opponents from appointing an unworthy replacement for Unila.⁵⁷ Together these three letters show John's continuing involvement with the Crimea, his concern for strong leadership of the Gothic church, and his use of monks in missionary work.

The only reference to John's involvement with mission to the Danubian Goths occurs in Theodoret's *Church History*. After describing Chrysostom's role in the mission to Phoenicia and his linguistic strategy in winning over the Goths in Constantinople, Theodoret turns to the "nomads along the Danube." Learning that they were "thirsty for salvation but had none to bring them to the stream," he explains, John sought men "who were zealous for the apostolic way of life" [τὴν ἀποστολικὴν φιλοσοφίαν ἐζηλωκότας] and entrusted them with the task of evangelization.⁵⁸ Theodoret claims that he learned of this missionary activity from a letter written by Chrysostom to Leontius, bishop of Ancyra, asking him to find suitable men to continue the work. John himself does not refer to this mission among the Danubian Goths, yet there is little reason to doubt his request to Leontius, given the latter's status as a leading monk-bishop, well-situated to recruit missionaries from the monasteries of the region.⁵⁹ Moreover, several aspects of this brief description fit the pattern of missions to Phoenicia and the Crimean Goths and resemble missions conducted by Homoians and Audians. As bishop, John was motivated by the plight of unevangelized peoples beyond the frontiers. He supervised missionary work, identified as "apostolic" ministry both in his own letters and in Theodoret's description; and he tended to recruit

---

55 *Ep.* 207. On Promotus, see Gilbert Dagron, *Naissance d'une capitale: Constantinople et ses institutions de 330 à 451* (Paris: Presses Universitaires de France, 1974), 466. Kelly, *Golden Mouth*, 143, calls it a "training-school for Gothic clergy."
56 *Ep.* 9.5b. Malingrey, SC bis13, 238.
57 *Ep.* 206 and *ep.* 207.
58 Theodoret, *h.e.* 5.31; GCS 5.331.
59 See Theodoret *h.e.* 5.27 and Sozomen, *h.e.* 6.34.9 for descriptions of Leontius as an exemplary monk before becoming bishop. Chrysostom's letter must have been written before July 403 since Leontius had by then become part of the faction that deposed him at the Synod of the Oak. For further discussion see Stanfill, "Embracing the Barbarian," 220–223.

monks – from monasteries near Antioch or Constantinople – as missionaries. As his network of supporting bishops collapsed around him, his broader web of ascetics, clergy, and wealthy laypeople continued the work of mission he had initiated.

2 Christianizing Nubia: Monks, bishops, and episcopal networks

Over a century later we have a fuller account of missionary activity beyond east Roman frontiers. The Christianization of Nubia is most often associated with the imperial couple Justinian and Theodora, who allegedly sent rival missions to the African kingdom toward the middle of the sixth century. Notwithstanding the importance of this imperially-sponsored mission, described in colorful detail by John of Ephesus, recent work on this area has added significant nuance to the story. Scholars have pointed to evidence of Nubian contact with Christianity through bishoprics and churches in the christianized north and south well before the imperially-sponsored mission. And as one of the foremost scholars of ancient Nubia has put it, Nubia is an "El Dorado" for today's archaeologists of Christianity.[60] Though the limited sources all present interpretive challenges, symbols on grave goods, inscriptions, and several official letters indicate that Christians were present in Nubia and even held administrative posts in the fifth century.[61] In light of recent archeological advances, textual evidence for the earliest stages of Christian expansion in Nubia deserves renewed attention as well.

Even more engaging than the lively narrative of John of Ephesus, the Coptic account of the *Life of Aaron*, translated as Paphnutius's *Histories of the Monks of Upper Egypt*, describes Christian missionary activity in this area in the fourth century highlighting the role of a network of monks and monk-bishops.[62] This text raises at least two major debates relevant to its interpretation: first, the ques-

---

[60] Siegfried G. Richter, "The Beginnings of Christianity in Nubia," in *Christianity and Monasticism in Aswan and Nubia*, eds. Gawdat Gabra and Hany N. Takla (Cairo: The American University in Cairo Press, 2013): 48. The essay summarizes research from 1938 to 2013.

[61] See Jitse H.F. Dijkstra, "Qasr Ibrim and the Religious Transformation of Lower Nubia in Late Antiquity," in *Qasr Ibrim, Between Egypt and Africa. Studies in Cultural Exchange*, eds. Jacques van der Vliet and J.L. Hagen (Leiden: Peeters, 2013), 111–22.

[62] Edited by E. A. Wallis Budge, *Coptic Texts V. Miscellaneous Texts in the Dialect of Upper Egypt* (New York: AMS Press, 1915); *Paphnutius. Histories of the Monks of Upper Egypt and the Life of Onnophrius*, Translation and Introduction by Tim Vivian (Kalamazoo, Mich.: Cistercian, 1993).

tion of its date, with estimates ranging from around 425 to 700, and second, the historical value of hagiography for the study of Christianity in late antique Egypt.[63] Despite these unresolved problems, the multifaceted evidence of earlier layers of Christianization in this area combined with the interaction between monks, bishops, and Nubians presented in this account make it well worth examining on the subject of bishops and mission. *Life of Aaron* is set in the Dodekaschoinos, the frontier area around the first cataract that served as a buffer zone between Roman Egypt and Nubia encompassing Aswan (ancient Syene) and the temple island of Philae, center of the Isis cult.[64] The second section of the work deals with the first four bishops of Philae highlighting their involvement in several episodes of outreach to pagan Nubians.

The first reference to Nubians shows the monk-bishop Macedonius training his new disciples, the pagan priest's two sons, Mark and Isaiah, who would in turn replace him as bishops of Philae.[65] The episode concerns a dispute between two Nubian camel owners. A stronger camel had broken the leg of a weaker one, and the owner of the injured camel demanded retribution. When Mark related this altercation to Macedonius, the bishop asked the two men to present their respective sides of the story. He then instructed Isaiah to sprinkle water on the camel's badly broken leg and make the sign of the cross over it; Isaiah did so, and the leg was immediately healed. The Nubians "were amazed, for they did not know God;" and when passersby from Philae saw what had happened, they "went to their town and spread the fame of the holy bishop." (19b, §47) Though serving as Bishop of Philae, Macedonius had distributed his possessions and allegedly lived among the pagan population not "with the authority of a

---

[63] For various positions in this debate see David Frankfurter, "Hagiography and the Reconstruction of Local Religion in Late Antique Egypt: Memories, Inventions, and Landscapes," in *The Encroaching Desert: Egyptian Hagiography and the Medieval West*, eds. Jitse Dijkstra and Mathilde van Dijk (Leiden: Brill, 2006): 13–37.

[64] On the Dodekaschoinos as a frontier zone see Jistse H.F. Dikstra, *Philae and the End of Ancient Egyptian Religion. A Regional Study of Religious Transformation (298–642 CE)* (Leuven: Peeters, 2008), 23–36 and Jacques van der Vliet, "Contested Frontiers: Southern Egypt and Northern Nubia, AD 300–1500. The Evidence of the Inscriptions," in *Christianity in Aswan and Nubia*, eds. Gabra and Takla, especially 63–65.

[65] *Monks of Upper Egypt*, 19b, §47; Vivian, 94. Section numbers (§) and English translation are from Vivian, who follows Budge's edition. On Macedonius see James E. Goehring, "Imagining Macedonius, The First Bishop of Philae," in *Christianity in Aswan and Nubia*, eds. Gabra and Takla, 9–20. Though we know almost nothing about these bishops, all three appear on episcopal lists from this period. On bishoprics in the first cataract area, see Dijkstra, *Philae*, 53–56, and Appendix 4, 359–360, for a list of the first bishops of Syene and Philae with relevant sources and dates.

bishop" but "as one who was the least among them." (31, §13a) He dwelt in the desert near a road on which traders, travelers, and camel herders passed, and he was clearly known to the Nubians as one who could be trusted to mediate disputes. His missionary activity involved listening patiently to two sides of a dispute; reconciling two friends, i.e., serving as a peacemaker; and healing the leg of a camel, probably the main source of the Nubians' livelihood.

The second reference to Nubians explicitly concerns mission. It occurs after the death of Macedonius when his disciple, Mark, who had been serving as a priest, became the people's choice for bishop. Like his predecessor, Mark was consecrated Bishop of Philae by Athanasius of Alexandria; but before the consecration, he has a long conversation with the archbishop about his commission to continue Macedonius's work, including mission to the Nubians. (26–29b, §60–68) Athanasius takes this opportunity to instruct Mark about the love of God, the mission to the gentiles, and the importance of acting out of love for the pagan Nubians. He cites a long series of biblical passages from both the Old and New Testament illustrating God's concern for the "nations." He continues with a series of local parables concluding with the exhortation that Mark should cultivate love for his pagan neighbors who, Athanasius assures him, "will come to believe in God after awhile." (29b, §68) While Athanasius's role in creating new bishoprics for Egypt and the frontiers is attested in other sources, his mini-sermon to Mark about the missionary call is distinctive. It contains a whole biblical theology of mission, which is echoed by the words and actions of the leading missionaries in the text. The missionary bishops in these episodes are not fiery preachers or iconoclasts. Their "mission" consists in reading and explaining the gospels, arbitrating disputes, and caring for the poor and needy. In short, they were engaged in the kind of everyday encounters that would have characterized life in this borderland, where Nubians lived alongside Egyptians and Romans and where travel and trade might well be vehicles for exchange of religious ideas and beliefs.[66]

Whatever the nature of missionary activity in the late fourth or fifth century, imperially-sponsored missions were certainly sent to Nubia in the sixth century; and episcopal networks were central to their success. The story of these missions is recounted by the Miaphysite historian and bishop, John of Ephesus, writing

---

[66] While acknowledging the problems of using Egyptian hagiographical texts as evidence, Peter Van Minnen, "Saving History? Egyptian Hagiography in Its Space and Time," in *Encroaching Desert*, eds. Dijkstra and van Dijk, 57–90, argues for the plausibility of such accounts of how "christianizers" saved others individually as opposed to "saints" converting entire communities of pagans.

c.580 and resident in Constantinople at the time the events unfolded.[67] According to John, missions to Nubia took place over several decades during the reigns of Justinian and his successor, Justin II, and comprised three main stages.[68] The first phase of the mission was initiated in Constantinople. From 535/6, numerous non-Chalcedonian monks, exiled bishops and clergy were resident in the imperial capital, housed in the old palace of Hormisdas, ostensibly under the protection of Empress Theodora.[69] An elderly monk-priest named Julian, one of the retinue in attendance on the exiled patriarch, Theodosius of Alexandria,[70] was "filled with spiritual zeal on account of the wandering people" who inhabited the eastern borders of the Thebais beyond Egypt. These tribes had never been subject to the Roman Empire, John explains, and "even receive a subsidy on condition that they do not enter or pillage Egypt."[71] This description of the Nubians points to earlier contact with Roman authorities suggesting the bestowal of federate status, which is also supported in other sources.[72]

---

67 See Jan Jacob Van Ginkel, *John of Ephesus. A Monophysite Historian in the Sixth Century* (Groningen: Rijksuniversiteit, 1996). Siegfried G. Richter, *Studien zur Christianisierung Nubiens*, SKCO 11 (Wiesbaden: Reichert, 2002), offers the fullest treatment of John's account of the Nubian missions placing them in the context of Byzantine ecclesiastical politics and assessing both written and archaeological evidence. For missionary themes in John of Ephesus's *Lives of the Eastern Saints*, see Jeanne-Nicole Mellon Saint-Laurent, *Missionary Stories and the Formation of the Syriac Churches* (Berkeley: University of California Press, 2015), especially 72–95.

68 The main narrative of Nubia's Christianization occurs in Part III, Book 4 of John of Ephesus's Church History: *Iohannis Ephesini historia ecclesiasticae pars tertia*, ed. and trans., E.W. Brooks, CSCO 105, 106 (Louvain: L. Durbecq, 1935–36); German translation (with commentary): Richter, *Studien*, 42–98; English translation: *The Third Part of the Ecclesiastical History of John of Ephesus*, R. Payne Smith (Oxford: Oxford University Press, 1860), 251–252 and 315–324. Translations here are from Payne Smith, sometimes modified. John starts Book 4.6 with a summary explaining that this chapter is "about the barbarian people of the Noubades who were converted to Christianity and about the cause of their conversion." *h.e.* 3.4.6: Brooks, 183; Richter, 46. Payne Smith's translation omits this statement.

69 Volker L. Menze, *Justinian and the Making of the Syrian Orthodox Church* (Oxford: Oxford University Press, 2008), 187, 217–218, 222.

70 Considered an "ecumenical patriarch" by his followers, Theodosius felt particularly responsible for the church of Alexandria and was concerned to fill the vacant Egyptian sees. See Alois Grillmeier, SJ with Theresia Hainthaler, *Christ in Christian Tradition*, 2/4: *The Church in Alexandria with Nubia and Ethiopia after 451*, tr. O.C. Dean, Jr. (Louisville, KY: Westminster John Knox Press, 1996), 53–54. For Theodosius's role in ecclesiastical politics in Constantinople, see Menze, *Syrian Orthodox Church*, 189, 190, 203–204, and 225; also T. Orlandi, "Teodosio di Alessandria nella letteratura copta," *GIF* 23 (1971): 175–85.

71 John of Ephesus, *h.e.* 3.4.6.

72 On the use of Blemmyes and Noubades as federates see Jitse H.F. Dijkstra, "Blemmyes, Noubades, and the Eastern Desert in Late Antiquity: Reassessing the Written Sources," in *The History*

Julian impressed upon Empress Theodora his concern for the salvation of these people and his longing to bring the gospel to them; and the empress promised to do everything in her power for their conversion. We then hear of an elaborate race between Justinian and Theodora in which the empress allegedly devised a plot to ensure that her mission should reach Nubia first.[73] Whether or not this competition actually took place, Julian's mission arrived with gifts and a letter from the empress explaining the purpose of their mission, and the kings and princes of the Noubades are said to have received the envoys with joy. The king and people abjured their errors and "confessed the God of the Christians," and Julian gave them "much instruction" in the faith. Julian remained in Noubadia for two years, though "suffering greatly from the extreme heat." He "endured it patiently," John comments, "and taught them, and baptized both the king and his nobles, and many of the people with him."[74]

The elderly bishop Theodore of Philae had accompanied Julian to Noubadia, and after Julian had instructed the people, he left the new Noubadian Christians to Theodore's care. Julian then departed for Constantinople, where he was received honorably by Theodora and related his experiences while John of Ephesus himself was present.[75] Bishop Theodore of Philae remained involved in Noubadia until 551. Though John of Ephesus says very little about him, he surely played a more significant role than John would lead us to believe.[76] First of all, Philae was the last stop on the Roman side of the frontier en route to Noubadia, and any Roman imperial or ecclesiastical embassy would have certainly sought the support of the city's bishop. Theodore had also been involved in the Christianization of the region in other ways through the course of his long episcopate. A series of inscriptions carved on the walls of the temple of Isis at Philae attest to the conversion of the temple in 535–537, and Theodore is mentioned in three of them as the bishop who "transformed this shrine into a place for Saint Stephen."[77] Moreover, Theodore accompanied Julian on his mission, stayed in Nou-

---

of the Peoples of the Eastern Desert, eds. H. Barnard and K. Duistermaat (Los Angeles: Cotsen Institute of Archaeology, 2012), 238–247.

73 Dijkstra, "Religious Transformation," 116, and idem, *Philae*, 295–298, places these events between 536 and 548. On the alleged rival missions, see Dijkstra, *Philae*, 286–289. See also Menze, *Syrian Orthodox Church*, 262–265 on relations between Justinian and John of Ephesus.

74 John of Ephesus, *h.e.* 3.4.7

75 John of Ephesus, *h.e.* 3.4.7; Brooks, 186: "in our presence he was received by the queen in great honor."

76 On Theodore's important role in the Christianization of Nubia see Dijkstra, *Philae*, 299–304, 324–333.

77 Philae. Greek graffiti commemorating the conversion of the temple of Isis. Ca. 535–537, no. 324 in *Fontes Historiae Nubiorum. Textual Sources for the History of the Middle Nile Region*

badia (specifically Qasr Ibrim) for some time after Julian's departure, and continued to visit the fledgling church for years. A Coptic inscription also refers to Theodore as the one who established the church in Dendur, 77 kilometers south of Syene, transforming it from a pagan temple to a Christian place of worship.⁷⁸ This was clearly Nubian rather than Roman territory. Known as the inscription of Eirpanome, it suggests that this was the name of the Nubian king who converted under Julian's ministry. While Bishop Theodore returned to Philae, he continued to oversee this missionary territory and was only replaced upon the arrival of Longinus, by which point he was a very old man.

We know very little about the Nubian Christians whom Julian left behind or how the process of Christianization continued in Lower Nubia under Bishop Theodore. In the next chapter of his *Ecclesiastical History*, however, John of Ephesus picks up the story again in Constantinople, where a second phase of mission began some 18 years later.⁷⁹ John reminds his readers that Patriarch Theodosius of Alexandria, still resident in the capital, maintained oversight of this missionary region and had not forgotten the new converts. On the very day of his death he remembered them, John explains, as their first teacher, Julian, had recently passed away and Theodora had given orders that Longinus be appointed bishop over the region.⁸⁰ John describes Longinus as "a zealous man who could more fully convert [the Noubades] and strengthen them in Christian faith."⁸¹ Thus, immediately after Theodosius's death in 566, Longinus was ordained bishop of the Noubades and commissioned to complete the work that Julian had begun.

By this point both Theodora and Justinian were dead, and Justin II attempted to prevent the mission altogether. Convinced by Longinus's enemies that the new bishop would stir up the Nubians against the Romans, the emperor had him detained in Constantinople for three years under constant watch; indeed he only managed to escape by disguising himself with a wig. After his arrival in Noubadia, Longinus immediately began to instruct the people afresh. What is more, John adds, "he built them a church, and ordained clergy, and taught them the order of divine service and all the ordinances of Christianity."⁸² Longinus remained in Noubadia approximately six years, until c.575, when he was unwitting-

---

between the Eighth Century BC and the Sixth Century AD. Vol. III: From the First to the Sixth Century AD, eds. Tormod Eide et al. (Bergen: University of Bergen, 1994), 1177–1178.
78 *Fontes Historiae Nubiorum*, no. 330. For the date and circumstances, see 1195–1196.
79 John of Ephesus, *h.e.* 3.4.8.
80 In an earlier chapter (*h.e.* 3.4.5) we learn that Theodosius had appointed Longinus to administer the eucharist in his place due to his feebleness in the later years of life.
81 John of Ephesus, *h.e.* 3.4.8: Brooks, 187.7–8.
82 John of Ephesus, *h.e.* 3.4.8.

ly drawn into an internal ecclesiastical dispute.[83] The next thirty chapters of Book 4 describe the conspiracy of certain Alexandrian clergy to place their own party on the patriarchal throne. In chapter 49, however, John returns to the situation in Nubia saying that he will now relate the conversion of the people "the Greeks call Alodiae." He immediately connects this account with Empress Theodora, who had earlier sent Julian to Nubia. Before relating further details of the mission to the southernmost kingdom, he reviews the first stages of the imperially-sponsored mission to Nubia – highlighting the roles of Julian, Theodore, and especially Longinus, who "instructed, exhorted, and taught them anew and baptized those among them who still remained unbaptized."[84]

Longinus's missionary activity did not end there, however, for he also evangelized the Nubian kingdom of Alodia, though not without considerable suffering and a new set of intrigues. In this phase it was neither the emperor nor any priest or bishop in Constantinople who prompted a mission but rather the request of the Alodian king himself. He had appealed to the king of the Noubades for the bishop who had instructed and baptized them to do likewise among the Alodiae. Yet a party of Alexandrian clergy attempted to thwart the mission and turn the Alodiae against Longinus. As with the first Nubian mission, rival missions were allegedly sent; yet it was not a matter of Chalcedonian versus non-Chalcedonian missionaries but a division between non-Chalcedonians themselves.[85] Meanwhile, Longinus was "stirred up" in spirit to go to the Alodiae, and John describes his departure, circuitous journey, and eventual arrival. Longinus and his companions fell ill due to heat and privations and lost seventeen camels accompanying them with baggage. Moreover, they had to contend with the hostile tribe of Makouria, situated between Noubadia and Alodia, which sought to prevent this mission to its southern neighbors. But God intervened, John explains, and Longinus and his company arrived safely at the borders of Alodia, where the people received him honorably and the king went out personally to meet him. Longinus "spoke the word of God" to the king and his nobles, instructed them for several days, then baptized the king, leading figures, and "gradually" many of the people as well.[86]

---

[83] John of Ephesus, *h.e.* 3.4.9.
[84] John of Ephesus, *h.e.* 3.4.49: Brooks, 233.15–234.5. In conclusion, John repeats that the Noubadian king sent envoys to Constantinople and that he was himself often in their company as they praised Longinus for his ministry.
[85] See Richter, *Studien*, 80–81 on this competition.
[86] John of Ephesus, *h.e.* 3.4.51: Brooks, 237.15–22. John's word choice here emphasizes a longer-term process.

At this point John inserts into his narrative parts of three letters which give further details about Longinus's mission, its results, and the setting in which these events took place. First he includes "a letter of thanks" from the king of Alodia to the king of the Noubades.[87] He then inserts an extract of a letter from Longinus in Alodia to the king of Noubadia describing the challenges of the mission and requesting that he forward it to Bishop Theodore of Alexandria, whom Longinus himself had appointed patriarch. He ends this letter with encouragement to send bishops who will be able to continue the flourishing work in Alodia, for "there are a thousand here who are hastening to salvation."[88] A third missive, the Noubadian king's letter to Theodore of Alexandria, echoes much of what Longinus had already written and explains the Noubadian king's own role in the mission.[89] John ends his account of the Alodian mission by citing Jesus' words in Matthew 24:14 that "this good news of the Kingdom shall be preached unto all the nations, and then shall the end be."[90]

A focus on diplomatic or confessional factors in John of Ephesus's account, though certainly important, may obscure other aspects of the missionary process. The early monk-bishops involved in mission to Nubia were described in *Life of Aaron* as having lived among the people – mediating disputes, intervening in crises, and helping in practical aspects of daily life. Amid political and ecclesiastical intrigues surrounding the sixth-century Nubian missions, little attention has been paid to the missionaries themselves – the elderly monastic priest, Julian, who proposed and led the first delegation, Bishop Theodore of Philae who regularly visited the fledgling church over 18 years, and especially Longinus, who continued the work in Noubadia and moved on to lead the Alodian mission. Delightful details of John's account, even if exaggerated, give some perspective on what mission to this region might entail, for example, the blistering heat that Julian escaped only by spending seven hours a day undressed in caverns of water.[91] We hear too of arduous journeys through the desert, sickness of men and animals, the baptism and training of disciples, the building of churches, and exchanges of letters between missionaries, bishops, and African kings.

---

87 John of Ephesus, *h.e.* 3.4.51.
88 John of Ephesus, *h.e.* 3.4.53.
89 Ibid. Specifically, he sent Longinus to the Blemmye king for help in avoiding the hostile Makouritae.
90 John of Ephesus, *h.e.* 3.4.53. He adds that these things were accomplished in the year 580.
91 John of Ephesus, *h.e.* 3.4.7.

3 Conclusion

Late antique Gothia and Nubia serve as case studies of the diverse roles that bishops played in the spread of Christianity on the eastern frontiers. Though church historians tended to emphasize imperial sponsorship, bishops themselves often initiated or supervised mission in these border areas. While evangelization of pagan populations might involve proclamation of the gospel, instruction in the faith, or translation of the Scriptures, mission also entailed a broad range of practical ministries and acts of compassion. Moreover, those already involved in missionary activity, whether as monks or priests, were more readily ordained as bishops for the people they served – like Ulfila and Audius in Gothia or Longinus in Nubia – or for other unevangelized areas. The Syrian ascetic Abraham of Carrhae provides a good example.[92] Having successfully evangelized a village in the Lebanon by his care for the social needs of this poor community, Abraham served for a time as their priest, trained a monk to replace him, and returned to his monastic dwelling–only to be called soon after to serve as bishop of the largely pagan city of Carrhae on the Mesopotamian frontier. There too the missionary-monk-turned-bishop allegedly converted many pagans to the Christian faith.[93] Though linked to Emperor Theodosius II in Theodoret's account, Abraham's missionary efforts were clearly self-initiated. In fact, he seems to have been selected as bishop on the basis of his proven apostolic ministry in the Lebanon.

The centrality of a physical church and the liturgy is also common to many accounts of mission in Late Antiquity. Chrysostom's letters repeatedly sought news of the building of churches in missionary territory.[94] Longinus built a church and instructed the people in the liturgy as soon as he arrived in Nubia. In other eastern mission narratives we find similar patterns. Abraham's evangelistic activity in Lebanon began with the quiet singing of the liturgy, which initially enraged the villagers, and continued with his insistence on building a church. Missionary work among the Hephthalite Huns also involved building a church

---

[92] Theodoret, *Historia religiosa* 17.
[93] However, Procopius, *Wars* 3.13.7 indicates that Carrhae was still largely pagan in the sixth century.
[94] His connection of church buildings with religious identity surely relates to this emphasis in missionary contexts he addresses. On Chrysostom's efforts to redefine the topography of Antioch see Christine Shepardson, "Controlling Contested Places: John Chrysostom's *Adversus Iudaeos* Homilies and the Spatial Politics of Religious Controversy," *JECS* 15 (2007): 483–516.

and instruction in the liturgy,[95] not only proclamation but calling people to the Christian community in a visible, concrete form. To these late antique missionary bishops, or the historians and hagiographers who recounted their deeds, mission entailed engagement in society, presence as much as preaching, and liturgy as both a method and goal of their evangelistic witness.

Mission was clearly a multi-layered affair in terms of personnel, strategy, and activity. Within this process, "episcopal networks" included not only bishops but a diverse cast of characters too easily dismissed as "accidental" evangelists. The reality of unofficial missionaries working both with and without episcopal oversight helps explain the rapid spread of Christianity in late antiquity, even when emperors showed little interest in mission to barbarians and bishops were preoccupied with doctrinal disputes.[96] Yet alongside the work of missionaries from below, apostolic work was the domain of bishops; and for some, the conversion of unevangelized peoples beyond their borders justified extra-jurisdictional engagement. Without denying the imperial dimensions of mission in late antiquity, the examples of Gothia and Nubia show that missionary bishops and their networks were critical agents in this process.

---

95 For two phases of mission to the Huns under the leadership of Armenian bishops see *The Chronicle of Pseudo-Zachariah Rhetor. Church and War in Late Antiquity*, ed. Geoffrey Greatrex, trans. Robert R. Phenix and Cornelia B. Horn (Liverpool: Liverpool University Press, 2011): 452–454.

96 Regarding the former see Ivanov, *"Pearls before Swine"*; on the latter, Andrew Fear, "Bishops, Imperialism and the *Barbaricum*," in Andrew Fear, José Fernández Ubiña and Mar Marcos (eds.), *The Role of the Bishop in Late Antiquity. Conflict and Compromise* (London: Bloomsbury, 2013): 223.

Bibliography

Primary Sources

Auxentius of Durostorum. *Vita Ufilae*. Edited by Roger Gryson. *Scolies ariennes sur le Concile d'Aquilée*. SC 267. Paris: Cerf, 1980. *Scripta arriana Latina*. Corpus Christianorum Series Latina 87. Turnhout: Brepols, 1982. Translated by Peter Heather and John Matthews. *The Goths in the Fourth Century*, 137–143. Translated Texts for Historians 11. Liverpool: Liverpool University Press, 1991.

Basil of Caesarea. *Epistulae*. Edited by Yves Courtonne. *Saint Basile: Lettres*. 3 vols. Paris: Les Belles Lettres, 1957–66.

Epiphanius. *Panarion* [= *Adversus haereses*]. Edited by Karl Holl. 3 vols. GCS 25, 31, 37. Leipzig: Hinrichs, 1915–33. Translated by Frank Williams. *The Panarion of Epiphanius of Salamis*, Books II and III, 2nd revd. ed. NHS 63. Leiden: Brill, 2013.

Eusebius, *Vita Constantini*. Edited by Friedhelm Winkelmann. GCS. Berlin: Akademie-Verlag, 1975.

Greatrex, Geoffrey, Sebastian P. Brock, and Wiltold Witakowski, eds. *The Chronicle of Pseudo-Zachariah Rhetor: Church and War in Late Antiquity*, trans. Robert R. Phenix and Cornelia B. Horn. Translated Texts for Historians 55. Liverpool: Liverpool University Press, 2011.

John Chrysostom. *Epistulae 1–17 ad Olympiadem*. Edited by Anne-Marie Malingrey. *Lettres à Olympias*. 2nd ed., SC 13 bis. Paris: Éditions du Cerf, 1968.

John Chrysostom. *Epistulae 18–242 ad diversos*. Edited by J.-P. Migne. *Patrologia graeca*. Vol. 52. Paris, 1857–66.

Life of Aaron. Edited by E. A. Wallis Budge, *Coptic Texts* V. *Miscellaneous Texts in the Dialect of Upper Egypt*, 432–495 (text), 248–1011 (translation). New York: AMS Press, 1915. Translated by Tim Vivian, *Paphnutius. Histories of the Monks of Upper Egypt and the Life of Onnophrius*, 73–141. Kalamazoo: Cistercian Publications, 2000.

Palladius. *Dialogus de vita Joannis Chrysostomi*. Edited by Anne-Marie Malingrey and Philippe Leclercq. *Dialogue sur la vie de Jean Chrysostome*. 2 vols. SC 341, 342. Paris: Éditions du Cerf, 1988.

Passio S. Sabae Gothi. Edited by Hippolyte Delehaye. "Saints de Thrace et de Mesie." *Analecta Bollandiana* 31 (1912): 216–21. Translated by Peter Heather and John Matthews. *The Goths in the Fourth Century*, 104–110. Translated Texts for Historians 11. Liverpool: Liverpool University Press, 1991.

Philostorgius. *Historia ecclesiastica*. Edited by Friedhelm Winkelmann and Joseph Bidez. *Kirchengeschichte*. 3rd ed. GCS. Berlin: Akademie Verlag, 1981. Translated by Philip R. Amidon. *Church History*. Atlanta: Society of Biblical Literature, 2007.

Photius. *Bibliotheca*. Edited by René Henry. 8 vols. Paris: Les Belles Lettres, 1959–77.

Socrates of Constantinople. *Historia ecclesiastica*. Edited by Günther Christian Hansen. Translated by Pierre Périchon and Pierre Maraval. 4 vols., SC 477, 493, 505, 506. Paris: Éditions du Cerf, 2004–7.

Sozomen. *Historia ecclesiastica*. Edited by Joseph Bidez and Günther Christian Hansen. *Kirchengeschichte*. GCS 50. Berlin: Akademie Verlag, 1960.

Theodoret of Cyrrhus. *Historia ecclesiastica*. Edited by Leon Parmentier and Günther Christian Hansen. *Kirchengeschichte*. 3rd ed. GCS, Neue Folge; Band 5. Berlin: Akademie Verlag, 1954.
Theodoret of Cyrrhus. *Historia religiosa*. Edited by Paul Canivet and Alice Leroy-Molinghen. *Histoire des moines de Syrie*. SC 234. Paris: Éditions du Cerf, 1977. Translated by R.M. Price. *A History of the Monks of Syria*. Kalamazoo: Cistercian Publications, 1985.
Jordanes. *Getica*. Translated by Charles C. Mierow. *The Origin and Deeds of the Goths*. Princeton, 1908.
John of Ephesus. *Iohannis Ephesini historia ecclesiasticae pars tertia*. Edited by E.W. Brooks, CSCO 105, 106 (Louvain: L. Durbecq, 1935 – 36) Translated by R. Payne Smith. *The Third Part of the Ecclesiastical History of John of Ephesus*. Oxford: Oxford University Press, 1860.
Fontes Historiae Nubiorum. Textual Sources for the History of the Middle Nile Region between the Eighth Century BC and the Sixth Century AD. Vol. III: From the First to the Sixth Century AD. Edited by Tormod Eide et. al. Bergen: University of Bergen, 1994.

Secondary Literature

Berndt, Guido M., and Roland Steinacher, eds. *Arianism: Roman Heresy and Barbarian Creed*. Burlington, VT: Ashgate, 2014.
Coman, J. "Saint Basile le Grand et l'Église de Gothie: Sur les missionaires cappadociens en Scythie Mineure et en Dacie." *The Patristic and Byzantine Review* 3 (1984): 54 – 68.
Dagron, Gilbert. *Naissance d'une capitale: Constantinople et ses institutions de 330 à 451*. Paris: Presses Universitaires de France, 1974.
Delmaire, Roland. "Les 'lettres d'exil' de Jean Chrysostome. Études de chronologie et de prosopographie." *RechAug* 25 (1991): 71–180.
De Wet, Chris L. "John Chrysostom and the Mission to the Goths: Rhetorical and Ethical Perspectives." *HTS Teologiese Studies / Theological Studies* 68/1 (2012): 1–10.
Fear, Andrew. "Bishops, Imperialism and the *Barbaricum*." In *The Role of the Bishop in Late Antiquity. Conflict and Compromise*, edited by Andrew Fear, José Fernández Ubiña and Mar Marcos, 209–27. London: Bloomsbury, 2013.
Dijkstra, H.F. "Blemmyes, Noubades, and the Eastern Desert in Late Antiquity: Reassessing the Written Sources." In *The History of the Peoples of the Eastern Desert*, edited by H. Barnard and K. Duistermaat, 238–47. Los Angeles: Cotsen Institute of Archaeology, 2012.
Dijkstra, H.F. "Qasr Ibrim and the Religious Transformation of Lower Nubia in Late Antiquity." In *Qasr Ibrim, Between Egypt and Africa. Studies in Cultural Exchange*, edited by Jacques van der Vliet and J.L. Hagen, 111–22. Leiden: Peeters, 2013.
Dikstra, Jitse H.F. *Philae and the End of Ancient Egyptian Religion. A Regional Study of Religious Transformation (298 – 642 CE)*. Leuven: Peeters, 2008.
Dijkstra, Jitse, and Mathilde van Dijk, eds. *The Encroaching Desert: Egyptian Hagiography and the Medieval West*. Leiden: Brill, 2006.
Falluomini, Carla. *The Gothic Version of the Gospels and Pauline Epistles. Cultural Background, Transmission and Character*. Berlin/Boston: de Gruyter, 2015.

Frankfurter, David. "Hagiography and the Reconstruction of Local Religion in Late Antique Egypt: Memories, Inventions, and Landscapes." In *The Encroaching Desert: Egyptian Hagiography and the Medieval West*, edited by Jitse Dijkstra and Mathilde van Dijk, 13–37. Leiden: Brill, 2006.

Gabra, Gawdat and Hany N. Takla, eds. *Christianity and Monasticism in Aswan and Nubia*. Cairo: The American University in Cairo Press, 2013.

Goehring, James E. "Imagining Macedonius, The First Bishop of Philae." In *Christianity and Monasticism in Aswan and Nubia*, edited by Gawdat Gabra and Hany N. Takla, 9–20. Cairo: The American University in Cairo Press, 2013.

Grillmeier, Alois, SJ, with Theresia Hainthaler, *Christ in Christian Tradition*, 2/4: *The Church in Alexandria with Nubia and Ethiopia after 451*, trans. O.C. Dean, Jr. Louisville, KY: Westminster John Knox Press, 1996.

Ivanov, Sergey. *"Pearls Before Swine": Missionary Work in Byzantium*. Paris: ACHCByz, 2015.

Kelly, John Norman Davidson. *Golden Mouth: The Story of John Chrysostom: Ascetic, Preacher, Bishop*. Ithaca: Cornell University Press, 1996.

Knorr, Uwe Walter. "Basilius der Grosse. Sein Beitrag zur christlichen Durchdringung Kleinasiens." PhD diss., Tübingen, 1968.

Lankina, Anna. "Reassessing Historiography in Late Antiquity: Philostorgius on Religion and Empire." PhD diss., University of Florida, 2014.

Leemans, Johann. "The Martyrdom of Sabas the Goth: History, Hagiography, and Identity." In *Christian Martyrdom in Late Antiquity (300–450 AD): History and Discourse, Tradition and Religious Identity*, edited by Peter Gemeinhardt and Johan Leemans, 201–23. Berlin/Boston: de Gruyter, 2012.

Lenski, Noel. "The Gothic Civil War and the Date of the Gothic Conversion." *Greek, Roman and Byzantine Studies* 36/1 (1996): 51–87.

Mathisen, Ralph W. "Barbarian Bishops and the Churches 'in barbaricis gentibus' during Late Antiquity", *Speculum* 72 (1997): 664–97.

Mathisen, Ralph W., "Barbarian 'Arian' Clergy, Church Organization, and Church Practices," in *Arianism: Roman Heresy and Barbarian Creed*, edited by Guido M. Berndt and Roland Steinacher, 145–192. Burlington, VT: Ashgate, 2014.

Mayer, Wendy. "The Bishop as a Crisis Manager. An Exploration of Early Fifth-Century Episcopal Strategy." In *Studies of Religion and Politics in the Early Christian Centuries*, edited by David Luckensmeyer and Pauline Allen, 159–71. Strathfield, Australia: St. Paul's Publications, 2010.

Mayer, Wendy "Patronage, Pastoral Care, and the Role of the Bishop in Antioch," *VigChr* 55 (2001): 58–70.

McLynn, Neil. "Little Wolf in the Big City: Ulfila and his Interpreters." In *Wolf Liebeschuetz Reflected: Essays Presented by Colleagues, Friends, and Pupils*, edited by John Drinkwater and Benet Salway, 125–35. London: Institute of Classical Studies, 2007.

Menze, Volker L. *Justinian and the Making of the Syrian Orthodox Church*. Oxford: Oxford University Press, 2008.

Orlandi, T. "Teodosio di Alessandria nella letteratura copta." *GIF* 23 (1971): 175–85.

Purvis, Paul, "Sabas: 'Orthodox' or 'Arian'?," in *Arianism: Roman Heresy and Barbarian Creed*, edited by Guido M. Berndt and Roland Steinacher, 67–85. Burlington, VT: Ashgate, 2014.

Richter, Siegfried G. *Studien zur Christianisierung Nubiens*. SKCO 11. Wiesbaden: Reichert, 2002.
Richter, Siegfried G. "The Beginnings of Christianity in Nubia." In *Christianity and Monasticism in Aswan and Nubia*, edited by Gawdat Gabra and Hany N. Takla, 47–54. Cairo: The American University in Cairo Press, 2013.
Saint-Laurent, Jeanne-Nicole Mellon. *Missionary Stories and the Formation of the Syriac Churches*. Berkeley: University of California Press, 2015.
Shepardson, Christine. "Controlling Contested Places: John Chrysostom's *Adversus Iudaeos* Homilies and the Spatial Politics of Religious Controversy." *JECS* 15 (2007): 483–516.
Sivan, Hagith. "Ulfila's Own Conversion." *HThR* 89 (1996): 373–86.
Stanfill, Peter Jonathan. "Embracing the Barbarian: John Chrysostom's Pastoral Care of the Goths." PhD diss., Fordham University, 2015.
Sterk, Andrea. "Representing Mission from Below: Historians as Interpreters and Agents of Christianization." *ChH* 79:2 (2010): 271–304.
Stevenson, Walt. "John Chrysostom, Maruthas and Christian Evangelism in Sasanian Iran." *StPatr* 47 (2010): 301–07.
Thompson, E.A. *The Visigoths at the Time of Ulfila*. Oxford: Clarendon, 1966.
Van der Vliet, Jacques. "Contested Frontiers: Southern Egypt and Northern Nubia, AD 300–1500. The Evidence of the Inscriptions," in *Christianity and Monasticism in Aswan and Nubia*, edited by Gawdat Gabra and Hany N. Takla, 63–65. Cairo: The American University in Cairo Press, 2013.
Van Ginkel, Jan Jacob. *John of Ephesus. A Monophysite Historian in the Sixth Century*. Groningen: Rijksuniversiteit, 1996.
Van Minnen, Peter. "Saving History? Egyptian Hagiography in Its Space and Time." In *The Encroaching Desert: Egyptian Hagiography and the Medieval West*, edited by Dijkstra and van Dijk, 57–90. Leiden: Brill, 2006.
Wolfram, Herwig. *History of the Goths*. Berkeley: University of California Press, 1998.
Wolfram, Herwig, "Vulfila, Bishop and Secular Leader of His People but not Their Apostle," in *Arianism: Roman Heresy and Barbarian Creed*, edited by Guido M. Berndt and Roland Steinacher, 131–144. Burlington, VT: Ashgate, 2014.
Wood, Ian. *The Missionary Life: Saints and the Evangelisation of Europe, 400–1050*. Harlow: Longman, 2001.
Zuckerman, Constantine. "Cappadocian Fathers and the Goths." *Travaux et Mémoires* 11 (1992): 473–86.

List of Contributors

Ariane Bodin studied Roman history and received her doctorate with a specialization in the consequences of the conversion to Christianity of the late antique Romans from Africa and Italy (fourth to sixth centuries) at the University of Paris Nanterre in 2014. She published with Tiphaine Moreau *Réseaux sociaux et contraintes dans l'Antiquité tardive* (*Revue des études tardo-antiques*, Supplément 1, 2014) and *Becoming Christian in the Late Antique West (3rd-6 centuries)* (*Studia Patristica* 77, 2017) with Camille Gerzaguet and Matthieu Pignot. More recently, her research focuses on the christianisation of the roman family in Italy, Africa and Gaul.

Gillian Clark is Professor Emerita of Ancient History, and Senior Research Fellow, at the University of Bristol, UK. She studied classics and ancient history at Oxford (D.Phil. 1972). She was a research fellow of Somerville College, Oxford, then taught for the universities of Glasgow and St Andrews, Manchester and Liverpool, before her appointment to Bristol. Publications include *Christianity and Roman Society* (CUP 2004), *Late Antiquity: A Very Short Introduction* (OUP 2011), *Monica: An Ordinary Saint* (OUP 2015), and many papers on Augustine. She co-edits *Oxford Early Christian Studies / Texts* (OUP) and *Translated Texts for Historians 300–800* (Liverpool University Press). She is a Fellow of the British Academy.

Carmen Angela Cvetković studied Classics and Theology at the universities of Durham and St. Andrews. She has obtained her PhD in 2010 from the University of St. Andrews. Since 2013 she is a postdoc at Georg-August University Göttingen, currently affiliated to the 'Forum for Interdisciplinary Religious Studies' (FIRSt). She is the author of *Seeking the Face of God: The Reception of Augustine in the Mystical Thought of Bernard of Clairvaux and William of St Thierry* (Brepols 2012). More recently her research focuses on Latin Ancient Christianity, in particular Niceta of Remesiana, Paulinus of Nola and Ambrose of Milan.

Jakob Engberg studied History and Classics at Aarhus University and obtained his PhD in 2005 from the University of Southern Denmark. After postdoctoral fellowships at the Faculty of Theology of Aarhus University and a term as guest professor in Kiel he became associate professor of church history at Aarhus University in 2010. Since 2009, he has been chairing the MA-programme "Religious Roots of Europe" (a joint programme offered by four Nordic universities) and, since 2012, he has been the chair of the Centre for the Study of Antiquity and Christianity. His research focus is on the relationship between Christians and Roman authorities, on apologetics and conversion.

Peter Gemeinhardt studied Theology at the universities of Marburg and Göttingen. In 2001, he received the degree of Dr. theol. from the University of Marburg and was awarded the habilitation by the University of Jena in 2006. Since 2007, he holds the Chair of Church History (patristics) at the University of Göttingen; since 2015, he acts as director of the DFG-funded Collaborative Research Centre 1136 "Education and Religion in Cultures of the Mediterranean and Its Environment from Antiquity to Medieval Times and the Classical Period of Islam." Recent publications include: *Die Kirche und ihre Heiligen: Studien zu Ekklesiologie und Hagiographie in der Spätantike* (Tübingen 2014); *Education and Religion in Late Antique Christiani-*

ty. *Reflections, Social Contexts, and Genres* (ed. with Peter van Nuffelen and Lieve Van Hoof; London/NewYork 2016); *Was ist Kirche in der Spätantike?* (ed.; Leuven 2017); *Athanasius von Alexandrien: Vita Antonii. Leben des Antonius* (introduction, translation and notes; FC 69; Freiburg et al. 2018).

David M. Gwynn studied Classics at Massey and Auckland Universities in New Zealand, before completing his doctoral thesis on Athanasius of Alexandria at Oxford in 2003. He was appointed Reader in Ancient and Late Antique History at Royal Holloway, University of London, in 2012, specialising in the study of religion in Late Antiquity with a particular interest in the transformation of Christianity and the Christian controversies of the fourth-sixth centuries. Recent publications include *Athanasius of Alexandria: Bishop, Theologian, Ascetic, Father* (Oxford University Press, 2012) and *Christianity in the Later Roman Empire: A Sourcebook* (Bloomsbury Publishing, 2014).

Daniel K. Knox is a PhD candidate at Central European University in Budapest, Hungary. His research is focused on the study of historic networks in sixth-century Italy. For his thesis he is conducting a study of the corpus of the sixth-century clergyman Ennodius of Pavia, which combines methods from social network analysis and text analysis to identify and understand the social discourses present in the preserved collection of texts.

Johan Leemans obtained his PhD in 2001 from the Catholic University of Leuven (Belgium) and is currently Professor for Christianity in Late Antiquity and Vice-dean of Research at the Faculty of Theology and Religious Studies of KU Leuven. In his research he focuses mainly on the fourth and fifth centuries in the "Greek East" (e.g. the Cappadocian Fathers and John Chrysostom). Transmission of the Christian faith and the construction of Christian identities in a religiously plural world are key terms in his research. Within this perspective, his main research topics are patristic homilies and the phenomenon of martyrdom. Johan Leemans is also editor-in chief of *Sacris Erudiri* and serves on the boards of the *Revue d'histoire ecclésiastique* and *Vigiliae Christianae*.

Erika Manders is currently postdoctoral researcher at the Department of History at the Radboud University Nijmegen and coordinator of the research project "Constraints and Tradition. Roman Power in Changing Societies (50 BCE – 565 CE)." She obtained her PhD in Ancient History from the Radboud University in 2008 and was a member of the Nijmegen research team "Emperors and Ancestors: the creation of an imperial image" from 2009 to 2013. From 2013 until 2017 she worked at the Georg-August-Universität Göttingen where she led the junior research group 'Religion' at the Graduiertenschule für Geisteswissenschaften (GSGG). Her research interests focus on modes of transmitting imperial ideology in general and religious representation of Roman and Byzantine emperors in particular.

Volker Menze is Associate Professor of Late Antique History at the Central European University (CEU) in Budapest. His publications include *Justinian and the Making of the Syrian Orthodox Church* (Oxford 2008); he is currently working on ecclesiastical politics in the fifth-century Roman Empire.

Sigrid Mratschek is Professor of Ancient History at the University of Rostock, Member of the Council of the International Association of Patristic Studies and Consulting Editor of the *Jour-*

nal of Late Antiquity. Her books *Der Briefwechsel des Paulinus von Nola* on the worldwide web of Christian intellectuals (Göttingen 2002) and *Divites et praepotentes* on wealth and social standing under the Principate (Stuttgart 1993) were recognised with a DFG award and the Bruno Heck Prize. Her present research focuses on visual culture and literary interactions of the creative elites in the Roman Empire and Late Antiquity. A special area of interest is reflected in numerous essays on epistolography written during and since her Visiting Fellowship at All Souls College, Oxford. Their topics include the construction of history (Louvain 2013), the letter collection of Sidonius Apollinaris (Oakland 2017), the unwritten letters of Augustine (Turnhout 2017), a dispute between Augustine and Paulinus on moving the monastery (Göttingen 2014), strategies of visualisation and social practices of renunciation in Paulinus of Nola (Louvain 2015; Stuttgart 2018), and self-definition through intertextual discourses in Pliny and Martial (Cambridge 2018).

Daniëlle Slootjes took her PhD at the University of North Carolina at Chapel Hill (USA), which was published in 2006 entitled *The Governor and his Subjects in the Later Roman Empire* (Brill, Leiden). Since 2004 she is a member of the Department of History of the Radboud University. She specializes in the field of Late Antiquity, Early Byzantine and Early Medieval History. Her presentations and publications have a particular focus on late Roman administrative structures, early Christianity and crowd behavior. Currently, she works on two research projects, one on urban crowd behavior in antiquity, and the other on the functioning of dioceses in late antiquity.

Andrea Sterk is Associate Professor of History at the University of Minnesota. Her publications include *Renouncing the World Yet Leading the Church. The Monk-Bishop in Late Antiquity* (Harvard, 2004) and the co-edited volumes *Readings in World Christian History. Origins to 1453* (Orbis, 2014*)* and *Faithful Narratives. Historians, Religion, and the Challenge of Objectivity* (Cornell, 2014). Her current book project is a study of apostles, evangelists, and missionaries "from below" from 300 to 1000. She is also co-editor of the journal *Church History. Studies in Christianity and Culture*.

Madalina Toca holds a BA in Classics from Babes-Bolyai University, Cluj-Napoca, and MA degrees from CEU Budapest (Late Antique and Medieval Studies) and KU Leuven (Theology and Religious Studies). She is currently completing a PhD at KU Leuven working on the epistolary collection of Isidore of Pelusium and the network it projects in fifth century Egypt, tackling issues related to the historicity of the addressees, to the formation of the corpus, and to its Greek, Latin, and Syriac receptions.

Jamie Wood studied Medieval History at the University of Manchester, before going on to do his PhD in Classics and Ancient History in 2007. Since then he taught at the universities of Manchester, Sheffield, Warwick and Liverpool, in addition to holding a Leverhulme Trust Early Career Postdoctoral Fellowship at the University of Manchester from 2009–2011. He has worked in the School of History and Heritage at the University of Lincoln since 2013, where he researches and teaches on the social, religious and cultural history of the Iberian Peninsula in the late antique and early medieval periods. He has worked extensively on Isidore of Seville and his present research focuses on monasticism and episcopal power in Visigothic Iberia.

Index of Authors and Texts

a) Bible

Psalms (according to Vulgate)
4:7	118
66:2	118
118:105	118

Jeremiah
13:23	98

Ecclesiastes
1:2	170

Matthew
22:35–40	10
24:14	331
25:35	153
28:19	314

Acts
20:15–17	278
28:11–15	278
28:11–16	278

1 Corinthians
9:16	140
15:23–28	157

Philippians
4:1	140

Ephesians
4:11	117

Colossians
1:24–2:5	270

1 Thessalonians
2:19	140

1 Timothy
3:2	149
5:14	131

b) Ancient Writers and Texts

Acta Carpi, Papyli et Agathonicae
4	267

Acta Maximi
1	267

Acta Sanctorum
sept. VI	54

Ambrose of Milan
De Abrahamo
1.5.34	154, 165

De excessu fratris Satyri
1.17	53
1.24	53
1.32	56
1.54	50

De Nabuthae
13.54	51

De officiis
1.20	149
1.139	149
2.21	149
2.64	149

De viduis
15.88	49

De virginibus
1.59	53
3.1	47

Exhortatio virginitatis
12.82	51

Epistulae
2 (Maur. 65)	57
7 (Maur. 37)	57
8 (Maur. 39)	57

11 (Maur. 29)	57
15 (Maur. 69)	57
18 (Maur. 70)	57
20 (Maur. 77)	57
25 (Maur. 53)	57
34 (Maur. 45)	57
35 (Maur. 83)	57
40 (Maur 32)	57
45 (Maur. 52)	57
46 (Maur. 85)	57
48 (Maur. 66)	57
49 (Maur. 59)	44
52 (Maur. 16)	57
56 (Maur. 5)	57
57 (Maur. 6)	57
58 (Maur. 60)	57
59 (Maur. 84)	57
62 (Maur. 19)	57
67 (Maur. 80)	57
68 (Maur. 26)	57
72 (Maur. 17)	57
74 (Maur. 40)	57
75 (Maur. 21)	56
77 (Maur. 22)	47, 57

Expositio evangelii secundum Lucam

5.35	167

Ammianus Marcellinus
Res gestae

14.10	252
17.7	262
21.16	2

Ammon
Epistula Ammonis 141

Athanasius of Alexandria
Apologia contra Arianos

71	102
78	107

Apologia de fuga sua

7	141

De incarnatione verbi

57	142

Epistula ad Afros

10	113

Epistula ad Dracontium

1	141
3	139–141
4	140
5	139
7	141
8	141
9	139, 140
10	140, 141

Epistulae ad Serapionem

1	108, 110
2	106

Epistulae festales

6	105, 110
10	104, 105
12	106, 108, 110
13	104
19	106, 107, 108, 110–112
37	111
39	111, 112
40	106, 107, 110–112
41	111

Historia Arianorum

1	252
72	141

Index festalis

2	103
4	103
12	104

Tomus ad Antiochenos

10	141

Vita Antonii

2	140, 142

Augustine of Hippo
De beata vita

1	75

De catechizandis rudibus

9.13	123

De civitate Dei

1	121, 165
1–3	77

Confessiones

3.6	74
3.9	123
4.5	72
5.23	72, 73

6.3	150	151	170–172
6.16	77	153	77
6.18	73	154	77
6.19	63, 73	155	77
7.8	72	162	68
7.13	74	162	66, 67
8.14	72	186	72
10.3	63	214	66

Contra Cresconium
3.56	75

Contra Faustum
5.5	73

De cura mortuorum
1	161

De ordine
1.11	75

De peccatorum meritis et remissione
1	77

Enarrationes in Psalmos
99	286

Epistulae
1 A	171
3–14	69
10	67
16	68
24	70
25	164
27	71, 164
31	71, 164
32	71
80	165
86	170, 171
95	72, 166
97	76
100	76
112	76
113	168
114–116	168
124	164
132	122–124
134	77
135	122, 124
136	77
137	122, 123, 125, 126
138	125
139	77
143	77

224	64, 65, 69
233	69
234	69
235	70
258	76
268	169

Retractationes
1.2	75
1.21	76
2.20	65
2.67	65

Sermones
48	286
173	154
302	75
355	149

Aurelius Victor
Liber de Caesaribus
28	267

Auxentius
Vita Ulfilae
33[53–54]	315
35[56]	315
37[59]	315

Apuleius
Metamorphoses
11.28	276, 286

Basilius of Caesarea
Epistulae
54	26
59	27
60	27
94	159
154	318
155	318

164	318	13	276
165	318	14	272
		18	270
Braulio of Zaragoza		19	267, 268, 276, 277
Epistulae		21	268–274, 278, 279, 285
3	233		
5	236	22	268, 269, 272–275, 279, 286
31–32	236		
		24	276
Breviarium Melitii	102	25	274
		27	268
Cassiodorus		37	269, 270, 272, 274–276
Institutiones divinarum et saecularium litterarum			
		38	274–276
1.16	180, 197	39	268, 269, 272, 274–276, 286
Cicero		40	272
Academica		55	268, 272
1.3	165	59	276
De officiis		60	274
1.139	167	66	274, 276
2.64	161, 165		
		Cyril of Alexandria	
Clement of Alexandria		*Epistulae*	
Stromateis		75	95
4.9	270	76	95
Cyprian of Carthage		**Cyril of Scythopolis**	
De lapsis		*Vita Euthymii*	
2	274, 276, 282	16	30
3	268	20	30
8	273		
11–12	276	*Didache*	
13	268, 274, 277	11	150
17–20	270	12	151
24	273		
28	268	**Dio Cassius**	
29–32	271	*Historiae*	
35–36	271	75.2	287
36	270	78.36	287
De unitate ecclesiae			
1	286	**Dioscorus of Alexandria**	
19	268	*Vita Dioscori*	24
Epistulae			
5	272	**Ennodius**	
8	272, 282	*Opuscula*	
10	277, 282, 285	5	219

Index of Authors and Texts — **347**

49	217	Gaudentius of Brescia	
77	219	*Sermones*	
139	219	8.25	130
225	220	17.14	156
226	220		
227	220	Gelasius I of Rome	
228	220, 221	*Epistulae*	
271	223	12	216
283	219		
300	219	Gennadius of Marseille	
301	221	*De viris illustribus*	
358	222	22	180
368	221		
370	223	Gerontius	
408	223	*Vita Melaniae*	
413	223	21	151
415	223	22	164
426	222, 223	34–35	164
		50	126
Epiphanius of Salamis		53	126, 164
Adversus haereses (Panarion)		55	126
70.1	316	57–58	164
70.2	316		
70.9	316	Gregory of Nazianzus	
70.14	316	*Epistulae*	
70.15	317	7	27
73.37	27	*Orationes*	
		18	158
Epitome de Caesaribus		21	108
1.6	283	43	159
Eusebius of Caesarea		Gregory of Nyssa	
Historia ecclesiastica		*Homiliae in Canticum Canticorum*	
5.24	24	Prol.	132
6.39	267	*Vita Gregorii Thaumaturgi* 267, 282	
6.40	282		
6.41	286	Gregory of Tours	
6.43	272, 284	*Historia Francorum*	
7.11	33, 272, 282	5.49	22
7.15	286		
7.20	103	Herodian	
Vita Constantini		*Historiae*	
3.19	305	3.8	287
3.36	305		
4.24	313	Hieronymus	
		Adversus Rufinum	
		3.17	150

Commentarius In Ezechielem
　11.36　　　　　　　162
Commentarius in Titum 149
De viris illustribus
　131　　　　　　　　196
Epistulae
　14　　　　　　　　　157
　45　　　　　　　　　50, 51
　47　　　　　　　　　158
　53　　　　　　　　　158
　57　　　　　　　　　156, 158
　64　　　　　　　　　158
　66　　　　　　　　　159, 160
　71　　　　　　　　　157, 158
　77　　　　　　　　　158–160
　108　　　　　　　　151, 157, 163
　112　　　　　　　　120
　145　　　　　　　　158
Vita Hilarionis
　20　　　　　　　　　141

Hilary of Poitiers
Fragmenta
　B 12　　　　　　　　179
Liber adversus Valentem et Ursacium
　1.2.1–29　　　　　　107

Hilarius of Rome
Epistulae
　15　　　　　　　　　21

History of the Patriarchs of the Coptic Church of Alexandria 32

Homer
Odyssea
　2.268　　　　　　　118

Ildefonsus of Toledo
De viris illustribus
　Praefatio　　　　　　232
　1　　　　　　　　　　232
　2　　　　　　　　　　232
　4　　　　　　　　　　232
　5　　　　　　　　　　232
　6　　　　　　　　　　232
　7　　　　　　　　　　232
　8　　　　　　　　　　232
　9　　　　　　　　　　232
　10　　　　　　　　　232
　11　　　　　　　　　232
　12　　　　　　　　　232
　13　　　　　　　　　232

Innocentius I of Rome
Epistulae
　1　　　　　　　　　　198
　2　　　　　　　　　　198
　16　　　　　　　　　179, 180, 199
　17　　　　　　　　　179, 180

Itinerarium Antonini Placentini
　23　　　　　　　　　152

Itinerarium Egeriae
　3.1　　　　　　　　152
　4.3　　　　　　　　151
　7.6　　　　　　　　152
　10.7　　　　　　　151
　19.5　　　　　　　151
　20.12　　　　　　　153
　25.7　　　　　　　152

Iuvenal
　3.180　　　　　　　286

Isidore of Pelusium
Epistulae
　23　　　　　　　　　96
　25　　　　　　　　　92
　26　　　　　　　　　93
　28　　　　　　　　　93
　30　　　　　　　　　93
　35　　　　　　　　　91
　119　　　　　　　　93
　151　　　　　　　　93
　178　　　　　　　　90
　199　　　　　　　　86
　201　　　　　　　　86
　204　　　　　　　　86
　205　　　　　　　　86
　215　　　　　　　　93
　250　　　　　　　　93
　281　　　　　　　　86, 89, 90

299	88	1448	86
300	88	1478	85
303	96	1492	86
310	33, 92, 94, 95	1493	86
311	91, 92, 95	1503	97
323	92, 96	1515	86
324	92, 96	1528	95
330	86	1582	92
331	86	1776	85
341	93	1818	86
351	89, 90	1822	93
352	89, 90	1901	97
370	92, 95	1902	93
393	92	1931	97
405	96	1949	86
430	89	1982	86
483–487	89		
484	90		
485	90		
486	90		
487	90		
489	90		
489–490	89		
490	89, 90		
497	92		
544	93		
572	97		
613	93		
627	92, 93		
681	86		
682	86		
766	97		
890	93		
898	97		
1025	97		
1027	97		
1028	97		
1035	93		
1048	93		
1106	92		
1124	97		
1249	86		
1290	93		
1303	97		
1324	85		
1328	90, 92, 93		
1346	95		

Isidore of Seville
De ecclesiasticis officiis
    2.5   149, 230
De viris illustribus
    21–22   241

John of Biclaro
Chronica
    58   233

John Chrysostom
Epistulae 1–17 ad Olympiadem
    7   136, 167
    8   133, 136, 156
    9   156, 321–323
    12   136–138
    17   137
Epistulae 18–242 ad diversos
    21   321
    28   321
    51   321
    53   321
    54   321
    69   321
    123   321
    126   321
    175   321
    206   322, 323
    207   322, 323
    221   320

Homiliae in Eutropium
1	169, 170
2	170
3	169
5	170

Homiliae in Genesim
8	167

John of Ephesus
Historia ecclesiastica
3.4	327–331
4.6	327

John of Nikiu
Chronica
79	31

John of Rhodes
Passio Artemii 262

Jordanes
Getica
25.133	316

Flavius Josephus
De bello iudaico
2.382–386	283

Vita
15	284

Julian 'the Apostate'
Orationes
1.33	262

Lactantius
De mortibus persecutorum
4	267

Divinae Institutiones
6.11	154
6.12	154

Laterculus Veronensis 305

Leo I of Rome
Epistulae
9	35

Libanius of Antioch
Orationes
59.94	253

Liber Pontificalis
41	197

Liberatus of Carthage
Breviarium 35

Life of Aaron 324

Lucian of Samosata
De morte Peregrini
11–16	272

Macrobius
In somnium Scipionis 59

Martyrium Pionii
3	267

Martyrium Polycarpi
7–8	270

Martyrologium Hieronymianum 54

Minucius Felix
Octavius 278, 284

Oracula Sibyllina
13.87–88	267

Origen
Exhortatio ad Martyrium
30	270

In Leviticum homiliae
9	270

Orosius
Historiae adversus paganos
7.42	171

Palladius
Dialogus de vita Ioannis Chrysostomi
4	184
6	31, 167

7	167	54	48
10	136		
12	168	Paulinus of Nola	
16	133, 134, 320	*Carmina*	
17	131–134	17	10, 179, 182–184, 186–190

Historia Lausiaca

Praef.	164	18	10, 160, 163
7	152	21	160, 161, 165
46	156	23	160, 163
54	156	26	165
55	156	27	160, 162, 163, 179, 183, 187–190
56	131, 132		
61	163, 164	*Epistulae*	
66–68	158	1	154
		2	150

Papyrus London 1914	103	3	70, 192
		4	71, 164
Passio Maximini et Isaac		5	160, 161
12	282	6	71
		11	189, 192
Passio Perpetuae et Felicitatis		13	150, 154, 160, 192
3	272	18	160
4	272	27	10
7–8	270	28	160
18	270	29	160, 161, 179, 182, 187, 193, 198
21	270		
		31	156
Passio Sabae		32	160, 161
2	317	42	192
3	317	50	67, 117, 118
4	317		
7	317	Persius	
8	318	*Saturae*	
		5.24–25	123

Pastor Hermae
Mandata

		Philostorgius	
8.10	149	*Historia ecclesiastica*	
Similitudines		2.5	315
9.27	149		
9.28	270	Photius	
		Bibliotheca	
Paulinus of Milan		59	135, 167
Vita Ambrosii		273	322
3	44	508a	168
4	47, 48, 50, 53		
9	52		
46	24		

Pliny the Elder
Naturalis historia
 18 283
 34 273

Pliny the Younger
Epistulae
 10.68 249

Possidius
Vita Augustini
 3–4 63
 22 77
 27 149

Procopius
Bella
 3.13 332

Pseudo-Martyrius
Oratio funebris in laudem Sancti Iohannis Chrysostomi
 130 133

Sidon Apollinaris
Epistulae
 4.1 167
 7.9 37

Socrates Scholasticus
Historia ecclesiastica
 2.7 252
 2.13 252–254
 2.16 255
 2.22 255
 2.26 256
 2.27 257–259
 2.28 257
 2.38 258–261
 4.33 315
 4.37 30
 5.8 28
 5.9 256
 5.23 316
 6.5 170
 6.12 196
 6.18 196
 6.19 28
 7.7 32
 7.8 322

Sozomenos
Historia ecclesiastica
 3.3 256
 3.4 252
 3.7 252–254
 3.9 255
 4.2 256, 257, 259
 4.20 257, 258, 260
 4.21 257, 258, 260, 261
 6.19 30
 6.34 159, 323
 6.37 315
 7.8 28
 7.17 316
 7.28 150, 196
 8.7 170
 8.16 322
 8.18 31
 8.23 28
 8.24 131, 133
 8.27 138

Strabo
Geographica
 7.3 186

Suetonius
Claudius
 18–19 283
 23 280

Sulpicus Severus
Dialogi
 1.7 158
 1.8 158, 162
 1.25 149
 3.17 162, 199
Vita Martini
 25 151

Synesius of Cyrene
Epistulae
 4 284

Symmachus
Epistulae
1.15	69, 73
1.46	56
1.63	53, 55, 56
1.64	73
1.94	73
1.99	72
3.23	54
3.30–37	55
3.50	73
4.30	56
5.4–16	74
5.16	56
5.32	72
5.87	54
6.26	56
6.34	56
6.35	56
6.37	56
6.81	54
7.66	54
7.109	56
8.57	56
9.51	73
9.130	54

Tertullian
Ad uxorem
1.4	272
2.3–5	289
2.5	288

Apologeticum 274
De baptismo
16	270

De pudicitia
22.4–6	270

Theodoret of Cyrus
Epistulae
60	35

Historia ecclesiastica
4.9	316
4.15	27
5.27	323
5.28–31	322
5.29	320
5.31	323
5.40	28

Historia religiosa
17	332

Uranius
Epistula de obitu Paulini
3	162

Valerius
Epistulae
5	151

Vergilius
Aeneis
7.115	159

Vetustissimae epistulae romanorum pontificum
9	180
14	180

Vita Olympiadis
2	131
5	134
6	134
8	134, 135
9	135
14	134
15	132

Vita Pachomii bohairice scripta
189	112

Vitas Sanctorum Patrum Emeritensium
Praefatio	231
4.1	242
4.3	242
4.4	242
4.5	242, 243
5.5	238
5.6	238, 239
5.8	238, 239, 241

Zacharias Rhetor
Historia ecclesiastica
   3.1   35
Vita Severi Antiocheni 25

Zeno of Verona
Tractatus
   1.2   128, 129
   1.3   129
   1.25   129

   1.32   129
   1.35   130
   1.59   129
   2.1   128, 129

Zosimus
Historia nova
   1.21   267
   2.32   262
   5.8   156

c) Synodical and Juridical Texts

Canones Apostolorum
   Canon 76   23, 29, 36

Codex Theodosianus
   1.5.13   304
   1.15.12   304
   2.26.1   304
   3.17.4   49
   6.13.1   304
   7.6.3   304
   7.10.1   304
   9.2.6   168, 169
   9.40.17   170
   9.45.1–4   168
   10.19.7   304
   10.19.12   304
   11.1.5   45
   11.30.62   170
   12.1.97   304
   12.12.9   304
   16.1.3   304
   16.2.32   38
   16.5.55   172

Constitutiones Apostolorum
   2.26   127

Constitutiones Sirmondianae
   3.12   304

Council of Aachen (814)
   Canon 9   149

Council of Antioch (341)
   Canon 23   23

Council of Arles (314)
   Canon 2   298

Council of Constantinople (381)
   Canon 2   167

Council of Épaone (517)
   Canon 5   307
   Canon 8   307

Concilium of Nîmes (394)
   Canon 5   152

Council of Merida (666)
   Canon 13–14 243
   Canon 16   243
   Canon 18   243
   Canon 20–21 243

Council of Neocaesarea (315)
   Canon 11   180

Council of Nicaea (325)
   Canon 4   302
   Canon 5   167, 302
   Canon 6   101, 303, 306
   Canon 7   102
   Canon 15   297

Council of Orléans (538)
   Canon 21   307

Council of Orléans (541)
   Canon 33   307

Council of Serdica (343)
   Canon 1   298
   Canon 5   168
   Canon 11   196
   Canon 12   196

(First) Council of Toledo
Exemplar definitivae sententiae translate de gestis   235

Council in Trullo (692)
   Canon 33   24

Digestae
   48.22.7   280
   48.22.18   280

Index of Ancient Places

Africa   12, 13, 48, 53, 54, 59, 63, 67, 70–73, 75–77, 117, 142, 162–166, 168–172, 268–286, 288, 290, 331
Alexandria   9, 28, 30–36, 38, 39, 83, 87, 88, 93, 94, 96, 101–104, 107–109, 111–113, 138, 141, 143, 158, 167, 251, 256, 284, 303–307, 327, 330
Alodia   330, 331
Ammoniaca   103
Ancyra   158, 323
Antinoopolis   106, 107
Antioch   23, 25, 29, 30, 38, 74, 101, 102, 135, 163, 167, 168, 251, 252, 254, 303–306, 319, 320, 324, 332
Apamea   28
Aphroditon   6, 106
Apollon   106
Aquileia   47, 184
Arabia   317, 320
Arabissus   131
Arles   208, 298
Arsenoitis   106
Asia Minor   158, 162
Asiana   304, 307
Aswan   325
Augustamnica Prima   83, 89
Aulona   184

Baetica   231, 236, 237
Beroea   150, 167
Bethlehem   156–159, 162
Bithynia-Pontus   249
Bucolia   106

Caesarea   27, 143, 156–158
Cappadocia   8, 14, 26, 27, 32, 38, 89, 132, 155, 255, 314, 317, 318
Capua   195
Carrhae   28, 152, 332
Carthago   12, 47, 53, 64, 67, 70–72, 74, 75, 77, 122, 170, 268, 270, 272–277, 279, 282, 284, 286, 290, 291
Cherchell   53

Cilicia   321
Cirta Fortunatus   168
Clermont   22
Clysma   106, 109
Constantia   163
Constantinople   10, 14, 27, 33, 34, 39, 87–90, 96, 121, 131–135, 137, 138, 142, 151, 156, 163, 164, 167–169, 179, 184, 193–196, 216, 251, 252, 254–257, 259, 261, 262, 303–305, 307, 319, 320, 322–324, 327–330
Coptos   106
Crimea   322, 323
Cucusus (Göksun)   131, 133, 156, 255, 320
Cyprus   163, 170, 317
Cyrenaica   102, 107
Cyrene   74, 298

Dacia   162, 163, 179, 180, 182, 183, 186, 194
Dacia Mediterranea   179, 182, 186
Dacia Ripensis   186
Dalmatia   184, 195
Dardania   182
Dendur   329
Der-el-Arbein   152
Diospolis   106
Dorylaeum   28
Durrachium   184, 185

Écija   233
Edessa   8, 28, 29, 33, 38
Egypt   6, 8, 9, 87, 88, 95, 98, 101–113, 139, 140, 142, 162, 167, 168, 283, 303, 305, 307, 324–327
Emesa   46
Ephesus   24, 28–33, 35, 85, 91–94, 96
Epirus   182
Euphrates   151, 317

Garyathis   106
Gaul   22, 36, 44–47, 59, 74, 152, 158, 162, 163, 235

Gerona   232
Gothia   13, 14, 313–319, 322, 332, 333

Haemus   185
Har(r)an   28, 152
Helenopolis   163
Hermopolis Parva   111, 139
Hippo   63, 68, 71, 73, 76, 77, 164, 165, 168, 169, 298
Hispania   11, 44, 227, 228, 230, 231, 233–235, 237, 244
Hydruntum   182
Hypsele   106, 109

Iberia   11, 14, 227–232, 243, 244
Iconium in Lycaonia   26
Illyricum   14, 162, 184, 185, 193–195, 197, 199, 200
Iol Caesarea   73
Italia   11, 25, 76, 104, 128, 162, 182, 193–195, 199, 208, 280

Jebel Musa   152
Jerusalem   8, 102, 108, 127, 140, 152, 156–158, 160, 164, 251, 303, 304

Kochanes/Qudshanis (Hakkâri)   19, 39

Langres   22
Laton   106
Libya   101, 102, 104–108, 113, 303
Lower Egypt   142
Lower Nubia   324, 329
Lupiae   182
Lusitania   231, 237, 243
Lycopolis   106
Lyon   22

Macedonia   182, 184, 185, 194
Makouria   330
Mantinium   258–261
Marmarica   102, 106, 107
Marmoutier   152
Mauretania   53, 54, 73
Maximianopolis   106
Mérida   230, 231, 233, 236–239, 241–243
Mesopotamia   316, 321, 322

Milan   9, 44, 48, 53, 54, 63, 64, 71–74, 76, 150, 184, 195, 207, 208, 211, 217–219, 221, 223
Moesia   267, 315
Moesia Superior   267
Mopsuestia   28
Mount of Olives   156–158, 163, 164

Nag Hammadi   112
Naissus   195, 196, 199
Nantes   22, 23
Nazianzus   26
Neocaesarea   26, 29, 180
Nicaea   102, 305, 320
Nicomedia   253, 262
Nilopolis   106, 109
Nisibis   153
Nitrian Desert   32, 84
Nola   10, 160–163, 165, 166, 179, 180, 182–184, 187, 188, 190, 192, 193, 198
Noricum   195
Noubadia   328–331
Nubia   13, 14, 314, 324–333
Numidia   168, 171
Nyssa   26

Osrhoene   28
Ostia   278, 282–284, 290
Oxyrynchus   6, 106

Palencia   232
Palestine   27, 32, 156, 158, 162, 164, 317
Palmyra   46
Panephysis   87
Pangaion Mountain   185
Pannonia   195, 267
Panos   106
Paralus   106
Pavia   11, 207, 208, 211, 220
Pelargus   258, 259
Pelusium   9, 83–85, 89, 90, 92–94, 98
Pentapolis   101, 103, 107, 303
Persia   19, 153, 253, 314, 321, 322
Philae   325, 326, 328, 329
Philippi   182, 184
Phoenicia   319–323
Pityus   131

Podanus 158
Pollentia 165
Pontica 305, 307
Pontus 26, 322
Portus 159, 278, 282–284, 290
Prosopitis 106
Ptolemais 284, 298

Qasr Ibrim 329

Ravenna 75
Remesiana 179, 183, 184
Resafa 25
Rhodope Mountain 185
Rhynocoruron 106
Rome 10, 12, 13, 22, 30, 32, 47, 49–55, 58–60, 64, 69–77, 101, 102, 121, 142, 155, 158–161, 163, 166, 168, 180, 182, 184, 185, 193–200, 210, 211, 216, 219, 221, 243, 249, 268–285, 288–290, 303, 304

Saiton 106
Samosata 27
Sarepta 10, 150
Sarug 29
Sasima 26, 27, 158
Scupi 182, 193, 196, 197
Scythia 183–185, 194, 196, 316, 322
Scythia Minor 182, 318
Scythopolis 30
Sebaste 26, 156
Serdica 107, 195, 196, 254, 255, 298
Sethroitis 106
Seville 232–234, 240

Sicily 53, 54, 283
Sozopolis 25
Spania 234
Stathma 106
Stobi 183, 193
Syene 106, 325, 329
Syria 28, 321

Tanis 106, 107
Tarraconensis 236
Tarragona 235, 236
Tella 28
Tentyra 106,
Thagaste 63, 70, 71, 74, 164, 298
Tarraconensis 236
Thebais 106, 327
Thessalonike 182–185, 193, 194, 196, 198
Thracia 185, 267, 307, 322
Ticinum 208
Tomi 182–184, 193, 196, 200
Tours 22
Trier 46, 47, 49, 59, 255

Ur 153
Urmia 20

Verona 267

Wadi-el-Leja 152

Xois 106

Zaragoza 232, 233, 235, 236
Zeugma 320

Index of Modern Authors

Adamiak, Stanisław   149, 169, 170
Adkin, Neil   50, 51
Allen, Pauline   65, 113, 119, 131, 209, 320
Althoff, Gerd   207
Amidon, Philip R.   113
Amory, Patrick   208, 216
Anatolios, Khaled   105
Ansell, Christopher K.   223
Arterbury, Andrew   149, 150, 153
Ayres, Lewis   195

Balsdon, John P.V.D.   288
Banev, Krastu   113
Barnes, J.A.   3
Barnes, Timothy D.   45–47, 50, 57–59, 101, 104, 109, 251, 252, 254–256, 295, 296, 304
Bartlett, Richard   209, 223
Basson, André   179
Baudrillart, Alfred   54
Baum, Wilhelm   20
Beard, Mary   249
Beeley, Christopher A.   303
Benson, Edward White   274, 286
Beresford, James   186
Bird, Isabella L.   19, 20, 39
Birley, Anthony R.   230, 236
Bleckmann, Bruno   268
Blowers, Paul M.   157
Blumell, Lincoln H.   107
Bobertz, Charles A.   275
Bodin, Ariane   6, 8, 9, 14
Boissevain, Jeremy   3, 5, 181
Borgatti, Stephen, P.   210
Bott, Elizabeth   3
Bourdieu, Pierre   154
Bowersock, Glen   151, 250
Brakke, David   105, 106, 109, 111, 138–141
Brändli, Adrian   64
Braudel, Fernand   4, 5
Brooks, Ernest W.   327–330
Brown, Peter   1, 50, 75, 153, 154, 156, 163, 179, 199, 284, 299

Brughmans, Tom   78
Brunt, Peter A.   287
Buchanan, Mark   4
Budge, E.A. Wallis   324, 325
Burgess, Henry   104, 106, 262
Burke, Peter   151
Burn, Andrew E.   180, 183, 187, 193, 194, 197
Burns, J. Patout   267, 271
Bury, John B.   304
Bush, Archie C.   55

Cain, Andrew   65, 157, 159, 163
Cameron, Alan   45, 66, 67, 170, 208, 217, 249, 250
Cameron, Averil   151, 287
Camplani, Alberto   104, 109–111
Caner, David   152
Casson, Lionel   278, 283
Castellanos, Santiago   231, 232
Cazier, Pierre   227
Cerutti, Steven   55
Chadwick, Henry   236, 303
Christiansen, Erik   287
Clark, Elizabeth   5, 65, 164
Clark, Gillian   8, 9, 14, 69, 74, 119, 149, 161, 165, 170, 171, 288
Clarke, Graeme W.   267, 268, 271–276, 280, 282, 284, 286
Coakley, James F.   20
Collar, Anna   78
Collins, Roger   231, 237
Coman, J.   318
Conybeare, Catherine   7, 64, 66, 68, 153, 188, 191
Corbier, Mireille   56
Coward, Fiona   78
Cureton, William   104
Cvetković, Carmen   8, 10, 14, 19, 149, 185, 197

Dagron, Gilbert   169, 170, 254, 295, 323
Davis, Stephen J.   101

De Rossi, Giovanni Battista 44, 55
De Wet, Chris L. 320
Delehaye, Hippolyte 273
Delmaire, Roland 320, 321, 322
Demacopoulos, George 119, 120, 138, 142
Devos, Paul 156
Dey, Hendrick W. 239
Diefenbach, Steffen 250
Dijkstra, Jitse H.F. 324, 325, 327, 328
Dijkstra, Roald 249
Divjak, Johannes 68, 120
Dixon, Suzanne 288
Domagalski, Bernhard 32
Downey, Glanville 262
Drake, Harold 250
Drijvers, Jan Willem 27
Duch, Michał 287
Dümler, Bärbel 128, 129
Dunn, Geoffrey D. 180, 194, 197, 229
Duval, Yves-Marie 43, 53, 158, 183

Ebbeler, Jennifer 66, 68, 72, 73, 78, 159
Eco, Umberto 155
Elm, Susanna 250, 250, 261
Elsner, Jaś 155
Engberg, Jakob 6, 11, 12, 14, 268, 279–281
Erdös, Paul 4
Escribano, Victoria 236
Everett, Martin G. 210
Évieux, Pierre 84–90, 92–94, 96

Fabre, Pierre 180, 186, 188
Falluomini, Carla 315, 316
Fear, Andrew 227, 333
Fedwick, Jonathan 26
Feissel, Denis 295
Finn, Richard 154
Fitschen, Klaus 103
Forlin Patrucco, Marcella 120, 134
Fox, Robin Lane 71, 74, 274
Francis, E.D. 164
Frank, Georgia 2
Frankfurter, David 325
Freeman, Linton, C. 210
Frend, William H.C. 274

Gaddis, Michael 258

Gatier, Pierre-Louis 25
Geerlings, Wilhelm 122
Gemeinhardt, Peter 8, 9, 19, 101, 111, 118, 124, 127, 128, 130, 139, 141, 149, 150, 156, 187, 189
Gibson, Roy 66
Giebel, Marion 165
Gilliard, Frank D. 299
Gioanni, Stéphane 44
Girardet, Klaus M. 250
Gnilka, Christian 125
Goehring, James E. 325
González Fernández, R. 235, 241
Gorce, Denys 150, 151, 153
Gradel, Ittai 268
Granerød, Gard 150, 153
Granovetter, Mark S. 4, 213
Grant, Michael 267
Graumann, Thomas 29, 35
Greenslade, S.L. 194
Greenwood, Timothy 24
Greschat, Katharina 131–133, 136
Grig, Lucy 154
Grillmeier, Alois 327
Gryson, Roger 187
Gülzow, Henneke 269
Gwynn, David M. 8, 9, 14, 101, 105, 109, 111, 138, 139, 251, 252, 261, 303

Haas, Christopher 93
Haensch, Rudolf 19, 25, 302
Hagl, Wolfgang 250
Hahn, Johannes 250
Hainthaler, Theresia 149, 327
Hansen, Günther Christian 27
Hardy, Edward Rochie 31
Harmless, William 120, 127
Harries, Jill 154
Hauben, Hans 102
Heather, Peter 315, 317, 318
Heinzelmann, Martin 22
Henck, Nick 254
Henig, Martin 287
Hermanowicz, Erika 68, 75
Herrmann-Otto, Elisabeth 296, 298, 302, 306
Hess, Hamilton 196

Hillgarth, Jocelyn N.   239
Hillner, Julia   2, 6, 7, 8, 280
Hiltbrunner, Otto   150, 152–154
Hirschmann, Vera   257
Hombert, Pierre-Marie   69
Honigmann, Ernst   27
Hugo, Victor   19
Humbert, Michel   48
Hunt, David   150, 151–153, 157, 158, 163, 164, 301, 306
Huttner, Ulrich   268

Isele, Bernd   251, 257, 258, 261, 262
Ivanov, Sergey   313, 314, 333

Jacobs, Ine   239
Jakab, Attila   101
Jenott, Lance   112
Jensen, Robin M.   267, 271
Jerg, Ernst   187
Jones, Arnold Hugh Martin   31, 38, 47, 48, 63, 170, 171, 295, 304
Junkelmann, Marcus   287
Jussen, Bernhard   37
Just, Patricia   250, 251, 257

Kahlos, Maijastina   130, 260
Kelly, Christopher   189
Kelly, David   59
Kelly, John Norman Davidson   320, 322, 323
Kennell, Stefanie A.H.   208, 209, 211, 219, 220, 222, 223
Keough, Shawn W.J.   228
Keppie, Lawrence   287
Key Fowden, Elizabeth   185
King, Anthony   287
King, P.D.   341
Kirstein, Robert   179, 182, 183, 185, 186, 188
Kleinschmidt, Anika L.   161
Knipfing, John R.   267
Knorr, Uwe Walter   319
Knox, Daniel K.   11, 14, 211
Kolb, Anne   151
Kolbet, Paul R.   126
Konstan, David   64, 150
Kritzinger, Peter   21, 296

Kulikowski, Michael   227
Kunst, Christiane   286

Lake, Kirsopp   84
Lane Fox, Robin   71, 74, 274
Lanéry, Cécile   52
Lankina, Anna   319
Larsen, Lillian   84, 92, 95
Latham, Jacob A.   239
Lauwers, Michel   306, 308
Lazzati, Giuseppe   43
Leemans, Johan   8, 9, 14, 65, 84, 97, 228, 317
Lefort, Louis-Théophile   104
Lehmann, Tomas   160
Lenski, Noel   164, 314, 315, 318, 319
Leone, Anna   70
Leppin, Hartmut   259, 260
Lewis, Naphtali   286, 287
Leyerle, Blake   2
Leyser, Conrad   64
Lhuillier-Martinetti, Dominique   48
Liebeschuetz, Wolf   65, 163, 254, 296, 298, 299, 302, 315
Lienhard, Joseph   71, 182
Lizzi Testa, Rita   1, 2, 188
Llewellyn, P.A.B.   217
Long, Jacqueline   170
Lorenz, Rudolf   104, 260
Lorgeoux, Olga   127
Löw, Martina   153
Lundhaug, Hugo   112

Machado, Carlos   52
MacMullen, Ramsay   260
Malkin, Irad   155
Manders, Erika   11, 12, 14, 249, 250
Mango, Cyril   164, 261
Marrou, Henri-Irénée   22
Marucchi, Horace   52
Martin, Annick   101, 102, 106, 107, 109, 110, 139
Martin, Céline   227
Martindale, John R.   48, 208
Mathisen, Ralph W.   314, 317, 318, 320
Matthews, John   161, 315, 317, 318
Mauss, Marcel   154

Mayer, Wendy   119, 131, 135, 136, 319, 320
Mazel, Florian   306–308
Mazzarino, Santo   45, 46
McCormick, Michael   239
McEnerney, John I.   95
McGuckin, John   34
McLynn, Neil   43, 50–53, 55, 56, 59, 74, 75, 77, 149, 168, 170, 171, 253–255, 257, 262, 263, 315
Meijer, Fik   267, 283, 284
Menze, Volker L.   8, 14, 241, 327, 328
Meredith, Anthony   26
Merendino, Rosario P.   105
Meyendorff, John   216
Meyer, Reinhold   286, 287
Migl, Joachim   295, 296, 304
Miles, Richard   72
Milgram, Stanley   4
Millar, Fergus   249, 267, 274, 275, 282, 302
Mitchell, J. Clyde   3, 4, 5
Molthagen, Joachim   267
Moore, Michael E.   300, 301, 303
Moorhead, John   43, 210, 216, 217, 221, 222
Moreau, Tiphaine   6, 7
Morgenstern, Frank   120
Morris, John   48
Mratschek, Sigrid   5, 8, 10, 67, 70, 76, 150–152, 154–156, 158, 160–166, 181, 191, 199
Mullet, Margaret   5, 7, 14, 181

Natal, David   2, 227, 230, 235
Neil, Bronwen   65
Ng, Nathan K.-K.   105
Nicolaye, Carla   228
Noethlichs, Karl Leo   38, 39, 295
North, John   249
Norton, Peter   21, 23, 35, 228, 235, 254, 256, 257

O'Daly, Gerard   77
O'Donnell, James J.   63, 64, 75
O'Keefe, John J.   113
Ohme, Heinz   23, 29
Orlandi, Tito   327

Padgett, John F.   223

Palanque, Jean-Rémy   43, 44, 47, 48
Palme, Bernhard   295, 296
Paredi, Angelo   43
Parker, H.M.D.   287
Patrich, Joseph   157
Patzold, Steffen   22
Peltzer, Jörg   228
Pietri, Charles   21, 194, 195
Pietri, Luce   21, 22
Pohl, Christine Dorothy   153
Powell, Walter W.   223
Price, Simon   249
Purvis, Paul   317
Puzicha, Michaela   149

Rammelt, Claudia   28, 38
Ramsey, Boniface   44, 47, 48, 52
Rapp, Claudia   21, 73, 110, 121, 188, 227, 241, 242, 299
Rebenich, Stefan   64, 157, 158, 189
Rebillard, Éric   68, 155
Reimitz, Helmut   244
Reinhard, Wolfgang   21, 286
Reis, David   280
Renfrew, Colin   155
Reynolds, Paul   242
Richter, Siegfried G.   324, 327, 330
Riedinger, Utto   85
Rousseau, Philip   26, 27
Ruffini, Giovanni   4, 6
Russell, Norman   31, 92, 94, 95, 113

Saint-Laurent, Jeanne-Nicole Mellon   327
Salomies, Ollies   45
Salzman, Michele R.   58
Sanchez, Mar Marco   227
Satlow, Michael L.   154
Savon, Hervé   43
Schindler, Alfred   121
Schmid, Andreas   96
Schöllgen, Georg   33
Schor, Adam   5
Schwaiger, Georg   20
Scott, John   212, 213
Seeck, Otto   57
Settipani, Christian   58
Shaw, Brent D.   72, 75, 76, 149, 170, 171

Shepardson, Christine   332
Siebig, Gereon   39
Siems, Harald   168
Sivan, Hagith   179, 184, 193, 194, 315
Skinner, Alexander   253
Slootjes, Daniëlle   11, 13, 14, 249, 295, 299, 300, 302, 303
Smith, Morton   84
Smith, R. Payne   327
Sogno, Christiana   65, 72, 73
Soroceanu, Alina   184, 196, 197
Sotinel, Claire   21, 22, 65, 70, 78, 150, 151, 155, 182, 184, 198, 298
Stanfill, Jonathan Peter   319, 322, 323
Stepper, Ruth   249
Sterk, Andrea   11, 13, 14, 110, 111, 120, 299, 313
Stevenson, Walt   251, 322
Stocking, R.L.   227, 232–234, 237
Storin, Bradley   65
Strogatz, Steven   4
Sullivan, Daniel D.   272
Szaivert, Wolfgang   286

Thompson, E. A.   233, 234, 241, 313, 314
Tiersch, Claudia   131, 133–135, 168
Toca, Mădălina   8, 9, 14, 19, 65, 84, 86
Tornau, Christian   122, 124, 125
Tränkle, Hermann   183
Treu, Ursula   84, 85
Trout, Dennis   71, 161, 181
Turner, Cuthbert Hamilton   84

Ulrich, Jörg   6, 282
Urbiña, José Fernández   227

Vallejo Girvés, Margarita   237, 279
Van Dam, Raymond   26, 27, 29, 155, 159
Van der Vliet, Jacques   325
Van Espelo, Dorine   249
Van Ginkel, Jan Jacob   327
Van Minnen, Peter   326

Van Nijf, Onno   283, 284
Van Nuffelen, Peter   228, 256
Velázquez, Isabel   230
Vessey, Mark   68, 71
Veyne, Paul   288
Viard, Paul   150
Vickers, Michael   164
Vinel, Nicolas   84
Vives, José   235
Vivian, Tim   324, 325
Von Campenhausen, Hans   274, 275
Von Domaszewski, Alfred   287

Wallraff, Martin   257, 259
Walsh, P.G.   117, 184
Walter, Conrad   22
Watson, George R.   287
Watts, Duncan J.   4
Watts, Edward J.   65
Webster, Graham   287
Wessel, Susan   32, 92, 94
Whelan, Robin   64
White, Carolinne   131, 190–192
White, L. Michael   5
Williams, Daniel H.   197
Williams, Michael S.   64
Williams, Rowan D.   102
Wilson, J.P.   55
Winkler, Dietmar W.   20
Wipszycka, Ewa   25, 31, 36, 93, 101
Wolfram, Herwig   315, 317, 319
Wolters, Reinhard   286
Wood, Ian   314
Wood, Jamie   11, 12, 14, 227, 230, 232, 235
Woods, David   262
Worp, Klaas A.   107

Yarnold, Edward   27

Zeiller, Jacques   196
Zuckerman, Constantin   295, 305, 317, 318

www.ingramcontent.com/pod-product-compliance
Lightning Source LLC
Chambersburg PA
CBHW031752220426
43662CB00007B/374